COLVILLES AND THE SCOTTISH STEEL INDUSTRY

BY

PETER L. PAYNE

CLARENDON PRESS · OXFORD

1979

Oxford University Press, Walton Street, Oxford OX2 6DP

OXFORD   LONDON   GLASGOW

NEW YORK   TORONTO   MELBOURNE   WELLINGTON

KUALA LUMPUR   SINGAPORE   JAKARTA   HONG KONG   TOKYO

DELHI   BOMBAY   CALCUTTA   MADRAS   KARACHI

IBADAN   NAIROBI   DAR ES SALAAM   CAPE TOWN

© *Peter L. Payne* 1979

British Library Cataloguing in Publication Data
Payne, Peter Lester
    Colvilles and the Scottish steel industry.
    1. Colvilles Ltd—History
    I. Title
    338.7'66'9109411   HD9521.9.C/   78–41147
    ISBN 0-19-828278-8

*Printed in Great Britain by
Butler & Tanner Ltd,
Frome and London*

To my wife, Enid,
and my children,
Simon and Samantha

Preface

This book had its genesis as long ago as 1960, within a few months of my appointment to the newly created Colquhoun Lectureship in Business History at the University of Glasgow. One of the major contributors to the fund by which this unique appointment was founded was Colvilles Ltd. Moreover, the Chairman of the Glasgow Junior Chamber of Commerce who, with the Senior Chamber, had sponsored the Colquhoun Appeal was Ralph A. Hillis, at that time Personal Assistant to Sir Andrew McCance, Chairman and Managing Director of Colvilles. In addition to being of help in providing contacts among the business community of the Glasgow region and so greatly facilitating the survey of historical business records of Clydeside, which was properly regarded as the lecturer's primary task, Mr. Hillis suggested to Professor S. G. Checkland that as Colvilles were approaching their Centenary, the University of Glasgow might consider the possibility under-taking a history of the Group.

However welcome, this suggestion merely reinforced my con-viction that my initial research effort should be an investigation of the Scottish iron and steel industry, without more detailed knowledge of which the economic development of the Scottish economy during the past century could not, I felt, be properly understood. Hence, the Colquhoun Survey proceeded in tandem with a systematic examination of the surviving records of the heavy industries of the West of Scotland.

Two years passed before any attempt was made by Colvilles Ltd. formally to commission the University of Glasgow to pro-duce a history of the Colville Group. By this time, considerable research had already been undertaken into the manuscript material which would necessarily constitute the basis for such a study. Helped by financial support—which served to pay the salary of a part-time research assistant—the work of analysing the voluminous records and examining the trade press pro-ceeded more rapidly. By 1966 the major phases in the evolution of the Scottish iron and steel industry were reasonably clear and a preliminary study of nineteenth century developments had been drafted. Already, however, problems of confidentiality had arisen, and it was by no means certain that the way in which I envisaged the completed monograph met with the entire approval of the Board. While it was agreed that my objective should be a study of the Colville Group in depth, it became apparent that this was not quite what the Board had in mind to celebrate the Company's Centenary. It was therefore decided that I should make a full investigation of the post-1945 period. Only if such a study of 'contemporary history' received approval, could I be confident that the work would eventually be published.

In 1969, some time after the second nationalization of the industry, when the Company had become the major constituent of the Scottish and Northwest Group of the British Steel Corporation, a lengthy manuscript devoted to an examination of the years 1945 to 1960 was presented to Colvilles. The nature of its reception would, I believed, provide me with some guidance as to the acceptability of the approach I had adopted, and this would determine my future commitment to the Centenary volume. In the event, the delivery of the manuscript aroused no response at all. It simply disappeared into the Company's Head Office at West George Street, Glasgow, without producing a ripple. By this time I had moved to the University of Aberdeen, where my attention was fully occupied with the establishment of the Department of Economic History. Not until 1970 was any attempt made by the senior members of what had been Colvilles Ltd. to resuscitate the project. The late Mr. R. C. Dymock, sometime Special Director and Chief Labour Officer of the Colville Group, was appointed to liaise between myself and those who were interested in the completion of the study. Even then, repeated requests for observations on the manuscript and for further information of a kind that did not appear in the written records went largely unanswered. Nevertheless, as so much time and effort had already been invested in the undertaking, I determined to complete it. From 1970 onwards, I conducted a detailed correspondence with Mr. Dymock and met him at regular intervals. Periodically, a wide range of questions was discussed with Sir Andrew McCance. Eschewing any further financial support, the acceptance of which, I believed, might involve my agreement to a timetable which the exigencies of other work would render unrealistic, I completed my coverage of the remaining period of the firm's history, c. 1895–1945. Drafts of each chapter were submitted to Mr. Dymock and Sir Andrew McCance who subjected the manuscript to searching criticism. I wanted to be reasonably certain that my interpretation of the plethora of documentary evidence was both accurate and properly cognizant of the technological possibilities open to the firm which, as a layman, I could judge but imperfectly. So the work proceeded. The manuscript grew enormously. This caused me little anxiety since it had always been my intention to reduce its length once I was confident that a comprehensive treatment of several issues contained no major flaws. Only the reader can judge how far I succeeded in this. It is enough to emphasize that every word has been read by Sir Andrew McCance and Mr. R. C. Dymock, for whose enthusiastic support I will always be grateful.

What I believed to be the final draft was completed early in 1977. It took the form not of an orthodox company history, for I had no wish slavishly to record each and every aspect of the development of the Colville Group of companies, which the absence or destruction of certain sources would in any case have rendered impossible. Instead, I concentrated on a number of important themes. The early chapters, which rely heavily on the records of the Steel Company of Scotland, attempt to explain why this pioneering concern lost its hegemony of the steel industry in Scotland to David Colville & Sons; Part II is therefore concerned with business rivalry. Part III examines the impact on the industry of the First World War and the manifold problems that had to be overcome by those who sought to achieve some degree of rationalization in the inter-war years. Part IV is devoted to post-merger strategy and structure and to the impact of the Second World War; and Part V to what is, in effect, an illustration of the difficulty of reconciling the interests of private enterprise and public policy in this most vital and complex of industries. If the book possesses a unifying theme beyond the evolution of the Scottish steel industry, it is that of the influence of personality on industrial development. The way in which Colvilles grew and the strengths and weaknesses of the firm reflect the characters, motives and ideals of a handful of ambitious, single-minded, powerful and gifted men : David Colville, the founder, his sons, Archibald and David, Jnr., Sir John Craig and Sir Andrew McCance.

In the 1977 manuscript several sections dealt with early industrial relations but, compared with other issues, the documentary basis for this theme was inadequate, resting far too heavily on the records of the Board of Conciliation and Arbitration of the Manufactured Steel Trade of the West of Scotland. Consequently, in the version accepted for publication by Oxford University Press, and written during my tenure of a Sherman Fairchild Distinguished Scholarship at the California Institute of Technology, these sections were, after considerable heartsearching, excised. To some readers this may appear to be yet another manifestation of the workers being sacrificed : a confirmation of all that is bad in both capitalism and its chroniclers. I regret this omission, but without it the book may never have appeared at all. Heavy casualties among the private soldiers were necessary to attain the author's primary objective. The only consolation that can be offered is that the footsloggers are not dead, only sent to reserve. They will fight another day.

Several reasons prompted this brief account of the conception and protracted gestation of this book. First, it illustrates some of the pitfalls confronting those who venture into this most hazardous branch of economic history. Second, it may explain to the many persons who have helped me along the way why my formal thanks to them has been so belatedly recorded. Third, I wish to emphasize that while this book may have started life as a commissioned history, it ceased to be so many years ago and that any potential or actual restrictions on what I wished to say were thereby removed. Sir Andrew McCance was always ready to assist my interpretation and deepen my understanding, never to impose his own views or to suggest tactful omissions. Fourth, even when certain members of the Board expressed reservations about my approach, at no time was I denied access to any of the known records of either the parent or subsidiary companies, even when such records concerned contemporary events.

Despite every effort to explain to several generations of

students the basic technology of iron- and steel-making, a disconcerting number remain wedded to the belief that steel comes out of a blast furnace. For those readers who share this misconception and, indeed, for all those who possess but a hazy idea of metallurgical processes, it may be appropriate to mention that some parts of this book necessitate an elementary knowledge of iron- and steel-making. Numerous specialized studies exist from which such information can be acquired, but it would be difficult to improve upon the illustrated brochures produced by the Information Services Department of the British Steel Corporation (*Making Steel, The Open Hearth Furnace, The Basic Oxygen Furnace, Plate, Sheet and Coil* are representative titles), worthy successors to the British Iron and Steel Federation's *Simple Guides*. More detailed information on technique may be gained from consulting the works of W. K. V. Gale (*The British Iron and Steel Industry: A Technical History* [Newton Abbot: David & Charles, 1967], *The Iron and Steel Industry: A Dictionary of Terms* [Newton Abbot: David & Charles, 1971]), but perhaps the finest brief introduction for economic historians and economists to the processes in use for the greater part of the period covered by this book remains that of P. W. S. Andrews and Elizabeth Brunner, *Capital Development in Steel: A Study of the United Steel Companies Limited* (Oxford: Blackwell, 1952), Chapter 2.

Finally, I must record my thanks to the many who have helped in the production of this book. It would be tedious—and for one with a fallible memory, even impossible—to list all those who have contributed by answering questions, assisting in the location of source material, granting access to records, and commenting on parts of the manuscript, but I cannot conclude without expressing my special indebtedness to the following: Sir Andrew McCance, for reading and re-reading every word and whose comments were uniquely revealing; the late R. C. Dymock for resurrecting the project in 1970 and without whose enthusiasm, advice and help, it might never have come to fruition; Ralph A. Hillis for numerous kindnesses; Lord Clydesmuir; T. R. Craig, the last Chairman of the Colville Group; T. S. Craig, the Company Secretary; W. Gillies, General Manager, Lanarkshire Steel Works; A. R. McInnes; David Muir; the late W. J. Storey, Works Manager,

Glengarnock; James Kerr, director of the Etna Iron and Steel Co.; John Beresford; Adam Humphries; William McKay; D. D. Ramsey, Works Manager, Clydebridge Steel Works; David Bennett, Works Manager, Blochairn Steel Works; H. A. Lear, Divisional Secretary to the British Steel Corporation's Tubes Division; Jim Kelly, Scottish Area Training Officer of the Iron and Steel Industry Training Board, for many years of friendship and constructive help; Alastair Borthwick, the last editor of *Colvilles Magazine*, and his predecessors who made that house journal a most valuable source of information and ideas; Derek Charman, Archivist to the British Steel Corporation; Miss Jill Hampson, the Corporation's Scottish Regional Archivist at Glasgow, and P. Emmerson, the Corporation's East Midlands Regional Archivist at Wellingborough.

Academic colleagues to whom I owe grateful thanks are Sidney Checkland for encouragement and help from the very beginning and who kindly read an earlier draft of Parts I and V; Tony Slaven, whose friendship has been of great value to me since together we breathed the dust and grime that once covered the records of 'Dixon's Blazes' and the Goven Collieries, and who subsequently read the early drafts of Parts I and V of this book; Derek H. Aldcroft, who from his unrivalled knowledge of the trade press brought many references to Colvilles to my attention; Charlotte Erickson for providing me with unpublished information on the first David Colville and his family drawn from the files she prepared for her regrettably still unique study of *British Industrialists: Steel and Hosiery*; Ken Warren whose studies on many aspects of the steel industry have proved invaluable and whose help has been much appreciated; I. F. Gibson who, many years ago, lent me a copy of his Ph.D. thesis on the Scottish iron and steel industry and so greatly eased the way into this present study; Leslie Clarkson for collecting statistics for me on Belfast ship launchings; Peter N. Davies, who answered questions about Lord Kylsant and helped in other ways; Neil Buxton and Donald McKay who let me read their unpublished study of the Scottish steel industry between the wars; R. H. Campbell for help and encouragement from the moment I first arrived at Glasgow University almost completely innocent of knowledge of Scottish economic history; T. J. Byres for letting me use several statistical series drawn from his Glasgow B.Litt. thesis; Robert Irving for providing several illuminating clues to the tangled history of W. Beardmore & Co.; Miss Helena Sokolowski, who collected some figures for me during the course of her work on the files of the early Scottish joint stock companies; R. F. Dell, the Strathclyde Regional Archivist, and his staff for many helpful references to source material; Sir Alec Cairncross for reading the penultimate manuscript and introducing it to Oxford University Press; and John Hume and Michael Moss for numerous kindnesses over the years, including sharing with me their knowledge of William Beardmore & Co. (the majority of whose records I had been told, many years before their more successful enquiries, had been destroyed) and for reading and commenting upon Part III of this book.

It gives me great pleasure to thank the Governor and Company of the Bank of England for granting me access to, and permission to quote from, the Bank's archives relating to the Scottish steel industry; H. Gillett of the Bank's archival staff for his help when I consulted these papers; Anthony R. Thomas for lending me the post-production script of his 1973 ATV television programme 'Where Harry Stood: A History of Our Times as seen Through the Eyes of a Working Man' who had been employed in Stewarts & Lloyds' Clydesdale Works from 1917 to 1933 and in the Corby Works thereafter; and the staff of the Oxford University Press for unfailing courtesy and assistance.

The task of transforming many hundreds of pages of execrable handwriting into a respectable typescript has been cheerfully borne by numerous departmental secretaries both at Glasgow and Aberdeen. For their patience, ingenuity and plain hard work, I would especially like to thank Mrs. Margaret E. Davies, who did so much for me at Glasgow, and Mrs. Patricia A. Smith, my incomparable secretary at Aberdeen.

Lastly, I must record my indebtedness to my wife, Enid, for many years of labouring among the records of the Colville Group and the trade journals and for living with this book for so long. At times, the burden must have been almost intolerable. My long absences in an incredibly untidy study surrounded by notes, minute books, files, and bundles of correspondence aroused little comment from my children. Their response to those who asked after me was simply that, 'He's doing Colvilles'. 'Colvilles' is now done; and my dedication of this book to my wife and children can but inadequately express my everlasting gratitude to them.

November 1978   Peter L. Payne

Contents

PART IV

RECOVERY AND WAR AGAIN

PART V

PROGRESS UNDER PLANNING

Tables

Figures

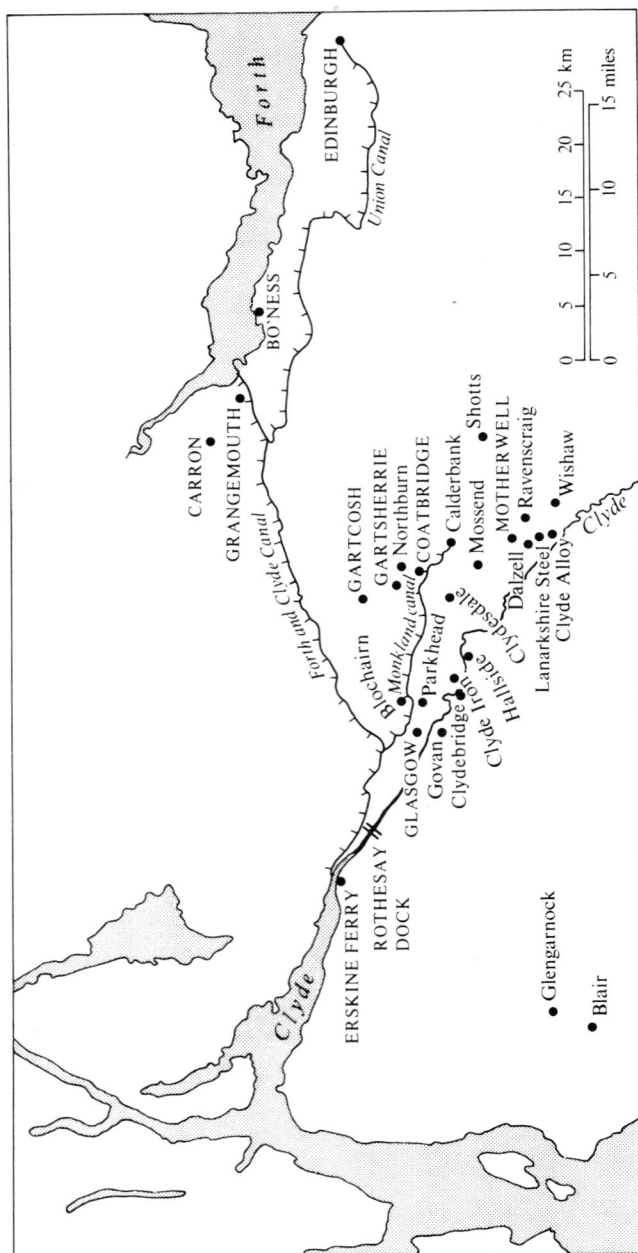

FIG. I. *The Scottish Steel Industry: Principal Locations.*

PART I

Birth and adolescence

I

Prelude

In 1861, when David Colville and his partner Thomas Gray erected the Clifton Iron Works in Coatbridge for the manufacture of finished malleable iron, the annual production of Scottish pig iron had just reached one million tons. In the previous three decades the number of furnaces erected in Scotland had increased sixfold, from 27 in 1830 to 171 in 1861 (122 in blast), and Scotland's proportion of the total British output had risen from 5–6 per cent to 25–6 per cent.[1]

The great expansion in the Scottish pig iron trade—'one of the most striking industrial transformations of the nineteenth century'[2]—was based on the exploitation of the blackband ironstone. This ferrous ore lay in the coal measures of north Lanarkshire, Ayrshire, and Stirlingshire, but was particularly rich in iron in the area around Airdrie and Coatbridge.[3] Discovered at the beginning of the century by David Mushet, its great value was not immediately recognized, and for several years he alone used it, mixed with poorer clay ironstones, at the Calder Iron Works, where he was the manager. Later Mushet's Black Band was partially employed at the Clyde Iron Works, but elsewhere it was neglected, for its richness made it unsuitable for the low furnace temperatures then in use, and the ironmasters entertained a strong prejudice against it. Not until the success of the Monkland Company in using it alone, unmixed with any other material except limestone for a flux, did its worth come belatedly to be appreciated, and with the invention of the hot-blast by James Beaumont Neilson in 1828, the Scottish iron

[1] R. H. Campbell, 'Statistics of the Scottish Pig Iron Trade, 1830 to 1865', *Proceedings of the West of Scotland Iron and Steel Institute*, lxiv (1956–7), 283, 285, 287.
[2] Ibid., p. 282.
[3] A. Miller, *The Rise and Progress of Coatbridge* (Glasgow, 1864), pp. 7–10; David Mushet, *Papers on Iron and Steel* (London, 1840), p. 121; J. Cunnison and J. B. S. Gilfillan (eds.), *The City of Glasgow* (*The Third Statistical Account of Scotland*, vol. V) (Glasgow: Collins, 1958), pp. 153–4.

industry entered upon a phase of such rapid growth that by the
mid-forties some ninety furnaces were producing pig at an
annual rate of over half a million tons.[4]

Neilson's hot-blast—the technical foundation of this enormous expansion—was first used at the Clyde Iron Works, and
so great were the fuel economies which ensued that by 1833
the same amount of fuel was producing three times as much
iron as it had done previously. So admirably was the process
adapted for smelting blackband ironstone that its widespread
adoption rapidly followed, and by 1835 hot-blast working was
an integral part of Scottish practice.[5] In the next five years the
number of furnaces in Scotland doubled, and by May 1841 in
Lanarkshire alone there were no fewer than sixty-four furnaces
in blast and eight new ones in process of erection.[6] The development of the Scottish smelting industry at this time was dominated 'by a group of some two dozen men, the great majority
of whom were originally tenant farmers or small coal masters
in the Coatbridge and Glasgow areas'.[7] Among these proprietors were the Bairds of Gartsherrie, John Wilson of Dundyvan, James Merry and Alexander Cunninghame of Carnbroe,
Glengarnock, and Ardeer, the Neilsons of Summerlee, the
Dunlops of Clyde, Robert Addie of Langloan, and the Dixons
of Calder and Govan.

These men were all intensely active in the management of
their concerns, and under their control steady technical advance
was achieved. This 'took the form of progressive improvements in points of furnace construction, plant layout and furnace working . . . adding up to an increase in efficiency scarcely
less important than the introduction of the hot-blast itself'.[8]

---

[4] I. F. Gibson, 'The Economic History of the Scottish Iron and Steel Industry, 1830–1880' (University of London, Ph.D. thesis, 1955), pp. 117 ff.,
168–85; R. D. Corrins, 'The Great Hot-Blast Affair', *Industrial Archaeology*,
vii (1970), 233–63, see also his 'William Baird & Company, Coal and
Iron Masters, 1830–1914' (University of Strathclyde, Ph.D. thesis, 1974);
W. K. V. Gale, *The British Iron & Steel Industry* (Newton Abbot: David &
Charles, 1967), pp. 54–8.

[5] John Percy, *Metallurgy: Iron and Steel* (London: Murray, 1864), p. 398;
Mushet, *Papers*, p. 127; Henry Hamilton, *The Industrial Revolution in Scotland*
(Oxford: O.U.P., 1932), pp. 179–83.

[6] Campbell, 'Statistics', p. 283.

[7] Gibson, 'Economic History of the Scottish Iron and Steel Industry', p. 541.

[8] Ibid., p. 186.

In 1830 the *per capita* consumption of iron in Scotland was still relatively low, however, and the industry's growing output found its greatest markets in England and Wales and abroad. It has been estimated that in the mid-forties well over 50 per cent of the total Scottish make of pig was exported, and for many years the commercial bases of the Scottish industry were English and foreign markets and the easy access to tide water which the Scottish industry enjoyed.[9]

The dependence of the Scottish pig iron industry on the vagaries of the export trade might have been lessened had the later processes of iron manufacture grown commensurately with the production of pig, but 'the Scots rarely showed much interest in processes subsequent to smelting'.[10] Although growing quantities of iron were absorbed by the increasing number of foundries that were being established in and around Glasgow (the composition of 'Scotch' pig made it highly suitable for castings), malleable iron production lagged behind. The neglect of this branch of the industry was to have important consequences. Indeed, it has been argued that the later 'failure of the Scottish ironmasters to enter quickly into steel-making can best be understood by seeing why they failed long before to enter the malleable iron trade'.[11] The reasons for this deserve further examination.

Some decades before the enormous relative expansion of the Scottish pig iron industry, attempts had been made to expand the production of malleable iron. As soon as Carron's first furnace was in blast it was 'decided to erect, as soon as possible, a forge of three furnaces and two hammers'.[12] This forge was subsequently to be the scene of unsuccessful experiments by John Roebuck to use coke in the production of bar iron and the object of an abortive agreement with Henry Cort, who was

[9] Campbell, 'Statistics', pp. 286–7; Wray Vamplew, 'The Railways and the Iron Industry: A Study of their Relationship in Scotland', in M. C. Reed (ed.), *Railways in the Victorian Economy* (Newton Abbot: David & Charles, 1969), p. 72; J. H. Clapham, *An Economic History of Modern Britain*, vol. 1: *The Early Railway Age, 1820–1850* (Cambridge: C.U.P., 1926), p. 426.

[10] R. H. Campbell, 'Early Malleable Iron Production in Scotland', *Business History*, iv (1961–2), 22.

[11] Ibid., p. 23.

[12] R. H. Campbell, *Carron Company* (Edinburgh: Oliver & Boyd, 1961), p. 35.

to have leased the forge for experimental purposes. However, this branch of the business was but little developed and malleable iron made at Carron was of such poor quality that it was mainly used for conversion into rails. At Clyde Iron Works too the forges erected in the early nineties by Thomas Edington in the hope of dispensing with the need for Swedish bar iron proved unsuccessful. Even the technical successes attained at the Muirkirk Iron Works, where Edington, John Gillies of the Dalnotter Iron Works, and William Robertson of the Smithfield Iron Company, joined together in order to produce bar iron for their works at Cramond, Dalnotter, and Glasgow, did not bring commensurate financial rewards. 'To Robert Napier, the engineer, at one time a partner at Muirkirk, it was "always one of his Sinking-Funds".'[13]

These early failures discouraged later Scottish ironmasters, and malleable iron production languished. Not until the late eighteen-thirties and early forties can the trade be said to have taken root in Scotland. It was during this period that Murray and Buttery of the Monkland Iron & Steel Company equipped their Calderbank Works to produce 220 tons of malleable iron per week; William Dixon—who had abandoned his tentative efforts to make bar iron at St. Rollox—built forty-two puddling furnaces capable of a similar output at Govan; Colin Dunlop and John Wilson erected plant with a weekly capacity of about 300 tons at Dundyvan; and the Mossend Iron Company set up puddling furnaces and rolling mills at Holytown. Scotland's output of malleable iron was thereby increased from substantially less than 5,000 tons in 1830 to around 35,000 tons in 1845, by which time the demand for railway iron was emphasizing Scotland's lag in this branch of the industry. In England and South Wales, ironmasters were using large quantities of Scottish pig, mixed with other brands, in the rolling mills, and some even went abroad to be manufactured into rails in the mills of Pennsylvania. Yet in Scotland, in 1845, the malleable iron works were consuming the output of only about fifteen of the country's 94 furnaces in blast, and the *Mining Journal* expressed

[13] Campbell, 'Early Malleable Iron Production', p. 24; and see Hamilton, *Industrial Revolution*, pp. 166–7.

surprise 'that this branch of the trade has hitherto escaped the attention of our capitalists'.[14]

Belatedly recognizing the advantages to be gained by providing a local market for Scottish pig iron, a number of prominent ironmasters co-operated to establish three joint-stock companies expressly for the manufacture of malleable iron: the West of Scotland Malleable Iron Company, whose prospectus was issued during the last stages of the railway boom, the East of Scotland Malleable Iron Company, formed in the Autumn of 1846, and the Ayrshire Malleable Iron Company, floated a year later. The founders and major shareholders of each of these companies were the leading ironmasters in each area, and it was hoped that the various concerns that they represented would supply the pig required for the manufacture of the malleable iron.

Apparently well organized and soundly based, all of these companies might have been expected to fulfil the hopes invitingly set down in their prospectuses. Yet within five years they had all failed. The Ayrshire Malleable Iron Company was the first to go. Having merged with Alexander Alison's Blair Iron Company in 1847 to form the Ayrshire Iron Company in order to produce an integrated iron works of the type conspicuously lacking in Scotland, the new concern became a victim of the commercial crisis of 1847–8, when Alison became bankrupt as a result of railway speculation and the company crashed with him. The West of Scotland Company, after a most encouraging start, soon outran its capital resources and thereby placed itself in such a vulnerable position that when prices fell and interest rates rose it was able neither to conduct the business without loss nor to raise sufficient additional capital to weather the depression following the collapse of the railway boom. Thus, in 1850, a number of the leading shareholders (the Bairds, the Houldsworths, and Merry & Cunninghame) insisted on the dissolution of the company. It is hardly surprising that the third concern, the least favourably placed and much smaller East of Scotland Malleable Iron Company, shared a similar fate. The enthusiasm which generated its flotation was soon dissipated

[14] Campbell, 'Early Malleable Iron Production', p. 26, quoting the *Mining Journal*, 20 Dec. 1845.

by consistent losses, and when its calls on shareholders met with no response, this company too petered out.

These three abortive attempts by Scottish ironmasters to emulate the malleable ironmasters in England and Wales were unfortunately timed. The decision to invest in forges was taken when prices were high and construction costs heavier than anticipated, and production of malleable iron for the market first became possible during the period of low prices following the end of the railway boom. In the meantime, each company had saddled itself with a burden of debt which proved insupportable in the unfavourable conditions of the late forties. An additional difficulty was that Scotch pig iron was basically unsuitable for use in the forge, however admirable it may have been in the foundry.

But less important than the reasons for these discouraging failures is their possible influence on the future course of the Scottish iron and steel industry. It has been argued that the collapse of these early attempts by the leading Scottish ironmasters to manufacture malleable iron on a large scale seems to have convinced many of them to concentrate on smelting, a branch of the industry in which vast profits were still to be made, and to lose interest in subsequent processes. If this argument is sound, it would partially account for the marked lack of enthusiasm with which the great Scottish ironmasters greeted the coming of cheap steel. It may well be that 'these early failures had a much more lasting adverse effect on the Scottish economy than has generally been credited to them'.[15]

These fiascos, far from heralding the end of malleable iron manufacture in Scotland, simply retarded the advent of large-scale fully-integrated works. Nevertheless, the fortunes of several existing puddlers did little to inspire confidence in this branch of the industry. Following the death of their founder, John Wilson, in 1851, the Dundyvan works began to decline and were eventually closed and demolished in the early eighteen-sixties. Part of the William Dixon's Govan plant was taken down in 1856–7 to make way for his vain attempt to manufacture Bessemer steel from Scottish pig iron. And even the well-

---

[15] Campbell, 'Early Malleable Iron Production', p. 33. Campbell's article forms the basis of the previous five paragraphs.

equipped Monkland Iron & Steel Company ran into difficulties
in the late fifties and was obliged to suspend payment in 1861.[16]
Other concerns, however, were more successful. The Mossend
Iron Company's plant at Holytown, near Coatbridge, which
when erected in 1840–1 comprised eight puddling and two
reheating furnaces, grew steadily under the ownership of the
energetic Neilson family, and its early specialization in the production of plates and angles for the expanding iron shipbuilding
industry, paved the way to prosperity in the malleable iron
trade.[17] Similar products were soon being made by the Glasgow
Iron Company, established in 1845, at its works at St. Rollox
and Motherwell. Beginning with the manufacture of merchant
bar and railway iron, this firm soon diversified its output to
include ship and boiler plates, hoop-iron, angle- and tee-iron,
and other sections. By the mid-seventies the Glasgow Iron Company, operating 102 pudddling furnaces, numerous reheating
furnaces, and four rolling mills, was the largest maker of
puddled iron in Scotland, its capacity having meanwhile been
considerably expanded by its purchase of the Motherwell works
of the ill-fated West of Scotland Malleable Iron Company.[18]

But lesser firms too could maintain themselves by supplying
the needs of the iron shipbuilders, and new and aggressive
entrepreneurs saw in the rapidly expanding Clydeside market
potentially profitable opportunities for the establishment of independent units catering for specialized demands. Already by
the late 1840s a number of concerns had gained a wide reputation for their skill in the production of heavy forgings, and
'when malleable iron came into general use for the hulls and
decking of ships as well as for crankshafts and other engine
parts, a number of the largest Scottish forgers found it worth
while to set up their own malleable iron departments so they
could at once undertake the production of puddled iron needed

[16] Gibson, 'Economic History of the Scottish Iron and Steel Industry', p.
412; T. R. Miller, *The Monkland Tradition* (London: Nelson, 1958), p. 34.
[17] A. Miller, *Rise and Progress of Coatbridge*, pp. 120–1; St. John V. Day, 'The
Iron and Steel Industries', in British Association, *Notices of Some of the Principal
Manufactures of the West of Scotland* (Glasgow, 1876), pp. 55–6; T. R. Miller,
The Monkland Tradition, p. 32.
[18] Day, 'The Iron and Steel Industries', pp. 49–51; George Thomson (ed.),
The County of Lanark (*The Third Statistical Account of Scotland*, vol. viii) (Glas-
gow: Collins, 1960), pp. 51–5.

10   *Prelude*

for their large forgings and enter new fields by adding ship plates to their other products'.[19] Foremost of such enterprising concerns in the eighteen-fifties were the Parkhead and Lancefield Forges. Both Parkhead, established by the eminent shipbuilders and marine engineers, Robert Napier and Sons, and at this period controlled by William Rigby, Napier's son-in-law, and his partner, William Beardmore, and Lancefield, erected by David Napier in 1821, were equipped with steam hammers, cranes, rolling mills, lathes, slotting and boring machines, and numerous puddling, scrap, and forge furnaces. At these works, and at the less well-known Dennystoun Forge, opened at Dumbarton in 1855, large marine fittings were produced in the form of crank- and propeller-shafts, stern and rudder posts, and high grade boiler and ship plates. Armour plates of a quality acceptable to the Admiralty and foreign governments were rolled at Parkhead in the sixties, but inadequate transport facilities inhibited the full development of this promising trade until the mid-seventies.[20]

The success of these large plants added substantially to the productive capacity of the Scottish malleable iron trade, and such achievements as the forging of the stern-frame and the propeller- and crank-shaft of Brunel's *Great Eastern* at Lancefield, and the production of similar heavy and intricate forgings for the early Cunard, P. & O., and Royal Mail steamers and for warships of the Royal Navy, enhanced the reputation of this branch of the Scottish iron industry at home and abroad. With favourable market conditions created by the growing demand of both the Clyde shipyards and the expanding engineering concerns of Glasgow and the West of Scotland, who contracted to build bridges, gasometers and gaswork plant, floating docks and iron landing and promenade piers throughout the world, the time was opportune for lesser firms to establish themselves. Large numbers of small entrepreneurs, frequently grouped into partnerships, promoted a series of small malleable iron works,

[19] Gibson, 'Economic History of the Scottish Iron and Steel Industry', p. 416.
[20] Ibid., p. 417; C. Ferdinand Kohn, *Iron and Steel Manufacture* (Glasgow and Edinburgh: William Mackenzie, 1869), pp. 152–6; Day, 'The Iron and Steel Industries', pp. 51–3; David Bremner, *The Industries of Scotland. Their Rise, Progress and Present Condition* (Edinburgh: A. & C. Black, 1869), pp. 54–7.

many of them on or near the banks of the Monkland Canal, close to the blast furnaces of Coatbridge from which they obtained their raw materials.[21] Hence, the historian of Coatbridge records the erection of the Merryston Iron Works by Hugh Martin and Sons in 1851, with six puddling and two heating furnaces capable of a monthly production of about 300 tons of finished malleable iron; the Coats, by Thomas Jackson in 1854, with approximately double this capacity; the Rochsolloch Iron Works, near Coatdyke, in 1858; the Drumpeller, by Henderson and Dimmock in 1859; and John Spencer's Phoenix Iron Works, with furnaces, engines, and machinery capable of producing about 250 tons of finished iron monthly, which was laid down in 1861, the same year as Colville and Gray's Clifton Iron Works.[22]

Ronald's Forge, established in 1840 by Alexander Ronald to produce forge-castings for axles, wheel tyres, and forged iron boiler plates, was also converted to a malleable iron works about this time and renamed the 'Phoenix'. Shortly afterwards it passed into the hands of Thomas Ellis & Son, who changed the name yet again to the North British Iron Works. In 1866–7 James Miller bought the plant in order to set up his sons, Alexander and Thomas, in the iron industry. The firm then became known as Alexander & Thomas Miller, Globe Iron Works.[23] Such frequent changes of ownership and name were not uncommon, and this example serves to illustrate the difficulties of tracing the early histories of the numerous small concerns which burgeoned in and around Coatbridge in the mid-nineteenth century. In the same area, there were also established tube works, foundries, tin plate works, and bolt and rivet manufacturers.[24] Further west, near the junction of the Monkland and Forth and Clyde Canals

[21] Gibson, 'Economic History of the Scottish Iron and Steel Industry', p. 416.
[22] A. Miller, *Rise and Progress of Coatbridge*, pp. 60–1, 64; see also G. Thomson, *The County of Lanark*, p. 51, and Day, 'The Iron and Steel Industries', p. 50. It is worth noting that in discussing these small malleable iron companies, Gibson, 'Economic History', p. 419, comments on the unreliability of the information relating to them. The official returns—the *Mineral Statistics*—contain numerous inaccuracies and omissions, and there is no consistency among the contemporary accounts and the later authorities concerning the spelling either of the names of the works or their proprietors.
[23] T. R. Miller, *The Monkland Tradition*, p. 36.
[24] A. Miller, *Rise and Progress of Coatbridge*, p. 60.

and in Glasgow itself, similar developments were taking place, though with a lesser degree of concentration. Among the many firms that sprang up on the outskirts of Glasgow were the Blochairn Iron Works at St. Rollox, established in the fifties, and the Clyde Galvanising Company at Mavisbank, which was founded in 1852.

The Blochairn Iron Company, soon in financial difficulties resulting from the 1857 crisis, operated on a small scale until 1867, when it passed into the hands of Hanney & Sons. Robert Hanney, who held a substantial interest in the Barrow Hematite Steel Company Ltd.—a firm created by the fusion of the Barrow Steel Company, Schneider & Hanney, and the Furness Railway in 1865–6—saw that the development of the Blochairn works might provide a means of breaking into the rapidly expanding market for malleable iron created by the pressing demands of the booming Clyde shipbuilders, who, for want of local capacity, were being forced to place large orders for high quality ship plates with leading English firms in Sheffield and Cleveland. The Hanneys immediately embarked on a costly development programme, erecting large banks of puddling furnaces on both sides of the Monkland Canal, together with elaborate finishing equipment, so that by the seventies the Blochairn works had become the largest establishment of its kind in Scotland, with a weekly capacity of around 15,000 tons.[25]

The other concern, which exemplifies the secondary metal trades being established in the Glasgow area in the buoyant decades of the mid-nineteenth century, had a more typically modest beginning. Founded by the firm of McGavin & Thompson, the Clyde Galvanising Company laid down plant at Mavisbank in 1852. Five years later an interest in the company was acquired by Richard Smith. Smith, a manufacturing chemist, came to Glasgow in 1841 and, in a chemical works erected in the grounds of his country house at Tradeston, began the manufacture of the basic acids (sulphuric, hydrochloric, and nitric),

[25] Gibson, 'Economic History', pp. 423–4; John Hodge, *Workman's Cottage to Windsor Castle* (London: Sampson Low, Marston, & Co., 1931), pp. 12–13; J. D. Marshall, *Furness and the Industrial Revolution* (Barrow-in-Furness: Barrow-in-Furness Library and Museum Committee, 1958), pp. 205, 220–2, 252–3, 342–3, 414; C. Erickson, *British Industrialists: Steel and Hosiery, 1850–1950* (Cambridge: C.U.P., 1959), pp. 152–3; Day, 'The Iron and Steel Industries', p. 49.

together with such products as nitrate of iron and chloride of iron and a number of tin compounds. Smith believed that by purchasing an interest in the Clyde Galvanising Company he would secure an outlet for the products of his chemical works. One of the customers of the Mavisbank firm was Charles McLean, a prominent merchant and ironfounder, and in 1861 he joined with Richard Smith to purchase the Clyde Galvanising Company as a going concern for the sum of £5,000. The partnership of Smith and McLean was short-lived, being terminated in 1865 by the death of Richard Smith. Charles McLean continued to direct the firm until 1867 when it passed into the hands of Charles C. Jardine, who appointed Edward Yates, an engineer at the time in the employ of P. & W. MacLellan, as works manager in 1869. With Yates in charge of the manufacturing processes and with greatly enhanced capital funds provided by Jardine (£24,000) and his cousin, Charles C. Mowbray (£9,000), who was brought in as a junior partner in 1870, this firm too began rapidly to expand, taking over a small sheet rolling and bar mill at Gartcosh in northern Lanarkshire in 1872.[26]

[26] *Colvilles' Magazine*, Summer 1961, pp. 2–3. This article was prepared by the author on the basis of the early manuscript records of Smith & McLean and Richard Smith & Co. See also Kenneth Warren, *The British Iron and Steel Sheet Industry since 1840* (London: Bell, 1970), p. 34, and George Beard, obituary notice, *Journal of the West of Scotland Iron and Steel Institute*, xx (1912–13), 241.

II

The Foundation of David Colville & Sons, 1861

This then was the economic environment in which David Colville embarked on his career as an ironmaster. The time was propitious. By taking advantage of the steadily increasing and massive demands of the Clyde shipbuilders, who required at least 10 cwt of malleable iron for every ton of shipping launched,[1] and the expanding needs of the complex of engineering concerns growing up in the West of Scotland, an energetic man might make his fortune.

David Colville was born in Campbeltown in the Mull of Kintyre in 1813. His first acquaintance with the world of business was gained in assisting his father in the ownership and control of a number of coasting vessels and in the management of various small-scale local enterprises, of which the most important was the distilling of whisky. Some time in the late forties, however, he decided to strike out on his own, perhaps because his strong temperance convictions made the family interest in distilling abhorrent to him, perhaps because of the realization that, as the youngest in a family of eleven, his scope would be somewhat limited by the prior claims of his elders.[2] Endowed with some capital by his father, he moved to Glasgow and set up as a provision merchant in the Trongate. The business was modestly successful but it became apparent to this able and ambitious man that the buoyant iron trade presented much greater opportunities. Within a few years of his migration to Glasgow he had resolved to abandon dealing in tea and coffee, his principal activity, and to embark on the manufacture of

---

[1] British Iron Trade Association, Annual Report, 1879, p. 83; and see T. J. Byres, 'The Scottish Economy during the "Great Depression", 1873–1896, with Special Reference to the Heavy Industries of the South-West' (University of Glasgow, B.Litt. thesis, 1962), i. 322–3.

[2] Gibson, 'Economic History', pp. 425–6; David Colville & Sons Ltd., Souvenir booklet, *Jubilee of David Colville & Sons Ltd., 1871–1921* (hereinafter cited D.C. & S., *Jubilee* booklet).

malleable iron, despite his complete ignorance of ironmaking processes.

Accordingly David Colville began to mobilize his capital and seek a partner possessing the necessary technical expertise. Such a partner he found in Thomas Gray, a skilled operative who had risen to be manager of a small malleable iron works at Coatbridge and who was anxious to establish himself as an independent ironmaster. The assets of the two men were complementary. By joining together, commercial acumen could be wedded to technical knowledge, and so on 11 June 1861, in the offices of Smith and Wright, a formal contract of co-partnery was signed which established the firm of Colville and Gray for carrying on the business of malleable iron manufactures. The 'capital stock' of the new company was to be £6,500, of which £5,000 was to be provided by David Colville. Initially, Gray was to advance only £1,000 and pay in the remainder when he found it convenient to do so, presumably out of his share of the expected profits, amounting to one-quarter of the whole. The partnership was to last for fifteen years. David Colville was to 'take charge of the Books and cash transactions' of the concern and Thomas Gray was to be responsible for 'the working department of the Co-partnery'. Each partner was entitled to an annual salary of £150, of which Thomas Gray's 'shall begin to run' from the date of the contract, and David Colville's when manufacturing actually started, since he was still engaged in winding up his provision business. Each partner was to be allowed 5 per cent interest on his capital balance, which could be augmented by the retention of profits in the business or by additional advances. In the event of any dispute between the partners, Walter MacLellan, iron merchant and manufacturer, and partner in the Glasgow firm of P. & W. MacLellan, was to be sole arbiter.[3]

The legal preliminaries completed, a suitable site was obtained on the Coats estate having ready access to both the

---

[3] Clydesmuir Papers: 'Contract of Co-partnery between David Colville, Junior, and Thomas Gray, 1861'. This contract is reproduced in Gibson, 'Economic History', Appendix I. The firm of P. & W. MacLellan was established in 1811 as an ironmongery business. Manufacturing started in 1840 when a smithy was opened in the Old Wynd, Trongate, Glasgow. Cunnison and Gilfillan, *The City of Glasgow*, p. 226.

Monkland Canal and the Monkland and Kirkintilloch Railway, and adjacent to the Atlas Foundry, the North British, Phoenix, and Coats Iron Works, and the Caledonian and Britannia Tube Works.[4] Thomas Gray immediately set about the task of superintending the erection of the plant. Ten puddling and three heating furnaces were put up together with ancillary machinery. The Clifton Iron Works was soon in commission. The manufacture of malleable iron began in February 1862 and the capacity of the plant was estimated to be some 600 tons of finished malleable iron per month.[5] The works had cost some £7,000, 'clear evidence of the relatively limited capital then required by entrepreneurs ready to enter the industry on a small-scale'.[6]

Very little is known of the Clifton Iron Works but they were evidently successful. Profits were not withdrawn from the company but were used to increase the number of furnaces and steadily improve the finishing machinery. Relations between the two partners, however, began to deteriorate in the late sixties. The reasons for this are obscure but it is said that David Colville increasingly objected to Gray's drinking habits, though whether this was because the efficiency of the works was adversely affected or whether the objection stemmed solely from Colville's deep-rooted antipathy towards alcoholic drink is unknown. At all events, by 1870 the two men had resolved to dissolve their partnership, though neither was willing to surrender his claim to the ownership of the prosperous and well-equipped works. It was therefore decided that each of them would submit sealed tenders to the arbiter, the highest bidder to buy out his partner and so become sole owner. David Colville, eager to obtain control of the Clifton Works and confident that his financial resources would permit him to out-bid Gray, submitted a most generous offer. He was therefore mortified to learn that when Mr. Peter MacLellan had opened the sealed envelopes Gray had put in a much higher bid. Unknown to his partner, Gray had received financial backing from Mr. Wylie, a licenced grocer and ex-Provost of Hamilton, to whom the Clifton Works represented both a sound investment and a

---

[4] A. Miller, *Rise and Progress of Coatbridge*, pp. 60–2.
[5] Ibid., p. 61.
[6] Gibson, 'Economic History', p. 427.

going concern in which his sons, William and John, could become interested.[7]

Unexpectedly provided with ample funds from the sale of his three-fourths share in the company, and incomparably more experienced in the iron trade than he had been a decade earlier, David Colville, now nearly sixty years of age, determined to set up another malleable iron works entirely under his own control, in the management of which he would be assisted by his two elder sons, John and Archibald, born in 1852 and 1854, respectively. John Colville had already gained a knowledge of iron manufacture at the Clifton works and Archibald had received commercial training in Glasgow.[8]

The first task was to find a suitable site. There is little doubt that a works could have been located in the Coatbridge district, but characteristically this possibility was rejected, as the great industrial development of the area made it impossible to obtain an area large enough to permit of future expansion. While engaged in the search for a location that met this basic condition, David Colville was approached by the agents of the Hamiltons of Dalzell, who were then anxious to develop their estates around the small burgh. Colville was offered land at Motherwell on very favourable terms. Situated between the Clyde and the Calder, on a coalfield, with abundant supplies of pig iron available in the neighbourhood, near the Caledonian Railway's Clydesdale Junction line (opened in 1849) which provided direct access to Glasgow, and with ample room for subsequent expansion, this site admirably fulfilled Colville's requirements. He seized the opportunity and, on 22 August 1871, was granted two feus by Lord Hamilton of Dalzell: one, of just over 10 acres, 'for the purpose of erecting a Malleable Iron

[7] Colvilles Ltd., 'Reply to a Question by Mr. J. C. Carr', undated document among the Colville Archives; T. R. Miller, *The Monkland Tradition*, p. 62. Mr. Peter MacLellan succeeded his brother as sole arbiter under the partnership contract. Wylie eventually bought out Gray and became senior partner in the company in association with his sons. The Clifton Iron Works were incorporated into the Scottish Iron & Steel Company in 1912. T. R. Miller, op. cit., pp. 56–8 and see below, pp. 99–100. Dr. Charlotte Erickson has revealed the 'interesting and significant fact that no other business, apart from industries closely related to iron and steel, provided so many links with steel investment as food, drink and fuel distribution'. Erickson, *British Industralists*, p. 15.

[8] D.C. & S., *Jubilee* booklet, p. 1.

Works', at the rate of £10 per acre, and another, at the same rate, of just over half an acre, 'for a pumping station on the River Calder with the right to take water from the river'. As an added inducement Lord Hamilton agreed to permit Colville to lay water pipes through the land between the two feus and to pay £500 towards the cost of doing so. Furthermore, he bound himself 'not to work the minerals under the two pieces of land' and promised 'that if the law of entail be altered so as to enable him to do so he [would] also bind himself his heirs and successors not to work them'. In return, Colville was to erect buildings on the site to the value of 25 years' feu-duty and forbid the sale of spirits therein, a clause which could hardly have proved onerous to him.[9]

Even before the formal granting of the feus the erection of the plant had already begun, work on the foundations having been started on 17 February 1871.[10] It is said that David Colville and his sons not only personally supervised every item of the construction but even shared in the physical labour involved.[11] Despite many difficulties encountered in obtaining the necessary equipment, building materials, and skilled manpower, brought about by the boom conditions prevailing in the economy generally and in the iron and engineering industries in particular, and hindered by unfavourable weather, the Dalzell Works were practically completed and ready to begin operations in the spring of 1872. Substantially larger than the average Coatbridge malleable iron works, the basic plant consisted of twenty puddling furnaces, two ball furnaces, and two mills, one of 18 inches and the other of 12 inches. The puddling furnaces were put into commission on 18 March 1872, and rolling began two weeks later. The works occupied barely one-tenth of the land feued and employed about two hundred men. The firm of David Colville and Sons had begun: from these comparatively modest beginnings the company was eventually to dominate the Scottish iron and steel industry.

[9] D.C. & S., Register of Documents, Nos. 1 and 2: Feu-Charters granted by John Glencairn Carter Hamilton of Dalzell to David Colville, 22 Aug. 1871; No. 3: Letter from John Glencairn Carter Hamilton of Dalzell to David Colville, 22 Aug. 1871.
[10] *Iron and Coal Trades Review* (hereinafter cited *I.C.T.R.*), v. 42, cited by Gibson, 'Economic History', p. 428.
[11] D.C. & S., *Jubilee* booklet, p. 1.

III

The Establishment of the Scottish Steel Industry

1 The Reception of the Bessemer Process

Small quantities of sword steel had been made in Highland bloomeries in the sixteenth century; blister and shear steel by the Cadells at Cramond in the 1770s, and high carbon steel by Aitken, Fleming, and McGregor, and their successors at the Monkland Iron and Steel Works, Francis Murray and John Buttery, during the Napoleonic Wars. Production of crucible steel continued in the West of Scotland even after the Monkland Company had abandoned its manufacture in favour of malleable iron, but the toolmakers and forgemasters who used the process operated on a very small scale. Under these conditions, steel was expensive and its use highly specialized.[1]

The era of cheap steel began only some five or six years before David Colville and Thomas Gray established the Clifton Iron Works. In 1855 Henry Bessemer had taken out the first of his many patents for improvements in the manufacture of iron and steel. Within a few months he had devised 'a method of converting pig iron into steel . . . by forcing into and among the particles of a mass of molten iron currents of air'.[2] In August 1856 Bessemer was persuaded to read a paper concerning this process to the mechanical section of the British Association, meeting that year at Cheltenham. Subsequent events were to reveal that much costly developmental work was necessary before the process described by Bessemer was of general applicability, but it

[1] I. F. Gibson, 'The Establishment of the Scottish Steel Industry', *Scottish Journal of Political Economy*, (1958), 22–3. See also A. Miller, *Rise and Progress of Coatbridge*, pp. 107–8; Hamilton, *Industrial Revolution*, p. 165.
[2] Henry Bessemer, 'Improvements in the Manufacture of Iron and Steel', Pat. No. 356, 12 Feb. 1856. Percy, *Metallurgy*, pp. 815–16, provides an eye-witness account of Bessemer's spectacular experiments at Baxter House during which the converter was devised. See also J. C. Carr and W. Taplin, *A History of the British Steel Industry* (Oxford: Blackwell, 1962), pp. 19–20.

is from the epoch-making Cheltenham paper that the birth of the modern steel industry is usually dated.

The interest aroused by Bessemer's discovery was intense, and within a few weeks enterprising iron makers throughout the country were conducting trials of the new process. In Scotland the first recorded experiments were made by Thomas Jackson of the Coats Iron Works.[3] Having had his attention 'drawn to the subject by drawings in the *Illustrated News*', Jackson rigged up a primitive apparatus based on 'these drawings and the accompanying letterpress'.

> ... An old locomotive cylinder attached to the engine of the turning-lathe served as a blast-cylinder. The foundry cupola and Bessemer furnace were lengths of old boiler tube lined with brick and erected close together. The charges varied from 5 to 10 cwts; the pig iron used, Eglington, No. 1, in those days a very superior brand. From a charge of this iron drawn off in the state of refined metal, which was then puddled and rolled, and afterwards re-rolled into merchant bars, the result was B-best iron ... Analysed by Dr. Penny, Professor of Chemistry in the Andersonian University, Glasgow, [it was discovered] that the substance was chemically pure iron, but commercially valueless, being what the workmen usually style burnt iron. It seemed to be impossible to hit the point when the iron could be run from the converter to produce good malleable iron.[4]

This and similar experiments by Jackson and other far-sighted ironmasters all failed: in every case useless 'red-short' metal was the result. Among those who were prepared to conduct more systematic and elaborate trials was the vigorous proprietor of the Govan Iron Works, William Dixon, whose company was one of the most powerful concerns in the industry. Having paid a royalty of £10,000 for the use of the patent in Scotland, 'a small, but ... complete plant was erected under the personal supervision of the inventor and operations conducted for some time, Scotch iron being used in the "converter". Owing to the amount of phosphorus present the

[3] The Coats Iron Works were to become the largest of the Coatbridge malleable iron works and the scene of many experiments 'for economising the cost of production and for minimising labour' in the production of iron. See Day, 'The Iron and Steel Industries', p. 54.

[4] James Riley, 'The Rise and Progress of the Scotch Steel Trade', *Journal of the Iron and Steel Industry*, 1885, pp. 395–6, quoting remarks made to him by Thomas Jackson. A paper describing the experiment was read by William Cockey to the Philosophical Society of Glasgow on 11 Feb. 1857. See *Proceedings of the Philosophical Society of Glasgow*, iv (1857), 81–2.

resulting steel was unsatisfactory, and as this could not
be reduced when dealing with their own pig iron, the licensees
abandoned the process, Mr. Bessemer returning the sum
paid by them for the licence.'[5] It was widely believed that
where Dixon had failed others could hardly hope to succeed.
Scottish interest in the process rapidly evaporated and, as in
England and elsewhere, Bessemer was denounced as a wild
enthusiast.[6]

Bessemer persevered, however, and gradually overcame the
problems revealed by these disappointing failures. Continuous
and costly experiments made it clear that his process was practicable only when phosphorus-free pig was employed, and that
the addition of manganese greatly improved the quality of
metal produced in his converter.[7] He demonstrated that these
discoveries made his process fully practicable and commercially
viable by setting up his own steel works at Sheffield in 1858.
Within a few years he was making handsome profits. Interest
was reawakened. The great Sheffield firms of John Brown and
Charles Cammell took up the process; in Lancashire the Bolton
Iron & Steel Company installed converters; and in South
Wales, works were soon under erection at Dowlais, Ebbw Vale,
and Blaenavon.[8]

In Scotland the great ironmasters remained sceptical.
'Doubtless the unsuitability of the pig iron of the district had

[5] Riley, 'Rise and Progress of the Scotch Steel Trade', pp. 396–7.

[6] Carr and Taplin, *History of the British Steel Industry*, p. 21. An interesting
account of the technical difficulties encountered by the pioneers of the Bessemer process is that by Ernest F. Lang, 'The Old Lancashire Steel Company', *Memoirs and Proceedings of the Manchester Literary and Philosophical Society*,
lxxxii (1937–8), 82–7.

[7] Carr and Taplin, *History of the British Steel Industry*, pp. 20–4. Bessemer
induced a Glasgow firm, William Henderson & Co., to produce a ferro-
manganese alloy (containing 25–30 per cent manganese) at the Phoenix
Foundry for the use of himself and his licensees. Kohn, *Iron and Steel Manufacture*, pp. 76, 108–10; and see John Ferguson, 'Chemical Manufactures of
Glasgow and the West of Scotland', in British Association, *Notices of Some of
the Principal Manufactures of the West of Scotland* (Glasgow, 1876), pp. 224–5;
S. G. Checkland, *The Mines of Tharsis* (London: Allen & Unwin, 1967), pp.
94–5.

[8] Carr and Taplin, *History of the British Steel Industry*, pp. 27–8. See also K.
Warren, 'The Sheffield Rail Trade, 1861–1930: An Episode in the Locational
History of the British Steel Industry', *Transactions and Papers of the Institute
of British Geographers*, Publication No. 34 (1964), pp. 132 ff.

a good deal to do with the want of interest,'[9] and the contemporary well-being of the pig iron trade was not conducive to further possibly costly experimentation that might involve a diminution of pig iron capacity.[10] An additional factor *may* have been a slackening of the entrepreneurial energy that characterized the activities of the Scottish ironmasters earlier in their careers.[11] Whatever the reasons, only one firm in Scotland, J. M. Rowan & Company, was prepared to make further trials of the Bessemer Process. John M. Rowan, a forgemaster, who was described as possessing 'great energy and determination of character in the adaptation of anything new in engineering or applied science',[12] had equipped his Atlas Works as a general engineering and millwright's establishment and had gained a European reputation for the manufacture of railway wheels and axles.[13] For this purpose he had installed elaborate machinery built to his own designs, including several steam hammers, bending machines, a vertical tyre mill, and a whole range of ingenious supplementary plant, much of which represented improvements on existing machinery.[14] This talented engineer and far-sighted businessman—a rare combination—quickly appreciated that tyres and axles of steel would eventually supersede those of iron on the world's railways and, seeking to assure himself of a ready and relatively cheap supply of the metal, obtained a license from Bessemer in December 1861. He then 'commenced the erection of what were then considered to be

[9] Riley, 'Rise and Progress of the Scotch Steel Trade', p. 398. Lang makes the point that the lack of technical knowledge which 'was to blame for many of [the] initial uncertainties with Bessemer Steel ... were seized upon and magnified in every possible manner by ... powerful vested interests'—those who had invested large sums in the manufacture of wrought iron and who feared its supersession by mild steel ('The Old Lancashire Steel Co.', p. 90). It may be surmised that among such vested interests were many of the malleable iron manufacturers of West-Central Scotland.

[10] It will be recalled that Dixon had dismantled part of his Govan plant to provide a site for his abortive experiments with Bessemer's process. See above, p. 8.

[11] Byres, 'The Scottish Economy', pp. 751–910; a shortened version of Byres's argument may be found in P. L. Payne (ed.), *Studies in Scottish Business History* (London: Cass, 1967), pp. 250–96. See below, pp. 48–55.

[12] F. H. Thompson, 'The Workshops of Glasgow', *Proceedings of the Philosophical Society of Glasgow*, vi (1865–8), 145.

[13] Kohn, *Iron and Steel Manufacture*, p. 84.

[14] Rowan's steam hammer principle is illustrated and described in detail by Kohn, ibid., p. 166 and Plate 40, opposite p. 165.

the most perfect Bessemer works, having two 3-ton converters, and the necessary apparatus for working them on an economical and practical scale'.[15] Despite the fact that the pig iron used at the Atlas Works was chiefly Cumberland Hematite, considerable difficulties were experienced in steel-making, and it was fully two years before satisfactory results were obtained.[16] Even in 1866 the proprietor's son, who supervised this branch of the Atlas Works, was still complaining that 'when cut in large blocks, the Bessemer steel [was] rather uncertain in its quality'. Nevertheless, fine steel was produced 'at best iron prices' and made into tyres, axles, and forgings which rapidly gained 'a very high character' in European markets.[17] However, Rowan's ingot output rarely exceeded 40 tons a month—'principally [for] want of demand'[18]—and the converters were in operation only once or twice a week. Perhaps it was this limited demand for Bessemer steel, despite its much publicized *potential* value in shipbuilding, that dissuaded other Scottish entrepreneurs from taking up the process. Although the high phosphoric content of local pig iron militated against its adoption on the part of the well-established Scottish ironmasters, there seems to have been a paucity of enterprise in the West of Scotland at this time.

Meanwhile, the Atlas Works continued to flourish, and in the boom period of the early seventies was fully engaged in the manufacture of general steel forgings, steel tyres for locomotives and railway rolling stock, steel rails for Russia (a market which the firm long served), and work sub-contracted to it by Krupp's of Essen. But even before reaping the rewards of their earlier efforts in this way Rowan's, characteristically progressive, were among the very first companies to conduct trials with Siemens's open-hearth process in the late sixties.[19] It was perhaps for this reason that the Atlas Works were to be the scene of experiments

[15] Riley, 'Rise and Progress', p. 397. Detailed drawings of the Bessemer plant erected by Rowan are given by Kohn, *Iron and Steel Manufacture*, pp. 78–81, Plates 21–5, between pp. 78–9. A description of the works in operation is given by F. H. Thompson, 'The Workshops of Glasgow', pp. 145–6.
[16] F. H. Thompson, 'Workshops of Glasgow', p. 145; Riley, 'Rise and Progress', p. 397.
[17] F. H. Thompson, 'Workshops of Glasgow', pp. 146–7.
[18] Riley, 'Rise and Progress', p. 397.
[19] Kohn, *Iron and Steel Manufacture*, p. 131.

that culminated in the establishment of the first of the great Scottish steel companies.

2 The Siemens Process and the Formation of the Steel Company of Scotland

In 1866 the Tharsis Sulphur & Copper Company was promoted by a group of businessmen headed by John and Charles Tennant, proprietors of the famous chemical works at St. Rollox founded by Tennant, Knox, & Company at the beginning of the century.[20] Being major manufacturers of sulphuric acid, Charles Tennant, Sons, & Company were, by the late fifties, importing vast quantities of Spanish cupriferous pyrites which had recently become the major source of oil of vitriol.[21] Initially this ore was purchased from Mason, Barry, & Company's mines on the river Guadiana, but such was the demand for sulphuric acid that it was readily apparent that supplies from their San Domingo mine might profitably be supplemented. At the instigation of the Tennants, the Tharsis Company was founded to work the mines at Huelva and these soon became the major source of Spanish pyrites.[22] On delivery at St. Rollox, the ore was first roasted to drive off the sulphur for conversion into sulphuric acid and then the residue, rich in copper and iron, was treated to obtain the copper.[23] This second operation took place at either the Tharsis Company's own Garngad Works or those of the British Metal Extracting Company Ltd., a firm created to work several of the patents taken out by the talented chemist, William Henderson, the manufacturer of ferro-manganese for Bessemer's process. As a by-product of these processes, the Tharsis Company accumulated many thousands of tons of slag, known as 'Blue Billy' or 'Purple Ore', which was, in fact, 'an oxide of iron purified from all its admixtures'.[24]

[20] The history of the Tharsis Sulphur & Copper Company has been told by S. G. Checkland, *The Mines of Tharsis*.

[21] See J. Mactear, 'On the Sources of Sulphur used in the Manufacture of Oil of Vitriol or Sulphuric Acid', *Proceedings of the Philosophical Society of Glasgow*, vi (1865–8), 339.

[22] Ibid., p. 342; Checkland, *The Mines of Tharsis*, pp. 92–3, 102–10.

[23] Ferguson, 'Chemical Manufactures', pp. 228–9. See also Checkland, *The Mines of Tharsis*, pp. 95–6.

[24] Kohn, *Iron and Steel Manufacture*, pp. 108–10.

As early as 1866, the indefatigable William Henderson was conducting experiments for the conversion of this 'ore' into steel in a furnace specially designed for him by Charles William Siemens, who was convinced that 'the direct conversion of iron ore into malleable iron and steel would ultimately be accomplished', thereby rendering the blast furnace, in which raw materials became 'contaminated', completely redundant. Henderson's experiments came to nothing, but Siemens persevered. He designed and built new furnaces for the 'direct process' at his 'Sample Steel Works' in Birmingham, took out patents covering the invention in 1867, 1868, and 1869, and explained his ideas to the Chemical Society of London in May, 1868.[25] There seemed to be every reason to expect ultimate success and, undaunted by Henderson's failure, Charles Tennant approached Siemens to discover whether the mounting stock of 'Blue Billy' 'might be converted into steel in a modified form of the Siemens furnace'. Siemens believed that the prospects were favourable and he personally supervised the erection of a direct rotary furnace at J. M. Rowan's Atlas Works in order to conduct trials with the 'purple ore'. Although the results were apparently adverse, it is clear that 'the opinion was strongly entertained that success would be achieved both practically and economically'.[26]

Tennant and his closest colleagues persisted. They determined to organize a company for the manufacture of steel on a large scale in a works designed by Siemens, whose technical guidance was secured by his appointment as consulting engineer.[27] Envisaged as a private company with a capital of £100,000 in twenty shares of £5,000 each, by January 1872 it had been decided to incorporate the new concern as a public company. Thus, on 9 February 1872, the Steel Company of Scotland came formally into existence, and with its creation the modern Scottish steel industry was born. The majority of the original body of twenty-eight shareholders of the Steel Company of Scotland were men already closely connected with

[25] Ibid., pp. 130–1; W. Pole, *The Life of Sir William Siemens* (London: John Murray, 1888), pp. 148–51, 196–7.

[26] Riley, 'Rise and Progress', pp. 398–9.

[27] Steel Company of Scotland (hereinafter S.C. of S.), Letter Book I, Michael Scott to C. W. Siemens, 3 Oct. 1872.

the chemical, iron and heavy engineering industries of the West
of Scotland. The leading spirits in the enterprise were members
of the board of the Tharsis Company: Charles and John Tennant, Archibald S. Schaw, the Glasgow merchant, David and
John Wilson, Archibald Arrol, the construction engineer, and
John Moffat, an eminent civil engineer.[28] The only outsider on
the original board of the Steel Company was Henry Dübs, proprietor of the Glasgow Locomotive Works. From the very beginning the firm was controlled and managed by men with
diverse interests. With the benefit of hindsight later critics of
the company have commented that in comparison with David
Colville & Sons the Steel Company of Scotland was never run
by steel men, only by men who had an interest in steel.[29]

The promoters showed great energy in establishing the company. Even before the formal incorporation, detailed surveys
were being made of numerous possible sites to determine the
best location for a large steel works. The first recorded letter
of Michael Scott, appointed Acting Manager of the company
on 1 August 1871 and Interim Secretary on 14 February 1872,
was to C. W. Siemens requesting details of the quantity of
imported ore, imported or native pig iron, coal, and dross required to produce one ton of steel, so that accurate calculations
could be made of the comparative costs of materials and carriage for operations at Coatbridge and at Ardrossan on the Ayrshire coast.[30] The problem of choosing the correct site was of
critical importance. Siemens was taken on tours of inspection
of all the locations which Scott's own investigations and reports
by landowners' agents had suggested were at all feasible. It was
imperative that 70–100 acres be obtained and 'that the ground
should be solid—no coal or other workings underneath at least
30 acres out of the 100—that the surface should be level or
nearly so—that there should be a plentiful supply of water.
That there should be communication by rail with coal and iron
districts and shipping ports. That large steel works should not

[28] S.C. of S., Minute Book I, 14 Feb. 1872, and Tharsis Sulphur & Copper
Co., Minute Book I, 17 Apr. 1872.
[29] This point will be developed later (see below, pp. 62–5); it is a
comment repeatedly made to the author by officials and past employees of
firms within the Colville group.
[30] S.C. of S., Letter Book I, Michael Scott to C. W. Siemens, 4 Aug. 1871.

be considered a nuisance, and that there should be dwellings for workmen within a mile or two.'[31]

Initially, it appeared that these criteria might best be met by a site on the Ayrshire coast, but when the calculations necessary to determine the best of the possible alternatives were already far advanced, James Dunlop, a nephew of Colin Dunlop of the Clyde Iron Works and himself a substantial coal- and ironmaster, suggested that it might be worth while to examine 'the ground ... at Hallside', belonging to the Duke of Hamilton.[32] Only a few miles to the south-east of Glasgow, and favourably situated in relation to the Tharsis Works, the River Clyde, and to suppliers of coal and pig iron, the potentialities of this site clearly deserved careful assessment. Having made exhaustive inquiries, Scott was soon convinced that Hallside met the various criteria in almost every respect. Only one serious problem remained before the site could unreservedly be recommended to the board: the underlying coal would have to be purchased to prevent it from being worked. This was 'a serious matter for the cost would be almost £750 per acre for coal alone',[33] but, after Siemens had determined the minimum area that must remain perfectly solid, James Dunlop, the coal lessee, agreed that his claim for coal would not exceed £3,120.[34] Thus, when the Caledonian Railway was persuaded to grant especially favourable rates for the company, it was decided to purchase the site for £14,000.[35]

Work began almost immediately. A month after the company was formed, the railway had to put a workmen's carriage on trains from Glasgow, and within another month a special workers' train was required.[36] Large quantities of bricks, sleepers, and rails were ordered locally, and numerous contracts arranged for earthworks, buildings, and the supply of heavy equipment and machine tools. A chemist, John Robinson, of Clifton College, Bristol, was appointed after being interviewed by Siemens, on condition that 'before joining [he gave] some

---

[31] Ibid., Michael Scott to A. Finnie, 7 Sept. 1871.
[32] Ibid., M. Scott to S. Robertson, 30 Aug. 1871.
[33] Ibid., Michael Scott to C. W. Siemens, 23 Sept. 1871.
[34] Ibid., Michael Scott to C. W. Siemens, 10 Oct. 1871.
[35] S.C. of S., Minute Book I, 4 Sept. 1872.
[36] S.C. of S., Letter Book I, Michael Scott to Caledonian Railway Co., 4 Mar. 1872, 2 Apr. 1872.

time to the acquirement of a special knowledge of the particular branch of chemistry connected with the company's business' by attendance at the School of Mines in London. In the next two months, a forge manager, Joseph Rodger, formerly of the Barrow Steel Works, and a resident manager, Charles Blayden, also joined the staff.[37]

The surviving correspondence of this period creates an impression of immense drive and energy. Yet no major decision was made without the prior approval of Siemens himself, who, in addition to being responsible for the original designs of the plant (which provided for the erection of four hammer furnaces, two steel-melting furnaces, two ingot furnaces, and ancillary workshops), was constantly consulted on the analysis of the raw materials that would be necessary when production commenced, the choice of contractors for furnace ironwork and machinery, and the selection of senior officials. Every effort was made to hasten the erection of the works. The agreement between the company and William Lancaster, who had been engaged to construct the railway sidings, the main drains, and the reservoir, was revoked on the grounds that he had failed to meet the time clauses. Michael Scott repeatedly urged brick-makers to speed deliveries. Even Siemens was chided for delays in supplying specifications. Unforeseen difficulties were encountered 'in procuring men', but the major factor in retarding progress was 'the exceptionally unfavourable weather'. So continuously wet through the year that 'outdoor work was often at a standstill'. by September Scott was reluctantly forced to advise some suppliers of heavy plant that the works 'were not yet sufficiently advanced to allow of our taking delivery'.[38]

Nevertheless, by taking advantage of every hour of dry weather, and by continuous appeals to drainage and building contractors to engage more men in order to expedite the works, significant headway was made. Although the directors were able to report this progress to the first General Meeting of the Company held in September 1872, they made 'no attempt to

[37] Ibid., Michael Scott to John Robinson, 3 Apr. 1872, 5 Apr. 1872; Michael Scott to Joseph Rodger, 15 May 1872; Michael Scott to Moncrieff, Paterson, Forbes, and Barr, 27 June 1872.

[38] Ibid., Michael Scott to C. W. Siemens, 8 Aug. 1872; Michael Scott to I. Ireland, Manchester, 26 Sept. 1872; Michael Scott to Claridge, North, & Co., Bilston, 7 Aug. 1872, 12 Sept. 1872.

conceal the fact that the advanced price of labour and materials [had greatly augmented] the cost of the undertaking'. Despite the fact that this would necessitate an increase in the firm's capital, the directors were unanimous in their belief that the construction of the works should be pushed ahead at all possible speed. By the end of August 1872, the contractual obligations of the company totalled approximately £97,000. The major items comprised £14,000 for land at Hallside; £12,000 for earthworks, roads, culverts, railway lines, and foundations for the shops and foundries; and £20,000 for a mill and smelting shop being constructed by W. E. Jackson of Newcastle-on-Tyne, who was also building retaining walls, boiler settings, chimneys, coal bunkers, and ore bins. Thwaits and Carbutt were to provide the mill engines and three eight-ton hammers (£6,500); Claridge, North, & Company, a 26-inch Rolling Mill (£2,400); William Arrol & Co., twelve steam boilers (£4,450); and various contractors, ironwork for ten Siemens furnaces and ten blocks of gas producers.[39] Significantly, an offer by the Tharsis Sulphur & Copper Company to supply 20,000 to 25,000 tons of 'purple ore' during 1873 at 22/6 per ton had already been accepted.[40]

Despite 'unpropitious weather' throughout the spring and summer of 1873, Scott's continuous pressure on contractors and staff brought results. The production of steel began in the autumn when four 6-ton Siemens furnaces fired by gas producers came into operation. By this time 'the whole of the extensive workshops, including the Foundry, Loam Mill, Smithy, Machine Shop, Carpenters' and Patternmakers' Shops, the offices, stores, and chemical laboratory' had been completed, and the directors were able to congratulate themselves that the company was 'now reaping the benefit in superior facilities and diminished cost of production. When the time arrives for extension, renewals, or repairs of the works, the possession of these workshops will enable the company to execute them economically and quickly, whilst in the event of an accident to the machinery—the patterns being on the spot—delay will be avoided in re-starting'. The shareholders were doubtless also

[39] S.C. of S., Minute Book I, 'Report of the Directors to the First General Meeting', 4 Sept. 1872.
[40] Ibid., 31 July 1872.

encouraged by the fact that shortly after steel production commenced, the 26-inch rolling mill was started and the manufacture of steel rails begun, the Caledonian Railway already having placed an order for 1,000 tons.[41]

As the directors had warned at the first General Meeting, the delays caused by the weather, the mounting cost of labour, plant, and raw materials, and the ambitious plans to lay-out and equip the extensive works to permit well-balanced growth in the future, soon exhausted the provisional capital of £105,000. In June 1873 a special resolution was passed to convert the 10,500 original shares, fully paid up, into 21,000 shares, of which £5 was deemed to have been paid, and to issue an additional 4,000 shares.[42] The directors had also arranged a loan of £20,000 at 4½ per cent from the trustees of William Dixon, on the security of a further 5½ acres of land purchased from the Duke of Hamilton, in order to build 110 workmen's houses, since it was becoming imperative to have 'the officers and men residing in the immediate vicinity of the works'. It was expected that rentals of 2s. 6d., 4s., and 6s. per week would return 10 per cent on the cost of the necessary buildings, roads, and drains.[43]

By the end of August 1873, £136,000 had already been spent, and the directors believed that 'the growing importance of the steel rail trade' justified further expansion.[44] But the boom, which had so enhanced the anticipated costs of both construction and operation, was about to collapse, and this, coupled with the contemporary sharp expansion of steel railmaking capacity in Britain and abroad, meant that although 'the cost of manufacture [was, within a year, to be] reduced to a point which contrasts favourable with that of any other steel rail works',[45] the company's steadily rising output could not readily be sold at remunerative prices.[46] Nor was the com-

[41] Ibid., 'Report of the Directors to the Second Annual General Meeting', 29 Oct. 1873.

[42] Ibid., 'Special General Meetings', 17 June 1873, 2 July 1873.

[43] Ibid., 25 Apr. 1873, 10 Sept. 1873.

[44] Ibid., 'Reports of the Directors to the Second Annual General Meeting', 29 Oct. 1873; Balance sheet of the Steel Company of Scotland, Ltd., 31 Aug. 1873.

[45] Ibid., 'Report of the Directors to the Third Annual General Meeting,' 27 Oct. 1874.

[46] The vicissitudes of the steel rail trade have been carefully examined by

pany able to improve its relative position by manufacturing pig iron more cheaply than the going market price by the direct reduction of 'Blue Billy' purchased from the Tharsis Company, the profitable utilization of which had been a prime motive in the establishment of the firm. Extensive trials of Siemens's revolving furnace, two of which were erected, were carried out during the closing months of 1874, and although 170 tons of excellent puddled ball iron was made 'from a mixture of half purple and half other ores', the cost of production was so high that the experiments were suspended in January 1875, and the furnaces dismantled.[47] Henceforth, the company relied conventionally on external supplies of pig iron and scrap to become a simple steel-melting and rolling concern.

Although the first full year's working had not been profitable—the balance sheet for 31 Aug. 1874 showed a loss of £27,000—it was felt that there was 'no cause for uneasiness regarding the future success of the company'. Eight steel-melting and eight heating furnaces were now in operation. The average weekly make of steel had progressively increased as the furnaces came into service, and production was running at the rate of about 18,000 tons per year, sufficient to supply half the quantity of steel capable of being handled by the heating furnaces, rail mill, and steam hammers with which the works had been equipped.

During the year ended 31 Aug. 1874, 8,400 tons of rails had been rolled, the bulk of them being delivered to the Caledonian, the Glasgow and South Western, and North British Railways. But such was 'the unfortunate state of the iron and steel rail

Dr. K. Warren, *The Sheffield Rail Trade*, pp. 131–57. The tremendous boom in this trade at the close of the sixties and early seventies is associated with feverish American railway construction which reached a peak in 1871. As a response, many British works were extended (John Brown & Co.'s Atlas Works, Charles Cammell & Co.'s Penistone Works, and Samuel Fox's Stocksbridge Works in the Sheffield area, and the Barrow Works which was more than doubled in capacity over the period 1869–74), and eight new works established, three of them being open-hearth works (in addition to the Steel Co. of Scotland's Hallside Works, there were those at Landore and Panteg in South Wales) and the others, Bessemer concerns, the most important being the West Cumberland Works at Workington. The Hallside Works came into production at the very same time that the steel rail trade collapsed: not until 1879 was there to be a marked revival.

[47] S.C. of S., Minute Book I, 'Report of the Directors to the Third Annual General Meeting', 27 Oct. 1874. Riley, 'Rise and Progress', p. 399.

trades',[48] that the directors proposed to diversify the company's output by going into the manufacture of plates, bars, forgings, and castings. So great was their confidence that these branches of business would prove profitable that eight additional melting furnaces were planned, thus increasing the annual output of steel to between 36,000 and 40,000 tons and reducing the cost of production. The construction of a merchant bar mill was begun, and experiments were made to ascertain the best and most economical method of casting. In the next three years a cogging mill was constructed (1875), a plate mill and annealing furnace laid down (1876), additional hammers and cranes erected for the production of light forgings (1875), and a steel foundry (1876) and a wheel-moulding machine installed, together with a whole range of ancillary equipment. By October 1877 the total expenditure on the works exceeded £220,000. This had necessitated a doubling of the firm's authorized capital to £500,000, and the issue of debenture bonds to the value of £100,000 in order to enable the directors to pay off advances from the Bank of Scotland.[49]

3 Steel and Shipbuilding

Whereas the timing of rail manufacture had been unfortunate for the Steel Company, these new plans were destined to come to fruition at a most auspicious period. In shipbuilding and engineering, 'iron had scarcely established supremacy over timber, when mild steel arrived to replace it'.[50] Steel for the construction of marine boilers was first used by the Admiralty in 1857. The results were far from satisfactory, and although a number of commercial steamships were fitted out with steel

[48] Ibid., 'Report of the Directors to the Third Annual General Meeting', 27 Oct. 1874.

[49] Ibid., 'Special General Meetings', 16 June 1874, 7 July 1874.

[50] D. S. Cormack, 'An Economic History of Shipbuilding and Marine Engineering (with Special Reference to the West of Scotland)' (University of Glasgow, Ph.D. thesis, 1929), p. 150. Professor Donald N. McCloskey's discussion of the substitution of steel for iron in shipbuilding is extremely valuable. See his study *Economic Maturity and Entrepreneurial Decline: British Iron and Steel, 1870–1913* (Cambridge, Mass.: Harvard U.P., 1973), pp. 46–54. It is interesting to compare McCloskey's arguments with the careful contemporary calculations of J. H. Biles, of J. & G. Thomson, Clydebank, 'Notes on Shipbuilding', *Engineering*, xl (1885), 264–5.

boilers at about the same time, the experiments failed to demonstrate any convincing superiority for this material. Later, it became clear that the failures that occurred were caused by imperfections in the Bessemer steel employed and by the lack of experience of the workmen in manipulating the new material. Both faults were eventually eradicated, the former largely by the advent of open-hearth steel—free of the embrittling impurity, nitrogen, which Bessemer steel contained as an inevitable consequence of blowing atmospheric air through the molten metal—and by the late seventies many prominent engineers and shipbuilders were wholeheartedly advocating the use of steel for marine purposes.

In the late fifties steel was successfully employed in constructing the hulls of a number of small or medium-sized vessels. One of the first—if not the very first—was the *Ma Robert* in which David Livingstone ascended the Zambezi River in 1858,[51] but it was not until Samuda Brothers and Money, Wigram, & Sons built five steel-hulled Dover Mail packets for the London, Chatham, and Dover Railway Company in 1860–61 that the doubts and suspicions of the shipbuilding industry began to ebb.[52] Only the substantially greater cost of steel compared with malleable iron militated against the more rapid substitution of the former for the latter, so convinced had the shipbuilders and engineers become of the 'greater rigidity, greater ductility and greater strength' of steel.[53] Indeed, when a deputation of naval architects visited Glasgow for the Naval and Marine Engineering Exhibition in 1881, 'they found a general feeling to prevail ... that the present use of steel, both for ships and boilers, was only limited by the existing powers of production',[54] and, presumably, by the consequent price differential in favour of iron.

[51] Cormack, 'Economic History of Shipbuilding', p. 151; and see A. C. Kirk, discussion in *Transactions of the Institution of Naval Architects*, xxi (1880), 219.

[52] J. R. Ravenhill, 'The Increased Use of Steel in Shipbuilding and Marine Engineering', *Trans. Inst. Nav. Arch.*, xxii (1881), 38–9.

[53] Benjamin Martell, discussing the paper by W. Parker 'On the Peculiarities of Behaviour of Steel Plates Supplied for the Boilers of the Imperial Russian Yacht *Livadia*', read at the 22nd Session of the Institute of Naval Architects, 6 Apr. 1881. *Trans. Inst. Nav. Arch.*, xxii (1881), 31. The prohibitive price of steel for private shipbuilders was emphasized by N. Barnaby, Chief Naval Architect of the Royal Navy, in 1875. See his paper 'On Iron and Steel for Shipbuilding', *Trans. Inst. Nav. Arch.*, xvi (1875), 131.

[54] Ravenhill, 'The Increased Use of Steel', p. 38.

Despite the fact that the price of steel plates fell from £20 per ton in 1876 to around £9 12s. 6d. in 1881, their cost to the shipbuilder was still about 50 per cent higher than iron plates, the price of which had fallen in comparable fashion.[55] Nevertheless, the use of steel was rapidly increasing. In 1878, when William Parker, the Chief Engineer Surveyor of Lloyd's Register, foresaw that mild steel would eventually replace iron in the construction of marine boilers,[56] he could hardly have expected that his prediction was to be fulfilled so quickly. Yet by the spring of 1881 no fewer than 1,100 steel boilers had been installed in steamships, representing a total weight of over 17,000 tons of mild steel.[57] More remarkable still was the use of steel in ship construction. In 1875 the Chief Naval Architect of the Royal Navy, Nathaniel Barnaby, after emphasizing 'the uncertainties and treacheries of Bessemer steel' had challenged the British steel manufacturers to produce a thoroughly reliable and homogeneous material which was capable of being worked up 'without fear and trembling'; to produce, in fact, the sort of steel that he had seen demonstrated in 1874 during a visit to L'Orient and Brest where the French were building warships of mild steel manufactured at Creusot and Terre-Noire.[58] The

---

[55] J. Price, 'On Iron and Steel as Constructive Materials for Ships', *Proceedings of the Institution of Mechanical Engineers*, 1881, p. 557; Riley, 'Rise and Progress': 'Prices of Steel Plates', Chart VI, between pp. 546 and 547.

[56] W. Parker, 'Use of Mild Steel for Marine Boilers', *Trans. Inst. Nav. Arch.*, xix (1878), 172–81.

[57] W. Parker, 'On the Peculiarities of Behaviour of Steel Plates', p. 12. J. R. Ravenhill, 'Increased Use of Steel', p. 41, gives the following figures of steamships fitted with boilers made either wholly or partially of steel:

	No. of steam vessels	Approx. tons of steel
1 May 1878–30 Apr. 1879	120	3,000
1 May 1879–30 Apr. 1880	160	4,000
1 May 1880–31 Mar. 1881	280	10,000

[58] N. Barnaby, 'On Iron and Steel for Shipbuilding', pp. 135–6. Lang's comments on this episode are extremely interesting. He implies that Barnaby was guilty of exaggerating the uncertainties of Bessemer steel in order to justify the prejudice and conservatism of the Admiralty and to divert public criticsm when the public discovered that the French government 'had built, or were building, four large ironclads with Bessemer steel'. See Lang, 'The Old Lancashire Steel Company', pp. 88–9. William Denny used Bessemer steel in the construction of several paddle steamers intended for blockade-running during the American Civil War. 'The material as then made was far from satisfactory, and its behaviour did not encourage us to extend its use.' W. Denny, 'On Steel in the Shipbuilding Yard', *Trans. Inst. Nav. Arch.*, xxi (1880), 185.

Landore Siemens-Steel Works rose to the challenge, and within a few months had produced a mild steel of such quality that in 1875 the Admiralty contracted to purchase from Landore the plates, angles, and beams 'for two armed despatch vessels, the *Iris* and *Mercury*, to be built at Pembroke Dockyard'.[59]

In the following year the Steel Company of Scotland was given its first Admiralty order for ship plates at a price of £17 10s. per ton,[60] and in 1877 John Elder & Company built two paddle steamers at Govan for service in the English Channel using steel plates and angles produced at Hallside. In 1878 James and George Thompson completed the steel paddle steamer *Columbia*,[61] and in 1879 William Denny, who had previously launched several small steel vessels, built the *Rotomahana* for the Union Steamship Company of New Zealand. This was the first ocean-going steamer to be built of mild steel; steel, moreover, manufactured by the Steel Company of Scotland.[62] Besides setting an example in the adoption of this material, William Denny became a leading protagonist of the use of mild steel. In papers read before various societies, 'he dealt in an effective and persuasive manner with existing misgivings on the score of safety and economy'.[63] In 1880 he addressed the Institution of Naval Architects on 'Steel in the Shipbuilding Yard', in which he described the experiences of his firm in using steel for ship construction and endeavoured to meet the remaining doubts concerning the reliability of the material for this purpose.[64] To support his argument he was able to cite the case of the *Rotomahana* which in January had 'struck a sunken rock with considerable force'. The only damage sustained was a severe indentation of her plates and considerable buckling of seven frames, all of which were able to be repaired within seventy-two hours, despite the fact that the worst damaged plate had to be removed, heated, and re-rolled. 'The experience has shown clearly', wrote the Manager of the Union Steamship

[59] J. Riley, 'On Steel for Shipbuilding as Supplied to the Royal Navy', *Trans. Inst. Nav. Arch.*, xvii (1876), 135–6.
[60] S.C. of S., Minute Book II, 10 Oct. 1876.
[61] The *Columbia* was also built of steel manufactured at Hallside. Riley, 'Rise and Progress', p. 400.
[62] 'Official Report of an Accident to the *Rotomahana*', pamphlet published by S.C. of S., *c.* 1880.
[63] A. B. Bruce, *The Life of William Denny* (London, 1888), p. 151.
[64] W. Denny, 'On Steel in the Shipbuilding Yard', pp. 185–207.

Company, 'the immense superiority of Steel over Iron. There is little doubt that, had the *Rotomahana* been of iron, such a rent would have been made in her that she would have filled in a few minutes . . . yet there did not appear one crack anywhere.'[65]

Denny's arguments, reinforced by his continued use of mild steel—in 1880 he built the *Buenos Ayrean*, of just over 4,000 tons, the first steel ship for transatlantic service[66]—convinced other shipbuilders of its immense value, and the widespread adoption of Siemens steel rapidly followed, especially as its price fell. This transition was particularly marked on the Clyde, where between 1879 and 1889 the proportion of steel-built vessels rose from 10·3 per cent to 97·2 per cent, a phenomenal development unequalled by any other shipbuilding area of Britain.[67] This large and growing demand for steel for shipbuilding was the critical factor in the creation and growth of the Scottish steel industry. Henceforth, the fortunes of the two industries were wedded indissolubly.[68]

4 The Steel Company of Scotland: The Years of Monopoly, 1873–1880

It was not altogether a coincidence that the Steel Company of Scotland paid its first dividend in 1879, the year in which plates and angles made at Hallside were used in building the *Rotomahana*. The accident to this vessel was given the widest publicity by the firm, and considerable emphasis given to those parts of the official report which mentioned 'the splendid ductile material' of which the steamer was constructed. The decision of the directors to lay down a plate mill in 1876 was both courageous and far-sighted, and their statement to the shareholders that 'steel plates . . . will soon, to a large extent—like

[65] 'Official Report of an Accident to the *Rotomahana*', part of which is reproduced as an appendix to the paper by William Denny, 'On Steel in the Shipbuilding Yard', pp. 206–7.

[66] D. Pollock, *Dictionary of the Clyde* (Glasgow, 1888), p. 107.

[67] Ibid., p. 264; Byres, 'The Scottish Economy', p. 775; A. M. Robb, 'Shipbuilding and Marine Engineering' in J. Cunnison and J. B. S. Gilfillan (eds.), *Glasgow*, p. 181. In 1885, Biles, 'Notes on Shipbuilding', p. 264, could see no reason 'why another iron cargo-carrying ship should be built upon the Clyde'.

[68] See below, pp. 147–50.

steel rails—supersede iron'[69] proved to be fully justified by subsequent events.

Nevertheless, before even twelve months had elapsed, the dangers of too great a dependence upon the shipbuilding industry were to be demonstrated. In 1877 and 1878, when the plate mill might have been expected to have been increasingly busy, the yards along the Clyde were all but paralysed by a depression in shipbuilding coupled with a series of bitter and lengthy strikes by the shipwrights.[70] So slack was demand for steel ship plates that in 1878 it was 'impossible to keep the plate mill fully employed, even when working single shift'.[71] Yet in that year too the solution to undue specialization was to be indicated, for it was during this depressed period that the company began 'the manufacture of heavy angles, of large tee-bulbs, and of tin plate bars, and ... entered into arrangements for working the Terre-Noire process of making steel castings'.[72]

The directors never lost faith that their company had a great future, and if 1878 was 'a depressing one in many respects',[73] one event took place which in retrospect may be seen to have immeasurably strengthened the company and contributed profoundly to its world-wide reputation. This was the appointment of James Riley as General Manager. Born in Halifax in 1840, the son of a porter, Riley was the one of the only two men of working-class origin to come to the fore as managers of limited companies in the 'innovating' period (1865–85) of the British steel industry.[74] He first went to work as a millwright in his native town without apparently serving an apprenticeship. He soon left Halifax for Middlesbrough, where eventually he became a foreman with Cochrane & Company. From there, at the age of 29, he went as manager to the Askam Iron Works at Barrow, where he became acquainted with Sir William

[69] S.C. of S., Minute Book II, 'Report to Fifth Annual General Meeting', 24 Oct. 1876.
[70] See Pollock, *Dictionary of the Clyde*, p. 263; Byres, 'The Scottish Economy', pp. 479–80.
[71] S.C. of S., Minute Book II, 'Report to the Seventh Annual General Meeting', 30 Oct. 1878.
[72] Riley, 'Rise and Progress', p. 400.
[73] Ibid.
[74] Charlotte Erickson, *British Industrialists*, pp. 13, 168–9. The other man was Richard Williams, a millwright's son, who became general manager of the Patent Shaft and Axletree Company at the age of 49.

Siemens, who subsequently appointed him blast-furnace manager at Landore, South Wales, the first works constructed to exploit the Siemens process. Within three years, during a period in which the works were experiencing grave difficulties, Riley had been appointed general manager at Landore. As mass production methods were increasingly adopted in its manufacture, Bessemer steel became progressively cheaper than open-hearth steel. Indeed, rails made of Siemens steel were fast being priced out of the market. It was recognized that the lengthy open-hearth process permitted more scope for quality control, but in 1875 neither makers nor potential buyers 'found much in actual results to justify its higher cost'.[75] Deprived of its major market—the manufacture of rails—the Landore Works seemed doomed to 'a lingering, miserable existence'.[76] It was imperative that alternative outlets be found for the company's products. Riley found the solution in the manufacture of special quality steel utilizing ferro-manganese, the employment of which was apparently better suited to the open-hearth furnace than to the converter.[77] It was steel made by this method which had so impressed Barnaby when he visited the French dockyards in October 1874,[78] and, indeed, it was French metallurgists who had first successfully used ferro-manganese, although, somewhat ironically, it was first manufactured commercially by the Glasgow chemist William Henderson, associated with the Tharsis Company![79] By adopting the Terre-Noire process, Riley saved the Landore Works from extinction. Plates and angles of 'the new material' for shipbuilding purposes and for boiler and bridge construction soon found a ready market.

Identical problems to those of Landore were confronting Hallside. Extremely well situated to exploit the potential market for Siemens steel among the Clydeside shipyards, the Steel

[75] Duncan Burn, *The Economic History of Steel Making, 1867–1939* (Cambridge: C.U.P., 1940), p. 51. Compare McCloskey, *Economic Maturity*, p. 49.

[76] James Riley, 'On Recent Improvements in the Method of Manufacture of Open-Hearth Steel', *Journal of the Iron and Steel Institute*, 1884, No. 2, pp. 443–4.

[77] Burn, *Economic History of Steel Making*, p. 54.

[78] Barnaby, 'On Iron and Steel for Shipbuilding', pp. 131–2, and *Trans. Inst. Nav. Arch.*, xvii (1876), 149.

[79] See above, p. 24; W. T. Jeans, *Creators of the Age of Steel* (London, 1884), pp. 65–6.

Company of Scotland's need for a manager of Riley's experience and ability led Siemens to recommend that he be appointed to fill the vacancy caused by Michael Scott's departure.[80] Hence Riley moved from South Wales to Scotland at the very time, as one Glasgow journal put it, when 'the fortunes of the concern required a man of mettle in every sense of the term'.[81]

Under Riley's vigorous leadership the Steel Company overcame its initial difficulties, and the plans and schemes initiated by the directors were pushed rapidly ahead. The company soon earned a very high reputation for the excellence of its boiler and ship plates, which were singled out for special mention by many eminent shipbuilders and engineers in papers delivered to the learned societies of the late seventies and eighties.[82] Such was the demand for the company's steel for shipbuilding, boilers, and bridge and construction work that by 1880 the plant at Hallside became 'quite inadequate to the business offered, and large orders [were], in consequence, placed in Iron which would have been placed in Steel had it been procurable'.[83] Although further improvements and extensions were made at Hallside 'by remodelling the [melting] shop and ... by largely increasing the capacity of the melting furnaces', demand continued to outrun the company's maximum output.[84] The directors made a bold decision. They determined to purchase the Blochairn Works, idle for the past six years, and move the plant to Hallside.[85]

Only nine years earlier, the Blochairn Works had been

---

[80] Michael Scott resigned in 1874. Until his replacement by James Riley, William Lorimer, Henry Dübs's partner at the Glasgow Locomotive Works, acted as General Manager.

[81] *The Bailie*, 23 Jan. 1884, which, in its profile of James Riley in the series 'Men You Know', provides a brief summary of Riley's early career.

[82] Innumerable instances could be cited, but taking the meetings of the Institution of Naval Architects held in 1881 as an example, boiler and ship plates made by the Steel Company were praised by, among others, William Parker, Sir Spencer Robinson ('[their] steel has never failed under any particulars'), A. C. Kirk, and M. Marc Berrier-Fontaine, *Trans. Inst. Nav. Arch.*, xxii (1881), 16, 32, 53, 88.

[83] S.C. of S., Volume of Printed Notices, p. 63, Letter to Shareholders, 14 Jan. 1880.

[84] Riley, 'On Recent Improvements', p. 444.

[85] S.C. of S., Minute Book III, 9 Dec. 1879, 17 Dec. 1879, 19 Dec. 1879; Letter to Shareholders, 14 Jan. 1880.

described as 'the most extensive and most complete finished Ironworks North of the Tweed', with 'scientific equipment [which]
bids fair to surpass every other finished Ironworks in the
Kingdom'.[86] In 1873, at the height of the boom, the Hannays,
owners of Blochairn since 1867 and responsible for its great
expansion, sold the works to a new company for the sum of
£377,020. They retained a major share in the firm, holding two
of the seven directorships. The managing director was the
nephew of James Beaumont Neilson, Walter Neilson of the
Mossend Iron Works. Neilson immediately condemned the gas
furnaces erected by the Hannays—the regenerator chambers
of which were subject to damp—and replaced them by the old
system of heating by the grate fire,[87] thus adding to the lavish
expenditure already incurred. This capital burden was exacerbated by the continuing high rates of wages. The costs of the
concern, coupled with heavy interest charges, raised the
expense of malleable iron production so greatly that sales fell
off and profits dwindled. The financial position of the firm was
already precarious when Colin Campbell, sole partner in the
firm of Wilson & Campbell, the Glasgow iron merchants, failed
for over a quarter of a million pounds. The Hannays and the
Blochairn Company had had extensive dealings with Campbell's firm and both were severely affected by his bankruptcy.
A few days later the Hannays themselves failed, and the
Blochairn Company was dragged down with them. Feverish
attempts to raise additional capital and keep the plant in operation proved unavailing, and for six years the works lay idle.[88]

Created at a cost conservatively estimated at £250,000, the
works were purchased by the Steel Company for the sum of
£60,000. A thorough examination was made of the plant by
James Riley, whose report convinced the directors that rather
than dismantle the works for removal to Hallside, as had originally been intended, it would be better to convert and re-equip
them for steel-making. It was calculated that this could be done

[86] Gibson, 'The Establishment of the Scottish Steel Industry', p. 30, n. 18,
and see his unpublished thesis, pp. 424–5. Compare this description with John
Hodge, *From Workman's Cottage to Windsor Castle*, pp. 12–13. Also, see above,
p. 12.
[87] Hodge, *Workman's Cottage to Windsor Castle*, pp. 12–13.
[88] The foregoing paragraph draws heavily on Gibson's thesis, pp. 424–5.
See also J. D. Marshall, *Furness and the Industrial Revolution*, pp. 342, 414.

for about £85,000, when Blochairn would be 'capable of turning out nearly an equal quantity of steel to that made at Hallside'.[89] The whole operation was to be financed by selling unissued shares at a premium, and it was believed that 'when both works [were] completed, their power of production [would] be sufficiently great to enable them to meet the probable demand for steel in this district for many years to come'.[90]

This prediction proved to be wildly inaccurate. The growing Scottish demand for steel was soon to outrun the capacity of the combined Hallside and Blochairn Works, estimated in 1880 to be 'not less than 80,000 tons of ingots per annum'.[91] The directors were, however, correct in believing that steel would eventually displace malleable iron in the heavy industries of the West of Scotland. The Scottish malleable iron-makers were becoming equally conscious of this probability, and the more far-sighted of them realized that 'they were faced with a direct choice between conversion to steel-making or eventual extinction'.[92] One of these firms was that established by David Colville who, soon after the erection of Hallside 'had sent his younger son to Newton [the alternative name for Hallside] to undergo a lengthy training and obtain by first-hand practical experience a thorough understanding of the processes employed'.[93] Thus, in 1880, the year in which the Steel Company doubled its capacity by purchasing Blochairn, David Colville, his Dalzell Iron Works now firmly established, decided to go into steel.

[89] S.C. of S., Letter to Shareholders, 14 Jan. 1880, p. 2.
[90] S.C. of S., Minute Book III, 'Report to the Ninth Annual General Meeting', 27 Oct. 1880.
[91] Ibid.
[92] Gibson, 'The Establishment of the Scottish Steel Industry', p. 34.
[93] D.C. & S., *Jubilee* booklet, p. 2.

PART II

Competition and maturity

IV

The Rise of Competitors, 1880–1895

1 The Malleable Iron Producers and the Ironmasters

At the same time as David Colville made his momentous decision to go into steel production, others also determined to follow the lead of the Steel Company of Scotland. Indeed, William Beardmore, owner of Parkhead Forge, had already made his move. In May 1879, when it was fast becoming clear that the shipbuilders would transfer their allegiance from malleable iron to steel (Lloyds issued its first set of steel rules in 1877), Beardmores began the construction of three 10-ton open-hearth furnaces and forced through their completion with such speed that the first cast steel was made less than four months later.[1] In the same year, John Williams & Co., a medium-sized malleable iron firm engaged principally in the production of sheets and plates, laid down three open-hearths at their Excelsior Iron Works at Wishaw. In 1880, when David Colville's plant was approaching completion,[2] William Beardmore added two more furnaces at Parkhead, and the Mossend Iron Company, a malleable iron firm which produced up to 50,000 tons of finished plate and bar iron each year for the shipyards, put down five open-hearths. The Neilsons, who largely controlled both Mossend and the Summerlee Iron Company, thereby moved into steel. In the next three years extensions to all the existing plants were made and, in addition, five other firms— four malleable iron-makers and one iron-founder—installed open-hearth furnaces and began to turn out rolled steel products and steel castings.[3] Within two years, the annual output of acid steel in Scotland had increased by over 250 per cent. By 1885—when total production exceeded 240,000 tons—some

---

[1] Riley, 'Rise and Progress', p. 401, described this as 'a feat which ... is almost unparalleled'.

[2] See below, pp. 55–7.

[3] Gibson, 'The Establishment of the Scottish Steel Industry', p. 34.

42 per cent of the British make of Siemens Steel was coming from 73 Scottish furnaces. These were operated by ten firms. In that year Merry & Cunninghame erected four 10-ton basic furnaces at Glengarnock, and in 1886 the Glasgow Iron Company laid down three 7-ton Bessemer converters at Wishaw.

Why did the malleable iron-makers not move into steel rather more quickly than they did? Why was it that the Steel Company of Scotland enjoyed a virtual monopoly throughout the seventies? In answer to the first question, Dr. I. F. Gibson[4] emphasizes first, that 'it was only natural, after the failure of the various attempts to work the Bessemer process in Scotland, and the initial difficulties encountered by the Steel Company of Scotland in introducing the manufacture of Siemens open hearth steel, that other firms in the district should hang back until such time as the practicability and profitability of the latter process had been clearly established'. Second, that 'the unsuitability of the pig iron made from local ores, which, in the early 1870s, still accounted for some 85 per cent of the charges of the Scottish blast-furnaces, meant that the introduction of steel-making tended to lag behind developments in those areas where a haematite pig iron was locally available'. Not until the Scottish ironmasters became more dependent on imported ores—a development which began to accelerate during the later half of the seventies with the rapid exhaustion of blackband ore and splint coal—were local supplies of pig iron made, largely from Spanish ore, suitable for the manufacture of acid steel.[5] Third, 'the general depression experienced throughout the iron trade of the world in the mid-1870s, a depression accentuated in Britain by the excess capacity which arose in the malleable iron trade as a result of the rapid growth of Bessemer steel production in England, naturally made Scottish malleable iron producers hesitant of embarking upon new and risky developments which of necessity involved heavy capital expenditure.'

Gibson's fourth, and most important, point is that initially the principal uses for Bessemer and open-hearth steels were in

---

[4] Ibid., pp. 32–4.
[5] See R. D. Corrins, 'William Baird & Company, Coal and Iron Masters, 1830–1914', pp. 109, 114. Bairds were producing hematite for steel-making at Gartsherrie in 1877 (after a false start in 1868) and at Eglinton in 1881.

the manufacture of rails and of high-grade tools and castings. But the Scottish puddlers had never been deeply involved in the manufacture of rails.[6] Their major market was provided by the demands of the iron shipbuilders. 'Thus so long as the use of steel was confined to high quality goods of the type made by the Sheffield firms and to the production of rails, Scottish firms had no real incentive to begin the manufacture of steel. To them the rise of the new English steel firms was reflected only indirectly in the increased competition which resulted from the entry of English and Welsh malleable iron producers displaced from the production of railway iron into the market for ship plates, angles, bars and other rolled products.'

Although it was imperative that the Scottish makers of malleable iron reduced their production costs if they were to escape the bankruptcies which were so common in England, as long as malleable iron retained its supremacy in ship- and bridge-building, they were under no great pressure to go into steel. Not until the Steel Company of Scotland was forced to diversify its output in the second half of the seventies, and seek to market rolled steel products among local consumers, did the malleable ironmakers of the West of Scotland become seriously alarmed. As Gibson puts it:

as soon as it became clear that steel could with advantage be used for boiler- and ship-plates, and that, because of rapidly rising furnace capacities and rapidly falling costs, the new material was bound to displace malleable iron in the shipbuilding and allied trades in the near future, the Scottish malleable iron firms mainly concerned with these markets were faced with a direct choice between conversion to steel-making or eventual extinction.

However convincing these arguments may be in elucidating the reasons for, and the timing of, the movement of the more far-sighted malleable iron producers into the steel trade, they fail to explain why the firms in the primary or blast-furnace section of the industry, although substantially larger and better endowed than the malleable iron-makers, stood aloof from the new developments. Even with the entry of Merry & Cunninghame and the Wishaw Iron Company, and the tangential integration effected by the Neilsons, who in large measure controlled the blast furnaces of the Summerlee Iron Company as

[6] This argument has subsequently been confirmed by Wray Vamplew. See his paper 'The Railways and the Iron Industry', pp. 45–7.

well as the open-hearth at Mossend, the old-established Scottish pig iron-makers seem to have been curiously reluctant to go into steel. Was there a failure of entrepreneurship? It is by no means certain that an unqualified affirmative answer can be given to this question. Once again, Dr. Gibson has addressed himself to the problem. He explains that

... in the middle and late 1870s, the Scottish smelting industry was passing through a period of very real strain. For while the general demand for pig iron had declined sharply from the boom levels of the early '70s, the Scottish smelters found their costs of production rising steadily, and this at a time when they had lost some of their main markets overseas and had to encounter very severe competition, first in England and Wales, and later even in the Scottish home market, from Cleveland pig iron selling at prices from 10 to 20 per cent below the Scottish level. These difficulties were accentuated by the fact that by the late 1870s most of the pioneers of the great expansion of the Scottish smelting industry had died or retired, leaving their firms in the hands of less able or less courageous men. Since most of the Scottish smelting firms had only a limited direct interest in the forge and foundry branches of the industry, they tended to concentrate on attempts to strengthen the position of the blast-furnace section and to leave the building of steel-furnaces to others.[7]

That Gibson's argument is essentially accurate is undeniable: this much is borne out by the statistics presented in Table 4.1, which reveal, *inter alia*, the significant impact that Cleveland pig iron was having on the Scottish home market.[8] But whether the Scottish smelters were culpable of entrepreneurial failure in not integrating forward into steel deserves further investigation.

The 'giant' of Scottish iron-making was William Baird & Company, a firm said to be producing about a quarter of Scottish pig iron output in 1882.[9] It was during the fifties that the seven Baird brothers gradually relinquished the active control of this great firm to others. Not to their own children, whom they brought up to be cultivated gentlefolk, but to their nephews Alexander Whitelaw, David Wallace, and William Weir, all of whom were admitted to the partnership between

    [7] 'The Establishment of the Scottish Steel Industry', p. 35.
    [8] On this subject, see H. W. Macrosty, *The Trust Movement in British Industry* (London: Longmans, 1907), pp. 57 ff.; Byres, 'The Scottish Economy', pp. 415–18; G. A. North, *Teesside's Economic Heritage* (Middlesbrough: County Council of Cleveland, 1975), pp. 17–29.
    [9] Macrosty, *The Trust Movement*, p. 58.

TABLE 4.1

Statistics of the Scottish Pig Iron Industry, 1870–1896

Year	(1) Output ('000 tons)	(2) Stocks 31 December ('000 tons)	(3) Sales ('000 tons)	(4) Exports as %age of (3)	(5) Mean price of G.M.B. warrants (per ton)	(6) Furnaces	(7) Av. no. in blast	(8) Imports of English pig iron ('000 tons)	(9) Col. (8) expressed as %age of Scottish output
1870	1,206	665	1,161	34	59·3	160	n.d.	110	9·1
1871	1,160	490	1,335	38	62·2	154	127	n.d.	—
1872	1,090	194	1,386	45	110·0	154	127	n.d.	—
1873	993	120	1,067	37	130·5	152	119	125	12·6
1874	806	96	830	36	99·0	157	96	200	24·8
1875	1,050	170	976	38	65·8	155	117	220	21·0
1876	1,103	363	910	33	58·5	154	116	285	25·8
1877	982	505	840	33	54·3	155	103	353	35·9
1878	902	679	728	32	48·4	154	90	325	36·0
1879	932	745	866	39	50·3	154	88	315	33·8
1880	1,049	739	1,055	42	54·5	152	106	335	31·9
1881	1,176	940	975	37	49·1	150	116	420	35·7
1882	1,126	836	1,230	35	50·3	148	108	345	30·6
1883	1,129	835	1,130	37	46·8	145	110	432	38·3
1884	988	821	1,002	32	42·2	145	95	369	37·3
1885	1,003	1,051	773	35	41·8	143	90	465	46·4
1886	936	1,183	804	28	39·9	141	83	410	43·8
1887	932	1,228	887	32	42·3	141	80	434	46·6
1888	1,028	1,244	1,012	24	39·9	140	84	427	41·5
1889	978	1,036	1,107	22	47·8	140	84	394	40·3
1890	737	613	1,221	19	49·5	140	66	n.d.	—
1891	674	580	707	n.d.	47·2	124	51	n.d.	—
1892	972	444	1,113	n.d.	41·8	125	77	n.d.	—
1893	793	381	846	n.d.	42·3	122	53	n.d.	—
1894	642	358	678	n.d.	42·7	122	45	n.d.	—
1895	1,049	480	974	n.d.	44·4	109	74	n.d.	—
1896	1,114	508	1,152	n.d.	46·8	109	80	n.d.	—

Source: T. J. Byres, 'The Scottish Economy during the "Great Depression", 1873–1896', pp. 574–81. (Cols. 1–4, 7–8 are based on the circulars of Wm. Connal & Co., Col. 5 on the *Mineral Statistics*.)

1860 and 1862. The most recent historian of the firm, Dr. R. D. Corrins, has characterized their leadership as 'unimaginative though not incompetent';[10] but this second generation was, in turn, succeeded by a group of men—Alexander Fleming, James Baird Thorneycroft, William Baird, Robert Angus, John Alexander, and Andrew Kirkwood McCosh—who 'represented the arrival in power of the professional bureaucrats who had been for some years past, gradually increasing the extent to which the running of the firm depended on them'.[11] This third generation all joined the partnership in February 1878 and, with the exception of J. B. Thorneycroft, none of them was related to the Bairds.

Is the history of William Baird & Company, then, a variant of the so-called Buddenbrooks syndrome? Apparently not. 'The [new] leaders of William Baird & Co., if anything, displayed greater initiative during the adverse years during the close of the century than had been shown by their predecessors during the mid-Victorian Golden Age.'[12] This they did by closing down unprofitable works and concentrating production of pig iron on the remaining sites, where the old furnaces were entirely replaced by more efficient ones situated in replanned works with the latest ancillary plant, much of it for the recovery of by-products. Coupled to this policy of doing supremely well what the firm had always done, they integrated not forwards but *backwards*. Not only were the Bairds 'among the first British companies to own ore mines in Northern Spain and the first to exploit supplies in the South of the country', but they became the largest concern in the Scottish coal industry, in which they were pioneers in the development and use of coal-cutting machines. 'They sank many new, deeper mines; they were the first in Scotland to manufacture briquettes and they led in the adoption of many of the new developments in coke manufacture.'[13]

Baird's increasing involvement in the coal industry was ex-

[10] R. D. Corrins, 'William Baird & Company, Coal and Iron Masters', p. 292. This thesis provides much of the information for this and the following paragraphs.
[11] Ibid., p. 294.
[12] Ibid., p. 304.
[13] Ibid., pp. 304–5.

tremely profitable, far more so than the making of pig iron, and in this they *may* have been typical of the majority, if not all, the Scottish ironmasters. Giving evidence before the Tariff Commission in 1904, 'Witness No. 3', almost certainly Andrew K. McCosh, managing director of William Baird & Company, drew special attention 'to the fact that the profits of Scottish ironmasters . . . were not all due to iron'. 'I find that of the income tax which our firm has paid during the past five years, 36·69 per cent was for profit on iron; 12·53 per cent for profit on by-products for the blast furnaces, and 50·78 per cent for profit on coal and other things . . . I believe those figures of percentages given will be something like a fair approximate average of the Scottish iron trade. A neighbouring ironmaster, a partner in one of our largest firms, told me that 55 per cent of their profits, assessed in the last five years, was profit on coal. The whole of the Scottish ironmasters as a body have increased their output of coal very considerably in recent years.'[14]

In the following year, 1905, the *Iron and Coal Trades Review*, commenting on the impression 'in the minds of a certain number of half-fledged economists . . . that if a man has any special ambition to become a Crœsus, he has only to embark on an iron-making career', drew attention to the fact that only seven iron and steel concerns of the thirty whose recent results were tabulated had achieved a 10 per cent dividend in 1904. 'One of them—the Harvey United Steel Company—is not a manufacturing concern at all. Others, again—including Guest, Keen & Company, the Coltness Iron Company, the Shotts Iron Company, the Consett Iron Company, and Merry and Cunninghame—have made their profits mainly through coal, and not as manufacturers . . . Manufacturing, indeed, has, so far as steel is concerned, been given up by the Summerlee and Mossend Company, at what must have been a very serious loss, because it was so difficult to carry on the business with profit, and yet they are shown as paying excellent average dividends over the last four years—again, of course, mainly founded on

[14] *Report of the Tariff Commission*, vol. i: *The Iron and Steel Trades* (London: published for the Tariff Commission by P. S. King, 1904), paragraphs 565, 569. Cf. Burn, *Economic History of Steel Making*, pp. 286–8.

TABLE 4.2

Scottish Pig Iron Producers, their Blast Furnaces in 1872 and 1900, and the Coal Mines they Owned and Operated in 1894

(1) Name of company	(2) Name and location of iron works		(3) Number of blast furnaces			(4) Number of coal mines owned, numbers employed, and size ranking, 1894		
			1872	1900 Owned	1900 In blast	Mines	Employees	Ranking
William Baird & Co.	Gartsherrie: Old Monkland, Nr. Coatbridge	L	16	12	12	39	7,424	1
Eglinton Iron Co.	Eglinton: Muirkirk	A	8	6	5			
	Lugar: Lugar	A	4	5	5			
	Muirkirk: Muirkirk	A	3	3	2			
	Portland: Portland	A	6	—				
Merry & Cunninghame Ltd./Glengarnock Iron & Steel Co.	Glengarnock: Kilbirnie	A	14	7	5	12	3,199	2
	Ardeer: Stevenston	A	5	5	3			
	Carnbroe: Bothwell	L	6	5	4			
William Dixon & Co.	Govan: Glasgow	L	5	6	5	7	2,148	7
	Calder: Old Monkland, Nr Coatbridge	L	8	6	6			
Coltness Iron Co.	Coltness: Cambusnethan, Nr. Wishaw	L	12	9	9			
Dalmellington Iron Co.	Dalmellington	A	8	6	5	25	2,952	3
	Calder Bank: Old Monkland, Nr. Coatbridge	A						
Monkland Iron & Steel Co.	Chapelhall: Old Monkland, Nr. Coatbridge	L	9	—	3	—	—	—
Robert Addie & Sons/Langloan Iron Co.	Langloan: Old Monkland, Nr. Coatbridge	L	8	5	3	5	1,705	11

Company	Works and location	Col. 2						Col. 4
Wilson & Co./Summerlee & Mossend Iron & Steel Co.	Summerlee Works: Old Monkland, Nr. Coatbridge	L	8	7	6	9	1,697	12
Shotts Iron Co.	Castlehill: Carluke	L	3	—	6 ⎫	n.d.	n.d.	
	Shotts	L	4	6	4 ⎭			
James Dunlop & Co.	Clyde Iron Works: Old Monkland, Nr. Coatbridge	L	6	5	4	6	1,362	15
Colin Dunlop & Co.	Quarter Iron Works: Hamilton	L	4	—	—	—	—	—
George Wilson & Co.	Kinniel Works: Borrowstonness	Lin	4	—	—	—	—	—
Lochgelly Iron Co.	Lochgelly	F	4	—	—	2	1,238	18
Carron Iron Co.	Carron, Nr. Falkirk	S	4	4	4	3	1,167	20
Glasgow Iron & Steel Co.	Wishaw: Cambusneathan, Nr. Wishaw	L	3	4	4	8	1,848	10
Others			2	—	—	396	54,619	
Total			154	101	86	512	79,359	

Notes and Sources: Col. (1) The Eglinton Iron Co. was the collective name for the Baird's operations in Ayrshire; of those concerns given two names, the second was that employed in 1900. The Coltness Iron Co. and the Dalmellington Iron Co. are grouped together because of their common ownership by the Houldsworth family interests.

Col. (2) The information on name and location is based largely on George Thomson (ed.), *The County of Lanark*, vol. viii of the *Third Statistical Account of Scotland* (Glasgow, 1960), p. 47, supplemented by Kenneth Warren, 'Locational Problems', Pt. I, *Scottish Geographical Magazine*, vol. lxxxi (Apr. 1965). L. indicates Lanarkshire; A. Ayrshire; F. the Kingdom of Fife; Lin. Linlithgow, and S. Stirlingshire.

Col. (3) Number of Furnaces owned in 1872: Report in the *North British Daily Mail*, 28 Dec. 1872, quoted by T. J. Byres, 'The Scottish Economy during the "Great Depression"', p. 370, supplemented by St. John V. Day, 'The Iron and Steel Industries', pp. 30–47, who gives the number of blast furnaces in Scotland in 1876 as 163, of which 116 were in blast (123 in blast in 1874). Number of furnaces owned and in blast in 1900: A. McLean (ed.), *Local Industries of Glasgow and the West of Scotland* (Glasgow, 1901), pp. 21–3.

Col. (4) The size ranking is by numbers employed. In 1894, there were in Scotland, 318 firms owning a total of 79,359 men. The figures are derived from a calculation by T. J. Byres, op. cit., pp. 391–2, based upon a Parliamentary Return, 'List of Mines in the United Kingdom for the year 1894'.

coal.'[15] Is this the answer to the conundrum? The ironmasters, having weighed up the relative merits and potential profitability of moving forward into steel or intensifying their backward linkages with coal, chose the latter path. In retrospect, they *may* have been wrong to do so;[16] there are so many unknown variables in the equation that it is currently impossible to say with certainty. But no one can deny the energy that was expended in following their chosen course. By the early nineties, approximately one-third of all Scottish colliers worked in mines owned by ironmasters, whose position in the industry was exceptionally important. Ranked by numbers of employees at the pits, ten of the largest twenty coal producers in Scotland, including the three largest concerns in the industry, were ironmasters (see Table 4.2). 'Most of them, in addition to meeting their own needs, sold in the open market. Indeed, "coal ousted iron from first place in the Coltness Iron Company's activities in the nineties"; though this was not a general phenomenon.'[17]

It was not that the great ironmasters completely ignored steel. By 1900, half of the largest ten iron-making concerns in Scotland were directly involved in steel production, but the effort was somewhat half-hearted. Of the five companies involved only two—Merry & Cunninghame and the Glasgow Iron & Steel Company—were fully integrated concerns. The other three (the Coltness Iron Company, James Dunlop & Company, and the Summerlee and Mossend Iron & Steel Company) possessed blast furnaces and steel works, but in different places.[18] To have integrated forward into steel with more conviction would evidently have utilized funds more profitably employed

[15] 'The Profits of the Iron and Steel Industry', *I.C.T.R.*, 1 Apr. 1905. H. W. Richardson and J. M. Bass have shown the great importance of backward integration—particularly into coal—in sustaining Consett's prosperity. See 'The Profitability of the Consett Iron Company before 1914', *Business History*, vii (1965), 81–2.

[16] In 1869, the seven largest Scottish concerns in mining coal were all iron producers. They were William Baird & Co., Merry & Cunninghame, William Dixon & Co., the Shotts Iron Company, the Glasgow Iron Co., James Dunlop & Co. and the Monkland Iron & Steel Co. See A. J. Youngson Brown, 'The Scots Coal Industry, 1854–1886' (University of Aberdeen, D.Litt. thesis, 1952), p. 97.

[17] Byres, 'The Scottish Economy,' p. 379, quoting J. L. Carvel, *The Coltness Iron Company* (Edinburgh, 1948), p. 61. See also Augustus Muir, *The Story of Shotts* (Edinburgh: Shotts Iron Co. Ltd., n.d. [*c.* 1953]), pp. 26ff.

[18] Byres, 'The Scottish Economy', p. 380.

in coal-getting. It is not impossible that the ironmasters realized more clearly than has hitherto been recognized that, as indigenous supplies of blackband ores and splint coal became increasingly scarce after 1870, the Scottish smelting industry was in irretrievable relative decline, and that if they were to go into steel it would have to be on the same basis as those who were currently making the running, the Steel Company of Scotland, William Beardmore & Company, and David Colville & Sons, that is, as melters of pig iron purchased at the lowest possible market price, with all the risks inseparably associated with such a course. They chose not to do so. They chose to postpone the inevitable curtailment of their iron-making activities by reducing costs by the adoption of by-product recovery plant and to intensify their efforts in the mining of coal. This was a branch of the heavy industries with which they had long been acquainted and in which they possessed heavy investments and enviable technical expertise. Who can blame them?

2 Colvilles Enter the Steel Trade

It is apparent that by the late seventies David Colville had little to lose by going into the production of steel. He decided to put down open-hearth furnaces. His instincts and experience told him that mild steel, manufactured by the Siemens Martin process, would enjoy the greater demand in the markets of Clydeside, and it was with this process that his son, David, had become fully conversant at Hallside. This decision made, site operations, the acquisition of the necessary licence from Siemens, and the search for additional capital proceeded simultaneously.

An insight into the progress of the work at Dalzell is provided by the Steel Works Erection Account Book opened in November 1879, the first entries in which concern the wages of drawing office staff, the purchase of plans, and the employment of labourers. Within a few weeks an agreement had been made between David Colville & Sons and James Smith Napier, a Glasgow iron merchant, whereby the latter loaned £33,000 to the Colvilles[19] specifically for the purpose

---

[19] At this time the partnership consisted of David Colville and his sons, John and Archibald, trading under the name 'David Colville'.

of establishing a steel works. This sum was equivalent to the total capital then employed in the business. In return, Napier was to receive a half-share in the net profits.[20] The arrangement was to run for ten years from 20 July 1880, when the loan was to be repaid.[21] Three weeks later, Charles William Siemens granted the firm a licence for the manufacture of steel under various of his patents or those assigned to him by the Martins. For this David Colville paid £100 down and agreed to pay a royalty of 2s. 6d. per ton on all merchantable articles produced by the Siemens Martin process during the terms of the patents.[22]

The way was now clear to erect the steel works. It was pushed on rapidly. In the first eighteen months some £50,000 had been expended. Of this sum about 10 per cent represented direct wage payments. Vast quantities of bricks, cement, lime, timber, pipes, tubes, bolts, castings, and rails were purchased in small lots from a great variety of suppliers, and many small contracts were made with joiners, bricklayers, and slaters. What is remarkable is the relatively small number of large individual capital expenditures and contracts. It is, in some ways, all very reminiscent of the earlier Industrial Revolution. A locomotive was purchased from Shearer & Pettigrew for £500 in March 1880, four steam boilers from A. & W. Smith & Co. for £1,750 in August, a ten-ton steam hammer from Robert Harvey & Co. for £1,300 in October, and unspecified 'machinery' from Turnbull, Grant & Co., to whom over £10,000 was paid between July 1880 and March 1881. A major contractor was Laidlaw, Sons, & Caine, who was paid £1,500 for roofing in May 1880. But in the Steel Works Erection Account Book these major items of expenditure were almost lost in innumerable small purchases, the majority of which involved sums below £30, and payments to dozens of tradesmen whose monthly accounts rarely exceeded £20.

[20] There were to be no deductions for interest on the existing capital although 5 per cent interest was to be allowed on any further capital contributed by the Colvilles, who were to receive £1,000 per annum as salary for their personal management of the business.

[21] David Colville & Sons, 'Agreement between James Smith Napier and David Colville', 22 Jan. 1880.

[22] D. C. & S., 'Licence Granted by Charles William Siemens to David Colville to use Patents for the Manufacture of Steel by the Siemens Martin Process at Dalzell Iron Works, Motherwell, North Britain', 13 Feb. 1880.

By this means, under the close supervision of David Colville, jun., there were erected at Dalzell five Siemens open-hearth furnaces, each of ten tons capacity, and a steam hammer, plate mill, and shearing plant. It was always intended that the works should concentrate on the manufacture of ship and boiler plates. The first melt of steel was made in 1881 and by the end of the year 12,524 tons of ingots had been produced.[23] 'Dalzell Steel' rapidly gained a wide reputation both at home and abroad. It is said that the first plates rolled in the United States were made from slabs supplied by Dalzell and that the first

TABLE 4.3

The Steel/Iron Price Ratio and the Share of Steel Tonnage in Scottish Shipbuilding, 1880–1890

Year	Price of steel ship plates ÷ price of iron ship plates	Share of steel in net tons of ships built in Scotland
1880	1·43	0·15
1881	1·48	0·14
1882	1·39	0·25
1883	1·36	0·31
1884	1·34	0·44
1885	1·21	0·39
1886	1·24	0·62
1887	1·18	0·75
1888	1·06	0·91
1889	1·06	0·96
1890	1·06	0·96

Source: D. N. McCloskey, *Economic Maturity and Entrepreneurial Decline*, p. 51.

Atlantic liner constructed in Germany was built entirely of steel manufactured by David Colville & Sons.[24] Be that as it may, there is no question that the Dalzell steel works could hardly have been commissioned at a more auspicious time. It was during the eighties when mild steel drove wrought iron from the Clydeside ship yards. This substitution may be ascribed partly to quality differences but mainly to price. It was a period when the price of open-hearth ship plates relative to wrought iron

[23] D. C. & S., *Jubilee* booklet, pp. 3–4, 8.
[24] Ibid., p. 4.

ship plates fell sharply, and by the end of the decade steel was overwhelmingly dominant (Table 4.3). Furthermore, such was the very high tonnage of ship launchings during the first part of the decade that the demand for plates and angles from the Clyde yards could readily absorb—though at a diminished price—the greatly enhanced output of Scottish mild steel. The principal statistical series are given in Table 4.4.

Any doubts which may have lingered in the minds of the Colville family were swept away by the reception given to steel plates of their manufacture and by the almost feverish ship-

TABLE 4.4

Scottish Production of Acid Steel, Price of Scottish Steel Ship Plates, and Clyde Steam Ship Launchings, 1880–1895

Year	(1) Scottish production of acid steel ingots (tons)	(2) Price of Scottish steel ship plates (in shillings per long ton)	(3) Tonnage of steam ships launched on the Clyde
1880	84,500	254	226,891
1881	166,200	222	292,175
1882	213,000	221	314,737
1883	222,000	200	347,434
1884	213,887	175	228,906
1885	241,074	144	92,940
1886	244,900	139	113,238
1887	334,314	136	149,840
1888	442,936	129	221,511
1889	437,605	156	258,506
1890	481,668	165	270,299
1891	478,602[a]	132	222,098
1892	458,568	124	163,176
1893	443,013	112	169,707
1894	433,166	114	261,524
1895	505,850	105	304,146

Notes and Sources: Col. (1): M. L. Simpson, 'Steel Works—A Twenty-One Years' Review', *Journal of the West of Scotland Iron and Steel Institute*, xxx (1913–14), 56.

[a] For the year 1891 the figure given is that of acid and basic ingot tonnage. No separate records exist to determine the tonnage of basic ingots, but it is unlikely to have exceeded 3,000–4,000 tons.

Col. (2): McCloskey, *Economic Maturity and Entrepreneurial Decline*, pp. 135–6, based on J. Riley, 'Rise and Progress of the Scotch Steel Trade' (1880–2) and *I.C.T.R.* (1883–95). See McCloskey's observations, op. cit., p. 138.

Col. (3): J. Cunnison and J. B. S. Gilfillan (eds.), *Glasgow*, p. 839. Cf. Table 4.3 above.

building activity on the Clyde. Hardly had the Dalzell steel mill been commissioned than it was decided to enlarge it. In November 1882, James Smith Napier, who had already loaned the Colvilles £33,000 under the agreement of January 1880, advanced a further £23,000, a sum expected to cover about half the costs of the proposed extensions.[25] By the end of 1883, a further 15 acres of land had been feued from Lord Hamilton of Dalzell,[26] and the total expenditure under the 'Steel Works Erection Account' exceeded £120,000. Thereafter, the pace of investment slowed down. Although nearly £20,000 was expended in 1888, in the ten years following 1883 the average annual sum spent on the steel works was only half this figure. At the termination of the agreement with James Smith Napier, the total expenditure on the steel works was about £215,000.

3 The Steel Company of Scotland: The Pioneer Weakens

While newcomers like David Colville and William Beardmore strove to establish their steel works, the Steel Company of Scotland pushed confidently on. Having in 1880 purchased Blochairn for £60,000, they anticipated investing a further £85,000 to bring its future steel capacity to a level roughly comparable to that of Hallside, where massive plant extensions and improvements were already under way.[27] These were designed to raise the annual productive capacity of the original works to not less than 80,000 tons in order to exploit the burgeoning demand for ship plates, bridge-building angles, and plates for land and marine boilers. A notable addition to the plant— which in 1880 comprised a large open-hearth steel melting shop, cogging and forge hammers, and rail, plate, bar, and

[25] D. C. & S., 'Supplementary Agreement between James Smith Napier and David Colville', 15/16 Nov. 1882. The loan was to be on the same terms as the earlier agreement, the total sum of £56,000 to be repaid on 20 July 1893.

[26] 'Feu-Charter granted by John Glencairn Carter Hamilton of Dalzell to ... the firm of David Colville & Sons, 8 December 1883', D. C. & S., Register of Documents.

[27] Secretary of the S.C. of S. to all shareholders in the company, 14 Jan. 1880, a copy of which is contained in a volume of printed notices of, and press cuttings relating to, the Steel Company of Scotland (subsequently referred to as 'S.C. of S.: Printed Notices'), p. 63. See also S.C. of S., Minute Book III, 27 Oct. 1880.

guide mills—was a 26-inch reversing combination section and plate mill. Intended primarily for the production of rails and heavy sections, it was capable of rolling plates and in this respect anticipated several later developments. Of further historical significance was the fact that it was driven by one of the first twin tandem compound reversing engines to be built for mill duty.[28]

Blochairn had been fully converted to steel-making by late 1881 at a cost of over £100,000. It was here that Riley introduced, and was to develop, a whole range of special mechanical equipment for use in the manufacture of steel plates, and to conduct pioneering work in the application of open-hearth steel to shipbuilding and engineering purposes. Methods of casting and handling ingots, originally devised at the early Bessemer plants, were adopted; reheating furnaces were replaced by soaking pits, on Gjers's principle, in 1884, thereby reducing costs and improving ingot quality; a 32-inch reversing slabbing mill, the first in existence, was installed; and an impressive collection of ingenious ancillary equipment—often inspired by attempts to economize on, and reduce the power of, labour—evolved.

In the year ended mid-July 1882, the Steel Company's ingot output was 157,678 tons; by 1890, the firm's productive capacity was over 260,000 tons and total annual sales were running at well over £1 million. Despite 'the great depression in the iron and steel industries'[29] in the mid-eighties, the directors had still been able to declare a dividend, albeit a small one, and profits had sufficiently recovered by the end of the decade to warrant a distribution of $12\frac{1}{2}$ per cent. (See Table 4.5.) This was the last dividend to be paid on the ordinary shares for many years and when, in 1894, the company attempted 'to put its finances on a more satisfactory footing' by offering the public £150,000 of 5 per cent First Mortgage Debenture Stock and £100,000 of 6 per cent Second Mortgage Debenture Bonds, one periodical, *Today*, commented that 'it is to be hoped that English folk have left the issue to their good friends across the

---

[28] J. A. Kilby, 'The Production of Steel Plates in Scotland', *Journal of the Iron and Steel Institute*, clxvi (1950), 63, 65.

[29] S.C. of S., Minute Book V, 16 Sept. 1885; 8 Sept. 1886.

TABLE 4.5 *Steel Company of Scotland: Capital Structure and Dividend Payments, 1871–1895*

Year ending	(1) Nominal Ordinary capital in £10 shares	(2) Number of £10 shares issued	(3) Amount called on each share (£s)	(4) Total issued capital (£s)	(5) Annual Dividend (%)	(6) Debentures Authorized (£s)
31 Aug. 1872	105,000	10,500	4	42,000	Nil	None
31 Aug. 1873	250,000	25,000	5	125,000	Nil	None
31 Aug. 1874	500,000	25,000	8	200,000	Nil	None
31 Aug. 1875	500,000	34,480	8	275,840	Nil	None
31 Aug. 1876	500,000	34,480	8	275,840	Nil	None
31 Aug. 1877	500,000	34,480	8	275,840	Nil	None
31 Aug. 1878	500,000	34,480	8	275,840	Nil	None
31 Aug. 1879	500,000	34,800	8	275,840	6	150,000
31 Aug. 1880	500,000	39,958	8	317,566	9	150,000
14 July 1881	500,000	43,221	8	345,767	5⅜	250,000
13 July 1882	500,000	49,560	8	396,480	7	250,000
12 July 1883	500,000	49,560	8	396,480	11	250,000
17 July 1884	500,000	49,560	8	396,480	7½	250,000
16 July 1885	500,000	49,560	8	396,480	4	250,000
15 July 1886	500,000	49,560	8	396,480	4	250,000
14 July 1887	500,000	49,560	8	396,480	3½	250,000
12 July 1888	500,000	49,560	9	446,040	5	250,000
14 July 1889	500,000	49,560	9	446,040	10	250,000
17 July 1890	500,000	49,560	9	446,040	12½	250,000
16 July 1891	500,000	49,560	9	446,040	Nil	250,000
14 July 1892	500,000	49,560	9	446,040	Nil	250,000
13 July 1893	500,000	49,560	9	446,040	Nil	250,000
12 July 1894	500,000	49,560	9	446,040	Nil	250,000
11 July 1895	500,000	49,560	9	446,040	Nil	250,000

Notes: (1) For certain years, the number of shares issued (Col. 2) and the total issued capital (Col. 4) have sometimes been estimated from fragmentary information, though in years when dividends are paid, they have been calculated from accurate balance sheet data.

(2) Col. (6): Until 1895 all debentures issued were short-term terminable stock and were subject to fluctuating rates of interest. During the year ended 11 July 1895, the directors were authorized to issue £150,000 in 5 per cent 'A' or First Debenture Stock and £100,000 in 6 per cent 'B' or Second Debenture Stock.

Source: S.C. of S., Minute Books of the Board of Directors, vols. I–IX, and Printed Notices.

border',[30] and many years later the *Statist* was to recall that in 1894 the company had been 'on the verge of bankruptcy and practically moribund'.[31] What had gone wrong?

Although any answer must be conjectural, it is certainly many-sided. Following their careful study of the British iron and steel industry, Burnham and Hoskins concluded that 'If a business deteriorates it is of no use blaming anyone except those at the top'[32] and it is appropriate that speculations should begin with the Board of Directors. The point has already been made that the Steel Company of Scotland was established and controlled by those with an oblique interest in steel and by users, rather than by makers, of iron and steel and perhaps this was the root of the problem. For the first twenty years of the existence of the company, the board was composed of those whose primary interests were in chemicals (Charles Tennant, Archibald S. Schaw, David Wilson, John Wilson, and, later, James Couper),[33] locomotive building (Henry Dübs and, later,

[30] *Today*, 17 Nov. 1894, a copy of which is included in S.C. of S., Printed Notices.

[31] *Statist*, 19 Sept. 1914. The *Statist* was presumably referring to the crisis in the firm's affairs occasioned by the initial failure of the new Debenture issue of 1894, which promised to make it impossible to redeem the outstanding terminable Debentures which fell due at Martinmas (11 Nov.) 1894. Only £30,000 had been subscribed by 16 Oct. which was quite inadequate to meet the £46,000 of debentures falling due. Yet the basic financial position of the company was perfectly sound. By 1894, four years of no dividends on the ordinary shares had produced a crisis of confidence. It took all of Sir Charles Tennant's oratorical and business skill to avert a complete disaster. He told the shareholders that he was ready to take up £10,000 in B Debenture stock himself and appealed to their patriotism: 'To go into liquidation now would be unworthy of Scotchmen. (Cheers.) They ought to stick together and pull together, and, thus acting, he had no doubt whatever, the Company would again become a successful concern. Making 4,000 to 5,000 tons of steel a week, as they could do, a good profit should be realized. (Cheers.): By the end of the meeting a committee of shareholders had been created (consisting of Lord Overtoun, Mr. Holms Ivory, Mr. James Templeton, Mr. William Houldsworth, and Mr. Thomas Reid of Kilmardinny) and a 'considerable number' of shareholders had 'signed a paper agreeing to take debenture stocks'. *Glasgow Herald*, 31 Oct. 1894.

[32] T. H. Burnham and G. O. Hoskins, *Iron and Steel in Britain, 1870–1930* (London: Allen & Unwin, 1943), p. 271.

[33] For Charles Tennant, see S. H. Checkland, *The Mines of Tharsis*, particularly pp. 99–103, 268–9, and W. J. Reader, *ICI. A History*, vol. i, *The Forerunners, 1870–1926* (London: O.U.P., 1970), pp. 76, 104–5, 182. Archibald Shanks Schaw, a close associate of Tennant's, was a Glasgow ore merchant and dealer in minerals. Instrumental in forming various metal extraction

William Lorimer),[34] and civil engineering (John Moffat and
Archibald Arrol).[35] It is difficult to resist the conclusion that
the Steel Company of Scotland, like Nobel's Explosives Company, 'was firmly welded to the wide-ranging group of interests
centred on the person of Charles Tennant, of the family which
owned the great chemical business based on St. Rollox
Works'.[36]

This is not to say that the meetings of the board were poorly
attended. Nor is there any evidence that its members neglected
the affairs of the Steel Company, but inevitably they could
not—nor perhaps did they ever expect to—give it their un-
divided attention. What apparently they did do, after Michael
Scott's resignation in 1874 and the death of Henry Dübs in
1876, was to allow—indeed, encourage—power to pass to
James Riley, who rapidly became identified with the firm's
early success. Indeed, it was later said of him that 'no one who
was associated with him in the early days of the introduction
of mild steel but admired him for his indominable energy and
the manner in which he impressed shipbuilders, boilermakers,
and others as to the superiority of mild steel for all the purposes

companies, he was also the second chairman of Nobel's Explosives Company
Ltd., the British company formed in 1877, with head offices in Glasgow, to
exploit Nobel's patents. David Wilson joined the board of Nobel's at the same
time as Schaw; Tennant became a director in 1885. John Wilson, of the Hur-
let and Campsie alum works, had long been associated with the chemical
industry and was a partner of the Glasgow chemist William Henderson (see
above, p. 24). He, like Schaw and, of course, Tennant, was a director of the
Tharsis Sulphur and Copper Company. See Checkland, op. cit., pp. 90, 95,
104, 124, 158; Reader, op. cit., pp. 32, 71. James Couper, who joined the
board of the Steel Company in 1882, following the death of John Moffat,
was associated with the St. Rollox Chemical Works.

[34] Henry Dübs was the founder of the Glasgow Locomotive Works, and
William Lorimer, his partner in Dübs & Co. William Lorimer joined the
board of the Steel Company in 1878 two years after Dübs's death. He acted
as General Manager of the Steel Company in the latter part of the interregnum between Michael Scott's resignation (1874) and the appointment of
James Riley (1878). William Lorimer became first chairman of the North
British Locomotive Co. when that company was founded in 1903.

[35] Gibson, 'The Establishment of the Scottish Steel Industry', p. 27, de-
scribes John Moffat as 'an eminent civil engineer'. He was appointed Deputy
Chairman of the Steel Company in 1879 and died in 1882. Archibald Arrol
was a member of the Arrol family of bridge and structural engineers, four
members of which were among the original 28 shareholders in the Steel Company.

[36] Reader, *ICI. A History*, i. 32.

required in construction of ships . . . [He] was rightly recognised . . . as the father of the mild steel trade in Scotland.'[37]

Of his technical ability, there is no question. It was primarily due to Riley's efforts that when Sir Henry Bessemer visited the works in 1885 he remarked, 'I have not seen during the whole of my experience such excellent material and finished work as I see here today.'[38] It was Riley who introduced, adopted, and improved upon the plant employed at Hallside and Blochairn. It was he who first recognized that although much could be learned from the production methods employed by the iron-masters, heavy equipment of a specialized nature was essential to deal with steel in the quantities required and for which entirely new plant for heating, rolling, and finishing needed to be developed. Hallside and—even more so—Blochairn became vast experimental laboratories for new techniques. It was all very exciting and very expensive. Inevitably, mistakes were made. The enormous 300-ton twin tandem compound reversing engine installed at Hallside in 1878 to provide motive power for the 26-inch reversing combination and plate mill, was 'not too successful, and it was ultimately rebuilt as a simple high-pressure unit'.[39] In 1882 the 'dead' soaking pit was invented by Gjers and rapidly adopted by Riley at Blochairn,[40] but the difficulties of maintaining an even flow of ingots from the open-hearth melting shop soon led to its abandonment in favour of the 'live' soaking pit or vertical heating furnace.[41] Riley even installed a single-stand Lauth three-high plate mill at Blochairn in 1888, but its performance was disappointing and it was abandoned in the early nineties because of frequent gearing breakages.[42] Furthermore, many of Riley's lesser innovations

[37] 'James Riley', obituary notice in the *Journal of the West of Scotland Iron and Steel Institute*, xviii (1911), 233.

[38] Reported by George Beard, *Journal of the West of Scotland Iron and Steel Institute*, i (1892), 16.

[39] Kilby, 'The Production of Steel Plates in Scotland', p. 65, and James Riley, 'Notes on Modern Steel-works Machinery', *Proceedings of the Institution of Mechanical Engineers* (1895), pts. 3–4, p. 437.

[40] See above, p. 60.

[41] Kilby, 'The Production of Steel Plates in Scotland', p. 38. Hodge, *Workman's Cottage to Windsor Castle*, pp. 29–30, 76–7 gives a good idea of the potential disadvantages of 'dead' soakers.

[42] Kilby, 'The Production of Steel Plates in Scotland', p. 47. The breakdowns were referred to by F. W. Paul, sometime manager of Blochairn, in the discussion of Andrew Lamberton's paper 'Improvements in Plate Rolling

encountered lengthy 'teething troubles' and took longer to contribute to increased productivity than had been anticipated.

At every stage in the various productive processes, Riley sought to work at the known technological limits. This not only involved rapid obsolescence but a rate of capital formation apparently far higher than many contemporary works, much of it financed by endlessly troublesome short-dated terminable debentures which had either to be renewed or paid off at inconvenient times.[43] By 1890 the production of ship plates—overwhelmingly the most important item of manufacture in the Scottish steel trade—had been abandoned at Hallside, which thenceforth was devoted to the making of forgings, sections, rails, and bars. To Riley the potential economies of scale dictated a massive increase of productive capacity. By 1890 the works were said to be capable of producing well over a quarter of a million tons of finished steel. But, by so pushing ahead, Riley rendered the Steel Company extremely vulnerable to trade fluctuations and to competition from those firms able to work to a higher proportion of capacity. Thus when, in the early nineties, the Steel Company of Scotland's sales fell away and the firm was badly affected by trade disputes—involving not only the steelmen's unions but the coalminers—Hallside and Blochairn were reduced to working at about 50 per cent of capacity and experienced relatively high unit costs. Driven along by Riley, whose ambitions were but loosely restrained by a compliant board, the members of which were essentially unversed in steel-making technology, the Steel Company of Scotland had, almost fatally, over-reached itself. Riley—frustrated and bitterly disappointed—resigned from the General Managership in 1895. His tenure of office at the Steel Company is perhaps an object lesson in the dangers of allowing technology to outweigh commercial considerations. It is possible to detect

---

Mills' delivered before the Iron and Steel Institute in 1908. In the course of this discussion, it was said by E. J. Duff, Riley's assistant, when the mill—the first to be erected in Great Britain—was put down, that 'if Mr. Riley's directors had had the nerve to spend the money in eliminating these defects, and had gone on with the principle of three-high rolling, they would have made a success of it'. *Journal of the Iron and Steel Institute*, lxxvi (1908), 39–40, 45, 51.

[43] Sir Charles Tennant, address to the shareholders of the Steel Company, 30 Oct. 1894. *Glasgow Herald*, 31 Oct. 1894.

elements of irony and sadness in a passage from his Presidential Address to the West of Scotland Iron and Steel Institute in 1894: 'It is not always the finest equipped plants that achieve the best results; on the contrary, quite a number of blast furnace managers (in America), who have attained enviable reputations, have furnaces with but moderate equipment.'[44]

But an indulgent board, a brilliantly ingenious, if adventurous, general manager, a period of labour troubles, a temporarily aberrant capital structure—all these would have had little immediate adverse effect on the long run future of the Steel Company had it retained its geographical monopoly. The root cause of the company's difficulties was the growth of vigorous local competition. In the span of only a decade David Colville & Sons, William Beardmore, the Clydebridge Steel Company, the Glengarnock Iron & Steel Company, and others captured many of the markets which, in their absence, might have been supplied by Hallside and Blochairn; and from the north-east coast of England there poured into Scotland good quality, low-priced finished steel products that further eroded the Steel Company's position, forcing it to work well below its optimum technical and economic capacity. Under these conditions, mistakes in policy—however minor and however tolerable in the past—were shortly to bring about the downfall of the Steel Company from its premier position in the Scottish steel industry.

4 Technique and Competition

But were these competitors simply taking advantage of a temporary weakening in the position of the pioneering concern? What factors permitted them to succeed where the Steel Company seemed to have failed? Indeed, how far and in what way *did* they succeed?

One thing is certain: James Riley and the Steel Company possessed no monopoly of technical innovation. At Dalzell, David Colville jun. strove unceasingly to discover what was taking place elsewhere. In time, he was to visit America, Germany, and France to acquaint himself with the most advanced

[44] James Riley, Presidential Address, *Journal of the West of Scotland Iron and Steel Institute*, i (1894), 7.

methods, and it was said of him that 'there was nothing in the industry with which he did not make himself fully conversant. He adopted everything that he considered likely to improve the manufacture of steel within the Dalzell ... works.'[45] At first, he operated within severe financial constraints, but with the growing profitability of the firm he was able to substitute the most sophisticated slab rolling facilities for the earlier method of hammer cogging and cutting the steel ingots produced by the open-hearth furnaces. The reversing slabbing mill installed in 1894 was the first of its kind to be equipped with power-operated side carriages for positioning the great slabs of steel laterally on the working roller tables. But if this was the most important of Colville's early innovations, its efficiency was much enhanced by his rapid adoption of the most modern practice for those processes immediately preceding the initial rolling of ingots. Colville endeavoured to discover all he could about Riley's use of Gjers, or 'dead', soaking pits from John Hodge, who had once been a third hand melter at Blochairn.[46] Having obtained the required information, such pits were installed in 1889, only to be superseded within but a year by vertical heating furnaces, or 'live' soaking pits. Following the next process, during which the ingots were forged down and cut to size under steam hammers, the slabs were reheated in 'in-and-out' hearth type regenerative furnaces fired with producer gas before moving on to the slabbing mill. There was a beauty and order about these arrangements which impressed all contemporary observers and it was manifestly clear that Colville always planned the layout and designed the equipment in such a way and on such a scale that it constantly anticipated future

[45] *Transactions of the Institute of Engineers and Shipbuilders in Scotland* (1915–16), pp. 401–2.

[46] Hodge, *Workman's Cottage to Windsor Castle*, p. 29. When properly employed, Gjers' Soaking Pit system saved the wages of a furnaceman and a great deal of incidental labour and fuel. Previously, steel ingots, having been removed from the ingot moulds, had been permitted to cool. They were then reheated in a furnace before passing through the primary rolling stage in a cogging mill. Gjers devised the method of placing steel ingots immediately after they had been stripped of their moulds into a battery of bricked holes in the ground covered by lids. In these soaking pits, as they were called, the casting heat became uniformly diffused throughout the ingot as it solidified. At the appropriate time the ingot could be rolled in the cogging mill without the necessity of reheating. See *Journal of the Iron and Steel Institute* (1884), p. 467.

demands, particularly concerning the growing weight and size of individual plates.

At Clydebridge, too, considerable thought had been devoted to the method of dealing with the ingots from the casting bay to the soaking pits and slabbing mill to ensure an uninterrupted material flow and minimum fuel consumption. Established in 1887 by the Clydebridge Steel Company Ltd., the original plant, installed in the following year, was laid out with the soaking pit and slabbing mill building arranged at right angles to the casting bay and positioned centrally so that the ingots could be transferred to the pits with a minimum of movement.[47] There appears to have been little possibility of adopting such a careful layout at Parkhead, where William Beardmore put down melting furnaces in 1879. To some extent a captive of earlier technology, Beardmore initially produced steel plates by the same methods as those already in use for wrought iron; that is, the slabs were hammer cogged and rolled into plates on existing pull-over and reversing mills. Not until the early eighties were slab rolling facilities installed and Parkhead was never technically in the forefront in the manufacture of commercial plates and sections. Beardmore's strength was in the production of armour plates and Parkhead's contribution to developments in this field came later. Clydesdale's experience was much the same as Parkhead's. Established in 1872 for the manufacture of wrought iron, open-hearth furnaces were not introduced until 1884, when the ingots were initially processed by methods almost identical with those at Parkhead. Not until 1894 were slab rolling facilities added to the existing plant.[48]

[47] Kilby, 'The Production of Steel Plates in Scotland', p. 61.

[48] Accounts very similar to that of Parkhead could be given of the Calderbank works of the Calderbank Steel & Coal Co. and the Mossend works of the Summerlee and Mossend Iron & Steel Co. Both works were of some antiquity and both had chequered histories. Indeed, the works at Calderbank had their genesis in a small foundry and forge established in 1794. This early concern was taken over by the Monkland Steel Co. in 1805 for the production of tool steel by the cementation process. The company also produced nail rod, forgings, and boiler plates and, in 1819, the hull plates for the first iron boat built in Scotland, the *Vulcan*. During the mid-thirties two blast furnaces were erected, and in 1839–40 the Monkland Co. erected a battery of twenty-four puddling furnaces. Rapid expansion followed. In 1845 four more blast furnaces were built at Calderbank and forty-two more puddling furnaces. The company flourished until 1861 when, almost without warning, it suspended payments and the works ceased operations. Resuming

So far attention has been directed to concerns that were heavily involved in the production of ship and boiler plates. These exhibit a range of technical progressiveness from the pioneering (the Steel Company of Scotland and David Colville & Sons) to simple imitative competence (Clydesdale). The Scottish firms that concentrated on the exploitation of other sectors of the total market for finished steel products displayed a similar range of technical adventurousness in the closing decades of the nineteenth century.

At Glengarnock, where increasing difficulty was being experienced in selling the product of the blast furnaces originally erected in the eighteen-forties, the Cunninghames decided to put down four 8-ton basic Bessemer converters in 1884.[49] It had been intended to concentrate on the manufacture of steel plates, angles, and tinplate blooms, a 30-inch reversing rolling mill being installed for this purpose, but since at the time the plant was under consideration, some doubt still existed concerning the technical wisdom of using rolled slabs for special duty plates, a 10-ton steam hammer was also erected. This had an anvil block of 215 tons, the heaviest in Scotland at the time. After a promising start, the imposition of the McKinley tariffs virtually killed the trade in tin plate bars for South Wales and,

---

on a smaller scale, all the creditors had been paid off by 1872. A second company at Calderbank enjoyed even less success, failing in 1887, when most of the blast furnaces and much of the puddling plant were demolished. Resuscitated in 1890 by yet another company, the Calderbank Steel & Coal Co., open-hearth furnaces were laid down but their output was initially processed by methods more appropriate for the manufacture of wrought iron than Siemens steel. Mossend was established by the Neilson family—already associated with the Summerlee iron works at Coatbridge—in 1840, and rapidly became one of the largest units in the Scottish malleable iron trade. By 1876 two reversing plate mills were in operation, one of which was capable of rolling plates up to 6 ft. wide. In 1880, open-hearth steel furnaces were laid down and, after the merging of the Mossend and Summerlee companies, slab rolling facilities were installed in 1889. The historical background of these two companies is taken from George Thomson (ed.), *The County of Lanark*, pp. 222–3, 291. See also Kilby, 'The Production of Steel Plates in Scotland', pp. 33–4; A. Miller, *The Rise and Progress of Coatbridge*, pp. 39–40, 107–8, 120–1.

[49] A detailed description, together with a plan, of the Glengarnock Steel Works was given in *Engineering*, xl (1885), 175–7. The ore which Merry & Cunninghame were using was 'pre-eminently suitable for the basic process, for while the pig iron made from it contains an abundance of phosphorus—the *bête noir* of the steel manufacturer—it is very low in silicon and exceedingly rich in manganese' (cf. p. 71 below).

following reorganization, the firm moved rapidly into the market for joists or 'H' beams for structural and bridge-building purposes,[50] installing the equipment needed for this branch of the steel trade and extending it in order to meet the related demand for rails, sleepers, and fishplates. The blast furnaces were reconstructed to give a higher weekly output (250–300 tons per furnace) and in 1892 an entirely new melting shop comprising three 25-ton acid-lined Siemens-Martin furnaces was commissioned. A slag mill was installed to grind the basic slag from the Bessemer process for sale as fertilizer and in 1894 the company joined with R. & J. Dempster[51] of Newton Heath, Manchester, to form the Glengarnock Chemical Company, who built extensive plant sited on a levelled blaize to recover by-products, such as sulphate of ammonia and tar from the blast furnace gases. Technically, the Glengarnock Iron & Steel Company appears to have been highly efficient. It gave special attention to the preparation and testing of its products, even employing a chemist for whom a properly equipped laboratory was provided.[52]

The Wishaw works of the Glasgow Iron & Steel Company—established in 1859 when Robert Bell erected the three blast furnaces of the Wishaw Iron Works[53]—were, like Glengarnock, initially equipped with basic Bessemer plant. Under the direction of Maximilian Mannaberg, the company moved into steel in 1885 when three 7-ton converters were put up and hot metal was conveyed by means of an inclined railway direct to the Bessemer vessels. But the venture was not completely successful. The company, in adopting the Thomas-Gilchrist process, sought to utilize the many thousands of tons of cinder produced

[51] This firm was very experienced in the design and erection of plant for the recovery of tar and ammonia from blast furnace gases. See the paper by William Jones, 'The Present Position and Prospects of Processes for the Recovery of Tar and Ammonia from Blast Furnaces', delivered to the Iron and Steel Institute meeting in Glasgow in 1885. *Engineering*, xl (1885), 409.
[52] This and the previous paragraph, are based upon A. Humbolt Sexton, 'Use of Mild Steel for Marine Boilers', *Trans. Inst. Nav. Arch.*, xxi (1880), 27; Kilby, 'The Production of Steel Plates in Scotland', p. 33; and on the fragmentary pre-1916 manuscript sources that have survived.
[53] These blast furnaces were acquired by the Wishaw Iron Co. in 1864 and by the Glasgow Iron Co. (later the Glasgow Iron and Steel Co.) in 1866. Thomson, *The County of Lanark*, p. 330.

by the blast furnaces. It was believed that this could be converted into a marketable product by mixing it with local iron
ore and producing basic iron at the blast furnaces and then converting it into basic steel by the basic Bessemer process. Despite
consultation with Percy Gilchrist, who had invited Mannaberg
to come to Britain to build and operate the works, this belief
proved to be erroneous. The cinder was too low in phosphorus
for the manufacture of basic pig and too high in silicon for basic
steel. The works could be kept going only by the purchase of
appropriate brands of basic pig, the conversion of which was—
such was the heavy loss in blowing—highly expensive. Moreover, basic steel

did not find favour in Scotland, either for shipbuilding or boiler-making purposes. Engineers, shipbuilders, and boilermakers had a dread of it, owing to
various circumstances that had transpired at other places, and inspectors
looked upon it with doubt and suspicion, knowing that the material was sometimes irregular in hardness, on account of the uncertainty in thoroughly eliminating the phosphorus and sulphur during the conversion process . . .

There was nothing for it but to abandon the works or to have
them reconstructed and converted to the open-hearth process.[54]
This was carried out under the direction of Thomas Williamson
in 1894. There was nothing particularly remarkable about the
new plant, which was designed to produce rails, angles,
channels and tees as well as plates. The works were, however,
well laid out and were expected to be capable of manufacturing
about 160,000 tons per annum (130,000 tons of Siemens open-
hearth steel and 30,000 tons of acid Bessemer). The company
had responded positively to its somewhat disappointing introduction to steel-making. In appointing Thomas Williamson as
engineer and manager of the steel works,[55] they had acquired

[54] In 1888 Mannaberg went—also at Gilchrist's suggestion—to the Frodingham Iron & Steel Co., whose managing director he remained until his
retirement in 1920. Carr and Taplin, *History of the British Steel Industry*, p.
400n. See also below, p. 84.
[55] Thomas Williamson was trained by Tulloch & Denny at Dumbarton
and subsequently worked at Neilson's Locomotive Works, Dübs, and
Rowan's Marine Engineering Works. He was appointed works manager at
the Hallside works of the Steel Company of Scotland in 1875 and was responsible for the conversion of Blochairn to steel-making when that works was
acquired by the Steel Company in 1879. Before going to Wishaw, he superin-
tended the erection of the Clydebridge works and those of John Spencer &
Co. at Newburn, Newcastle-on-Tyne.

an exceptionally experienced and resourceful man to direct their activities: the great days of the company were to come with the appointment of James Riley as general manager in 1895.[56]

The Lanarkshire Works, situated at Flemington, between Motherwell and Wishaw, were established in 1889 by the Lanarkshire Steel Company Ltd. Superbly laid out to provide ample room for subsequent expansion, five acid open-hearth furnaces had been built by August 1893, the products of which were rolled into bars, angles, and sections in plant initially comprising a 27-inch reversing blooming and bar mill and a number of small section and guide mills. Apparently completely orthodox in its original choice of plant, which embodied the best contemporary practice, the works got off to an encouraging start. In 1895 the ingot output exceeded 41,000 tons and the cost per ton of finished materials was tending steadily downwards. The Lanarkshire was to be the last steel-making company to be formed in Scotland. In this sense the commissioning of its plant marked the end of an era: two decades during which the modern Scottish steel industry had come into being.

Not all of these infant concerns were destined to survive. Some went quickly, others enjoyed but a sickly existence, a few reached adult status. Yet, as has been seen, initially none was technically backward, some may justly be described as pioneers. Technical modernity, simple 'best practice', was not enough for long-run economic success.

The Calderbank Steel & Coal Company, floated only in 1890, was the first to go. In the seven and a half years of its existence its steel works were operated altogether for less than two years, despite the directors' claim to have continued to adopt the latest improvements. In 1899 it was succeeded by the Calderbank Steel Company, which went into liquidation in 1900. Calderbank was an ill-starred works, though precisely what was the root of the trouble is not known.[57] Nor is it possible

[56] The foregoing account of the Wishaw Works is heavily based on a series of articles in *Engineering*, lix (1895), 427–9, 535–9, 623–4, 755–7, 822. The quotation is from p. 535.

[57] Thomson, *The County of Lanark*, p. 233; Report of the directors of the Calderbank Steel & Coal Co. for the period 1 July 1895 to 30 June 1896, published 21 Oct. 1896.

to do much more than speculate on the possible weaknesses of the Mossend works of the Summerlee and Mossend Iron and Steel Company. An anonymous writer in *Engineering* provides one clue: '... as in some other old-established concerns, sufficient reconstruction work was not undertaken to keep the plant in line with modern invention. As a consequence the degree of efficiency which characterised the early history of the establishment waned until the commercial results became disappointing.'[58] But there was probably more in the company's failure than this. There was certainly a history of bad labour relations. 'Mossend', John Hodge wrote, 'had an evil tradition so far as iron and steel works were concerned.'[59] The company lasted barely ten years.

Clydebridge was fortunate not to suffer a similar fate. Established in 1887 with a nominal capital of £90,000 of which £60,000 was taken up by a group related to the Neilson family, the original manager was James Neilson. By general agreement 'the most vindictive anti-trade union employer in the Scottish iron and steel industry',[60] within a few months of the creation of the firm, Neilson was beset with labour problems and strikes which shut down the furnaces for months on end. Wages were said to be some 20 per cent below those customarily paid in the district and even then the men claimed that they were cheated in the calculation of piece-rate payments.[61] Despite a change of management, labour troubles continued to plague the company, morale was poor and efficiency low.

It can hardly be imagined that the sorry state of the Steel Company of Scotland in the mid-nineties was caused by the puny efforts of these last three companies, enfeebled as they were by defective management and corrosive labour relations. Nor could Parkhead and Clydesdale have constituted much of a challenge at this early stage of their development: only inasmuch as they contributed to the general weakening of the Steel Company's monopolistic position were they significant. In the first half of the nineties even the competitive power of

---

[58] *Engineering*, lxxxvi (1908), 666.
[59] Hodge, *Workman's Cottage to Windsor Castle*, pp. 286–7; see also Sir Arthur Pugh, *Men of Steel* (London: Iron and Steel Trades Confederation, 1951), pp. 114–16.
[60] Pugh, *Men of Steel*, p. 217.
[61] Hodge, *Workman's Cottage to Windsor Castle*, pp. 45, 283–4.

Glengarnock and Wishaw was potential rather than real. They were in no position to seize a sizeable part of the Steel Company's market until they had converted their plant from basic to acid processes. However, the future of the former works looked exceptionally promising after a reorganization of Merry & Cunninghame in 1890 whereby the Ayrshire interests of the firm were formed into the Glengarnock Iron & Steel Company. J. C. Cunninghame remained as chairman of the board of the Glengarnock company and among the directors was the renowned iron- and steelmaster, E. Windsor Richards, whose brother, Edgar J. Richards, became general works manager.[62] Lanarkshire, off to a good start—it was already paying dividends on its ordinary shares in 1894[63]—was taking part of the market for bars, angles, and sections, but its impact on the Steel Company was inevitably reduced by its directors' decision not to enter the market for ship plates.

It is clear that the Steel Company had been brought almost to its knees by its own weaknesses exacerbated by fierce competition from the North of England and from the rapidly growing firm of David Colville & Sons. Already, by 1890, John Cronin was able to tell the Royal Commission on Labour that at Consett, ship plates

are heated and rolled for 2s. 3d. per ton, while in Scotland we are paying from 4s. 6d. to 4s. 9d. for the same class of work. We have put down the same machinery, or something very like the machinery, which is put down at Consett, but our employers tell us that certain firms can send their ship plates into the Clyde at 7s. 6d. a ton less than we can make them in Scotland ... They say such-and-such works in England are cutting us out of our own markets; they are not paying the same price for labour that we are paying, and hence they are enabled to send their plates into our markets and beat us. That is a common argument used by the employers.[64]

Questioned further on this point, Cronin was adamant that 'a great deal lower wages [were] paid in England than [were] paid

---

[62] Sometime manager of the Bolckow Vaughan works at Eston and a leading spokesman for the steel industry, Windsor Richards had supported Gilchrist and Thomas in their early experiments which led to the discovery of the basic process of steel making. See Carr and Taplin, *History of the British Steel Industry*, pp. 97, 100–1, 124.

[63] See below, p. 116.

[64] *Minutes of Evidence taken before the Royal Commission on Labour*, Group A, Q. 16,000.

in Scotland'.[65] Furthermore, 'better machinery' used at Consett permitted a reduction in the labour force. 'Labour', observed Edward Trow, the ironworkers' leader and a member of the Royal Commission, was 'dispensed with', and higher productivity resulted. The Consett mills turned out over 100 tons per shift with five men at the rolls; in Scotland, six to eight men worked only 80 tons. Asked if it was fair 'to single out one large mill, and not consider the rates of ... other mills when they are doing work of a similar nature ...?', Cronin replied: 'The principal part of the work is done in the large mill at Consett. It is supposed to turn out the most material of any other mill in the trade, and does it.' His statement was not denied: Trow remained silent. The result was, Cronin observed, that 'whereas the Consett Iron & Steel Company can pay $33\frac{1}{3}$ and 20 per cent dividends, we have firms in Scotland who have lost through the past year as much as £50,000'.[66]

In this part of his evidence to the Royal Commission on Labour, Cronin was lamenting a very recent phenomenon. During the seventies, when the Steel Company of Scotland was the only producer of open-hearth steel in Scotland, South Wales had been the leading British region for this material. Not until 1881 did Scotland surpass South Wales and enjoy supremacy in the British open-hearth steel industry. But by 1889, barely five years after entering the trade on a large scale, Cleveland had not only almost matched Scottish output but had done so with a smaller number of active furnaces (see Table 4.6). These furnaces had been put down in the mid-eighties by the Consett Iron & Steel Company, Bolckow Vaughan & Company, and Palmer's Shipbuilding Company.[67]

Of these firms, not only was Consett the most efficient—in 1890 its output per furnace, for example, was the highest in

[65] Confronted with Edward Trow's argument that rollers at Consett were, in fact, paid more highly than their Scottish counterparts, Cronin countered with the observation that 'at Consett the mill is sub-contracted; the roller has a certain number of men to pay out of [his earnings of £16–£18]; how do we know he is not putting this amount of money into his pocket'. Ibid., Qs. 16,160–7. See also Burn, *Economic History of Steel Making*, p. 127.

[66] *Minutes of the Royal Commission on Labour*, Qs. 16,151–8; 16,137–8; 16,116. That Cronin was not exaggerating the 'prodigious' profitability of Consett has been shown by Richardson and Bass, 'The Profitability of the Consett Iron Company', pp. 71–93.

[67] British Iron Trade Association, Annual Report for 1886, p. 40.

TABLE 4.6

Output of Open-Hearth Steel, Output per Active Open-Hearth Furnace, and Market Price of Steel Ship Plates, by District, 1879–1895

	(1)	(2)	(3)	(4)	(5)	(6)	(7)	(8)	(9)	(10)	(11)
	Output of open-hearth steel ('000 tons)				Output per active open-hearth furnace ('000 tons)				Market price of steel ship plates		$\frac{(9)-(10)}{(10)}$ %
Year	Scotland	S. Wales	Cleveland	Britain	Scotland	S. Wales	Cleveland	Britain	Scotland £ s. d.	Cleveland £ s. d.	
1879	50	85	1	175							
1880	85	116	3	251							
1881	166	102	6	338							
1882	213	130	6	436							
1883	222	136	10	456							
1884	214	151	16	476	4,551	3,509	1,822	3,573			
1885	241	173	76	584	4,464	3,601	n.d.	3,518			
1886	245	195	124	694	4,898	3,740	4,432	n.d.			
1887	334	226	248	981	5,685	4,100	6,055	4,419	6 12 9	6 4 0	7
1888	443	275	353	1,293	6,513	5,970	7,425	5,608	7 0 10	6 14 7	4
1889	438	243	437	1,429	6,028	5,274	7,285	5,772	7 17 9	7 7 7	7
1890	482	282	470	1,564	6,468	5,426	7,549	5,964	7 16 11	7 2 7	10
1891	479	256	439	1,515	n.d.	n.d.	n.d.	n.d.	6 11 7	6 0 6	9
1892	459	224	428	1,419	7,362	4,562	7,512	6,019	6 1 8	5 13 0	8
1893	443	234	482	1,456	8,128	4,679	8,766	6,501	5 9 5	5 1 0	9
1894	433	237	546	1,575	n.d.	n.d.	n.d.	n.d.	5 10 4	4 19 9	10
1895	506	217	703	1,755	8,457	7,241	9,094	7,531	5 2 9	4 17 1	6

Sources: Col. (1): British Iron & Steel Federation, Statistics Department, tabulated by Byres, 'The Scottish Economy', p. 621.

Cols. (2)–(8): Annual Reports of the British Iron Trade Association, tabulated by Byres, op. cit., pp. 621–3.

Cols. (9)–(11): 'Report on Wholesale and Retail Prices in the United Kingdom in 1902, with Comprehensive Statistical Tables for a Series of Years' (1903), tabulated by Byres, op. cit., p. 624. Col. (11) expresses the percentage by which the price of

TABLE 4.7

David Colville & Sons: Capital Account and Net Profits, at the End of Various Biannual Accounting Periods, 1881–1895

Half year ending	(1) Amount of capital contributed by J. S. Napier (£s)	(2) The Colvilles (£s)	(3) Total capital (£s)	(4) Net profit (£s)	(5) Amount credited to Napier and the Colvilles (£s)	(6) Amount credited to reserves (£s)
2 Jan. 1882	33,000	30,788	63,788	8,700	6,960	1,740
21 July 1883	56,000	46,433	102,433	20,000	16,000	4,000
1 Jan. 1884	56,000	53,200	109,200	18,000	14,400	3,600
19 July 1884	56,000	58,486	114,486	23,500	18,800	4,700
1 Jan. 1886	56,000	75,022	131,022	24,500	19,600	4,900
20 July 1886	56,000	80,364	136,364	17,700	14,160	3,540
1 Jan. 1887	56,000	84,771	140,771	1,400	1,120	280
20 July 1887	56,000	79,062	135,062	22,200	17,760	4,440
20 July 1888	56,000	91,369	147,369	28,000	28,000	Nil
1 Jan. 1889	51,533	99,594	151,127	32,000	25,600	6,400
1 Jan. 1890	n.d.	128,590	n.d.	50,000	n.d.	n.d.
1 Jan. 1891	1,490	184,070	185,560	6,500	5,200	1,300
1 Jan. 1892	1,492	200,627	202,119	11,200	8,960	2,240
20 July 1892	8	218,541	218,549	23,200	n.d.	n.d.
20 July 1893	8	243,938	243,946	9,000	9,000	Nil
20 July 1895	Nil	239,063	239,063	14,128	To private company	

Notes: 1. The horizontal gaps in the table indicate periods for which balance sheets have not survived.
2. The amounts credited to 'the partners' were equally divided between J. S. Napier (50 per cent) and David Colville, sen., John Colville, and Archibald Colville (50 per cent).
3. For three twelve-month periods, it is possible to use the data in the above table to make a crude comparison of the net profit on the capital employed in David Colville & Sons and the dividend on the Ordinary shares of the Steel Company of Scotland (see top of next page).

| | David Colville & Sons | | | S.C. of S. |
Year ending	Total capital employed at end of period (£s)	Amount credited to 'Partners' (£s)	Approximate 'Dividend' (%)	Dividend on ordinary shares (%)
mid-1884	114,486	33,200	29	7½
mid-1886	136,364	33,760	25	4
mid-1887	135,062	18,880	14	3½

Source: D. C. & S., Balance Sheets.

Great Britain—but it specialized in the production of ship plates.[68] It was, moreover, a backwardly integrated concern enjoying considerable economies in raw material and fuel costs. Cautious in the adoption of new techniques, William Jenkins, the general manager from 1869 to 1894, always kept the plant up-to-date by periodic reconstruction and the ruthless replacement of obsolete equipment:[69] Jenkins, an exceptionally shrewd and able man, especially in his judgement of commercial possibilities, possessed none of the pyrotechnic virtuosity of James Riley. He was firm but fair with the men and although he thought that labour was too highly paid, he would always concede to wage claims 'if he thought that justice and the company's honour required it',[70] and in this policy he doubtless received the full support of his chairman, David Dale, one of the great pioneers in industrial arbitration. These, and other factors—not the least important of which was the avoidance of over-capitalization[71]—largely explain the competitive power and the almost breathtaking profitability of Consett.[72] This was

[68] This paragraph is based upon Richardson and Bass, 'The Profitability of the Consett Iron Company, *passim.*
[69] Gross capital expenditure on fixed assets over the quarter century of his management averaged £56,000 per year. Ibid., p. 79.
[70] Ibid., p. 80.
[71] This was partly due to the 'paltry' sum for which the original works and estates of the Derwent & Consett Iron Co. were purchased in 1864: for £295,318, the Consett Iron Co. acquired 18 blast furnaces with blowing engines, plate, rail, angle, and bar mills with puddling furnaces, coke ovens, 500 acres of freehold land, more than 1,000 freehold cottages, and Managers' houses and offices. Ibid., pp. 83–4.
[72] Over the period 1864–1914, the *average* dividend on the Ordinary shares was about 23½ per cent. Ibid., pp. 82, 91–2.

the firm with which the Steel Company of Scotland had primarily to compete in the early nineties, not its Scottish neighbours nor overseas concerns.[73] This it manifestly failed to do and was, thereby, chronically weakened.

Yet David Colville & Sons, facing the very same competition, successfully met the challenge and, in the two decades remaining before the First World War, emerged as the undisputed leader of the Scottish steel industry. Untroubled by shareholders, David, John, and Archibald Colville, after putting aside an amount sufficient to pay off the loan from J. S. Napier, retained their share of the net profits in the firm and by so doing permitted David Colville jun. constantly to improve the plant at Dalzell and keep the growing firm at peak efficiency. A much smaller firm than either the Steel Company or Consett in the early nineties,[74] like the latter it concentrated on the production of ship and boiler plates, was very carefully managed and what disadvantages, compared with Consett, it suffered from a lack of backward integration, were at least partially offset by Dalzell's nearness to the Clyde shipyards.

Whatever the precise reasons for the firm's success and continuous growth during the eighties and early nineties, David Colville & Sons was able to produce a much more handsome

---

[73] Asked by the Royal Commission on Labour about foreign competition, Cronin replied: 'I do not know of any competition so far as Scotland is concerned, although I have heard that there has been a little iron and steel imported from Belgium, but I cannot say, as far as we are concerned, we are the least frightened of foreign competition.' *Minutes of the Royal Commission on Labour*, Group A, loc. cit., Qs. 16,043–4.

[74] Accurate figures are unobtainable and comparisons potentially misleading but, by 1891, the total capital employed, the number of melting furnaces built, and the ingot outputs for each of the three firms was approximately as follows:

	S.C. of S.	D.C. & S.	Consett
Total capital employed	£550,000	£200,000	£1,044,000
No. of steel melting furnaces	28	13	18
Steel ingot output (tons)	130,000	85,000	170,000

These figures are *estimates* from data drawn from S.C. of S.: Minute Books and published descriptions of the Hallside and Blochairn works in the mid- and late eighties; D.C. & S.: Balance sheets and printed descriptions of the Dalzell works; Consett: Richardson and Bass, 'The Profitability of the Consett Company', *passim*. Consett's capital was employed in a much wider range of activities than either of the Scottish firms.

profit on its capital than either the Steel Company or the other Scottish concerns in the mild steel trade (see Table 4.7) and to do so at prices that undercut Consett.[75] This is perhaps the best measure of Colvilles' comparative efficiency and the most reliable guide to its immediate future.

[75] In 1893, William Jenkins admitted in a letter to David Dale, his chairman, that Consett was being undersold by Colvilles. Richardson and Bass, 'The Profitability of the Consett Company', p. 77.

V

Growth and Maturity, 1895–1914

During the two decades preceding the First World War, the output of the Scottish Steel industry increased nearly threefold (see Table 5.1). Essentially, this was in response to the massive growth of the shipbuilding industry, although a substantial demand for finished steel came from the heavy engineering trades, the bridge-builders, and the tube-makers. Despite this rapid rate of growth, no new steel-melting firms were created[1] and, superficially at least, the structure of the Scottish steel industry underwent little change. Yet the fact that the firms that existed in 1895 produced the bulk of Scotland's output of steel ingots on the eve of the First World War is somewhat misleading. Significant developments took place in ownership and control, in backward and forward integration, and in techniques.

1 Ownership, Control, and Structure

Important changes took place in the ownership and control of the major Scottish steel firms in 1895. The leading firm, the Steel Company of Scotland, having narrowly escaped bankruptcy in 1894, lost its original chairman when Sir Charles Tennant resigned in the following year.[2] It may be that he was finding the wearisome and profitless affairs of the Steel Company an irksome brake on his ambitions to move to 'greater things'

---

[1] Seen in its British context, the increase in output is, however, much less dramatic: Scotland's percentage share of British acid open-hearth steel production and of total British steel production (acid and basic by both open-hearth and Bessemer processes) is as follows:

Year	1895	1900	1905	1910
Acid open-hearth	32·3	33·6	37·0	35·2
All processes	16·3	19·7	21·8	18·9

[2] Although he retained his place on the board and was appointed Honorary President of the company, after 1895 Tennant played very little active part in its activities.

TABLE 5.1

Scottish Steel Production, Price of Scottish Steel Ship Plates, and Clyde Steam Ship Launchings, 1895–1914

	(1)	(2)	(3)	(4)	(5)
		Ingot output (tons)		Price of Scottish ship plates (shillings per	Tonnage of steam ships launched
Year	Acid	Basic	Total	long ton)	on the Clyde
1895	505,850	26,920	532,770	105	304,146
1896	583,266	2,613	585,879	108	352,737
1897	809,311	3,384	812,695	114	282,284
1898	n.d.	n.d.	948,120	118	429,440
1899	936,836	3,399	940,235	146	462,600
1900	960,581	2,764	963,345	167	451,232
1901	948,659	1,038	949,697	124	511,990
1902	999,994	21,186	1,013,180	118	518,270
1903	865,953	38,897	904,850	115	446,869
1904	986,674	105,331	1,092,005	113	417,870
1905	1,126,428	140,158	1,266,586	124	539,850
1906	1,147,833	158,760	1,306,593	146	598,841
1907	1,131,179	155,025	1,286,204	152	619,919
1908	899,215	129,985	1,029,200	127	355,586
1909	916,570	115,235	1,031,805	123	403,187
1910	1,063,250	138,381	1,201,631	128	392,392
1911	1,120,078	136,469	1,256,547	138	630,583
1912	884,457	162,422	1,046,879	152	640,529
1913	1,186,130	245,010[a]	1,469,451[c]	164	756,976
1914	1,052,685	255,438[b]	1,326,489[d]	n.d.	653,332

Notes: [a] includes 57,020 tons of Basic Bessemer ingots: [b] includes 35,400 tons of Basic Bessemer ingots; [c] includes 38,311 tons of 'other ingots and castings'; [d] includes 18,366 tons of 'other ingots and castings'.

Sources: Cols. (1)–(3): M. L. Simpson, 'Steel Works—A Twenty-One Years' Review', *Journal of the West of Scotland Iron and Steel Institute,* xxi (1913–14), 56; the data for 1913 and 1914 were kindly supplied by the Statistics Department of the British Iron and Steel Federation.
Col. (4): McCloskey, *Economic Maturity,* p. 136, based on *Iron and Coal Trades Review.* The figure given is an average of the prices for the week of the *I.C.T.R.* closest to the middle of the months of January, April, July, and October.
Col. (5): Cunnison and Gilfillan (eds.), *Glasgow,* pp. 839–40.

in the metropolis and in international big business. Certainly, for some years he had been becoming increasingly detached from his inherited interest, St. Rollox, in his efforts to attain the status of a cosmopolitan and international businessman.[3]

[3] This idea was suggested to the author by Professor S. G. Checkland (also, see his *Mines of Tharsis,* pp. 97–103, 263–9), who pointed out that Tennant

The departure of Tennant in 1895 probably had little effect on the practical operations of the Steel Company, but his resignation coincided with that of the general manager, James Riley, who left to go to the Glasgow Iron & Steel Company at Wishaw. Control of Hallside and Blochairn thus passed to Sir William Lorimer. Lorimer's principal interest was in locomotive building—he had been Henry Dübs's partner at the Glasgow Locomotive Works and was to become the first chairman of the North British Locomotive Company when that company was founded in 1903—but the fact that he had been acting general manager of the Steel Company in the latter part of the interregnum between Michael Scott's resignation in 1874 and the appointment of James Riley in 1878[4] is some indication of his knowledge of steel-making. If it was to survive, what the Steel Company needed was sound—even conservative—management. This Lorimer provided. Confidence in this tottering concern had to be restored, the flow of dividends had to be re-started. With a measure of good fortune, Lorimer was able to achieve these related objectives. His grasp of the Steel Company's affairs was thereby consolidated. From the mid-nineties until 1920 he remained in indisputable command of the enterprise. Of his board only Wallace Thorneycroft, elected in 1900, appears to have attained any real power: none of the senior officials was given the opportunity to emulate Riley.

In the two decades preceding the First World War, the Steel Company of Scotland, like its competitors, repeatedly found that its efforts to maintain technical modernity and so stabilize or even reduce costs were more than offset by unprecedented increases in the costs of raw materials, particularly fuel. By 1904 Lorimer told the shareholders that in the constant quest to reduce the consumption of coal, the Company 'had almost touched bottom'; two years later 'to his surprise and certainly to his great delight, he found that during [the year 1905–6] coal consumption was reduced . . . by something like 4 per cent

probably exemplifies those businessmen who, having made, or consolidated, the family fortunes in the provinces, widened their horizons by moving to London and participating in the great outflow of capital and expertise from late Victorian Britain. This activity was often detrimental to many local family firms and may have involved the 'creaming' of the provinces of entrepreneurial talent. This is an issue that deserves further investigation.

[4] See above, p. 39n.

on the amount per ton of steel made'. Economical working could go no further. Unless the demand for the Company's products was to be chocked off by the necessity of covering increased input prices, backwards integration was imperative. As he told the annual meeting:

> Ever since they came into existence as a company they had bought their fuel from coalmasters, and although occasionally they thought of the expediency of acquiring a colliery, up to the present they had never considered the advantages were such as to induce them to take this step. But circumstances had changed, and, of course, they changed with them. The report of the Royal Commission on Coal Supplies had revealed what they knew fairly well before, that the thick and cheaply-worked seams of coal in their district were rather rapidly approaching exhaustion.

It was for this reason that the Steel Company had purchased a mineral field, already partly developed, lying north and south of the Monkland Canal, 'and a sufficient supply for the Blochairn Works would be got from it'.[5] By 1909, after expensive development, the collieries at Garthamlock and Queenslie began to contribute to the firm's profits.

A further step towards reducing its dependence upon outside sources of raw materials was taken in 1913 when the Steel Company purchased 50,000 shares of the Appleby Iron Company Ltd., of £1 each, fully paid, and 125,000 shares of £1 each on which the sum of 6*d.* per share had been paid. This constituted a half interest in the Appleby company: the other half being held by the Frodingham Iron & Steel Company, who were the vendors. This was the culmination of a search by the Steel Company, extending over many years, for an interest in a suitable source of iron ore or pig iron.[6] In 1910, Wallace Thorneycroft— who by this time had gained a powerful position in the Steel Company—and Maximilian Mannaberg, of the Frodingham Company, visited Algiers together to examine a number of iron ore properties.[7] This attempt to secure ore reserves was un-

[5] Steel Company of Scotland: report of the Annual General Meeting, 1906. *Glasgow Herald*, 6 Sept. 1906.

[6] As early as 1886 the Steel Company was involved in examining the commercial potentialities of ore deposits in Spain. S.C. of S., Minute Book V, 15 Sept. 1886; VI, 7 Feb. 1888; VII, 9 Oct. 1889; XII, 14 Apr. 1905 (a joint venture with the Glasgow Iron & Steel Co.)

[7] The Steel Company of Scotland and the Frodingham Iron & Steel Co. were associated in a syndicate, known as the Olga Iron Ore Co., set up to prospect for oxide ores which would be suitable substitutes for the Swedish

successful, but from it sprang the connection between the two companies. Thus when, in 1912, the Frodingham Iron & Steel Company took over the Appleby Iron Company,[8] and proposed to enlarge and modernize the iron works and to erect a steel-making plant and plate rolling mill on the site, it was decided to sell half the shares in the iron company to the Steel Company of Scotland. The latter's experience in the manufacture and sale of plates would be invaluable to Frodingham, and, in return, the Scottish concern would gain its long-sought interest in both an iron ore property and a pig-iron producer. Furthermore, Lorimer believed it was imperative to move into the manufacture of basic steel plates: 'these were being made in Germany and much of the export trade built up during the past forty years was being taken from the Steel Company of Scotland as a result . . . The company could not afford to neglect this side of the trade, it was constantly growing and passing the manufacture of acid steel rapidly. [Moreover] the great American industry had been built up on basic steel . . .'[9] The shareholders agreed with these sentiments and it was agreed to create 40,000 new £10 Cumulative Preference shares to pay for the Appleby Iron Company's shares. The venture seemed extremely promising. Under Lorimer, the *Statist* had commented a year earlier, the Steel Company had remedied the mistakes of the past and had transformed 'a derelict concern . . . into one of the most important and successful concerns in Scotland'.[10]

At Dalzell, changes were less dramatic but, in the long run, even more important. They concerned the control of the company. In 1895, the founder of David Colville & Sons, now aged 82, had for some time allowed effective control of the firm to pass to his sons: John, Archibald, and David, jun. The eldest

---

ores generally used in open-hearth furnaces. Ibid., XIV, 13 Apr. 1910; P. W. S. Andrews and Elizabeth Brunner, *Capital Development in Steel* (Oxford: Blackwell, 1951), p. 112; Sir Frederick Scopes, *The Development of Corby Works* (privately printed for Stewarts & Lloyds, 1968), p. 15.

[8] The Frodingham company had earlier advanced money to the Appleby company when the latter concern got into financial difficulties earlier in the century. Andrews and Brunner, *Capital Development in Steel*, p. 112.

[9] *Glasgow Herald*, 5 Feb. 1914; *Scotsman*, 5 Feb. 1914.

[10] *Statist*, 6 Sept. 1913. It was emphasized that 'nineteen years ago the shares were selling at less than £1 for the £10 share; today's price is $11\frac{3}{16}$'.

son, John, however, became known 'not for his conspicuous business ability ... but for his unceasing labours for the good of his fellow-men'.[11] There is ample evidence that he played an important role—especially on the financial and commercial side—in establishing the steel works at Dalzell, but increasingly his energies were absorbed by public works. 'It would be hard to name any religious or benevolent enterprise in the town [of Motherwell] to which he was not a tower of strength ... As Volunteer Officer, School Board Member, Burgh Commissioner, County Councillor, and Provost [from 1888 to 1895], he served the community', and to promote 'the causes that lay nearest his heart, especially those of religion, temperance and social reform', he 'responded to the call to represent the constituency in Parliament', being elected the Liberal member for north-east Lanarkshire in 1895. This event, coinciding with the paying off of the loans made to the firm by J. S. Napier in the early eighties, prompted the conversion of the original partnership to a private limited liability company in the same year.

Although the change was more apparent than real—the control of the enterprise remained firmly in the hands of Archibald and David Colville, jun.—it permitted the firm to continue to develop and grow with no perceptible hesitation when David Colville, the founder, died in 1897 and John—who immediately assumed the chairmanship of the company—died suddenly only four years later. The potentially disruptive effects of death on a small partnership had been avoided, and the establishment of family trusts in the names of David and John Colville served, in the event, merely to increase the power of the surviving brothers. On the establishment of the company all the Ordinary shares were allocated to the founder and his sons who held all but six of the 25,727 £10 Preference shares. The Ordinary shares were even more tightly held when the founder died, since not only were most of David Colville's shares transferred to Archibald and David, jun., but they were among the trustees under their father's Trust Disposition and Settlement.[12] All the

---

[11] Anon., *Glasgow and Lanarkshire Illustrated* (Hamilton: Hamilton Herald Printing & Publishing Co. Ltd., 1904), p. 90. The following quotations, typical of the many eulogistic obituary notices which followed John Colville's death in 1901, are taken from the same source. A factual profile of John Colville was given in the first volume of *Colvilles' Magazine*, pp. 22–3.

[12] David Colville, Trust Disposition and Settlement, dated 21 Dec. 1897.

other shareholders, with the exception of George B. Douglas and the two partners of the firm's solicitors, Maclay, Murray, & Spens, were members of the family.[13]

Ownership of the firm was slightly widened when, on the death of John Colville, 500 Cumulative Preference shares were allotted to William Currie, the Company Secretary, who was promptly made a director.[14] Two months later, certain of John Colville's Ordinary shares were transferred to members of the prominent firm of Glasgow iron merchants, Napier and McIntyre, whose senior partner, James Smith Napier, had figured so prominently in the establishment of the steel works. What is remarkable, however, was the directors' decision, in 1902, to offer shares in David Colville & Sons to several 'young men in the employment of the Company'. It is true that certain limitations were imposed on the sale and transfer of such shares,[15] but such a step was clearly unusual and remarkably progressive in the context of the British steel industry at the turn of the century. As a result the leading officials acquired a personal interest in the fortunes of the firm and many were subsequently to become members of the Board, and one, John Craig, its chairman.[16] It is not impossible that this policy—modestly

[13] Alexander Bilsland and John Lusk were David Colville's sons-in-law.
[14] D.C. & S., Directors' Minute Book I, p. 136, 1901.
[15] The conditions were set down in a special resolution passed at an Extraordinary General Meeting of the shareholders held on 11 June 1902. D.C. & S., Directors' Minute Book I.
[16] By the original decision of 10 April 1902, shares were offered at par to the following managers or employees:

David Mowat Maclay (Works Manager, Dalzell)	250
James Gillespie (Chief Engineer for Maintenance and Upkeep)	250
John Lennox (Plate Sales Manager)	250
John Craig (Colville's representative on the Glasgow Royal Exchange)	250
James B. Allan (Company Secretary, successor to William Currie)	250
William Currie (Sometime Company Secretary)	200
James Hamilton	200
Daniel Jack	200
Thomas Mackenzie (Drawing Office Manager, subsequently Chief Engineer for all new work)	200
John Thorburn	150
David Lockhart	150

Where the information is available the appointment held by the manager or employee *in 1902* has been given in brackets. D.C. & S., Directors' Minute Book I, 10 Apr. 1902.

begun but actively encouraged throughout the prewar years[17]—constitutes an important element in the success of the firm during the difficult years of the twentieth century. Certainly its implications were momentous. Until 1916 real power remained with the Colville brothers and their relatives, but within a decade and a half it was to pass to those enfranchised by the decision of 1902.

More orthodox[18] changes were taking place elsewhere in the Scottish steel industry. In 1899 William Beardmore developed a patent armour plate, laying down a cogging and armour plate mill at Parkhead. In the following year, finding his market unduly circumscribed by the control exercised by the existing armour firms, Beardmore took over the famous shipbuilding firm of Robert Napier & Sons, with a yard at Govan and an engine works at Lancefield. In 1902 90 acres of land was purchased at Dalmuir, Dunbartonshire, where a 'naval construction works' was laid out, with berths designed for building capital ships. To service Dalmuir, plant for making large naval guns was put down at Parkhead in 1905. This included a 12,000 ton hydraulic press and a gun tempering shop. And, only a year later, Beardmores bought the Mossend Steel Works from the Summerlee and Mossend Iron & Steel Company for £50,000 in order to provide additional plate and section capacity for their shipyards.[19] More remarkably, in 1903 the firm took over

---

[17] For example, the trustees of John McIntyre transferred 500 of his Ordinary shares to various officials in 1908. D.C. & S., Directors' Minute Book I, 18 Feb. 1908. In 1911, when it was decided to issue 3,000 £10 Ordinary shares in Colvilles, the directors wrote to the shareholders: 'Under Article 39, you, as an Ordinary Shareholder are entitled to be offered —— Shares of the Allotment, but the Managing Directors think it is in the interests of the Company to stand aside to some extent in this instance so as to allow heads of departments to have a larger interest in the business ... [thus] the Managing Directors trust that you will assist them to further their purpose by not applying for more than at the outside about one half of your *pro rata* proportion . . .' In the event, not only were the senior management allotted 1,710 shares of the issue, but—'as it was considered undesirable for them to borrow outside for this purpose'—facilities were provided for them to borrow part of the purchase price (at 5 per cent interest) from the company. D.C. & S., Directors' Minute Book II, 8 May 1911, 17 May 1911.

[18] That is, 'orthodox' in the sense that a number of firms participated in the combination movement that characterized British industry at the turn of the century. See P. L. Payne, 'The Emergence of the Large-Scale Company in Great Britain', *Economic History Review*, 2nd Series, xx (1967).

[19] The Mossend Steel Works had been advertised as being for sale by

the Mo-Car Syndicate, makers of the Arrol Johnston motor car.[20]

This massive expansion and diversification—nearly £250,000 was spent on buildings at Parkhead alone between 1884 and 1914—was financed partly out of profits and partly by the conversion of the original partnership to a limited company and the issue of Ordinary shares. The latter took place in 1902 and nearly one-half of them (£749,997)[21] was taken up by Vickers, Sons, & Maxim, in order, it was said, to keep Beardmores 'out of ordnance', or at least to prevent the Parkhead firm from directly competing with the products of Barrow.[22] Whatever the *precise* reason for the combination, Vickers' directors, 'after the most careful investigation [had] come to the conclusion that . . . the two firms should have a community of interest'.[23] This was achieved by the acquisition of Beardmores' Ordinary shares by Vickers and the issue as fully paid to William Beardmore of 400,000 Ordinary shares in Vickers. Beardmore was appointed Chairman and Managing Director of the new company of William Beardmore & Company Ltd., and he was joined on the board by his brother, Mr. Joseph Beardmore, and two directors of Vickers, Albert Vickers and Lieutenant A. J. Dawson. In turn, William Beardmore was appointed a director of Vickers, Sons, & Maxim.[24]

the Summerlee and Mossend Iron & Steel Co. in the local press as early as 1902. Its major plant was then said to consist of 12 melting furnaces (2 of 40, 3 of 30, 2 of 25, and 5 of 20 tons capacity), a 45-inch cogging mill, 2 reversing and one pull-over plate mill, a 26-inch reversing and a 17-inch pull-over bar mill, and a 10-inch guide mill. The plate mills were said to have a monthly capacity of 6,000 tons. An undated [1902] cutting, almost certainly from the *Glasgow Herald*, is included in one of David Colville & Sons' early books of 'Newspaper Cuttings'.

[20] The foregoing paragraph and much of the subsequent data on Beardmores are based upon John R. Hume and Michael S. Moss, *Beardmore: The History of a Scottish Industrial Giant* (London: Heinemann, 1979), an early draft of which the authors very kindly permitted me to read.

[21] £1·5 m of Debentures were issued in 1904–5.

[22] In 1897, Vickers had acquired the Naval Construction and Armaments Company of Barrow, the capacity of which they promptly doubled. See J. D. Scott, *Vickers: A History* (London: Weidenfeld & Nicolson, 1962), pp. 44, 46, 48–9.

[23] Letter from J. R. Heckley, Secretary of Vickers, Sons, & Maxim to all shareholders, 18 Jan. 1902. The circular is reproduced in full in the *Glasgow Herald*, 20 Jan. 1902.

[24] Ibid.

In acquiring a half share in the Ordinary capital of Beardmores, Vickers may have tightened their grip of the potentially
lucrative armaments business, but they rapidly became dis-
enchanted with William Beardmore's style of management. In
the years following 1902, Beardmore's ambitions for Parkhead,
Dalmuir, and Mossend proved to be very expenisve. Parkhead
managed to show a healthy profit, but this was more than offset
by massive losses at the Dalmuir Yard and by the expensive
reconstruction of Mossend. The opening of the enormous
engine and boiler works, built by Sir William Arrol & Company, at Dalmuir was, as the directors' statement of accounts
for the year 1907 delicately put it, 'attended by a slackness of
orders and low prices, consequent upon the state of the shipbuilding industry' which meant that it was impossible fully to
employ the new plant at Mossend.[25] Worse was to come. The
debt burden continued to grow, trade remained dull, and funds
were drained away in ill-defined 'experimental ventures'. The
reactions of the financial press were vitriolic. None more so than
that of the *Syren*:

There is not a single redeeming feature in the report and accounts of
William Beardmore & Co. Limited—even their issue is late. Here we are
in the autumn of 1909, and Mr. Beardmore and his friends calmly come along
with accounts for the year ended December 31, 1908. Is it bashfulness or
shame that has caused this lingering by the way? The report tells us that
'the profits for the year are £66,433.' They are nothing of the sort, for there
are numerous charges to be deducted which result in there being a balance
of loss to carry forward of £72,400, and this is without making any allowance
for depreciation, or taking into account the £50,000 cumulative preference
dividend accrued and unpaid at the year's end. An interesting light is thrown
on the methods of management by the statement in the report that 'the losses
arising from investments in subsidiary and other companies have been unusu-
ally heavy.' The impression this gives is that such losses are regarded as regular
events, like the coming of buttercups and daisies, or the shooting season, or
rent day. We gather that at the date last year to which the accounts were
made up, the Company owed for loans and interest £17,483, sundry debtors
(including bank overdrafts, the amount of which is not stated) £175,430, and
on bills payable, £4,723. Do the directors not believe in giving bills? The
assets are of the assorted character. Land, buildings, fixed plant and
machinery, goodwill (!) and patent rights, figure at £3,185,312, £74,330 of
which was added during 1908. Investments, loans, etc., stand at £141,704,
and of this the auditors say: 'The investments are chiefly in subsidiary com-

[25] William Beardmore & Co., Statement of Accounts for the year ended
31 Dec. 1907.

panies for which there is no market value.' Pleasant for the shareholders. Sundry debts due to the Company are £236,246 (we trust they are all good), and, thank heaven, there are some bawbees in good red gold—at least, let us hope so! Scots notes are not nice handling—the amount is £433 13s. 2d. We note, by the way, that 'interest on debentures and loans amounted to £74,561', or £8,128 more than the so-called profits. And yet we find 'goodwill' figuring as an asset![26]

Goodwill was evidently also lacking in the boardroom. There is some evidence that Vickers sought to replace Beardmore as Chairman of the firm that bore his name and having failed to do so attempted to induce their arch-rivals, Armstrong, Whitworth, & Company Ltd., to take a share in the Beardmore business. Let the historian of Vickers, J. D. Scott, take up the story: 'By 1910 Armstrongs had twice declined to entertain a proposal from Vickers that they should buy Beardmore shares, and when Vickers approached Armstrongs for a third time on this score, it was on the grounds that only by this means could Sir William Beardmore be restrained from regaining full control of "his great enterprise" and extending its manufacture. In May 1910 Albert Vickers wrote to Sir Andrew Noble [Armstrongs' chairman]:

I feel that your Board is doing your Company a serious future injury by so lightly refusing the offer I have made ... The Beardmore Company is now in such sound condition comparatively, that I have grave fear that he may get someone to find the money to buy back his shares and thus get control of the Beardmore Company ... Even if Beardmore does not buy the shares back, we shall, as I explained to you, be compelled to push the Beardmore business to the detriment of your Firm and so render amicable and consequently profitable working together difficult if not impossible.

But [Lord] Rendel [Armstrongs' largest single shareholder] was very much opposed to this proposal. He warned Saxton Noble [Sir Andrew's son] not to listen to "loose talk" about Vickers' inability to restrain Beardmore any longer; he regarded this statement with scepticism, saying that it was no more than another effort of Vickers to unload their bad bargain with Beardmore upon Armstrongs.' And Rendel's view eventually prevailed.[27]

[26] *Syren and Shipping*, 6 Oct. 1909.
[27] Scott, *Vickers*, p. 92. Scott is incorrect in believing that the Armstrong Board agreed to the Vickers proposal. After considering the proposal in great detail they eventually turned it down. I am indebted to Dr. R. J. Irving for information concerning Armstrongs' reception of the Vickers proposals.

Unabashed by the ululations of the financial press, by the growing discord of his Board, by the suspicions of the Armstrongs and the clamour of the shareholders, Sir William Beardmore forged on. He personally bought shares in, and became a director of, the firm of Merry & Cunninghame. And nothing was too good for his own works, which were steadily integrated, and his firm, the products of which were increasingly diversified.[28] But whatever the technical or even the medium-term economic merits of the growth of the firm that had originated at Parkhead, the ambitions of Sir William Beardmore effectively blunted the competitive edge of his firm in the market for commercial steels. The rolled products of Parkhead and Mossend were primarily intended for the other parts of the Beardmore empire, not to compete with the similar products of the Steel Company or David Colville & Company Ltd. Beardmore was losing sight of his bread and butter: it was to have disastrous results.

No such mistake was made by the firm established by Andrew Stewart. His concern, the Clyde Tube Works, began modestly in St. Enoch's Wynd, Glasgow, but so successful was it that seven years later a new and larger works of the same name was built at Coatbridge specifically to manufacture buttweld and lapweld tubes. In 1872 Andrew Stewart took his brother James into partnership and the name of the firm was changed to A. & J. Stewart. Ten years later the partnership was converted into a private limited company in order, it was said, to give the principal heads of the departments an opportunity of acquiring a permanent 'interest' in the rapidly-growing firm.[29] but no less an important motive was, it may be conjectured, to take over the Sun Tube Works, Coatbridge, and the Clyde Pipe Foundry, Glasgow, where cast iron pipes were made. Within a decade the firm was employing about 1,200 hands and its products enjoyed an international reputation.[30]

[28] In 1913, Beardmores took a out a licence to build Austro-Daimler aero engines and increased the scale of its commitment to motor cars. John R. Hume and Michael S. Moss, *Beardmore: The History of a Scottish Industrial Giant*.

[29] Stewarts & Lloyds, Ltd., special number of the *S. & L. Review*, entitled *Stewarts & Lloyds, 1903–1953* (privately printed, undated, *c.* 1954), pp. 6–7. The statement is based on a report in the *Glasgow Weekly Herald*, 19 Apr. 1902. I am indebted to Mr. H. A. Lear, Divisional Secretary, Tubes Division, British Steel Corporation, for this reference.

[30] These were principally marine and locomotive boiler tubes, steam, water,

In 1889, J. G. Stewart and T. C. Stewart, Andrew Stewart's
sons, established their own firm, Stewart Brothers, and began
making lapweld tubes at the British Tube Works, Coatbridge.
This firm was not destined to enjoy a long independent existence. In 1890 it was merged with A. & J. Stewart and the Clydesdale Iron & Steel Company of Mossend, which, since 1871,
had specialized in making iron strip for tube making and, since
1884, steel strip from a battery of open-hearth furnaces and rolling mills. Designed principally to ensure that the Stewart concerns enjoyed control of the major raw materials of tube manufacture, this amalgamation could have proved ruinous.[31] The
fact was—as the Chairman of Stewart & Clydesdale Ltd. had
to admit at the third annual general meeting of shareholders
in 1893—that the Clydesdale Works were 'not in the efficient
condition in which Messrs M'Corkindale & Bain [had] represented them to be'. Certainly, 'part of the plant was old-
fashioned and part of it almost worn out, and it was not making
the profits which it ought to make'. The open-hearth furnaces
were efficient enough, it would appear, 'but this is not the case
as regards the steel-producing plant. The rolling mills we have
found to be neither modern nor of an approved type. They were
erected for working iron plates, and are not of the weight or
power required for steel plates.' Furthermore, there was no cogging mill: all the ingots were hammered preparatory to rolling.
This produced a high quality product but one which was very
expensive.[32] Andrew Stewart then made the remarkable admis-
sion that before the merger he had never been in the Clydesdale
Works. 'Some of my co-directors, no doubt, had visited the

gas, oil, and artesian well tubes, and a comprehensive variety of ancillary fittings.
[31] Incorporated under the Companies Acts as A. & J. Stewart & Clydesdale
Ltd., the total capital was to be £700,000 divided into 25,000 6 per cent
Cumulative Preference shares of £10 each and 45,000 Ordinary shares of
£10 each. The original board of directors was Andrew Stewart (Chairman)
and John Wotherspoon (of A. & J. Stewart Ltd.), Sir William Arrol, James
L. Mitchell, Dugald M'Corkindale, and Andrew Bain (of Clydesdale Iron
& Steel Co.), and John G. Stewart (of Stewart Bros.) *Glasgow Herald*, 16 Mar.
1890.
[32] In the very heated debate which ensued, Andrew Bain produced letters
from both James Neilson of Mossend and David Colville & Sons testifying
to the very high quality of hammered plates and, with a *'limited production
of steel'*, the relative economy of hammering as compared with cogging.

works on ordinary business, but none of them had ever gone there for the purpose of going over the plant and ascertaining its completeness and efficiency. I had long known the works in connection with the production of iron and steel for tube making, and had found their quality satisfactory. Of the cost of production I knew nothing. I have never had anything to do with plates ...'

This statement incensed the shareholders, one of whom rightly accused the directors of A. &. J. Stewart and Stewart Brothers of failing 'to take sufficient pains to verify ... the condition of the works' and another of whom argued that far from the shareholders having to sacrifice part of their dividends in order to remedy the defects discovered at Clydesdale, 'the directors, the vendors, [who had] got a good price for their works, [should] amongst themselves put in [a] cogging mill'. A cogging mill which, it was said, would cost £30,000 and save up to 4s. 6d. per ton in the cost of producing steel. In the end—after 'Sir William Arrol [had] said he did not think it was for the advantage of the company to discuss all these petty details'[33]—Dugald M'Corkindale resigned from the Board; the five directors who remained (including Andrew Bain) were, amazingly, voted an additional £2,000, and the firm was committed to a thorough modernization at Clydesdale.[34]

In the years following this meeting, the steel smelting and heating furnaces were rebuilt and three new rolling mills put down at Clydesdale,[35] and the company's prosperity boosted by the introduction of welded-on flange joints for high pressure steam installations. In 1898 the business of James Menzies & Company of the Phoenix Tube Works, Rutherglen—manufacturers of solid-drawn (seamless) steel tubes—was purchased[36]

[33] A sentiment greeted with cries of 'Hear, hear!'
[34] Stewart & Clydesdale Ltd., Report of the Third Annual General Meeting, 28 Mar. 1893. *Glasgow Herald*, 29 Mar. 1893.
[35] 'From 1890 to 1900 Clydesdale contributed little or nothing to the profits of the Company. Mr. P. N. Cunningham (General Manager of Clydesdale from 1890 to 1920) told [Sir Frederick Scopes] that 1900 was the first year when Clydesdale made a profit. Mr. Cunningham remembered with pleasure that when Mr. Andrew Stewart was very ill not long before his death in 1901 he was able to cheer him up by telling him that Clydesdale had contributed to the profits of the Company for the first time.' Scopes, *The Development of Corby Works*, p. 13.
[36] In announcing this move at the eighth Annual General Meeting, Andrew

and the name of the firm changed to A. & J. Stewart & Menzies Ltd.[37] Two years later, the Imperial Tube Works were erected at Airdrie for the manufacture of large diameter steel pipes by the lapweld process, and, on an adjacent site, the process of integration was continued by the building of the Climax Engineering Works for the manufacture of machine tools required by the various works within the group. By the end of the century finished output averaged some 36,000 tons a year compared with about 16,000 tons in 1890. It was a remarkable achievement. Financially, the company was extremely sound. The dividend policy was, by the standards of the time, conservative.[38] So much so that when, in 1900, one shareholder attending the tenth ordinary general meeting pointed out that 'the directors wanted to put aside something like £80,000— nearly one-half of the whole earnings of the concern, which, in ordinary honesty should have been divided among the Ordinary shareholders . . .', a rebellion among his fellow aggrieved shareholders was averted only by the time-honoured practice of drawing attention to the handsome dividend of 10 per cent declared in that year and hinting that this might well be endangered if the point was pressed.[39]

And, indeed, it might have been. Stewart & Menzies had to retain a high proportion of its earnings in order to maintain its very high efficiency if fierce competition in the tube trade,

---

Stewart commented that for the last few years James Menzies & Co. had been Stewart & Clydesdale's 'principal rivals'. Questioned about the terms the directors had made with Menzies & Co. by one of the same shareholders (Hugh Begg) who had caused such an uproar five years earlier, the Chairman—learning from past experience—refused to be drawn. It would, he said, be 'unwise' and 'premature' to go into such questions now.

[37] The capital of the new company, £850,000, divided into 35,000 6 per cent Cumulative Preference shares of £10 each and 50,000 Ordinary shares of £10 each, was soon enlarged by the issue of £200,000 in 3½ per cent Debentures of £100 each. The directors were Andrew Stewart (Chairman), Sir William Arrol, John G. Stewart, Walter Menzies, John R. Cassels, Thomas C. Stewart, and James Menzies.

[38] The average dividend on the Ordinary shares for the twelve years of the company's existence was 8½ per cent and by 1902 the reserve fund stood at £209,000. Stewart & Menzies, Report of the annual general meeting, *Glasgow Herald*, 28 March 1902.

[39] See P. L. Payne, 'Industrial Entrepreneurship and Management in Britain, c. 1760–1970', in P. Mathias and M. M. Postan (eds.), *The Cambridge Economic History of Europe*, Vol. VII, *The Industrial Economies: Capital, Labour, and Enterprise* (Cambridge: C.U.P., 1978), Pt. 1, p. 205.

both at home and abroad, was successfully to be met. The firm's greatest rivals were undoubtedly Lloyd & Lloyd, of Birmingham. Established in 1859 by Samuel Lloyd and his cousin, Edward Rigge Lloyd, to make boiler tubes, within a decade this firm had come to specialize in the manufacture of wrought iron and, later, steel screwed and socketed tubes and fittings. Always in the forefront of technical innovation,[40] this highly progressive firm, having been converted to a private limited company in 1898, decided two years later to manufacture seamless tubes in the Glasgow district, purchasing the Clydeside Tube Company Ltd. at Whifflet. Competition between Stewart & Menzies and Lloyd & Lloyd promised to become intolerable: late in 1902 agreement was reached to amalgamate the two firms. The express reason was explained by Henry Howard, Chairman of Lloyd & Lloyd:

> In the past, they had continually crossed each other's paths in most corners of the globe. The fight had been severe, and victory had sometimes been secured by one side and sometimes by the other, but there had been one uniform result from all this fighting to the shareholders of both companies, that whether victorious or not it had diminished their profits. This competition would for the future cease to exist, and this concentration of practical experience should enable home and foreign competition to be more easily dealt with.[41]

Stewarts & Lloyds came into being on 1 Jan. 1903, with a share capital of £1,750,000. It was, commented Macrosty, writing in 1907, 'the embryo of an "efficiency" trust',[42] and, indeed, for the next decade consolidation and progress continued steadily, the large-scale manufacture of steel castings by the Tropenas process being undertaken in 1906 and new uses for tubes being continually pioneered.[43] New works were erected and existing ones purchased,[44] usually for the manufacture of

[40] Lloyd & Lloyd introduced the Albion Loose Flange Joint for gas, water, air and steam pipes in 1893, the process of gas welding for large tubes, and, following visits to Russia by Henry Howard in 1890 and 1892, secured the European patents under the Benardos process of electric welding. *Stewarts & Lloyds, 1903–1953*, pp. 10–11.

[41] H. W. Macrosty, *The Trust Movement in British Industry*, pp. 46–7.

[42] Ibid.

[43] *Stewarts & Lloyds, 1903–1953*, pp. 19–23.

[44] For example, in 1912 the Vulcan Works, where pipes up to 72-inch diameter were manufactured, were acquired by the purchase of the British Welding Co. Ltd. of Motherwell; and, in the following year, a new works was laid down at Tollcross for the purpose of making seamless tubes up to 4-inch diameter, particularly for locomotive and stationary boilers.

specialized tubes and pipes, and in 1908, Stewarts & Lloyds acquired a controlling interest in Robert Addie & Sons' Collieries Limited.[45] But Macrosty's use of the word 'efficiency' was—at least at the outset—somewhat misleading. Admittedly, on-cost charges and selling prices were reduced almost immediately, but the 'considerable internal administrative adjustments' consequent upon the amalgamation 'took time'. Management remained only loosely centralized and radical organizational change was slow. Only the possession of a high degree of monopoly power permitted the continuous payment of handsome dividends.[46] The situation prevailing at the Works Office of the Clyde Tube Works is illuminating:

> The only piece of modern office equipment was the telephone, with a private line to the Glasgow Office ... But there was no other office machinery of any kind—no typewriters, adding machines, comptometers, pay-roll listing machines, etc. There were no women in the office. Everything was handwritten and the only duplication was by letter press copying ... No one trained in a modern office can have any idea of the crudity of office methods and organization at that time.[47]

Not surprisingly, some years after the merger John Graham Stewart, the first chairman of the company, commented that 'the weld between A. & J. Stewart & Menzies Ltd. and Lloyd and Lloyd Ltd. had not been made in one heat. I do not know how many heats were required but ... traces of the weld were visible for years ...'[48]

---

[45] Scopes, *The Development of Corby Works*, gives the details, p. 14, see also pp. 141–7.

[46] In commenting on the circular to the shareholders of Stewart & Menzies announcing the amalgamation (issued 2 Dec. 1902), the *Glasgow Herald* noted that the output of the amalgamated companies would be about 50 per cent of the total output of iron and steel tubes in Great Britain and that, with the exception of the U.S. Steel Corporation, the company would be the largest producer of tubes in the world. The total labour force would be about 8,000 and a staff of about 450 clerks would be employed in the different offices and warehouses at home and abroad.

[47] *Stewarts & Lloyds, 1903–1953*, p. 20.

[48] Ibid., p. 19. This was not unexpected. At the very outset of the company John Graham Stewart told the shareholders '... the subject of unification of management of all the works was being fully considered and was steadily progressing, although it could not be expected that a problem so complicated, owing to the varied methods and systems, which in each case were the result of many years' working experience, could be harmonised in a day, a month, or even a year ... The beneficial results of the amalgamation might therefore take some little time to fully develop.' Stewarts & Lloyds, report of the ordinary general meeting of the shareholders of Stewarts & Lloyds to consider

By the eve of the First World War, Stewarts & Lloyds' output of tubes and fittings had risen from some 80,000 tons in 1903 to 152,000 tons, just under half of which was exported.[49] In 1913 the company's make of steel at Clydesdale was approximately 161,000 tons.[50] This would have made Stewarts & Lloyds a serious competitor of the other Scottish steel makers had it not been for the fact that the overwhelming bulk of the company's ingot output was destined for further processing in its own works. The sheer success of Stewarts & Lloyds in the tube trade had effectively removed Clydesdale from the market for commercial steels. The implications of Clydesdale's unique position could not be foreseen.

Developments elsewhere in the Scottish steel industry were more mundane. The Calderbank Steel Works, following the liquidation of the Calderbank Steel Company in 1900, was acquired by James Dunlop & Company, proprietors of the Clyde Iron Works and a number of collieries. Little is known of James Dunlop & Company under the chairmanship of W. A. Donaldson. Its dividend record was good, if unexciting— averaging over $7\frac{1}{2}$ per cent on the Ordinary shares for the first eight years of its existence as a limited company (i.e. 1899– 1907)—and would have been even better had it not been for the board's conservative financial policy and constant efforts to keep the works and collieries at a high level of efficiency.[51] Like David Colville & Sons, the Lanarkshire Steel Company

---

the accounts of A. & J. Stewart & Menzies to 31 Dec. 1902. *Glasgow Herald*, 27 Mar. 1903.

[49] In an effort to retain a significant proportion of the tube market, a group of eight partnerships and companies on Clydeside merged their interests in 1912 to form the Scottish Tube Co. The constituent companies were the Caledonian Tube Co., Caledonian Works, Coatbridge; Coats Tube Co., Coats Works, Coatbridge; James Eadie & Sons, Clydesdale Works, Rutherglen; Chisholm & Henry Ltd., Saracen Works, Garnkirk; John Marshall & Sons, Glasgow Works, Dalmarnock; David Richmond & Co. Ltd., City Works, Gorbals, Glasgow; Tradeston Tube Co., Tradeston Works, Glasgow; Wilsons & Union Tube Co. Ltd., Union Works, Coatbridge and Govan Works, Glasgow. T. R. Miller, *The Monkland Tradition*, p. 79; Thomson, *The County of Lanark*, p. 61.

[50] *Stewarts & Lloyds, 1903–1953*, pp. 25–6.

[51] In 1970 the company possessed 'something like £160,000 or £170,000 in liquid assets', and its accounts always provided for substantial depreciation and relatively heavy capital outlays. See, for example, report of the annual general meeting. *Glasgow Herald*, 28 Feb. 1908.

remained simply a steel-melting and rolling firm. Reconstructed in 1897—the new company was incorporated on 27 April—Lanarkshire made nothing but standard sections.[52] The chairman, John Strain, would have nothing to do with backward and forward integration. Its marketing policy was extremely aggressive and although, by rigorous control of costs, it was usually able to pay its Preference dividend, its Ordinary shareholders received very little, a dividend being paid on only six occasions before the First World War. The leading spirit in the enterprise was John Strain: the other directors appear to have contributed little.[53] At least, Strain kept the company afloat and his thunderous statements to the annual general meetings, its name before the public.

This survey of developments in the structure of the Scottish steel industry would be incomplete without some mention of the malleable iron firms that managed to survive into the twentieth century. Faced with a declining demand for their traditional products, the majority of them began to use their plant to re-roll semi-finished steel goods, dependent for their supply of billets on the steel manufacturers: 'a weak position to hold, like an army with no base to fall back upon', as one of them commented later.[54] Those who continued to make wrought iron attempted to reduce costs—gas furnaces were substituted for coal-fired furnaces at a number of works—but fierce competition to obtain a share of the shrinking market made the position desperate for all of them. The fundamental problem was that 'no mechanical processes had been evolved to replace

[52] See *Report of the Tariff Commission*, vol. i: *The Iron and Steel Trades*, evidence of Witness No. 6 (John Strain, Chairman of the Lanarkshire Steel Co.), para. 628.

[53] An article in the *Motherwell Times*, 18 June 1902, took pains to emphasize that although the Lanarkshire Steel Co. was, in respect of its nominal capital of £450,000, 'the largest of all Motherwell's numerous companies . . . its shares are held almost exclusively by persons residing outwith Motherwell . . . There are only some three or four Motherwell people in the extensive list of shareholders, and their holdings are merely nominal. Some of the shareholders are resident in England, in Egypt, and even in South Africa.' At that time the board of directors were John Strain, John Ross, Alexander Watt, Alexander Rose, all of Glasgow; Hugh Steven, of the Milton Iron Works, Glasgow, and William Dickson of Uddingston.

[54] T. R. Miller, a director of A. & J. Miller's Globe Iron & Steel Works, in his study *The Monkland Tradition*, p. 60. This brief account of the genesis of the Scottish Iron and Steel Co. draws heavily on this source, particularly pp. 56–61.

successfully the hand labour of the puddler',[55] and further cost reduction was possible only if the malleable iron-makers agreed to limit the range of sizes of finished iron produced in each works, thus saving the time and labour involved in the frequent changing of rolls. Fruitless discussions to achieve this objective were held in 1902–3 and again in 1910. Not until financial disaster was imminent in 1911–12 were the malleable iron-makers prepared to sink their differences and agree to a scheme of amalgamation drawn up by a small committee composed of representatives of four of the largest firms: William Downs of the Coats Iron & Steel Works, Colin F. McLaren of the Stenton Works, Arthur J. Spencer of the Phoenix, and T. R. Miller of the Globe Iron & Steel Works. Thirteen malleable iron firms operating fifteen works agreed to the scheme,[56] firms who had in 1911 produced between them about 225,000 tons of malleable iron and steel. The outcome was the formation of the Scottish Iron and Steel Company Ltd., registered on 31 Dec. 1912, with a share capital of £750,000 augmented by £300,000 of 5 per cent Redeemable Debenture Stock.[57]

With so many firms involved in the amalgamation, some of which had three or four active partners or executive directors, lengthy and delicate negotiations had been necessary before the question of post-merger control could be settled:

> It was essential to give confidence to those who had for years controlled a business, as their feelings were sensitive to an appointment which might appear to lower their status. One of the partners of an old-established firm reconciled himself to the changing times when he told the committee that it was better to be one of a number in a large prosperous business than to be slowly starved out with his retainers like some impoverished landowner living in his cold, empty castle.[58]

Despite the care with which the merger had been organized, difficulties remained. Within a year it became necessary completely to reorganize the entire internal structure of the com-

---

[55] Thomson, *The County of Lanark*, pp. 30–1.

[56] They were Archibald Baird & Son, Downs & Jardine, Thomas Ellis Ltd., Glencairn Iron & Steel Co., C. F. McLaren & Co., Hugh Martin & Sons, A. & T. Miller, John Spencer (Coatbridge) Ltd., William Tudhope & Son Ltd., the Victoria Iron & Steel Co., the Waverley Iron & Steel Co., Wylie & Co., and the Woodside Steel & Iron Co.

[57] Clapham's comment on the amalgamation is interesting. See his *Economic History of Modern Britain*, iii. 271–2.

[58] T. R. Miller, *The Monkland Tradition*, p. 57.

pany, but unlike two of the four firms remaining outside 'the Combine',[59] it survived to play a significant, if relatively minor, role in the subsequent history of the Scottish steel industry.

2 Associations and Foreign Competition

Under an agreement with the Scotch Steelmasters' Association, Clydebridge was closed down in 1907.[60] This was perhaps the most significant combined action taken by the firms in the Scottish steel industry to regulate competition and maintain prices. They had initially combined to try to control the local market in 1885, and in the course of the year prices were, in fact, raised by 10s. a ton; but in the winter the English makers, notably Consett, undercut the combine severely and prices fell again. 'This was the beginning of a warfare frequently to be repeated in later years. In May, 1886, the Scotch Steelmakers' Association was dissolved, prices being then lower than before its formation.'[61] In later years all manner of 'agreements and understandings', usually applying to specific branches of the trade, were in operation. They all enjoyed some measure of success—particularly the Scotch Boiler-plate Association—but invariably they broke up because of the external pressure of English, German, or American competition or, more obviously, because of intense local rivalries.[62] Glengarnock and Lanarkshire always pursued highly individualistic policies and their withdrawal from several schemes—when, in fact, they had

[59] The Motherwell Iron & Steel Co. and the Pather Iron & Steel Co. both went down in the inter-war period. The Etna Iron & Steel Co. and the Dundyvan Iron Works of William Martin enjoyed a somewhat precarious existence as simple re-rollers.

[60] In 1912, when a number of shipbuilders, angered by the workings of a deferred rebate scheme under which firms agreeing to purchase only from association members received a discount on their purchases at the end of each year, threatened to resuscitate Clydebridge, the 'Scotch Steel Manufacturers' decided to forestall them by purchasing the works themselves and keeping them closed. When this proposal was discussed by Colvilles board, 'it was pointed out that it would be cheaper to purchase the works at a reasonable price than continue to pay the subsidy of £12,000 a year now being paid'. *Glasgow Herald*, 29 Oct. 1912; D.C. & S., Directors' Minutes II, 15 Apr. 1912.

[61] Macrosty, *The Trust Movement*, p. 66.

[62] Macrosty, op. cit., pp. 67–72, provides a good picture of the situation at the turn of the century, and Carr and Taplin, *History of the British Steel Industry*, pp. 257–60, survey the pre-First World War position.

been induced to join in at all—usually marked the beginning of periods of dissolution, particularly when technically
progressive firms, like David Colville & Sons, believed that
they had been making the greatest sacrifices to keep the
various associations together.

The impermanence of several of the territorial arrangements
can often be ascribed to 'the independent line' taken by Lanarkshire. The response of the North-east coast makers to Lanarkshire's efforts to undercut them in the sale of angles on the Tyne
was to invade the Scottish market: 'The only gainers by this
singular rivalry are the railway companies, who earn handsome
returns by facilitating a competition which leaves no profit to
the freighters.'[63] But Lanarkshire's concentration on sections
left them little alternative to persistent attempts to break out
of the confines of a purely Clydeside market, especially when
that market was adversely affected by German dumping.[64]

That there was German 'dumping' is undeniable: it forms
a constant theme in the annual statements of the chairmen of
the Scottish steel companies from about 1903, when attempts
were made—by Strain, for example—to estimate the degree to
which the German f.o.b. Antwerp prices were below the manufacturing costs. But, although 'dumping' was the expression still
being employed ten years later, the prices asked by German
manufacturers of steel ship plates for delivery to the Clyde or
Belfast in 1913, may well, by then, have more truly reflected
differences in production costs, despite the suspicion that the
'knockout prices' being asked by the Germans were motivated
by a desire 'to secure cash for the needy bankers, into whose
hands a large number of the German works [had] fallen'.[65]
Once foreign made plates of basic steel were accepted by
Lloyds, the protection once enjoyed by the Scottish acid steel-
makers disappeared and, as the *Shipping World* emphasized,
since shipbuilders had no sentiment in these matters, they preferred to buy German and Belgian plates at prices approximately 20*s.* per ton less than the prices of home makers.[66]

[63] Sir Charles McLaren, *The Times*, 11 Apr. 1906.
[64] This was one of Strain's constant refrains. See his evidence to the Tariff
Commission, *The Iron and Steel Trades*, para. 627, and *Glasgow Herald*, 4 Feb.
1908; 15 Feb. 1910; 19 Feb. 1913.
[65] Unidentified press cutting among the Colville records, dated 1 Nov. 1913.
[66] *Pall Mall Gazette*, 14 Feb. 1913.

Thus, although associations were frequently to be found in the Scottish steel industry before 1914, they reflected the national picture, being loose in form, embracing but a limited number of products, and only rarely loyally observed for more than short periods. On the eve of the First World War, only the British Tube Association appeared to be working in a satisfactory manner and that was undoubtedly because the trade was dominated by Stewarts & Lloyds.[67] The tube trade's demonstration of the necessity of structural change as a prerequisite for successful price control associations was a lesson not lost on John Craig, the youngest of David Colville & Sons' directors.[68]

3 Technique

This is not a technical treatise, nor can the author pretend to any metallurgical expertise, but as the economic historian often makes international—or even interregional—technological comparisons (usually in order to substantiate or even to 'prove' his judgements on entrepreneurial performance),[69] a brief and necessarily selective survey of the *major* developments in steel works' plant in Scotland during the decades immediately preceding the First World War may be permitted. Such a survey has several purposes. The first is simply to make the historical record reasonably comprehensive; the second is to reveal the differing progressiveness of individual units in the industry in the hope that this will contribute to fuller understanding of the relative success of the competing firms; and the third is to indicate (no stronger word is appropriate) whether that part of the

---

[67] See Carr and Taplin, *History of the British Steel Industry*, pp. 261-2.

[68] In the relatively small collection of newspaper cuttings kept by David Colville & Sons before 1914, Stewarts & Lloyds and its antecedent and constituent companies is the best covered of all the firms in the Scottish steel industry.

[69] Some years ago, the author tried to synthesize the existing literature that attempted to demonstrate and explain the relative decline of Britain's iron and steel industry in the decades before the First World War in his paper 'Iron and Steel Manufacturers' in D. H. Aldcroft (ed.), *The Development of British Industry and Foreign Competition, 1875–1914* (London: Allen & Unwin, 1968, pp. 71–99). Since then D. N. McCloskey has published his most important pioneering study, *Economic Maturity and Entrepreneurial Decline: British Iron and Steel, 1870–1913* (Cambridge, Mass.; Harvard U.P., 1973).

Scottish steel industry with which this study is primarily concerned illustrates McCloskey's contention that the British iron and steel industry 'exploited well the potential of world technology before World War I'.[70]

If one important conclusion may be anticipated, it would appear that whatever was happening in the British iron and steel industry as a whole, there is little evidence of any technological sluggishness in the open-hearth and plate rolling works of Scotland, where the rate of adoption of new techniques responded rapidly to economic incentives. Not only did Scottish output of Siemens steel expand rapidly to meet the demands of the shipbuilding industry but the timing of major investment programmes, whether they were directed to enlarging melting or rolling capacities, accords with fluctuations in shipbuilding activity. Opportunities were seized with alacrity. There were no hesitations here: even the slow adoption of the basic open-hearth steel-making process was a perfectly rational response to consumer demand. The shipbuilders distrusted basic steel;[71] furthermore, until the introduction of the Talbot tilting furnace at the turn of the century, it was more expensive.[72] Where the Scottish works could claim technological equality—even primacy in some respects—with the best American and German practice was in rolling mill plant, particularly that concerned with the manufacture of ship and boiler plates.

Admittedly, the Steel Company of Scotland—following Riley's departure after five profitless years of operation—never regained its technological adventurousness and was thenceforth content to follow its local competitors rather than lead them,

[70] D. N. McCloskey, 'A Summary of Economic Maturity and Entrepreneurial Decline: British Iron and Steel, 1870–1913', Ph.D. thesis, University of Chicago, April 1970, p. 6.

[71] So, indeed, did other potential consumers. In 1902, 'Mr David Colville mentioned that the name "Basic Steel" did not sufficiently designate the process by which the Company's Open Hearth Basic Steel was manufactured, and might prove very misleading to those who were only acquainted with the earlier Bessemer Basic process. It had been suggested to him that some distinguishing name other than the word "Basic" should be used. It was decided to consider this matter . . . Mr A. Colville reported that "Dalzell O.H.B. Steel" was meantime being used.' D.C. & S.: Board Minute Book I, 7 Apr. 1902.

[72] McCloskey, *Economic Maturity and Entrepreneurial Decline*, pp. 71–2, explains why this was so. See also Carr and Taplin, *History of the British Steel Industry*, pp. 216–18.

Table 5.2

Gross Capital Investment in Steel-Making Plant by Three Scottish Firms, 1894–1914

Year	(1) Steel Company of Scotland (£s)	(2) David Colville & Sons (£s)	(3) Lanarkshire (£s)
1894			467
1895	9,330	6,946	1,300
1896	16,426	4,759	3,819
1897	17,262	25,022	19,188
1898	22,878	53,769	43,476
1899	34,441	33,810	130,815
1900	23,913	48,189	73,033
1901	16,340	36,345	21,383
1902	21,603	34,905	15,171
1903	21,105	23,091	16,094
1904	22,645	19,094	10,588
1905	33,010	21,447	7,977
1906	34,359	65,249	17,428
1907	34,559	64,155	6,924
1908	33,785	37,524	10,604
1909	24,940	7,736	3,639
1910	24,182	25,438	2,114
1911	32,946	33,305	7,258
1912	24,815	83,402	9,743
1913	27,551	267,808	25,926
1914	31,661		9,267
Total	507,751	625,186* 892,994	436,214
No. of years	20	17½* 18½	21
Annual Average	25,388	35,725* 48,270	20,772

Notes and Sources: (1) S.C. of S., Directors' Minute Books. The figures are those for 'Improvements to Plant [i.e. Steel works]', the expenditure on collieries has been omitted. Each financial year ends in mid-July.
(2) D.C. & S., Annual Balance Sheets. The figures are those for the 'Steel-works Erection A/c'; other minor capital expenditures (e.g. those on the iron works) have been omitted. The figure for 1895 is for the period 20 July 1895 to 31 December 1895; figures marked * exclude 1913.
(3) Lanarkshire, Statistical Records: 'Additions to Capital A/c including Wages', the wage element never represented more than a minor proportion of the total.

but, under Lorimer, it consciously sought to keep abreast of the most recent *proven* developments by investing an annual average of £25,000 in plant improvements (see Table 5.2) even in the most dispiriting prewar years. The pioneering role it had once assumed now passed to others.

Following the conversion of the original family partnership to a private limited liability company, David Colville, jun. pursued a policy of continuous modernization and improvement at Dalzell, a policy which reached its apogee in the four years immediately preceding the First World War. The furnaces erected during the eighties were systematically reconstructed and enlarged, and all manner of devices for the handling and manipulation of ingots and semi-finished products were introduced. Throughout the works, efforts were constantly being made to conserve heat, reduce the amount of labour at the rolls, and speed up the movement of the sequential processes.

The cutting-up of large, heavy plates had always been a source of difficulty since the days when few or no mechanical aids were available and all plates had to be dealt with manually. The plates were brought to the shear on bogies and manipulated during the shearing process by a large squad of men with forks. Even when it was possible to utilize the assistance of cranes, shearing remained a tedious and expensive business, and with the steady increase in the size and weight of individual pieces, some change in the methods of handling the plates became imperative. At first, castor beds were introduced, and although this simple device greatly eased the problem of manipulation, its use continued to require large numbers of men. The first workable alternative was the development of a mechanical shearing table consisting of a number of driven rollers, mounted on a carriage which could be power-traversed past the shear in a line parallel to the blades. This was designed and introduced at Dalzell in 1901 and anticipated what became known as the Ennis Table by many years and (apart from the plate-gripping mechanism, which made use of pneumatic cylinders instead of magnets) was almost identical with it. For reasons that remain obscure, this original table appears never to have been fully completed, but it did represent a remarkably early and ingenious attempt to grapple with the problems involved in the precise shearing of large pieces of steel.[73]

Although this was the most novel of David Colville's technological innovations,[74] it must not be allowed to obscure the less dramatic but very real progress he made in raising the entire scale of the operations at Dalzell. The size of the melting furnaces was kept perpetually under review. In 1895, three old furnaces were enlarged to 25 tons capacity; two additional 40-ton furnaces were erected in 1896 and another in 1897; by the end of the century, five 50-ton furnaces had been built—there were now 20 furnaces in all—and within a few years some of the older, smaller furnaces had been replaced by furnaces of 60 tons capacity. Two 75-ton furnaces had been installed in No. 3 Melting Shop by 1905 and by 1910 the two largest furnaces there were rated at 100 tons capacity. With their erection it was claimed that Colvilles had 'gone further ... than any other firm in the world—British, American, and German manufacturers not excepted'.[75]

[73] This paragraph is based upon Kilby, 'The Production of Steel Plates in Scotland', pp. 54–5, 58, 60.

[74] Early in 1901, the board accepted David Colville's arguments in favour of a trial of the Bertrand-Thiel process of basic open-hearth steel-making. A licence was obtained from John H. Darby of Brymbo; David Colville visited Germany to study the process, and the necessary plant was put down. Two furnaces were involved, 'the charge being partially refined in the first and then tapped into the second for finishing. This [it was claimed] would reduce costs by over 25 per cent and increase output as much as 70 per cent' (Carr and Taplin, *History of the British Steel Industry*, p. 215). Production of basic steel by this method began at Dalzell in October 1901, and within a few months had been accepted by the Admiralty and Lloyd's 'for ship plates and bars of all thicknesses and sections'. But within a year the Bertrand-Thiel experiment had been discontinued and four open-hearth furnaces at Dalzell were making ordinary Thomas basic steel. In reporting to the board, David Colville asserted that 'The Bertrand-Thiel process made first class steel but it delayed output and was a failure without a supply of hot metal.' (D.C. & S.: Board Minute Book I, 11 Mar. 1901, 17 Apr. 1901, 9 Sept. 1901, 8 Oct. 1902.) Partly as a consequence of this experiment, the board went into the question of erecting blast furnace plant. Plans were drawn up by the firm's engineer, Thomas B. McKenzie, but nothing came of the idea which was again considered in 1905. (Ibid., 11 Mar. 1901, 20 Nov. 1903, 2 Oct. 1905, 23 Oct. 1905.)

[75] So claimed the *Glasgow Evening News*, 6 Jan. 1910, under the headline: 'A Monster Furnace. Largest in the World. Erected at Motherwell'; somewhat later in the article the newspaper did acknowledge, 'It is to be noted that the furnaces referred to are of the stationary regenerative type. Larger—much larger—furnaces are in existence, but they are of a different type.'

The increasing size of the open-hearth furnaces was in part a cause of improvements and growing scale elsewhere in the productive processes, in part a consequence. With each addition in melting capacity, the entire range of ancillary equipment in the melting shops had to be enlarged or extended. In 1903 the firm purchased a Wellman open-hearth charging machine for No. 3 Melting Shop,[76] a decision which involved the subsequent purchase of two new double cantilever electric stockyard cranes.[77] Such was the capacity of the Wellman charger that, within a few months, it became necessary to purchase additional bogies and boxes for cold pig, ore, and scrap, and so satisfactory was the machine in operation that it. was 'saving thirty men in the working of the furnaces'.[78] The increase in ingot output that ensued necessitated putting down additional soaking pits 'to meet the congestion at the heating furnaces when too many melting furnaces were tapped at the same time',[79] and, within a few months, the installation of an entirely new gas producer plant.[80]

Such were *some* of the repercussions of enlarging the capacity of the melting shops, the incentive for which was provided by the increasing demand for the firm's finished products. Continuous improvements were made in the mill plant and, as with the melting shops, each major increase in capacity involved consequential changes throughout the entire range of related equipment. There was, of course, nothing unusual in this constant 'balancing upwards'; what is noteworthy is the advantageous way in which the opportunities implicit in this situation were exploited. David Colville appears never to have ceased to experiment with new processes and devices in order to improve quality, to increase labour productivity, and reduce costs. The power of the mill engines and the capacity of the overhead cranes were always being increased; electric power

[76] David Colville arranged for its purchase from the Wellman-Seaver-Morgan Engineering Co. of Cleveland, Ohio, though their London representatives, Jerimiah Head & Sons, with a guarantee that if its use caused a diminution of the output of No. 3 Melting Shop, a second machine would be provided free of charge. D.C. & S.: Directors' Minute Book I, 24 June 1903. For the Wellman charger, see Burn, *Economic History of Steel Making*, p. 201.

[77] D.C. & S., Directors' Minutes I, 10 Nov. 1903.

[78] Ibid., 25 Jan. 1905.

[79] Ibid., 3 Mar. 1904.

[80] Ibid., 29 June 1904.

was introduced whenever possible; and, periodically, particularly at periods of peak demand, an entire collection of interrelated processes was modernized. In 1905, for example, the directors agreed to a £50,000 plan for the extension and improvement of the plate cooling floors, the shearing department, and the fitting shop: 'It was estimated that these improvements would deal with 20 to 25 per cent more material and at the same time save over 100 men ... the two new pairs of shears should be hydraulic shears with steam intensifiers as designed and made by the Maschinenfabrik Sack, Germany ...'[81] The largest scheme of this kind before the First World War involved an expenditure of well over £250,000.[82] Its major constituents were ten melting furnaces, a new foundry, bar mill, 14-ft plate mill, cogging mill, and several reheating furnaces. Perhaps its most significant element was a 36-inch × 10-foot reversing slabbing mill, installed in 1913, whose capacity, measured by the size of ingots and slabs to be rolled, 'has probably not been exceeded by any mill in the world'. It was designed to roll ingots up to 50 tons in weight and was provided with devices for turning and manipulating pieces of this size.[83]

By the eve of the First World War, the Dazell Works had an ingot producing *capacity* of well over 350,000 tons per annum. David Colville & Sons was the largest firm in the Scottish steel industry and one of the largest in Great Britain: its output had expanded much faster than the average.[84] A Scottish firm that conformed more to the norm in its speed of growth, despite constant innovation, was the Glasgow Iron & Steel Company. Converted to the open-hearth process under the

[81] Ibid., II, 18 Dec. 1905, 1 Feb. 1906.
[82] The original plans were approved by the directors in June 1912. Ibid., 7 June 1912.
[83] Kilby, 'Production of Steel Plates', p. 60. The motive power of the mill was provided by a massive pair of horizontal engines, 48-inch diameter × 60-inch stroke.
[84] Precise comparisons are difficult. Burn provides the most reliable guide (op. cit., pp. 335–6): 'it is doubtful whether any ... [British] firm save Dorman's had an annual output above 500,000 tons [in 1913], and it is unlikely that more than six firms all told had outputs exceeding—in most cases barely exceeding—300,000 tons.' Colvilles known ingot output in 1914 was 318,000 tons; its sales of finished materials were 244,360 tons (see Table 5.5). In both 1912 and 1913, Colvilles sales exceeded 278,000 tons and the firm's ingot output was probably about 360,000 tons in each of these years.

direction of Thomas Williamson in 1894,[85] the Wishaw Works were the scene of constant experiment, especially during James Riley's brief tenure as general manager between 1895 and 1899.

Always interested in the possibility of using hot metal practice in the Siemens process—or, as he put it, 'the use of fluid metal taken directly from the blast-furnace to the open-hearth furnace'—but prevented from making trials because the Steel Company of Scotland possessed no blast furnaces, immediately on his new appointment Riley attempted to obtain permission from his new directors to make provision for hot metal practice at Wishaw. Eventually, after considerable prevarication—'for want of confidence in success, and the passive resistance often met with in such cases'—this permission was 'reluctantly' given, but

only to the extent that the railways were laid down so that the ladles which had [once] been used to convey ... fluid metal [from the blast furnaces] to the [Bessemer] converters might be brought to the door of [a Siemens open hearth] furnace, and by means of improvised tackle and manual labour be tipped up into shutes on runners to let their contents run into the furnace.

The first experiments using these crude methods were made in March 1898 and although 'the time occupied in working the first charge was longer than ordinary . . . in other respects the results were encouraging. Especially was this the case in the important matter of yield'. With the refusal of the directors of the Glasgow Iron & Steel Company to sanction the additional 'considerable' expenditure required to perfect the apparatus, and Riley's constant anxiety that the use of his relatively inefficient appliances would suddenly fail and cause some dreadful accident, further experiments were postponed until May 1898, when fourteen charges were worked during the course of a week. This intensive trial, carried out under the immediate supervision of Mr. Mills, the manager of the steel works, was a triumphant technical success.[86] The data collected indicated that 'with proper arrangements', the large-scale adoption of hot metal practice would result in very significant savings in

[85] See above, p. 71.
[86] The full details are provided by Riley in his paper to the Iron and Steel Institute, 'The Use of Fluid Metal in the Open-Hearth Furnace', *Journal of the Iron and Steel Institute*, lvii (1900), 22–32, on which this paragraph is based. The original paper has been summarized by Burn, *Economic History of Steel Making*, pp. 202–3.

materials and labour,[87] especially if a hot metal 'mixer' were to be interposed between the blast furnaces and the melting furnaces. Riley's directors were convinced, and although it was decided not 'to incur the considerable expenditure involved' in the construction of a mixer—at least not immediately—in all other respects hot metal open-hearth practice was adopted at Wishaw. Riley, who left the employ of the Glasgow Iron & Steel Company to make steel on his own account at the Richmond Works, Stockton-on-Tees, in 1900, was convinced that 'eventually this will be the process which will prevail'. But such was the fragmented structure of the British iron and steel industry in 1900 that for the majority of the biggest plants any change to hot metal practice was 'out of the question'.[88]

Another manifestation of Riley's prescience was his rapid adoption of B. H. Thwaite's gas engine at Wishaw. Thwaite, one of the pioneers in the utilization of blast furnace waste gases as motive power, took out a patent (No. 8670) for an engine directly driven by blast furnace gas in 1894. He advocated its use both for driving blowing engines and for the generation of electricity. Thwaite first approached Lothian Bell, who emphasized the difficulties involved; only James Riley immediately saw the merits of the proposal and promptly installed a 30-horsepower blast furnace gas engine at Wishaw in February 1895. But no one else in Britain was interested until the use of much larger engines of several hundred horsepower, built by the Belgian firm of Cockerill's at Seraing, aroused attention. Even then British progress in this field was hesitant.[89]

---

[87] So good was the 'yield' that it appeared to Riley that the saving in metal inputs alone would be worth some 10*d.* a ton.

[88] Burn, *Economic History of Steel Making*, p. 203, who estimates that only 'twenty-one firms out of seventy-two making open-hearth steel in 1902, with 25 per cent of the British "make", owned adjacent blast furnaces'.

[89] For the early history of Thwaite's gas engine in Britain, see Burn, *Economic History of Steel Making*, pp. 208–9, and Carr and Taplin, *History of the British Steel Industry*, pp. 212–13, the two sources on which this paragraph is based, and *Journal of the Iron and Steel Institute*, lxxvi (1908), 231. As late as 1925, Sir Frederick Mills, in his Presidential Address to the Iron and Steel Institute, was still able to ask: 'Are we quite sure we were correct in our policy of rejecting, for the most part, the use of large gas-engines using coke-oven and blast-furnaces gases'—the discovery of B. H. Thwaite, and first employed at Wishaw in 1896. 'The process is nearly universal on the Continent . . . but in most of our establishments [gas engines] are entirely absent.' Ibid., cxi (1925), 39.

The other plant installed at Wishaw about this time, while not so revolutionary, represented the most modern practice. Much of the rolling equipment was built by Lamberton & Company of Coatbridge, probably the leading firm in this field, and incorporated the fruits of Andrew Lamberton's 'careful and prolonged study . . . of the machinery used in the manipulation of steel'.[90] The 30-inch × 8-foot and 40-inch × 12-foot reversing plate mills put down in 1893–4, which comprised three stands of two-high rolls in train with a pinion housing unit, were capable of producing boiler, ship, and merchant plates in a wide variety of sizes, and the 30-inch × 6½-foot tandem reversing plate mill put down in 1906 embodied a number of unconventional features designed to eliminate the usual loss of time involved in transferring the slab being rolled from the roughing to the finishing stands. This latter mill was, in fact, 'the forerunner of most modern light and medium plate mills'.[91]

It will be noticed that the mills at Wishaw, like those elsewhere in Scotland—and, indeed, in Britain—at the turn of the century, were two-high reversing rather than three-high plate mills. For this the British have been criticized. Had not Riley himself experimented with a three-high mill at Blochairn in 1880?[92] And were such mills not 'capable of doing more work in a given time, and probably at less cost, than the reversing mills so commonly used here'?[93] If the Americans could use them so successfully, why were the British so reluctant to adopt them? The answer lay not so much in entrepreneurial ineptitude as in the demand situation facing the British steel-makers. As E. Windsor Richards emphasized:

. . . there was of course a great deal of difference in the plates turned out in America and in England. For the limited range of sizes of plates made in America the best form of mill undoubtedly was the three-high non-revers-

[90] James Riley's words, used in the discussion of Andrew Lamberton's paper, 'Improvements in Plate Rolling Mills', *Journal of the Iron and Steel Institute*, lxxvi (1908), 39.

[91] The details are given by Kilby, 'Production of Steel Plates', pp. 34, 64–5, 68. Riley described the earlier reversing plate mills as 'excellent illustrations of present practice', J. Riley, 'Notes on Modern Steel-Works Machinery', *Proceedings of the Institute of Mechanical Engineers* (1895), p. 444. The equipment is illustrated in Plates 132 and 133.

[92] See above, p. 64.

[93] Riley's words, 'Notes on . . . Machinery', loc. cit., p. 446.

ing mill with fly-wheel. *The American mills had not yet been called upon to produce the diversity of work required in England* ...[94]

And, as Riley himself confessed, that 'variety [of plates], as all engineers knew, had been largely increased during the last few years'.[95] Even William Garrett, an outspoken critic of British rolling-mill practice, supported the British preference for two-high reversing mills in his comparative review of the subject before the Iron and Steel Institute in 1901,[96] and seven years later Andrew Lamberton emphasized that even the finest three-high mill could not produce plates with the high surface finish and close adherence to gauge thickness required by British consumers.[97]

Such mills were, in fact, erected in two Scottish works before the First World War. In 1905, William Beardmore & Company Ltd., having taken over the Mossend Works from the Summerlee and Mossend Iron & Steel Company, began a comprehensive programme of reconstruction. This involved, *inter alia*, the abandonment of the existing plate mills[98] and the erection of a Lauth-type three-high mill in 1908.[99] This in itself was notable but equally significant was the fact that its motive power was provided by a direct-coupled slow-speed engine.[100] Furthermore, the mill was the first in Scotland to be equipped with a

[94] Discussion following Riley's paper, ibid., p. 451. Emphasis supplied.
[95] Ibid., p. 459. For those interested in the influence of demand on the speed of diffusion of technological innovation, the entire discussion of Riley's paper (ibid., pp. 451–61) is of considerable significance. At one point (p. 447), Riley acknowledged that 'the use of three-high mills ... should be limited to the production of plates of light or medium weight and of medium width'. Few British rolling mills could concentrate on work of this description at the end of the nineteenth century. The arguments used echo those of earlier discussions. See Burn, *Economic History of Steel Making*, pp. 57–9.
[96] See Carr and Taplin, *History of the British Steel Industry*, pp. 222–3.
[97] 'Here surface finish must be first-class, and adherence to gauge thickness must be within 2½ per cent over or under. In America steel-plate makers are not under such stringent conditions, and the writer has seen thin plates being rolled in which a margin of 15 per cent variation in thickness was accepted. Were it not for the stringency of [these] conditions, ... the probability is that plate rolling mills of the American three-high type would have been adopted in this country before this time.' Lamberton, 'Improvements in Plate Rolling Mills', p. 31.
[98] These comprised a 29-inch × 8-foot and 26-inch × 6½-foot reversing plate mill, driven by beam engines!
[99] A full description was given in *Engineering*, 13 Nov. 1908, 27 Nov. 1908.
[100] Clean gas was supplied by a Mond producer plant which also fed the soaking pits and the slab reheating furnaces. The engine was of the Oechell-

fully-mechanized cooling and inspection bank.[101] In 1909, James Dunlop & Company, having taken over the Calderbank Steel & Coal Company and embarked upon an extensive programme of modernization of the Calderbank Works,[102] also erected a Lauth-type three-high mill. Built by Lamberton & Company of Coatbridge, it was 'unique in having as prime mover a Parsons mixed-pressure turbine, operating on exhaust steam from the slabbing and heavy mills and/or live steam'. Despite considerable teething troubles, the mill attained a high standard of performance in both output and quality.[103]

These, then, were some of the major developments in steel manufacture in Scotland in the two decades preceding the First World War. The survey could have been considerably expanded and much could have been said of the many minor modifications to plant and machinery that 'greatly stimulated output and enormously reduced manual effort'.[104] There is no question that productivity would have been greatly enhanced had the Scottish works not had to cater to the often perverse requirements of marine and locomotive engineers whose specifications possessed a highly individualistic character, necessitating constant roll changing and machinery adjustments,[105] but

---

haueser type. This gas engine was chosen following the successful application of a similar unit at Parkhead, where a pull-over type light plate and sheet mill were driven in this way. Kilby, 'Production of Steel Plates', p. 66.

[101] Ibid., pp. 66–7, where Kilby provides a useful summary of the details.

[102] James Dunlop & Co., newspaper report of the Third Annual General Meeting, *c.* September 1902.

[103] Kilby, 'Production of Steel Plates', pp. 68–70, who gives additional details including general arrangement drawings. A full description of the mill was given in a paper to the West of Scotland Iron and Steel Institute in 1911 by A. Quintin Carnegie. See his paper 'The Application of a Geared Steam Turbine to Rolling Mill Driving', and the subsequent discussion, in the *Journal of the West of Scotland Iron and Steel Institute*, xviii (1911), 193–204, 217–32.

[104] T. H. Hand, 'Progress in British Rolling-Mill Practice', *Journal of the Iron and Steel Institute*, cxi (1925), 52.

[105] Fred Clements made the point in the correspondence arising from T. H. Hand's paper that 'In Great Britain the demand was in the main made up of a mass of relatively small orders, which often, though the sizes called for might be identical, varied in the quality of even the steel required. British mills, therefore, had to have a degree of flexibility and adjustment which was not called for in mass production plants designed to roll large quantities of material similar in size and quality.' Ibid., pp. 99–100. The expense and trouble involved in roll changing was a perpetual refrain in the annual reports of the Steel Company of Scotland.

it is clear that where demand conditions warranted the adoption of new methods in both melting and rolling, these appear to have been fully exploited. In his review of the alterations in steel works during the twenty-one years' existence of the West of Scotland Iron and Steel Institute, M. L. Simpson concluded that 'great ingenuity and engineering skills have been exercised in modifying plant to suit modern requirements, but wherever economies can be effected by the installation of new plant it [has been] quickly undertaken'.[106] It was a just verdict.

4 Changing Relative Positions

By the first decade of the twentieth century the Steel Company of Scotland had lost its pre-eminence in the Scottish steel industry. It had been overtaken by David Colville & Sons in terms of efficiency, profitability (see Table 5.3), and finished output (see Tables 5.4, 5.5), while, snapping profitlessly at its heels, was the Lanarkshire Steel Company.

By 1913, David Colville & Sons was one of the half a dozen firms in the United Kingdom with an ingot output in excess of 300,000 tons (it was, in fact, 318,000 tons); only the Dorman Long group of plants, the biggest producing group in 1913, with an output in three plants of 700,000 tons, was substantially larger.[107] Moreover, Colvilles were investing very heavily in

[106] M. L. Simpson, 'Steel Works—A Twenty-One Years' Review', p. 55. In moving a vote of thanks to the author, Andrew Lamberton (a Past President of the Institute) commented that 'there seemed to be no resting-place for the steel manufacturers, for as soon as one important improvement appeared and was adopted, something new came along and superseded it, and they had again to address themselves to new problems and methods, and there seemed to be no escape from the necessity of dealing with these as they from time to time arise.'

[107] Burn, *Economic History of Steel Making*, pp. 335–6. The figures given in Table 5.5 are annual 'assigned tonnages' or 'Deliveries of Finished Materials'. In the few cases where ingot tonnages are known, comparisons may be made with these finished weights. Such comparisons indicate that in the period under discussion it took one ton of ingot steel to produce about 15–16 cwts of finished products. That is, 4–5 cwts of ingot steel in every ton were either lost in the heating and rolling processes or, overwhelmingly, ended up as scrap, scrap which was re-cycled in the melting furnaces. Thus to obtain an approximate idea of the annual ingot outputs of the firms represented in Table 5.5, it is necessary to increase their annual consigned tonnages by 30 per cent. On this basis, their deliveries of finished products in 1913, which totalled 858,227 tons (in the case of the Steel Company of Scotland an average has

TABLE 5.3

Scottish Steel Companies: Dividends Paid on Ordinary Shares, 1894–1915

	(1) S.C. of S.[a]	(2) D.C. & S.[b]	(3) Lanarkshire	(4) J. Dunlop & Co.[c]	(5) Stewarts & Lloyds[d]	(6) W. Beardmore & Co.	(7) Merry & Cunning- hame[e]
1894	Nil	—	5			n.d.	7½
1895	Nil		10		7	n.d.	10
1896	3		15		8	n.d.	10
1897	5		7½		8	n.d.	15½
1898	6		10		10	n.d.	50
1899	5		7½		10	n.d.	60
1900	1⅔		Nil	10	9	n.d.	10
1901	2½	5	Nil	5	10	n.d.	10
1902	2½	5	Nil	6	10	Nil	20
1903	2½	5	Nil	4	10	7½	20
1904	5	10	Nil	4	10	6	10
1905	7½	20	8	7	10	6	20
1906	7½	22½	8	10	10	6	20
1907	7½	22½	5	12½	10	Nil	10
1908	7½	7½	Nil	5	35	Nil	10
1909	6	7½	Nil	5	5	Nil	5
1910	6	15	Nil	6	5	Nil	5
1911	10	17½	Nil	6	5	5	20
1912	10	25	Nil	10	10	5	20
1913	5	7½	Nil	6	12½	5	Nil
1914	7½	12½	Nil	Nil	12½	5	10
1915		20	10	6	12½	6	

Notes: [a] The financial year of the Steel Company of Scotland ended on 31 August.
[b] Before the reorganization of the capital in 1901, the capital structure of David Colville & Sons consisted of £10 5 per cent Cumulative Preference shares, £10 5 per cent Preference shares and 700 £1 Ordinary shares. The number of C.P. shares rose from 10,000 in 1895 to 18,500 in 1901; the number of Preference shares remained unchanged at 13,930 throughout the period 1895–1901, and the dividend on the £1 Ordinary shares was as follows:

1895	1896	1897	1898	1899	1900
£5	£10	£20	£26	£120	£65

[c] James Dunlop & Co., proprietors of the Clyde Iron Works and a number of collieries, went into steel production when they acquired the Calderbank Steel Works in 1900.
[d] The dividends shown are those for A. & J. Stewart & Clydesdale up to 1898; A. J. Stewart & Menzies Ltd., 1899 to 1902 inclusive; and Stewarts & Lloyds thereafter.
[e] The Glengarnock Iron & Steel Co. was a private joint stock company and it has been impossible to obtain dividend data. It was closely associated with Merry & Cunninghame (J.C. Cunninghame was chairman of Glengarnock), and dividend figures for this firm, whose profits were mainly derived from coal mining, have been provided for comparison with the dividends paid by the steel companies. The financial year of Merry & Cunninghame ended in the Spring.

Sources: Col. (1) S.C. of S., Directors' Minute Books.
(2) D.C. & S., Annual Balance Sheets.
(3) Lanarkshire: Statistical Records.
(4), (5), and (7) Published annual reports supplemented by various editions of the *Stock Exchange Year-Book.*
(6) W. Beardmore & Co.: Information kindly provided by Mr. John Hume and Mr. Michael Moss.

---

new plant on the eve of the First World War—plant which had yet to be fully worked up. It was, conceivably, the fastest growing concern in the British steel industry, and it owed its growth largely to the daemonic energy and drive of David Colville, jun., ably supported by those very managers who had taken a stake in the firm some ten years earlier. The weakness of the firm—and, in this, it exemplifies the Scottish steel industry generally—was its alarming dependence upon the notoriously fickle shipbuilding industry[108] and its almost complete lack of integration either backwards towards its raw materials or forwards towards its major customers. It was, simply, an extremely efficient steel-melting and -rolling concern.

---

been taken of the 'Deliveries' for the years ended mid-July 1913 and 1914), represented an ingot tonnage of 1,115,695, or about 76 per cent of the total Scottish ingot output for 1913 (see Table 5.1).
[108] This can be seen from Table 5.6. Over 60 per cent of the products (by weight and by value) of the Scottish Steel Makers' Association in 1912 and 1913 consisted of ship and marine boiler plates; a high proportion of the sections was also destined for the shipyards.

The Steel Company of Scotland, recognizing the dangers implicit in such a position, was taking steps to integrate backwards, gaining control of collieries and acquiring an interest in pig iron production. Beardmores, firmly attached to Vickers, had moved forwards to the manufacture of armaments and into shipbuilding and motor car manufacture. Dunlops, controlled by the Lithgows, were linked with shipyards but owed the bulk of their profits to coal; Glengarnock was connected with collieries and chemicals; Stewarts & Lloyds were, essentially, tube-makers. Only Lanarkshire, concentrating on the manufacture of boiler plates and angles, was as vulnerable as Colvilles. It is interesting to speculate on what might have happened to this fiercely competitive collection of firms had the war not intervened, but whatever the results of such speculations, they could hardly be more dramatic than what actually transpired.

TABLE 5.4

Steel Company of Scotland: Sales of Finished Materials and Average Net Prices at Works, 1897–1915

	All finished material				Plates and bars only			
Year ending July	Tonnage	Value (£s)	Average net price £ s. d.		Tonnage	Value (£s)	Average net price £ s. d.	
1898	163,458	922,611	5 12 11		134,574	697,402	5 3 8	
1899	175,434	1,119,398	6 7 8		143,537	850,381	5 18 6	
1900	177,425	1,360,211	7 13 4		139,131	1,023,511	7 7 1	
1901	155,458	1,196,439	7 13 11		115,709	834,544	7 4 3	
1902	187,898	1,171,376	6 4 8		134,074	788,311	5 17 7	
1903	193,343	1,182,618	6 2 4		139,698	807,400	5 17 7	
1904	186,210	1,097,623	5 17 10		145,869	813,203	5 11 6	
1905	188,121	1,127,224	5 19 10		142,863	811,359	5 13 7	
1906	212,933	1,378,340	6 9 5		167,272	1,020,043	6 1 11	
1907	212,033	1,542,114	7 5 6		159,297	1,097,824	6 17 10	
1908	182,655	1,413,768	7 14 9		135,912	982,734	7 4 7	
1909	159,606	1,073,520	6 14 6		118,016	739,574	6 5 4	
1910	184,768	1,256,813	6 16 0		134,929	870,792	6 9 1	
1911	188,812	1,367,631	7 4 10		140,616	958,839	6 16 4	
1912	199,638	1,484,013	7 8 8		150,728	1,047,024	6 19 0	
1913	224,598	1,802,039	8 0 6		168,183	1,265,861	7 10 6	
1914	171,017	1,376,311	8 0 11		116,700	848,754	7 5 6	
1915	172,418	1,536,163	8 18 2		131,870	1,087,183	8 4 11	

Source: S.C. of S., Sales Records.

TABLE 5.5 Scottish Steel Companies: Deliveries of Finished Materials, 1892–1915 (in tons)

Year	(1) S.C. of S.	(2) D.C. & S.	(3) Lanarkshire	(4) Clydebridge	(5) W. Beardmore & Co.: Parkhead	(6) W. Beardmore & Co.: Mossend	(7) Stewarts & Lloyds
1892	i.d.	102,986	26,324	n.d.	n.d.	n.d.	—
1893	i.d.	99,644	31,366	n.d.	n.d.	n.d.	—
1894	i.d.	75,804	27,033	n.d.	n.d.	n.d.	—
1895	i.d.	108,197	38,437	n.d.	n.d.	n.d.	—
1896	i.d.	127,629	43,551	n.d.	n.d.	n.d.	—
1897	163,458	131,215	48,507	n.d.	n.d.	n.d.	—
1898	175,434	136,689	50,021	n.d.	n.d.	n.d.	—
1899	177,425	171,573	49,148	n.d.	n.d.	n.d.	—
1900	155,458	172,132	51,054	n.d.	n.d.	n.d.	—
1901	187,899	160,588	74,010	n.d.	55,239	n.d.	—
1902	193,343	178,588	107,330	n.d.	59,410	n.d.	80,000
1903	186,210	176,996	114,244	n.d.	53,907	n.d.	n.d.
1904	188,121	201,462	123,277	n.d.	52,232	n.d.	n.d.
1905	212,933	218,550	152,784	n.d.	62,925	n.d.	n.d.
1906	212,003	211,524	147,404	79,324	62,202	32,775	n.d.
1907	182,655	216,354	147,644	70,500	63,005	21,884	n.d.
1908	159,606	179,305	113,936	nil	45,465	46,225	n.d.
1909	184,768	193,455	114,733	nil	45,178	45,607	n.d.
1910	188,812	248,285	127,577	nil	52,313	42,846	140,000
1911	199,638	244,948	107,516	nil	53,852	60,350	n.d.
1912	224,598	278,039	124,186	n.d.	66,044	50,410	n.d.
1913	171,017	278,785	128,306	n.d.	71,481	29,847	152,000
1914	172,418	244,360	112,016	n.d.	66,086	49,869	n.d.
1915		359,458	127,135	n.d.	65,612	47,082	n.d.

Sources: (1) Table 5.4, the S.C. of S.'s financial year ended in mid-July. The figures are of 'Deliveries of Finished Materials'. The data for 1892–7 are incomplete (i.d.).
(2) D.C. & S. Dalzell Steelworks Output 'Consigned Tonnages'; the figures for the early years almost certainly include major quantities (i.e. *c.* 7,000–8,000 tons) of ironwork.
(3) Lanarkshire Steel Co., Statistical Records, 'Output of Finished Materials'.
(4) Sir John Craig's Personal Papers; 'Statements Made Regarding C. B. Coy', undated.
(5) W. Beardmore & Co.: Finished Weight (in tons) sold by Parkhead. These figures represent a summation of the finished weights of armour plates, steel plates (about 40–60 per cent of each annual total), steel castings, steel tyres, slabs, ingots, forgings, nickel steel, gun forgings, axles, and rolled keel bars. These data were kindly supplied by John Hume and Michael Moss. Some annual totals include estimates of individual items. No output figures are available for 'railway wheels and axles' and there is no reliable method of estimating these; this item is, therefore, excluded. It should be noted that the average value per ton of finished materials produced at Parkhead was considerably higher than comparable figures for the other works and the *only* justification for adding the 'finished weights' of individual items is that this appears to have been the common practice of Scottish steel works in arriving at annual outputs.
(6) William Beardmore & Co.: Mossend Works: Output (in tons) of plates and slabs. Until 1915, the output was overwhelmingly of plates; slabs constituted less than 1 per cent of the totals given. These data were kindly supplied by John Hume and Michael Moss.
(7) Stewarts & Lloyds, *Stewarts & Lloyds, 1903–1953*, pp. 20, 25–26.

TABLE 5.6

Products of the Scottish Steel Makers' Association,[a] 1912–1913

Products Year	Plates Tons	%[b]	Value[c] (£s)	%[d]	Sections[e] Tons	%	Value (£s)	%	Steel rails and accessories[e] Tons	%	Value (£s)	%	Steel joists Tons	%	Value (£s)	%
1912	590,460	60·8	4,423,006	63·0	240,362	24·7	1,689,906	24·1	28,446	2·9	170,300	2·4	56,880	5·9	379,001	5·4
1913	589,375	60·6	4,751,622	62·9	230,762	23·7	1,772,193	23·5	46,476	4·8	300,143	4·0	64,494	6·6	438,377	5·8

Year	Other items[f] Tons	%	Value (£s)	%	Total Tons	Value (£s)
1912	55,350	5·7	356,740	5·1	971,498	7,018,953
1913	41,543	4·3	293,249	3·9	972,652	7,555,584

Source: 'Memorandum of Replies by the Scottish Steel Makers to the Questions formulated by the Shipping and Shipbuilding Committee of the Board of Trade, and sent to the Secretary on 16 March 1917.'

Notes: [a] The Association comprised the following firms: William Beardmore & Co., D. C. & S., James Dunlop & Co., the Glasgow Iron & Steel Co., the Lanarkshire Steel Co., the S.C. of S., and Stewarts & Lloyds.

[b] i.e. percentage of total tonnage of all products cited.

[c] Value given is the Invoice Value for Home and f.o.b. nearest Ports for Exports.

[d] i.e. percentage of total value of all products cited.

[e] Steel sections, include rounds, squares, and flats.

[f] This category includes ingots, billets, blooms, etc.

Meanwhile, the strength of the Scottish steel industry— whatever the specializations, however great the vitality of its constituent firms—was being eroded by the failure of the Scottish ironmasters to take advantage of the relative buoyancy of their home market (despite the reduction of export sales, the annual make of pig reached an all-time peak of 1,400,000 tons in 1910) to undertake the radical overhaul of the location, plant, and techniques of the Scottish smelting industry. There was, at this time, more money in coal, and so 'the old, and by contemporary standards, extremely small blast furnaces remained in operation in their old locations, and, as the competitive strength of the Scottish smelting industry progressively declined, it came in time to act as a positive incubus on the steel-making and iron-founding trades, and indirectly, on all the metal-using industries of the Glasgow conurbation.'[109]

[109] Gibson, 'The Establishment . . .', pp. 37–8.

PART III

War, depression, and rationalization

VI

The Impact of the First World War, 1914–1920

The rapid acceleration in the growth of David Colville & Sons on the eve of the First World War had carried the Motherwell firm far beyond its neighbours in terms of productive capacity, but at this stage few could have foreseen that Colville's were to become almost synonymous with the Scottish steel industry. The pressing demands of war and the inducements of the Ministry of Munitions provided considerable impetus to these developments.[1]

1 The Growth of David Colville & Sons

Appreciating apparently earlier than most iron and steel companies that it would be necessary not only to turn over its entire plant to war production[2] but to increase its capacity, David Colville & Sons acted to safeguard certain of the firm's sources of supply. One major weakness was a reliance on ingot moulds and bottoms manufactured in the Midlands and in Wales, many thousands of tons of which were required annually. Thus, when it was proposed to establish a foundry for their production at Fullwood in 1915, it was agreed to subscribe 60 per cent of the total ordinary share capital (£15,000 out of £25,000) to give Colvilles a controlling interest. This would enable the firm

---

[1] Valuable general surveys of the impact of the First World War on the iron and steel industry are provided by Burn, *Economic History of Steelmaking*, pp. 350–92, and Carr and Taplin, *History of the British Steel Industry*, pp. 299–336. For a brief semi-official history of the Iron and Steel Production Department of the Ministry of Munitions, see F. H. Hatch, *The Iron and Steel Industry of the United Kingdom under War Conditions* (London: published privately, 1919). See also M. S. Birkett, 'The Iron and Steel Trades During the War', *Journal of the Royal Statistical Society*, lxxxiii, Part III (May 1920), pp. 351–91.

[2] See Birkett, 'The Iron and Steel Trades', p. 353. For several months after its outbreak, Lorimer of the Steel Company of Scotland appears to have been almost completely unaware of the implications of the war on the steel industry. See S.C. of S., Minute Book XVI.

to obtain essential moulds and heavy melting shop furnace castings with a minimum of delay and would permit Colvilles to exercise adequate quality control. Significantly, Mr. John Craig was appointed the company's representative on the Board of Directors.[3]

This was but a beginning. Increasingly feverish appeals by the Ministry of Munitions to increase Scottish steel output led to Colvilles absorbing both the Clydebridge Steel Company and the Glengarnock Iron & Steel Company. Although it had been closed under subsidy from its fellow members of the Scottish Steelmakers Association since 1908, the plant at Clydebridge[4] was said to be in good condition and fully equal to the task of producing steel at the level attained before the closure.[5] It was believed that all that was needed for this unhappy concern to make a useful contribution to the war effort was proper direction and control. This, argued the Ministry of Munitions, could be provided by David Colville & Sons, and it was suggested that Clydebridge be leased to Colvilles.[6] It was on this basis that the negotiations began, but the owners of Clydebridge could not agree to the terms of a lease. Colvilles board therefore decided to purchase all the 600 £100 Ordinary shares of the Clydebridge Iron & Steel Company outright at par after a thorough inspection of the works and the account books had proved satisfactory. The transaction was completed in October 1915, and the Debenture Bonds purchased some six months later. By the end of 1916 it was arranged that the Clydebridge Steel Company be put into voluntary liquidation, and the business completely absorbed by David Colville & Sons.[7] It was

[3] D.C. & S., Minute Book II, 18 Mar. 1915 and 2 Aug. 1915; W. M. Marshall to John Craig, 14 June 1915. The control of Fullwood Foundry would also permit David Colville & Sons to obtain a supply of ingot moulds outside the Ingot Mould Association.

[4] For Clydebridge, see above, p. 68.

[5] Sir John Craig's Private Papers, 'Statements made regarding Clydebridge Company' (undated). The report concerning the state of the plant had been made by the eminent heavy machine maker, John Lamberton.

[6] It is not without significance that a leading member of the Iron and Steel Department of the Ministry of Munitions was W. T. MacLellan, of the Glasgow firm of P. & W. MacLellan, long associated with the Colville family. Sir John Hunter, head of the Department from mid-1916, was, until his appointment, Managing Director of Sir William Arrol & Co.

[7] D.C. & S., Minute Book II, 20 Sept. 1915, 11 Oct. 1915, 10 May 1916, 18 Dec. 1916.

the first important step in the creation of what was to be known as the Colville Group.

Simultaneously, Colvilles attempted, again at the instigation of the Ministry of Munitions, to lease the Glengarnock Iron & Steel Company's works. By mid-1914 these had virtually come to a standstill; all the blast furnaces had been blown out and the steel furnaces and the finishing mills were being utilized at well below their rated capacity. In March 1915, the proprietors granted a six months' lease of the steel-making plant to Colvilles, as the ageing J. C. Cunninghame, Glengarnock's chairman, did not feel equal to the task of coping with the problems involved in meeting the demands of war. In October 1915, the lease was extended for a further period, and in January 1916, the Glengarnock board agreed to a five-year lease of the *entire* works, with an option which gave David Colville & Sons the opportunity of purchasing them at the balance sheet valuation of March 1915, calculated at £328,744.[8] Initially, a five-year lease of all the blast furnace and steel-making plant was obtained, but subsequent difficulties caused by a prewar agreement between the Glengarnock Iron & Steel Company and its partially-owned subsidiary, the Glengarnock Chemical Company, which threatened to prevent the lessees obtaining the maximum output of pig iron from the blast furnaces, induced Colvilles to buy the Glengarnock company and its controlling interest in the chemical company outright, a course encouraged by the Ministry of Munitions. The purchase agreement was signed in June 1916.[9] The price paid was £400,000, payable half in 6 per cent Debentures and half in cash.[10] For the first time Colvilles were committed to the production of pig iron and to the revival of Bessemer steel production in Scotland.

Even before the acquisition of Clydebridge and Glengarnock, it was becoming increasingly evident to Colvilles that the company should safeguard its vital supplies of fuel; with the

[8] Ibid., 18 Mar. 1915, 2 Aug. 1915, and 24 Jan. 1916; *Colvilles' Magazine,* Winter 1961–2, p. 10.

[9] D.C. & S., Minute Book II, 13 June 1916. Under the agreement between the Glengarnock Iron & Steel Co. and the Glengarnock Chemical Co., the latter could insist that practically the whole fuel burden of the blast furnaces should be of coal, so that the chemical plant would obtain rich gases. The more economic use of coke was thus barred. See also *Colvilles' Magazine,* Winter 1961–2, p. 12.

[10] D.C. & S., Minute Book II, 19 June 1916, 4 July 1916.

purchase of these two firms, it became imperative. Detailed investigations into the current availability of coal were conducted and several 'trial mineral leases' obtained during 1916. It was soon discovered, however, that at this time the Ministry of Munitions did not consider it to be in the national interest to employ labour to open up *new* coal fields, and thereafter attention was confined to the possible purchase of one or a number of going colliery companies.[11] The colliery company which best met Colvilles requirements was Archibald Russell Ltd. Founded in 1843 by Archibald Russell, this firm had expanded during the latter half of the nineteenth century until it owned half-a-dozen collieries. Converted into a private limited liability company in 1904, its leading members were four grandsons of Archibald Russell. These directors, and also the manager of the company, T. G. Hardie, welcomed David Colville's overtures, and a scheme of amalgamation was drawn up. A purchase price of £650,000 for the 500,000 Ordinary £1 shares of Archibald Russell was finally agreed upon, £500,000 of which was to be in cash instalments apread over ten years and £150,000 by the issue of 15,000 Ordinary £10 shares of David Colville & Sons Ltd. A further condition of the agreement between the two companies was that three directors of Archibald Russell be given seats on the board of David Colville & Sons.[12] Still the search for coking coal continued. In August 1917, Archibald Russell Ltd. acquired control of the Murdostoun Colliery Company, whose pits were located at Cleveland, Lanarkshire; and in July, 1918, they bought the Ross Colliery, Hamilton.

It was one thing to acquire Clydebridge and Glengarnock, it was quite another, as the Ministry of Munitions recognized, to turn their neglected works into economic producers of iron and steel rapidly enough to make a useful contribution to the war effort. Although both plants were quickly brought into operation, enabling Colvilles to increase their weekly output of steel by some 5,000–6,000 tons (the bulk of which was destined for the production of shells), the Ministry requested the

[11] Sir John Craig's Private Papers, 'Report by R. W. Dron to David Colville and Sons, 17 October 1916'.
[12] Archibald Russell's first representatives on the Colville Board were William Russell, a Barrister-at-law, Jackson Russell, and Thomas G. Hardie.

company to undertake large extensions, primarily to prepare for an expected increased demand for shipbuilding materials. Plans were immediately prepared, and the enlargement of the melting and rolling capacity of both works began in October 1916. At Dalzell, too, additional furnaces and ancillary equipment, much of it specifically designed for the manufacture of armaments, were installed.[13] In physical terms, the result of all this feverish endeavour was that during the war years David

TABLE 6.1
David Colville & Sons: Ingot Output, 1914–1918
(in tons)

(a) *By Qualities*:

Year	Open-Hearth		Bessemer	Total
	Basic	Acid	(Glengarnock only)	
1914	55,811	262,189	—	318,000
1916	61,357	616,643	—	678,000
1918	217,395	505,633	69,316	792,344

Source: D.C. & S., *Jubilee* booklet, p. 14.

(b) *By Works:*

Year	Dalzell	Glengarnock	Clydebridge	Total
1914	318,000	—	—	318,000
1915	467,037	34,848	8,991	510,876
1916	490,166	99,454	88,308	677,928
1917	516,482	142,754	119,286	778,522
1918	469,557	151,612	171,019	792,169

Sources: 1914–16: Sir John Craig's Private Papers, 'Report by J. C. Davies to John Mann, Ministry of Munitions, 13 November 1917'. 1917–18: Estimated from D.C. & S., 'Consigned Tonnages', given in 'Dalzell Steelworks Output' and 'Clydebridge Steelworks Output'.

[13] D.C. & S., *Jubilee* booklet, pp. 10–12; Minute Book II, *passim*.

Colville & Sons increased their ingot steel output by about 250 per cent (see Table 6.1). They turned out a considerable variety of finished and semi-finished materials to increasingly sophisticated specifications, and, in addition, a useful quantity of pig iron was made at Glengarnock.

In financial terms, the impact of war was equally dramatic. The purchase of Clydebridge and Glengarnock (including the outstanding shares of the Glengarnock Chemical Company), their commissioning, and the extensions undertaken at both these works and at Dalzell, may be estimated at nearly £2½ million.[14] The huge advances made to Colvilles by the Ministry of Munitions to affect this transformation were subject to a complex formula of writing-off and repayments. In addition, there was the purchase of Archibald Russell and Company for some £650,000, a move towards vertical integration which necessitated the issue of 15,000 Ordinary shares in David Colville & Sons to members of the Russell family. It was therefore proposed to increase the company's share capital so as to reduce the floating liability and to bring the issued capital more into line with the value of the company's assets. Thus, the reserve fund was capitalized by issuing a further 30,000 Ordinary shares to the shareholders and these, added to the 15,000 Ordinary shares issued to the Russell interests, brought the Ordinary share capital of Colvilles up to £750,000. In addition, £300,000 Second Preference shares were created and were taken up principally in payment of existing cash loans. The shares remained very closely held. The company continued to be 'strictly private', and even after the merger with Russells there were not more than forty shareholders. These were almost entirely either members of the original founders, or the senior executives of the Colville or Russell enterprises.[15]

[14] The calculation of this figure is extremely complex. It is based on various agreements with the Ministry of Munitions (those dated 16 Jan. 1916, 10 Oct. 1916, and 18 Oct. 1916) and their subsequent amendment by mutual consent. The details were codified in a financial agreement between the Ministry and Colvilles, dated 21 Sept. 1920. Additional data have been gathered from various reports and calculations among Sir John Craig's personal papers. The enlargement of Glengarnock and Clydebridge alone cost over £1½ million.

[15] D.C. & S., Balance Sheets; Moores, Carson, and Watson to the Secretary to the Treasury, 28 Dec. 1916; Agreement between the Ministry of Munitions and David Colville & Sons, 21 Sept. 1920.

2 David Colville & Sons: New Personalities and New Prospects

In the long run, more important than either the physical or financial impact of war on David Colville & Sons was its effect on the personalities who guided the company's growth and development. When the war began the direction of the firm was largely in the hands of the founder's sons, Archibald and David Colville. It was they who willingly agreed to meet the Government's request for a massive increase of Scottish steel output; it was they who decided to take control of Clydebridge and Glengarnock, and, as a later independent report to the Ministry of Munitions phrased it, convert two 'practically obsolete and unremunerative works into profitable commercial propositions';[16] it was they who conceived the idea of safeguarding the firm's supply of ingot moulds by acquiring a controlling interest in Fullwood Foundry. They made a formidable team. David possessed a magnetic personality. He captured the imagination of the men by his flamboyance and his grand manner. He was *the* master: everyone, from the board to the office-boy, knew it. He was the driving force behind the growth of Colvilles. His ambitions for the firm were contained by his elder brother, Archibald, the firm's chairman, the only person who could withstand David's violent temper and harness his incredible energies in order to attain realistic objectives. Archibald was shrewd, calculating, and cool; reputed, as John Hodge put it, 'to have an absolute knowledge of how many beans make five'.[17] The demands of war—and the beneficence of the Ministry of Munitions—gave David his chance. There was no restraining him. Everything seemed to come within his purview. The physical and mental strain was too great. In October 1916, David Colville collapsed and died. He was fifty-six. Two months later, Archibald, utterly exhausted with the effort of implementing his brother's plans, succumbed to a brief illness at the age of sixty-two.

Thus ended the second generation of command. It was undoubtedly a critical point in the development of Colvilles, the point at which the firm could have foundered. Whoever was

[16] Sir John Craig's Private Papers, J. C. Davies, 'Report to John Mann, Ministry of Munitions, 13 June 1917'.
[17] Hodge, *Workman's Cottage to Windsor Castle*, pp. 33–44.

to assume the chairmanship of the company would have to take over at a most difficult period. The enormous sums being expended at Glengarnock and Clydebridge had yet to produce any tangible results; the negotiations with the Russells were at a delicate stage; the acquisition of raw materials was a constant anxiety. Who was to be appointed to bear a burden which, it was unanimously agreed, had killed the senior Colvilles?

One possible course, that of electing one of their sons to the chairmanship, was out of the question. Not only had they little or no executive experience within the firm, but they were all serving in the army. Unless a complete outsider was to be brought in, which was unthinkable, the choice lay between James B. Allan, John Craig, John Lennox, and David M. Maclay. It was unanimously agreed that John Craig be appointed, though it is probable that had Captain James Lusk not been fatally wounded near Amiens on Christmas Day, 1915, he would have succeeded to the chairmanship of the company. A grandson of David Colville, the founder, Lusk was born in 1878. After his education at Uddingston School and the West of Scotland Technical College, Glasgow, he served a five-year apprenticeship in engineering with Sir William Arrol & Company. In 1901 he worked in the engineering shops at Dalzell, but left two years later to take a degree in the Mechanical Science tripos at Cambridge. In 1905 he returned to Dalzell to become Assistant Works Manager, and together with John Craig and J. B. Allan was made a director when the board was enlarged to six members in 1910.[18] A clear and incisive thinker, he possessed a rare combination of technical expertise and commercial judgement. He was, moreover, uniformly respected and liked by the workmen. His direct descent from the company's founder, coupled with his considerable talents, made him the obvious successor to Archibald and David Colville. His death on 28 December 1915 was perhaps the greatest of the company's wartime losses.[19]

The choice of John Craig as chairman and managing director was a momentous decision.[20] He was to become the architect of the modern Scottish iron and steel industry. Born at Clydes-

18 D.C. & S., Minute Book II, 2 Feb. 1910.
19 *Colvilles' Magazine*, i (1920), 93–4.
20 D.C. & S., Minute Book II, 18 Dec. 1916.

dale, New Stevenston, on 11 December 1874, John Craig was the son and grandson of ironworkers. His father, a strict Presbyterian, was a furnaceman who came to work at Colvilles in 1882, where six years later, after an education at Dalzell Public School, John Craig was taken on as an office-boy at five shillings a week. After fifteen months in the general office, he became an order clerk concerned with the purchase of pig iron. It is said that his motto was 'never leave today's work till tomorrow', and so hard would he work that James McSkimming, the office manager, had to limit the number of tasks that were given to him to perform. Indeed, his prodigious energy made it impossible for his superiors to fail to notice him, and he was quickly marked out for promotion. When John Colville entered Parliament in 1895, John Craig, then aged only twenty-one, was entrusted with his duties at the Royal Exchange in Glasgow, and it is apparent that he soon gained the complete confidence of the Colville brothers, who appointed him Iron Works Salesman in 1905, and invited him to become a member of the board five years later. The puddler's son was then only thirty-six, and when he was elected chairman in the fateful year of 1916, he was, in years, the board's most junior member.[21]

As his vice-chairman, Craig had J. B. Allan, also a managing director. Unhappy in his father's clothing and drapery business, in 1881 he replied to an advertisement in the *Glasgow Herald* and successfully applied for an assistantship in the 'testing department'. He was soon in full charge of the department. In 1901 he became the Company Secretary and, nine years later, director with special responsibility for the purchase of iron ore and pig iron. The two other directors responsible for John Craig's election were David M. Maclay and John Lennox. The former was the son of David Thompson Maclay, the founder of the legal firm of Maclay, Murray, and Spens. Born in Glasgow, David Maclay was educated at Glasgow Academy and Loretto. In 1887 he was appointed assistant to Hugh Neilson at Clydebridge Steel Works, where he gained a thorough general knowledge of steel-making. He worked in the melting shop, the rolling mills, the shearing department, the test house

[21] This paragraph is based on a brochure by David Murray, 'Sir John Craig: sixty-seven years with Colvilles'; *Colvilles' Magazine*, i (1920), 129–30; ibid., Spring 1957, p. 4.

and, finally, the laboratory. Meanwhile, he attended evening classes. He left Clydebridge in 1894 to become Works Manager of the Steel Nut & Tube Company in Manchester, resigning in 1898 to visit the United States to familiarize himself with American steel-making practice. In the following year, he was appointed Works Manager at Dalzell, a post he held for seventeen years. Made a director in 1913, at the same time as John Lennox, he continued to manage Dalzell, and with the deaths of David Colville, jun., and Captain James Lusk, he was the sole member of the board with technical knowledge.

John Lennox, like the new chairman, was a salesman, and his early career is curiously similar to that of John Craig. As soon as he had left school, his father applied on his behalf for the first vacancy to occur in the general office at Dalzell. Lennox was taken on in 1880. He too was an office-boy whose devotions to his work took him to the top. Soon transferred to the invoice department, he was subsequently appointed to deal with John Colville's correspondence. So efficiently did he perform this task that he was given charge of plate sales, and in 1900 he became, with John Craig, one of the company's representatives on the Glasgow Royal Exchange. When Lennox was made a director in 1913, he continued to specialize in the commercial side of the business. He was, it was said, 'a great Sales Director'.[22]

It seems improbable that the Ministry of Munitions would have chosen *this* board of directors to be the vehicle for the great expansion of Scottish output that took place during the war. Individually, its members were as yet little known. Two had risen from the post of office-boy, three had gained their experience largely on the commercial side. So far they had been completely overshadowed by the Colville brothers to whom they clearly owed their positions. They all acknowledged this; not least the new chairman. Few could have foreseen John Craig's immense strength of purpose; few would have imagined that he would fashion and lead the company to its overwhelming dominance in the Scottish iron and steel industry. His one great resource in 1916–17 was the immense loyalty to the firm that

[22] The information on the careers of J. B. Allan, David Maclay, and John Lennox has been drawn from *Colvilles' Magazine*, i (1920), 147–8, 166, supplemented by some sparse details in D.C. & S., Minute Books, *passim*.

the founder's sons, particularly David, had inspired in workmen and management alike.[23] Indeed, for some time John Craig regarded himself simply as a trustee acting for the Colville family. He was, at this stage, perfectly prepared to hand over the company to the founder's grandsons as soon as they were sufficiently experienced to assume command.[24] Significantly, the first decision of the new board was to invite Captain David Colville, Archibald's elder son, to become a director.[25]

But others, outside Colvilles, were showing interest in the rapidly-growing and apparently rudderless iron and steel company. Within two months of the creation of the new board, both Lord Pirrie, chairman of Harland & Wolff, and Mr. Russell Ferguson, of Barclay, Curle & Company Ltd., had approached John Craig with proposals 'for a closer alliance' between their shipbuilding concerns and David Colville & Sons.[26] After further discussions, negotiations with Barclay Curle's were broken off when Lord Pirrie made an informal offer for the purchase of Colvilles by means of an exchange of shares with John Brown & Company Ltd., another of his shipbuilding interests.[27] These negotiations were suspended in May 1917,[28] but when Lord Pirrie visited Dalzell later in the year, he repeated his invitation to John Craig 'to consider the question of being linked with Harland & Wolff Ltd. in some way'.[29] This invitation was followed by numerous informal discussions

[23] A point repeatedly emphasized in conversations with old employees and those who became senior officials in the company. I am particularly indebted to Mr. R. C. Dymock, who joined the company as a pay clerk at Dalzell in 1906, and who subsequently became Chief Labour Officer of the Group's works and a Special Director, for recreating the spirit of these times.
[24] I am indebted to Mr. T. R. Craig, Sir John's son, for this information.
[25] D.C. & S.: Minute Book III, 18 Dec. 1916. Born in 1890, David Colville was educated at Fettes College and Pembroke, Cambridge. In 1912 he entered business in Moores, Carson, & Watson, Glasgow, and in the following year was appointed assistant to D. M. Maclay and James Lusk at Dalzell, where he was chiefly engaged in the construction of Number Four melting shop and bar mill. In 1914 he joined the Fife and Forfar Yeomanry and served in Gallipoli and Egypt. He was allowed to relinquish his commission on his father's death, when he took over at Glengarnock. The large new melting shop and bar mill plant known as 'Scheme B' was completed under his supervision. *Colvilles' Magazine*, iii (1922), 111–12.
[26] D.C. & S., Minute Book III, 13 Feb. 1917.
[27] Ibid., 17 June 1917.
[28] Ibid., 15 May 1917. The reason is obscure; the scheme may have failed to secure Treasury consent.
[29] Ibid., 11 Sept. 1917.

between John Craig and Lord Pirrie culminating, early in January 1918, in a decision by the board of Colvilles, now enlarged by the Russell representatives, Captain David Colville and Sir Henry Robertson,[30] that 'it would be of advantage for the company to have an alliance with Harland & Wolff Ltd. . . . provided satisfactory terms and the approval of the shareholders could be obtained'.[31] Various schemes were considered during the following twelve months but all were rejected as being either impractical or unacceptable. There the matter stood when the First World War ended.

3 Other Firms in Scotland

Of all the Scottish steel companies, the war of 1914–18 had the greatest impact on David Colville & Sons. In a sense, the decisions of the Ministry of Munitions simply confirmed and consolidated the growing relative importance of the Dalzell firm. In making their plans to achieve a rapid expansion in steelmaking capacity, the Ministry backed a winner. By 1917 David Colville & Sons were producing over 40 per cent of the Scottish make of steel (see Table 6.2): Dalzell itself was turning out well over half a million ingot tons (see Table 6.1), far more than any other plant in Scotland.

Colvilles' major competitors expanded, but not on this scale or in this way; their shares of the increasing total make remained relatively stable and what increases in output were achieved were as much due to the hard-driving of existing plant as to the installation of new equipment. Four new melting furnaces were built at Lanarkshire; at the Steel Company, major extensions to the Hallside steel foundry were undertaken, although the work did not begin until 1918; and at Parkhead and Dalmuir, Beardmores created new facilities for gun-making. Outside Colvilles, the most important increase in melting capacity was the extension of Beardmores' Mossend plant in 1917, specifically to make shell bars and ship plates. But Beardmores had never concentrated on the manufacture of com-

---

[30] Sir Henry Robertson was appointed a director in October 1917, apparently as a representative of the Ministry of Munitions. Ibid., 'Minutes of an Extra-Ordinary General Meeting', 8 Oct. 1917.
[31] Ibid., 15 June 1918.

TABLE 6.2

The Contribution of Various Companies to the Scottish Output of Steel, 1914–1919

	(1) Scotland	(2) D.C. & S.		(3) S.C. of S.		(4) W. Beardmore & Co		(5) Lanarkshire		(6) Stewarts & Lloyds		(7) Other companies
Year	Ingot output	Ingot output	Prop. of col. (1)	Est. ingot output	Prop. of col. (1)	Est. ingot output	Prop. of col. (1)	Ingot output	Prop. of col. (1)	Approx. ingot output	Prop. of col. (1)	Approx. share of col. (1)
	(tons)		(%)		(%)		(%)		(%)		(%)	(%)
1914	1,326,489	318,000	24·0	229,891	16·2	154,607	11·7	140,189	10·6	140,000	10·6	27
1915	1,516,211	510,876	33·7	281,515	17·4	150,259	9·9	155,318	10·2	150,000	9·9	20
1916	1,718,790	677,928	39·4	326,731	18·2	163,452	9·5	157,262	9·1	150,000	8·7	15
1917	1,874,959	778,522	41·5	305,412	16·1	202,555	10·8	168,092	9·0	150,000	8·0	13
1918	1,923,499	791,169	41·1	276,712	15·7	174,179	9·1	175,324	9·1	150,000	7·8	17
1919	1,597,200	742,837	46·5			186,524	11·7	139,907	8·8	n.d.	—	10

Notes and sources: Col. (1) British Iron and Steel Federation, Statistics Department.

(2) Table 6.1(b). The figure for 1919 has, like those for 1917 and 1918, been estimated from D.C. & S., 'Consigned Tonnages' given in 'Dalzell Steelworks Output' and 'Clydebridge Steelworks Output'.

(3) Estimated from S.C. of S., 'Deliveries of Finished Materials'. The Steel Company's financial year ended in mid-July, and the proportions given are calculated on an average of the Scottish output for the two years in which the Steel Company's 'year' falls. That is, for example, the S.C. of S.'s estimated ingot output for the year ending mid-July 1915 is assessed as a proportion of the average Scottish output for the years 1914 and 1915.

(4) Estimated from finished weights kindly provided by John Hume and Michael Moss. See note (5), Table 5.5.

(5) Lanarkshire Steel Co.: Statistical Records: 'Ingot Outputs'.

(6) Stewarts & Lloyds: Estimated from an isotype chart in *Stewarts & Lloyds, 1903–1953*, p. 31.

(7) This column is intended primarily to provide a rough indication of the coverage of columns (2)–(6). That is, it is a residual produced by subtracting the known or estimated proportions from 100. The most important companies whose output figures are not known are the Glasgow Iron & Steel Co. and James Dunlop & Co.

Additional note: Where it has been necessary to estimate the ingot outputs from 'consigned tonnages' (Cols. (3) & (4)), the estimates have been based on the assumption that it took one ton of ingot steel to produce 15 cwts of 'finished material'.

mercial steels. The output of its furnaces was intended primarily
for internal consumption: for warships at Dalmuir, for Arrol-
Johnson motor cars at Dumfries, and, during the war, for aero-
engines at Tongland and airship building at Inchinnan. Beardmores had become a veritable arsenal: involved in the production of armaments of every description.[32] If Colvilles had been
urged by the Ministry of Munitions to make more steel, Beardmores may be said, in contrast, to have been encouraged to
use more steel in the most diversified ways. The roles of the
two firms were diverging rapidly.

When the Government first became fully conscious of the
magnitude of the steel problem the highest priority was given
to the expansion of steel-making capacity, and the extensions
planned for Scotland, because of the overwhelming importance
of Clyde shipbuilding, was, in the British context, dispropor-
tionately high.[33] It was not the task of the Iron and Steel Department of the Ministry of Munitions and its predecessors to
rectify imbalances in productive capacities which had grown
up before hostilities began, nor was it within its remit—or even
within its consciousness—to attempt to moderate the compel-
ling needs of war in order to ease the eventual transition to
peacetime conditions. Hence, while Scottish melting capacity
was substantially expanded, it is noteworthy that in Scotland
no *new* blast furnaces were planned. 'There were, it is true, some
improvements in the auxiliary equipment of the existing Scots
[blast] furnaces which slightly added to their power of production; but this amounted to little.'[34] In the light of domestic
sources of iron ore, this neglect of smelting was undoubtedly
justified, but it meant that Scotland emerged from the war with
the imbalance in its iron and steel industry exacerbated rather
than remedied. It was an unfortunate legacy.

This made the sudden relinquishment by the Steel Company
of Scotland of its half interest in the Appleby Iron Company
Ltd. all the more depressing. This had seemed a most promising prewar development, but when, in 1917, following the
fusion of Samuel Fox & Company and Steel, Peech, & Tozer,

[32] The details are given in Hume and Moss, *Beardmore*.
[33] See Burn, *Economic History of Steel Making*, p. 359; Hatch, *The Iron and Steel Industry*, p. 41.
[34] Burn, *Economic History of Steel Making*, pp. 356–8.

this Sheffied group (the genesis of the United Steel Companies) absorbed the Frodingham Iron & Steel Company,[35] the Steel Company felt it could not continue with the arrangement. The shares were sold to United Steel for £250,000.[36]

4 Immediate Postwar Developments

Events in the Scottish iron and steel industry immediately following the Armistice are an integral part of the impact of the war. Once an iron and steel company is committed to major extensions—inevitably of a long gestation period—these must perforce be completed unless very heavy losses are to result. Once under way, fundamental structural and organizational changes possess a similar, temporarily irresistible, momentum. This was certainly so in the case of both Colvilles and Beardmores, the Scottish steel firms most affected by wartime planning.

If the possibility of an alliance with Harland & Wolff greatly occupied the minds of the members of the board of Colvilles throughout the last twelve months of the war, other important matters were not neglected. It is apparent that Colvilles eagerness to come to some arrangement with a large shipbuilding concern was powerfully motivated by a desire to secure an outlet for the company's greatly enhanced steel output.[37] But the blandishments of Lord Pirrie did not blind them to other possibilities. Thus, in October 1918, when Archibald Mowbray, the Managing Director of Smith & McLean Ltd., the Glasgow firm of sheet rollers, and one of the largest galvanizing concerns in the country, mentioned to John Craig that he and his friends, who held approximately seven-eighths of the total share capital,

[35] S.C. of S., Minute Book XVII, 24 Oct. 1917.
[36] See Burn, *Economic History of Steel Making*, pp. 371–2; Andrews and Brunner, *Capital Development*, p. 117. Apart from the bald statement in the 'Directors' Report to the Shareholders for the year ended 11 July 1918', that 'During the year circumstances arose which resulted in your Directors disposing of the Company's interest in the Appleby Iron Co. Ltd.' (S.C. of S.: Minute Book XVII, 23 Oct. 1918), the Minute Books of the Steel Company of Scotland are infuriatingly silent on this, as in so many other matters. It is not impossible that there was a clash of personalities, but perhaps the Steel Company feared being drawn into this Sheffield-inspired grouping.
[37] Most studies have emphasized the desire of the shipbuilders to integrate backwards in the great postwar boom; few have given the same attention to the equally powerful desire of many steel-makers to integrate forwards.

might be prepared to consider selling a controlling interest in his firm to Colvilles, the matter was taken up with alacrity.[38] Smith & McLean purchased a large quantity of semi-finished steel from Colvilles in the forms of bars, billets, and plate cuttings for processing at their four works at Mavisbank (Glasgow), Gartcosh, Milnwood (Mossend), and Port Glasgow, and thereby constituted an important outlet for the company's products that was not markedly affected by fluctuations in shipbuilding activity. It was too great an opportunity to be ignored. Within a year Colvilles had acquired nearly all the equity capital of Smith & McLean, two of the directors had been 'asked in a friendly way to retire at an early date', and the board reconstituted to include John Craig, chairman, Archibald Mowbray, D. M. Maclay, and John Lennox.[39]

At about the same time that Archibald Mowbray first mentioned to John Craig that Colvilles might wish to purchase control of Smith & McLean, J. B. Allan received a similar approach by the senior partner of Cox & Danks. Mr. Cox told Allan that he wished to sell his small iron works at Craigneuk, Motherwell, together with some 5,000 tons of steel billets and scrap. After the great acquisitions of the past three years, this was but a minor proposition. Nevertheless, its ultimate significance can hardly be exaggerated. Cox wanted £15,000 for the almost derelict Inshaw Works, and the board decided to make the purchase. Three factors influenced Colvilles. It was felt that buying the works would obviate any 'possibility of [their] being started by some other company', the steel scrap that was to be sold with the works would be a useful supplement to Colvilles' stocks, and the plant might serve to roll down war material when there was capacity working elsewhere.[40] In the event, the 20,000 tons of steel billets purchased from the Ministry of Munitions which it had been intended to re-roll at Inshaw were used at Dalzell:[41] the Inshaw Works was destined to be started for a much more momentous purpose. In April 1919, John Craig and David Maclay were approached by 'two expert metallurgists in regard to starting a small work to manufacture

[38] D.C. & S., Minute Book III, 15 Oct. 1918.
[39] Ibid., 11 Nov. 1919, 9 Dec. 1919, 13 Jan. 1920.
[40] Ibid., 9 Dec. 1918, 14 Jan. 1919, *Jubilee* booklet, p. 20. The steel scrap was purchased at £6 10s. a ton.
[41] Ibid., 11 Feb. 1919.

special steel castings, magnet steel and other qualities. They suggested that the Inshaw Works, buildings and plant ... would suit them admirably. They desired [Colvilles] to consider the matter and perhaps take an interest in the proposed company.'[42] The 'two expert metallurgists' were Dr. Andrew McCance and T. M. Service.

The future Sir Andrew McCance was born at Cadder near Glasgow in 1889, and educated at Morrison's Academy, Crieff, Alan Glen's School, Glasgow, and the Royal School of Mines in London. In 1910 he returned to Scotland determined to make steel-making his career. With some prescience, Beardmores gave him the run of their melting shop at Parkhead, unpaid until a vacancy was found for him six months later as an assistant chemist at 30 shillings a week. After discovering how to prevent cracks in armour plate ingots, he was moved to the armour shop where he conducted far-reaching experiments into the annealing process. As a result he was made Assistant Armour Manager. Soon after this promotion, he was examining steel samples behind a portable crane when the crane moved and crushed him, breaking his breast bone and five ribs and puncturing a lung. This accident left him with no permanent disability but it kept him from work for five months and caused him to be rejected on the two occasions when he tried to enlist with the colours. In 1916 he received the degree of Doctor of Science from the University of London.[43]

Dr. McCance stayed in the armour shop at Parkhead until 1919, though shortly before the end of the war he had been sent to Dalzell by Sir William Beardmore to give Colvilles technical assistance in the production of bullet-proof steel plates.[44] It was clear to him that with the Armistice signed there would be no great demand for armour steel, and equally clear that in times of peace there would be a growing market for alloy steels and high quality steel castings. He therefore decided to set up on his own, and it was a consequence of this decision that he and T. M. Service, the manager at Beardmores who had first promoted him in the Armour Shop, approached John

[42] Ibid., 15 Apr. 1919.
[43] This paragraph draws on an article in *Colvilles' Magazine*, Spring 1965, pp. 2–7.
[44] D.C. & S., Minute Book III, 18 Sept. 1918.

Craig and David Maclay in April 1919 with their proposition
to convert the Inshaw Works to a steel foundry. Colvilles decided to support the scheme. A new company, the Clyde Alloy
Steel Company Ltd., was to be created with a capital of
£60,000 in Ordinary £1 shares.[45] It was registered on the 13
November 1919. David Colville & Sons took up 40,000 of these
shares together with 8,000 which were to be held for sale to
Dr. McCance and T. M. Service until they were in a position
to purchase them.

One other development took place as a consequence of the
purchase of the Inshaw Works. Even before Dr. McCance had
put proposals forward to convert the old works into a steel
foundry, it had been decided to float a small subsidiary concern,
called the Motherwell Machinery & Scrap Company, for the
purpose of starting a scrap yard on an unoccupied part of the
ground attached to the works. The total subscribed capital was
fixed at £10,000 in £1 Ordinary shares of which David Colville
& Sons took up 60 per cent, and William Muir, a former
employee of Colvilles who was to manage the scrap yard, 40
per cent.[46] Initially, only half the capital was called up. Later
in 1919, Mr. Bernard Cohen of George Cohen & Company
called on William Muir and asked if his company could be
associated with the enterprise. Since William Muir believed
that, if such an arrangement were not made, Cohens would
'start a place of their own which would [represent] further competition in the [Lanarkshire] district',[47] Colvilles board decided
to negotiate with the London company, and in 1920 2,500 shares
(10 shillings paid) were transferred to George Cohen's nominees
at the price of 42 shillings each. It was subsequently agreed to
increase the company's share capital to £20,000 divided in
such a way that Colvilles held £7,000, George Cohen & Sons &
Company, £7,000, William Muir, £4,500, and employees of
the company, should they wish to take up the shares, £1,500.[48]

[45] Sir John Craig's Private Papers: John Craig to Maclay, Murray and
Spens, 12 Sept. 1919, A. Moore to John Craig, 6 Sept. 1919; D.C. & S.,
Minute Book III, 9 Sept. 1919, 14 Oct. 1919, 11 Nov. 1919.
[46] Ibid., 14 Jan. 1919; Sir John Craig's Private Papers, John Craig to
Maclay, Murray, and Spens, 20 Jan. 1919.
[47] Sir John Craig's Private Papers, William Muir to John Craig, 8 Sept.
1919; D.C. & S., Minute Book III, 9 Sept. 1919.
[48] Sir John Craig's Private Papers, undated memorandum on the Motherwell Machinery & Scrap Co.

With the exception of the purchase of the foundry belonging to John Frew & Company Ltd., Hamilton, by the Fullwood Foundry Company for £30,000 in November 1920, Colvilles' last major acquisiton during the heady postwar days was the Carnlough Lime Company of Carnlough, County Antrim, Ireland, as 'it was imperative to secure . . . a better supply of limestone for the works'. The price paid for the works, plant, and lease of the quarries, together with the steamer *Olderfleet*, was £32,000.[49] The company, established about 1853, was reconstructed under the original name in August 1920, with a capital of £40,000, and was placed under the responsibility of Archibald Russell Ltd.[50]

In five years David Colville and Sons had grown from a single works at Dalzell, Motherwell, turning out just over 300,000 tons of steel ingots, to a group of companies, linked horizontally and vertically, which annually melted about 800,000 tons of steel ingots; produced some 80,000 tons of pig iron and a range of by-products;[51] mined over a million tons of coal a year; quarried thousands of tons of limestone; and manufactured an ever-increasing range of finished and semi-finished rolled products and special steel castings. The growth in the scale of the enterprise is indicated by the expansion of the labour force. This rose from approximately 2,800 at Dalzell in 1914, to about 18,000 in 1920, 10,000 of whom were involved in the manufacture of iron and steel (5,000 at Dalzell, 3,000 at Glengarnock, and 2,000 at Clydebridge), 6,500 were at the collieries, and 1,500 in the rolling mills of Smith & McLean Ltd. The issued nominal capital of the group had increased commensurately, from £600,000 in 1914 to about £3½ million in 1920.[52] By any standards of measurement, this represented a remarkable acceleration in the growth of the firm: it had perhaps all taken place *too* rapidly, for whereas by 1920 Colvilles was undoubtedly able to enjoy certain of the *commercial* economies of scale, the *technical* economies, which are the reward of greater physical integration of plant, were still remote. It could be

[49] D.C. & S., Minute Book III, 11 May 1920, 8 June 1920.
[50] Ibid., 13 July 1920, 10 Aug. 1920, 14 Sept. 1920.
[51] The more important by-products were sulphate of ammonia, basic slag, and fuel oil; D.C. & S., *Jubilee* booket, p. 13.
[52] In May 1920 the book value of David Colville & Sons alone was about £6 million.

argued that the collection of companies and works brought together so hastily by David and Archibald Colville and John Craig *possessed* but limited potential for integrated production, and that from a purely economic viewpoint it would have been better, once the war was over, to undertake radical reorganization involving, *inter alia*, the phasing out of the geographically distant Glengarnock works. Why this did not take place is difficult to determine. Perhaps the explanation lies in the character of the company's chairman, whose incredible energy and co-ordinating ability kept the entire edifice together. John Craig was greatly influenced by commercial considerations, and on these grounds the structure of the Colville group of companies in 1920 was perfectly defensible. But his actions are not to be understood simply in terms of the economic text-book or the accounting manual. Initially at least, he felt himself to be a trustee of the Colville family interests. Having brought the plans of David and Archibald Colville to fruition, he wished to pass their heritage on to their sons intact. But, even more important, the deeply religious John Craig was supremely conscious of his social responsibilities. Systematic rationalization inevitably involved throwing men out of work. To close down Glengarnock, for example, would have meant the murder of an isolated community. This he would not countenance; neither in 1919 nor later.

Of one thing he was sure, to keep his 'big combine' going he had to have a market. Colvilles' largest customer was Harland & Wolff. What then could be more natural than to pursue the negotiations with Lord Pirrie for some form of alliance? These continued throughout the first nine months of 1919, when, after special resolutions by both bodies of shareholders, it was agreed that Harland & Wolff be allocated 15,000 Ordinary £10 shares in Colvilles in exchange for 300,000 6 per cent Cumulative Preference shares of £1 each in Harland & Wolff, 'thus sealing a long friendship and close working connection of many years'.[53] In March 1920 the bonds between the two firms were tightened, when Lord Pirrie made an offer on behalf of Harland & Wolff to purchase the whole or the largest part of Colvilles' Ordinary shares. After he had agreed to retain the

[53] D.C. & S., *Jubilee* booklet, p. 16; Minute Book III, 14 May 1919; 9 Sept. 1919.

services of the current board for a period of at least five years, this offer was accepted by the members of the board and the shareholders alike.[54] The formal transfer of the bulk of the shares took place in April, and within a month Harland & Wolff held 85,442, or 95 per cent, of Colvilles' 90,000 £10 Ordinary shares.[55] Ultimate control of Colvilles had passed into the hands of Lord Pirrie,[56] though in the following four years it is clear that he left the effective direction of this part of his industrial empire to John Craig, whose power, far from being diminished, seems actually to have increased following the absorption of David Colville & Sons by Harland & Wolff.

The firm of William Beardmore & Company Ltd. did not have to affiliate itself to a major shipbuilding concern.[57] At Dalmuir Beardmores already possessed its own yard, from the berths of which a vast tonnage of naval vessels had been launched during the war years. Furthermore, even before 1914 the firm had become diversified and this tendency was given additional impetus by military demands. Considerable new capacity had been created for light and medium engineering—for example, during the closing months of the war Beardmores purchased the Sentinel Works of Alley & MacLellan and the Scottish Ice Rink at Crossmyloof, the latter for the assembly of ABC 'Dragon Fly' aero-engines—and this capacity had to be kept employed. Consequently Sir William Beardmore, by nature an expansionist, introduced motor car manufacture at Anniesland and Tongland (in Glasgow), revived motor car manufacture at Dumfries, and continued the promising development of aeroplanes started during the war. Diesel engines were also developed for marine use and for vehicles, airships, and locomotives. Indeed, a locomotive works was built at Dalmuir.

[54] Ibid., 9 Mar. 1920. The Russell interests accepted Lord Pirrie's offer on condition that their loan to Colvilles of £350,000 (that is, the outstanding portion of the purchase price to Archibald Russell & Co.) was repaid by seven half-yearly instalments of £50,000 each.

[55] Ibid., 13 Apr. 1920; D.C. & S., 'Memorandum on the capital of David Colville and Sons and affiliated companies', dated 13 May 1920.

[56] It is significant that in the Minute Books of David Colville & Sons, Harland & Wolff Ltd. are usually referred to only in the matter of share transfers. Until his death in 1924, decisions are referred to, and suggestions for action come from, Lord Pirrie.

[57] See Hume and Moss, *Beardmore*. The authors have kindly provided the information on which this paragraph is based. See also J. M. Reid, *James Lithgow, Master of Work* (London: Hutchinson, 1964), p. 144.

Mossend was further improved and, joining with Swan, Hunter, & Wigham Richardson, Beardmores purchased the Glasgow Iron & Steel Company of Wishaw, once the scene of experiments by James Riley.[58] All this activity—estimated to cost nearly £4 millions—was to be financed by a £5 million share issue. It was designed to exploit 'the general expansion of trade consequent on the victorious terminatiom of the war'.

The boom in the iron and steel trade which set in shortly after the end of the First World War was fundamentally psychological. It was rooted in the belief that, with the abandonment of government controls in the early months of 1919, prices and profits would rise in response to sustained pressure of demand on iron- and steel-making capacity which could not quickly be further expanded. Such was the postwar optimism that the disquieting features in the situation—uncertainties in export markets, substantial cost increases in labour and raw materials—while not ignored, were assumed to be surmountable.

Whatever misgivings were entertained by the steel-makers, they were not shared by the shipbuilders. Confident of full order books for the foreseeable future, and conscious of competing demands for steel by those who sought to make good the ravages of war and the reconversion of industry to peacetime purposes, the shipbuilders attempted to ensure their necessary supplies by acquiring control of steel-making companies. Harland & Wolff's purchase of the Ordinary shares of David Colville & Sons was but one example of this strategy; the takeover of the Glasgow Iron & Steel Company by Beardmores and Swan, Hunters, another. In 1920, Lithgows of Port Glasgow acquired a controlling interest in the firm of James Dunlop & Company; the Steel Company of Scotland was purchased by a consortium of Clyde shipbuilders;[59] and the Lanarkshire Steel Company was brought into the Sperling group by the purchase of its

[58] The Glasgow Iron & Steel Co. was purchased jointly by William Beardmore & Co. Ltd. and Swan, Hunter, & Wigham Richardson. Each of the purchasers paid £750,000 for their 50 per cent holding of the 6,000 £100 Ordinary shares, or £250 for each share of £100 denomination.
[59] The consortium comprised Alexander Stephens & Sons Ltd. of Linthouse; the Greenock Dockyard Co., Greenock; Yarrow & Co., Scotstoun; the Blythswood Shipbuilding Co., Whiteinch; the Ardrossan Shipbuilding Co., Ardrossan; James Little & Co., Glasgow; the Campbeltown Shipbuilding Co., Campbeltown; and the Lloyd Royal Belge (Great Britain), Glasgow. *Shipping and Shipbuilding Record*, 22 Apr. 1920.

shares by Workman, Clark & Company Ltd. of Belfast.[60] With
the exception of the Clydesdale Works of Stewarts & Lloyds
at Mossend, the entire steel-making capacity of Scotland was
in the hands of the shipbuilders, and those who seek to discover
the inadequacies of the Scottish iron and steel industry in the
interwar period must constantly recognize the fact. In retrospect, the action of the shipbuilders seems touched with mad-
ness. At the time, its economic irrationality was far from
apparent. Between the end of the war and mid-1920, the prices
of ship plates quadrupled; few could have foreseen their subsequent collapse (see Table 6.3).

Nevertheless, whoever *owned* the Scottish steel works, their
products were almost inevitably destined to be absorbed by the
shipbuilders. The nature of the various markets that the Scottish steel industry depended upon cannot be determined with
any exactitude. Indeed, not until long after the First World
War is there any evidence that the Scottish steel-makers made
any formal attempt to discover *precisely* where their output was
going. Perhaps they felt no need to do so. It is apparent that
their thinking was principally in terms of acquiring the largest
possible share of the ramified demands arising from shipbuilding. Other markets—while recognized as being of some importance—were apt to be regarded as of marginal significance. Nor
is this surprising. From the 1880s the Scottish steel industry had
grown largely in response to the requirements of the Clyde.
Admittedly, Glengarnock was a major rail maker; the bulk
of the output of the Clydesdale Works was destined to be converted into tubes; the Steel Company of Scotland and Beardmores supplied the needs of the railway locomotive and rolling
stock producers, and all the works were called upon to provide
the sections and joists demanded by the large structural
engineers and heavy tool-makers; but the economies of all the
steel-making firms in the West of Scotland were dominated by
the manufacture and sale of the steel plates needed by the
thirty-nine shipbuilding yards grouped along the Clyde from

[60] The Sperling group brought into working agreement Workman, Clark
& Co. Ltd., the National Shipyards (later the Monmouth Shipbuilding Co.
Ltd.), William Doxford & Sons Ltd., and the Northumberland Shipbuilding
Co. Ltd. *Stock Exchange Gazette*, 6 May 1920. For Workman, Clark & Co.,
see W. E. Coe, *The Engineering Industry of the North of Ireland* (Newton Abbot:
David & Charles, 1969), pp. 84–6.

Table 6.3

Price of Ship Plates and Sections (in £s per ton) for Delivery in Scotland, 1919–1930

Date	Ship Plates	Sections	Comments
1 July 1919	18·25	17·75	English makers: plates, 17·75; sections, 17·25
1 Aug. 1919	18·75	18·25	English makers: plates, 18·25; sections, 17·75. Boiler plates: 22·00
21 Nov. 1919	19·75	19·25	Boiler plates: 24·00
15 Jan. 1920	21·00	20·50	—
9 Feb. 1920	22·00	21·50	—
8 Mar. 1920	24·00	23·50	—
3 May 1920	25·00	24·50	—
12 May 1920	26·00	25·50	—
15 Nov. 1920	24·50	23·50	—
10 Jan. 1921	23·50	23·00	Boiler plates: 30·00
20 Jan. 1921	22·50	21·00	Boiler plates: 29·00
19 Feb. 1921	21·00	19·00	Boiler plates: 28·00
19 Mar. 1921	19·00	17·50	Boiler plates: 25·00
14 Oct. 1921	12·50	12·00	English makers: plates, 10·50; sections, 10·00
10 Nov. 1921	10·50	10·00	Boiler plates: 15·50, 'all free to quote'
9 Jan. 1922	10·00	9·50	—
3 Aug. 1922	9·00	8·75	—
27 Mar. 1923	9·75	9·25	'Min. basic price, all free to quote'
17 Jun. 1923	10·25	10·00	Export prices lower
24 Oct. 1923	10·00	9·75	'Members free to lower prices if in competition with English makers'
20 Nov. 1923	9·75	9·50	Rails: 9·00; exports free to quote
7 Dec. 1923	10·25	10·00	—
13 Nov. 1924	9·50	9·00	'North-East Coast Makers lower'
17 Apr. 1925	9·50	9·00	Boiler plates: 12·50. Free pricing
8 Oct. 1925	8·00	7·50	These prices are a guide, pricing free 'North-East Coast competition damaging'
9 Feb. 1926	7·375	6·875	North-East prices lower
25 Mar. 1926	7·50	7·00	—
15 Apr. 1926	7·625	7·125	—
17 June 1926	7·875	7·375	—
12 Nov. 1929	8·625	8·125	Subject to rebate of 0·50 per ton
14 Jan. 1930	8·75	8·375	Subject to rebate of 0·50 per ton

Source: S.C. of S., Minute Books XVII–XIX.

TABLE 6.4

Ingot Steel Output in Scotland, Output by Colvilles, and Tonnage of Ships Launched on the Clyde and in Northern Ireland, 1920–1938

Year	(1) Scotland: Total ingot output	(2) D.C. & S./Colvilles' ingot output	(3) Ships launched on Clyde (tonnage)		(4) Ships launched from yards in N. Ireland (tonnage)	(5) Cols. (3) + (4)
			Merchant	Naval		
1920	2,074·4	829·5	672·4	None	84·7	757·1
1921	583·4	267·6	511·2	None	63·1	564·3
1922	768·1	267·4	388·5	None	94·3	482·8
1923	1,252·9	501·9	175·5	None	129·3	304·8
1924	1,241·4	588·6	538·0	None	116·3	654·3
1925	1,074·6	455·5	523·3	None	57·5	580·8
1926	423·7	166·4	275·1	11·2	92·0	389·5
1927	1,587·6	694·5	441·4	21·2	111·1	594·9
1928	1,425·1	626·3	583·1	25·2	75·7	701·8
1929	1,581·6	697·6	558·1	7·7	144·0	717·5
1930	1,212·9	496·5	526·6	3·3	168·1	701·3
1931	676·2	349·4	152·1	0·6	77·3	230·6
1932	552·7	275·5	63·8	2·9	5·7	74·9
1933	799·3	386·4	55·1	1·3	14·2	71·9
1934	1,220·3	693·2	238·3	29·8	87·4	385·3
1935	1,326·0	736·9	162·0	9·9	97·0	278·8
1936	1,636·9	897·3	296·4	30·5	62·4	419·8
1937	1,895·1	1,029·1	344·2	36·9	74·4	492·4
1938	1,601·5	881·8	415·1	28·5	69·6	541·7

Notes and sources: Col. (1) Scotland: ingot output, 1920–34, statistics provided by B.I.S.F. Statistics Department; 1935–40, B.S.C. Statistical Services.

(2) D.C. & S./Colvilles Ltd., Miscellaneous statistical records and Board Meeting Papers. The figures represent the steel ingot outputs of Dalzell, Clydebridge, and Glengarnock. No steel was ever melted at Calderbank after David Colville & Sons merged with James Dunlop & Co. to form Colvilles Ltd. in 1931. The first full calendar year in which the Steel Company of Scotland's Blochairn and Hallside Works, and the Lanarkshire Steel Co.'s works at Flemington, were within the Colville Group was 1937.

(3) J. Cunnison and J. B. S. Gilfillan (eds.), *Glasgow*, p. 841.

(4) Net tonnage figures, 1920–1 inclusive; gross tonnage, thereafter. Merchant vessels only. Sources: various issues of the *Ulster Yearbook*. Figures kindly provided by Dr. Leslie Clarkson.

(5) In arriving at total tonnage launched, naval output on the Clyde was multiplied by a factor of 2 in order to convert *all* shipbuilding output to its equivalent in mercantile tonnage.

Greenock to Govan and the two large yards on the Lagan at Belfast. This much is apparent from a comparison of the industry's output with that of the gross registered tonnage launched on the Clyde and on the Lagan (see Table 6.4). More sophisticated calculations indicate that variations in shipbuilding output 'explain' some 60 per cent of the variations in steel output. Hence the difficulties of the twenties and thirties facing Colvilles and the steel-makers of the West of Scotland generally were an inevitable consequence of the ill-fortunes of the shipping and shipbuilding industries of the inter-war period. Not surprisingly, the response of the steel-makers was to attempt once more to take refuge in conference agreements relating to prices and quotas, to participate in endless and frustrating negotiations with continental competitors, and, when all else failed, to seek a solution in various forms of rationalization.

VII

The Decade of Frustration, 1920–1930

1 The State of the Companies, 1920–1923

At the first meeting of the board of David Colville & Sons in 1921, it was reported that despite price reductions 'the orders on the books were very poor and the outlook was depressing'.[1] The completion of several large contracts kept much of the plant in operation for the first three months of the year, but the coal strike which began early in April produced an almost immediate shut-down, and for four months the works stood idle. Thereafter, only a partial resumption of activity was possible, and this was conducted in an atmosphere made cheerless by rapidly falling prices and a collapse in the value of trading stocks which amounted to no less that $£\frac{3}{4}$ million.[2] The depression which set in acutely in 1921 continued throughout 1922. Acute competition was encountered, especially after the Association of Scottish Steel Makers ceased fixing prices in August 1922.[3] Prices promptly fell below production costs and it was determined to undertake only that work necessary to retain market connections. Some benefits were, however, derived from the wartime diversification of interests. Archibald Russells experienced a rapid recovery in the second half of the year, and were able to contribute to Colvilles' income. At Gartcosh, Smith & McLean—despite a generally unsatisfactory year—largely remodelled the works, and were able to take advantage of the upswing in the market in the closing months of

[1] D.C. & S., Minute Book IV, 11 Jan. 1921.
[2] Ibid., 'Annual Report for 1921', 14 Mar. 1922.
[3] On 3 Aug. 1922, a meeting of English and Scottish steel-makers to consider prices had been unable to arrive at any agreement, and prices were 'declared free'. Immediately, the Scottish makers attempted to fix prices for their district at £9 per ton and £8·75 per ton for ship plates and sections respectively, but 'William Beardmore & Co. . . . declined to be parties to any agreement for fixed prices of steel for Scotland so long as free prices obtained in England', and the arrangements were abandoned. S.C. of S., Minute Book XVIII, 4 Aug. 1922 and 31 Aug. 1922.

1922. Clyde Alloy steadily increased both their reputation and their market. They were 'making money towards the end of the year', and would probably have been able to pay a dividend had it not been for severe price cutting by the Sheffield makers. Only Fullwood Foundry failed to experience any relief from the depression.[4]

The growing optimism of the directors during the winter of 1922 was boosted by the French occupation of the Ruhr. Orders came flowing in once more, but labour troubles began in the shipyards in April 1923. These were destined to last for seven months, seriously to curtail the demands of Colvilles' major customers, and to give rise to such fierce competition for the available business that the steel-makers reintroduced a national price-fixing arrangement in November.[5] This produced little or no benefit since the official selling price for ship plates was fixed at a level below production costs. 'Dumping' by continental manufacturers exacerbated the position. Refuge was taken in product diversification (special qualities of steel being produced), ruthless fuel economies, and the concentration of work on the most efficient plant. Productivity had, in fact, never been higher. The subsidiaries continued to do relatively well and although after 1920 Colvilles paid no ordinary dividend, it was possible to keep up the payments on the Cumulative Preference shares. The business was basically healthy.

Superficially, a similar verdict could have been reached on the condition of the Steel Company of Scotland. Taken over in 1920 by a consortium of shipbuilders—the new directors, under the chairmanship of Frederick J. Stephen of Linthouse, assumed office in April[6]—the company promptly concentrated

[4] D.C. & S., Minute Book IV, 'Annual Report for 1922', 13 Mar. 1923.

[5] In November 1923, the prices of ship plates, sections, and rails were fixed at £9·75, £9·50, and £9, respectively. No arrangement could be made for export prices, and Cargo Fleet and South Durham declined to participate in any price agreement. Indeed, both companies resigned from all Associations. S.C. of S., Minute Book XVIII, 30 Nov. 1923.

[6] Among the new directors were Mr. Emile Aitken-Quack of Ardrossan, James Napier and Donald Bremner of Glasgow, Harold E. Yarrow of Scotstoun, and August B. J. Cayzer, the representative of the Clan Line. Walter G. Gray was appointed managing director. S.C. of S.: Minute Book XVIII, 28 Apr. 1920. The consortium had purchased 49,885 Ordinary £10 shares at £35 each. The price of these Ordinary shares had fluctuated between 14½ and 16⅞ in 1919, had risen sharply to over 30 in January, and before the offer was known had advanced to 33¼. *Investors' Guardian*, 20 Mar. 1920.

on fulfilling the requirements of its new owners. Several agencies at home and abroad were terminated, the company's shares were removed from the official list of the Glasgow Stock Exchange, and the Glasgow office closed down.[7] The Steel Company was to become principally a supplier of ship plates to the members of the consortium; the demands of other customers were to take second place. This was not irrational when the postwar boom was at its height, and when the price of ship plates had stood at £26 per ton, but the boom was about to collapse, and steel prices begin that unremitting decline to unremunerative levels which they were to reach within two years. Despite the efforts of Walter G. Gray, the new managing director, to keep the plant in efficient condition, a loss of £62,262 was incurred on the manufacturing account during the financial year ended 12 July 1923, and the general outlook seemed bleak. The collieries owned by the company were nearing the end of their profitable lives; there had been a loss of goodwill when long-standing customers of the Steel Company had been unable to secure supplies during the hectic postwar boom and, understandably, the members of the new board of directors were primarily interested in their shipbuilding and shipping activities. This, above all, was the greatest weakness of the Steel Company's position.

But if in 1923 the affairs of the Steel Company inspired little confidence, the futures of some of the other companies in the industry engendered acute pessimism. At Flemington, the Lanarkshire Steel Company—now part of the Sperling group—had failed to make money even during 1920, when a loss of 1s. 6d. per ton of consigned output was recorded. This was undoubtedly due in part to high labour costs, the corollary of hard-driven and antiquated equipment, but a contributing factor may have been that at the time of the Sperling group's take-over, it was imagined that its members would be able to secure their supplies of ship plates from Flemington, only to discover—such was the hysteria of the time—that the Lanarkshire Steel Company, for which £25 for each fully-paid £10 share had been paid, did not, and never had, rolled plates![8]

[7] S.C. of S., Minute Book XVIII, 5 May, 23 June, 14 July, 28 Oct. 1920.
[8] The author was told this story by Sir Andrew McCance. By 1921, the Sperling combine, acting through the Northumberland Shipbuilding Co.,

This inevitably led to confusion. Throughout the whole of 1921 the melting shops were closed down. Four furnaces put out 73,365 tons of basic ingots in 1922, during the course of which year six of the nine acid furnaces were scrapped; and in 1923, when 112,638 tons of ingots were produced, four of the nine basic furnaces were demolished. Only the balance carried forward from the war years saved the directors from declaring a loss. No dividend on either the Preference or Ordinary shares could be paid.

If things at Lanarkshire were bad, at Beardmores they were fast becoming desperate. The remarkable extension and diversification of their activities during and after the war had had an appalling effect on the firm's capital structure, always somewhat shaky. In 1923, there were outstanding £1·44 million in 6 per cent Cumulative Preference shares, an issue of nearly £½ million debentures, loans amounting to £1·4 million, and, as if all this were not crippling enough, £1 million of 8 per cent Notes redeemable on or before 1 January 1928. These Notes had been issued in 1920, following the high profits of the war years,[9] but heavy losses after the poor year of 1922 threatened to make this burden insupportable.[10] Something had to be done.

---

owned the Furness interest in the Irvine Shipbuilding & Dry Docks Co., the whole of the share capital of Doxfords, 85 per cent of the capital of Fairfields, the Clyde shipbuilders, the whole of the share capital of the Monmouth Shipbuilding Co., and all the capital of Workman, Clark in addition to a controlling interest in another Clyde yard, the Blythswood Shipbuilding Co. J. R. Parkinson, *The Economics of Shipbuilding in the United Kingdom* (Cambridge: C.U.P., 1960), p. 35. Information on the Lanarkshire Steel Co. has been mainly derived from Sir John Craig's Private Papers and from a comprehensive collection of statistical data collected by an official of the Lanarkshire Steel Co. With the take-over of the Lanarkshire Steel Company by Workman, Clark in 1920, the existing board was augmented by the addition of R. A. Workman, who became Chairman, Sir E. Mackay Edgar, Sir John Esplan, and W. O. Workman. The price paid for the Lanarkshire shares in December 1919 emerged during the course of a valuation appeal. *Motherwell Times*, 3 Oct. 1921.

[9] Gross profits for the five years 1916–20 were just over £4m., although after deduction of depreciation, 'management commissions' and dividends, this was reduced to under £2m., of which £1·1m. was put to reserve. Information kindly provided by John Hume and Michael Moss.

[10] D. C. & S., Report by Sir William Plender to Lord Invernairn, 14 May 1923. Appendix B, p. 2; Carr and Taplin, *History of the British Steel Industry*, p. 445; Sir John Craig's Private Papers, Memorandum on 'Capital Structures' (undated, *c.* 1923).

2 Lord Invernairn and the Plender Report, 1923

Appropriately, the initiative was taken by Lord Invernairn.[11]
In January 1923, he wrote to James Strain, Vice-Chairman of
Lanarkshire Steel, R. M. Donaldson, of James Dunlops (the
owners of Clyde Iron Works, and since 1919 controlled by Lithgows), F. J. Stephen, Chairman of the Steel Company of Scotland, J. G. Stewart, Chairman of Stewarts & Lloyds, and John
Craig, inviting them to a meeting at Parkhead to 'examine the
possibility of an amalgamation of Iron and Steel Interests in
Scotland'. Invernairn was 'gravely concerned' about the future
of the Scottish steel industry. He believed that 'it is necessary
at once to consider plans *not merely for revival but for the survival
of the Trade*, and if the important North East Coast Group are
of the opinion that this can best be done by the amalgamation
of the firms engaged in the Industry in their district, then it
behoves us to consider carefully whether a similar project is not
also the best solution for our district'.[12] To the steel-makers who
attended the meeting—only Stewarts & Lloyds stood aside
because 'their steel manufacture [was] purely incidental to, and
only for the purpose of, supplying their own particular requirements'—Lord Invernairn emphasized 'the unfortunate
position in which the Scottish Steel Trade now finds itself'.[13]
There existed 'cut-throat competition' in both the acquisition
of raw materials ('we are being played off, the one against the
other, by the suppliers') and in selling finished steel products,
and this was leading to a massive prodigality in capital expenditures—for fear that unless new assets be acquired 'one will gain
some advantage over the other'—and the uneconomic utilization of plant, particularly in the rolling of sections, for which
'we take orders for all sizes . . . irrespective of tonnages involved'.
This state of affairs could not continue for it could 'only be a
comparatively short time before the industry is bankrupt'.
There was only one solution: 'a combine of our several interests
into an amalgamated whole'. And if this resulted in even keener

[11] Sir William Beardmore had been raised to the peerage, assuming the
title Lord Invernairn, in 1921.
[12] Invernairn to John Craig, 29 Jan. 1923. Emphasis supplied.
[13] A copy of Invernairn's statement was sent to Craig on the following day.
A. B. MacDuff to J. Craig, 21 Feb. 1923. It is from this copy that the quotations are taken.

competition with similar groups in England, 'surely we would be in a better position to face such competition combined than individually?' Of the ensuing discussion little is known, John Craig's scribbled notes indicate that only Strain, of Lanarkshire, was in complete agreement with Lord Invernairn. The others offered various criticisms and suggestions. But whatever transpired, it may be imagined that, although no one present doubted the sincerity of Invernairn's attempts to restore prosperity to the Scottish steel industry, it could not but have occurred to the steelmasters that his proposals did not exclude a certain self-interested calculation. Beardmores, whatever the state of their plant—which was generally acknowledged to be relatively efficient—were in a parlous financial position.

Lord Pirrie, on receiving an account of the meeting, doubted whether much would come of the scheme. Indeed, he soon came out against it, but he was interested to learn how it developed if only because, in collaboration with Sir Robert Horne, he was hatching a project of his own involving a merger between a collection of Scottish and English makers. Thus, at a further meeting of Scottish steel-makers held at Parkhead, Craig stated categorically that 'his Directors were not prepared to consider a scheme of amalgamation of Scottish makers alone, as they did not see in such a scheme a practical solution of the problem with which the Steelmasters were faced'. Nor were James Dunlops any more enthusiastic. Dunlops' board, represented by Henry Lithgow and R. M. Donaldson, were not prepared to consider a merger. Nor would they enter 'any other working arrangement' unless 'their shipyards were assured of steel supplies'. Significantly, the Steel Company of Scotland did not even send a representative to the meeting. The only real encouragement that Invarnairn received came from Strain of Lanarkshire, whose company, somewhat desperately, was prepared 'to examine *any* proposal . . . which would lead to the betterment of the Steel trade in Scotland'. It was finally agreed that the whole matter be submitted to Sir William Plender, the eminent accountant, who was to be asked to formulate a scheme of amalgamation or some lesser arrangement conducive to the 'better working and administration of the Steel trade in Scotland'.[14]

[14] Based on D.C. & S., 'Notes re meeting of Steelmakers held at Parkhead Works, on 20 March 1923'.

Plender presented a lengthy report to Lord Invernairn in May. It was general in tone and couched in financial terms. This is not surprising, since Plender confessed that he was 'not at present intimately acquainted with any unusual conditions attaching to the industry, or with any peculiar circumstances which may affect the various Companies'. Yet without the detailed examination of specific problems confronting the individual companies and the industry as a whole, it was doomed to remain little more than an elegant series of variations, lacking in depth and unconvincing in its recommendations. True, it touched upon matters of great importance. Plender recognized that any scheme, 'the objects of which are confined to the elimination of competition among the Scottish makers alone, might not of itself fully overcome the evil it is designed to relieve, if, in spite of such an arrangement, ... keen competition would still have to be faced on the part of the English makers', and he suggested that the choice of scheme should be at least partially determined by the long-run necessity of either expanding it 'so as to embrace the English makers', or of placing the Scots in the most favourable competitive position to combat English competition. Since the latter appeared the more feasible, everything pointed to the desirability of a Scottish merger, 'despite the strong feeling against an amalgamation that apparently exists'. Sensing the many personal animosities that would have to be smoothed over, and appreciating the conflicting interests that would have to be reconciled before any agreement was possible, Plender appealed to the Scottish steelmasters:

... to approach the matter in a broad-minded way ... It is not improbable that each concern may, in its own opinion, see excellent reasons for special consideration being given to it under a number of heads in arriving at the purchase price to be paid for its business. But it is obvious that it would be impractical to weigh all these considerations mathematically—in other words, there must be a certain amount of 'give and take'. If the amalgamation is worth consummating, it is to be assumed that the advantages which the owners of any one concern will reap should be very material and should therefore more than outweigh any detriment which such owners may suffer as compared with other concerns by reason of the application of the financial terms of the scheme.

It is probable that certain of the steelmasters did not quite see the issue in this light. It was already quite plain that Colvilles, Dunlops, and the Steel Company of Scotland had already set their faces against a merger, and nothing came of Invernairn's initiative.

3 Lord Pirrie's Scheme, 1923

This first scheme was, in any case, superseded by a much more ambitious plan instigated by Lord Pirrie himself. In July, discussions took place between the representatives of six major groups of steelmasters. They were Sir Robert Horne and Sir William Charles Wright of Baldwins; Viscount Furness, Ethelbert Furness, and Benjamin Talbot of Cargo Fleet; Sir Arthur Dorman and Col. Byrne of Dorman, Long & Co.; Sir J. E. Johnson-Ferguson of Bolckow, Vaughan & Company; Lord Invernairn of William Beardmores; and John Craig of Colvilles. No record of these discussions seems to have survived. All that is known is that once again Sir William Plender was 'asked to prepare a scheme for the purpose of carrying out the views which seemed to be those favoured by the majority of those present',[15] and that such a scheme—which is 'one of the most secret and confidential character'—was presented to Lord Pirrie on 11 October 1923. Although the report cannot be found, it apparently envisaged a mammoth holding company. Discussions of the plan went on throughout October and November, by which time Pirrie had already confessed that he did 'not consider that the matter [would] develop further, at least in the meantime . . .'[16]

But 'in the meantime', Lord Pirrie died[17] and with his death—on 7 June 1924—the steel amalgamation scheme too passed away. While he lived, there was always the possibility that the fiercely-competitive iron- and steelmasters could be brought together: without his immense reputation, energy, experience, and financial power, there was very little chance. Only faint echoes of the scheme continued to reverberate. In the summer of 1925, Sir Charles Wright of Baldwins, harking back to the negotiations with Pirrie, discussed with John Craig the possibility of a fusion of interests between his company, Col-

---

[15] Lord Pirrie to John Craig, 15 Oct. 1923.
[16] J. Philp to John Craig, 27 Nov. 1923.
[17] Herbert Jefferson, *Viscount Pirrie of Belfast* (Belfast: Wm. Mullan, [1949]), pp. 283–4.

villes, and Dorman Longs, 'as it was recognized that the three companies by combining would control about one-third of the output of steel of the United Kingdom'. Lord Kylsant—Pirrie's successor—was enthusiastic, and had his solicitors draft a Memorandum and Articles of Association and apply for registration of a company with the name 'The British Steel Company Ltd.' But nothing came of it. Arthur Dorman, Colvilles board minutes tersely reported, was 'committed to another proposition'.[18]

4 Safeguarding and the Committee on Civil Research, 1925

It is difficult to determine John Craig's personal attitude in this long and abortive series of negotiations. First Invernairn, then Pirrie, and subsequently Sir Charles Wright, appear to have initiated the discussions. Amalgamation was in the air: the government continually emphasized that it was 'in the interests of the Trade'.[19] Exactly what benefits were to accrue from large mergers was rarely made explicit. Clearly, costs—efforts to reduce which had been 'unabated'—had to be forced down. But would amalgamation achieve this objective? John Craig did not think so. His evidence to the Civil Research Committee investigating the industry's application for safeguarding duties in the Autumn of 1925 is of considerable interest.[20] Asked by Sir P. Cunliffe-Lister, the President of the Board of Trade, 'To what extent it would be possible, either by amalgamation or by some working arrangement, to concentrate whatever orders are available in the plant which can turn them out cheapest?', Craig answered:

A good deal has been done in that way. Mr. Dorman has done a lot on the North-East Coast. My own Company in Scotland have done the same thing. We have bought up two steel works, some collieries and sheet works. We have

[18] D.C. & S., Minute Book IV, 13 July 1925, 11 Aug. 1925, 9 Oct. 1925.
[19] Ibid., 17 Nov. 1925.
[20] No minutes of evidence relating to this committee were published (*Hansard*, 1924–5 (189), col. 1946). The following account of Craig's evidence is based on a printed transcript sent to him by Sir William Larke on 7 Oct. 1925.
     The Safeguarding of Industries Act is discussed by Carr and Taplin, *History of the British Steel Industry*, pp. 378–9.

a fair idea of the benefits to be derived from such a scheme or extension of such a scheme, but they could not be a cure of the ills today. There would be benefits in course of time ...

This point was taken up by Lord Balfour, to whom Craig replied '... because of the bad state of the trade in the last four years we have not got the full benefit of the amalgamation which was begun in 1916, but I should mislead the Committee if I said that that in itself would put the British steel trade today in a position to bridge over the difference between the Continent and ourselves'. Again and again, this point was reiterated, even after Arthur Dorman stated that 'Mr. Craig is right; you must not mislead yourself into thinking that if there was one centralized works it would make much difference. It would not make very much difference—about 1s. 6d. a ton perhaps. That is the most you could hope for.' Indeed, Craig argued that 'if you had amalgamation tomorrow, you would have to keep a very strong personnel and a big staff of more highly-paid men, and unless you are going to get a bigger output of steel I am not sure that these things do not add to your costs unless you wipe out many of the existing personnel and scrap much of the machinery.'

To Craig the root of the problem was that 'the world consumption of steel was currently too small' coupled with the fact that too much steel was being imported. 'Can we not have the privilege of making that ourselves?' he asked the Committee. Not, he hastened to add, by erecting high tariff walls behind which the inefficient might shelter, but by temporarily safeguarding the industry sufficiently to ensure that some part of the $2\frac{1}{2}$ million tons currently being imported be made domestically. This would permit a higher utilization of capacity, which would substantially lower the general cost of steel, the benefits of which would partially be passed on to the consumer. To those cynics who doubted this, Craig's answer was:

... you may take it that our application ... would not hurt our customers. If it did, we would not put it forward. We debated it with some of our customers. There are some ... who believe in dumping so far as imports are concerned, and who will die believing that this country should be the dumping ground for all steel, but others are waking up to the fact that unless you can make the heavy steel trade of this country efficient, they too will go under; and an application for safeguarding is, in the opinion of heavy steel makers, the only protection for those who use iron and steel in this country. If we

hurt our customers, in a year or two we should be put out of business ...
The galvanized sheet trade use a million tons of [imported] steel, and some
of them recognize that unless we can maintain the steel trade in an efficient
condition in this country, even they will then find their source of supply is
a dangerous one. I was in a foreign country the other day, and took a look
into some new buildings in a steel works, and I asked to see them. They said:
'These are our safeguarding mills. You might get safeguarding, and if you
get it, we are ready to ship the finished goods.' They are doing that today,
and we think our customers' safest position is to build their important industry
on the steel trade in Britain and not to rely upon the foreigner for his raw
materials.

Sir Hugo Hirst, Chairman and managing director of G.E.C.,
a member of the Committee, remained unconvinced. He asked
what guarantee the steel-makers would give that the finishing
trades would not be exploited if the steel-makers were to be
protected. A chorus of suggestions came from Craig, Lloyd,
Dorman, and Sir William Larke, and it was agreed that a
guarantee 'might take the form of a clause or a binding condition
that we are to supply these goods at cost price plus a small percentage to be certified by an independent accountant failing
mutual agreement'. That was all very well, Sir Hugo
countered, but what if the cost price of steel was, under protection, to remain high? Could the steelmasters promise that semi-
finished steel prices would come down? To Arthur Dorman
much depended on the price of coal. The point was elaborated
upon by John Craig.

The conversion costs, and therefore the amount between the raw materials
and the price at which we sell, would, we believe, be substantially reduced
... If we were to roll 2 million tons of steel we would require, roughly speaking,
7 to 8 million tons of coal. The effect of that upon the market might be to
stiffen it, but ... on the whole it is our considered view that we could supply
the consumers in Britain with cheaper steel than we can today, cheaper in
cost of production ... We are only working a fraction of our time. Given
full time we could, I believe, [provide] cheaper steel .... You know the argument of the re-roller. His fear is that the Continental maker would say, if
we were successful in our application: 'What am I going to do with 2 million
tons of steel?' and he would go into the finishing trade and become a competitor. Make him go to New York for his money at 12 per cent, put down his
finishing mills now rather than over the next two or three years, rush him
into a big capital cost now, and when he has to face the capital cost of his
new mills we shall be able to fight him possibly without any help. He will
have to find new capital. We consider therefore that immediate help of a
temporary nature is necessary. We believe that in this way we are going to

have cheaper steel, more efficient works, the men better employed; and we hope to take 50,000 to 100,000 men off the streets. Our case is safeguarding; we are not asking for subsidies, nor are we asking for money. If you stop that stuff coming in by any method you can adopt we will make the steel industry in our country more efficient with cheaper costs, and, on the whole, I think, make the country a better exporting country than it has ever been. If we do not and the steel trade goes a little further down, all these big machine builders, structural steel makers, locomotive builders, will have to look to the Continent for all their steel, and the day they do that it is all up with them.[21]

Such was Craig's case in support of Sir William Larke's request for a duty of 30 per cent *ad valorem*. It is clear that Craig did not see amalgamation of itself being the panacea of the industry's ills, nor did he want more than temporary assistance from the government. Given a 'fair' chance, the iron and steel industry could solve the problems that beset it, and in so doing confer considerable social benefit. He, perhaps more than any of the other witnesses, had faith in the future of the iron and steel trade. Even the conflicting interests within the industry could be reconciled by rational argument and compromise. He was even prepared to consider the possibility of entering into a treaty with the shipbuilders, embodying a fixed basis price for ship plates for a period of years, similar to the scheme designed to placate the re-rollers. But all these possibilities, all these hopes, depended upon a favourable response by the government to the steel-makers' plea for tariff protection. This was not forthcoming. Although the Prime Minister acknowledged that the evidence presented to the Committee of Civil Research had revealed a serious situation, and that a strong— indeed, 'complete'—case for safeguarding had been made, the government felt unable to take any action. This was because it was impossible to protect a basic industry like iron and steel

[21] Cf. the words of Windsor Richards in 1902: 'Is it probable that America and Germany will continue to exercise their good nature, and supply us with bars and billets and rails and plates at a price below their cost of production, when they find our works are stopped and we are unable to supply ourselves? They will most certainly not do so, but will increase the price as much as possible, and we shall regret our folly when too late, and when at their mercy.' Quotation from the *Western Mail* by C. Wilkins, *History of the Iron, Steel, and Tinplate and other Trades of Wales* (Merthyr Tydfil: Joseph Williams, 1903), pp. 203–6.

without abandoning the government's pledge not to introduce a general tariff.[22]

However disappointing this outcome was, to Craig the prolonged discussions and conferences in which he had participated in preparing and submitting the steel-makers' case were not without value. They had convinced him that an amalgamation of Scottish makers alone was insufficient. If Colvilles were to become a party to amalgamation, 'a stronger combination would result from makers in South Wales and the North-East Coast joining with us', he explained to his board, who agreed that: 'If the question of amalgamation was to be pressed, we should first seek to combine with Makers in the two districts referred to, and failing that, with a Maker in the North-East Coast, the *question of combining with the other Scottish Makers to be considered only if similar groupings took place in other districts.*'[23]

5 A National Scheme or a Regional Grouping?

By November 1926, all hopes of an amalgamation with any of the makers on the North-East coast or in South Wales had evaporated, as they had 'decided to confine the negotiations to themselves'. At the same time John Craig was being approached by representatives of both Beardmores and the Steel Company of Scotland to consider 'a fusion of interests', and by 'parties acting on behalf of the Lanarkshire Steel Company' who sought to sell the concern to Colvilles outright. For Lanarkshire, Craig offered £150,000 for the share capital (it had a nominal value of £435,000) which was, the Lanarkshire directors complained to Lord Kylsant in breaking off the negotiations, less than the break-up value of the works. Within a few months, Beardmores had offered to sell their Mossend Works, and the Scottish Iron & Steel Company[24] their

[22] *Hansard*, 1924–5 (189), cols. 1944-5; the entire episode is clearly explained by Carr and Taplin, *History of the British Steel Industry*, pp. 378–80.

[23] D.C. & S., Minute Book IV, 17 Nov. 1925. Emphasis supplied.

[24] The Scottish Iron & Steel Co., formed in 1912 by an amalgamation of thirteen Lanarkshire companies engaged in producing malleable iron bars, rods, and sections (see above, pp. 99–100), sensing that the days of malleable

Northburn Works, to Colvilles. Both offers were rejected. The asking prices were much too high.[25]

Again, the question of Lanarkshire Steel arose. The works at Flemington were carefully inspected by John Craig and G. P. West who found them 'unbalanced in lay-out with insufficient furnace capacity', weaknesses which would involve a capital expenditure of at least £50,000 to recitify. Nevertheless, a price of £200,000 was agreed upon;[26] but the negotiations were once again brought to an end when Lloyds Bank—holders of the Prior-Lien Debentures of Workman Clark & Company, who had gone into liquidation the previous year—refused to agree to the terms of payment proposed by Kylsant: 'that Lloyds Bank should advance the price required and that D.C. & S. should undertake to repay over a period [not exceeding] five years'.[27]

With every board meeting came reports of discussions, correspondence, proposals, and offers of sale relating to various amalgamations. From London, Sir William Larke informed Craig that 'important financial interests, realizing the great difficulties in securing complete amalgamation at this time ... [had suggested the creation of] a separate operating company,

---

iron were numbered, gradually began either to dismantle its constituent works or to convert them to re-rolling. 'In defence of the company's very existence', William Downs, the chairman, decided to put down a steel works on a site adjoining the company's Waverley Works. After protracted negotiations during 1918, Downs finally obtained permission to do so from Sir John Hunter, the finances being largely supplied by the Ministry of Munitions. Technically very advanced (the consulting engineer for the new plant was James Smith, of the William Smith Owen Engineering Corporation), production began in 1920 with three 50-ton furnaces giving a weekly output of some 1,500 tons. See Thomson, *The County of Lanark*, pp. 51–5; T. R. Miller, *The Monkland Tradition*, pp. 88–90.

[25] D.C. & S., Minute Book V, 15 June 1926, 13 July 1926, 9 Nov. 1926, 11 Jan. 1927, 15 Mar. 1927.

[26] J. H. Stephens to Sir William McLintock, 10 Feb. 1927. The figure of £200,000 was reached only after prolonged and involved negotiations. Craig was always reluctant to go beyond £180,000, but as he wrote to Kylsant (11 Feb. 1927): 'We are still fully alive to considerable advantages which would accrue from our control of these Works. They have been troublesome competitors for years, and we are satisfied ... that the organization could be very much improved and considerable economies effected in general management.'

[27] Kylsant to Sir William McLintock, 31 Dec. 1926; Sir William McLintock to J. Craig, 11 Feb. 1927; Sir William McLintock to J. H. Stephens, 14 Feb. 1927; D.C. & S., Minute Book V, 15 Feb. 1927.

the stockholders in which would be the principal steel producers':

> This operating Company would lease the constituent concerns for a term of not less than five years; the basis of rental to be their fixed charges; the management of the existing concerns to be unaffected; the operating Company to control production and commercial policies, but as each firm would retain its organisation and its identity, in the event of the agreement not being as satisfactory as expected, each would be able to resume its identity at the expiration of the Agreement.[28]

Because this scheme, the brain-child of F. A. Szarvasy of the British, Foreign and Colonial Corporation, was supported by National Federation of Iron and Steel Manufacturers[29] and was strongly suspected of being inspired by powerful banking interests who could not be ignored,[30] it was given very careful consideration by the group of steel-makers to whom it was addressed. For several months the plan and all its implications were discussed by Henry Bond of Richard Thomas & Company, Albert Peach of United Steel, Benjamin Talbot of South Durham & Cargo Fleet, Sir John Davies of Baldwins, Roland Kitson of Bolckow, Vaughan & Company and John Craig; whose firms represented a potential annual output of five million tons of steel ingots.[31] But nothing came of it. From the very beginning Craig was unenthusiastic:

> ... any scheme which merely operated for a number of years [and involved leasing] could not be looked upon with much favour as the retention of the personal interest in any business would rob it of the benefits of a whole-hearted amalgamation ... I do feel that in any real organization of the Steel Trade there must be entirely eliminated the personal equation and all concerned should have only one object in view and that is the prosperity of the new Company and the fearless dealing with the Plants for the good of the Company without any fear of complications arising as to individual interests.[32]

[28] Sir William Larke to John Craig, 3 Jan. 1927. D.C. & S., Minute Book V, 11 Jan. 1927. A detailed outline of Szarvasy's scheme was sent to Craig by Sir William Larke, 25 Feb. 1927.
[29] Indeed, there is some evidence that the seeds of the idea may have been planted by Sir William Peat, Secretary of the National Federation. Sir William Peat to John Craig, 11 Oct. 1926.
[30] John Craig to Lord Kylsant, 20 Jan. 1927, 9 Feb. 1927.
[31] Henry Bond to John Craig, 8 Feb. 1927. Of all the manufacturers invited only one, Arthur Dorman, declined to participate. Idem, 3 Mar. 1927.
[32] John Craig to Sir William Larke, 6 Jan. 1927.

It is clear that the other active participants also had doubts and by May 1927, Henry Bond—who had been acting as chairman of the informal group of steelmasters—felt that as there were no prospects of bringing the negotiations to a successful conclusion they should be terminated.[33] 'At the same time', he wrote to Craig, 'I personally feel that the Iron and Steel Industry of this country will have to be reorganized—we cannot fail to be impressed with the extraordinary success which has followed the reorganization of the Industry in Germany. So I hope that the time spent on these negotiations will not have altogether been wasted and that even if this particular scheme is not practicable we shall in process of time be able to evolve some other scheme which will have more general support'.[34]

Craig acknowledged this letter, expressed his disappointment, and, a week later, after thinking over the situation, suggested that

the leaders of the Industry should not await developments from the outside . . . six or seven of the leading Makers, who have expressed sympathy with the idea of larger units in the trade being formed, should go into the country somewhere to a quiet Hotel, make up their minds they would sit down for a few days to discuss in all its aspects the present position of the Industry, and in an undisturbed manner set themselves the task of endeavouring to evolve a practical scheme. It seems to me that if those in the Industry cannot overcome the difficulties of working together that no scheme suggested by outsiders can hope to be successful unless they secure sufficient power to dictate a policy . . . . I learned recently from one of the Cabinet that they were largely influenced in their recent attitude to the Trade by the feeling that those responsible . . . had not shown sufficient leadership and, frankly, as I think you and I agree, our attempts to get the matter even seriously discussed have revealed a spirit not quite worthy of our great Industry.[35]

This idea of a quiet get-together by representatives of the leading steel firms in order to evolve a coherent policy for the steel industry was enthusiastically taken up by W. H. Peat, who offered his services to further the idea. Without some measure of amalgamation or, at the very least, agreement to co-operate, Peat believed that any application under the Safeguarding of Industries Act, would have 'very little prospect of success'.[36]

[33] H. Bond to F. A. Szarvasy, 5 May 1927.
[34] Henry Bond to John Craig, 5 May 1927.
[35] John Craig to Henry Bond, 14 May 1927.
[36] W. H. Peat to H. C. Bond, 1 July 1927, copy sent to John Craig, 1 July 1927.

But Bond was 'quite convinced that it is no use for Sir Harry Peat, or Szarvasy or anybody else to put their oar in at this stage', the initiative must come from within the industry.[37] Craig agreed. Sir Harry Peat was, he reported to Lord Kylsant, secretly acting on behalf of the Rothschilds, but 'no outsider can render much help. The attitudes of the makers to the outsider has so far been one morely of criticism, and I do feel that unless the makers themselves can put forward a constructive policy, any amalgamation created by pressure would not have great hopes of success.'[38]

Over the next six months further talks took place between those steel-makers who had discussed Szarvasy's scheme, but nothing came of them. The plans put forward were too ambitious, too much of a gamble. Always there were highly cogent objections to one or other element in the multitude of proposals, and compromise floundered on the abrasive characters of the major participants in the discussion.[39]

Craig, once again, was forced back to regional rationalization. In April 1928, he was approached by 'Lord Weir and Sir Harry McGowan, who, on behalf of the newly-formed Anglo-American Finance Corporation, had opened conversations involving the Scottish Steel Trade as a whole'. Almost simultaneously, Craig was 'surprised to learn that [Lord Invernairn] was pressing for amalgamation on the basis of [obtaining] American Finance through Sir Harry McGowan'.[40] But for Invernairn it was too late. Beardmores' losses had steadily mounted in the early twenties.[41] In 1924 they had amounted to just over £½ million; in 1926, only a year before the 8 per cent Notes were due for redemption, they exceeded £¾ million, and Beardmores asked the government for financial assistance.

[37] H. C. Bond to J. Craig, 7 July 1927.
[38] J. Craig to Lord Kylsant, 7 July 1927.
[39] Some inkling of the problems can be derived from John Craig's correspondence with the participants, dated July 1927–Jan. 1928.
[40] D.C. & S., Minute Book V, 12 June 1928; Craig to Kylsant, 24 May 1928. For McGowan, see W. J. Reader's monumental *Imperial Chemical Industries: A History*, vol. ii, *The First Quarter Century, 1926–1952* (Oxford: O.U.P., 1975), *passim*.
[41] It is noteworthy that from 1921 onwards the Glasgow Iron & Steel Co., owned jointly with Swan, Hunters, made a succession of losses. During the period 1921 to 1928 inclusive these amounted to £276,335. Figures kindly supplied by Mr. Michael Moss.

Montagu Norman, the Governor of the Bank of England, strongly advised the government against providing help, on the grounds that the Parkhead firm, like Baldwins, Armstrong, Whitworth, & Company, and others 'needed new blood, new management and economies which could be secured only by a receiver'. Furthermore, 'the Exchequer could ill-afford such assistance and would find it very difficult to limit its amount. He suspected the [iron and steel] industry of refusing to face the need of drastic reorganization because it was sitting waiting for protection.'[42] Denied immediate help, Beardmores had to appoint an advisory committee which at once realized that urgently-needed capital could never be raised in priority to mortgages and bank charges.[43] An agreement was reached for the banks to postpone their charges, while the Treasury remitted £100,000 and postponed the major part of the first mortgage which it held on Beardmores' Mossend Works.

This was not enough. A scheme put foward by the advisory committee in October 1928,[44] failed because Beardmores were unable to raise the £1 million of 7 per cent debentures on which the entire plan depended, and in June 1929 the firm was in danger under Scottish law of immediate liquidation. After some deliberation, Lord Norman came to the rescue by proposing that the Bank of England invest £710,000 in First Mortgage Debentures; that the capital structure be amended so that the ratio of loan capital to share capital be reduced from four to one to two to one; that, while the debenture stock was outstanding, the voting control of the company be vested not in the trustees for the stock but in a committee of three persons, including, at the outset, Mr. Frater Taylor (Chairman), Mr. L. C. Ord, and Mr. W. W. Paine (joint general manager of Lloyds Bank); and that the board include seven directors, all

[42] Sir Henry Clay, *Lord Norman* (London: Macmillan, 1957), p. 323. This episode is considered more fully by Hume and Moss, *Beardmore*, Chapter 6.
[43] The advisory committee consisted of Mr. F. A. Szarvasy, Sir Gilbert Garnsey of Price, Waterhouse, & Co., Chartered Accountants, Mr. W. W. Paine, joint general manager of Lloyds Bank, and Mr. P. E. Marmion. *Economist*, 20 Oct. 1928.
[44] The full details are given in: William Beardmore & Co. Ltd., 'Scheme for Reorganization of Share and Loan Capital', 15 Oct. 1928, a copy of which is in the Colville archives: 'S.I.S.M.: S. & L. and B. Reports'. See also, Carr and Taplin, *History of the British Steel Industry*, p. 445; *Economist*, 20 Oct. 1928.

nominated by this committee with the approval of the Governor of the Bank of England. A grateful government, alarmed at the possibility of the closure of Beardmores, and the ensuing augmentation of Clydeside's unemployed, welcomed this new plan and postponed its claims on the company. Lord Invernairn and his fellow directors promptly retired; the quality of their management condemned.[45]

With Invernairn gone, the collapse of the Weir/McGowan proposals—those proposals which in the summer of 1928 had seemed to offer the only lifeline to Beardmores—because of premature press publicity;[46] the capital reconstruction of Baldwins; and the failure of yet another appeal for Safeguarding;[47] Craig plunged back into negotiation with his neighbours.[48] The Steel Company of Scotland sought only an alliance with Colvilles—Gray, their managing director, wanted nothing to do with a comprehensive Scottish grouping;[49] Stephens threatened to open negotiations for the sale of Lanarkshire 'in another quarter';[50] G. A. Mitchell of Stewarts & Lloyds suggested that his firm and Colvilles might combine and then create a new blast furnace plant;[51] and Mr. Thirlaway, chairman of Swan, Hunter, & Wigham Richardson—joint owners with Beardmores of the Glasgow Iron & Steel Company—suggested that Colvilles might acquire Beardmores' interest in this concern.[52]

Not until the close of 1928 did this highly confused situation begin to clarify. In December discussions took place between Lord Weir, Sir James Lithgow, and John Craig, during which

[45] *Economist*, 29 July 1929; Clay, *Lord Norman*, p. 325; Carr and Taplin, *History of the British Steel Industry*, pp. 445–6.
[46] Craig to Kyslant, 11 June 1928; D.C. & S., Board Minute Book V, p. 200, 9 July 1928.
[47] This was the subject of a detailed correspondence between Craig and Kylsant. Lord Weir, it was said, believed that the Cabinet had rejected the fresh appeal for tariff protection 'largely because the [steel] Makers had not shown a sufficient spirit of co-operation amongst themselves' (Craig to Kylsant, 20 Apr. 1928), but Kylsant felt this to be merely 'an excuse' (Kylsant to Craig, 21 Apr. 1928), 'Winston Churchill and Balfour still block progress [towards safeguarding], and they seem to carry more weight with the Prime Minister than Joynson-Hicks and Amery' (Kylsant to Craig, 30 July 1928).
[48] See Carr and Taplin, *History of the British Steel Industry*, p. 446.
[49] D.C. & S., Board Minute Book V, p. 200, 9 July 1928.
[50] Ibid., V, p. 208, 14 Aug. 1928.
[51] Ibid., V, p. 224, 16 Oct. 1928.
[52] Ibid., V, p. 249, 15 Jan. 1929.

Lord Weir 'urged the importance of creating modern Blast Furnaces in Scotland, [and indicated] that Government money would be available at a low rate of interest provided a suitable combined scheme was submitted'. The result was that on 5 February 1929 a meeting took place between Lord Weir, Sir James Lithgow, Sir Adam Nimmo,[53] A. K. McCosh, F. J. Stephen, and John Craig at which it was decided that 'full consideration might be given to the possibilities of a single unit for the production of Iron and Steel in Scotland'. As an essential preliminary step should be a review of technical possibilities, Lord Weir was authorized to engage the services of the internationally-known firm of consulting engineers, H. A. Brassert & Company, of Chicago, to make a comprehensive survey of the Scottish iron and steel industry, 'the cost not to exceed £10,000'.[54] Within a few weeks the investigation was under way;[55] not even the blandishments of Clarence Hatry—who sought to absorb Colvilles into his ambitious scheme to control about half the steel industry's total capacity—were to disturb it.[56]

6 The Brassert Report, 1929

Brasserts submitted their report to Lord Weir on 16 May 1929, and copies were immediately transmitted to the directors of the five participating companies.[57] These companies had in 1927 manufactured approximately 64 per cent of the plate, and over 70 per cent of the heavy section and heavy rail tonnage of Scotland, together with about 50 per cent of the light sections. It

[53] Managing director of James Nimmo & Co., Chairman of the Fife Coal Co., and a director of Shotts Iron Co.

[54] D.C. & S., Minute Book V, 12 Feb. 1929. Sir John Craig's Private Papers, 'Notes of a Meeting held at Eastwood Park on 5 February 1929'.

[55] D.C. & S., Minute Book V, p. 267, 19 Mar. 1929.

[56] References to meetings between Craig and Hatry are made in the Board Minute Book V, pp. 288, 299, 14 May and 11 June 1929, respectively. The details of the discussion and notes on Hatry's activities were transmitted to Lord Kylsant in a series of letters dated April–June 1929. For Hatry, see Carr and Taplin, *History of the British Steel Industry*, p. 448.

[57] Report to Lord Weir of Eastwood on the Manufacture of Iron and Steel by William Baird & Co. Ltd., David Colville & Sons Ltd., James Dunlop & Co. Ltd., Steel Company of Scotland, Stewarts & Lloyds Ltd. By H. A. Brassert & Co. of Chicago and London, 16 May 1929. The report was never published.

is a remarkable document. In ten weeks, Brassert's team had laid bare the fundamental weaknesses of Scottish iron and steel and had submitted recommendations designed to rehabilitate the industry. The analysis is impressive, the argument persuasive, and the solution proposed, convincing. This was no accountant's nostrum but a practical guide to economic steel-making in Scotland.[58]

A detailed survey of the blast furnaces operated by Bairds at Gartsherrie, Dunlops at Clyde Iron, and Colvilles at Glengarnock found that since their plant—like that elsewhere in Scotland—was the 'result of many years experience in the peculiar metallurgy of iron resulting from the use of [blackband and clay ironstones and of] splint coal, which influenced the size and particularly the height of the furnace and also the rate of operation', it was not 'adapted in design or capacity to present day conditions of competitive iron manufacture' utilizing imported ores and coke. Not only did the existing blast furnace plant 'lack future usefulness', but 'the present installations for manufacture of by-product coke [were] also unsuitable for future requirements'.[59] These uncompromising conclusions were based on the fact that in 1928 average pig iron production costs were 74s. 4d. per ton, a figure that could be reduced by nearly 19s. by the installation of modern equipment integrated with steel manufacturing.[60]

Since Brasserts believed that the primary requirement of the steel industry was cheap pig iron, the construction of new blast furnace capacity was an essential requirement for the rehabilitation of the Scottish iron and steel industry. Detailed calculations indicated that *on the basis of the industry's experience in 1927*, Scotland's total pig iron requirement was some 1,050,000 tons. But this figure was dependent upon the use of a very high proportion of scrap in the melting furnaces. Such a high level of scrap usage—over 70 per cent—could not be expected to

[58] In writing to Lord Kylsant about a discussion he had had with Lord Weir, Craig mentioned that J. H. Thomas, Lord Privy Seal in MacDonald's Second Labour Cabinet, 'had been making enquiries regarding the position in Scotland. Mr. Thomas ... was not much impressed with the amalgamations which were taking place in England and this evidently was also the opinion of Lord Weir who described them as balance sheet amalgamations and not product amalgamations'. John Craig to Lord Kylsant, 26 June 1929.

[59] Brassert Report, p. 51.

[60] Ibid., p. 51.

continue. Moreover, in the future it would clearly be desirable for Scotland to produce the steel products currently being imported. In 1927 these amounted to 616,000 tons. To produce these finished and semi-finished products domestically would require Scotland's ingot output to be increased by about 720,000 tons over the 1927 figure of nearly 1,587,500 tons or, say, 2,300,000 tons. On the assumptions that both the practice regarding and the output of acid open-hearth steel remained unchanged, and that the proportion of pig iron used in the charging of the basic melting furnaces rose from about 29 per cent to some 50 or even 65 per cent, then to manufacture all the steel *used* in Scotland would require the annual production—if consumption remained at the 1927 level—of between about 1,250,000 and 1,500,000 tons of pig iron.

Having determined what pig iron capacity was required, the more fundamental question arose of where it should be located. In arriving at an answer it was recognized that an attempt should be made to fulfil certain conditions:

1. The possibility of assembling at the site of manufacture a supply of suitable raw materials at minimum cost.
2. A furnace plant which permits a regular and large-scale production with minimum use of fuel and of hand labour, and with the most direct and economical handling of materials.
3. The use of by-product coke under circumstances of production which make possible the full use of the gases of distillation, either for manufacturing purposes or for sale.
4. Full use of the blast furnace gases, after fine cleaning, in the under-firing of the coke ovens, in steel melting and heating, and for power, the latter being preferably used in connection with the manufacturing operations of the producing company, rather than generated for sale.
5. Proximity to market or point of use and, where steel-making pig iron is produced, the largest possible use of hot metal in the steel-making furnace.
6. Recovery of the values contained in the blast furnace slag.[61]

[61] Brassert Report, pp. 52–3.

TABLE 7.1

Comparative Costs of (a) Assembly of Materials to make One Ton of Pig Iron at Various Scottish Locations, and (b) Distribution of Pig Iron to the Steel Works of the Four Steel Producing Companies

Location of Iron Works	Elements in Cost	With Ore through Clyde (s. d.)	With Ore through Grangemouth (s. d.)	Average Freight on Pig to Steel Works (s. d.)	Total, with Ore through Clyde (s. d.)	Total, with Ore through Grangemouth (s. d.)
Motherwell	Harbour dues	1 7·65	9·0			
	Freight on ore at 3s.	5 3·0	at 2 10·5 5 0·4			
	" " coal at 1s. 10·8d.	2 6·1	2 6·1			
	" " stone at 3s.	1 0·6	at 3 0 1 0·6			
		10 5·35	9 4·1	1 9·6	12 2·95	11 1·7
Mossend	Harbour dues	1 7·65	9·0			
	Freight on ore at 2s. 9d.	4 9·75	at 2 7·5 4 7·12			
	" " coal at 1s. 8·8d.	2 3·46	2 3·46			
	" " stone at 2s. 9d.	11·55	at 2 9 11·55			
		9 8·4	8 7·1	1 7·0	11 3·4	10 2·1
Gartsherrie	Harbour dues	1 7·65	9·0			
	Freight on ore at 2s. 2·5d.	3 10·4	at 2 3·9 4 0·8			
	" " coal at 1s. 4·8d.	1 10·2	1 10·2			
	" " stone at 2s. 2·5d.	9·3	9·3			
		8 1·55	7 5·3	2 1·2	10 2·75	9 6·5
Erskine Ferry	Harbour dues	1 4·65				
	Freight on ore	—				
	" " coal at 2s. 6d.	3 3·6				
	" " limestone	—				
		4 8·25		3 2·75	7 11·0	

Source: Brassert Report, pp. 86–91.

The inescapable conclusion drawn by Brasserts from a detailed analysis of each of these conditions was that *only* a fully integrated iron- and steel-making plant with the most modern ore dock facilities would permit the rehabilitation of the Scottish iron and steel industry. Only thus could costs be reduced sufficiently to restore Scotland's competitive vitality.

But where should such plant be located? A prerequisite for an increased make of pig in Scotland was a massive rise in ore imports, and on the basis of a comparison of costs, Grangemouth possessed very real merits, but it is clear that the ultimate selection of the port of entry for *ore* was dependent on the conclusions which were reached with respect to other major policy decisions.

There are manifest advantages in a scheme which contemplates the location of coke ovens and blast furnaces, together with sufficient open hearth and mill capacity to utilise the surplus gases of coke and iron manufacture at the waterfront, with the idea that all new construction and large-scale modification of equipment shall be concentrated at this point. Such a scheme involves a heavy outlay of capital beyond that required for docks, coke plants and blast furnaces alone. It has, however, the great advantage of avoiding all inland freight on ore and limestone, together with the return carriage on steel products to the Clyde either for use there or for export.[62]

When *all* the costs involved in the assembly of materials and the distribution of pig iron, semi-finished and finished steel products, were considered, it was possible to recommend no other location than one on the Clyde. But if a Clydeside location were to be chosen, would it not be possible, even more economic, to utilize an existing plant as the primary unit of a new programme of integrated manufacture? Brasserts were emphatic in rejecting this solution:

None of the existing units is well-suited to this purpose. Some of them are not correctly located with regard to other plants or to costs of carriage. Some are unit plants, too good to alter and not adapted as they stand to large expansion. Others are unfitted for development by reason of the fact that their existence has extended over many years and that the improvements which have been made from time to time have contemplated an ultimate result very different from that which is now apparently necessary, with the result that a correct layout of new construction is impossible. If major expenditures are made in such a plant, the difficulties of reconstruction during operation and the limitations imposed by lack of space are certain to produce a much less

[62] Brassert Report, pp. 84–5.

favourable result than if construction is undertaken on a new site ... The companies at present face a decision between temporary convenience combined with a future unfavourable situation and a relatively drastic present step which will permit the future conduct of the business to be carried on in accordance with definitely correct principles. While realizing the temporary difficulties involved in initiating manufacture in a new location, we give as our considered opinion, that no full realization of the possible economies of the situation can be obtained in an inland location selected with reference to existing plants, and we recommend the location of the proposed new plant on a site to be selected along the river Clyde.[63]

A two-stage construction programme was recommended. It was designed to supply the tonnage of pig iron necessary for current needs and for a considerable extension to the existing business, and to provide an economical steel unit which would put the production of steel on a comparatively sound basis. The first part of the programme envisaged 'the construction of two blast furnaces with a capacity of 750 tons per day each, with the necessary by-product coke plant and vessel docks, an open-hearth steel plant of six furnaces of 125 tons capacity each, a 42-inch blooming mill, and a Lauth-type plate mill capable of rolling plate up to approximately 9 feet in width and a 24-inch mill capable of rolling finished sections, billets and sheet bar'. It also included a power station for the generation of electric current required within the works. This plant would, it was estimated, make possible the annual production of a nominal 547,500 tons of pig iron, of which it was proposed to allocate approximately 317,700 tons to existing works and 229,800 tons to the new works. The second stage of the programme called for a third blast furnace, additional coking capacity and a seventh open-hearth furnace.[64] Its completion would establish a balance between open-hearth and finishing capacity in the new works and would provide all the pig iron necessary for current steel requirements plus a surplus of some 200,000 tons. It was estimated that the costs of this programme would be approximately £5½ million, but such were the savings in operating costs that the total investment would be entirely recovered in less than five years.

While recognizing that 'any attempt to state accurately the future earnings of a business so complex as that under

[63] Ibid., pp. 118, 120–1.
[64] Ibid., pp. 123–4.

consideration must be approximate only', the statistics were 'sufficiently well based on present and possible [future] costs of operation, costs of construction, markets and the known principles of steel manufacture to enable the programme ... to be recommended as entirely sound, and as the one practicable method of placing the manufacture of the interested companies on a basis which [would] permit eventual complete rationalization, and the fullest realization of the possibilities of the Scottish situation'. Furthermore, such a plant 'on the Clyde should form the nucleus for the eventual centralisation of Scottish iron and steel production, and owing to its advantages will not need to fear competition from any source at home or abroad'[65]

A summary can hardly do justice to the analytical depth of the Brassert Report. The statistical underpinnings command enormous respect. The recommendations, while radical, were realistic. The Report was taken very seriously by the companies concerned: meeting after meeting was held to examine the figures; the viability of the contemplated production balances upon which it was dependent; the costing systems involved, especially those concerned with the transfer of materials between plants; and the financial implications for the associated companies, both jointly and individually, of the implementation of the programme.

The expert advice of accountants was sought to find a suitable basis for capitalizing the value of existing works, a problem made extremely difficult because past profits had 'not been commensurate with [real asset] values' and because it was almost impossible to assess the *exact* effect that an entirely new integrated works would have on the future value of existing plant.[66] This problem, and there were many of a similar nature, was not simply one of accountancy—not simply an echo of the Plender enquiries—but of very real concern to the directors of the participating companies, who had, at all stages, to protect the interests of their own shareholders and private lenders. Whatever economists and engineers might have advised them, they could not judge Brasserts' proposals solely on technological grounds, they had always to consider the financial realities. In

---

[65] Ibid., pp. 155, 162.
[66] 'Memorandum re Steel Trade', dated 2 Oct. 1929.

the event they might, in retrospect, be condemned as short-sighted but one thing is certain: in their consideration of the Brassert Report, they were neither negligent nor particularly selfish. The initial discussions, if one can judge from what documentary evidence has survived, evince a genuine desire for co-operation on the part of the majority of the participants; a healthy awareness of the necessity for change.

Again and again, Brasserts were asked to amend their figures, elaborate upon points of obscurity, and revise the programme to take account of possible alternatives. Detailed drawings were submitted; statistics were adjusted to conform with new arrangements and new evidence.[67] Estimates were made of cash flows under various conditions.[68] In mid-October, a special committee appointed by the steel-makers reported in detail on the Brassert proposals. This committee concurred with the majority of Brasserts' findings and recommendations. The site recommended for the new integrated steel works was approved, though it was felt that Brasserts were optimistic in believing that a fully-equipped dock at this site would cheapen the c.i.f. price of ore by over 2s. a ton. Brasserts' calculation relating to the acquisition and treatment of coking coal were accepted 'by those familiar with the subject' with the reservation that the cost of washed dross—the principal burden of the coking ovens—were underestimated by 2s. per ton. The pig iron production programme—one of the fundamental elements in the scheme—was accepted as economically and technically sound: it was agreed that basic pig, of a quality best suited for steel-making, *could* thereby be delivered at the melting furnaces at the estimated 70s. a ton, but whether basic steel ingots—using about 50 per cent hot pig and 50 per cent scrap—could be produced at Brasserts' original estimate of £4 12s. 7·23d. per ton was doubted—'no existing works in Scotland with pig at 70s. and scrap at 68s. [the estimated figures] can produce basic ingots at this cost'. Nevertheless, an offsetting factor was that rolling mills existed in Scotland which could and did manufacture

[67] The most far-reaching amendments were embodied in a supplementary report by Brasserts entitled 'Manufacture of Semi-Finished Steel', dated 3 Oct. 1929. The revised estimated costs of production of various major products are given in Table 7.2.

[68] Anon., 'Notes from Brasserts' Reports', 4 Oct. 1929.

ingots into finished steel at less than Brasserts' estimates.[69] Only the elaborate and ingenious plan for the commercial sale of surplus coke oven gases could not be endorsed.

TABLE 7.2 *Estimated Costs of Production, including all Fixed Charges, under Brassert Programme (as revised October 1929)*

Product	Estimated manufacturing costs			Fixed charges			Total cost of production		
	£	s.	d.	£	s.	d.	£	s.	d.
Coke		15	2·23		3	2·08		18	4·31
Basic pig iron	2	18	0·10		7	10·60	3	5	10·70
Ingots	4	1	11·94		8	4·61	4	10	4·55
Billets and sheet bar	4	15	7·28		14	10·69	5	10	5·97
Tube strip	5	14	7·20	1	0	3·16	6	14	10·36
Tube strip (wide)	5	11	8·99		15	7·74	6	7	4·73

Source: H. A. Brassert & Co., 'Scheme for Programme suggested by Committee of Steel Manufacturers in Scotland, 3 October 1929'.

When adjustments had been made to Brasserts' estimates on the basis of the Committee's deliberations, it was calculated that the net profits arising from the full implementation of the scheme would be about £157,745.[70] *The* 'question to be decided' was 'whether this £157,745 surplus [was] sufficiently attractive to bring together some or all of the Ironmasters and Steelmasters, having regard to the present state of affairs [especially when] out of the surplus some compensation would have to be paid to close certain works in whole or in part'.[71] Again, the figures were examined and memoranda on a variety of technical and financial questions by A. J. H. Mowbray, of Colvilles, and T. Thorneycroft, of Bairds, considered. An interesting question discussed at the end of October was 'the savings that might be expected to be secured if all the works were under one control, or, in other words, Rationalized';[72] and, within

[69] See Table 7.3.
[70] See Table 7.3.
[71] The foregoing is based on a document entitled 'Draft Review of Brasserts' Report by the Committee appointed for the Purpose'. It is dated 16 Oct. 1929.
[72] 'Brassert: Minutes of Meeting of 30 October 1929', p. 2.

Part One: Calculations of Profit and Manufacturing Account

Product	Output in tons	Disposal	Cost (per ton)	Realized (per ton)	Profit (per ton)	Totals (£s)
Coke	475,162	Transferred (Trans.)	22s. 10d.	22s. 10d.	—	—
Pig Iron	547,500	229,800 (Trans.)	70s.	70s.	—	
		317,700 (Sold)	71s. 9·25d.	71s. 9·25d.	1s. 9·25d.	28,129
Ingots	469,665	Trans.	92s. 7·23d.	92s. 7·23d.	—	—
Blooms, slabs	427,395	Trans.	103s. 5·30d.	103s. 5·30d.	—	
Plate	154,930	Sold	144s. 6·05d.	157s. 6d.	12s. 11·95d.	100,672
Sections	211,000	100,000 (Billets, sold)	120s. 10d.	112s. 6d.	−8s. 4d.	−41,666
		111,300 (Bars, sold)	137s. 4d.	147s. 6d.	10s. 2d.	56,577

	143,712
Interest and Depreciation provided for in costs	471,758
Interest alone provided for in costs	42,825
Total Sum available before charging income tax, interest, and depreciation	658,295

Part Two: Calculation of Capital Requirements and Proposed Capital Structure

Capital Required:

Plant and Buildings	£4,764,000	spent in 2 years?
Site and Railway connections	£200,000	,, ,, first year
Interest during construction	£250,000	,, ,, 2 years
Working Capital	£82,000	,, ,, third year
TOTAL	£6,034,000	

Capital Provisions:

£5,000,000 Debentures yielding at £95 net £4,750,000
1,284,000 Cum. Pref. shares 7% at par issued at end of 2nd year £1,284,000

TOTAL £6,034,000

Part Three: Result of first year's working excluding Income Tax

	(£s)	(£s)
Gross Profits		658,295
5% Interest on Debentures	250,000	
(?) 7% Interest on Pref. Shares	89,800	
Depreciation 3¼% on £4,764,000	155,000	
1% on site £200,000	2,000	
1½% on interest during construction (= 31 years to redeem)	3,750	
Balance	157,745	
	658,295	658,295

Source: John Craig's Private Papers, 'Draft Review of Brasserts' Report by the Committee For The Purpose', dated 16 October 1929.

ten days, these had been calculated at some £30,000.[73] This amendment, and other adjustments, both up and down, indicated that the surplus previously estimated was too conservative, that the annual amount available for distribution and compensation might realistically be expected to be perhaps three or even four hundred thousand pounds.

7 The Creation of Colvilles Ltd., 1931

There is no question that Colvilles vigorously supported Brasserts' scheme throughout these lengthy proceedings. Craig was aware that 'leading members of the [second Labour] Government' were sympathetically disposed towards the plan and that financial assistance would be forthcoming if only the steelmakers would agree on united action to implement it.[74] Lord Norman had promised that 'the present position of Messrs. Beardmore and the Lanarkshire Steel Co. would not be allowed to impede possible developments'.[75] By mid-October, however, Craig, growing impatient with his fellow-steelmasters, had a series of meetings with Peter Baxter, managing director of James Dunlop & Co., proprietors of the Clyde Iron Works and Calderbank Steel Works, 'with a view to effecting a closer relationship between the two companies'. Colvilles' board was enthusiastic. Lord Kylsant fully approved. It was recognized that 'a definite connection with Messrs. Lithgow, through Dunlops, was desirable'.[76]

[73] 'The total amount expended in administration by the Scotch Steel industry (excluding Beardmores and Scottish) is about £237,000, of which about one-third is the cost of selling. It is estimated that, under one control, this could be satisfactorily done at a cost of £207,000.' Memorandum on points of agreement by the Committee, dated 8 Nov. 1929.

[74] This was reported by Craig to Kylsant in a letter dated 26 June 1929. His informant was Lord Weir who had discussed the Brassert scheme with the Governor of the Bank of England and with J. H. Thomas. Kylsant evidently became rather annoyed by Craig's repeated references to 'Lord Weir, who is so fond of intervening between the steelmakers and the Government as if he was a great expert on the subject.' Kylsant to John Craig, 5 Sept. 1929. See also John Vaizey, *The History of British Steel* (London: Weidenfeld & Nicolson, 1974), pp. 50–2.

[75] D.C. & S., Minute Book V, 9 July 1929.

[76] D.C. & S., Board Minute Book V, p. 336, 11 Oct. 1929. Craig later wrote to Sir William McLintock: '... we have always been conscious that, in our amalgamation with Dunlop, the principal attraction was the influence—personal and commercial—of the Lithgows. In our earlier discussions with the Steel Makers in Scotland, it never did appear as likely that we could obtain

Thereafter, consideration of the wider Brassert scheme and the more limited possibilities of either a full amalgamation of Scottish steel-makers or a Colville/Dunlop merger proceeded in tandem. Brasserts' radical reorganization was clearly preferred, but by November, investigations were already under way to determine what advantages 'might be *immediately* derived from a simple merger of Scottish Steel Makers'. The possibility of taking this less far-reaching step was resurrected after conversations between Craig and the general manager of the Tata Iron & Steel Company of Calcutta had indicated that one million tons of Indian pig iron might be delivered to Colvilles over the next ten years at a price even less than the cost of production envisaged for the new tidewater plant.[77] The force of the Brassert proposals was seriously weakened by this development and the sharp recession of trade in the autumn of 1929 enhanced the financial difficulties involved in their implementation.[78] The board of Colvilles resolved to push ahead with plans for a merger, recognizing that an amalgamation 'would result in immediate benefits of a substantial nature and [constitute] an essential preliminary step towards consideration of the larger scheme as outlined in the Brassert Reports'.[79]

---

from the Lithgows an agreement whereby they would undertake to confine their purchases of Steel to any Company but ultimately this was found possible and, of course, proved a very big attraction to me. Indeed, personally I indicated to our own people time and again that Colville would gladly pay £15,000 a year to secure the Lithgows' orders for Steel: they would make all the difference in running Clydebridge and be a great help to Glengarnock.' J. Craig to Sir William McLintock, 16 June 1930.

[77] D.C. & S., Board Minute Book V, p. 342, 15 Nov. 1929.

[78] Had the associated companies pushed ahead with the Brassert scheme, such were the terrible market conditions in the following two–three years, the investment required might have brought them all to their knees (like Invernairn and Beardmores).

[79] D.C. & S., Board Minute Book V, p. 350, 20 Dec. 1929. Sir James and Henry Lithgow 'held practically all the ordinary shares' in Dunlops. (Confidential Memo in Colvilles' files dated 3 June 1930.) Earlier in December, Craig had written to Kylsant: 'It is a certain amount of satisfaction to us to find that, as a result of exchange of costs of production, our Company's figures are favourable as compared with the other Makers' in Scotland ... A question might arise in your mind as to whether, in view of Colvilles' relatively favourable position, we should not allow matters to drift to their economic conclusions but it is to be remembered that the constitution of the Steel Trade in Scotland is of a unique nature. Two of the other Steel Works are entirely controlled by Shipbuilders and while they have not derived any profit from them and, in some cases, have had to meet losses, still they have

The plan for a full merger of Scottish steel-makers soon foundered. Stewarts & Lloyds, having already insisted on special safeguards to protect their tube-making interests in discussions of the Brassert Reports—safeguards which involved formidable questions both of production facilities and control—dropped out of the negotiations at an early stage. A. C. Macdiarmid, infuriated by the arguments of the Scottish makers, was said to have stormed out of one meeting declaring that he would 'go on by himself' and promptly commissioned H. A. Brassert to examine the special problems facing Stewarts & Lloyds: an action which proved to be the genesis of the Corby Works and Stewarts & Lloyds' greatly-diminished interest in developments in South-West Scotland.[80] The representatives of the Steel Company of Scotland, lukewarm on the Brassert scheme, would not be drawn into any alternative arrangement, partly because of a personal animosity towards John Craig,[81]

---

looked upon the actual possession of the Works as an asset and will, we believe, continue to operate them irrespective of their results.

'We feel therefore satisfied that, if any improvement in the present position is to be realized, it can only be by merging the Scottish Steel Works . . . There is one difficulty which we have not faced and that is the question of control in the future. Colville would, in all probability, possess over sixty per cent of the combined capital and we feel that the other Shipbuilders might consider it too great a risk to be at the mercy of our Company, so that there would require to be some form of assurance to them whereby their supplies of Steel would be guaranteed. I have no doubt, however, that this point could be arranged to the mutual satisfaction of the Various parties, as I think the present mood of the Makers is to recognize the importance of co-operation and the necessity for a change in the present unfortunate conditions.

'While it is true . . . . that a merger would have immediate benefits, it cannot be overlooked that some portion of the Brassert Scheme would become ultimately essential if the Trade is to be placed in a sounder position for the future and this may be the most opportune time for considering it in view of the fact that we are led to believe the Government are most anxious to give assistance to any scheme which would help unemployment and, at the same time, be of real value in fostering an existing industry. I think some members of the Government feel that they have gone as far as they dare go in Road making, etc. and it would be a great achievement for them if they could get our Industry interested in some scheme of development.' J. Craig to Lord Kylsant, 5 Dec. 1929.

[80] Scopes provides a detailed account of these developments, *Development of Corby Works*, pp. 55–97. Macdiarmid's attitude is based on a conversation between the author and Sir Andrew McCance.

[81] D.C. & S., Board Minute Book VI, p. 16, 11 Apr. 1930. It is possible that the Steel Company of Scotland's attitude was influenced by the fact that Stephens of Linthouse—a member of the consortium which owned the Steel Company—was controlled by Lord Inchcape who personally held 51 per cent

and Bairds, under A. K. McCosh, were unwilling to co-operate.
The fact was that a full amalgamation of Scottish steel-
makers—like the acceptance of Brasserts' scheme—was be-
devilled by the abrasive personalities of the major participants
in the discussions. Without exception, 'they all hated each
other'.[82]

Undeterred, Craig pushed on. In February 1930, Beardmores, having previously informed Colvilles that it was their
intention to break up the Mossend Steel Works,[83] transferred
their business in plates, sections, and rails to Colvilles in return
for an undertaking by Colvilles to supply the Parkhead firm
with their requirements of axle billets, blooms, and slabs and
not to enter into the manufacture of heavy forgings. Meanwhile, negotiations continued with Sir James Lithgow, Mr.
Peter Baxter, and Mr. MacHarg of Dunlops.[84] By mid-April
agreement had been reached on a whole range of issues, not
the least important of which was that the board of the new company—to be called Colvilles Ltd.—would consist of four directors to be nominated by David Colville & Sons Ltd. and two
by James Dunlop & Company. Lord Kylsant was in favour of
the arrangements, and both Harland & Wolff and Lithgows
had agreed to take their supplies of steel from the amalgamated
companies for a period of years.[85] Certain concessions had won
over those members of the Colville family who represented the
cash lenders,[86] and the directors of the National Bank of

---

of the shipbuilding company's Ordinary shares and 50 per cent of the Preference shares. It may be that Inchcape did not wish to become too involved
with a company controlled by Kylsant either because he was aware of structural weakness of the Royal Mail Group, or because he had a personal antipathy towards Kylsant. For the financial structure and Inchcape's holdings,
see Paul L. Robertson, 'Shipping and Shipbuilding: The Case of William
Denny & Brothers', *Business History*, No. 1 (Jan. 1974), p. 43, note I.

[82] Based on a conversation with Sir Andrew McCance. This explanation
may not fully satisfy my fellow economic historians. One can but say that
it is consistent with the facts; that economic historians should understand
that business behaviour cannot be fully understood with reference solely to
the abstractions of economists, statisticians, and accountants; and that when
amalgamations are contemplated, the problem of post-merger control—
which rests primarily on the psychological make-up of the executive body—
is a matter of overwhelming practical relevance.

[83] D.C. & S., Minute Book V, 20 Dec. 1929.

[84] Ibid., 14 Feb. 1930, 21 Mar. 1930.

[85] Ibid., VI, 11 Apr. 1930, 9 May 1930, 19 May 1930.

[86] Ibid., VI, 11 June 1930.

Scotland—who would have preferred '... a more comprehensive scheme of amalgamation to include also the Steel Company of Scotland and ... the Lanarkshire Steel Company'—had stated that they were 'sympathetically disposed towards the scheme';[87] a sympathy which did not inhibit them from imposing the most stringent conditions on the grant of a credit of £800,000 for the new company![88]

All seemed to be going well when a totally unexpected event occurred which threatened to bring the entire proceedings to a halt and severely damage not merely David Colville & Sons but the entire British steel and shipbuilding industries. In 1929 there had begun that depression in world trade which was to cause enormous losses to British shipping companies. Between March and October of that year the shares of the Royal Mail Group—the supreme figure in which (by virtue of his personal shareholdings) was Lord Kylsant—had fallen in value by no less than sixteen million pounds. An integral part of the Royal Mail Group was Elder Dempster & Company, whose principal ordinary shareholder was Lord Kylsant. It was through Elder Dempsters, and the other companies over which Kylsant had almost complete authority, that the Royal Mail Group controlled Harland & Wolff, and hence Colvilles (see Figure II). The general loss of confidence in Royal Mail shares which took place during 1929 could not but have repercussions throughout the Kylsant empire. By March 1929, 'new and ominous cracks began to appear in the financial edifice of the Royal Mail'.[89] These were first seen in the accounts of Lamport and Holt which revealed a discrepancy of 50 per cent between the book and market values of the company's reserve investments. Further disclosures indicated extremely serious financial diffi-

[87] Ibid., VI, 9 May 1930. It is worth noting that the National Bank of Scotland, the Royal Bank of Scotland, and Lloyds Bank were at this time acting in concert to solve the manifold problems confronting Beardmores and the Lanarkshire Steel Co.; that since 1918 the entire capital of the National Bank of Scotland had been owned by Lloyds (S. G. Checkland, *Scottish Banking*, pp. 562–3), and that Lord Weir was a director of Lloyds. I am indebted to Mr. Michael Moss for drawing my attention to this point.

[88] Ibid., VI, 19 May 1930. See Table 7.4.

[89] This, and part of the following paragraph, is based on P. N. Davies, *The Trade Makers. Elder Dempster in West Africa, 1852–1972* (London: Allen & Unwin, 1973), pp. 251–60. See also P. N. Davies and A. M. Bourn, 'Lord Kylsant and the Royal Mail', *Business History*, xiv, No. 2 (July 1972), pp. 103–23.

TABLE 7.4
David Colville & Sons: Credits Granted by National Bank of Scotland, 1921–1930

Date	Overdraft limit (£s)	Conditions of Credit and Comments
29 Dec. 1921	800,000	D.C. & S. had requested £1m; Bank could not agree because 'a standing unsecured credit to that extent [would] practically equal the Bank's capital'.
14 July 1922	800,000	Interest payable: Bank Rate (B.R.) to 5 per cent; below 5 per cent, ½ per cent above B.R. Minimum 4 per cent.
20 July 1922	800,000	Interest: minimum payable reduced to 3½ per cent.
15 Mar. 1923	800,000	D.C. & S. request £1m. Bank insists upon security: 30,000 £10 shares in Archibald Russell (A.R.). D.C. & S. to make no material repayment to private lenders.
14 July 1925	800,000	Bank requests additional security. D.C. & S. refuse but agree that no security would be granted to any other creditor while Bank overdraft limit remained at £800,000.
14 July 1927		Bank suggests overdraft limit of £550,000.
20 Sept. 1927	800,000	Additional security granted: total now £½m: 50,000 £10 shares in A.R. D.C. & S.'s cash lenders increasingly restive: any reduction in overdraft insisted upon by Bank should be followed by repayment of similar amount to cash lenders who also argue for 'equal security with the Bank'.
29 Sept. 1927		From this date onwards Bank repeatedly hints at reduction of credit and presses D.C. & S. to make a Debenture issue to clear off cash loans and Bank overdraft.
18 Oct. 1928	700,000	With temporary excess of £20,000.
2 May 1929		Bank suggests £600,000 maximum and protests that balance due cash creditors had been reduced by £93,000 during the past year.
16 May 1929	700,000	Bank agree to £700,000 *only* because a reduction of the overdraft limit by £100,000 would involve a similar reduction in the volume of cash loans which, it was recognized, would seriously reduce D.C. & S.'s working capital. Bank insists that (i) no security to be granted to any other creditors without Bank approval; (ii) no repayment to cash lenders without Bank approval. Cash lenders protest, but asked to be patient since 'more money is being withdrawn from [the Company's] floating capital than we are able to afford'.
3 Apr. 1930	670,000	Overdraft limit reduced as result of repayment of £30,000 to one of the Company's cash creditors. That is, Bank insists on imposing conditions of May–June 1929.
1 May 1930		D.C. & S. request limit of £800,000 in view of Colville/Dunlop amalgamation. Request initially refused because Bank directors believe that merger with S.C. of S. and Lanarkshire Steel Co. essential to success of new company.

(continued on page 186)

Date	Overdraft limit (£s)	Conditions of Credit and Comments
20 June 1930	800,000	Credit granted with extreme reluctance ('it must be recorded that the Directors had the greatest difficulty in reconciling the granting of such a large advance to one customer with sound principles governing Banking advances', 15 May 1930).
		Conditions imposed: (i) Massive *increase* in security: 49,450 £10 shares in A.R.; 17,501 £10 shares in Smith & McLean (giving voting control); 250,000 £1 First Preference shares in Colvilles Ltd. ('Even this cover [is] not of the readily marketable nature so desirable against such a large advance', 8 May 1930.)
		(ii) No repayment to private cash lenders without Bank's consent.
		(iii) No further security to that arranged in the course of the formation of Colvilles Ltd. to be granted to the cash lenders.
		(iv) D.C. & S. not to borrow money from any source whatsoever other than the Bank without Bank's consent.
		(v) Increase in interest payable: when B.R. is 5 per cent or over, $\frac{1}{2}$ per cent above B.R.; when B.R. below 5 per cent, 1 per cent above B.R. Minimum payable $4\frac{1}{2}$ per cent.

Sources: Correspondence between J. B. Allan and the National Bank of Scotland Ltd.; correspondence between J. B. Allan and the trustees for the cash creditors; D.C. & S.: Minute Books, 1920–30.

culties, and in May Kylsant announced the creation of a committee to confer with the directors of the Royal Mail Steam Packet Company on matters of management, administration, and finance.

Thus, at the very time when it became imperative for Craig to obtain the Treasury's approval of the proposed Colville/Dunlop amalgamation—a step made necessary because Colvilles had still not completed the repayment of the wartime loans granted by the Ministry of Munitions—the Royal Mail Group was rapidly disintegrating, and the object of acute and growing suspicion. Not surprisingly, the Treasury placed the entire matter in the hands of Sir William McLintock, who was a member of the Special Committee set up to inquire into the affairs of the Royal Mail Group, and who, within a few days, was to be appointed one of three trustees with voting control of the Royal Mail Steam Packet Company, and hence the destinies of its subsidiary and associated companies, one of which was Harland & Wolff, owners of 95 per cent of the ordinary shares of David Colville & Sons.

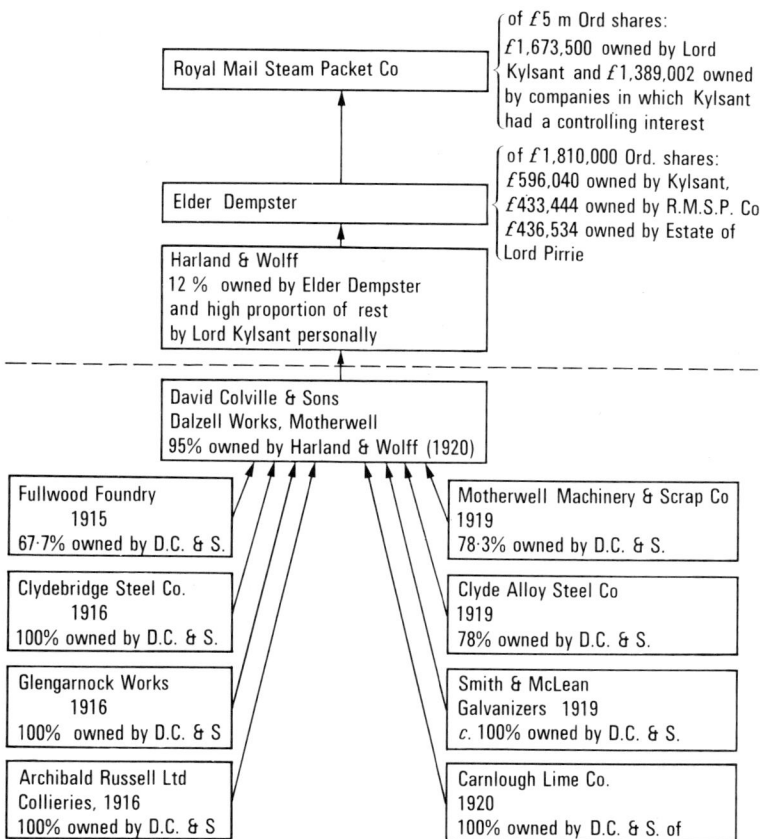

```
┌─────────────────────────────────┐        ⎧ of £5 m Ord shares:
│ Royal Mail Steam Packet Co      │        ⎪ £1,673,500 owned by Lord
└─────────────────────────────────┘        ⎨ Kylsant and £1,389,002 owned
                 ↑                          ⎪ by companies in which Kylsant
                                            ⎩ had a controlling interest

┌─────────────────────────────────┐        ⎧ of £1,810,000 Ord. shares:
│ Elder Dempster                  │        ⎪ £596,040 owned by Kylsant,
└─────────────────────────────────┘        ⎨ £433,444 owned by R.M.S.P. Co
                 ↑                          ⎪ £436,534 owned by Estate of
┌─────────────────────────────────┐        ⎩ Lord Pirrie
│ Harland & Wolff                 │
│ 12 % owned by Elder Dempster    │
│ and high proportion of rest     │
│ by Lord Kylsant personally      │
└─────────────────────────────────┘
```

Royal Mail Steam Packet Co

of £5 m Ord shares:
£1,673,500 owned by Lord Kylsant and £1,389,002 owned by companies in which Kylsant had a controlling interest

Elder Dempster

of £1,810,000 Ord. shares:
£596,040 owned by Kylsant, £433,444 owned by R.M.S.P. Co £436,534 owned by Estate of Lord Pirrie

Harland & Wolff
12 % owned by Elder Dempster and high proportion of rest by Lord Kylsant personally

- -

David Colville & Sons
Dalzell Works, Motherwell
95% owned by Harland & Wolff (1920)

Fullwood Foundry 1915 67·7% owned by D.C. & S.	Motherwell Machinery & Scrap Co 1919 78·3% owned by D.C. & S.
Clydebridge Steel Co. 1916 100% owned by D.C. & S.	Clyde Alloy Steel Co 1919 78% owned by D.C. & S.
Glengarnock Works 1916 100% owned by D.C. & S	Smith & McLean Galvanizers 1919 c. 100% owned by D.C. & S.
Archibald Russell Ltd Collieries, 1916 100% owned by D.C. & S	Carnlough Lime Co. 1920 100% owned by D.C. & S. of

Sources: Below broken horizontal line: Colville Archives. The percentages given represent the proportion of
the Ordinary Shares owned

Above broken horizontal line   P.N. Davies, *The Trade Makers, Elder Dempster in West Africa.*
1852–1972. (London: Allan & Unwin, 1973), pp. 251 – 60.

FIG. 11. *Financial Structure of David Colville & Sons, c. 1920, and the Relevant
Part of the Royal Mail Steam Packet Company, c. 1927.*

John Craig was summoned to London to discuss the Colville/
Dunlop merger proposals with the members of the Special
Committee of Inquiry. Although it was felt that the new company would be both over-capitalized and burdened with a disproportionate volume of Cumulative Preference shares,[90] Craig
was subsequently informed that the Committee would permit
the amalgamation to take place, and Colvilles Ltd. to come into
being, *only* on condition that the Second Preference shares
which it was proposed to issue would be non-accumulative for
the first five years and that the voting trustees of the Royal Mail
Steam Packet Company be represented on the board of the new
company, a condition that they were prepared to waive 'so long
as Mr. Craig was Chairman or Managing Director'.[91] Satisfied
on these points—agreement to which had first to be obtained
from Dunlops,[92] the Colville cash lenders, and the National
Bank of Scotland—the Special Committee gave its approval to
the scheme and the voting trustees promised to grant any necessary proxy in respect of Harland & Wolff's shareholdings.

[90] Writing later in his capacity as a voting trustee of the Royal Mail Steam
Packet Company, McLintock was much more critical: '. . . you will appreciate that [the] consent [of the voting trustees] was given largely owing to the
special circumstances of the case, and as a result of the negotiations having
been carried to such an advanced stage before the matter came under the
Trustees' consideration. As you are aware, the Trustees do not like the scheme
. . . I note . . . that both you and Sir James Lithgow do not think that the
completion of this scheme will create any difficulties in connection with the
larger amalgamation at present under consideration. I want to make it quite
clear that in my view, particularly having regard to the present obscure outlook, the proposed capital of Colvilles Ltd. is too high, and I should have
preferred a scheme which provided for a much lower capitalization. I am
afraid I cannot agree with your view that this excessive capitalization will
not cause difficulties later, but I take it that you and Sir James Lithgow both
appreciate that the present Scheme cannot form the nucleus of the larger
Merger, and I must put it clearly on record that when I come to advise on
the larger question, I must in no way be held as having expressed approval
of the present capitalization of Colvilles Ltd.' Sir William McLintock to J.
Craig, 30 Oct. 1930. McLintock's criticisms were not new to Craig who had
evidently tried to get the Lithgows to agree to a lower capitalization and
a smaller proportion of Cumulative Preference shares, but the Lithgow
brothers would not budge on the question of the capital structure of Colvilles
Ltd., and had they been pushed any more there was a very real 'risk of [them]
going off altogether' (J. Craig to Sir William McLintock, 30 June 1930; idem,
8 July 1930.)

[91] Sir William McLintock to J. Craig, 28 June 1930. D.C. & S., Board
Minute Book VI, p. 49, 11 July 1930.

[92] D.C. & S., 'Memorandum on discussion between the Directors of James
Dunlop & Co. Ltd., and Mr. John Craig . . . 10 October 1930'.

Furthermore, Sir William McLintock, acting on behalf of the
Treasury, agreed to postpone further repayments in reduction
of the Ministry of Munitions loan, subject to security being
granted and the payment of interest on the same terms as those
demanded by the National Bank of Scotland.[93]
The way was now clear for the amalgamation to take place.
On 10 October 1930, complete agreement was reached by the
boards of David Colville & Sons and James Dunlop.[94] The voting trustees gave their consent to the proposals on 30 October,[95]
and a month later the scheme to form a new company,
registered as Colvilles Ltd., to acquire the Dalzell, Clydebridge,
and Glengarnock Works from David Colville & Sons and the
Clyde Iron Works at Tolcross and the Calderbank Steel Works
at Airdrie from James Dunlop & Company, together with their
associated collieries, was ratified by an Extraordinary meeting
of the shareholders of David Colville & Sons.[96] Colvilles Ltd.
came into being on 1 January 1931, only two weeks after John
Craig had reported to the board of David Colville & Sons that
the 'general [steel] situation was critical, with acute depression
throughout the industry . . . there was [moreover] no indication
whatsoever of any signs of improvement'. Indeed, within a few
months, David Colville & Sons, now a holding company, had
become so 'seriously embarrassed financially' that it became
'absolutely necessary' for the company's cash creditors to agree
to a Moratorium, the effect of which was that they could not
recall their advances (which in September 1931 stood at over
£1½ million) nor be *entitled* to any interest payments for the
period 1 July 1931 to 31 December 1933.[97] The new company of
Colvilles Ltd. could hardly have had a less auspicious beginning.

[93] D.C. & S., Board Minute Book VI, pp. 48–51, 11 July 1930.
[94] Ibid., p. 79, 10 Oct. 1930.
[95] Sir William McLintock to J. Craig, 30 Oct. 1930; D.C. & S., Board
Minute Book VI, p. 89, 14 Nov. 1930.
[96] D.C. & S., Board Minute Book VI, pp. 100–2, 28 Nov. 1930.
[97] R. A. Murray to the Trustees for Cash Lenders of Messrs. David Colville
& Sons Ltd., 13 Oct. 1931. The Moratorium generated an enormous correspondence and a series of legal agreements with the private cash lenders, the
National Bank of Scotland, and the Treasury. The essence of the arrangement
is contained in D.C. & S. Ltd., 'Suggested basis for negotiating proposed
Moratorium . . .', 27 Oct. 1931. On 21 Sept. 1931, the total amount due to
the Cash Creditors stood at £1,579, 832, and another £118, 375 had been
borrowed from subsidiary companies. D.C. & S., 'Summary of Cash Position
as at 21 September 1931'.

VIII

The Turning Point, 1931–1936

1 Colvilles' Inheritance

In retrospect, the amalgamation of David Colville & Sons and James Dunlop & Company seems scant reward for a decade of almost ceaseless negotiations by John Craig. From the point of view of productive assets, the union of the two firms can hardly be said to have greatly strengthened the more powerful partner, but it did constitute a first step in the achievement of Craig's grand design for the Scottish steel industry. Craig never lost sight of the desirability of a complete merger of the Scottish steel-makers; only by this means could the proper rationalization of the industry be achieved. He had made his position clear in discussing the Szarvasy scheme, which he had rejected because it would mean the 'retention of the personal interest' and the impossibility of concentrating production on the most economic plant. It is evident that Sir James Lithgow shared this opinion. He too believed in *one* Scottish steel-making firm: not simply because it would be 'big', but because of its potentialities for greater efficiency.[1] The most important consequence of the Colville/Dunlop merger was that it brought these two determined, like-minded personalities together.

In acquiring Dalzell, Clydebridge, and Glengarnock from David Colville & Sons, Colvilles Ltd. took over three relatively efficient steel works. Much of the plant was comparatively new, either having been commissioned almost immediately before the war or erected during or soon after it. When, through ill-health, David Maclay (who had been responsible for the general supervision and control of all three works since the death of David Colville, jun.) had to resign from active participation in Colvilles' affairs in December 1920, John Craig was left without a single colleague on the technical side. A replacement for Maclay was urgently needed, and within a few weeks he was succeeded by G. P. West, who had only just been

[1] Personal communication from Sir Andrew McCance.

appointed General Manager at Glengarnock. West, trained at Chatham Dock Yard, had previously been principal Admiralty Overseer for Scotland, a post to which he had been promoted in 1900 at the age of 32. Thoroughly conversant with every aspect of steel manufacture, and well known to Colvilles' senior officials, he was appointed to the board in 1921 and made General Works Manager.[2] With the assistance of the company's chief engineers, Thomas B. Mackenzie, a leading expert in fuel conservation and waste heat utilization, and James Gillespie, it was West who was responsible for the technical efficiency of the works during the twenties: a period which, although capital expenditure totalled only £60,000,[3] was remarkable for the dismantling of several plants, the concentration of production on the most economical units within the group, and the improvement of many aspects of steel-making practice.[4] Thus, when the merger took place in 1930, there is no reason to question the essential validity of Colvilles' oft-reported claim that

[2] *Colvilles' Magazine*, ii (1921), 39; March–April 1948, p. 22.

[3] Personal communication from Sir Andrew McCance.

[4] Although many of the improvements (including, for example, greater care of furnace bottoms (fettling), more precise control of saturation and gas temperatures at the gas producers, and a whole range of minor but cumulatively important modifications in furnace charging and slag control), were relatively inexpensive to implement, they brought about a marked improvement in furnace outputs and fuel consumption. This may be illustrated by the following statistics:

Basic Practice at No. 2 Melting Shop, Clydebridge

	1919	1923	1927	1931
Average weekly no. of charges per furnace	8	11·7	12·7	13·1
Average weekly tonnage of ingots per furnace	500	914	1,041	1,130
Best week: Ingot tonnage for a furnace	748	1,154	1,306	1,297
Fuel Consumption: lbs per ton of steel	n.d.	678	547	569
Lime Consumption: cwt per ton of steel	n.d.	0·81	0·74	0·55

Average Weekly Output (in tons) per Furnace at Glengarnock

1919	1921	1923	1925	1927	1929	1931
537	734	850	872	916	985	1,103

Cwts of Coal Consumed per Ton of Ingots Produced, Glengarnock

1919	1921	1923	1925	1927	1929	1931
n.d.	8·3	6·7	6·8	6·0	5·7	5·1

J. G. Fairgrieve and J. Gibson, 'Basic Open Hearth Practice in Scotland', in Iron and Steel Institute, *Special Report*, No. 22 (1938), pp. 18–19, 28.

despite, or perhaps even because of, pinch-penny methods, the plant at Dalzell, Glengarnock, and Clydebridge was in 'a high state of efficiency'.[5] With limited resources, West, a martinet, had done his job well.[6]

By contrast, Dunlops, as a collection of iron- and steel-making plant, was of doubtful value to the Colville group. The Calderbank Steel Works—with its six relatively small furnaces—had a smaller capacity than Dalzell, Clydebridge, or Glengarnock, and was almost immediately closed down.[7] Its five small hand-filled open-topped blast furnaces were obsolete and wasteful of fuel. They seemed to possess little potential, and, in any case, Craig's experience at Glengarnock had convinced him that the economic production of pig iron in Scotland was all but impossible. This meant that the 80,000 tons of iron ore at Calderbank seemed to have about as little value as Tennant's piles of 'Blue Billy' had had sixty years earlier. Moreover, Dunlops had £107,000 of Preference share interest outstanding, and the firm was indebted to Lithgows for £335,000.[8] This was what gave James Lithgow the power to enforce the merger, but in terms of physical assets the successful conclusion of the negotiations can have given little positive satisfaction to either of the two parties.

2 The McLintock Proposals, 1931

Certainly, the union of Colvilles and Dunlops gave little satisfaction to Sir William McLintock. He had grave misgivings about the capital structure of the new company which he believed would make a more comprehensive amalgamation scheme even more difficult to achieve. In September 1930 Sir William had been called in with encouragement from Montagu Norman to advise the Scottish ironmasters and steel-makers on

[5] This phrase, or some variation of it, was invariably employed in the Annual Reports from 1924–9, D.C. & S., Minute Books IV and V.

[6] West was highly regarded by his immediate colleagues; to his subordinates he was, the author has been informed by older employees of Colvilles, 'a tyrant and a bully'. Perhaps the times needed such a man.

[7] Brassert Report, p. 42. Calderbank was roughly the same size as the Hallside Works of the S.C. of S.; its steel works lost money throughout 1920 and an important motive for the Colville/Dunlop merger was to close them down. John Craig to Sir William McLintock, 21 June 1930, 23 June 1930.

[8] *The Economist*, 6 Dec. 1930.

the methods whereby a merger involving William Baird & Company, the Steel Company of Scotland, Stewarts & Lloyds, Colvilles, and Dunlops might take place.[9] Since serious joint consideration of the Brassert proposals had only recently been abandoned, the likelihood of securing any agreement on this new plan was optimistic, although not impossible. Conditions had changed, even in the past year.

It is unanimously believed that the twenties constituted a 'black decade'[10] for the steel-makers, a decade in which, despite the revival following the 1921 slump, 'things got worse rather than better'. Burdened with suffocating debts, recklessly assumed in the short postwar boom, the majority of firms could pay their Ordinary shareholders virtually nothing, many were hard pressed to pay dividends on their Preference shares (which were often cumulative), and some were unable even to pay their Debenture holders. The result was that between 1920 and 1925 a considerable number of firms fell into the hands of the joint-stock banks, and one, Armstrong, Whitworth, & Company, into the hands of the Bank of England. Montagu Norman was forced to devise a solution for Armstrongs, as later he was for Beardmores and Baldwins. Soon the problems of other ailing giants in iron and steel were brought to him, and, along with the problems, came a surfeit of advice and plans for the resuscitation of the industry. Until the end of 1929, there was no formal organization at the Bank to deal with these matters which were handled personally by Norman, relying for advice on a small group of specialists. For iron and steel he called in Brasserts and then, through Sir Andrew Duncan, secured the services of Charles Bruce Gardner, managing director of the Shelton Iron, Steel, & Coal Company, a subsidiary of John Summers. Gardner was promptly commissioned to make another study of the industry. Correctly anticipating that Brasserts, Charles Bruce Gardner, and the sub-committee of the Committee on Civil Research, which under Lord Sankey was set up in July 1929 to inquire into 'the present conditions and prospects of the iron and steel industry', would propose fundamental reorganization and modernization, Norman formed a company for

[9] D.C. & S., Minute Book VI, 9 Sept. 1930.
[10] The indelible phrase used by Burn, *Economic History of Steel Making*, p. 393.

'the purpose of examining schemes [in iron and steel and other industries] and, if approved, carrying them through'. This company was registered as the Securities Management Trust in November 1929 and it promptly spawned the Bankers' Industrial Development Company in order 'to examine, assist, and finance the amalgamation, reconstruction, and reorganization on an economic and rationalized basis of groups of British Companies engaged in important industries'.[11]

Brasserts reported first, in January 1930.[12] The American firm recommended concentrating the British iron and steel industry 'on six pivotal centres where integrated plants existed or were to be built', each one of which was to be allocated a share of the total national tonnage (13 million tons in 1929, three million of which was imported) in such a way as to justify 'the operation of large integrated units equal to any existing in Europe or in America'. The centres in being were Partington in Lancashire, Dorman Longs at Middlesbrough, and Guest, Keen, & Nettlefolds at Cardiff; the three to be built were at Frodingham, Kettering, and on the Clyde.[13] Lord Sankey's sub-committee reported next. The committee—to whom Norman had given evidence two months after receiving Brasserts' 'Memorandum'—found that the basic ills of the iron and steel industry were a consequence of a lack of co-ordination among

[11] Clay, *Lord Norman*, p. 329; Leslie Hannah, *The Rise of the Corporate Economy* (London: Methuen, 1976), pp. 73–4. For authoritative statements concerning the genesis, purpose and policies of the Securities Management Trust and the Bankers' Industrial Development Co., see the evidence of Sir Ernest Harvey (S.M.T.) and Sir W. Guy Granet (B.I.D. Co.) to the Macmillan Committee, Committee on Finance and Industry, *Minutes of Evidence* (1931, 2 vols.), qq. 828–60, 9027–184. See also R. S. Sayers, *The Bank of England, 1891–1944* (Cambridge: C.U.P., 1976), i, 314–30. Bruce Gardner joined the board of directors of S.M.T. early in 1930 and became Managing Director in March 1930. He remained for eight years. The relationship between S.M.T. and B.I.D. Co. has been most succinctly expressed by Sayers, op. cit., p. 327: 'Effectively . . . there was most of the time only one organization: the group of experts in S.M.T. who investigated and discussed among themselves schemes of industrial reconstruction.'

[12] H. A. Brassert & Co. Ltd.: 'Memorandum on the Rationalization of the British Iron and Steel Industry', dated 10 Jan. 1930, and forwarded to J. Frater Taylor on 20 Jan. 1930. Vaizey, *History of British Steel*, p. 51, gives the details, which are expanded in his *Notes and Sources to the History of British Steel* (London, privately printed, 1974), p. 16. J. Frater Taylor was one of Norman's group of advisers. See Clay, *Lord Norman*, p. 327.

[13] Vaizey, *Notes and Sources*, p. 16; the second quotation is taken from Brasserts' 'Memorandum', p. 6.

steel-makers. Protection was not desirable until the industry had been reorganized 'in the nature of vertical combinations owning sources of supply of raw materials and producing finished steel goods'. It was recommended that 'five or six units' be erected—each being 'confined to one district' and substantially representing 'the whole of that district'—which should 'make arrangements with one another for the development of the industry on national lines'.[14] Nine months later, C. Bruce Gardner's report was published.[15] This emphasized that '*though there are other matters of serious importance which affect manufacturing costs and should be dealt with*, it is absolutely essential ... *that rationalization and re-organization of the iron and steel industry should be carried through without further delay*'.[16] This principal objective could be achieved by the creation of four regional districts: (a) Scotland; (b) North-East Coast; (c) Midland and North-West Coast; and (d) South Wales. In Scotland 'the steel producing companies' should 'be amalgamated so that, under unified control, the work may be regulated and allocated in the most efficient manner'. In addition, 'new complete coke oven and blast furnace equipment [should] be installed in such a situation as to produce the cheapest pig iron for the new steel company, having in view future developments and further concentration of the steel output into fewer units'.[17]

These three influential reports all seemed to confirm the correctness of Craig's plans for the industry in Scotland. Whereas, in the late twenties, he appears to have been almost alone in voicing his belief in a regional grouping, the impact of his con-

[14] Vaizey, *History of British Steel*, p. 51, citing P.R.O. Cab. 58 File 131, Economic Advisory Council, Iron and Steel Committee, Draft Report (March 1930), E.A.C. (I. and S.), 99, p. 36.
[15] C. Bruce Gardner, *Report on the Structure of the Iron and Steel Industry of Great Britain incorporating Plans for Rationalization*, 31 Dec. 1930.
[16] Ibid., p. 94.
[17] Ibid., p. 95. These recommendations were based on a complete survey of the Scottish iron and steel industry (pp. 24–30), most of the information for which was provided by John Craig in a memorandum entitled 'The Iron and Steel Industry of Scotland'. J. Craig to C. B. Gardner, 15 Aug. 1930. Craig subsequently read and amended those parts of Gardner's *Report* relating to Scotland. C. B. Gardner to John Craig, 9 Dec. 1930. It is noteworthy that a number of directors and senior officials of Colvilles' competitors—Walter G. Gray of the Steel Company of Scotland and Andrew Gray of Lanarkshire were typical examples—bitterly resented Craig's leading role in official and semi-official inquiries, especially when they themselves were completely ignored. Personal Communication by Sir Andrew McCance.

troversial views was now given additional weight by the findings of inquiries sponsored by the government and the City.
But this was not the only factor that promised to ensure a sym-
pathetic reception to whatever plan Sir William McLintock
might devise for Scotland. Whereas, throughout the twenties,
the joint-stock banks had displayed an unyielding loyalty to
what *The Times* characterized as a 'policy of benevolent but in-
ert orthodoxy', refusing to take a positive role in the reconstruction of British industry, by 1930 this attitude was weakening.[18]
The conviction was slowly spreading that some modification
must be made in time-honoured banking policies: that the
banks could and should use their financial powers to evolve constructive measures for relief and, if necessary, to enforce the
adoption of such measures by the threat of bankruptcy.[19] The
lead had already been taken by the Bank of England. The commercial banks, somewhat reluctantly, followed. Indeed, by taking up 'A' shares in the Bankers' Industrial Development Company,[20] twenty major joint-stock banks manifested their sympathy towards the objectives of the Development Company in
a tangible form. There was, then, a much stronger likelihood
than had hitherto existed that the banks might be prepared to
bring pressure to bear on their impoverished clients in the Scottish iron and steel industry to agree to McLintock's recommendations.

[18] *The Times*, 3 Feb. 1930, p. 13. An extended discussion of the traditional
relationship between industry and banking in Britain may be found in the
Report of the Committee on Finance and Industry [the Macmillan Report]
(1931. Cmd. 3897), Part I, Chapter XI, Section 5, and Part II, Chapter IV.
[19] Sir Arthur Salter rightly commented that 'The industries most needing
reorganization are to a large extent living on frozen overdrafts, which are
terminable at short notice and give great power to the banks if they care
to exercise it.' *The Times*, 9 Dec. 1930, p. 15.
[20] The Bankers' Industrial Development Co. Ltd. had a capitalization of
£6 million, divided into 60 shares of £100,000 each. These shares were of two
types, 'A' and 'B'. Forty-five 'A' shares were alloted to important banking
and investment houses, including 20 joint-stock banks. The 'B' shares were
retained by the Bank of England, 14 in the possession of the Securities
Management Trust and one held directly by the Governor. Since the 'A'
shares carried only one vote each and the 'B' shares had three, the Securities
Management Trust and the Governor were able to deploy the same number
of votes as the other shareholders combined. The Governor of the Bank of
England was also the chairman of the Development Co. See Arthur F. Lucas,
'The Bankers' Industrial Development Company', *Harvard Business Review*,
xi (1933), pp. 273–5, and above, n. 11.

The third factor which made for the possibility of greater co-operation among the major Scottish iron and steel companies to achieve the rehabilitation of the industry was the increasingly dismal economic climate. Having overcome the sharp depression of the early twenties and survived the complete dislocation caused by the General Strike in 1926, there had been three years of encouraging activity. The requirements of the shipyards had been at their highest level since 1920 (see Table 6.4), reaching a peak in 1929. There then began a sickening collapse in demand from this sector, which within three years was to drag Scottish steel output down to less than a third of the 1929 level. In 1931 the tonnage of vessels launched on the Clyde was at its lowest point since 1867 and, almost unbelievably, worse was to come. In such a situation, there seemed to be nothing to lose by acting together to save something from the wreck, especially when it was made known that any comprehensive amalgamation scheme embracing Bairds, the Steel Company, Stewarts & Lloyds, and Colvilles had tacit governmental encouragement and the vigorous support of the Securities Management Trust and the Bankers' Industrial Development Company.

Sir William's plan was to merge into an operating company the entire assets of Colvilles Ltd., the Steel Company of Scotland (including their collieries), the Gartsherrie Iron Works, collieries, coke ovens, by-product plants and limestone quarries of William Bairds, and the Clydesdale Works of Stewarts & Lloyds, together with Govan Shafting and Engineering Works (owned by the Steel Company of Scotland) and the subsidiaries of David Colville & Sons Ltd. Excluding the subsidiaries, McLintock's initial valuation of the fixed assets of the various works was £5,354,319, and the estimated working capital employed in their operations, £1,551,140. He proposed issuing 6 per cent Preference shares for the working capital, and Ordinary share capital in exchange for the fixed assets. In order that the total capital of the new company could be fixed at a reasonable amount, the value of the fixed assets was to be subject to an overall reduction of 20 per cent. This major writing down, together with a number of lesser adjustments, produced a total capitalization of £5,607,263, the average return on which—if the experience of the previous three years could be taken as a guide—would be equivalent to about 9 per cent on the proposed ordinary share capital of £4,283,456. Perhaps the most far-reaching aspect of the scheme was the proposal to discontinue the production of coke and to scrap all the existing blast furnace and the chemical plant at Gartsherrie, where an entirely new range of ovens, by-product recovery plant, and blast furnaces would be erected (at a cost of £1,200,000). This was to be designed to produce 438,000 tons of pig iron, representing over 89 per cent of the average annual quantity used by the Scottish steel industry over the three years ended 30 June 1930.[21]

Craig's reaction to the plan was critical; without his support it could not be implemented. The share of the fixed assets of the proposed new company to be provided by Colvilles and David Colville & Sons was over 50 per cent, on which the average annual net profits represented over about two-thirds of the total average annual net profits earned by the interested concerns. McLintock's scheme, based as it was on the valuation of capital assets, gave Colvilles a smaller percentage allocation of the total capitalization of the merger company than Craig believed was justified. The biggest problem was the Steel Company of Scotland. Not only was the Steel Company burdened by a loan of £179,304 at 5 per cent which was secured on their Fixed Assets and guaranteed under the Trade Facilities Act, but McLintock's carefully-collected figures indicated that the Steel Company had made only losses over the past three years (see Table 8.1). Surely, it was argued, their assets must be written down as a consequence? McLintock had to accept validity of this argument and in his Supplementary Report, issued in August, a deduction of 10 per cent was made from the value placed on the works of the Steel Company. Craig remained dissatisfied: 'No one I am sure, with any knowledge of the Works would support your valuation of the respective plants, even leaving the question of past profits out of account ... the attitude of my people is that they are not likely to support a scheme based on your figures. I repeat I am most anxious to see a development in Scotland but I do not think we would be justified in paying too big a price for it and that is what your suggestions would mean.'[22]

[21] The details are from Sir William McLintock's 'Report on a Scottish Iron and Steel Merger', 30 July 1931.
[22] J. Craig to Sir William McLintock, 24 Aug. 1931.

TABLE 8.1

Average Annual Net Profits (after Deduction of Depreciation and Interest on Working Capital) made during the Three Years ended 30 June 1930 by the Companies participating in the Scottish Iron and Steel Merger

Total	Colvilles		William Baird & Co.[a]		Steel Company of Scotland[b]		Stewarts & Lloyds		David Colville & Sons	
£	£	%	£	%	£	%	£	%	£	%
347,047	162,366	46·79	94,443	27·21	Loss of 11,107	−3·20	48,128	13·87	53,127	15·33

Notes:
[a] Figures for three years ended 31 May 1930.
[b] Figures for three years ended 17 July 1930.
Source: McLintock Report of 29 July 1931, Appendix 4.

Further meetings took place between representatives of the companies concerned and by September it had been decided that agreement should be reached on the 'steel' position before Bairds and the subsidiaries of David Colville & Sons could be properly considered and that of the total value of the assets of the steel-making concerns, amounting to £3,237,500, Colville should be allocated 67 per cent, the Steel Company, 18·5 per cent, and Stewarts & Lloyds, 14·5 per cent.[23] If satisfactory arrangements could be made on a number of supplementary points, the representatives agreed to recommend the acceptance of the proposed allocations to their respective boards.

This encouraging beginning served only to deceive the more optimistic proponents of amalgamation. Within a few weeks it was apparent that Stewarts & Lloyds would not participate in the amalgamation without the imposition of totally unacceptable conditions regarding the management of their Clydesdale Works;[24] while Colvilles could not agree to any of the solutions

[23] S.I.S.M., 'Minute of Meeting of the Parties to the Proposed Merger ...', 4 Sept. 1931, pp. 2–3. D.C. & S.: Minute Book IV, 11 Sept. 1931.
[24] The correspondence and papers on this issue are extensive and complex. The more important documents are 'Scheme for Leasing of Clydesdale Works to Stewarts & Lloyds by Combination of Steel Works', undated, early Sept. 1931; Sir William McLintock to John Craig, 2 Oct. 1931; 'Proposals by Stewarts & Lloyds for Clydesdale Works', 12 Nov. 1931; S.I.S.M., 'Notes of a meeting between Stewarts & Lloyds Ltd. and Colvilles Ltd.', undated, *c.* Nov. 1931; S.I.S.M., 'Suggestions [by S. &. L.] for Amendments to the Proposals by Stewarts & Lloyds for Clydesdale Works submitted 12 Nov. 1931', 11 Feb. 1932.

proposed either by McLintock or by the Steel Company to the problem of the Steel Company's Trade Facilities Loan, all of which contained elements prejudicial to the position of David Colville & Sons' cash lenders.[25]

3 John Craig's Independent Initiatives, C. Bruce Gardner's Helping Hand, 1931–1933

With remarkable resilience, Craig pushed on with independent negotiations. Possible blast furnace schemes at Clyde Iron Works and Gartsherrie were discussed with William Baird & Company.[26] Talks were held with A. C. Macdiarmid of Stewarts & Lloyds at which it was agreed that although the Clydesdale Works would not be part of the merger, Stewarts & Lloyds would act in such friendly co-operation with the combine that, 'from a public point of view, they would cease to exist as buyers and sellers of steel and merely use the Works for their own tube requirements'.[27] Craig had his colleague A. J. H. Mowbray investigate the possible economies which might be effected by a simple merger of Colvilles with the Steel Company of Scotland alone;[28] and he never ceased to work for the absorption of Lanarkshire Steel and Beardmores' Mossend Works.[29] Craig

[25] John Craig to Sir William McLintock, 27 Oct. 1931; D.C. & S.: Minute Book VI, 13 Nov. 1931. The precise position reached during the negotiations was summarized by Sir James Lithgow in a letter to Sir Andrew Duncan, dated 2 Nov. 1931, in which Lithgow asked: 'I should like your opinion as to how the Bankers' Industrial Development Trust now view the problem. Would they lend Colvilles Limited ... the necessary funds? And would they be prepared to say to Steel Company and Bairds that unless they joined in a scheme within a certain time they would get no financial assistance? Are there any conditions or suggestions which might be made? You will appreciate that I do not want to go personally to Bruce Gardner as it looks like getting behind the backs of other people who may think they are genuinely endeavouring to reach agreement with us, but obviously one of my temperament gets "fed up" with all these negotiations and talking, particularly when the characteristics of men like McCosh and Gray are known to us.' Bank of England Archives: S.M.T. 3/101.
[26] D.C. & S., Minute Book VI, 13 Nov. 1931, 10 Dec. 1931; Andrew McCance, 'Memorandum on New Blast Furances', 22 Feb. 1932.
[27] John Craig to Sir William McLintock, 31 Oct. 1931.
[28] D.C. & S., Minute Book VI, 9 Oct. 1931.
[29] Ibid., 3 Aug. 1931, 21 Mar. 1932. In March 1932, C. B. Gardner informed Sir Andrew Duncan of these facts, adding: 'It therefore comes to this—Colvilles are anxious and willing to join up with the Steel Company of Scotland, the Lanarkshire Steel Company, and Mossend. If they cannot

was indefatigable. Each new frustrating complication, each new legal impediment, seemed only to invigorate him. The millstone of David Colville & Sons' cash creditors, the perpetual wrangling by the shareholders of the Steel Company of Scotland, the intransigence of Stewarts & Lloyds, and the infuriating caution of the clearing banks: all were regarded simply as temporary obstacles in the way of his grand design. With prodigious energy he travelled repeatedly to London, to the various works, and to the banks. The sheer volume of his correspondence alone would have broken lesser men. His colleagues, carried along by his own momentum, supplied memorandum after memorandum on production capacities and balances, financial possibilities, legal technicalites, and market trends.

By the spring of 1932 the Boards of both Colvilles Ltd. and David Colville & Sons recommended that 'immediate steps . . . be taken to secure an amalgamation of Colvilles Ltd., the Steel Company, the subsidiaries of David Colville & Sons Ltd., the Lanarkshire Steel Company, and the Mossend Works of William Beardmore & Company Ltd.',[30] and that 'to avoid delay, the parties concerned, . . . should agree to accept, without further discussion, percentage allocations to be made by Sir William to each company'.[31] This forthright proposal was unacceptable to the Steel Company of Scotland. The Steel Company would proceed only on the basis of the original McLintock report valuations, which were, as Craig constantly fulminated, unjustifiably favourable to themselves. Meanwhile, William Baird & Company withdrew from the discussions concerning the manufacture of pig iron. David Colville & Sons' Minutes record, with massive understatement, that 'Mr. N. R. Colville commented on the protracted nature of the negotiations and referred to the continued serious depression in trade'.[32] Even

---

get the three of them, they are prepared to get two, and if they cannot get two, they are prepared to join up with one . . . it seems to me we have now got it down to a fairly simple proposition and between us we ought to be able to button this thing up pretty quickly.' C. Bruce Gardner to Sir Andrew Duncan, Bank of England Archives: S.M.T. 3/101.

[30] Colvilles Ltd., Board Minutes, 8 Apr. 1932; D.C. & S., Minute Book VI, pp. 221–2, 21 Mar. 1932.

[31] D.C. & S., Minute Book VI, pp. 222–4, 21 Mar. 1932.

[32] Ibid., p. 241, 4 July 1932.

John Craig might have despaired had he known that both were
to drag on for another year or more.

However fairly Craig might claim that Colvilles deserved *at
least* an 80 per cent interest in a merger company involving the
Steel Company of Scotland (14 per cent) and Lanarkshire (6
per cent), Bruce Gardner—who, as managing director of
S.M.T., had since 1930 been kept fully informed of all the developments that had taken place—was surely right in com-
mending 'the views expressed by Sir James Lithgow ... when
he [argued] that it did not matter much whether a few percentages more or less were obtained *provided one could only get something
done*'. Gardner considered

the Scottish position to be very acute and serious ... There is so much dead
wood that will have to be cut out. In order that the Scottish steel industry
may in the future be on a sound foundation, I see no possibility of avoidance
of cutting deeply with the surgeon's knife and performing a serious amputation ... It is going to be painful and pretty desperate. There are individuals
we all know who, rather than go through the painful operation of amputation,
will hang on with the desperate hope that a tariff will save their position.
I do not believe that, unless the Scottish Steel Industry is reorganized, a tariff
will have this effect, because without an enormous improvement in the near
future in the shipbuilding industry ... a great deal of Scotland's output will
have to come south, and this will bring them up against the most intensive
competition if they are to hold their output.[33]

Craig knew this, but he stubbornly refused to accede to any
diminution in Colvilles' interest in a merger company. Bruce
Gardner's suggestions of the following percentage allocations
(Table 8.2)—after numerous different formulas had been
devised and found unacceptable to one or other of the companies involved—was, as Craig had commented to McLintock

TABLE 8.2

*Bruce Gardner's Percentage Allocation of the Share Capital in Three
Possible Scottish Mergers, January 1933*

Colvilles	70·80	75·6	83·4
S.C. of S.	14·15	15·1	16·6
Lanarkshire	8·75	9·3	
Beardmores (Mossend)	6·30		

Source: C. Bruce Gardner to John Craig, 24 Jan. 1933.

[33] C. Bruce Gardner to J. Craig, 27 Feb. 1932.

two years earlier, asking Colvilles to pay too high a price for the rationalization of Scotland's steel industry. Was it then Craig's own obduracy on this point that was preventing the fulfilment of his own vision? In one sense it was. But consider his position. The one-time minor employee of David Colville & Sons now dominated the Scottish steel industry, but fundamentally he believed himself to be simply a trustee of that which had been created by the Colville family. Voluntarily to sacrifice part of this inheritance for whatever object was anathema to him. Furthermore, he felt that the almost desperate appeals for him to do so were both unfair and unjust. Why should the biggest unit make the largest sacrifice, when that unit had become the biggest *because* of its own sheer efficiency?

Colvilles based their claim for an 80 per cent interest in a merger involving the Steel Company and Lanarkshire on the grounds that 'important sections of their plant' belonged to the postwar period and were 'of modern and efficient design'; that 'their costs of production of ingots, plates, and sections [were] substantially lower than those of the other makers; that the relative profits of the 4½-year period ended 31 December 1931 [the McLintock period] more than [justified] the figures claimed', and that their case on this score would be even stronger were the results of developments during 1932 to be taken into account.

Significant developments had, indeed, taken place since the Colville/Dunlop amalgamation. Under Dr. Andrew McCance an intensive effort by Colvilles' technical staff had made it possible for the company to market stainless steel manufactured in

TABLE 8.3

Average Annual Net Profits (excluding Collieries) of the Proposed Scottish Merger Companies for the 4½ Years ended 31 December 1931

	£	
Colvilles	225,244	(86·5 per cent)
S.C. of S.	24,601	(9·5 per cent)
Lanarkshire[a]	10,374	(4·0 per cent)

Note: [a]Four-year period only.
Source: Colvilles Ltd., 'Memorandum to C. Bruce Gardner ...', 30 Dec. 1932.

the open-hearth furnace (Colvilles were the only company in
Britain to have done this successfully), a range of rust- and heat-
resistant steels, and alloy steel for superheater tubes, the whole
of the development expenses of which had been placed against
revenue. Glengarnock had been remodelled during the first half
of 1931, and the first year's working had produced economies
calculated at some £50,000 per annum. Despite diminished
output during the depression, new equipment and reorganization had reduced the wage cost of finished steel by no less than
4s. 7d. a ton at Motherwell, where their cogging mill—the
largest in Europe—had been electrified in order to effect further
economies when it came into operation in January 1933. Long-
term contracts had been entered into with Harland & Wolff
and the Lithgow group whereby these concerns undertook to
draw their entire supplies of steel from Colvilles at ruling market prices. And, of the greatest importance, since the initial
McLintock Report the company's blast furnaces at Clyde Iron
Works—which 'in common with Scottish blast furnaces generally' had been assessed as being obsolete, and of no more than
scrap value—had been modernized, increased in capacity, and
were producing basic pig of excellent quality that yielded a
profit even at the prices ruling in 1932.

Conversely, the Steel Company's claim to 25 per cent was
grossly inflated:[34] even 14 per cent was, Colvilles contended,
more than the profit figures of the past quinquennium would
justify. The Steel Company argued that their profits were unduly depressed because of the losses at Hallside—losses which
would no longer be incurred if Hallside was to be closed down
on the Steel Company's entry into the merger. This was only
partly admitted by Colvilles, who reasoned that the profits at
Blochairn would not have been as high as they were if Hallside
had not been bearing substantial overhead charges. Furthermore, only the continued operations at Hallside permitted the
Steel Company to accept general and mixed orders, including
rails, the price of which had been kept high by the Rail Association.

[34] The clearest statement of the Steel Company's claim is contained in a
'Memorandum by Mr. A. M. Stephen', dated 28 Oct. 1932, appended to
Colvilles Ltd., 'Notes of Meetings with the Steel Company of Scotland', 10
Nov. 1932.

TABLE 8.4

Steel Company of Scotland: Profits (excluding Collieries), before Interest and Depreciation, 1927–1931

Y/e 31 July	Blochairn	Hallside	Houses and Land	Govan Shafting	Total
1928	55,477	−24,158	975	−894	22,859
1929	41,718	−18,764	975	699	23,253
1930	79,153	−32,658	975	608	44,139
1931	38,929	−34,190	527	−1,408	5,713
July–Dec. 1931 (est.)	13,000	−11,500	250	−730	3,820
Annual Average	50,728	−26,949	822	−384	24,218

Source: As Table 8.3.

As for Lanarkshire's claim to 15 per cent, this was quite unreasonable since it was based on carefully selected statistics. Most of their rolling plant was thirty to forty years old; their conversion costs were considerably in excess of those current at Glengarnock; and their melting costs uniquely low in the year chosen to illustrate their claim (1931) because of abnormally cheap scrap (40s. per ton, compared with 67s. per ton basic pig) of which they were able to use a much higher proportion (95 per cent) in their furnace charge than Colvilles and the Steel Company, the nature of whose products precluded them from using more than 70 per cent scrap.[35]

Arguments such as this—and they were repeated, with variations, almost endlessly in innumerable discussions, in internal memoranda, in reports to Bruce Gardner and S.M.T., and in the board minutes of David Colville & Sons and Colvilles Ltd—inhibited further progress towards the rationalization of the Scottish steel industry. However valid, in both a book-keeping and technical sense, these arguments were, Craig's adamant refusal to agree to Colvilles receiving less than 80 per cent of the share capital of a merger company had, by 1933, become the major obstacle to its realization. Craig was conscious that while Colvilles were forging ahead in almost every sphere of operations, the Steel Company and particularly Lanarkshire were

[35] The argument in this, and the proceeding three paragraphs, is based on Colvilles Ltd., 'Memorandum to C. Bruce Gardner on Colvilles' Claim to an 80 per cent Interest in a Merger Company, 30 December 1932'.

declining both relatively and absolutely. In September—after further abortive meetings with directors of the Steel Company, in which they 'kept repeating that nothing less than 21 per cent would meet the situation',[36] and with James Strain of Lanarkshire, who, supported by Lloyds Bank, would countenance no reduction below 15 per cent[37]—Colvilles made one last attempt to keep negotiations with the Steel Company alive. They made what seemed to them to be a major concession. They agreed to a division of the capital between the three companies so that Colvilles received 73·5 per cent, the Steel Company 17·2 per cent, and Lanarkshire 9·3 per cent. It was to no avail.[38] The directors of the Lanarkshire Steel Company would not budge, and by the time this had become clear (December 1933), an important development had taken place which made Colvilles' directors conclude that 'it might be better for all concerned to abandon [the current negotiations] and review the situation a year hence'.[39]

4 Agreement with Stewarts & Lloyds, 1933

A year after it became clear that Stewarts & Lloyds would not permit the merger of their Clydesdale Works with those of the other Scottish steel-makers, they approached Craig with proposals for an agreement whereby Colvilles would undertake to supply their requirements of steel plates, so permitting them to remove their 48-inch Universal plate mill from Clydesdale for use as a blooming mill at their new Corby Works.[40] Sensing a major opportunity to salvage something from the wreck of the original McLintock negotiations, Craig immediately asked Dr. McCance to meet J. Mitchell of Stewarts & Lloyds to see if a price formula, based on the production costs at Clydesdale during the past five years, could be hammered out for adoption as the basis of a long-term agreement between the two

---

[36] John Craig to C. Bruce Gardner, 27 Feb. 1933.
[37] Sir James Lithgow to C. Bruce Gardner, 21 June 1933.
[38] John Craig to C. Bruce Gardner, 14 Sept. 1933; Colvilles Ltd., Board Minutes, 16 Oct. 1933.
[39] C. Bruce Gardner to John Craig, 8 Dec. 1933; John Craig to C. Bruce Gardner, 7 Dec. 1933.
[40] D.C. & S., Minute Book VI, p. 257, 11 Nov. 1932; Scopes, *Corby Works*, p. 86.

companies.[41] Within two months draft heads of an agreement had been drawn up, a remarkable achievement in the light of the commercial and technical complexity of the case.[42] Considerable difficulties remained. They revolved around three major issues. In return for the undertaking by Stewarts & Lloyds to cease all rolling operations at their Clydesdale Works, Colvilles were expected not to manufacture tubes in Britain, nor to sell tubes anywhere without the consent of Stewarts & Lloyds. An undertaking to this effect was regarded by Stewarts & Lloyds as the most important point in the agreement, and Colvilles naturally hesitated to commit themselves on it without the most detailed considerations. Secondly, there was interminable debate about the purchase price to be paid by Colvilles for Stewarts & Lloyds' outside business in plates both at home and for export.[43] Thirdly, Colvilles were anxious to gain some compensation from Stewarts & Lloyds for the fact that they believed that when the Corby plant started manufacturing, Stewarts & Lloyds would make the entire Tube Investments Group self-supporting with regard to tube billets, thereby substantially reducing the tonnage of the tube billets being manufactured and sold by Colvilles who were supplying nearly a quarter of the British tube-makers' requirements at the time (see Table 8.5).[44]

Broad agreement on these and other issues had been reached by May 1933. There was a refreshing element of 'give and take' about the negotiations and if Colvilles still felt themselves in a disadvantageous position on some points they had to remember, as J. Mitchell emphasized, that they were 'achieving concentration of production without having to buy up and close down a rival plant'.[45] By mid-June 1933, after Craig had had further meetings with Macdiarmid and A. G. Stewart, it was all settled. The preliminary agreement was signed on 17

[41] Colvilles Ltd., Board Minutes, 11 Nov. 1932.
[42] J. Craig to A. C. Macdiarmid, 12 Jan. 1933, including 'Draft Heads of Agreement between C. and S. & L.'
[43] That is, the business built up by Stewarts & Lloyds in the manufacture and sale of plates beyond their own internal requirements at Tollcross.
[44] Colvilles Ltd., 'Progress Report on Discussions with Stewarts & Lloyds Ltd., 15 March 1933'; Colvilles Ltd., 'Memorandum on Tube Steel Billets', 30 Dec. 1932.
[45] J. Mitchell to A. McCance, 17 Mar. 1933.

208   *The Turning Point, 1931–1936*

TABLE 8.5

Domestic Deliveries of Tube Steel Billets by the Associated Makers for the Four Years ended 31 March 1931

	Tons	% of total
Colvilles Ltd.	56,028	23·44
Steel, Peech & Tozer Ltd.	30,870	12·91
Steel Company of Scotland Ltd.	16,096	6·73
Dorman Long & Co. Ltd.	1,122	0·47
John Lysaght & Co. Ltd.	15,473	6·47
Lancashire Steel Corp. Ltd.	106,765	44·66
Earl of Dudley's Round Oak Works	12,695	5·31
	239,045	100·00

Source: Colvilles Ltd., 'Memorandum on Tube Steel Billets', 30 Dec. 1932.

October 1933; the formal agreement in March 1934. It was to run for fifteen years.[46] In return for the payment of £12,500, and for agreeing to supply the steel plates required for tubemaking by Stewarts & Lloyds' Scottish works (at a price not higher than the cost Stewarts & Lloyds might have been expected to have incurred had their Clydesdale works remained in operation), Colvilles took over Stewarts & Lloyds' plate business in Scotland and in world export markets, secured an important local outlet for their rolled products (thereby improving the load factor on their most efficient mills), and at last made a positive step towards the rationalization of the Scottish steel industry.[47]

5 Lithgows' Purchase of the Steel Company of Scotland, 1934

His hand thus strengthened, Craig refused to negotiate further with the Steel Company of Scotland. In vain did Bruce

[46] D.C. & S., Minute Book VI, p. 332, 9 Mar. 1934.
[47] This represents a summary of the 'Memorandum of Agreement between Stewarts & Lloyds and Colvilles'. One further point may be made. The price paid by Colvilles for Stewarts & Lloyds' plate business in Scotland and in world export markets was to be paid in five yearly instalments in the form of a reduction in the invoice price of steel supplied. The figure was reached after very hard bargaining. Stewarts & Lloyds had originally asked for

Gardner plead for greater flexibility; in vain did Murray Stephen, of the Steel Company, assert that valuable benefits would accrue to both companies if only Colvilles would be slightly more generous.[48] In April 1934, the almost interminable discussions were brought to an end. There was nothing more to be said.[49] Colvilles, he declared, would proceed to rationalize the Scottish steel industry without further wearisome debate. In April 1934, Colvilles' offer of £100,000 for the Mossend Works was accepted by Beardmores under strong pressure from Securities Management Trust.[50] Then, three months later, Sir James Lithgow, with the aid of C. Bruce Gardner, purchased 49,850 £10 Ordinary shares in the Steel Company of Scotland for £13 10s. each,[51] and immediately made it clear that Colvilles could have the shares for the price that he had paid for them whenever they wished. Craig was

---

£100,000, but calculations by Dr. Andrew McCance completely destroyed Stewarts & Lloyds' case on this point. The essence of this element in the negotiations is contained in Colvilles Ltd., 'Progress Report on Discussions . . ., 15 Mar. 1933'; Colvilles Ltd., Board Minutes, 26 June 1933.

[48] C. Bruce Gardner to J. Craig, 21 Mar. 1934. 'To go back today on your original expression of opinion that a Scottish merger was the right thing will undoubtedly create a bad impression, particularly as, rightly or wrongly, the change of heart will be put down to the beneficial results of tariffs relieving the pressure.'

[49] D.C. & S., Minute Book VI, p. 338, 27 Apr. 1934.

[50] On 6 Dec. 1933, Sir Andrew Duncan had proposed this sale in a memorandum to Montagu Norman. I am indebted to Michael S. Moss and John R. Hume for this information.

Colvilles Ltd., Board Minutes, 7 Mar. 1934, 5 Apr. 1934; D.C. & S., Minute Book VI, 27 Apr. 1934.

[51] The figures were given by Sir James Lithgow in a 'very personal' note to John Craig, 30 Nov. 1934; the acquisition was announced by Sir James Lithgow at D. Colville & Sons' board meeting of 6 July 1934, in the words: 'Mr. Chairman, I've bought you the Steel Company'. Sir Andrew McCance, personal communication to the author. The entire plan whereby Sir James Lithgow was to purchase the Steel Company of Scotland was discussed at length with C. Bruce Gardner during May–June, 1934, and was essentially endorsed by him. The correspondence on the subject makes it clear that Gardner agreed in principle to help Lithgow obtain £650,000 before the end of July 1934, in order to complete the purchase. *Exactly* how the financing of the purchase of the Steel Company of Scotland shares was carried out is, as yet, obscure. Suffice it to say that among the Chairman's (Montagu Norman's) Papers of the Bankers' Industrial Development Co., is a note (folio 457), dated 4 July 1934, which states, laconically, '*Steel Co. of Scotland*. Purchased by Sir James Lithgow: Valuation and negotiations between parties carried out by C. B. G. Offer has been successful.' (Bank of England Archives: S.M.T. 2/56.)

'a little bit piqued at this action'[52] since he felt that too much had been paid for the Steel Company,[53] but Sir James Lithgow was now in a very powerful position. If need be, he could—when the current agreement between the Lithgow Group and Colvilles Ltd. expired in 1938—have acquired the steel supplies required by his shipping interests from the Steel Company and not from Colvilles.[54] He was therefore able to insist that Colvilles Ltd. and the Steel Company develop 'a common policy as regards both output and capital expenditure'.[55] To this end Dr. Andrew McCance was asked to investigate the operations of the Steel Company in order that the performance of its two works at Blochairn and Hallside could be improved (see Table 8.6), and generally to act as if the Steel Company was already within the Colville Group.[56] Furthermore, Sir James was also able to insist that renewed efforts be made to absorb the Lanarkshire Iron & Steel Company.[57]

6 The Public Issue of Shares in Colvilles Ltd., 1936

At the same time as Colvilles withdrew from further negotiations with their fellow steel-makers in the spring of 1934, the problem of David Colville & Sons' 'private loans' was becoming acute. The Moratorium of July 1931, whereby the private cash lenders, the Treasury, and the National Bank of Scotland

[52] John Craig to F. E. Rebbeck, 7 Dec. 1934.

[53] Sir Andrew McCance, personal communication to the author; John Craig to F. E. Rebbeck, 7 Jan. 1935. Somewhat earlier, Sir James Lithgow had told C. Bruce Gardner that, whereas Murray Stephen and S. Turnbull, of the S.C. of S., wanted a minimum of £13 15s. for their shares, he considered them 'worth £10 in the ordinary course, but having regard to the savings which the other steelmakers might effect, £12 10s. [is] my utmost option'. Nevertheless, both Walter Gray and Murray Stephen proved to be 'hard bargainers, not to say greedy'. Sir James Lithgow to C. Bruce Gardner, 4 May 1934, 25 May 1934. Bank of England Archives: B.I.D. I/58.

[54] A fear acknowledged by Craig at the board meeting of D.C. & S., 30 Nov. 1934. Minute Book VI.

[55] Colvilles Ltd., Board Minutes, 26 Dec. 1934; D.C. & S., Minute Book VI, 14 Feb. 1935.

[56] Sir Andrew McCance, personal communication to the author; Colvilles Ltd., Board Minutes, 12 July 1934, 23 Mar. 1935. At Sir James Lithgow's request, Peter Baxter, a director of both Colvilles Ltd. and James Dunlops, joined the board of the Steel Company immediately after Lithgow's purchase of the shares.

[57] D.C. & S., Minute Book VI, 14 Feb. 1935.

TABLE 8.6

Comparative Costs of Similar Products: Colvilles and the Steel Company of Scotland, c. November 1934

Works	Company	Product	Average Cost (per ton)
Dalzell	Colvilles	Acid ingots	88s.
Hallside	S.C. of S.		94s.
Dalzell	Colvilles	Basic ingots	85s.
Hallside	S.C. of S.		88s.
Glengarnock	Colvilles		76s.
			Conversion Costs
Glengarnock	Colvilles	Sections and Rails	20s.
Hallside	S.C. of S.	Rails	28s.
Hallside	S.C. of S.	Sections	34s.
Dalzell	Colvilles	Semi-finished material	12s.
Hallside	S.C. of S.	e.g. wire and tube billets	26s.
Motherwell (No. 2 Bar Mill)	Colvilles		21s. 9d.
Motherwell (No. 1 Guide Mill)	Colvilles	'Fancy and small	35s.
Hallside (No. 4 Mill)	S.C. of S.	sections'	53s.
Hallside (No. 6 Mill)	S.C. of S.		54s.

Note: It is fully recognized that simple comparisons of this kind are, because of varying technical specifications, somewhat misleading. Whatever the inadequacies of the figures, however, they do reveal the much lower costs of Colvilles' operations compared with those of the Steel Company of Scotland.

Source: John Craig to Sir James Lithgow, 8 Feb. 1935, 9 Feb. 1935, based on Hallside Costs Sheets and those of Motherwell and Glengarnock for November 1934.

agreed to suspend the payment of interest and the repayment of principal, had expired on 31 December 1933. Although an extension of the agreement had reluctantly been granted by the cash creditors for a further year, their patient co-operation could not be expected to continue for ever.[58] Furthermore, the interest due on the debt of £1,680,948 represented a potentially crushing burden on the company's resources. The amount owing in interest payments to the cash creditors for the initial moratorium period was nearly a quarter of a million pounds (£229,706), and although occasional sums had been paid out of income to reduce the arrears, it was estimated that by the end of 1934, these alone would still stand at £167,132.[59] Meanwhile, no dividends could be paid on either the company's

[58] The extension to the Moratorium Agreement is clearly documented in D.C. & S., Minute Book VI, 8 Sept. 1933, 13 Oct. 1933, 8 Dec. 1933, 9 Mar. 1934.

[59] The essential figures are drawn from D.C. & S., Minute Book VI, pp. 341–3, 27 Apr. 1934. There is, needless to say, an enormous collection of records on this subject.

Preference or Ordinary capital and the sheer conservatism of the cash creditors tended to inhibit technical progress, since their representatives would agree to sanction only capital expenditure on the most vital and inescapable repairs. It was recognized that the reconstruction of the capital of the company was imperative, but despite feverish efforts during the early months of 1934, no one was able to come up with any universally acceptable scheme.

Yet time was running out. The forbearance of the cash creditors—certainly, the private lenders—could not be expected to survive another year. In the event the seemingly intractable difficulties were eased by the generosity of the National Bank of Scotland who, in June 1934, offered to accept 15 shillings in the pound in full settlement of their overdraft of £662,788,[60] and by the suggestion of Reginald McKenna, Chairman of the Midland Bank, that to provide David Colville & Sons with funds sufficient to discharge its cash indebtedness, it might be possible to dispose of some of the company's holding of Preference shares in Colvilles Ltd. McKenna's own plans for such an operation were rejected by both David Colville, representing the private lenders, and Sir James Lithgow. Instead, an offer by Cazenove, Akroyds, & Greenwood to issue 1,600,000 5½ per

TABLE 8.7

David Colville & Sons Ltd.: Debts Discharged to Cash Creditors, 1934

Date	Cash Creditors	Amount
9 Oct. 1934	National Bank of Scotland	£521,550
17 Oct. 1934	H.M. Treasury	124,669
17 Oct. 1934	Private Cash Lenders	816,549
17 Oct. 1934	Archibald Russell Ltd.	68,383
17 Oct. 1934	Carnlough Lime Co. Ltd.	15,140
	TOTAL	£1,546,291

Source: D.C. & S.: Minute Book VI, 30 Nov. 1934.

[60] D.C. & S., Minute Book VI, p. 347, 8 June 1934. In the event, the settlement resulted in the National Bank forgoing the sum of £165,697 (ibid., p. 385, 30 Nov. 1934). The Treasury would not accept a similar settlement in respect of the balance of the Ministry of Munitions' Loan.

cent Preference shares in Colvilles Ltd. to the public at 20*s.*
6*d.*, and to underwrite the issue for a commission of 1*s.* 1½*d.* per
share, was accepted. The issue took place in October,[61] and the
day after allotment David Colville & Company's cash loans
with all arrears of interest were repaid. A stultifying burden
was at last lifted from John Craig's shoulders. Whatever difficulties might be involved in public ownership of Colvilles'
cumulative Preference shares, it was improbable that they
would prove more onerous than the company's indirect dependence on a number of powerful private lenders.

7 The Final Stages of Rationalization, 1935–1936

The way was now clear to complete the process of rationalizing
the Scottish steel industry. Sir William McLintock and R.
McKenna, who as voting trustees of the Royal Mail Steam
Packet Company represented the main Ordinary shareholders
of David Colville & Sons, proposed to increase the Ordinary
share capital of Colvilles Ltd., publicly float the shares, and
with the proceeds purchase the subsidiaries of David Colville
& Sons, the Steel Company of Scotland, and eventually, it was
hoped, Lanarkshire.[62] Morgan Grenfell & Co. were prepared
to handle the issue; the Lithgows expressed their consent.[63] The

---

[61] Ibid., pp. 370–3, 25 Sept. 1934.
[62] Colvilles Ltd., Board Minutes, 31 May 1935. Sir William McLintock
said later 'You will appreciate my main interest in the matter is that the cutting of this particular knot by a realization of the Royal Mail Group Companies' interest in David Colville & Sons Ltd. will be of great assistance in
dealing with the reconstruction of Harland & Wolff's finances ...' Sir
William McLintock to John Craig, 26 June 1935.
[63] Not without some reservations. Sir James Lithgow was strongly in favour
of creating some Debentures 'so as to get the advantage of cheap money'.
Craig would have none of it, and he was supported by McLintock, '... a
great deal of the trouble and difficulties which have beset steel companies
in the past arose from ... creating large amounts of prior charge securities'.
John Craig to Sir William McLintock, 25 May 1935, Sir William McLintock
to John Craig, 27 May 1935. Lithgow's argument puzzled Craig, who was
vehemently against debentures, as was Rebbeck of Harland & Wolff. Not
until it became clear that the Lithgows were concerned with their power to
influence Colvilles' future policy was their attitude explicable. The issue of
debentures would reduce the volume of Ordinary shares necessitated by the
merger, thereby increasing the power attached to the Lithgows' existing and future holding of Colvilles Ordinary shares. John Craig to F. E.
Rebbeck, 1 June 1935.

plan involved creating an additional 1,500,000 Ordinary £1 shares in Colvilles Ltd. and selling 3,100,000 Ordinary shares to the public at the price of 29 shillings per share. The offer was made in March 1936 by the Midland Bank on behalf of Morgan Grenfell.[64] The issue was heavily over-subscribed.

It was now possible to purchase the Ordinary share capital of Smith & McLean, the Clyde Alloy Steel Company, Fullwood Foundry, and the Carnlough Lime Company—David Colville & Sons' subsidiaries—and the Steel Company of Scotland.[65] Only one obstacle stood in the way of Colvilles' virtually complete domination of Scotland's steel industry: the recalcitrance of the holders of the Ordinary shares of the Lanarkshire Iron & Steel Company.[66] They soon capitulated. Within a few days of Colvilles' public issue, Sir William McLintock learned from Sir Harry Peat that J. M. Strain and J. H. Stephens were prepared to negotiate the exchange of the entire Ordinary share

[64] The arrangements for the amalgamation and the sale of the Ordinary shares are outlined in detail in Colvilles Ltd., Board Minutes, 28 Feb. 1936. Morgan Grenfell acquired the 3,100,000 shares in Colvilles Ltd. at a price of 27s. 5d. Craig's private opinion is interesting: 'Quite frankly, one wishes that we could have carried a transaction like this through as a Company instead of selling our shares to Financiers, but I am afraid that this has gone too far and that Mr. Hyde and McLintock are now definitely committed to Morgan Grenfell.' John Craig to F. E. Rebbeck, 28 Dec. 1935. Craig's attitude was coloured by the fact that 'McLintock ... wanted to ... put a minimum price of 25s. net to the seller and was going to limit the price to the public to 27s. 6d. ... We were unanimous ... that, if the price to the public was to be 27s. 6d., then we would not sell at 25s.: in other words, that to ask for 2s. 6d. a share was ridiculous. It represented a sum of over £400,000.' Ibid., 27 Dec. 1935.

[65] The Lithgow brothers made a considerable profit on the sale of their Steel Company shares to Colvilles Ltd. As early as December 1935, Sir William McLintock 'had definitely made up his mind to offer 650,000 Colville shares to the Lithgows for the Steel Company of Scotland'. Craig argued that the Lithgows were not entitled to such a price, but he had to agree to the scheme, which was supported by Hyde of the Midland Bank. 'If it goes through', Craig wrote to Rebbeck, 'it is a very big bargain to Lithgow and I told him so.' (J. Craig to F. E. Rebbeck, 27 Dec. 1935.) The Lithgows had purchased the Steel Co. shares for £672,975 (49,850 £10 Ordinary shares at £13 10s. each); for these they received 650,000 Ordinary shares in Colvilles Ltd. which at the time of the arrangement had a market valuation of £956,750 (650,000 at £1 9s. 6d.). The entire profit was given to religious bodies in Scotland. Sir Andrew McCance in a personal communication to the author.

[66] The legal position was somewhat complicated, but at this time Sir Harry Peat and J. H. Stephens were Trustees of the First Debenture Holders of Workman, Clark & Co., holders of the Ordinary shares of Lanarkshire.

capital of Lanarkshire for an allotment of 155,000 Ordinary shares in Colvilles Ltd., and to arrange with the holders of at least half of Lanarkshire's 6 per cent Preference shares to exchange their shares for an equal number of Colvilles' $5\frac{1}{2}$ per cent Preference shares.[67] Craig was not impressed. He demanded information concerning Lanarkshire's current costs of production, and when this was not forthcoming commissioned a detailed investigation of the financial and technical position of the company.[68] This made it clear that the Lanarkshire shares were not worth the 155,000 Ordinary shares in Colvilles Ltd. demanded by the sellers. A counter offer was made: 130,000 Ordinary shares in Colvilles' for the total Ordinary share capital of Lanarkshire consisting of 100,000 £1 shares fully paid and 100,000 £1 shares, 17 shillings paid.[69] The offer was accepted.[70] With Colvilles' shares standing at about 33 shillings, it was worth approximately £215,000.[71]

The acquisition of Lanarkshire brought an end to negotiations that had their genesis in 1923, when the unfortunate Invernairn had called a meeting of his fellow steel-makers to examine the possibility of a Scottish merger. John Craig's sheer tenacity had, in the words of Sir William McLintock, 'achieved what no other district has done, ... the consolidation and rationalization of the Steel Industry in Scotland'.[72] John Craig's own view, expressed in a letter to David Colville, was that 'I hope we can now get a rest from further expansion, although it means that we shall have a busy time trying to improve the plant both at the Steel Company and

---

[67] Sir William McLintock to John Craig, 19 Mar. 1936.
[68] Colvilles Ltd., 'Memorandum on The Lanarkshire Steel Company Limited', 8 Apr. 1936.
[69] John Craig to J. R. Maskell, of Lescher Stephens & Co., Receiver for the First Debenture Holders of Workman, Clark & Co., 12 June 1936.
[70] J. R. Maskell to John Craig, 25 June 1936. As a further illustration of the labyrinthine nature of the whole long-drawn-out business, it was not discovered until mid-June that the actual owners of Lanarkshire's Ordinary shares were the British Canadian and General Investment Co. John Craig to Sir William McLintock, 12 June 1936; John Craig to Sir Andrew Duncan, 12 June 1936.
[71] Maclay, Murray & Spens to Colvilles Ltd., 15 July 1936.
[72] Sir William McLintock to John Craig, 16 June 1936. Sir Andrew Duncan echoed these words: 'I am glad to think that Scotland has now so completely led the way in consolidation of interests.' Sir Andrew Duncan to John Craig, 13 June 1936.

Lanarkshire, as well as what we still require to do in our own Works'.[73]

8 Capital Investment, 1931–1936

In the latter part of 1936, the situation facing Colvilles' board was in some ways comparable with that which faced John Craig and his colleagues in 1920. A further untidy collection of productive assets had been acquired: it was now necessary to weld them together into an efficient steel-producing complex. This posed problems of control, the optimum allocation of orders between works of different capability, capacity, and efficiency, and the acquisition and distribution of raw materials. Such problems were not new; they were simply bigger than those that had confronted the firm in the past and harder to solve. Their solution was, moreover, made more difficult by the severe slump through which the industry had recently passed. In the early thirties there had been little surplus for the improvement of plant and the exploitation of long-term technical and market possibilities. The board of Colvilles Ltd.—which, since the company's incorporation in 1931, had been composed of four directors nominated by David Colville & Sons (John Craig, John Lennox, David Colville, and Dr. Andrew McCance), the Lithgow brothers, and Peter Baxter—did everything possible to keep all the works 'adequately maintained', but severe financial constraints inhibited radical modernization. Not the least of these was the albatross of the cash creditors. In 1931 their grip on the company's finances had been rendered even stronger by the Moratorium: if the trustees had been suspicious of the investment of retained profits before, now that the incomes that the founder's kinsfolk derived from the various trusts had temporarily ceased, they tended to be even more difficult to convince of the necessity of all but the most vital repairs.

Thus Dr. McCance, who since the retirement of G. P. West in 1930 had been the outstanding 'technical' member of the board, had to employ most devious means to effect improvements. In doing so he was given invaluable assistance by Colvilles' chief mechanical and electrical engineers, T. W. Hand

[73] John Craig to David Colville, 12 June 1936.

and Lambert Rothera.[74] Hand and Rothera became expert in refurbishing second-hand engines, for the original installation of many of which they had been responsible. In one such case, McCance's plans called for a particular engine of 1,500–1,600 horsepower capacity. The purchase price of a new engine of this type was about £20,000, but Rothera knew that Mond Nickel was about to dispose of one. Indeed, he had installed it while Plant Sales Manager with English Electric. He was authorized to offer an almost derisory £500 for it and was, not unexpectedly, 'shown the door'. William Muir, of Colvilles' subsidiary the Motherwell Machinery & Scrap Company, subsequently bought the equipment for 'scrap' for £350. It was brought to Motherwell, completely reconditioned, and commissioned at Glengarnock. The cash creditors knew nothing of the transaction.[75] By such stratagems, every effort was made 'to ensure that the Company [would] be in a position to take full advantage of any revival in trade'.[76]

Some notable improvements were made at Glengarnock, the rolling mill for the production of sections was remodelled, and new plant for the production of steel sleepers brought into operation in an effort to force down the cost of production.[77] At Dalzell, the boiler range providing the motive power for the cogging mill was replaced by an electrified drive utilizing

[74] T. W. Hand's technical training was undertaken as an apprentice of William Jessop's in Sheffield and at the Sheffield Technical School. Subsequently he joined the technical staff of Davy Brothers Ltd., becoming Chief Engineer in 1915, a position he held until joining Colvilles as Chief Mechanical Engineer in 1930. While with Davy Brothers he was responsible for the design and construction of steel works plant throughout the world: in almost every European country, Canada, America, and, in his younger days, in Tsarist Russia. Among British specialists in this field, his experience was probably unique. He first impressed himself on John Craig through his work on the Clydebridge three-high plate mill. L. Rothera was an engineering student at Nottingham University College graduating with a London University external B.Sc. honours degree. He then became an apprentice with Siemens Bros. and after two years specialized in rolling mill drives and installations. From 1908 to 1928, when he joined David Colville & Sons, he was responsible for much pioneering work at Siemens and English Electric which fostered the use of electricity in steel works and metal rolling mills in Great Britain and abroad. *Colvilles' Magazine*, January–February 1947, pp. 12–13.

[75] Sir Andrew McCance, personal communication.

[76] The words quoted are from the Directors' Report for 1931.

[77] Report by Dr. Andrew McCance to John Craig, 'Glengarnock Works Sleeper Plant', 15 July 1931. It was expected that the new sleeper plant would reduce costs by 8 shillings a ton, or by some 45 per cent.

equipment purchased for £8,000 from the English Steel Corporation's Penistone Steel Works. It was estimated that new plant of similar quality and capacity would have cost £40,000. Colvilles were able to install the Penistone equipment in 1932 and make a whole series of consequential improvements for just over half that sum and recoup the total expenditure in reduced costs of production in approximately three to four years.[78] In the following year the 18-inch Merchant Mill was reconstructed and a comprehensive scheme for the modernization of No. 2 Plate Mill authorized. It was estimated that these changes would permit a reduction of no fewer than 65 men per shift at the mill and a much lower coal consumption per ton of plate output. It was believed that these economies would amount to approximately 28 per cent of the capital cost of the reconstruction even at the abnormally depressed production levels of 1932–3; in the event, the entire scheme had probably paid for itself within two years.

But perhaps the most significant development in the early thirties was the decision to reconstruct the blast furnaces at Clyde Iron. The genesis of this scheme went back to 1931, when Dr. McCance put forward a scheme to utilize the 40,000 tons of iron ore at Clyde Iron[79] which were inherited from James Dunlops.[80] But action on this and subsequent recommendations was inhibited by the endless negotiations with William Baird & Company, the massive capital cost (estimated at £720,000 in 1932), the depth of the depression, and the ready availability of imported pig iron[81] at abnormally low prices. Instead, piecemeal alterations—based on experimental work by Dr. McCance and David K. Glass—were authorized. These were designed to improve the efficiency of the blast furnaces at Clyde Iron and reduce costs so dramatically that the expense of the

[78] Colvilles Ltd., Board Meetings, Agendas and Papers, memoranda by Dr. A. McCance and by L. Rothera and T. W. Hand on the Electrification of Dalzell Cogging Mill, dated 18 Dec. 1931, and 7 July 1932. The period required to recoup the total capital expenditure in 'savings' has been calculated on facts presented in the above memoranda and the known output of Dalzell in the ensuing years.

[79] Colvilles Ltd., Board Meetings, Agendas, and Papers, Memorandum on 'Proposed New Blast Furnaces', by Dr. A. McCance, 5 Nov. 1931.

[80] Sir Andrew McCance, personal communication.

[81] See above, p. 181.

modifications would be rapidly recouped. It was also recognized that the alterations would make a useful contribution to any future, more radical, scheme of reorganization.[82] Thus at the close of 1932 Clyde Iron was producing high quality basic pig at a cost of around 53*s*. 2*d*. per ton (compared with the current market price for English iron of 58*s*. and for Indian pig of 58*s*. 6*d*.) with a coke consumption of just under 20 cwt per ton. More important, invaluable experience had been gained in iron production, John Craig's belief that blast furnaces could not be profitably operated in Scotland[83] proved groundless, and invaluable lessons learned in the practical difficulties of operating an integrated works.

During the first three years of the Colville/Dunlop regime, the Board had authorized capital expenditure of £210,000. With the sluggish revival of trade in 1934, it was decided to develop the production of semi-finished products and joists (part of the necessary plant coming from Mossend) at Glengarnock, and to raise the output of pig iron at Clyde Iron—by the reconstruction of another furnace—to 4,000 tons per week[84] (the surplus gas being destined for Clydebridge). But not until 1935–6 did the pace of capital expenditure really quicken (see Table 8.8). In February 1935 it was agreed to install a fast-running mill at Dalzell for the manufacture of small-diameter bars and the rolling of wire rod. Despite the fact that the engines for the finishing drive were purchased for only £6,000 from Palmers of Jarrow (they were probably worth about £80,000) and that much of the ancillary plant was moved from Beardmores' Mossend Works, the capital cost was relatively heavy (approximately £91,000), but this, it was believed, would be

[82] Colvilles Ltd., Board Meetings, Agendas, and Papers, 'Clyde Iron Works', 16 Mar. 1933; Report on Position at Works, 24 June 1933; Board Minutes, 20 Mar. 1933. The modifications to the Clyde Iron blast furnaces were partially determined by an attempt to make their dimensions conform as closely as possible to the blast furnace erected by Fords at Dagenham, the plans for which Fords lent to Dr. McCance, who had long been responsible for certain of their requirements of special steels. In the work involved Dr. McCance was greatly assisted by David K. Glass, the chief engineer at Clyde Iron. Sir Andrew McCance: personal communication, and see *Colvilles' Magazine*, xxiii (April 1942), 52.
[83] Colvilles Ltd., 'Proposals Regarding Blast Furnaces of Clyde Iron Works', 20 Sept. 1932.
[84] Colvilles Ltd., Board Minutes, 5 Apr. 1934.

TABLE 8.8

Colvilles Ltd.: Major Items of Capital Expenditure, January 1931– December 1937

Works	Year and Month Authorized	Brief Description	Amount Authorized
Dalzell	1932 July	Electrification of Cogging Mill	23,000
	1933 Sept.	18-inch Merchant Mill	8,000
	1933 Nov.	General Reconstruction	54,100
	1933 Dec.	No. 4 Bar Mill Heating Furnace	11,000
	1935 Jan.	Electric Supply	13,500
	1935 Feb.	Rod & Bar Mill	91,000
	1936 Jan.	No. 4 Bar Mill Conversion	55,000
	1936 Apr.	No. 2 Cogging Mill Ingot Soaker	12,000
	1936 May	Transporter Type Gantry Crane	11,000
	1936 Nov.	No. 2 Plate Mill Drive	18,000
		Total authorized in major schemes:	£296,600
Glengarnock	1931 Jan.	No. 3 Bar Mill Reconstruction	28,900
	1931 July	Sleeper Plant	10,000
	1935 June	Alterations at No. 3 Bar Mill	240,000
	1936 Feb.	Two Furnaces	44,000
	1936 Oct.	Two Roller Straightening Machines	18,000
		Total authorized in major schemes:	£340,900
Clydebridge	1933 Nov.	Slitting Machine	15,200
	1934 Feb.	Hydraulic Service and Blanking Press	7,700
	1936 June	Cogging Mill Plant	12,840
	1936 Nov.	New Plate Mill from Dorman Long	28,000
		Total authorized in major schemes:	£63,740
Clyde Iron	1932 Oct.	Blast Furnaces	13,500
	1934 Feb.	Gas Cleaning Plant	30,000
	1934 Nov.	Power Station	27,900
	1935 Oct.	New Blast Furnace Stoves	20,000
	1937 Jan.	Two New Blast Furnace Stoves	25,000
	1937 May	Pig Casting Machines	40,000
	1937 July	Bridge over River Clyde	30,000
	1937 Dec.	Fabricated Steelwork at Coke Oven & Blast Furnace Scheme	14,000
		Total authorized in major schemes:	£200,400

Actual expenditure on completed schemes, all works, 1 Jan. 1931–31 Dec. 1937:	£1,196,636
Actual expenditure on schemes not yet complete by 31 Dec. 1937:	102,960
Total Capital Expenditure:	£1,299,596
Estimated expenditure required to complete schemes authorized, 1 Jan. 1931–31 Dec. 1937:	136,767
Total sum committed in capital expenditure, 1 Jan. 1931–31 Dec. 1937:	£1,436,363

Source: Colvilles Ltd., Periodic Statements on 'Expenditure on Plant Schemes', Board Meetings, Agendas and Papers.

TABLE 8.9

Colvilles Ltd.: Consigned Tonnage per Man Employed at Dalzell, Clydebridge, Glengarnock, and Clyde Iron Works, 1930–1939

Year	Dalzell			Clydebridge			Glengarnock			Three Steel Works Combined			Clyde Iron Works		
	Av. No. of Men Employed	Consigned Tonnage	Av. Ton. per Man	Av. No. of Men Employed	Consigned Tonnage	Av. Ton. per Man	Av. No. of Men Employed	Consigned Tonnage	Av. Ton. per Man	Av. No. of Men Employed	Consigned Tonnage	Av. Ton. per Man	Av. No. of Men Employed	Consigned Tonnage	Av. Ton. per Man
1930	2,275	153,573	67·50	850	137,690	161·99	1,194	100,204	83·92	4,319	391,467	90·64	n.a.	n.a.	—
1931	1,778	104,809	58·95	636	87,392	137·41	844	65,267	77·33	3,258	257,467	79·03	208	55,152	265·15
1932	1,418	90,303	63·68	507	83,521	164·74	610	52,858	86·65	2,535	226,682	89·42	169	55,814	330·26
1933	1,528	114,475	74·92	705	108,816	154·35	713	82,130	115·19	2,946	305,421	103·67	302	88,238	292·18
1934	2,182	196,087	89·87	905	231,805	256·14	774	129,187	166·91	3,861	557,079	144·28	356	90,640	254·61
1935	2,231	219,656	98·46	958	232,824	243·03	821	146,349	178·26	4,010	598,829	149·33	356	120,739	339·15
1936	2,497	280,831	112·47	1,137	276,293	245·16	1,173	183,679	156·59	4,807	740,801	154·11	402	139,319	346·56
1937	2,776	365,919	131·82	1,141	297,729	260·94	1,293	227,396	175·87	5,210	891,044	171·03	444	154,802	348·65
1938	2,567	301,539	117·47	1,067	249,863	234·18	1,060	213,372	201·29	4,694	764,774	162·93	612	121,449	198·45
1939	3,354	333,284	99·37	1,320	259,557	196·63	1,222	284,168	232·54	5,896	877,009	148·75	622	122,777	197·39

Notes and Sources: 'Average number of men employed': The figure given is the average of the numbers employed at the various works during the last full week of each month in each calendar year where these statistics are provided in the 'Board Meeting Papers' or the 'Weekly Reports'.
'Consigned Tonnage': Colvilles Ltd., Output Statistics, Board Agendas and Papers, 1930–9. Since the object of the table is to give a crude measure of labour productivity, it was believed that the 'consigned tonnage' figure could provide a somewhat more realistic idea than the figure for 'ingot output' since the former might be expected to be the product of a larger proportion of the total labour force.
During the year 1930, the steel works were owned not by Colvilles Ltd. but by D. C. & S., and Clyde Iron Works by James Dunlop & Co.

offset by very low labour requirements. In June no less than £240,000 was committed to the creation of a new sheet, bar and billet mill at Glengarnock.[85] Then, in December, a carefully phased plan for further increasing the production of pig iron at Clyde Iron was submitted to the Board by Dr. McCance. In addition to the completion of plans already sanctioned, it envisaged the building of a new furnace with full ancillary equipment possessing a daily capacity of 400 tons and the complete remodelling of the ore-handling plant. By these and other means, production at Clyde Iron could be raised to 4,900 tons per week in 1937. A sketch of how a weekly output of 6,500 tons could be achieved was also put forward, this being the final stage in the long-term plan. The overall scheme recommended the grading of coke and the sintering of fine ores (which, it was observed, had permitted a marked economy in coke consumption at Corby and at Fords) and the construction of a bridge across the Clyde to permit hot metal working at Clydebridge.[86]

This was the major legacy of the Colville/Dunlop merger to Colvilles, the public company. Through a period of intense depression, of cruelly disheartening under-capacity working, and of seemingly endless negotiations, Craig, his old colleagues, and the Lithgow brothers, had by judicious capital expenditure kept the works in good heart, raised labour productivity (see Table 8.9), forced down conversion costs, and ultimately provided a blueprint for the future. Retrospective critics making comparisons with best international practice may belittle their efforts. They may point with scorn at the utilization of second-hand equipment purchased at scrap prices from those who went to the wall, and castigate Colvilles' short-term policy of determining priorities with reference to the time span required to recoup plant expenditure, but the Scottish steel industry— the future of which Bruce Gardner regarded with such well-founded pessimism in the early thirties—had at least survived. It was no mean achievement.

[85] Colvilles Ltd., Board Minutes, 24 June 1935.
[86] Colvilles Ltd., Board Meetings, Agendas and Papers, 'The Development of Pig Iron Output at Clyde Iron Works', undated, but considered at Board Meeting of 26 Dec. 1935.

PART IV

Recovery and war again

IX

Revival, 1936–1939

1 The New Environment

The concentration of the Scottish steel industry had taken place within an economic environment that was never less than sickly. The output of the industry reached its nadir in 1932; thereafter began a drawn-out revival which persisted until 1937 but so deep had been the depression that in its early stages the upswing is comparable more with the transference of a patient from the critical list to intensive care than the subsequent transition from sickness to convalescence. Certainly, the patient did not feel appreciably better until 1935, when the majority of the surviving furnaces and rolling mills were operating at around 85–95 per cent of what was deemed to be 'normal production' (see Table 9.1). Not until 1936 were the Directors' Reports of Colvilles at all optimistic: perhaps the fruits of rationalization were to be harvested.

There were other reasons for hopefulness. While Craig was engaged in apparently interminable negotiations with his immediate neighbours, the entire British steel industry had been undergoing a sort of transformation. Scotland may have 'led the way in the consolidation of interests', but other districts were slowly conforming to Bruce Gardner's plan.[1] They may not have done so with any enthusiasm but they had little option. Largely as a consequence of what in retrospect seems an almost suicidal prodigality of debenture and fixed interest bearing issues in the immediate postwar boom, by the late twenties nominees of the Bank of England, the clearing and merchant banks, and other financial institutions of the City either completely controlled or had attained an extremely powerful position in the conduct of the majority of iron and steel firms in Great Britain. Richard Thomas, John Summers, Dorman Long, South Durham, and Lancashire Steel had become prisoners of the financiers. This was quite fortuitous. The bankers

[1] See above, p. 195.

TABLE 9.1

Colvilles Ltd.: Percentage of 'Normal Production' Achieved in Furnace and Mill Outputs, and Average Number of Men Employed, during the Month of March, 1931–1939[a]

Output	No. of weeks ending: 4 / 28 Mar. 1931	5 / 2 Apr. 1932	5 / 1 Apr. 1933	4 / 31 Mar. 1934	4 / 30 Mar. 1935	4 / 28 Mar. 1936	5 / 3 Apr. 1937	5 / 2 Apr. 1938	5 / 1 Apr. 1939
Ingots (Dalzell, Glengarnock, and Clydebridge)	56·6	39·5	39·0	80·6	83·5	104·9	111·8	115·3	103·8
Dalzell Mills (No. 2 Plate, No. 4 Bar, No. 1 Guide, No. 2 Merchant, and No. 5 Guide Mills [No. 5 Guide Mill replaced by No. 5 Rod Mill in 1937])	50·9	37·4	40·4	70·4	91·0	84·7	93·7	105·0	70·3
Glengarnock Mill No. 3[b]	54·9	49·0	61·7	98·3	107·2	118·1	109·5	91·1	87·1
Clydebridge Mill No. 3	38·2	26·0	28·5	81·7	89·4	96·5	102·1	112·1	103·2
No. of Men Employed (All Works)	4,226	3,190	3,009	4,431	4,520	5,220	5,911	6,125	5,724

Notes:

[a] The phrase 'Normal Production' is first encountered in the records of the company in 1931. It is nowhere defined, but it clearly implies some concept of the output that past experience and/or the rated capacity of the plant suggest might be expected from the melting furnaces and the rolling mills. The periods chosen for this illustration have been determined by an attempt to 'cover' the month of March in each of the years 1931–9. There is nothing significant about the choice of this month other than the fact that it is one in which production appears not to have been influenced by holidays.

[b] The figures for 1938 and 1939 for Glengarnock Mill No. 3 are not absolutely comparable with those for the preceding years since a very minor proportion of the output of rolled products at Glengarnock was produced at No. 2 Mill during 1938 and 1939. The figures are not disaggregated.

Source: Colvilles Ltd., Output Statistics, Board Agendas and Papers, 1931–9.

appear to have been acutely embarrassed by the turn of events which gave them control of the iron and steel industry. They were at a loss to know what to do. They could, it is clear, have forced radical reconstruction upon the entire industry. This they were reluctant to do. Such a policy was quite foreign to their principles. But in the end the banks had to face the consequences of their past policies and it may be assumed that the majority of leading bankers were quite prepared, even relieved, to take their cue from Montagu Norman, who, when the full story is told, will be seen to have orchestrated much of what reconstruction and reorganization was achieved.[2] Working through Bruce Gardner and his other advisers in the Bank, Norman instigated far-reaching changes throughout the industry, often by putting pressure on the City's financial institutions. Norman, more than any other single person, knew what was going on in the nation's heavy industries.[3] To Sir Andrew McCance, it always seemed a great pity that C. Bruce Gardner, Norman's chosen instrument, was far 'too gentle' a person fully to employ his potential power to enforce more radical reconstruction.[4] Be that as it may, subtle moves were being made to resuscitate iron and steel, and with each development the likelihood of greater co-operation between regions, product associations, and individual firms was increased. This could not fail to ensure greater prosperity for Colvilles and the Scottish branch of the industry.

If the banks worked behind closed doors, other more observable factors were at work to ensure a similar result. Although the Safeguarding of Industries Act of 1921 was largely a dead letter throughout the twenties, the anguished cries of the steelmakers for protection were about to be answered. Following the overwhelming victory of the pro-tariff National Government in 1931, relief from foreign 'dumping' was at hand. With the passage of the Import Duties Act in 1932—which provided for a general duty of 10 per cent *ad valorem* on a wide range

[2] See, particularly, Hume and Moss's study of Beardmores.

[3] He was, for example, in constant contact with Sir James Lithgow concerning the state of shipbuilding. There are many hints of this among the Colville archives but, more explicitly, in the records of Beardmores and the Securities Management Trust. I am indebted to Mr. Michael Moss for valuable information on this matter.

[4] Sir Andrew McCance, personal communication.

of imported manufactured goods—and the creation of an Import Duties Advisory Committee, among whose tasks it was to recommend the imposition of higher duties where these were adjudged to be necessary and desirable, a potent weapon was placed in the hands of the government to further the reorganization of the iron and steel industry.

In its first recommendations on steel, which became effective in April 1932, the Import Duties Advisory Committee proposed that for an initial three-month period, the duties on railway material, tubes, wire, and a number of other of highly-finished products should be raised to 20 per cent, and that duties on all semis, heavy and light sections, and all forms of plates and sheet should be $33\frac{1}{3}$ per cent. Any continuance of these duties was, however, to be conditional upon 'satisfactory progress being made in the preparation of a scheme of reorganization and in putting the approved scheme into force'.[5] More specifically, the reorganization was to take the form of limiting capacity, greater co-operation between firms, and some form of closer link with overseas cartels. Sir George May, the chairman of the Committee, suggested that these objectives might best be achieved by the creation of a National Committee charged with the responsibility of formulating a reorganization plan.

The subsequent history of the reconstruction movement in the iron and steel industry[6] has been succinctly described as 'largely a record of repeated threats by the Government and the May Committee, of successive promises by the National Committee of the industry, and of the near breakdown of the reorganization programme in spite of the apparently sincere efforts on the part of the National Committee to fulfil its obligations'.[7] Two years elapsed before the National Committee produced a constitution for what had originally been intended to be a greatly strengthened Federation. Castigated by nearly everyone, given but lukewarm approval by the May Committee, and adopted without enthusiasm by the members of the

[5] Import Duties Advisory Committee, *Recommendations and Additional Import Duties (No. 8) Order 1932* (Cmd. 4181), p. 5.

[6] The details have been carefully set down by Carr and Taplin, *History of the British Steel Industry*, pp. 495–508.

[7] A. F. Lucas, *Industrial Reconstruction and the Control of Competition: The British Experiments* (London: Longmans, 1937), pp. 111–12.

National Federation (the voting was 90 in favour, 24 against,
and 79 abstentions), the new constitution was accepted and the
British Iron and Steel Federation brought into being in April
1934. Had it not been for the fact that the constitution provided for an 'independent chairman' for its Executive Committee, and that the man selected for this new post was Sir
Andrew Rae Duncan, vice-chairman of Securities Management Trust, the British Iron and Steel Federation might have
been a complete fiasco, confirming the complaints of those
critics who condemned the scheme as being little more than
a continuance of the old National Federation.[8] Under Duncan,
who took office in January 1935, the British Iron and Steel
Federation was gradually to assume the role intended for it by
Sir George May; that is, a powerful central body exercising
supervision of a group of strong affiliated associations through
a system of binding agreements regarding prices, quotas,
and loyalty rebates.[9] Within a few months of Duncan's
appointment, arrangements had been made with the European
Steel Cartel to set rigid limits to the volume of sales that both
British and continental producers might make in each other's
territories and to secure a 'fair' share of world markets for
British steel-makers.[10]

2 Expansion: Problems and Opportunities

In contrast with the depressing environment into which Colvilles Ltd. was born, the timing of the culmination of the consolidation movement in Scotland could hardly have been more
favourable. Now that the British iron and steel industry had

[8] It is significant that one of Duncan's major supporters was Montagu Norman. Carr and Taplin, *History of the British Steel Industry*, p. 503.
[9] How this transformation was achieved is explained by Carr and Taplin,
History of the British Steel Industry, pp. 503 ff.; and see B. S. Keeling and
A. E. Wright, *The Development of the Modern British Steel Industry* (London:
Longmans, 1964), pp. 9–23.
[10] For the details, see Carr and Taplin, *History of the British Steel Industry*,
pp. 520–4. It is worth noting that in order to carry out its agreement with
the Cartel, the Federation was obliged to exert strict control over the various
sectors of the steel industry. This greatly strengthened the Federation, since
as each section of the industry was to share in the total export quota, and
as the Federation determined the share of each, it was given a strong weapon
to enforce compliance with its policies. This point was made by A. F. Lucas,
Industrial Reconstruction, p. 119.

secured what the *Manchester Guardian* called 'a potential stranglehold' on the home market,[11] and Colvilles had all but monopolized the Scottish market, the question was, would the industry fulfil its responsibilities? In the long run, organizational change and protection could be justified only if there took place an improved economic response to mounting domestic demand. This home demand was created by rapidly-developing new industries, boom conditions experienced by the building sector, and the direct and indirect effects of rearmament.[12] Of these factors, the initial stimulus in Scotland was provided by the building boom. It was said, for example, that 'a decision of the Glasgow Corporation to build 20,000 houses is worth more to the steel industry than a Clyde order for a *Queen Mary*'.[13] And although Clyde launchings had been rising since 1933, the total tonnage which went down the slipways in 1936 was undramatic (see Table 6.4). Naval building resulting from the rearmament programme of 1935, did not reach the plating stage until the close of 1936, and rearmament did not apparently have a significant effect on Colvilles' output until 1937.[14] It is certain that Clyde Alloy did well out of the growing prosperity of motor-car and aircraft manufacture, and Smith & McLean benefited from the massive increase in galvanized sheet requirements, but for general steel products building construction constituted one of the biggest boosts.[15]

Colvilles were quick to take advantage of these opportunities, and new productive capacity at Motherwell, Glengarnock, and Clydebridge was pushed ahead. Even more important, Dr. McCance urged the board to raise the production of pig iron at Clyde Iron to 6,000 tons per week, and once again pressed for the construction of a bridge across the Clyde to permit hot

[11] *Manchester Guardian*, 10 June 1935, quoted Lucas, *Industrial Reconstruction*, p. 119.

[12] The influence of these various factors is outlined by Burn, *Economic History of Steel Making*, pp. 466–7.

[13] *Glasgow Herald Trade Review*, 28 Dec. 1937.

[14] The figures are difficult to interpret, but this is the impression created by the archival material. There is little question that structural steel was used in the construction of factories, workshops, and aircraft hangars, but it is impossible to disaggregate this from the steel used for dwellings.

[15] Colvilles Constructional Co., specializing in welded structural work, did well, and Dalzell benefited from the vastly increased demand by Stewarts & Lloyds for tube strip. John Craig's statement to the annual general meeting, 9 Mar. 1936, and see the *Financial Times*, 25 Apr. 1936.

metal working at Clydebridge.[16] In July 1936, within weeks of his carefully-argued case, a pipeline for conveying blast furnace gas from Clyde Iron to Clydebridge had been put into operation.[17] But expansion had hardly begun before severe supply constraints were encountered. McCance's ambitious plans for Clyde Iron/Clydebridge 'could only be effective provided [Colvilles] could secure adequate coke supplies which, in turn, involved the control of sufficient coal'.[18] Elsewhere in Scotland the existence of over fifty idle blast furnaces in Ayr, Stirling, and Lanark, held out little prospect of improved pig iron supplies since most of them had been 'out of commission for many years and [had to] be regarded as unserviceable'.[19] Moreover, within the Colville Group there was little reserve steel-making capacity and this prohibited the full utilization of new rolling plant.

Demand continued to rise. The second Cunarder, *Queen Elizabeth*, ordered from John Browns in 1936, was expected to require 40,000 tons from the rolling mills; Admiralty orders were fast approaching the plating stage; and the works of the Steel Company of Scotland (steel tyres) and Glengarnock (rails) were under great pressure from the main line railway rolling stock programmes.[20] The level of activity reached by the summer of 1936 could be maintained—given continued supplies of iron ore, pig iron from England (some of it from Fords of Dagenham), India, and Russia, and home and imported scrap—but not, it was thought, significantly or rapidly increased.[21] At this point, those who suffered most were the remaining independent iron and steel bar and sheet rollers in the Motherwell and Coatbridge district. With some 80 to 90 per cent of the heavy steel trade under Colvilles' control, they were starved of ingots: Colvilles' own mills required every ton produced within the Group.[22]

[16] Colvilles Ltd., Minute Book I, 19 May 1936.
[17] Ibid., I, 30 July 1936.
[18] Ibid., I, 11 Nov. 1936.
[19] *Financial Times*, 17 Aug. 1936.
[20] Careful assessments of the situation in Scotland were made by the *Financial News*, 29 Aug. 1936, and the *Scotsman*, 12 Oct. 1936.
[21] *Financial Times*, 14 Sept. 1936; *Scotsman*, 29 Sept. 1936.
[22] *Financial Times*, 21 Sept. 1936; *Scotsman*, 29 Sept. 1936; *Financial News*, 6 Oct. 1936.

Still the installation of new equipment went on. Record tonnages were produced everywhere but even this feverish activity could not prevent the informal rationing of some customers, the running down of stocks, and long delivery dates. Furthermore, increasing anxiety was experienced concerning the acquisition of raw materials. Coking coal had been a problem since 1935,[23] and pig iron—despite a massive increase in foreign imports—was a constant worry.[24] Scrap—so important to the Scottish steel-makers—had to be obtained wherever it could be found. Buyers were sent to America and in January 1937, Sir James Lithgow arranged for six ships to be provided for breaking up.[25] Scottish ingot output in 1936 had been pushed to a level about three times higher than that of 1932— indeed, it was the best year since 1920—and demand was still rising.[26] Not without some misgivings, Colvilles' Board was forced to acknowledge the necessity—so frequently urged by Dr. McCance—of an increase in overall capacity coupled with considerable reorganization. Ingenious 'patching' could go only so far; radical changes promised to solve many of the problems encountered in the boom of 1936–7 and to permit a further increase in productivity (see Table 8.9).

But the success of any such scheme depended on the prior solution of the fuel problem. In 1935 the constituent companies of the Colville Group consumed three-quarters of a million tons of coal, much of it of coking quality. But in that year David Colville & Sons had a prior claim to the output of their subsidiary, Archibald Russell, Ltd. In 1936 Russells were in the hands of the liquidators, being part of the assets of David Colville & Sons transferred to the Elder Dempster Realisation Company Ltd., and it was feared that the Russell collieries

[23] Colvilles Ltd., Agendas and Papers, 'Memorandum Regarding Coal', 11 May 1936.

[24] Colvilles Ltd., Agendas and Papers, 'Memorandum as Basis for Discussion on Future Requirements and Supply of Raw Material', 9 Apr. 1936; Burn, *Economic History of Steel Making*, pp. 467–8; *Financial Times*, 16 Nov. 1936.

[25] Colvilles Ltd., Minute Book I, 13 Jan. 1937.

[26] Many newspaper correspondents made the point that with the cessation of operations at North Motherwell, Mossend, Calderbank, Clydesdale, and Wishaw, during the years of deep depression, there was no possibility of surpassing the 1920 figures with current capacity, e.g. *Financial Times*, 21 Dec. 1936; *Financial News*, 29 Dec. 1936. Also see Burn, *Economic History of Steel Making*, p. 468.

might be acquired by William Baird & Company, who were believed to be trying to obtain control of all available supplies of coking coal in Stirlingshire and Lanarkshire.[27] Colvilles' Board felt that the company was in a very vulnerable position. The fuel problem was difficult enough in 1935; by 1936, with Dr. McCance pressing for the production of some 6,000 tons of pig iron per week at Clyde Iron, it promised to become insoluble. In mid-1936 Colvilles were drawing their coke supplies from James Nimmo & Company (1,000 tons per week) and William Dixon Ltd. (some 2,000 tons per week). Were the Board to sanction McCance's ambitious scheme, an additional 3,000 tons of coke—or 4,500 tons of coking coal—would have to be obtained. Unless the company could obtain control of an appropriate source, it was deemed to be too dangerous to lay down the coke ovens which formed an integral part of McCance's plans. Colvilles believed that they could not rely upon being able to purchase such a large quantity of coking coal in the open market. It was imperative to acquire Archibald Russells from the liquidators *and* to gain an interest in James Nimmo & Company[28] in order to secure adequate supplies of coking coal. At this point the record becomes fragmentary,[29] but it is apparent that within eight or nine months the fuel position had been secured. Russells were to remain within the Colville Group, and Colvilles Ltd. were to enter into a new holding company with Dunlops to acquire control of the collieries owned by James Nimmo & Company and James Dunlop & Company.[30]

[27] Bairds were understood to be very interested in acquiring the Alloa Coal Co.

[28] Only Russell's three Lanarkshire collieries—with a daily output of 1,650 tons—produced coal of metallurgical quality.

[29] This discussion of the fuel problem is based largely upon Colvilles Ltd., Agendas and Papers, 'Memorandum Regarding Coal', 11 May 1936; ibid., 'Notes Regarding Archibald Russell Ltd.', 19 May 1936; ibid., 'Memorandum on the Coke Position', 8 Jan. 1937; *Daily Telegraph*, 18 May 1936.

[30] Colvilles Ltd., Minute Book II, 28 May 1937, 29 July 1937. The exact arrangements are complex. Basically, the total capital of the holding company, Nimmo & Dunlop Ltd., was to be £750,000 in £1 Ordinary shares. The Ordinary shareholders of James Nimmo & Co. were to receive 287,500 of these shares in payment for their existing 250,000 Ordinary shares of £1 each and the Ordinary shareholders of James Dunlop & Co., 250,000 shares, in payment for their existing 250,000 Ordinary shares of £1 each; Sir James and Henry Lithgow—already proprietors of James Dunlop & Co.—were to purchase 125,000 shares, and Colvilles Ltd., 75,000 shares, leaving a balance

Only with the creation of Nimmo & Dunlop would the board of Colvilles countenance the full implementation of the Clyde Iron/Clydebridge coke oven and blast furnace scheme. Once the fuel problem had been solved, events moved rapidly. The full plan was submitted to the Federation in the spring of 1937. Indeed, it was one of the first major projects to be considered by the Federation's special committee on expansion proposals which had been established in December 1936.[31] Colvilles explained that the future supply of scrap was so uncertain and limited that even to maintain the company's current ingot output, it was essential to produce more pig iron within the Group. It was proposed to build two new 18-foot 3-inch diameter hearth blast furnaces with ore-handling plant at Clyde Iron (together with 68 coke ovens with their associated coal-blending and by-product plants) and a bridge over the Clyde to convey hot metal to Clydebridge. At the steel works, additional melting furnaces and a new plate mill would be laid down. The cost was estimated at some £2½ million. It was emphasized that all the coke oven and blast furnace gases would be utilized by the Clydebridge Steel Works.[32] This scheme, it was argued, 'would enable the best and most efficient practice in respect of coke, pig iron and plate production to be realized'.[33]

---

of 12,500 shares unissued. The board of the holding company would consist of four directors from each of the constituent companies, one of whom, because he was a director of James Nimmo & Co., would be John Craig. Sir Adam Nimmo would be Chairman, but it was recognized that voting control would rest with the Lithgow brothers.

[31] The genesis and role of the Federation's new consultative machinery is clearly explained by Carr and Taplin, *History of the British Steel Industry*, pp. 537–8. See also B. S. Keeling and A. E. G. Wright, *The Development of the Modern British Steel Industry* (London: Longmans, 1964), pp. 14–15, and the *Report of the Import Duties Advisory Committee on the Present Position and Future Development of the Iron and Steel Industry* (Cmd. 5507, H.M.S.O., 1937), pp. 35–7.

[32] This was a critical part of the plan. Repeated criticism of the blast furnace section of the Scottish iron and steel industry—which had but fifteen furnaces in blast even at the height of the boom—was invariably countered by the argument that modernization and expansion depended 'very largely, if not entirely, on a market being found for coke-oven gas'. The absence of such a market had constituted a major factor in inhibiting progress in the past.

[33] This paragraph is based on Colvilles Ltd., Agendas and Papers, 'Memorandum on Proposed Extension', 25 Jan. 1937; 'Memorandum for Board [on the proposals submitted to the Federation]', 23 Feb. 1937.

The Committee set up by the Federation to examine development proposals were completely satisfied as to the economic
desirability of Colvilles' scheme and, although there was some
debate about location, containing echoes of the Brassert Report
of 1929, gave it their unanimous approval. This was endorsed
by the Import Duties Advisory Committee.[34] Meanwhile, the
Colvilles' sub-committee on Finance (John Craig, Sir James
Lithgow, and Sir Steven Bilsland) was considering ways of raising the capital.[35] At first it had been intended to issue Ordinary
shares, John Craig said as much in his annual report of April
1937, but the Board was subsequently advised to issue
debentures. This plan too was quickly discarded. Craig never
lost his fear of this form of financing. Instead, it was decided
to borrow $£\frac{1}{2}$ million from the National Bank of Scotland (at
one-half of one per cent over Bank Rate, minimum 4 per cent)
and repay the principal over a period of five years, the rest of
the capital being met from existing resources. But even this
arrangement was abandoned.[36] Instead, the special bank loan
from the National Bank was employed to finance the company's
increased holdings in subsidiaries, and an agreement made
between Colvilles and the Royal Exchange Assurance (acting
for a consortium of insurance companies) which provided Colvilles with a loan of £1 million against the security of the herit-
able properties owned by the company at Clyde Iron and Clydebridge.[37] It was somewhat ironic, though hardly unexpected,
that by the time all these negotiations had been concluded and
construction was already well under way, Colvilles' directors
were presented with a detailed schedule of comparative costs
at the company's works to enable them to determine 'the best

[34] *Report of the Import Duties Advisory Committee on the Present Position and Future
Development of the Iron and Steel Industry*, pp. 37–8.

[35] Colvilles Ltd., Agendas and Papers, 'Blast Furnace and Coke Ovens Progress Report', 6 Sept. 1937; Minute Book II, 19 Oct. 1937.

[36] Colvilles' Ltd., Minute Book II, 2 Dec. 1937.

[37] This loan, interest on which was to be $3\frac{1}{2}$ per cent, would be made in
four equal quarterly instalments at 98 beginning on 14 July 1938. It was to
be repaid at £100,000 a year beginning on 31 Mar. 1941 up to and including
1946, the balance of £400,000 being repayable on 31 Mar. 1947. The full
details are given in Colvilles Ltd., Minute Book II, 14 July 1938; and Agendas
and Papers, 'The C.C. Scheme—Loan of £1,000,000', 3 Aug. 1938. The gist
of the arrangements was given in Colvilles' annual report for 1937, published
on 5 Apr. 1938, and attracted much favourable comment. See, for example,
Birmingham Post, 5 Apr. 1938.

plan to be adopted' in the event of 'a severe curtailment of production', such as was made probable by the contemporaneous sharp fall in the demand for steel.[38] Although the Clyde Iron/Clydebridge scheme was the most important element in Colvilles' expansion programme, it must not be allowed completely to overshadow developments elsewhere. During the winter of 1937–8 the main scheme at Glengarnock was completed; new melting furnaces were authorized at Lanarkshire (£65,000); extensions were begun at Fullwood Foundry to meet the increased requirements of both the parent group and Beardmores for ingot moulds and iron castings, and a massive new scheme was planned for handling imported ore on the Clyde at General Terminus Quay. In December 1937,[39] Colvilles agreed to an Admiralty request to undertake the manufacture of non-cemented armour plates and, so rapidly did such orders rise, that within a few months Colvilles were authorized by the Admiralty to spend nearly £400,000 on extensions to Mossend made necessary by the armour plate programme. The entire development scheme was completed by February 1939.[40]

Meanwhile, the steel industry had experienced a sharp downturn in activity. During 1938, Colvilles suffered severely from a dullness in shipbuilding—'empty berths are now becoming conspicuous', said the *Scotsman* in October—and Smith & McLean and Clyde Alloy reduced production as a consequence of 'lessened demand from English car factories'. Furthermore, it was feared that this branch of trade would suffer an absolute and irreversible decline when the new strip mill at Ebbw Vale went into full production.[41] The recovery did not come until the opening weeks of 1939 when—as the more optimistic commentators had continuously predicted—there was a sudden rise in demand, chiefly reflecting the Government's Air Raid Precaution programme.[42] To this boost was added a marked im-

[38] Colvilles Ltd., Agendas and Papers, 'Comparative Works Costs ...', 1 Aug. 1938.
[39] Colvilles Ltd., Minute Book II, 2 Dec. 1937, 24 Feb. 1938, 28 Apr. 1938; *Glasgow Herald*, 21 Mar. 1938.
[40] Colvilles Ltd., Minute Book II, 2 Mar. 1939.
[41] *Scotsman*, 31 Oct. 1938.
[42] Colvilles Ltd., Minute Book II, 2 Feb. 1939. It was estimated that Scotland's share of the first part of the A.R.P. programme was equivalent to 20,000 ingot tons. *Financial News*, 15 Apr. 1939.

provement in shipbuilding orders in the spring, following the announcement of a government building grant for the construction of cargo vessels. Even export demand revived strongly.[43]

John Craig was able to sound a cheerful note at the Company's Eighth Annual General Meeting in April 1939. Despite lower output, substantial economies in production had produced better results than had been obtained in the previous year. In November 1938, liquid pig iron had been used experimentally for the first time at Clydebridge in preparation for the completion of the new integrated iron and steel plant,[44] and in May 1939, the first blast furnace at Clyde Iron was to be blown in. Two months later the 68 coke ovens came into operation, and in February 1940, the second blast furnace was fired. It was a remarkably adventurous scheme. The feature which appealed most to the popular imagination was the way in which molten pig iron from the blast furnaces at Clyde Iron was conveyed across the Clyde to the steel-melting furnaces at Clydebridge.[45] But the most noteworthy feature of the project was its scale. In 1937, 'with demand at its peak and 16 Scottish blast furnaces working full time, output per furnace for the district as a whole averaged just over 31,000 tons a year but the two new furnaces [at Clyde Iron] had annual rated capacities of 182,500 tons each.'[46] And, as if to demonstrate the overall efficiency of the entire complex, a world record was claimed by Colvilles for Clydebridge when, in the week ended 22 July 1939, 7,090 tons of steel ship plates of varied thickness and length were sheared by a single mill.[47]

By the eve of the Second World War Scotland possessed a 'prosperous and progressive' steel industry.[48] It is true that much remained to be done. The London, Midland, & Scottish

[43] Colvilles Ltd., Minute Book II, 29 Mar. 1939; 27 Apr. 1939; 1 Apr. 1939; *News Chronicle*, 3 Apr. 1939.

[44] *Financial News*, 18 Nov. 1938.

[45] This and many other details of the scheme, were set forth in an illustrated article in the *Glasgow Herald*, 25 Oct. 1938.

[46] Carr and Taplin, *History of the British Steel Industry*, p. 540.

[47] Colvilles Ltd., Minute Book II, 3 Aug. 1939; *Financial News*, 24 July 1939. The previous record was also held by Clydebridge. This was a total of 5,238 tons turned out in January 1928.

[48] The adjectives are those of Carr and Taplin, *History of the British Steel Industry*, p. 540.

Railway Company was proving dilatory in approving rail links
to the proposed iron ore unloading wharf at General Terminus
Quay, Glasgow.[49] Colvilles still possessed an unacceptably high
scrap/pig iron ratio in the charging of the melting furnaces.
'Patching' was still going on at many of the works, particularly
at those of the Steel Company of Scotland, where the expenditure of over a quarter of a million pounds was authorized in
August 1939. But the board was aware of the weaknesses within
the Group and was making strenuous attempts to eradicate
them.

3 Structure, Personality, and Performance

The decisions made by Colvilles' board during the thirties were
taken within an environment which the founders of the firm
would probably have found irksome and inhibiting. It is not
difficult to imagine the reactions of the irascible David Colville,
jun. to the necessity of gaining the endorsement of the British
Iron and Steel Federation and of the Import Duties Advisory
Committee to the Clyde Iron Works/Clydebridge scheme. Yet
this was the price which John Craig, among many others, was
prepared to pay for the relatively orderly expansion of the industry during the thirties. Craig had long argued for 'safeguarding', and when the pleas of the heavy steel-makers for rejected
by Baldwin's Conservative Government of 1924–9, he was prepared to support by whatever means he could the industry's
attempts to secure some measure of price stabilization, joint selling in export markets, and the promotion of the use of British
steel at home. His belief in the necessity both for protection and
co-operation with his fellow steel-makers was strengthened by
the dismal events of 1930–1, and he welcomed the Import
Duties Act of 1932. He was, moreover, prepared to accept—
even welcome—the more powerful British Iron and Steel
Federation, whose difficult birth took place in April 1934, not
simply in return for the higher duties recommended by the
I.D.A.C., but because his experiences in the protracted negotia-

---

[49] This case is very fully documented in the Colville archives. Copies of
the most important exchanges between Craig and Lord Stamp, the Chairman
of the L.M. & S. Rly. Co., are included in the Agendas and Papers for the
meeting of 1 June 1939.

tions that resulted in Colvilles' dominance in the Scottish steel industry convinced him that voluntary co-operation, patience, and persuasion, where inadequate weapons in the struggle for the recovery of the British iron and steel industry. There had to be a body sufficiently powerful to overcome the obstacles to regeneration that stemmed from the ingrained competitiveness and jealousies of his fellow steel-makers, even if this meant the surrender of some degree of individual sovereignty over, for example, development plans, the level of prices, and marketing and acquisition policies.

He had always enjoyed friendly relations with Sir William Larke, the director of both the old National Federation of Iron and Steel Manufacturers and the new B.I.S.F., and his confidence in the new body was enhanced by the appointment of Sir Andrew Duncan as the Independent Chairman of its Executive Committee. Craig never ceased to give Duncan and the Federation his loyal, and often well publicized, support. In his address to the Eighth Annual General Meeting of Colvilles, he paid tribute to the constructive work of the B.I.S.F.:

> The British Iron and Steel Federation steadily grows in importance, and I think those of us who are intimately acquainted with it are bound to admit that it has proved of real benefit to the industry, not only in promoting a wider national outlook among the British steel-makers, but in maintaining a friendly and co-operating spirit with the steel-makers on the Continent and in America. . . . The Federation has kept also closely in touch with organizations representing the chief consumers of steel in the country, and has consequently been able to appreciate the point of view of the consumer, and this contact has enabled steel-makers to avoid taking too narrow a view of their responsibilities as a national industry.[50]

It has been argued that 'the degree of industry co-operation and the voluntary submission to Government price supervision to which the iron and steel industry assented in the 1930s was without precedent in the history of steel or of any other privately owned British industry'.[51] It is clear from John Craig's public statements and private communications that he was proud to have played a useful role in such a transformation.

But what of the Colville Group itself? In 1939 John Craig

[50] Colvilles Ltd., John Craig's statement to the Eighth Annual General Meeting, 27 Apr. 1939.

[51] B. S. Keeling and A. E. G. Wright, *Development of the Modern British Steel Industry*, p. 22.

had been connected with Colvilles for fifty years, for nearly thirty of them as a director. When he had been invited to accept a seat on the board of David Colville & Sons, the owners were managing the firm. The affairs of the Dalzell Iron & Steel Works were conducted by the founder's sons, Archibald and David Colville. Under their autocratic direction, Dalzell became the largest single unit in the British iron and steel industry. Employing the categories devised by A. D. Chandler,[52] the enterprise may be termed a *personal* one. The senior salaried managers may have been given the opportunity of buying shares, even rising to board level, but they were not expected to challenge the Colvilles' right to determine overall policy, long-term planning, and the allocation of resources. David Colville, jun. listened to the advice of his colleagues, but he determined the strategy. But with the deaths of the two Colvilles (John had died in 1905), control of the firm which they and their father had created passed suddenly and unexpectedly into the hands of the managers. The enterprise could properly be described as *managerial*. The owners—the trustees and the beneficiaries of the trusts established by the Colvilles—had not the information, experience, or commitment required to manage. By the accident of the premature death of the founder's sons and the youth of the third generation, David Colville & Sons missed a stage in the evolutionary pattern of the large-scale enterprise. Colvilles was never truly manager-manned but owner-controlled; it was never *entrepreneurial*, and any likelihood of a return to what might be called the orthodox pattern was rendered almost impossible by the events that took place during the war itself and the immediate postwar years, a period of forced, even unnatural, growth.

Under the Colvilles, when the firm operated a single works, Dalzell, every major aspect of the enterprise (purchasing, production, and sales) was personally supervised by the two brothers. They were assisted by a mere handful of managers, four of whom had been elevated to the board by the eve of the First World War. Under the senior managers there worked a

---

[52] The most succinct and relevant statement of Prof. A. D. Chandler's findings is his paper 'The Development of Modern Management Structure in the U.S. and U.K.', in Les Hannah (ed.), *Management Strategy and Business Development* (London: Macmillan, 1976), pp. 23–51.

hierarchy of operating staff. With the absorption of Clydebridge and Glengarnock in 1916 a more extensive middle
managerial staff was required, but essentially each unit was administered in a way which simply duplicated the arrangements
evolved at Dalzell. The general works manager, David Maclay,
and later G. P. West, was now responsible for not one but three
steel works and, like the directors with special responsibility
for purchasing and sales, had perforce to enlarge his departmental establishment to carry the greatly increased and more
complicated workload, involving as it did subtle questions of
balance and flows between works. At the top, the board made
the major decisions, and, indeed, many of the minor ones,
largely on the basis of detailed weekly reports. In administering
the three steel works, David Colville & Sons was slowly evolving
a centralized structure with departments divided by function.
But at the same time, Colvilles' relationship with its subsidiary
firms, Smith & McLean, Fullwood Foundry, Clyde Alloy,
Archibald Russell, and the Carnlough Lime Company, was
that of a holding company loosely administering a combination
of relatively autonomous operating units. Their activities were
co-ordinated with each other and with the steel works by the
chairman of the parent company, John Craig, acting with at
least one other director from the parent board. Thus, the board
of Smith & McLean consisted of Harry Yates, A. J. H. Mowbray (Managing Director), and Herbert Beard from the earlier
regime, and John Craig (Chairman), David M. Maclay, and
John Lennox from the board of David Colville & Sons; while
the two managing directors of Clyde Alloy, Dr. A. McCance
and T. M. Service,[53] had as fellow directors John Craig (Chairman), David Maclay, and Norman R. Colville. Each of the
subsidiaries in turn was administered by its own corps of middle
and lower level managers. In legal terms, David Colville & Sons
was both a trading and a holding company, and the entire Colville group was articulated by John Craig personally, chairman
of all the subsidiaries and the only single person to have direct,
as compared with reported, knowledge of every part of the
whole.

    With the purchase of Colvilles' Ordinary shares by Harland

[53] T. M. Service resigned as managing director of Clyde Alloy in September
1921, to return to Beardmores. D.C. & S.: Minute Book IV, 11 Oct. 1921.

& Wolff in 1920, ultimate control of the Group passed to Lord Pirrie, but because he and his successor, Lord Kylsant, were far more exercised by the problems of other parts of their ramified, loosely-federated shipping empire than by the relatively uncomplicated and efficient Colville Group, even more power devolved upon John Craig. It was through him and him alone that communication took place between Belfast, the head office of the Royal Mail Group at Cockspur Street, London, and Motherwell. Thus, although the firm of David Colville & Sons had itself been swept into a holding company, throughout the thirties this part of the Royal Mail Group enjoyed an almost independent existence. Craig's own power was constrained only by the rare demands of the ambitious Pirrie and the struggling Kylsant, the eagle-eyed cash creditors of David Colville & Sons, and the modification in policy suggested by his boardroom colleagues, of whom J. B. Allan, John Lennox, and G. P. West were paramount. These were all full-time salaried career managers who owned little or no stock.[54] The members of the Colville family—with the exception of Captain David Colville, Norman R. Colville, and John Colville (the last two of whom joined the board in 1920)—became mere *rentiers*, more concerned with the dividends than the operation of their company.

This was how matters stood until 1930 when, with the collapse of the Royal Mail Group and the creation of Colvilles Ltd., the structure of the Colville Group and the balance of power within its executive altered profoundly. The ultimate arbiter of the firm's strategy, Lord Kylsant, departed in ignominy,[55] and many of the Ordinary shares in David Colville &

[54] Indeed, in 1919 a committee appointed to consider the question of Directors' remuneration, recommended that 'in view of the very small shareholding of [the] local directors [i.e. John Craig, J. B. Allan, David Maclay, and John Lennox] we propose that between them they should have 6 per cent of any excess of profits *available for* distribution beyond £200,000. The 6 per cent to be apportioned as follows: Mr. C. 2 per cent, Messrs. A. M. & L. 1¼ per cent and Captain [David] Colville, ⅝ per cent. These rates are to be halved on any excess beyond £500,000.' D.C. & S.: Minute Book III, 11 Mar. 1919.

[55] The author has encountered considerable sympathy for Lord Kylsant among retired senior officials of Colvilles. He was regarded as a scapegoat in the condemnation of the policy of 'secret reserve' accounting apparently universally employed by shipping magnates—a policy for which some believed that there was considerable justification.

Sons, originally held exclusively by Harland & Wolff (see Figure II), passed into the hands of Sir William McLintock (acting for Lamport & Holt), the Union Castle Mail Steamship Company Ltd., Coast Lines Ltd., and the Duke of Abercorn and Sir Edward Scott (as trustees for the holders of the 5 per cent Debenture Stock of Elder Dempster & Company Ltd.).[56] It is unnecessary to dwell upon the crucial role of Sir William McLintock who, for the next four to five years, constantly cajoled and encouraged Craig into pushing on with his plans for the rationalization of the Scottish steel industry, except to emphasize that he made no effort to influence the internal workings of the new company. Because Craig possessed the complete confidence of the new 'owners' of the Ordinary shares,[57] there was little or no erosion of his dominating position.

But whereas Craig appears to have been all-powerful within David Colville & Sons, within Colvilles Ltd. he was forced always to consider, even act upon, the views of the two Lithgows. The creation of Colvilles Ltd. had the somewhat curious consequence of reversing the usual developmental pattern of ownership. David Colville & Sons had become a managerial enterprise in 1916; now in the thirties there took place a partial reversion to *personal* control, for the Lithgows expected to play a major role in the determination of the policy of Colvilles Ltd. Moreover, their power steadily increased as the firm pursued its long-run strategy of merger and consolidation. Not only did John Craig pay careful heed to the arguments that Sir James Lithgow advanced at board meetings but Sir James was often able to short-circuit Craig's carefully-planned negotiations with outside bodies by his close personal acquaintance with such persons as Montagu Norman, Charles Bruce Gardner, and Sir Andrew Duncan. His influence on the board of Colvilles Ltd., already considerable, was markedly increased when he purchased the Ordinary shares of the Steel Company of Scotland in 1934 and became chairman of Beardmores in 1936.

In addition to the changes that the advent of the Lithgow brothers made to the style of the management of the Colville Group, the formation of Colvilles Ltd. brought further structural

[56] D.C. & S.; Minute Book VI, 13 Oct. 1933.
[57] See above, p. 188.

changes. In 1930 David Colville & Sons became simply a holding company, concerned with the co-ordination of the activities of the relatively autonomous subsidiaries. Colvilles Ltd., by contrast, moved further in the direction of becoming a centralized, functionally departmentalized enterprise. While the board made the top level strategic and policy decisions, and the operating units (Dalzell, Clydebridge, Glengarnock, and Clyde Iron) continued to be run by a hierarchy of salaried officials at the top of each of which stood a plant manager having overall responsibility for a particular process or function (e.g. melting shop manager at Clydebridge, blast furnace manager at Clyde Iron, plate mill manager at Dalzell, etc.), there were appointed a group of specialists, often reporting to a specific member of the parent board, whose responsibilities extended to all the works. Thus T. W. Hand became chief mechanical engineer, L. Rothera chief electrical engineer, R. C. Dymock chief labour officer, and William Barr chief metallurgist.

By 1936, the Colville Group possessed a structure that had evolved pragmatically. At the top, the parent board of Colvilles Ltd. determined the strategic policy of the Group and directly controlled the iron and steel works at Dalzell, Glengarnock, Clydebridge, and Clyde Iron. Yet the head office staff also provided certain specialized technical, purchasing, and sales services for all the subsidiary concerns: the Steel Company of Scotland, Lanarkshire, Smith & McLean, Clyde Alloy, Fullwood Foundry, the Carnlough Lime Company, and Colville Constructional. These retained their own boards and were, within the limits established by the parent board, semi-autonomous units. As with the previous structure evolved in the days of David Colville & Sons, Colvilles' main board was represented on the boards of all the subsidiaries. John Craig was both Chairman and Managing Director of Colvilles Ltd. and (with the sole exception of the Steel Company of Scotland, whose chairman was Sir James Lithgow) was chairman of each of the subsidiary boards. At his right hand he had, on every board except Fullwood Foundry and the Carnlough Lime Company, Dr. Andrew McCance, managing director of Clyde Alloy (see Table 9.2). It is apparent that by this means every part of the Group, whatever its precise legal status, was carefully linked and

TABLE 9.2

Membership of the Boards of Directors of Colvilles Ltd. and its Subsidiaries, December 1938

	Colvilles Ltd.	S.C. of S.	Lanarkshire	Smith & McLean	Clyde Alloy	Fullwood Foundry	Carnlough Lime	Colville Constructional
John Craig	C. & M.D.	✓	C.	C.	C.	C.	C.	C.
Sir James Lithgow	✓	C.						
Henry Lithgow	✓	✓	✓					
Andrew McCance	✓	✓	✓		M.D.			✓
Peter Baxter	✓	✓		✓				✓
F. E. Rebbeck	✓							
H. Yates	✓			M.D.				
T. R. Craig	✓		✓	✓				
Sir Steven Bilsland	✓							
James Napier		✓						
S. M. Turnbull		✓						
A. M. Stephen		✓						
Sir H. E. Yarrow		✓						
J. M. Duncanson		✓						
H. Cunningham			✓					
A. J. H. Mowbray				✓				
Sydney G. A. Harvey				✓				
James Colville					✓			
James McArthur					✓			
John Hunter					✓			
T. A. Irvine						M.D.		
W. J. L. Cumming						✓		
H. W. Reid								
R. W. McBride							✓	✓
John Wright								✓

Notes: ✓ = Member of Board of Directors; C. = Chairman; M.D. = Managing Director.

Sources: Colvilles Ltd., Board Meetings, Agendas and Papers; Annual Reports of the various companies.

highly centralized. It might be asked why Colvilles did not go further and evolve some variant of the multidivisional form of organization.[58] Briefly, four interrelated explanations suggest themselves. First, few large-scale British companies had done so before 1950; second, in industries selling semi-finished products to a few large industrial consumers, the multidivisional structure is both inappropriate and unnecessary; third, 'of all industries, steel lends itself least to a delegation of decision-making',[59] and, fourth and last, Colvilles' internal organization appears to have worked satisfactorily.

It is, in fact, arguable that by the eve of the Second World War, Colvilles possessed one of the most efficient managements in the British steel industry. It would be difficult, if not impossible, to substantiate this suggestion, but certainly the main board appears to have been extremely vigorous and talented. The Chairman and Managing Director, John Craig, was exceptionally experienced in every aspect of the trade. Indefatigable, austere, ambitious for the firm for the growth of which he was so largely responsible, Craig kept tight control of the finances, and held himself responsible for Colvilles' relationship with outsiders, whether they were bankers or government bodies, the Federation or its affiliated associations, the firm's suppliers or its competitors. He never claimed expertise in iron-and steel-making; instead he was content to be advised by Dr. Andrew McCance, who was, in the late thirties, approaching the peak of his scientific and technical powers. These two men, who undoubtedly provided the driving force behind the development of Colvilles, were supported by a board each of whom made a very positive contribution to the firm's overall strategy. Foremost among them was Sir James Lithgow. Victorian in his convictions and the seriousness with which he shouldered his responsibilities, Lithgow, unlike many of his contemporaries, drew strength from his beliefs and with missionary zeal espoused the cause of rationalization. His prin-

[58] See Chandler, 'The Development of Modern Management Structure', *passim*; Derek F. Channon, *The Strategy and Structure of British Enterprise* (London: Macmillan, 1973), pp. 87–8, 119; Leslie Hannah, *The Rise of the Corporate Economy*, pp. 79–100; Leslie Hannah, 'Strategy and Structure in the Manufacturing Sector', in Les Hannah (ed.), *Management Strategy*, pp. 184–202.

[59] A. D. Chandler, 'Management Decentralisation: A Historical Analysis', *Business History Review*, xxx (1956), 158.

cipal concern was shipbuilding, but in seeking to restore health to this sickly branch of British industry, he extended his shipping interests and went into coal, iron, steel, and engineering. Energetic, impatient, apt to make sudden, but usually well-judged, decisions of far-reaching importance, he emerges from the Colville archives as mercurial in his enthusiasms, but forever sincere in his belief in the need for a soundly managed, strong, and progressive complex of heavy industries in the West of Scotland. In this work he was supported by his brother, Henry. More phlegmatic than James, more concerned with the detailed implementation of the schemes inaugurated by his brother, their relationship resembles that of the brothers David and Archibald Colville. What they brought to Colvilles was financial power (unparalleled in the West of Scotland), great knowledge of the heavy trades, and a very wide range of financial, industrial, commercial, and political contacts.[60]

With the formation of Colvilles Ltd. in 1930, the Lithgows brought Peter Baxter with them. Baxter's first important post had been in the Barrowfield Iron Works Company, a large Glasgow firm of constructional engineers who specialized in the erection of gas-holders. In 1913, after lengthy periods in the Middle East and Spain as one of the firm's overseas representatives, he was appointed Commercial Manager, in 1918 General Manager, and in 1921 Managing Director. In 1923, however, he joined James Dunlop & Company and was soon put on the board. With the Colville/Dunlop merger, he was appointed to the main board of Colvilles Ltd. and also to the board of Colvilles Constructional. When Sir James Lithgow purchased the Ordinary shares of the Steel Company of Scotland, he joined this board of directors too. Completely imperturbable, hard-working, and friendly, his particular concern on the parent board was the acquisition of raw materials: coal,

[60] Under Section 149 of the Companies Act of 1929, persons appointed company directors were required to enumerate those firms in which they were interested which had or might have business relations with the company to whose board they were appointed. Pursuant to this requirement, Henry Lithgow submitted a schedule to the Secretary of the Lanarkshire Steel Co. in 1936 which listed fifteen companies of which he was a director and a further twenty companies in which he was, either directly or indirectly, a major shareholder. Henry Lithgow to R. Ralston, 16 Oct. 1936, attached to Minute Book IV of the Lanarkshire Steel Co., p. 347.

iron ore, and pig iron; but he devoted much attention to those matters affecting the welfare of the company's employees.[61]

The other members of Colvilles' board in the late thirties were Sir Steven Bilsland, F. E. Rebbeck, H. Yates, and T. R. Craig.[62] By replacing David Colville on his resignation in February 1937,[63] Sir Steven Bilsland maintained the Colville family connection with the firm since he was the second David Colville's son-in-law. Moreover, he was a prominent banker and industrialist forever seeking ways of promoting economic growth in Scotland. He was, with Sir James Lithgow and Lord Elgin, one of the promoters of the Scottish Development Council, formed in 1931. As chairman of the Union Bank, Sir Steven had, by the late thirties, become much concerned with the provision of finance for Scottish industry. He was a member of the Scottish Advisory Board of Credit for Industry, formed in 1934 as a subsidiary of the United Dominions Trust, and in 1938 he advocated the establishment of a Scottish Development Finance Corporation which, with the aid of the Scottish banks, was intended to provide both finance and constructive ideas. This proposal proved unacceptable to the general managers of the Scottish banks at the time, but it is strong evidence of Sir Steven's attitude to economic affairs. Far greater success attended his efforts as Chairman of the first Scottish Industrial Estate Company, established in 1937. This body was responsible for setting up the Hillington estate, which within eighteen months had secured 67 tenants for the 103 factories built by the company. Since these were mainly representatives of small-scale light industries, the objective of diversifying the narrow economic base of Clydeside was attained. This initial success led to the creation of other estates at Carfin, Chapelhall, and Larkhall; these were factored by another company, Lanarkshire Industrial Estates Ltd., also under Sir Steven's chairmanship, incorporated in 1938. His breadth of vision,

[61] Much of the information on Peter Baxter is derived from a sketch in *Colvilles' Magazine*, xviii, No. 1 (Jan. 1937), pp. 1–2.

[62] John Lennox died in 1936. Colvilles Ltd.; Board Minutes, 11 Nov. 1936.

[63] Writing to F. E. Rebbeck about David Colville's resignation, Craig said, 'Personally, I will be sorry to see the name of David Colville go off the Board, but I recognize his position. He wants to go on a trip round the world and, quite frankly, he does not feel disposed to accept any responsibility about business and, knowing this, I think it would be wrong to press him to reconsider the matter.' John Craig to F. E. Rebbeck, 11 Jan. 1937.

business ability, and sound common sense made him a valuable member of Colvilles' board: his special contribution was to financial matters.[64]

Finally, there were three directors all appointed in April 1936. F. E. Rebbeck, whose apologies in the Minutes far outnumbered his appearances at meetings of the board, was appointed to cement the connection between Colvilles and Harland & Wolff. Rebbeck had been Chairman and Managing Director of the Belfast shipbuilding concern since 1930 and, although he was able to provide intimate knowledge of shipping developments when called upon to do so, had inevitably to devote his major energies to the yards on Queen's Island. Harry Yates, Managing Director of Smith & McLean since 1935, contributed a lifetime's knowledge of the sheet metal trades to Colvilles' board. A consummate negotiator, he had an unrivalled knowledge of the labyrinthine world of conference agreements and selling associations. And, lastly, T. R. Craig, John Craig's eldest son, whose entire training had been designed to make him a fitting director.

This, then, was Colvilles' board on the eve of the Second World War. There were no passengers here: no ornamental or guinea-pig directors. Their average age may have been disquieting, but no one could deny the immense experience and ability assembled at the monthly meetings; nor was there any gainsaying their enormous collective energy and voracious appetite for work. Yet none of them could be described as being purely economic men. The board possessed a very strong social conscience: it influenced every one of their major decisions. True, its members aimed at economic efficiency, but not at any price. Only by fully appreciating this fact can some of the decisions made in the thirties and later be understood.

It has been argued that the management of Colvilles Ltd. was efficient, emphasis being laid on the technical and organizational improvements apparent in the closing years of the thirties. To some, this argument may seem impressionistic, lacking

[64] The material on Sir A. Steven Bilsland as a banker is drawn from S. G. Checkland, *Scottish Banking: A History, 1695–1973* (Glasgow: Collins, 1975), pp. 572, 574; and his work for the industrial estates from A. Slaven, *The Development of the West of Scotland, 1750–1960* (London: Routledge & Kegan Paul, 1975), pp. 202–5. Lord Bilsland, as he became in 1950, was the subject of a 'Profile' in *Colvilles' Magazine*, Autumn 1955, pp. 6–7.

in rigour, and coloured by the almost inevitable sympathy that the historian of a firm comes to feel for his subject. This favourable verdict may, however, be buttressed by the firm's productivity record. The statistical data which can be employed to measure trends in productivity in the iron and steel industry have to be used with great circumspection. Buxton and McKay have illustrated the conflicting evidence of the *Census of Production* figures and those derived from the employment and output trends provided by the *Ministry of Labour Gazette*; and W. E. G. Salter has emphasized that 'a considerable discrepancy exists in the employment figures from census sources and the *Statistical Bulletin of the Iron and Steel Federation*'.[65] Any findings based on such data cannot fail to be tentative, but it would appear that in pig iron manufacture 'employment fell in Scotland by one-fifth between 1925 and 1938. Over the same period, output fell by only 5 per cent so that some increase in efficiency was achieved. This improvement was, however, much smaller than that in the rest of Britain where output rose by almost 10 per cent despite a fall of some 30 per cent in employment . . . Steel output increased in Scotland by one-half between 1925 and 1938, while employment remained static. This was matched by other British producers who reduced their labour force by one-tenth while raising production by 40 per cent'. Buxton and McKay conclude that 'it is clear that productivity *did* increase in Scottish iron and steel production. This increase was comparable to that achieved in the rest of Britain but not high enough to make good the relative inefficiency of the Scottish industry'.[66]

There seems to be no reason to dispute this finding as far as the relative performance of the *Scottish* iron and steel industry is concerned, but even allowing for statistical weaknesses, it would appear that during the thirties the firm did, in fact, quickly make good earlier deficiencies in steel-making, if not in the pig iron sector. Table 9.3 shows the increase in the volume of output per worker employed in the nation's blast furnaces compared with a similar index of productivity, derived from

---

[65] Neil K. Buxton and Donald McKay, unpublished paper on the Scottish Iron and Steel industry between the wars, pp. 24–5; W. E. G. Salter, *Productivity and Technical Change*, 2nd edition (Cambridge: C.U.P., 1969), p. 176.
[66] Buxton and McKay, op. cit., p. 25.

TABLE 9.3

Increase in Labour Productivity in the Manufacture of Pig Iron and the Melting and Rolling of Steel: United Kingdom compared with Colvilles Ltd. and Lanarkshire Steel Company, 1930, 1935, 1937

	(1) United Kingdom			(2) Colvilles Ltd.			(3) Lanarkshire Steel Co.		
	1930	1935	1937	1930	1935	1937	1930	1935	1937
Blast Furnaces	100	128(129)	133(132)	100	128	131	—	—	—
Steel Melting and Rolling	100	132(131)	136(156)	100	165	189	100	118	142

Notes and Sources:

Col. (1) The U.K. indices have been calculated from the Preliminary Report of the Import Duties Act Inquiry of 1937, published in the *Board of Trade Journal*, 1 June 1939. The indices in brackets have been calculated from Salter's figures for 'output per operative'. W. E. G. Salter, *Productivity and Technical Change*, Appendix A(4), p. 179.

(2) Colvilles Ltd.'s figures have been calculated from data presented in Table 8.9. Note that the Blast Furnace figures are those of the Clyde Iron Works and that in this case 1931=100, and that the steel melting and rolling figures are the total consigned tonnages of Dalzell, Clydebridge, and Glengarnock Steel Works. There is no reason to believe that the overall trend of those figures was significantly altered by changing inventory policies over the period concerned.

(3) The Lanarkshire figures have been calculated from data contained in the company's statistical records. In this case the calculation is based on the consigned tonnage of finished materials per man per week. Lanarkshire was taken over by Colvilles Ltd. in 1936.

The dates chosen have been determined by the available U.K. productivity data.

Table 8.9, which indicates the average consigned tonnage per man employed at Clyde Iron˚Works. The dates are those for which U.K. information is provided by the preliminary report of the Import Duties Act Inquiry of 1937. It will be remembered that Colvilles' first new blast furnace at Clyde Iron was not blown in until May 1939, so it is hardly surprising that Colvilles' performance in this section of iron and steel production shows no departure from the national trend. If anything, it is a matter of some surprise that Dr. McCance was able to get a sufficient improvement out of such obsolete equipment to match the national gain in productivity.

A much more favourable impression is given by Colvilles' performance in steel melting and rolling. Here, comparing the national trend with that revealed by the consigned tonnages of Dalzell, Clydebridge, and Glengarnock, it is apparent that whereas the U.K. increase in labour productivity between 1930 and 1937 was about 36 per cent (Import Duties Act Inquiry of 1937) or even 56 per cent (Salter), the increase in the productivity of the employees of the three major steel melting plants of Colvilles was 89 per cent. This is a remarkable improvement and although it is not denied that Colvilles were benefiting enormously from the higher loading of plant associated with a doubling of total output, it undoubtedly reflected the efforts of Colvilles board—and Dr. McCance in particular—to rectify technical imperfections and generally to improve plant design and layout as capital expenditure became easier following the desperate months of 1931–2 and the paying off of the cash creditors in 1936. Other data too are available, but their use in demonstrating increased efficiency is vitiated by the lack of comparable statistics for other concerns within the industry. It is, however, significant that Colvilles' conversion costs in nearly all the rolling mills were forced down during the thirties[67] but, here again, this partially reflected the fuller use of available capacity during the course of the decade (see Table 9.1). So too did the fall in establishment charges per ton of ingot production. Nevertheless, it is interesting that the growing salary bill inevitably associated with the creation of an increasingly centralized, functionally departmentalized structure, fell in terms of its costs per ton of consigned output, from 6*s.* 6*d.*

[67] Colvilles Ltd., Production and Cost Statistics, 1930–8.

in 1932 to 3*s*. 1*d*. in 1938. One's only regret is that comparable figures for such firms as Dorman Long, Stewarts & Lloyds, and United Steel are currently unavailable, but the data presented do, it is believed, go some way to confirming the impressionistic verdict on the quality of the management of Colvilles in the years immediately preceding the outbreak of the Second World War.

4 The Scottish Iron and Steel Industry: The Other Twenty Per Cent

By the late thirties the structure of the Scottish iron and steel industry would have been unrecognizable to the second David Colville. By 1937 the Colville Group dominated the industry, producing over 80 per cent of Scotland's ingot output. This he would have relished. He might also have derived a cynical pleasure from the decline in the power and influence of Dixon's Govan Iron Works, whose blast furnaces—Dixon's Blazes—once dominated the southern skyline of Glasgow. In 1922 Dixons had been the first to abandon the use of splint coal and revert entirely to coke fuel. This coke was obtained from the company's coke ovens at Wilsontown Colliery and by purchase from other coke makers. These outside sources began to dwindle as increasing quantities of coke were used at other iron works, and in 1934 a modern coking plant was laid down at Govan. This came into operation in 1936, by which time Dixons was fast becoming a satellite of the Colville Group: selling much of its pig iron and coke for charging the melting furnaces at Clydebridge, and increasingly dependent upon financial assistance from the B.I.S.F.[68] to maintain production of steel-making raw materials.

The once great iron-making firm of William Baird & Company had also fallen upon difficult days. Following the brief postwar boom of 1919–20, Bairds suffered severely from the depression, and their difficulties were exacerbated by the coal strike of 1921. It was during this prolonged strike that the company's Muirkirk furnaces were blown out, never to be relit. In 1924 the Eglinton Iron Works ceased production, and in 1928 Lugar too went out of blast. Had it not been for the availability

[68] *Financial News*, 6 Apr. 1938, 8 June 1939.

TABLE 9.4

Pig Iron Producers and Blast Furnaces in Scotland, 1937–1938

(a) *Blast Furnaces in Scotland: Average Number in Blast and Output per Furnace, 1937–1938*

	Average No. of Furnaces in Blast				Output per furnace per annum ('000 tons)	
	Hematite	Basic	Foundry, Forge, & Direct Castings	TOTAL	Scotland	U.K. (inc. Scotland)
1937	5·87	2·17	7·26	15·30	31·2	68·5
1938	5·65	1·15	5·65	12·45	32·8	68·6

(b) *Pig Iron Producers in Scotland, 1937–1939*

	Blast furnaces at 31 December 1937	In blast, March 1939	In blast, May 1939
W. Baird & Co. Ltd., Gartsherrie	5	3	4 { 3 on basic / 1 on foundry
Carron Co. Ltd., Carron	4	1	1 on foundry
Colvilles Ltd., Clyde Iron	3	0	0
William Dixon Ltd., Govan	12	3	3 { 2 on haematite / 1 on basic
Shotts Iron Co. Ltd., Shotts	4	3	3 on foundry
TOTAL	28	10	11

Notes and Sources:

(a) Iron and Steel Board and B.I.S.F., *Annual Statistics, 1955*, p. 22.

(b) *Glasgow Herald*, 20 Mar. 1939, 11 May 1939.

Colvilles' blast furnaces at Clyde Iron were temporarily stopped during most of 1939 for modifications during the building of the new furnaces that formed part of the Clyde Iron/Clydebridge scheme.

of coking coal at Kilsyth, the famous Gartsherrie works might have shared a similar fate. As it was, only five of its blast furnaces were active even at the height of the 1937 boom.[69] Under A. K. McCosh the firm repeatedly spurned Craig's overtures in the twenties and early thirties. Thus, when Colvilles Ltd.

[69] *Glasgow Herald*, 20 Mar. 1939. There is a full description of the blast furnace plant at Gartsherrie in the Brassert Report, pp. 3–4. The twelve furnaces—in two groups of six—had hearth diameters of 8 ft. 0 in. to 9 ft. 0 in. They were hand charged and were each capable of producing approximately 100 tons per twenty-four hours.

was formed, Baird's interests in iron-making were placed in a very vulnerable position, especially since their ambitious plans to erect a modern battery of coke-ovens in 1933 foundered with their failure to find a market for the surplus by-product gas.[70] Yet the firm's liquid reserves were very large, and the company possessed impressive coal-mining properties. Bairds also had a half interest in the Sierra Leone Development Company, which mined iron ore in West Africa, and, through a subsidiary, the firm owned iron ore mines near Seville and Santander, in Spain.

Down, Bairds were far from being out. Indeed, their trading profits for the year ended 31 May 1938, increased by £166,201 to £598,935, and, with war seemingly imminent in 1939, Bairds were clearly anxious to revive their fortunes. Belatedly, the firm integrated forward into steel; not by building steel-melting capacity, but by merging with the Scottish Iron & Steel Company, the only remaining Scottish steel concern outside the Colville Group. This amalgamation provided William Baird & Company with a steady and assured outlet for a proportion of their pig iron and a substantial part of their output of coke-oven gas, and the Scottish Iron & Steel Company with an abundant supply of essential raw materials. It was expected that coke-oven gas would be conveyed by pipeline from Gartsherrie to the Northburn steel works, the distance between the two plants being just over a mile. It was even conjectured that molten pig iron might be conveyed by rail to the steel works and that, since Northburn had a capacity of only 100,000 tons, additional steel plant might be laid down on the old site of Summerlee Iron Works.[71] These were the hopes that underlay the formation of Bairds and Scottish Steel. Some believed the merger to be the possible forerunner to building up of an organization resembling the Colville Group.

How would David Colville have seen what was left of the iron and steel industry? The Carron Company of Falkirk was still in being. It had survived the depression years better than most since the products of its foundries were much in demand

---

[70] Bairds offered coke-oven gas to Glasgow Corporation at a price with which the municipal undertakings could not compete, but the proposal was turned down by the Socialist majority in the city council. *The Economist*, 18 Mar. 1939; *Financial News*, 15 Mar. 1939.

[71] *Financial Times*, 24 Mar. 1939; *Financial News*, 15 Mar. 1939.

by the building trade, and it benefited from its interests in mines, ships, and estates. Indeed, these interests were expanded during the inter-war period. 'More mineral properties were acquired, notably the Bannockburn Colliery and the Carnock coke ovens and by-product plants from the Alloa Coal Company Ltd. in 1937. And at the works proper important changes were the increase in enamelling facilities and the continuous re-equipment of the engineering department.'[72] At one point at the depth of the depression, the only furnace in blast in the whole of Scotland was at Carron, busy producing foundry pig iron. Another firm that kept going, albeit with great difficulty, on foundry iron and coal production was the Shotts Iron Company. The centre of operations of Stewarts & Lloyds was now at Corby.[73] Clydesdale continued, drawing its supplies from Colvilles under the 1936 arrangement, and at periods of peak demand—at the end of 1936, for example—Stewarts & Lloyds temporarily re-started the butt welding furnaces at Phoenix Works, Rutherglen.[74] But the fact was that the Clydesdale Steel Works—once the nucleus of the firm—was now operated only on a standby basis and enjoyed but a precarious existence.[75] Beardmores, the once sickly giant, now slimmed down to Parkhead, was by the eve of the Second World War enjoying a new lease of life. Under the chairmanship of Sir James Lithgow (appointed in February 1936),[76] the firm increasingly co-ordinated its activities with Colvilles, and with the prospect of armament work, the Parkhead steel furnaces were relit in 1936 after standing idle for eight years.[77] The foundry department was modernized and new annealing furnaces installed. With the aid of an Admiralty grant, two new heavy forging presses were erected, and a large machine shop built. With the completion of these development schemes, the Parkhead works were capable of supplying heavy armour plates in bulk and of hand-

[72] R. H. Campbell, *Carron Company*, pp. 322–3.

[73] Augustus Muir, *The Story of Shotts: A Short History of the Shotts Iron Co. Ltd.*, pp. 43–53.

[74] *Scotsman*, 20 Dec. 1936.

[75] *Financial News*, 11 Feb. 1936.

[76] Sir James Lithgow first went on to the board of Beardmores in 1932 at the request of Sir Andrew Duncan. It was Duncan, as independent Chairman of the B.I.S.F., who appealed to Sir James to become the active head of the business in 1936. Reid, *James Lithgow*, p. 169.

[77] *Daily Mail*, 3 July 1936.

ling the very largest types of castings and forgings (particularly
for naval guns).[78] It remained only to reorganize Beardmores
capital structure completely to resuscitate the firm. This was
undertaken in May 1938, in an operation of considerable complexity involving a massive reduction in the issued share capital.[79] A dividend of $3\frac{1}{2}$ per cent was paid on the Ordinary stock
in March 1939, the first distribution of its kind since 1919.[80]
On the eve of the war, Beardmores were in a position to make
a valuable contribution to the national effort. Between them,
the Bank of England, Sir James Lithgow, and, unwittingly, the
unfortunate shareholders, Lord and Lady Invernairn, had
saved a concern of vital importance. It had been a near thing.

[78] *Scotsman*, 20 Dec. 1936.

[79] The full details were given in the *Financial Times*, 26 May 1938, together
with a statement by Sir James Lithgow, who made a further, much extended
statement to the annual general meeting of William Beardmore & Co. on
17 June 1939. *Financial Times*, 18 June 1938. The net result of the reconstruction was to reduce total debenture and share capital from £4,219,000 to
£2,479,000.

[80] *Financial Times*, 16 Mar. 1939.

X

The Second World War, 1939–1945

The Minutes of the first meeting of Colvilles' board following the outbreak of the Second World War, tersely record that the government had assumed control of the iron and steel industry as from 1 September 1939; that Sir Andrew Duncan had been appointed Controller of the industry; and that P. Baxter had been appointed Liaison Officer for the control of steel products in Scotland.[1] There was, apparently, no lengthy debate about these momentous developments: they were accepted as being inevitable and sensible, the product of emergency plans which had been evolving since Munich and which, essentially, built upon an administrative organization which had its genesis in the Import Duties Advisory Act of 1932. It is unnecessary to detail the machinery of wartime control.[2] Suffice it here to quote Duncan Burn, the most penetrating analyst of the industry's history and himself a member of the staff of the Iron and Steel Control of the Ministry of Supply:

> . . . it was a two-tier organization. The Raw Materials Department of the Ministry of Supply took the place (and much of the staff) of I.D.A.C., and had the job of formulating policy, or of interpreting and transmitting policies determined by higher authority—and of supervising and assisting the execution of policy. The Iron and Steel Control took the place (and most of the staff) of the Federation and was primarily conceived as an executive body to administer policies. In fact, it also often proposed, though it could not determine, the details of policy . . . The Federation itself continued to operate but on a very restricted scale, and there were regular meetings between the senior officials on the Steel Control and the President's Committee of the Federation.[3]

[1] Colvilles Ltd.; Minute Book II, 6 Sept. 1939.
[2] It has been described and analysed by Duncan Burn, *The Steel Industry, 1939–1959* (Cambridge: C.U.P., 1961), pp. 3–50, and Keeling and Wright, *The Development of the Modern British Steel Industry*, pp. 24–84.
[3] Burn, *The Steel Industry*, pp. 4–5. Sir Andrew Duncan became President of the Board of Trade in 1940; he was succeeded as Steel Controller by, successively, Sir Charles Wright, Sir John Duncanson, sometime commercial manager and, from 1936, a director of the Steel Company of Scotland, and Mr. C. R. Wheeler (Guest, Keen Baldwins). Among the Deputy Controllers

1 The Colville Group: Management and Control

The archives of the Colville Group, embarrassingly plentiful and comprehensive for certain periods, are frustratingly scanty for the years of the Second World War, but the board minutes indicate a wholeharted co-operation with the Iron and Steel Control, and a dedication to meeting the needs of the war economy.

There was little change in the administration of the Colville Group throughout the war years. The board retained tight control over the Group's manifold activities, and John Craig continued to dominate the board, although the growing power of Dr. Andrew McCance is increasingly evident. Advancing years, far from curbing the Chairman's energy, seemed merely to stimulate it. He was everywhere: frequently in London for discussions with Control and the President's Committee; at meetings of the boards of the subsidiary and associated companies (with the death of Sir Adam Nimmo in August 1939, John Craig assumed the chairmanship of both James Nimmo & Company and Nimmo & Dunlop);[4] at the various works, where his unhurried visits were welcomed by the managers and workmen alike: 'he always had time to address a word of greeting to the workers as he passed, calling them by their Christian names. He knew everybody—the fathers, the sons and the grandsons.'[5]

Yet because Craig's own peculiar skills were commercial, and the exigencies of war demanded mainly technical expertise, both the Chairman and the board became increasingly reliant on Dr. Andrew McCance. Awarded the Bessemer Gold Medal for 1940 by the Iron and Steel Institute and elected a Fellow of the Royal Society in 1943, McCance was perhaps at the height of his scientific powers during the war years. There were manifold problems for him to solve:[6] those posed by the substitution of home for foreign ores, the increasing complexity of producing

---

was Andrew McCosh, the Chairman of Bairds and Scottish Steel. He was in charge of Raw Materials. *Colvilles' Magazine* carried a biographical sketch of John M. Duncanson in vol. xix (Apr. 1938), p. 73.

[4] Colvilles Ltd., Minute Book II, 6 Sept. 1939, 5 Oct. 1939.

[5] David Graham, Dalzell Works, in *Colvilles' Magazine*, Spring 1957, pp. 6–7.

[6] See below, p. 263.

and handling ferro-alloys, and the difficulties inherent in the hard-driving of every kind of equipment when there was a chronic scarcity of spares, of facilities, and of time for proper maintenance. At several works the plant often began simply to wear out, and the repercussions of increasingly infrequent breakdowns disturbed the surprisingly delicate balance of integrated steel production processes. With the aid of the staff of the Metallurgical and Engineering Departments McCance met every demand made upon him. The requirements of the Ministry of Aircraft Production, the Admiralty, and the War Office for steels that had never previously been produced in bulk were satisfied by new specifications and original methods: 179,000 tons of tank armour and protective plating and over 10,000 tons of non-magnetic steel were dispatched during the war years.[7] It is not too much to say that during the period 1939–45 Colvilles became highly dependent upon the sheer scientific virtuosity of one man.

Other circumstances too strengthened the relative power of Sir John Craig (as he became in 1943) and Dr. Andrew McCance, who in 1944 was appointed Deputy Chairman and Joint Managing Director.[8] During the war, the board had to reach its decisions without the counsel of Sir James Lithgow, appointed Controller of Merchant Shipbuilding and Repairs in February 1940;[9] Sir Frederick Rebbeck, whose major energies had to be devoted to the shipyards at Belfast;[10] and T. R. Craig, mobilized with the 6th Cameronians in 1939 and A.A. and Q.M.G. of the 52nd (Lowland) Division from 1942 to 1945.[11] Peter Baxter, too, was often 'absent by arrangement', having temporarily relinquished his post as Scottish Liaison Officer in August 1941 to go, at Lord Beaverbrook's request, to the United States to take charge of the British Purchasing Commission for iron and steel products.[12] Thus, for long periods, the board was reduced to an effective membership of five. Of the directors, only Henry Lithgow, Sir A. Steven Bils-

[7] Colvilles Ltd., Chairman's Statement to the Fourteenth Annual General Meeting, 24 May 1945.
[8] Colvilles Ltd., Minute Book III, 4 May 1944.
[9] See J. M. Reid, *James Lithgow*, pp. 192–215.
[10] He was knighted in 1941.
[11] *Colvilles' Magazine*, Spring, 1965, p. 9.
[12] Colvilles Ltd., Minute Book II, 28 Aug. 1941.

land, and Harry Yates were able to attend regularly, and only
the last of these was able to give his whole time to the affairs
of the Group, being largely responsible for sheets and light
rolled products, the materials required for the production of
Nissen huts, Anderson and Morrison shelters, and bullet-proof
helmets.[13] Henry Lithgow—on the boards of no fewer than
twenty-four companies—had, in the absence of his brother at
the Admiralty, to carry 'alone the weight of wartime work at
Port Glasgow, where the Lithgow yards were pouring out stan-
dardized ships';[14] while Sir Steven Bilsland's manifold and
varied commitments prevented him too from playing a leading
role in the affairs of Colvilles Ltd.[15]

The resulting burden thrown on Sir John Craig and Dr.
McCance might well have proved insupportable had they not
been able to depend upon their fellow directors on the boards
of the subsidiary companies and the able co-operation of the
senior members of the staff. Of the directorate, increasingly important roles were played by A. J. H. Mowbray of Smith &
McLean, James Colville of Clyde Alloy, and John Wright of
Colville Constructional. But perhaps more important was the
Board's growing dependence on the senior members of the
staff: on William Barr, Chief Metallurgist, T. W. Hand, Chief
Mechanical Engineer, L. Rothera, Chief Electrical Engineer,
and R. C. Dymock, Chief Labour Officer, and on the works
managers, John McCracken of Clydebridge, Sam Thomson
of Lanarkshire, James Gibson of Glangarnock, James Ross
of Dalzell, James Bryden of Gartcosh, and Dr. J. M. Ferguson
of Mossend. That this was recognized is apparent from the
circulation among the members of Colvilles Board, of a
'Memorandum concerning Company Control', discussion of
which resulted, in March 1942, in an agreement that 'it would
be desirable to arrange occasional meetings of the Managers
of all the works in the Group'.[16] Thereafter, such meetings took
place regularly. Their value was so greatly appreciated that

[13] Ibid., II, 9 Sept. 1943.
[14] J. M. Reid, *James Lithgow*, p. 205.
[15] One of the hardest tasks of his career was said to have been that of District
Commissioner for Civil Defence in which office he was responsible for organizing three-fifths of the population of Scotland. *Colvilles' Magazine*, Autumn
1955, p. 7.
[16] Colvilles Ltd., Minute Book II, 5 Mar. 1942.

from them was to emerge the idea of an executive board, formally created within a year of the end of the war.[17] Yet the basic organizational structure of Colvilles was to be retained. At a meeting of the Board, held in January 1945, 'specially arranged to give the Directors an opportunity of reviewing the organisation of the Company and its subsidiaries', it was agreed that 'the present method of having separate Companies and separate Boards for all the subsidiaries was still desirable and that the present method of controlling finance on a Group basis should be continued'.[18]

2 Output, Maintenance, and Repair

During the war Colvilles Ltd. and its subsidiaries rolled over nine million tons of steel.[19] The precise contribution of each of the various works to this impressive total is not known, nor are the ingot equivalents, for only at the Lanarkshire Steel Works have the full details survived. The available information, including the *estimated* annual ingot outputs of the Colville Group, is given in Table 10.1. During the years 1939–45, Scotland produced approximately 15 per cent of the national product of ingots and of this the melting furnaces of the Colville Group supplied about 80 per cent. Steel ingots are, however, only an intermediate product. More important was the consigned tonnage of plates, rails, angles, sections and sheets, bombs and shells. These finished and semi-finished products were produced in mills whose efficiency ranged from the best in the country to those in which the plant was approaching obsolescence and whose shut-down was prevented only by the exigencies of wartime demand.

The Clyde Iron/Clydebridge complex—completed only in 1940—was of critical importance. No. 1 Blast Furnace at Clyde Iron was first put on blast in June 1939, and No. 2 Furnace in February 1940. The plant was designed to smelt high grade foreign ores and incorporated all the latest British and American innovations at the time of building, but with the cessation

[17] See below, pp. 313–15.
[18] Colvilles Ltd., Minute Book III, 5 Jan. 1945. 'It was also agreed to resume the practice of holding Board Meetings at the various Works.'
[19] Colvilles Ltd., Statement of Sir John Craig to Fourteenth Annual General Meeting, 24 May 1945.

TABLE 10.1
Ingot Output: United Kingdom, Scotland, the Colville Group, and Lanarkshire Steel Works, 1939–1945

(1)	(2)		(3)		(4)	
United Kingdom	Scotland		The Colville Group		Lanarkshire Steel Works	
(tons)	(tons)	$\frac{Scotland}{U.K.}$%	(tons)	$\frac{Colvilles}{Scotland}$%	*Tonnage of*	
					Ingots	Dispatches
12,936,400	1,872,800	14·5	1,544,415	82·5	196,021	151,569
12,586,200	1,998,800	15·9	1,608,385	80·5	230,827	194,162
11,881,000	1,763,200	14·8	1,445,824	82·0	211,181	192,871
12,730,100	1,773,400	13·9	1,454,188	82·0	227,261	207,346
12,415,300	1,893,100	15·2	1,533,411	81·0	254,014	218,276
11,553,500	1,754,200	15·2	1,403,360	80·0	236,415	196,206
11,821,000	1,747,200	14·8	1,380,288	79·0	237,069	n.d.
85,923,500	12,802,700	14·9	10,369,871	81·0		

and Sources:
1. (1) Lanarkshire Steel Co.: Statistical Records.
   (2) 1939–40, British Steel Corporation Statistical Services.
      1941–5, Lanarkshire Steel Co.: Statistical Records.
   (3) 1939–40, Colvilles Ltd., Directors' Minutes, 13 Feb. 1941.
      1941–5, *Estimated* on the basis of known figures for 1939–40 and 1947, details of the degree of capacity working provided by Colvilles Ltd.: Minute Books, and data on Lanarkshire Steel Works.
   (4) Lanarkshire Steel Co.: Statistical Records. 'Dispatches' represent consigned outputs of finished, rolled products; n.d. = no data.

of ore imports it was necessary to use low grade English ores from Northamptonshire. This involved a different operating technique and considerable difficulty was experienced before good results were obtained in the autumn of 1942. Even so, *maximum* output could not be obtained simply because the units of iron were not in the materials being smelted. Furthermore, the great variety of changes and varieties of ore to be charged often constituted a serious problem in proper stocking and furnace burdening. Despite these circumstances, the basic pig iron costs at Clyde Iron were repeatedly the lowest in the United Kingdom,[20] and by the end of April 1946 the two furnaces had between them produced nearly two million tons of pig iron at an average weekly rate of nearly 6,000 tons, a figure that might well have been 2,000 tons higher had high grade foreign ore been available.[21]

[20] Colvilles Ltd., Minute Book III, 7 Oct. 1943, 30 Mar. 1944.
[21] In other words, each furnace produced well over 150,000 tons of pig iron

At Clydebridge and Glengarnock, too, productivity was high, costs relatively low, and output often well in excess of the notional capacity when the new plant was laid down in 1938–9. At Dalzell, things were not so satisfactory. As early as February 1941, it was noted that 'owing to the heavy commitments for war purposes, it had been impossible to carry out urgent repair work and renewals, particularly [at] the melting shops'.[22] Not surprisingly, by 1943 the conditions at Dalzell were giving rise to considerable anxiety and the cost of melting was becoming excessive. Everywhere it was the same when older plant (which might well have been replaced had it not been for the war) was subjected to hard driving. This was particularly so at the Blochairn and Hallside Works of the Steel Company of Scotland. It was a case of making do: patching here and modifying there. The potential technical benefits of the inter-war mergers just could not be realized under wartime conditions when every melting shop and the majority of mills had to be kept going at whatever cost. The General Terminus Scheme was an early casualty: it was suspended in May 1940.[23] The new mixer at Clydebridge was converted to a melting furnace in order to increase productive capacity.[24] Vast sums of government money were poured into Blochairn and Hallside[25] with no real expectation of anything more than short-run boosts to output. Mossend No. 2 Mill was organized and equipped for rolling alloy bars at a cost of nearly £2 million, yet its capacity was never fully employed, and there were already discussions of its future redundancy in the summer of 1943.[26] Clearly, expensive misallocations of resources were made due to defective demand forecasts in the early years of the war. These were almost inevitable and little blame attaches to the mistakes of the planners at Control. The fact remains that many

per year, nearly five times the average Scottish rate in 1938 (see above, Table 9.3). This paragraph is based upon I. S. Scott Maxwell, 'Clyde Iron Works Blast Furnaces', *Colvilles' Magazine*, Summer 1946, pp. 6–7, and ibid., 'No. 1 Blast Furnace', Jan.–Feb. 1949, p. 3.

[22] Colvilles Ltd., Minute Book II, 13 Feb. 1941.
[23] Colvilles Ltd., Directors' Minutes, 9 May 1940.
[24] Ibid., 7 Dec. 1939.
[25] For example, increased plate capacity was laid down at Blochairn in 1942 at a cost of nearly £600,000. Ibid., 8 Jan. 1942.
[26] Ibid., 3 Oct. 1940, 29 July 1943.

of the inter-war weaknesses were exacerbated. Some plant, the products of which were urgently required, was often worked almost to destruction; elsewhere totally unexpected vicissitudes in demand, especially for special steels, left much costly equipment under-utilized: a hindrance to both current and future economical output.

Nevertheless, the iron and steel industry had been asked to maintain output at all costs and even when the Ministry of Supply seemed 'to be asking for the impossible'[27] the Colville Group—like the industry generally—responded positively. Rarely was there a failure to achieve the targets set by Control, even at times of 'acute demand'.[28] Sometimes, the targets were substantially exceeded. By mid-1943, the period of maximum pressure was over. The President's Committee of the B.I.S.F. believed that 'the peak of the demand for steel had been passed and that the position from now on would probably ease'. Indeed, by July 1943, 'the general tone in London was that ... we were now on the downgrade'.[29]

3 The Genesis of Postwar Planning

The time had come to devote some thought to the future. The war had come with Colvilles only halfway to realizing the full technical and economic potentialities inherent in the successful completion of its merger policy in the mid-thirties. Only the massive Clyde Iron/Clydebridge programme had been implemented by 1940:[30] lesser, albeit highly important, projects had had to wait their turn and had been overtaken by events beyond the control of the board. The expenditure of no less than $£4\frac{1}{4}$ million on government schemes by 1943—mainly for the production of armour and bullet-proof plate at Mossend, alloy steel

---

[27] Sir W. Charles Wright to John Craig, 18 Feb. 1943. The point is well made by Vaizey, *History of British Steel*, pp. 100–2.

[28] The Directors' Minutes make it clear that the greatest pressure on Colvilles' resources was experienced in the closing months of 1942 and early in 1943.

[29] John Craig, reporting the findings of the President's Committee to the board of Colvilles. Minute Book III, 20 May 1943, 29 July 1943. It was explained that 'Better deliveries were expected from America'.

[30] At a total cost which exceeded the amount authorized ($£2,199,000$) by less than $£30,000$. Colvilles Ltd., Accounts and Papers, 'Expenditure on C.C. Schemes', 29 Nov. 1939; Minute Book II, 8 Jan. 1940.

at Clyde Alloy and Hallside, and special aircraft steels throughout the Group—had exacerbated rather than remedied weaknesses in internal organization.[31]

The solution of these deep-rooted problems would have to await the return of peace. Meanwhile, early in 1943, it was permissible to think about what might happen 'after the war'. At this period, the company's managerial resources were too stretched to do more than introduce a few ideas at board level. The first topic of this kind to be discussed was 'the possibility of the development of plastics'. Inevitably, 'it was remitted to Dr. McCance to gather what information he could for [future] consideration',[32] and the subject was often to be raised again at future meetings. Nothing came of it, however; perhaps because the degree of diversification involved was too great to contemplate or perhaps because alternative by-products from the coke ovens were more valuable. Certainly, a small experimental plant for the production of carbon black (used in the manufacture of rubber) was installed in July 1943.[33] Greater success seemed to be promised by a whole series of discussions, inaugurated in March 1943, concerning the supply of sheet steel for 'postwar housing'.[34] Within a few months, light sections suit-

[31] The expenditures on government schemes are scattered throughout the Directors' Minutes but the principal summaries are those for the meetings of 3 Oct. 1940 and 2 Apr. 1942, at which it was mentioned that of the total expenditure of £4,159,950 authorized on government schemes *up to that date*, Colvilles were liable to meet only £362,000; some indication of the proportion of this vast investment which might prove to be of long-term benefit to the Group.

[32] Colvilles Ltd., Minute Book III, 30 Dec. 1942.

[33] Ibid., 1 July 1943.

[34] During 1923, Lord Weir established a factory at Cardonald which was planned to produce 2,500 houses annually. These houses were to be of composite construction of steel sheets (for the outer wall) attached to a strong wooden frame. The interior partitions, floors, and rafters were to be of wood; the foundations, concrete with bitumen damp course; and the roof, asbestos cement or clay tiles. Although some 3,000 Weir houses were put up, by the end of 1927 the entire scheme had been killed by the National Federation of Building Trades Operatives and the building employers, who threatened to disrupt the orthodox housing programmes of many Scottish local authorities if they persisted with their experiments with the Weir house. In 1943, Lord Weir—apparently under pressure from the Government—revived the idea of the steel houses as a contribution to solving the growing housing shortage. It is certain that Lord Weir discussed the possibilities with John Craig and Dr. McCance, with both of whom he had long been acquainted. For Weir's involvement with housing, see W. J. Reader, *The Weir Group* (London: Weidenfeld & Nicolson, 1971), pp. 100–3, 136, 146–7.

able for house construction had been designed though full-scale production might, it was thought, be inhibited because 'Scotland lacked a strip mill'.[35] Nevertheless, when 'Sir Steven Bilsland raised the question of the actual production of houses' in July 1943, it was agreed that 'when that stage was reached', Colvilles should take an interest in a separate company formed specifically for the supply of houses in Scotland, if this was what transpired.[36] Commercial considerations were also uppermost in several other developments. The agreements with Harland & Wolff for the supply of all their steel requirements and with Stewarts & Lloyds for the supply of the steel plates required for tubemaking at Clydesdale were extended for 'a period of time equal to the present emergency'. Planning for the future production of a special corrosion-resisting steel—known as Corten—for the British manufacture of which Colvilles had obtained exclusive rights from the United States Alloy Corporation on the eve of hostilities, was revived,[37] and the development of a process for impregnating mild steel with chrome—similarly suspended during the war—was actively resumed.[38]

More far-reaching ideas were prompted by the receipt of a letter from Sir Alexander Dunbar, chairman of the Federation's Post-War Reconstruction Committee, asking Colvilles to submit, 'without commitment, estimates of [their] probable capital expenditure in, say, the first five years after the European Armistice'.[39] But after 'extensive discussions', it was decided not to reply 'until the Board had further information on

[35] Colvilles Ltd., Minute Book III, 1 July 1943. In 1944, when Smith & McLean were considering the advisability of laying down plant for the production of sheets for housing, 'Harry Yates agreed that in our mills we could not produce sheets of the same finish as the new Strip Mills'. Ibid., 5 June 1944. This did not prevent him from assuring Lord Weir that in tonnage Smith & McLean would be able to meet all his requirements. Ibid., 6 July 1944.
[36] Ibid., 29 July 1943.
[37] Colvilles Ltd., Minute Book III, 4 May 1944, and Sir John Craig's Statement to the 14th Annual General Meeting, 24 May 1945.
[38] This process was covered by a patent held by Dr. Becker, a German. To work it a company, called the Metal-Gas Co. Ltd., was formed in 1938 with an authorized share capital of £48,250. The bulk of the issued capital was held jointly by Smith & McLean and Clyde Alloy, and hence Colvilles Ltd. Colvilles Ltd., Minute Book III, 16 Oct. 1944, 1 Nov. 1944, and Sir John Craig's Statement to the 14th Annual General Meeting, 24 May 1945.
[39] Ibid., 2 Dec. 1943. For the background, see Burn, *The Steel Industry*, pp. 52 ff., and Vaizey, *History of British Steel*, pp. 140–2.

what extensions had taken place in various categories of plant throughout Great Britain since the outbreak of war'.[40] This information Dunbar refused to supply and there, for the moment, the matter rested.[41] It was not resuscitated until August 1944, when, in response to another inquiry from the Federation requesting information on Colvilles' postwar plans (dated 4 August 1944), it was decided to press for a number of schemes that 'were urgently necessary for the replacement of plant and machinery to maintain the output and increase the efficiency of the Group'. These included an entirely new melting shop at Dalzell (£1,850,000), a continuous billet mill—together with three modern Venturi melting furnaces of 125–150 tons capacity—at Lanarkshire (£1 million), a light section mill at Glengarnock (£650,000), a wheel and axle plant at Hallside (£1 million), a medium plate mill at Clydebridge (£1,700,000), and a jobbing mill (£150,000). It was expected that the total expenditure involved would be between £5 million and £6 million.[42]

There was nothing radical about these proposals. They have been criticized as being far too conservative. Certainly, they did little to promote the ideal of 'the dramatic rather than the humdrum',[43] but they were, above all, realistic. It has been suggested that Colvilles' 1944 development programme reflected the competing interests of 'powerfully rooted local concerns',[44] and the distribution of major schemes does tend to lend credence to this view: something for Dalzell, something for Lanarkshire, something for the Steel Company, and so on. But this is a misleading impression. Criticisms of the 1944 proposals rest on the implicit assumption that they had been simply dreamed up to meet long-standing deficiencies with inadequate consideration being given to postwar demand patterns and the problem of congested sites. That this is not so is apparent from the lengthy report submitted to the Federation in mid-September 1944,[45] which set out the reasons for each part of the

[40] Colvilles Ltd., Minute Book III, 30 Dec. 1943.
[41] Ibid., 3 Feb. 1944.
[42] Ibid., 7 Sept. 1944, 16 Oct. 1944.
[43] Burn, *The Steel Industry*, p. 65.
[44] Vaizey, *History of British Steel*, p. 141.
[45] Colvilles Ltd., 'Report on Post-War Developments for the Colville Group', 4 Sept. 1944.

development programme. This closely-argued document explained, often in considerable detail, what changes were necessary, how they were related to demand projections, and how they improved site layouts and took account of existing transport facilities. It was emphasized that the implementation of the programme would permit the closure of five small mills at Dalzell, Glengarnock, Lanarkshire, and Hallside and the conversion of Hallside, one of the works of the Steel Company of Scotland, from melting and rolling operations to a solid wheel and axle plant. In effect, the entire scheme envisaged the completion of the prewar rationalization programme, a step made all the more necessary and urgent by the accelerated deterioration of hard-driven plant during the early years of the war.[46]

Two months after the submission of the main report— additional details covering costs and phasing were subsequently sent to the Federation—Dr. McCance reported to the board that he had attended meetings of the Economic Efficiency Committee,[47] of which he was a member, and it had been decided to arrange all the schemes submitted into four main groups:

(i) Deferred repairs;
(ii) Replacement of obsolete plant without expansion of output;
(iii) Replacement of obsolete plant with increased capacity; and
(iv) Capital expansion.

It was the intention to give priority to the schemes grouped under (i) and (ii) approved by the Committee.[48] After lengthy

[46] In the section of the Report concerned with the new Melting Shop at Dalzell—the most important element in the programme—it was stated that 'Before the war it was known that the cost of ingot production at Motherwell did not compare favourably with that at Clydebridge or Glengarnock, the average difference in 1937 being 10·0 shillings and in 1943 with increased cost of labour and fuel this difference had risen to 27·9 shillings'.

[47] The Economic Efficiency Committee was a standing committee of the B.I.S.F. It was charged with the duty of ' "making general surveys in order to co-ordinate modernization on a national basis". It was both to examine schemes put before it and to propose schemes . . .' and it began to advise Control and the Raw Materials Department of the Ministry of Supply on which schemes of capital investment they should sponsor under their existing powers in the Autumn of 1944. Burn, *The Steel Industry*, p. 66.

[48] Vaizey, *History of British Steel*, p. 141, gives the impression that this system of priorities was unique to Colvilles. It would appear rather that it was a

discussion, the board decided that the new melting shop at Dalzell must go into Group (i) and that Colvilles would be entirely responsible for its financing;[49] that the billet mill at Lanarkshire, the light section mill at Glengarnock, and the wheel and axle plant at Hallside should go into Group (ii), and that the medium plate mill at Clydebridge might be placed in Group (iv).[50]

After a further meeting of the Economic Efficiency Committee, the new Dalzell melting shop was formerly approved and recommended to Control, and authority was given to Colvilles to approach Control immediately for the necessary licences. The billet and light section mills were also approved in principle, but Colvilles made it plain that it would be some time yet before the firm would be in a position to take up these schemes.[51] More urgent, though not included in the original series of submissions, was the necessity of gaining the approval of the Economic Efficiency Committee to the construction of a third blast furnace at Clyde Iron. Although the two existing furnaces were working well and giving no cause for concern— even a year later the original linings appeared healthy and the monthly readings of casing and hearth cooling water temperatures were quite normal[52]—it was recognized that blast furnaces could begin to go seriously wrong very quickly. Furthermore, no one quite knew the deleterious effects of hard-driving under adverse conditions during which low grade and inferior raw materials had had to be employed. Colvilles were, therefore, conscious that the possibility existed of having both furnaces off for relining at the same time.[53] Consequently, their case for a third furnace at Clyde Iron rested on the argument that its

---

set of priorities designed by the Economic Efficiency Committee for the industry as a whole.

[49] It was calculated that the scheme would take eighteen months to complete.

[50] Colvilles Ltd., Minute Book III, 1 Nov. 1944.

[51] Ibid., 1 Dec. 1944. At an earlier board meeting, Dr. McCance had stated that 'we could not spend more than £1½ m. per annum and [even this rate of expenditure] would depend upon the staff available', ibid., 16 Oct. 1944.

[52] I. S. Scott Maxwell, 'Clyde Iron Works', p. 7.

[53] The Director of Plant Progress at Iron and Steel Control, Mr. Norman Iles, himself accepted that 'the safety margin [had] been exceeded'. '[Copy] Memo by Director for Plant Progress, Iron and Steel Control re The Installation of a new Blast Furnace at Clyde Iron Works', 8 June 1945.

installation was necessary to permit the relining of Nos. 1 and
2 Furnaces, without discontinuity of production which, should
it occur, would have disastrous consequences on steel plate production at Clydebridge. This was a very powerful case and it
was believed that its acceptance by Control would be eased by
its moderate cost. Only £300,000 was involved, largely because
of existing facilities at the proposed site, and this expenditure
had already been authorized by the board.[54]

Thus when the war 'petered out',[55] Colvilles Ltd. had not
only survived but had evolved a plan for the future. It may
not have been the most exciting plan submitted to the B.I.S.F.
Without doubt, it disappointed those who hoped for the revival
of the Brassert proposals of 1929, one of whom was Dr. T. P.
Colclough, the Technical Adviser of the Iron and Steel Control.
But it was technically feasible, financially practicable, and,
within its modest limits, economically efficient. Whether it
would be implemented only time would tell.

[54] Colvilles Ltd., Minute Book III, 1 Mar. 1945.
[55] The phrase is Vaizey's (*History of British Steel*, p. 118) and its accuracy
in relation to the iron and steel industry is amply justified if the records of
the Colville Group are at all typical. Thus, many operations were being
allowed to run down after mid-1943; massive orders for tank plates were can-
celled throughout the second half of 1943 ('the total production would only
be about one-third of the anticipated requirements'; the demand for shell
bars was already 'falling off' in July 1943; plate orders were 'slowing down'
early in 1944; and, at Mossend, No. 1 Cogging Mill was 'closed completely'
in July 1944, 'the last two electric furnaces' went out of commission in October
1944, and No. 2 Mill was stopped in November.

PART V

Progress under planning

XI

The First Development Plan, 1945–50: Clydeside Rejected

1 The Framework of Planning

'It was the almost universal acceptance of regular and co-ordinated development plans under central co-ordination, with
official government approval, which marked the period 1939
to 1945 as something of a watershed in the . . . history [of the
iron and steel industry].'[1] Whereas, during the thirties, the
wishes of the Federation had occasionally been ignored, even
thwarted, by individual firms, such recalcitrance became increasingly rare when the Federation's power was greatly strengthened by the superimposition of direct governmental control.
The government, operating through the Ministry of Supply,
and advised by the Iron and Steel Control—whose personnel
was recruited largely from the Federation—could now strongly
influence, even determine, programmes of capital investment.
Thus, the acceptability of each company's postwar development plan, however rational from the viewpoint of individual
firms, had to be assessed in the light of its contribution to the
national evolution of this key industry.[2]

To some of the leaders of the industry, more was involved
in this procedure than the elimination of conflicting elements
among the welter of individual schemes and the avoidance of
wasteful duplication: it implied more radical changes initiated
by the Federation itself. Firms must not be allowed simply
to patch; where necessary the Federation should supplement
the proposals of its members by its own schemes based on world-
wide surveys of market prospects and technical change. The
very structure of the industry should be altered by greater concentration and locational change. The logical consequence of
this line of argument was, of course, nationalization. But until

[1] Vaizey, *History of British Steel*, p. 120.
[2] Burn, *The Steel Industry*, p. 61.

this ultimate step was taken, the boards of individual companies had to be convinced of the desirability and, what was more, the potential profitability of the radical schemes evolved in the headquarters of the Federation or the offices of the Ministry of Supply. For a few more years boards of directors were to draw up development plans, and although they were prepared to amend and adjust them to conform to any national plan— essentially the summation of schemes of individual firms—they had to be convinced that the implementation of more far-reaching proposals emanating from outside were in the interests of their own companies. They might be pursuaded; they could not yet be dictated to. It is the object of this section to examine how this arrangement worked in practice: to investigate the nature of the postwar reconstruction of the Scottish iron and steel industry as revealed by Colvilles' development plans, the only coherent group of the firm's records that has survived from this period.

It will be recalled that it was late in 1943 when Colvilles were first asked by the Federation's Post-War Reconstruction Committee to provide estimates of their probable capital expenditure in the first five years after the European Armistice, a request which was repeated, with more urgency, in August 1944. To this request Colvilles and other members of the Federation responded within a few weeks. The returns of the various firms were pooled to be considered by the Federation's Economic Efficiency Committee, but there was little time for their proper co-ordination before a report was called for by the Minister of Supply. This report, which was presented in December 1944, recommended the licensing of schemes involving the expenditure of £20 million. Additional schemes, estimated to cost over £100 million, were under consideration. It was, as Burn observed, 'the first step towards a five years' plan'.[3] Such a plan was, in fact, formally called for by the caretaker government in May 1945. The resulting document, submitted in December 1945 and published in May 1946, has been rightly seen as marking a significant step in the public control of the industry.[4]

But between the time that Churchill's caretaker government had called on the British steel industry to provide a plan for

---

[3] Burn, *The Steel Industry*, p. 67.
[4] Andrews and Brunner, *Capital Development in Steel*, p. 294.

its postwar capital development and the submission of that plan, a Labour government had been elected pledged to nationalize the industry. Not surprisingly, no attempt was made to dismantle the controls that the government already exercised over the industry. Instead, the Iron and Steel Control—created to supervise the activities of the industry in wartime—was superseded by an Iron and Steel Board in September 1946, and the Control of Iron and Steel Orders remained in operation. The Board had no statutory powers, its function was simply to advise the Ministry of Supply. Patently a transitional scheme, the principal purpose of the Control Board was to bridge the gap between the wartime Steel Control and nationalization.[5]

This, then, was the national organizational framework within which Colvilles planned for the future in the immediate postwar years. Essentially, as Vaizey has emphasized, the wartime system was continued into the peace: it operated at four levels: the individual firms, the Federation, Iron and Steel Control and, after 1946, the Board, and the Ministry of Supply. Lurking in the wings, nebulous, its desirability and precise form the subject of fierce debate, was nationalization.[6]

2 The Development Plan of 1945

The basic concept underlying the plan that Colvilles submitted to the Federation in 1944 was the elimination of 'outstanding deficiencies in production facilities', and the most important of the detailed proposals was the construction at Dalzell of a completely new melting shop consisting of six 100-ton furnaces. The plan represented a further stage in the company's interrupted scheme of modernization and re-grouping drawn up before the war: it was intended to achieve a better, more economical internal balance rather than any significant increase in productive capacity.[7] In reviewing the outlook immediately after the war, however, it became increasingly clear that mere

[5] The basic details of the first Steel Board are given by Keeling and Wright, *The Development of the Modern British Steel Industry*, pp. 160–1; the finest analysis of its activities given, as always, by Burn, *The Steel Industry*, pp. 191–290.

[6] Vaizey, *History of British Steel*, pp. 121–8.

[7] Colvilles Ltd., 'Report on the Post-War Developments for the Colville Group', 4 Sept. 1944 (hereinafter cited 'Post-War Developments, 1944').

schemes of improvement would be insufficient if Scotland were to maintain its place in the British steel industry. Only by an expansion of Scottish steel output proportionate to the expected growth in national output could this be achieved.[8]

But Colvilles' projected expansion did not rest simply on a nationalistic desire not to fall behind the other regions: not to lose its place. As a review of Colvilles' developments sent in November 1945, to Sir John Duncanson,[9] the Commercial and

TABLE 11.1

Productive Capacity of the Colville Group as Envisaged in 1945 and 1947

Works	Production of Steel in Ingot Tons			
	1945[a]		1947	
	Existing	*Future*	*Existing*	*Future*
Dalzell	400,000	540,000	400,000	550,000
Clydebridge	400,000	400,000	350,000	600,000
Glengarnock	300,000	400,000	300,000	400,000
Lanarkshire	220,000	410,000	220,000	425,000
Blochairn	150,000	150,000	150,000	—
Hallside	175,000	—	175,000	—
TOTAL	1,645,000	1,900,000	1,595,000	1,975,000

Note: [a] It was emphasized that 'at the present time the figures given for existing production were very considerably reduced owing to war conditions'. Furthermore, no allowance was made for the production of electric furnace steel at the Clyde Alloy Works.

Sources: Colvilles Ltd., 'Post-War Developments, 1945'; 'Memorandum on Scottish Steel, 1947'.

[8] Colvilles Ltd.: 'Memorandum on the Scottish Steel Industry', 9 Apr. 1947, 'Introduction' (hereinafter cited 'Memorandum on Scottish Steel, 1947').

[9] At the outbreak of war Duncanson, a member of the board of the Steel Company of Scotland, was seconded to Iron and Steel Control, where he was shortly to be appointed Deputy Controller of Iron and Steel Supplies, becoming Controller of Iron and Steel in September 1942. Duncanson left the Iron and Steel Control—and resigned his position on the board of the Steel Company of Scotland—on his appointment as Commercial and Technical Director of the Federation in July 1945. Colvilles Ltd., Minute Book III, 28 June 1945; Keeling and Wright, *The Development of the Modern British Steel Industry*, pp. 33, 36, 160.

Technical Director of the Federation, emphasized: 'With the increase in labour costs and the cost of coal the scale of operations in Steelworks must be increased and mechanized to a greater extent than during the prewar period in order to compensate for these increased costs. We believe it is necessary to concentrate Steel production into works of not less than 4/500,000 ingot tons per annum, and our plans for postwar developments are based on this principle.'[10] Accordingly, it was envisaged that Colvilles' productive capacity would be increased by some 15 per cent and would be allocated as shown in the first part of Table 11.1. The total output of 1,900,000 ingot tons of steel would, it was anticipated, be devoted to the manufacture of the products shown in the first half of Table 11.2.

In putting forward this plan, modest though it appears in the light of subsequent events, Colvilles strongly emphasized that its realization 'must be spread over a number of years in order to avoid any social dislocation involved in the transfer of works or the closing of plants'. Indeed, while cogently argued, the tenor of the review was somewhat hesitant. The experiences of the inter-war period had left their mark. Colvilles fully realized that a larger proportion of the pig iron used in Scotland must be manufactured in Scotland, but no detailed figures could be submitted until the Federation had decided its policy concerning the importation of scrap. It was, moreover, recognized that 'during the period of reconstruction there should be no interruption in the supplies of steel to consumers in Scotland and elsewhere'.

Colvilles' concern over the supply of raw materials was well founded. As Dr. McCance had already pointed out to Sir John Duncanson, Scotland had always been a large scrap consumer and it was 'vital for the continuance of production . . . that the importation of scrap should be continued. Should anything happen to prevent this, then I can see a marked reduction in Scottish ingot production until such times as new Blast Furnaces and Coke Ovens have been created to offset the fall in scrap supplies. Under present conditions, such a change would take years to complete and I am afraid it would put the steel

---

[10] Colvilles Ltd., 'Post-War Developments of the Colville Group', 1 Nov. 1945, para. 1 (hereinafter cited 'Post-War Developments, 1945').

TABLE 11.2

Products of the Colville Group, by Works, as Envisaged in 1945 and 1947

	1945 (tons per annum)		1947 (tons per annum)	
Blooms, billets, sheet bars, etc.:				
Dalzell	150,000		150,000	
Lanarkshire	100,000		200,000	
Glengarnock	50,000		50,000	
Ingots required		375,000		500,000
Plates:				
Clydebridge	220,000		250,000	
Dalzell	180,000		180,000	
Blochairn	150,000		150,000	
Ingots required		800,000		850,000
Sections:				
Glengarnock	350,000		350,000	
Lanarkshire	150,000		150,000	
Ingots required		600,000		600,000
Merchant bars:				
Dalzell	100,000		—	
Ingots required		125,000		—
TOTAL INGOTS REQUIRED	—	1,900,000	—	1,950,000

Sources: Colvilles Ltd., 'Post-War Developments, 1945'; 'Memorandum on Scottish Steel, 1947'.

consumers of Scotland in a dangerously awkward plight.'[11] Supplementary calculations to determine the raw material requirements for various ingot outputs using different proportions of pig iron and scrap revealed marked deficiencies in both these metallic inputs (see Table 11.3). Even the position regarding the supply of coking coal smalls available from existing pits in Scotland gave rise to anxiety, though detailed estimates made by Capt. T. H. Thorneycroft of the Plean Colliery Company Ltd. indicated that fully adequate quantities were and could be made available.

Such were the difficulties involved even in attaining an increase in Scottish capacity of 500,000 ingot tons over 1937 pro-

[11] Dr. A. McCance to Sir John Duncanson, 16 Oct. 1945.

TABLE 11.3

Colville Group: Expected Raw Material Requirements under Different Conditions, 1945

	('000 tons)	
Ingot output	1,900	1,700
Material required: 108%	2,055	1,836
SCRAP (65%)	1,338	1,193
Circulating (25%)	516	459
Outside (40%)	822	734
Home	250	250
To be Imported	572	484
PIG IRON (35%)	717	643
Clyde Iron production	400	400
Deficiency	317	243
SCRAP (56%)	1,154	1,028
Circulating (25%)	516	459
Outside (31%)	638	569
Home	250	250
To be Imported	388	319
PIG IRON (44%)	901	808
Clyde Iron production	400	400
Deficiency	501	408

Source: Colvilles Ltd., 'Raw Material Requirements: Colville Group', Calculations dated 22 Oct. 1945 and 23 Oct. 1945.

duction (i.e. in reaching 2·3 million tons) that Colvilles were clearly reluctant to consider embarking on any radical schemes. They were particularly conscious of the fact that 'the unloading facilities at Glasgow Docks have always been quite inadequate to handle the quantities of ore required by the Scottish steel industry'.[12] Until this bottleneck had been overcome, it was unrealistic to expect any major changes in the company's manufacturing arrangements. Arguments such as these fortified Colvilles' belief that the company's immediate future lay in the

[12] Colvilles Ltd., 'Post-War Developments, 1945', para. 3. It will be recalled that an ambitious scheme to install modern unloaders at General Terminus Quay would probably have been implemented before the war had it not been for the dilatory attitude of the London, Midland, & Scottish Railway. See above, pp. 237–8.

improvement and development of Clydebridge and Clyde Iron,
Dalzell, Lanarkshire, and Glengarnock, detailed plans for
which had already been submitted to the Federation. Before
extensions to existing works were sanctioned, however, Colvilles
were pressed to give further consideration to the construction
of an entirely new steel works on a tidewater site in accordance
with the recommendations of the Brassert Report of 1929. Having done so, they argued against such a scheme in terms of the
factors that determined their decision to rebuild the Clyde Iron
Works, though they 'fully appreciated that if there is any
necessity in the future to erect a complete new Steelworks, the
Clyde site would have very definite advantages'.[13]

Colvilles' development plans of 1944–5 evoked a highly critical response from the Federation. It was implied that the firm's
anxieties over raw materials were groundless. 'The figure
quoted by Colvilles of 800,000 tons per annum of basic iron
will not be adequate to meet the steel-making requirements
under the anticipated conditions of scrap supplies. The figure
should be raised to 950,000 tons . . . The proposals [regarding
steel manufacture] submitted by Colvilles leave much to be
desired. While practically 75 per cent of the steel capacity is
to be rebuilt, 70 per cent of the steel production will be made
by the cold metal process and there will be little improvement
in the integration of coke plant, blast furnace, and steel plants.
The scheme still leaves the rolling mills out of balance with the
steel furnaces and involves the inter-works transfer of about
300,000 ingot tons per annum for further processing.' The
Federation's experts were alarmed at Colvilles' cautious policy.
The social considerations with which it was imbued were
ignored; the realistic economic statistics on which it was based,
swept aside. The measured terms of the company's arguments
were construed as mere advocacy of short-term expedients.
Instead, it was suggested

that the reconstruction programme of Colvilles should be based on an ultimate concentration into three works:

(a) Clydebridge to be extended to provide for the manufacture of all ship
plates, medium and light plates, and possible further extensions to flat
rolled products.
(b) A second works, *probably at Motherwell*, to take care of all special qualities

[13] Colvilles Ltd., 'Post-War Developments, 1945', para. 13 (ii).

and types of steel which are not suitable for mass production methods.
(c) A third works on a new site for concentration of billets, steel bars, rolled shapes, and ultimately rails. This works should be fully integrated with coke ovens and blast furnaces, so as to give maximum flexibility to take advantage of changing conditions in raw material supply . . . For economic reasons *this plant should be accessible to ocean-going vessels* for the reception of ore and limestone, and for the export of its products.

There followed detailed recommendations concerning the plant, capacity, and role of the new works, which 'should be erected on the south bank of the Clyde near the village of Inchinnan'. A glowing picture was painted of the significant savings, 'based on fundamental principles of manufacture and operating economics', which would follow its creation.[14] It is not without significance that the Federation's Technical Consultant was Dr. T. P. Colclough, formerly a partner in H. A. Brassert & Company, and responsible, under A. J. Boynton, for the preparation of the 1929 Report.[15]

Because the government had asked the Federation in May 1945 to submit its plans for the development of the iron and steel industry within six months, neither Colvilles' board nor the Federation's experts had time to refine their ideas further and it was impossible to arrive at a compromise. Inevitably, some features of that part of the plan presented by the Federation to the Ministry of Supply in December 1945 relating to Scotland were tentative, even negative in tone. The Scottish steel industry was to be modernized in order 'to make provision for the same proportion of the steel production of the country' as it had achieved in 1937. Its capacity was to be raised to about 2,300,000 tons but, as the Report recognized, the 1936 re-grouping 'had already secured the major economies to be obtained by concentration'.[16] The Hallside and Blochairn steel-making plants of the Steel Company of Scotland and part of the capacity of Clydebridge were to be scrapped. Although 'a limited expenditure' would be incurred at Glengarnock, Lanarkshire, and Clydebridge, the possibility of displacing one or more of these units existed. Whether this possibility was to

[14] B.I.S.F., 'Reconstruction of Scottish Steel Industry', undated, but apparently about October 1945. Emphasis added.
[15] Sir Andrew McCance, personal communication to the author.
[16] *Reports by the British Iron and Steel Federation and the Joint Iron Council to the Minister of Supply.* Cmd. 6811 (May 1946), pp. 18–20. The first of these is subsequently referred to as *B.I.S.F. Report*, 1946.

be realized depended upon whether or not new tidewater plant was subsequently created. Meanwhile, it was proposed 'to replace the basic open-hearth furnaces ... at Dalzell by a modern installation on a new site adjacent to the present works', and to erect additional blast furnace capacity of 200,000 tons at Clyde Iron. Dalzell was to be 'the only producer of the largest sizes of commercial plates', and because 'it is envisaged that this plant will continue to form an integral part of the steel industry for a considerable period [it] must be provided with adequate steel-making facilities' by the replacement of obsolete furnaces.

In a significant paragraph judiciously combining Colvilles' proposals, the views of the other Scottish iron- and steel-makers, and the hopes of the Federation's technical advisers, it was stated that these 'proposals regarding existing works are in line with the general policy adopted when the managements of the principal Scottish steel works came together in 1936. They provide a basis for a long-term policy based on constructing improved dock facilities for handling imported ore, ore preparation plant, new blast furnaces, and new and increased open-hearth capacity at a new plant on a riverside site.' This 'new Clyde plant' was to include a continuous billet and sheet bar mill ('to make the Scottish re-rolling and sheet industries self-contained'), to replace Colvilles' existing re-rolling capacity, and to include a four-high plate mill to roll all the light plate produced in Scotland. It was to be 'laid out as a nucleus around which the future developments of the Scottish steel industry will be planned as soon as economically practicable, having regard to the efficient balance and life of the existing plants on other sites'.[17]

3 Brassert Revisited: The Proposed New Tidewater Plant, 1945–1947

(a) *Colvilles' Memorandum on the Scottish Steel Industry.* Lack of time may have prevented proper reconsideration of a mill on

---

[17] *B.I.S.F. Report*, 1946, p. 19. Contemporary criticisms of the Scottish proposals (e.g. Brian Tew, 'Reports on the Iron and Steel Industry', *Economic Journal*, lvi (1946), 493–4) were somewhat muted by the expectation that the future tidewater plant implied that some of the schemes that were approved were simply to secure the greatest possible economies during what was believed to be a transitional phase of long-term development.

Clydeside *before* the submission of the *Report by the British Iron and Steel Federation*, but with Scotland's role in the nation's iron and steel industry in the immediate future now apparently settled, Colvilles were in a position to examine the relocation scheme with the thoroughness it deserved. There is little question that following the completion of the Clydebridge/Clyde Iron complex Colvilles had never welcomed the idea of a new plant on the Clyde. It had formed no part of their original proposals in 1944, and it is clear that the company resented the pressure that was being brought to bear upon them to proceed with such a scheme. Critics have implied that Colvilles' attitude was a compound of sheer perversity and reaction, pointing to the fact that the company never adequately justified the decision to ignore the recommendations contained in the 1946 White Paper. The records of the company reveal that this criticism cannot be sustained, though Colvilles were undoubtedly at fault in failing to publicize the full details of their exhaustive investigation of the advantages and disadvantages of a new works on a tidewater site.

The basic question that the company set itself to investigate was whether, in terms of the *economic* and *social* costs involved, the required output could best be attained by a new Clyde plant or by the modernization and enlargement of the company's existing capacity. To determine the answer inquiries were made of expert authorities in many relevant fields. Meetings were held with Sir Andrew Duncan.[18] Geologists, accountants, engineers, lawyers, fuel conservationists, ore shippers and railway officials were among those consulted. The Brassert Report was reconsidered; the *Report of the Scottish Coalfields Committee* studied. The evidence was carefully classified, the statistics tabulated and weighed, and drawings and maps prepared. Draft after draft of the findings were composed, circulated, discussed, and amended.

Not until April 1947, was the investigation complete and the

---

[18] In referring to 'the strong political support in favour of the new site proposals on Clydeside, Sir Andrew [Duncan] emphasized that any proposed scheme must be on a strictly economic basis'. Colvilles Ltd.: Minute Book III, 5 Dec. 1946. Sir Andrew Duncan, having been President of the Board of Trade or Minister of Supply throughout the war, was reappointed Independent Chairman of the B.I.S.F. in 1945.

findings embodied in a lengthy memorandum.[19] A review of the *raw material situation* revealed that Scotland's production of pig iron *could* be 1,200,000 tons per annum (cf. 496,700 tons in 1937, 'a representative year') which would give a ratio of pig iron production to steel ingot production of approximately 50 per cent when Scotland's share of the nation's production of steel rose to the 2·3 million tons envisaged in the White Paper. This proportion was believed to be a reasonable aim 'when account is taken of the scrap arising from the local engineering and shipbuilding industries and the probability that it will always be possible for some proportion of scrap to be imported'. Low though this pig iron/steel output ratio was, it represented a marked increase on previous levels: in 1937 the ratio had been only 26·2 per cent; in 1946, 31·5 per cent.[20]

Before a realistic appraisal could be made of the comparative costs of constructing and operating a new tidewater steel plant and the modernization and enlargement of the company's existing plant *designed to attain an equivalent increase in output*, Colvilles felt obliged to survey *the current state of their steel-making facilities*. The Clyde Iron Works (pig iron), Clydebridge Works (plates), and Glengarnock Works (heavy sections and billets) were technically efficient producers, and, with the electrification of the mills, so too was the Lanarkshire Works (rolled joists). It was recognized that the Dalzell Works, which produced the largest plates rolled in Great Britain, had an antiquated melting shop and a very poor layout. At the Blochairn Works of the Steel Company of Scotland, the cogging mill and plate mill, completely rebuilt at the request of the Ministry of Supply in 1942–3 to meet military demands, were capable of producing 150,000 tons of plate per annum, but the melting shop was obsolete and incapable of significant improvement. Production was therefore unbalanced and the long-term economic viability of the plant was doubtful. Consequently, the Blochairn Works was scheduled for closure. Similarly, the Hallside Works was 'too small for modern conditions' and site limitations made rebuilding impracticable. It too was ultimately to be abandoned.

---

[19] Colvilles Ltd., 'Memorandum on Scottish Steel, 1947'.

[20] Ibid., section 1–4, 12. Cf. the 1937 pig iron/steel output ratios of other countries: Great Britain, 65·2 per cent; U.S.A., 73·4 per cent; Germany, 80·4 per cent; France, 99·9 per cent; Belgium 99·9 per cent. Ibid., section 1.

In addition to weaknesses in certain works in the Colville Group, there were deficiencies in the supply of specific products. Although the internal demand for billets under 6-inch was estimated at 3,500 tons per week, and that of the local re-rollers in the Motherwell and Coatbridge areas at an additional 1,000 tons, Glengarnock was capable of meeting only a third of these requirements (1,500 tons per week). The four mills, producing a total of 2,000 to 2,500 tons of light section per week, were all obsolete and consequently wasteful of coal and manpower. Moreover, the Group had no plant capable of efficiently rolling the increasingly popular medium plates (between $\frac{1}{8}$-inch to $\frac{3}{8}$-inch).

Consideration of these factors—in the context of the company's 'considered opinion' that works producing ordinary mild steel in plates, sections, and bars, should not have a smaller annual production than 400,000–500,000 ingot tons[21]—meant that Colvilles conceived their 'ultimate aim' to be Clyde Iron Works producing 16,000 tons of pig iron per week and Dalzell, Clydebridge, Glengarnock, and Lanarkshire each producing 8,000–12,000 tons of ingots per week. Indeed, in productive capacity, their *1947 Plan* differed little from that presented to the B.I.S.F. two years earlier. This much can be seen from Tables 11.1 and 11.2. Consequently, the detailed components of the 1947 proposals were also similar to those put forward in 1945: the General Terminus Quay scheme to handle all Scottish requirements of imported ore was to be pushed ahead at an estimated cost of £500,000; another blast furnace, together with two additional batteries of coke ovens, was necessary at Clyde Iron in order to produce 800,000 tons of basic pig iron (£2,250,000); the manufacture of special steels was to be concentrated at Dalzell, where a third melting shop was to be erected on an entirely new site (£2,600,000); it was proposed to install a continuous billet mill at Lanarkshire and to increase the output of the melting shops by replacing the existing furnaces by two 150-ton fixed furnaces (£1 million); a light section mill was planned for Glengarnock (£1,250,000), and a light

[21] 'This is the minimum size necessary to achieve the economies of large scale operation. On the other hand, we do not believe there is much advantage in increasing the size beyond this, as our experience indicates that good management and efficient control of operations can best be achieved with a unit of this size.' Ibid., section 17.

plate mill at Clydebridge, which with its ancillary equipment would cost £2 million. On the assumption that labour and materials would be available, it was expected that these schemes would take not less than five to eight years to complete, but with their implementation the current inequality in the production costs for certain products would be eliminated and Scottish steel production would be brought up to a high standard of economic and technical efficiency.

Not until section 38 of the Memorandum was there any mention of the White Paper proposals for 'new blast furnace and steel plant to be built on the Clyde'. The company's object in giving primacy to its own schemes was that the hypothetical integrated plant on tidewater should be contrasted not with Colvilles' *existing* works but with the *potential* manufacturing arrangements purged of deficiencies and weaknesses. Not until these had been presented in detail was the company prepared to reveal the results of its thorough examination of the relocation scheme; results which were prefaced by the somewhat damping remark that 'it can be assumed that existing locations have not survived without sound reason and that only the strongest evidence for immediate and ultimate economy can justify a change which would create irrevocably a social upheaval of the first magnitude'.[22]

The capacity of *the new tidewater plant* was expected to be 700,000 ingot tons per annum and 600,000 tons of pig iron per annum, most of which would be used to produce steel. For the purpose of a preliminary estimate, it was assumed that the capital cost would be £40 per ingot ton of annual output, although it was emphasized that this figure was based on the somewhat unrealistic assumption that 'no more than an average amount of civil engineering work was involved'. On this basis the approximate cost of the new plant would be £28 million, of which £8 million was allocated to 'blast furnaces, coke ovens, docks, etc.' and £20 million to the steel works, from which the output of *finished* steel would be 600,000 tons equally divided between the three categories of billets, sections and plates. It was believed that plant of this capacity required a *site* of at least 600–700 acres of land, but if it was intended that the bulk of Scottish steel production—say, 1 million to 1½ million tons—

22 Ibid., section 39.

was ultimately to be concentrated on one site 'not less than 1,000 acres of land should be available'. Such considerations immediately ruled out the two sites suggested in the Brassert Report: those 'near the junction of the Cart and the Clyde opposite John Brown's shipyard [Inchinnan]' and 'the area of land west of Erskine Ferry on the Port Glasgow side'. Nevertheless, appreciating that the Federation's technical advisers might suspect Colvilles of sleight of hand, both these possible sites were re-examined 'for confirmation of their suitability'. It was discovered that, far from the 400 acres that Brassert had held were available at either of these locations, the Erskine site effectively contained less than half this area, while the Cart site, although somewhat larger, possessed variable and indeterminate subsoil,[23] with waterlogged mine workings, and was bounded on the south by Abbotsinch airport to the west of which running sand existed beneath the surface.[24] Only by moving inland away from the Clyde (but still alongside the Cart) might an adequate area of land be obtained, but in this case it would be necessary to convert the Cart, 'which can only be described as a shallow stream', into a deep-water canal for about a mile in length, and to include a large part of Abbotsinch airport which, in view of the expenditure already incurred in its construction, was not regarded as a practical possibility. Furthermore, both sites presented considerable transport difficulties.[25]

The possibilities of a site on the East coast of Scotland on the River Forth were also examined. Although this location had the advantage of being adjacent to an area of good coking coal in the Kinneil–Plean area, this was more than offset by the fact that the Forth was characterized by sandy banks, wide areas of sandy foreshore, and a limited navigational channel.

[23] Correspondence between Dr. McCance and Dr. Whitehead, Geological Survey of Great Britain, Edinburgh, March–April 1947.

[24] Among Colvilles' records there is a document (dated 14 Mar. 1947) referring to the report of a Special Committee on National Expenditure in 1940 in which it is stated that £250,000 was expended on a site near Abbotsinch in an endeavour to make a sound foundation for an Air Ministry repair establishment: 'it was found that piling was useless as the pile disappeared in a layer of running sand under the surface and the attempt was abandoned . . .'

[25] Cf. K. Warren, 'Locational Problems of the Scottish Iron and Steel Industry, Part 2', *Scottish Geographical Magazine*, vol lxxxi (September 1965), p. 89.

Furthermore, the only port available was Grangemouth, 'which can take in steamers of 7,000–8,000 tons and which we are advised would be difficult to deepen for larger vessels',[26] and any site adjoining Grangemouth Docks was honeycombed with old colliery workings. Even had a suitable site been available somewhere between Grangemouth and Carron, on balance the costs of assembling raw materials for the manufacture of basic iron and the distribution of finished products made any argument in favour of an East coast site untenable 'so long as the Clyde is the main centre of consumption'.

The inevitable conclusion was that: 'In a long term policy which involves the erection of a large and costly new Steel Works, the advantages of the site proposed should be obvious and overwhelming. That certainly cannot be said of either Erskine or Inchinnan.' Colvilles might have been justified in resting their case on these weighty arguments, but because Erskine 'is at least in a country district where freedom in planning for future development is possible if topographical disadvantages are disregarded', it was decided to make a detailed comparison between this site—typical of a tidewater site where imported ore could be discharged direct to the furnaces—and the Clydebridge–Clyde Iron Works site, around which all the company's development plans had hitherto been centred. The first stage in this comparison took the form of an analysis of the costs of assembling raw materials to make basic iron (see Table 11.4) and steel on each of the two sites and the costs involved in the subsequent distribution of the major categories of finished steel products.[27] This showed conclusively that in the matter of trans-

[26] This statement was based on conversations between Mr. Yeaman of the L.M.S. Railway and Dr. A. McCance. A. McCance to T. R. Craig, 9 Apr. 1947.

[27] Table 11.4 has been presented as an example of the calculations involved in comparing the transport costs involved. The figures for assembling raw materials at the steel works and the distribution of finished products are not readily reduced to tabular form. Furthermore, they are based on a whole series of further, albeit realistic, assumptions concerning the nature of the final products and the markets which they might have been expected to satisfy. No attempt has, therefore, been made to reproduce the statistical basis of Colvilles' argument that (a) the costs of assembling raw materials for steelmaking, and (b) the distribution of finished products (plates, sections, and billets) were either slightly in favour of Clyde Iron/Clydebridge or that the total sums involved, even at full production, were too small to influence the choice between Clyde Iron/Clydebridge or Erskine either way.

TABLE 11.4

Comparison of Railway Carriage Costs of Assembling Raw Materials to make One Ton of Basic Iron at Clyde Iron Works and Erskine, 1947

Material	Weight per ton[b]	CLYDE Rate per ton s. d.	Total d.	ERSKINE[a] Rate per ton s. d.	Total d.
Ore[c]	1·13	1 8	22·6	Nil	Nil
Sinter[d]	0·36	1 11	8·28	1 4	5·76
Residues	0·02	1 6	0·36	2 6	0·6
Cinder and Scale	0·13	2 0	3·12	3 0	4·68
Scrap	0·02	Nil	Nil	Nil	Nil
Basic Slag	0·15	Nil	Nil	Nil	Nil
Limestone	0·13	0 10	1·3	Nil	Nil
Coal	1·48	4 9	84·36	6 11	124·33
TOTAL			120·02d.		133·37d.

Notes:

[a] The figures for railway carriage to the Erskine site were estimated by the L.M.S. Railway Company.

[b] The actual consumption of iron ore, sinter, etc. at the two blast furnaces at Clyde Iron Works were selected from a typical week's production. Since both at Erskine and Clyde new unloading plant was required, neither cost was debited with any allowance for depreciation as the allocation in this case would obviously be the same. Similarly, where carriage costs are equal, these have been ignored.

[c] It was assumed that iron ore for the Clyde Iron Works would be discharged at General Terminus in accordance with the scheme already drawn up by Colvilles.

[d] The comparison of railway carriage costs of assembling raw materials to make one ton of sinter was based upon the following supplementary set of calculations:

Material	Weight per ton	CLYDE Rate per ton s. d.	Total d.	ERSKINE Rate per ton s. d.	Total d.
Ore	0·65	1 8	13·00	Nil	Nil
Residues and Cinder	0·26	1 6	4·68	2 6	7·8
Flue Dust	0·14	Nil	Nil	Nil	Nil
Borings	0·05	Nil	Nil	Nil	Nil
Coal	0·10	4 9	5·70	6 11	8·3
TOTAL			1s. 11·38d.		1s. 4·1d.

Source: 'Memorandum on Scottish Steel, 1947', section 56.

port costs Erskine possessed no advantages over the existing steel-making complex.

On the production side, it was argued (on the basis of a comparison between the expected conversion and manufacturing costs in an entirely new plant and those realizable from an expansion of existing facilities *to attain the same output*) that such was the relative efficiency of the present Clyde Iron Works for the production of pig iron, Clydebridge for plates, and Glengarnock for sections and billets (costs which, moreover, might be expected to have been lowered by any increase in scale), that there was little or no justification whatever for the much greater capital expenditure required for an entirely new integrated works, since it would bring no return. Proud of their existing low conversion costs,[28] Colvilles refused to admit that any new works was capable of effecting the *significant* cost reduction without which the case for transferring production was insupportable.[29]

However much care and objectivity may have gone into the compilation of the comparative transport and production costs of existing and potential sites (exemplified by Erskine), Colvilles' arguments were to some degree hypothetical. While the transport case appears unassailable, no one could accurately assess the lowering in conversion costs effected by a new integrated coastal steel plant, however much Colvilles might deny the possibilities of any significant reduction. So much depended upon the scale of the proposed new plant. At this point, Colvilles' critics might still feel confident of weakening or even destroying the company's case. There was, however, no gainsaying the strength of Colvilles' more general objections. It was pointed out that a steel works of the capacity contemplated in the White Paper would employ 3,600 men. 'There are no houses available near the site and a complete new township must be promoted. With the present slow progress in housing construction and with so many prior claims for houses, it is entirely conjectural when such a large scheme could be completed, and it would be very unwise to start the Steel Works and expect

[28] In a whole range of products, these were repeatedly reported as being the lowest in the United Kingdom. Colvilles Ltd., Minute Book III, 1944–7, *passim*.
[29] 'Memorandum on Scottish Steel, 1947', sections 68–80.

men to travel from their present houses, already convenient to Works, to a new plant many miles away.' Account was also taken of 'the social upheaval to Lanarkshire which any transfer of existing industries would create. We have seen in our own time the creation of special and distressed areas arise from this same cause, even when effected on a much smaller scale than that proposed.' 'Surely', the question was asked, 'it is better to prevent the creation of such distressed areas than to plead for the return of industry to revive them after they have been formed?' In the light of Britain's economic position, the final objection was equally formidable:

Many years would be required to construct so large a scheme involving such a vast change to the surrounding countryside. It will be evident that the time of completion would depend, not on the time it takes to construct the blast furnaces and steel works, but on the time required for the completion of roads, drainage, railways, houses, and for the creation of a new community. Even if the scheme justified itself economically, it would take probably at least ten years before it could be expected to come into full operation. At the present time it would seem wiser to proceed with such improvements to existing plant as will realize the same output objectives.

It was on the basis of these arguments that Colvilles expressed their firm intention of concentrating their steel manufacture into 'four large efficient units whose capacity [would] be increased in proportion as the national output increases to 15/16 million ingot tons per annum'.[30]

(b) *The Reactions to the Memorandum: The British Iron and Steel Federation and the Iron and Steel Board.* Colvilles felt that this was the last word on the subject of the tidewater site: the preparation of the Memorandum had confirmed their conviction that economically and socially the 'new Clyde plant' was impracticable. The Iron and Steel Board's technical adviser, Dr. J. P. Colclough, remained unconvinced. Completely unperturbed, he continued to press for a new works at Inchinnan, Colvilles' objections to which were almost contemptuously swept aside.[31] Agreeing with Colvilles that the company's modernization programme 'should have as a fundamental basis a concentration of products in as few units as possible so as to give the highest

[30] Ibid., section 90.
[31] T. P. Colclough to Dr. A. McCance, 27 May, 1947.

efficiency and lowest costs' and that Clydebridge and Glengarnock should be improved to permit the rolling of commercial plates and rails and heavy products, Colclough was adamant that 'the whole of the steel-making plant at Dalzell and all mills for rolling sections at Lanarkshire and Dalzell, require to be re-sited and modernized'. The existing sites were 'unsuitable' and already 'far too congested'. Instead, it would be 'far better to provide a new works which would take care of the whole of the semi-finished, medium, and light sections, and probably part of the heavy section tonnage, and which ultimately could be extended to replace the Glengarnock mills as and when they reach the end of their economic life'.

This last argument was critical to Colclough's case. If new and replacement capacity was to be laid down, its location would determine the site of the necessary additional blast furnace capacity. 'It is agreed that the present furnaces at Clyde Iron could provide up to 600,000 tons of iron per year. It is further agreed that an additional quantity of, say, 400,000 tons or more of iron is required. This additional capacity could be installed at Clyde Iron, *or equally well could be installed with the new steel-making and rolling capacity.* [Furthermore] while the Clyde Iron site would accommodate four large furnaces, the production of 1 million tons of pig iron per year would necessitate the rebuilding of the two present operating furnaces, involving not only the furnaces themselves but also stove capacity, blowing power and other ancillary equipment, and also probably a complete overhaul of the existing arrangements for the handling and preparation of ore.' Such radical reconstruction involved so great a capital expenditure that the difference in cost between the modernization of the existing works and the creation of an entirely new works would not be as substantial as Colvilles believed. For example, 'the cost of enlarging two blast furnaces with ancillaries and the erection of a fourth large unit at Clyde Iron, would go a long way towards the cost of erection of two new blast furnaces at another location'. It took but one further step to argue that in the long run a new site was infinitely preferable to making the best of Dalzell and Lanarkshire, and that its location should be at Inchinnan, Colvilles' objections to which, on both technical and social grounds, were dismissed as being exaggerated or based on erroneous assumptions.

Colclough's 'Steel Programme for Scotland' was considered
by the Federation's Development Committee on 15 July 1947,
alongside Colvilles' own scheme which was undergoing yet
further revision. The meeting proved to be 'rather heated'.[32]
Both Ellis Hunter, the President of the Federation, and Sir
Andrew Duncan, its Chairman, 'expressed concern that . . . Colvilles' scheme was inadequate as regards the use of hot metal.
This, of course, gave Colclough his opportunity of agreeing and
pointing out the necessity of going to a new site where hot
metal would be used.' Sir John Craig persevered. He agreed
to submit an even more detailed plan within two weeks and
to answer Colclough's document 'in detail'. Speed was imperative, 'the Minister [Mr. John Wilmot] personally was making
repeated applications to the Board for the Scottish Scheme to
be submitted to him and Sir Archibald Forbes had been urging
the Federation to submit schemes forthwith as the political
pressure was very great'. Immediately after the meeting Craig
circulated the latest version of the company's Development
Scheme and sent copies of Colclough's 'Programme' to all
members of the board of executive directors,[33] together with
Sir Andrew McCance's 'Comments'.[34] Point by point, Colclough's argument was refuted. The statistical basis of his calculations was questioned and doubt thrown on the objectivity of
his case: 'The combined area of Dalzell and Motherwell is 610
acres and not 400 acres as stated. It is rather amusing that while
400 acres at Motherwell is inadequate for a production of
900,000 tons per annum, 400 acres at Inchinnan is apparently
quite adequate for the new Steel Works to produce 1 million
tons per annum. In this, as in many of the other statements,
there is a regrettable absence of fairness in the conclusions stated.'[35] Downright disagreement was expressed on some issues.
Colclough's experience in cold metal scrap operations, it was
almost unanimously agreed, had led him into serious error.

[32] Sir John Craig to Dr. A. McCance, 16 July 1947, 'Notes on a Meeting
of the Development Committee, 15 July 1947'; Colvilles Ltd., 'Excerpt from
Minutes of the Development Committee Meeting held on 15 July 1947'.
[33] The Board of Executive Directors was established on 1 Jan. 1947. See
below, p. 313.
[34] Dr. Andrew McCance was knighted in June 1947.
[35] Sir Andrew McCance, 'Comments on Colclough's Steel Programme for
Scotland', 19 Aug. 1947, paras. 2(a), 5, and 7.

Further cogent arguments against a new plant at Inchinnan emerged. Item by item, the Colclough Programme was remorselessly demolished. It was left to A. K. McCosh, of Bairds and Scottish Steel Ltd., to express what was clearly the consensus of opinion within the Colville Group: 'The general impression I get from the [Colclough] Memorandum . . . is that the author has a preconceived idea and is trying to justify it largely by vague generalities, ignoring or slurring over all the difficulties and deprecating unduly the existing position and its possibilities.'[36]

The intensive research that went into the rejoinder to Colclough's recommendations was not animated by any personal hostility to the Board's technical adviser. Colvilles were becoming frustrated. Until the Iron and Steel Board and the Federation were convinced that a Clydeside plant was impractical, Colvilles' own development plans would not be approved. The ensuing deadlock was complicated by the fact that Bairds and Scottish Steel, who were to be responsible for a substantial proportion of the Scottish make of pig iron for Scottish requirements, were slow in submitting their proposals. In August, Sir John Craig sent a copy of the company's latest 'Scheme for the Development of Basic Pig Iron and Steel in Scotland' to Ellis Hunter.[37] Like its predecessors, the plan was based on the assumption that 'when the National steel production is increased to 15/16 million tons per annum, the Scottish production will be increased proportionately' to approximately 2·2 million tons per annum (i.e. 14 per cent of the national output). Of this, the Colville Group would produce 1·875 million tons per annum, and this clearly necessitated a substantial increase in pig iron production. To meet the criticisms made at the July meeting of the Development Committee, it was intended that a larger proportion of Scottish steel would be produced by the hot metal process. There followed detailed plans to attain this objective. Each interrelated part of the overall scheme was carefully balanced to achieve the most economical working practices, and high priority was given to the proposal for handling imported ore at the docks (the General Terminus Quay Pro-

---

[36] A. K. McCosh, Gartsherrie Iron Works, to Sir John Craig, 22 July 1947.
[37] Sir John Craig to Ellis Hunter, 20 Aug. 1947. The 'Scheme' itself is dated 18 Aug. 1947.

ject). The President's reply was unexpected and disappointing. Having examined the scheme 'with the Federation's Technical Officers', he proposed to submit to the Development Committee only those parts of it relating 'to the increased production of pig iron and an expansion of steel-making by the hot metal process', on which an earlier meeting of the Development Committee had *already* agreed in general terms. Several other features of the plan, including the location and capacity of the ore handling plant, were to be left 'for fuller examination later'.[38]

Despite an immediate appeal by Sir John Craig that the 'Ore Handling Plant at the General Terminus should proceed simultaneously with the development of pig iron production',[39] it was Hunter's version of Colvilles' plan—entitled 'Schemes for the First Stage Development of Basic Pig Iron and Steel in Scotland'—that was considered by the Development Committee on 16 September 1947. Asked to comment on the document, Sir John explained that it omitted what he considered to be 'a first essential to the development of iron-making in Scotland, i.e. the General Terminus Scheme'. Sir Andrew Duncan would have none of it. If the General Terminus Scheme were to be adopted 'at the moment', he argued, 'it would prejudice the whole development of iron and steel production in Scotland'. 'There was no room for both the General Terminus *and* the Deep-Water Scheme' to which the Committee, its advisers, and, indeed, the Minister of Supply himself remained abdurately attached, despite the fact that its implementation would, it was generally acknowledged, take between ten to fifteen years. Like the proceedings of so many committees, the debate revolved around an issue that was not, in fact, on the agenda at all; and so exhausted were the discussants that very little was said on the subject of Hunter's version of Colvilles' programme. This was unanimously recommended to the Iron and Steel Board as the first stage of the industry's development proposals for Scotland,[40] and

[38] Ellis Hunter to Sir John Craig, 5 Sept. 1947. Hunter appended an emasculated version of Colvilles' proposals on these lines.
[39] Sir John Craig to Ellis Hunter, 8 Sept. 1947.
[40] Sir John Craig, 'Notes of Meeting of Development Committee held in London on Tuesday 16 September 1947'; Colvilles Ltd.: 'Extract from Minutes of Development Committee Meeting held on 16 September 1947'.

subsequently 'approved in principle' by the Board itself.[41] Not until December was R. M. Shone able to inform Sir Andrew McCance that the Federation was prepared to try 'to clear up the position regarding long-term developments' in Scotland.[42] Sir Andrew's relief was obvious: 'I need not say that both Sir John and myself will be most willing to discuss [this] question ... at any time in the hope of being able to get a definite policy agreed. I confess that during the last two years I have felt frustrated by the atmosphere which prevents us from getting ahead with any schemes of development of our own by continued talk about developments which in our view are not practicable ... we feel we have been held back too long.'[43] If Shone's letter had raised hopes among the members of the board of Colvilles that an acceptable decision on the long-term development of the Scottish steel industry was shortly to be made, they were to be disappointed. Indeed, it is at this point that the correspondence between the Federation and the company begins to assume a nightmarish quality. Only three weeks after the completion of Colvilles' 'Scottish Steel Developments—Draft Report No. 2', Sir Andrew received a copy of a Memorandum prepared for the Federation by its technical advisers, Dr. T. P. Colclough and Mr. Bengtson, entitled 'Development of Iron and Steel Production in Scotland'.[44] Shone's covering letter, in which he spoke of it as 'an attempt to set out as clearly as possible in broad lines the basis of the proposal which incorporates development on a new site in Scotland',[45] must have engendered deep depression throughout the Group. Its thirteen closely argued pages led inexorably to the conclusion that a new integrated works, on a tidewater site at Inchinnan, was economically imperative. Colvilles' alternative

[41] A. C. Boddis, Secretary, Iron and Steel Board, to R. M. Shone, B.I.S.F., 24 Nov. 1947; R. M. Shone to Sir A. McCance, 27 Nov. 1947. R. M. Shone was Economic Director and Secretary of the B.I.S.F. from 1946 until 1950 when he became its Director, a post he held until he was appointed Executive Member of the Iron and Steel Board in 1953.
[42] R. M. Shone to Sir John McCance, 1 Dec. 1947.
[43] Sir Andrew McCance to R. M. Shone, 4 Dec. 1947.
[44] At some point during the second half of 1947, Dr. T. P. Colclough became technical adviser to the Federation; he had previously been with the Iron and Steel Board. It may be that he was acting for both bodies; his exact position is not clear.
[45] R. M. Shone to Sir Andrew McCance, 20 Jan. 1948.

proposals were stigmatized as unsound, misconceived, and, in the long run, thoroughly wasteful.

The essence of Colclough's case was that 'the policy adopted shall have first regard to the future needs and developments of the industry and must satisfy the fundamental change which will be made in the near future in the raw material position'.[46] Part of his argument may be reproduced:

During the last fifteen years, every steel-making company in this country, which has been faced with the problem of replacing obsolete capacity or creating new capacity for large tonnages of pig iron and ingots, has decided that the correct policy to adopt is that which secures the maximum possible integration of its various operations. Notable examples, taken in order of date of installation, are Irlam, Corby, Cardiff, Ebbw Vale, Clyde Iron, and the new works at Margam.

The position in Scotland today is in many respects parallel to that in South Wales in the 1930s. South Wales had been for many years based largely on the cold metal process, using large proportions of scrap. Most of the works were relatively of small capacity and obsolete in character. Presented with the necessity to modernize and increase capacity, the decision was made to abandon the traditional practice and to concentrate production in modern, composite works integrated from raw materials, coal and ore, to finished and semi-finished products. Completely new works were built at Cardiff, and the improvements at Margam and Port Talbot were made on the hot metal basis. Both works are based on the use of a high proportion of foreign ore and are located on seaboard. No question has arisen as to the soundness of this policy and its success has been demonstrated by the economic results and the decision to create further capacity on the same lines.

The concentration of sheet and tin plate production in a modern integrated works as contrasted with the improvement of a number of individual existing works by the Richard Thomas Company, has also demonstrated the economic soundness of the policy [Sir Andrew McCance's marginal comment was 'at what a cost £80 × 10⁶'] ...

The present position in Scotland offers a unique opportunity to adopt the same principles in so far as the works mainly involved in the necessary changes are overdue for replacement, and the new capacity required will consist of units, each of which is adequate for economic operation and together would give a well-balanced integrated unit.[47]

The implications of this argument were that of all the existing plant only the steel furnaces at Clydebridge were to be enlarged and supplemented by the installation of a new medium and light plate mill. Dalzell, Glengarnock, and Lanarkshire were to be renovated sufficiently to maintain economic production

[46] British Iron and Steel Federation, 'Development of Iron and Steel Production in Scotland' [The Colclough Report], 20 Jan. 1948, pp. 4–5.
[47] Ibid., p. 6.

at current tonnages, and Blochairn and Hallside were to be shut down as soon as possible. All new capacity was to be concentrated at a completely integrated works which 'should be laid down in such a manner as to permit easy expansion to a capacity of at least one million ingot tons per year'.

To Colvilles this modification to Colclough's earlier 'programme' was critical. Colclough was now arguing for a new tidewater plant on a scale larger than had hitherto been contemplated and the fact was that at this juncture Colvilles—acutely conscious of raw material difficulties, particularly coking coal and scrap, and not fully convinced of the existence of an effective demand for steel on the scale assumed by the national planners—did *not* anticipate expansion beyond 1,900,000 tons. Indeed, the correspondence reveals a subconscious anxiety—born perhaps of the experience of the inter-war years—that even this figure might be too high. Hence, the fourth draft of the company's latest submission to the Federation emphasized that 'within the production targets for Pig Iron and Steel for Scotland envisaged as part of the immediate expansion scheme for the United Kingdom, and as reaffirmed in the James Committee Report, adequate provision can be made to meet the immediate future demands by suitable concentration of production within certain of the existing Steel Works. The enlargement of these units will bring about useful economies and will make each Works an economic and efficient producer of its particular line of product judged by modern standards. There is consequently no justification for embarking at this time on the construction of another Steel Works on a new site.'[48] Nevertheless, Colvilles, acutely aware of the Federation's attachment to the tidewater plant and not wishing to create an impression of complete inflexibility, were careful to add: 'We have not excluded from our consideration the possibility that the demand for steel in Scotland may require at some future date an Ingot capacity in excess of that indicated in the White Paper, but should this be the case the quesion of whether a Steel Works on a new site was necessary must be considered in the light of the circumstances which then exist.'[49]

[48] Colvilles Ltd., ' Schemes for the Development of Pig Iron and Steel', 30 Jan. 1948, p. 12.
[49] Ibid., p. 13.

The positive part of Colvilles' fourth scheme closely followed previous proposals. The phasing of the overall plan, which would determine the future development of the Scottish steel industry over a period of seven to ten years, was explained and the capital expenditure estimated at about £17,000,000.[50] This was a large expenditure but substantially lower than that involved in building a new steel works with an annual output of 1,000,000 tons. Such a plant—which was, of course, the main feature of the Colclough Programme—would, the company had been advised from reliable sources in America, cost £55 per ingot ton of annual output, or £55 million, 'excluding the cost of land, housing, roads, and similar expenditure'. Furthermore, Colvilles were 'of the opinion that at the present time American prices for such construction are somewhat less than similar prices in this country'.[51]

These, then, were the two schemes. It was up to the Federation to decide which one would be submitted to the Board, or, alternatively, whether to try to attain some kind of compromise. Robert Shone was in a difficult position. To permit the Development Committee to 'judge as between the broad lines set out in the White Paper [Scheme A] and the subsequent suggestions put forward ... [by] Colvilles [Scheme B]', he deemed it necessary to try to 'set the two alternatives against one another as clearly as possible'.[52] Common to both plans were the increase in coke oven capacity to operate at least three blast furnaces; the extension of hot metal practice to a capacity of at least 600,000 ingot tons at Clydebridge; the development of the rolling of light plates at Clydebridge and the building of a new four-high plate mill; the concentration of heavy sections and rail production at Glengarnock and the elimination of ingot production at Hallside and Blochairn as expansion proceeded on the other sites. The main issues on which there was a clear difference in the alternative proposals were 'on the location of the blast furnace modernization and extension and on the location of a continuous billet plant and steel works'. Shone pointed out that: 'A decision on this issue is needed quickly

[50] Ibid., p. 11.
[51] Ibid., p. 12.
[52] R. M. Shone to Sir Andrew McCance, 9 Feb. 1948. Shone's statement, dated 9 Feb. 1948, was entitled 'Proposals for Pig Iron and Steel Development in Scotland'.

as the improvement of ore unloading in Scotland is urgent and depends on the location of future pig iron production. Also, the policy regarding steel furnace development and modernization at Lanarkshire and at Glengarnock must be largely determined by the long-term plan. It is desirable to undertake progressively the expansion and modernization of these works if Scheme B is adopted but not if Scheme A is proceeded with.'[53]

Using Colclough's estimate of the cost of a new plant, with which Colvilles vehemently disagreed, at £25,000,000, it was calculated that the cost of the White Paper scheme would be about £10,000,000 more than Colvilles'.[54] But against this had to be set the savings that would ensue from more integrated working in a new plant. These derived from greater economy in ore unloading, estimated at being between 6*d*. to 1*s*. 6*d*. per ton[55] (or between £50,000 and £150,000 a year); a better gas balance in having two integrated hot metal plants, estimated at about £275,000 per annum; and the greater use of hot metal. On the other hand, such savings—the magnitudes of which were vigorously denied by Colvilles—would melt away in the face of the high investment in social overhead capital associated with establishing a new site.[56] Moreover, there was no question that Colvilles' scheme would permit additional steel output much more rapidly than Colclough's radical proposals. These reflections led inevitably to an attempt to forecast 'the trend of Scottish steel demand':

The largest steel-consuming industry in Scotland is shipbuilding which takes about one-third of the total steel. If marine, constructional, and mechanical engineering is included with shipbuilding, about 60 per cent of the total steel consumption would be covered by this group. This is about twice as high as the proportion for the rest of the United Kingdom, and is reflected in the production of heavy plates in Scotland, representing about 32 per cent of the U.K. aggregate. For light products, however, the percentage in Scot-

[53] R. M. Shone, 'Proposals ...', section X.
[54] Ibid., section XI.
[55] The current cost of unloading at Rothesay Dock was 3*s*. 1½*d*. per ton. At a new site, using steel works' labour and unloading directly into bins at the blast furnaces, the cost could be reduced by at least 2*s*. 6*d*. per ton. Against this had to be set the savings that might be expected by the adoption of the General Terminus scheme. The difference between the two proposals was expected to be about 6*d*. to 1*s*. 6*d*. a ton in favour of 'the new site'.
[56] Ibid., sections XII, XIV.

land is no more than 8 per cent and for sheets only $5\frac{1}{2}$ per cent of the production in the country as a whole. As indicated previously, the main future expansion of demand is likely to lie with the lighter products and sheets.

In a recent broad appraisal of the future demand for steel undertaken by the Planning Department of the Government, a decline was expected in ship-building steel, even although the total future requirement of steel for all purposes was put at a considerably higher figure than was envisaged in the present Development Plan.

Attempts are being made to develop other industries in Scotland. Some of these, particularly bolts and nuts, tubes, and light engineering, will increase the demand for steel but the main emphasis of the development plans seems to be rather on chemicals, tobacco, non-ferrous metal manufacture, the food industry, and consumption industries generally. So far, therefore, there would not appear to be an overall basis for a big expansion in the consumption of steel. These considerations suggest that, while it may be appropriate to expand Scottish production on the basis of the present proportion of a 16 million ton capacity for the country as a whole, it would probably be undesirable to incur additional expenditure at this stage to facilitate still further expansion at a later date.[57]

Robert Shone's statement was presented to the Development Committeee on 17 February. No judgement was made on the relative merits of the alternative plans. Instead, the whole question was referred to a sub-committee, which, with refreshing realism, decided that, as the basic difference between the Colclough recommendations and those of the company was that the former would 'provide a nucleus for possible further expansion at a later date', while the latter made no claim to provide anything more than an efficient and economic means of providing for an ingot capacity of approximately 2·3–2·4 million tons, the choice of plan must be dependent upon demand factors.[58] These were, therefore, re-examined by the sub-committee. The evidence given by Sir Andrew McCance confirmed and amplified Shone's statement and his prediction that the 'expansion of demand in Scotland would rise to a level requiring a capacity of 2·4 million tons compared with 2 million tons prewar' received powerful support from an earlier examination made by the Statistical Department of the Federation which had concluded that 'the main expansion of production in the United Kingdom was likely to be in sheets and tinplate and

[57] Ibid., section XIV.
[58] R. M. Shone, 'Report from the Sub-Committee on Scottish Development', First Draft, 10 Mar. 1948, p. 2.

in the production of semi-finished steel to make good the large deficiencies, mainly in the Midland area, for the production of an increasing tonnage of the lighter steel products. On the other hand, shipbuilding in particular did not offer prospects of expansion, so that unless the character of Scottish demand changed radically, and of this there was little evidence, consumption would not be expected to expand so greatly as in the U.K. as a whole.' Even a report prepared for the Federation in 1945 by Mr. Bengtson—who with Dr. Colclough was the chief technical proponent of the tidewater scheme—had questioned whether it was 'right to figure ultimately on a steel output [for Scotland] higher than [that reached in] 1937'.[59]

This investigation was decisive. No one was prepared to visualize a significant overall increase in the demand for Scottish steel in the near future. To all intents and purposes the Federation finally jettisoned the White Paper proposals. It remained simply to examine whether Colvilles' proposals were as efficient as the company's spokesmen claimed, the primary issue being whether having only one integrated hot metal plant with a capacity of 650,000 tons in Scotland would deprive the company of certain economies available from hot metal practice. But on this subject, such was Sir Andrew's technical mastery and enormous experience, that his argument was sufficient to quell all but a few lingering doubts. Consequently, the sub-committee's recommendations almost completely vindicated the company's proposals. Nothing could have given Colvilles more satisfaction than the sub-committee's observation that 'it would appear that the best opportunity for prompt development of modern ore unloading facilities would be at the General Terminus site, which is a distance of just under 5 miles from the Clyde Iron Works', and no comment more relief than the reference to 'the new plant on a riverside site, which *would have involved* large scale requirements for housing, railway facilities and labour transfers [which] would inevitably have entailed serious delay'.[60]

---

[59] Both the findings of the Federation's Statistical Department and the Bengtson Report were set out in the 'Report of the [Federation's] Sub-Committee on Scottish Development', 10 Mar. 1948.
[60] R. M. Shone, 'Report from Sub-Committee on Scottish Development', Third and Final Draft, 11 Mar. 1948, p. 2. Emphasis added.

Nevertheless, the sub-committee's discussions with Sir Andrew McCance, Dr. Colclough, and Mr. Bengtson did result in one major modification of the company's original proposals. Hitherto, the plans for the further expansion of pig iron capacity had involved the construction of a *fourth* basic iron furnace at the Clyde Iron Works. It was now decided that, instead, 'the next stage in the development of pig iron production in Scotland should provide for the co-ordination of the Mother-well Steel Works (Lanarkshire and Dalzell) as completely integrated units by the erection of blast furnaces and coke ovens on an adjacent site'. Since the previous summer the scheme whereby Bairds and Scottish Steel were to have been responsible for the production of additional high phosphoric foundry iron, hematite, and low phosphoric basic iron in two furnaces at Gartsherrie, each of 200,000 tons capacity, had been 'indefinitely postponed'. Bairds and Scottish had never displayed much enthusiasm to undertake this part of the national plan, and Colvilles' repeated requests to the company to accelerate the submission of their scheme to the Iron and Steel Board had always been met with excuses and evasions.[61] Now that Bairds had finally withdrawn, Colvilles agreed to make provision at the new Motherwell site for two blast furnaces, one on high phosphoric foundry iron and one on hematite and low phosphoric basic iron.[62]

(c) *The Scottish Development Plan, 1948, and the Iron and Steel Board.* In April 1948, a report on 'Scottish Developments' was formally submitted to the Iron and Steel Board. It was based on the recommendations of the Federation's sub-committee and the Minutes of the meeting of the Development Committee.[63] The report went to some pains to set out the White Paper proposals

[61] Sir John Craig, 'Notes on a telephone conversation with Mr. McCosh', 7 Nov. 1947. There is little doubt that the dilatory attitude of Bairds and Scottish Steel on this issue had delayed the publication of a comprehensive development scheme for Scotland. This had resulted in strong press criticisms of the Scottish steelmasters, and because Colvilles constituted by far the largest single unit in the industry, it was erroneously assumed that it was Colvilles who were the major culprits in impeding progress. Sir John Craig, 'Notes on a visit by Mr. Richardson of the *Financial Times*', 7 Nov. 1947.
[62] R. M. Shone, 'Report from Sub-Committee . . .', Third and Final Draft, p. 1.
[63] R. M. Shone to Sir Andrew McCance, 6 Apr. 1948.

of 1945, the progress that had been made in putting them into effect and the new factors that had since 'come into play which made it desirable to make important changes in the policy then foreshadowed'. A critical paragraph read:

> Broadly the scheme now put forward is that the main pig iron plant be located on a site adjacent to the Lanarkshire steelworks instead of on a new riverside site to the West of Glasgow. The total pig iron capacity under this plan would be expanded to approximately 1,300,000 tons of basic and hematite iron, compared with 900,000 tons [envisaged in the White Paper proposals in 1945]. The increase is required as a result of the re-assessment of the overall scrap and pig iron position, and to meet the expanded steel capacity at Stewarts and Lloyds. The foundry iron modernization would also be carried out on the new Lanarkshire site. Total steelmaking capacity in Scotland would be approximately 2,400,000 tons.[64]

But if the Federation had finally capitulated to Colvilles' objections to a tidewater site, the Board was not prepared meekly to follow its lead. Having considered the latest report, the Board demanded 'a considerable amount of additional information', particularly 'an estimate of the relative costs of production on the basis of the present proposals and the costs of production at an integrated works on a riverside site'.[65] The resulting memorandum, 'The Future Development of Pig Iron and Steel Production in Scotland', was basically an elaborate version of the report on 'Scottish Developments' that had been submitted by the Federation to the Iron and Steel Board in April. There was but one significant difference. Colvilles had had second thoughts about undertaking responsibility for meeting Scotland's increased demand for low phosphoric iron suitable for tube making which had largely arisen from the extension of the Clydesdale Works of Stewarts & Lloyds. Because of the serious risk of contamination, there were inherent difficulties in making low phosphoric hematite and basic iron in the same blast furnace plant. The only way that contamination could be avoided was by having separate discharge facilities and separate conveyor belts for the two classes of ore required

---

[64] R. M. Shone, 'Scottish Developments', 10 Apr. 1948, section 3. This document was based on an earlier draft, dated 6 Apr. 1948, sent to Sir Andrew McCance for comments and partially amended in accordance with changes he suggested in a letter to R. M. Shone, 7 Apr. 1948.

[65] A. C. Boddis, Secretary to the Iron and Steel Board, to R. M. Shone, 3 May 1948; R. M. Shone to Sir Andrew McCance, 4 May 1948.

(low phosphorus hematite ore and high phosphorus basic ore), not only at the blast furnace plant but also at the docks. Colvilles therefore felt compelled strongly to 'recommend that the blast furnace plant for making hematite should be a separate unit'. The company was 'of the opinion that the Gartsherrie site could very properly be chosen for this purpose'.[66]

The 'essential problem' to which Colvilles' latest development plan was addressed was that of 'increasing pig iron production with some modernization of rolling mill equipment and a concentration of steel-making into fewer but larger units'.[67] The attainment of these objectives—which would cost £25 million—involved installing unloaders at the General Terminus to handle the 2,000,000 tons of ore required to expand the company's basic and foundry iron output to 1,180,000 tons. What this meant in statistical terms is shown in Table 11.5 and Figure III.

Early in 1949, Sir Archibald Forbes, Chairman of the Iron and Steel Board, held an exploratory meeting at Bush House to discuss the company's plan.[68] Several issues were given special attention. Sir Archibald was clearly concerned that the company had claimed no savings for an expenditure of £10·5 million on blast furnace plant at Motherwell, whereas the savings in production costs and increased profits arising from the increase in output of billets at Lanarkshire represented some £208,000 on a capital expenditure of £4,295,000 (or 4·95 per cent), and the savings in production costs to be expected from the expansion of Glengarnock and the re-allocation of heavy sections was £112,000 on a capital expenditure of £4,260,000 (or 2·36 per cent).[69] He was disturbed that the costs of production at the proposed works at Motherwell had not been estimated. Were there, he asked, no possible savings due to the larger hearth for the new furnace? And were there no possibilities of savings in assembling raw materials? Sir Andrew McCance

[66] Colvilles Ltd., 'The Future Development of Pig Iron and Steel Production in Scotland', 18 Nov. 1948, section 9.
[67] Ibid., section 7.
[68] Colvilles Ltd., 'Notes on a Meeting held in Bush House, London, 18 January 1949'.
[69] Colvilles Ltd., 'The Future Development . . .', 1948, Lanarkshire figures, sections 20 and 21; Glengarnock figures, sections 23 and 24. 'It must be appreciated that these savings are not substantial because Glengarnock already is an efficient producer.'

TABLE 11.5
The Statistical Bases of Colvilles' 1948 Plan

(a) *Pig Iron Requirements for Steel-making*

	Tons
Planned annual steel ingot production	2,200,000
Raw materials (Pig Iron and Scrap) at 108%	2,375,000

Scrap available:

		Tons
Circulating scrap		550,000
Uprising scrap—		
	Merchants	300,000
	Allied Firms	20,000
	Shipbreakers	130,000
Imported scrap		250,000
	TOTAL	1,250,000

Hematite and basic pig iron required	1,125,000

Hematite iron required from outside Colvilles:

Special West Coast iron	95,000
Ordinary hematite from Scottish sources	50,000
TOTAL	145,000

Basic quality iron to be produced by Colvilles	980,000
Clyde Iron Works existing capacity	600,000
Deficiency of basic iron to be produced by Colvilles	380,000

(b) *Total Pig Iron Production in Scotland and Production Units* (*Tons per Annum*)

Pig Iron Production		Production Units		Company
Basic Iron	980,000	Clyde Iron Works....	600,000	Colvilles
Foundry.......	200,000	Motherwell	580,000	Colvilles
Hematite.....	200,000	Gartsherrie...............	200,000	Bairds
	1,380,000		1,380,000	

(c) *Concentration of Colvilles' Steel Production Units* (*Tons per Annum*)

	Existing (1948)	Future	Speciality
Dalzell	400,000	475,000	Heavy plates and blooms
Clydebridge	350,000	600,000	Ship and light plates
Glengarnock	350,000	425,000	Heavy sections
Lanarkshire..........	220,000	400,000	Billets and light sections
Blochairn	130,000	—	—
Hallside	145,000	—	—
	1,595,000	1,900,000	

Source: Colvilles Ltd., 'The Future Development of Pig Iron and Steel Production in Scotland', 18 Nov. 1948; (a): section 8, p. 4; (b): section 11, p. 6; (c): section 13, pp. 7–8.

ORE

BASIC ORE
2 000 000

[GENERAL TERMINUS]

HEMATITE ORE
350 000

[ROTHESAY DOCK]

GARTSHERRIE
350 000

IRON

CLYDE IRON WORKS
1 020 000

BASIC IRON
600 000

FOUNDRY IRON
205 000

MOTHERWELL
980 000

IRON
580 000

375 000

WEST COAST HEMATITE

IRON
200 000

95 000

295 000

BASIC STEEL MAKING IRON
975 000

FOUNDRIES
20 000

MOULD FOUNDRIES
50 000

OTHER STEELMAKING IRON
225 000

STEEL

TOTAL STEELMAKING IRON
1 200 000

TOTAL SCRAP ALL SOURCES
1 284 000

RAW MATERIALS
2 484 000

CLYDEBRIDGE
SCRAP   162 000
HOT METAL 486 000
COLD METAL NIL

GLENGARNOCK
SCRAP   323 000
HOT METAL NIL
COLD METAL 137 000

DALZELL
SCRAP   225 000
HOT METAL 202 000
COLD METAL 85 000

LANARKSHIRE
SCRAP   302 000
HOT METAL NIL
COLD METAL 130 000

OTHERS
SCRAP   272 000
HOT METAL NIL
COLD METAL 160 000

RAW MATERIALS 648 000
INGOTS 600 000

RAW MATERIALS 460 000
INGOTS 425 000

RAW MATERIALS 512 000
INGOTS 475 000

RAW MATERIALS 432 000
INGOTS 400 000

RAW MATERIALS 432 000
INGOTS 400 000

BAIRDS & SCOTTISH STEEL LTD 120 000
W.M. BEARDMORE & COY. LTD. 130 000
STEWARTS & LLOYDS LTD   150 000
TOTAL   400 000

SLABS 535 000

BLOOMS 385 000

BLOOMS 400 000

BLOOMS AND SLABS 360 000

BLOOMS 400 000

FORGING INGOTS 5000

FORGING BLOOMS ETC 65 000

345 000

15 000

BILLETS 215 000

ROLLED PRODUCTS

CLYDEBRIDGE
SLABS 320 000

SMITH & McLEAN 345 000

BLOCHAIRN 192 000

RE ROLLING SLABS 23 000

RAILS AND HEAVY SECTIONS 313 000

BILLETS 37 000

FOR SALE 33 000

FOR WIRE RODS 4000

40 000

192 000

PLATES 150 000

SECTIONS ETC 115 000

128 000

80 000

FORGING BLOOMS 50 000
TUBE BILLETS 15 000
TOTAL   65 000

SALEABLE BLOOMS ETC 15 000

SHEET BARS 130 000

BARS AND LIGHT SECTIONS 200 000

PLATES 250 000

RAILS 85 000
SLEEPERS 8 000
JOISTS 79 000
HEAVY SECTIONS 141 000
TOTAL 313 000

PLATES 150 000

JOISTS 21 000
HEAVY SECTIONS 19 000
HEAVY BARS 25 000
WIRE ROD BILLETS 6 000
TUBE BILLETS 4 000
ALLOY BILLETS 40 000
TOTAL 115 000

BILLETS 5000
SLABS 4000
TUBE BILLETS 6000
TOTAL 15 000

LIGHT SECTIONS 90 000
LIGHT BARS 110 000
TOTAL 200 000

FIG. III. *Colvilles Ltd.: Annual Flow Chart illustrating 'The Future Development of Pig Iron and Steel Production in Scotland', dated 1 March 1949. (All figures are in tons.)*

replied that such savings would be 'fractional' and, in his opinion, 'not significant'. Sir Archibald was most perturbed by this answer. He was worried that there would be no savings available to take up the extra depreciation involved in the increase in costs of the new blast furnace plant compared with Clyde Iron Works.[70]

Another point to give rise to anxiety was the raw material position. Sir Archibald emphasized that the company's submission assumed a supply of 250,000 tons of imported scrap, and 130,000 tons of shipbreaking scrap (see Table 11.5). He felt that this was unrealistic. In future, such quantities of scrap would not be available. It would be necessary, therefore, to reconsider the pig iron capacity for steel-making. Neither Sir John nor Sir Andrew was prepared to accept this pessimistic view of future scrap supplies, but they did admit that financial factors, especially the supply of dollars, 'might distort the normal commercial position'. Although it was felt that the additional capacity 'could readily be made available' if the situation did develop as Sir Archibald feared, Sir Andrew expressed strong doubts that sufficient care was being taken to see that the additional ore and coke supplies would be available as soon as additional blast furnace capacity.[71]

The result of this meeting was that Sir Archibald Forbes demanded more data on a whole range of issues. Their preparation took considerable time. Not until May were Thomson McLintock & Company, the Iron and Steel Board's financial advisers, in full possession of all the facts they required and by this time the Iron and Steel Board had ceased to function.[72]

[70] Colvilles Ltd., 'Notes of a Meeting ... January 1949', paragraphs 13–17. 'On questioning, Sir Archibald stated that his opinion of a significant saving in pig iron production would be 5s. per ton. Sir Andrew replied that in that case he would not like to be bound to show savings of that amount on the present production costs at Clyde Iron Works, *which were known to be the lowest in the country.*' Emphasis added. On the question of hematite and low phosphorus iron (see above, p. 305), it was agreed that Gartsherrie was technically the most suitable site for the production of Scotland's requirements, and Sir Archibald was pressed to encourage Bairds and Scottish Steel to undertake this project (paragraph 24).
[71] Ibid., paragraphs 22–3.
[72] At a meeting held at Bush House on 29 March 1949, Sir Archibald Forbes had promised that although the Board was 'definitely demitting office at the end of the month ... he thought he could get his Board to meet for the special purpose of considering [Colvilles'] schemes, if the details were forthcoming,

The Board's original term of office had expired in the autumn of 1948. When the Minister of Supply[73] asked its members to serve an additional year, all but the trade union members (A. Callighan, General Secretary of the National Union of Blast Furnacemen, and Mr. Lincoln Evans, General Secretary of the Iron and Steel Trades Confederation) refused. Their explanation for so doing, according to the statement issued by Mr. George R. Strauss, was that 'in the changed circumstances likely in their view to arise from the Government's proposals for bringing sections of the iron and steel industry under public ownership', they could not carry on. The functions of the Board were transferred to the steel section of the Ministry of Supply.[74] Nevertheless, much of Colvilles' 1948 Development Plan was subsequently to be approved either by the permanent staff of the Iron and Steel Board, the Iron and Steel Corporation of Great Britain, or the Second Iron and Steel Board.

4 Hiatus in Planning: Progress in Production and Organization

The expansion of the melting shop at Clydebridge and the construction of an additional battery of 68 coke ovens to supply the coke required by the third blast furnace at Clyde Iron had, indeed, already been authorized before the completion of Colvilles' scheme for 'The Future Development of Pig Iron and Steel in Scotland' in November 1949.[75] The company had, in fact, 'continued their prewar policy of piecemeal improvement

---

say within a period of two months ...' Colvilles Ltd., 'Notes of a Meeting on Scottish Steel Development at Bush House, London, on 29 March 1949', section 4.

[73] John Wilmot had been replaced by George R. Strauss as Minister of Supply early in October 1949, following the Cabinet's decision to nationalize the iron and steel industry. Wilmot had identified himself with a less radical plan, strongly favoured by Herbert Morrison, of greatly strengthening the powers of direction and control of the Iron and Steel Board, and so providing a sort of half-way house between private ownership and 'full' nationalization. The story is told by George W. Ross, *The Nationalization of Steel* (London: MacGibbon & Kee, 1965), pp. 60–86.

[74] British Iron and Steel Federation, 'The Public Supervision of the Iron and Steel Industry', *Statistical Bulletin*, vol. xxiv, No. 10 (October 1949), p. 1; Ross, *Nationalization of Steel*, p. 86.

[75] The melting shop at Clydebridge was authorized on 29 June 1948; the coke ovens on 7 Oct. 1948.

to existing plant . . . on a fairly lavish scale'.[76] In describing Colvilles' policy in these words, Burn is somewhat misleading. Piecemeal though the changes may appear to have been, they each represented progress towards the completion of a consciously structured plan evolved on the eve of the war which attempted to meet both economic and social needs. However much Colvilles may in retrospect be criticized for its rejection of the possibilities inherent in a new tidewater site, the board was always realistic.

The raw material difficulties which played so large a part in shaping Colvilles' plan should not be ignored. Of all steelmakers in the United Kingdom, none was more dependent than Colvilles on scrap. Fear of a shortage of scrap and the anxiety that the company should obtain what it considered to be its proper share of imported scrap permeates the firm's major policy documents.[77] Furthermore, shortages of coking coal were so severe in Scotland that the newly-completed blast furnace at Clyde Iron was idle for three months waiting for assured fuel supplies.[78] Earlier, Colvilles had felt compelled to convert No. 4 Melting Shop at Dalzell to oil burning at a cost of £500,000.[79] Equally powerful in moulding the company's policy were economic and political pressures to meet the production targets set out in the White Paper of 1945.

[76] Burn, *The Steel Industry*, p. 262.

[77] Prewar, Scotland consumed between 50 and 60 per cent of all the scrap imported into Britain. Colvilles Ltd., 'The Future Development . . .', section 2. There are many supporting documents in the company's archives.

[78] Moreover, when coal was available, it was not only much more expensive than before the war (at one of the works the price of fuel delivered during 1947 was almost double that of 1938, compared with an increase in the selling price of steel over the same period of only 52 per cent), but it was markedly inferior in quality. 'In some of our works, we are actually using 20 per cent more fuel per ton of ingot output than we would have used if the sources of supply and the quality had been the same as in 1938.' Colvilles Ltd., Chairman's Statement, 26 May 1948.

[79] Ibid. Sir John Craig added: 'We completed a similar conversion at Clydebridge. Unfortunately, and quite unexpectedly, the price of oil was increased in September 1947 by £1 15s. per ton and again by £1 per ton in February of this year [1948]. These increases not only eliminated any benefit from the use of oil but added substantially to the fuel cost of steel melting as compared with the use of coal. We had commenced to convert the furnaces at Hallside Works in the same way when, after a considerable amount of money had been spent and the plant installed, we were informed that the amount of oil available was insufficient for our needs and this scheme had to be abandoned.'

One further factor is relevant in understanding Colvilles' policy. The senior members of the firm believed that any increase in the annual capacity of an individual unit much beyond 400,000 to 500,000 ingot tons could be achieved only at the cost of good management and efficient control. It may be inferred that they also recognized—perhaps subconsciously—some measurable size of a *group* of such units beyond which they felt that overall direction was subject to steeply diminishing returns. It might be conjectured that Sir John Craig, who by 1948 had already completed sixty years' service with Colvilles, and Sir Andrew McCance, who had carried such enormous responsibility for so long, both believed that the Group could grow no further under their personal supervision. Perhaps they could not face undertaking the radical changes that a new plant on the Clyde would inevitably have involved?[80] But subsequent events lend little support to this hypothesis. Undoubtedly, they had both been working under great strain during the war and immediate postwar periods, but the energies of neither Sir John nor Sir Andrew McCance appear to have reached their limits during the forties.[81] Although they were to lose the invaluable counsel of Sir James Lithgow, who had resigned from the boards of both Colvilles and the Steel Company of Scotland in 1946, and his brother, Henry, who died in May 1948,[82] the creation of an executive board, composed of senior members of the staff, served to ease many pressures upon the directors. Having its genesis in 1942, when 'occasional meetings of the managers of all the works in the Group' were formally inaugurated, the executive board was created on 1 January 1947.[83] It was made responsible for 'all

[80] This seems to be Vaizey's implication, *History of British Steel*, p. 142.

[81] In an interview with *Scope*, August 1947, Sir John emphasized: 'I say there is no joy in life to compare with work ... as I grow older, the pleasure work gives me becomes keener and ever keener. I would rather be at my desk or the works than anywhere in the world.' Quoted by Roy Lewis and Rosemary Stewart, *The Boss* (London: Dent, 1961), p. 131. In the same year, at a presentation by his fellow directors to Dr. Andrew McCance of a portrait of himself by James Gunn to mark his election to a Fellowship of the Royal Society, Mrs. McCance drily observed that 'the portrait would bring her joy if only because she would see her husband more often in the future'. *Colvilles' Magazine*, May–June 1947, p. 6.

[82] Colvilles Ltd., Minute Book III, 4 July 1946. *Colvilles' Magazine*, May–June 1948, p. 1.

[83] See above, pp. 261–2. The decision to create an executive board was

problems affecting works' operation, improvements in plant, maintenance of quality and the general technical and commercial development of the Works'.[84] In the formulation of the company's development plans, the work of the special directors, as they came to be called in 1955, was of inestimable value to the parent board.[85] But was the executive board not another manifestation of Colvilles' 'inherent caution'?[86] Would not some more radical reorganization of the firm's structure have been even more beneficial? It is highly improbable. The reasons why Colvilles did not evolve some variant of the multidivisional form in the late thirties has already been discussed.[87] The same factors militating against sweeping organizational change were still operative ten years later. Indeed, Sir John Craig had asked his fellow directors seriously to consider the possibility of more fundamental change—he suggested a complete amalgamation—in 1946, but 'it was unanimously decided to continue the present arrangement'.[88] His speech to the Extraordinary General Meeting to consider the amendments in the Articles of Association necessary to permit the creation of the executive board explained:

> The Company has followed a policy of leaving the Subsidiaries as separate legal entities to enable us to retain the goodwill associated with the established business of each Subsidiary. The Directors of Colvilles Ltd. have supervised the Colville Works and, at the same time, undertaken a general supervision of the Subsidiaries so as to ensure a common policy of finance and development. It has been felt desirable that we should constitute a Board which would

the subject of considerable debate by the Directors, and great care went into its constitution. The principal Minutes are those of 5 Jan. 1945; 1 Oct. 1945; 7 Feb. 1946. In 1944, Sir Ellis Hunter had introduced special directors— a similar arrangement—into the administration of Dorman Long & Co. Ltd. Charles Wilson, *A Man and His Times: A Memoir of Sir Ellis Hunter* (London: Newman Neame, n.d.), p. 5.

[84] Colvilles Ltd., Chairman's Statement, 26 May 1948.

[85] In addition to Sir John Craig, Sir Andrew McCance, and T. R. Craig from the parent board, the original executive board consisted of William Barr, Chief Metallurgist; R. C. Dymock, Chief Labour Officer; T. W. Hand, Chief Mechanical Engineer; John McCracken, Senior Works Manager (Clydebridge); Robert Marshall, Sales Manager; L. Rothera, Chief Electrical Engineer; T. J. Smith, Purchasing Manager; H. Griffin (Secretary). Colvilles Ltd., Minute Book III, 5 Dec. 1946. *Colvilles' Magazine* January–February 1947, pp. 11–14.

[86] Vaizey's expression, *History of British Steel*, p. 142.

[87] See above, p. 246.

[88] Colvilles Ltd., Minute Book III, 7 Feb. 1946.

have the responsibility of managing the Colville Works, thereby placing them in a position similar to the Subsidiary Companies. This would enable the Parent Board to deal with the Company and Subsidiaries as a whole and relieve it of some of the detailed control of the Colville Works. There was the alternative idea of putting all the Companies under one Board but . . . it is considered that the plan now proposed is in the best interests of the Company as well as of the Subsidiaries.[89]

The fact seems to be that if the joint managing directors saw a ceiling to the growth of Colvilles at this point it was related not to their managerial capacity but to their assessment of the effective demand for the firm's products. Their anxieties on this score have already been examined, and Sir John Craig returned to this theme in 1950 when he drew attention to the O.E.E.C. report on *European Steel Trends* which concluded that 'if all the schemes at present under way in many countries are completed, there may not be a sufficient demand to keep all the plants employed'. He warned the stockholders that although Colvilles 'had a good order book . . . some departments are experiencing a shortage of orders'.[90] In the same year, Sir Andrew McCance forecast a future national demand of 17,500,000 ingot tons[91] in 1960, and his assessment of Colvilles' own share of this figure was similarly based not on 'irrational guesswork' but on a careful calculation of past trends and present prospects coupled with estimates of the future supply of coking coal and scrap. Towards the end of the forties, Colvilles believed that in the predictable future the company's optimum output, from the viewpoint of both supply and demand, was about 1,900,000 ingot tons. That being so, this target could be most economically and efficiently attained by the scheme submitted to the Federation and to the

[89] *Colvilles' Magazine*, Summer 1946, pp. 2–3, January–February 1947, p. 1.

[90] Colvilles Ltd., Annual Report for 1949, Chairman's Statement, p. 15; *Colvilles' Magazine*, May–June 1950, p. 2.

[91] Sir Andrew McCance, 'Production in the Steel Industry: Its Growth, Distribution, and Future Course'. The Harold Wright Lecture, at the Cleveland Scientific and Technical Institute, Middlesbrough, 28 Nov. 1950, partly reprinted in the *Iron and Steel Review*, 12 Jan. 1951, pp. 75–8. Burn (*The Steel Industry*, p. 278) points out that this figure was actually surpassed in 1953, but, as Sir Andrew emphasized in his lecture, his mathematical formula for estimating future outputs could not 'take into account the fortuitous fluctuations that occur as between one year and the next as determined by the varying conditions of trade and demand'.

Iron and Steel Board. It is difficult, if not impossible, to prove that they were wildly inaccurate.

By spending some £3,200,000 on plant extensions and improvements in the first five years after the war,[92] Colvilles had

TABLE 11.6

Crude Steel Output:[a] United Kingdom, Scotland, and the Colville Group; and Pig Iron Production of the Colville Group, 1946–1967

	U.K.	SCOTLAND		THE COLVILLE GROUP		
Year	('000 tons)	('000 tons)	$\frac{\text{Scot.}}{\text{U.K.}}\%$	Crude Steel (tons)	$\frac{\text{Colvilles}}{\text{Scotland}}\%$	Pig Iron (tons)
1946	12,695·3	1,764·5	13·9	1,410,824	80·0	375,121
1947	12,724·5	1,878·9	14·8	1,489,513	79·3	341,640
1948	14,876·6	2,253·9	15·2	1,734,675	77·0	521,564
1949	15,552·9	2,381·8	15·3	1,853,650	77·8	511,142
1950	16,292·7	2,426·2	14·9	1,887,170	77·8	488,303
1951	15,638·5	2,114·8	13·5	1,664,922	78·7	546,335
1952	16,417·9	2,132·7	13·0	1,678,241	78·7	606,477
1953[b]	17,608·5	2,322·8	13·2	1,864,079	80·3	613,224
1954	18,519·7	2,231·9	12·1	1,818,491	81·5	625,936
1955	19,790·6	2,343·9	11·8	1,849,610	78·9	739,205
1956	20,658·9	2,518·9	12·2	1,973,568	78·4	741,764
1957	21,699·1	2,626·5	12·1	2,095,274	79·8	789,377
1958	19,565·7	2,115·6	10·8	1,847,063	87·3	918,942
1959	20,186·4	1,964·2	9·7	1,442,312	73·4	673,163
1960	24,305·0	2,700·6	11·1	2,056,467	76·1	963,586
1961	22,086·1	2,341·4	10·6	2,041,947	87·2	1,041,531
1962	20,491·0	1,895·0	9·2	1,611,415	85·0	739,245
1963	22,520·2	2,067·7	9·2	1,535,267	74·2	640,792
1964	26,229·9	2,974·2	11·3	2,361,848	79·4	1,232,427
1965	27,006·1	3,053·0	11·3	2,657,307	87·0	1,430,234
1966	24,315·3	2,677·6	11·0	2,219,834	82·9	1,240,946
1967	23,895·2	2,599·7	10·9	n.d.	—	n.d.

Notes:

[a]'Crude Steel Output' represents the total tonnage of steel produced by the open-hearth, Bessemer, and electric processes, together with all other ingots and castings, in each calendar year.

[b]In 1951 Colvilles Ltd. agreed to the request of the Iron and Steel Corporation of Great Britain to change their balancing date from 31 December to the Saturday nearest to 30 September in each year. One consequence of this change is that after 1952 the figures of Colvilles' annual outputs of steel and pig iron are those for the twelve months ending approx. 30 September. The column showing the percentage of total Scottish steel output produced by Colvilles is, as a consequence, only a guide, since the figures have been obtained by expressing Colvilles' output for each financial year as a percentage of Scottish output in each calendar year.

Sources: Crude Steel Outputs, U.K. and Scotland: British Iron and Steel Federation, subsequently Iron and Steel Board and the B.I.S.F., *Annual Statistics.*

Crude Steel and Pig Iron outputs of the Colville Group: Colvilles Ltd., Annual Reports and Accounts.

[92] Colvilles Ltd., Annual Report for 1949, Chairman's Statement. *Colvilles' Magazine*, May–June 1950, p. 2. A brief description of the company's major plants in 1949 is included in *Steel and Britain's Future*, a Special Issue of the *Iron and Coal Trades Review*, vol. clix, No. 4255A (1949), pp. 42–5.

all but attained their objectives by 1950 when 1,887,170 tons of steel ingots and 488,303 tons of pig iron were produced (see Table 11.6). Moreover, these record figures had been achieved without the full benefit of the Clydebridge/Clyde Iron extensions and despite raw material problems exacerbated by a chronic shortage of railway wagons. It is indisputable that in the short run Colvilles' policy had 'paid off' and, in so doing, had 'virtually decided the planning issue as Colvilles wished',[93] whatever reservations Sir Archibald Forbes still entertained in March 1949. The successors to the first Iron and Steel Board had little option but to agree, however reluctantly, with the board features of Colvilles' *Memorandum* of November 1948. After 1949, the controversy over the tidewater scheme was, to all intents and purposes, dead.[94] Colvilles' extensions, completed and approved, had made it so; and the growing relative cost of, and delay incurred in, constructing entirely new plant of similar capacity,[95] seemed to confirm the wisdom of Colvilles' policy.

One further point should be made. Sir John Craig's experiences during the dismal inter-war period had instilled in him a deep distrust of outside finance. Without in any way questioning the strength of his belief in the firm's social responsibilities, to have given way to the national planners, to have agreed to build a new integrated plant on Clydeside, would inevitably—if Richard Thomas's was any guide—have thrown Colvilles into the hands of the financial institutions. This he could not countenance. Colvilles would be crushed by the enormous fixed-interest debt burden, and power would pass to those with no sympathy for the sheer process of steel-making. This was anathema to him. He even begrudged paying dividends to the Ordinary shareholders—this represented a diversion of the life-blood of the firm. Had he been able, he would doubtless have retained *all* the profits within the firm. For some years before the war, financial commentators had repeatedly drawn attention, in words which combined respect and annoyance, to Colvilles' conservative dividend policy. In the five years

[93] Burn, *The Steel Industry*, p. 262.
[94] Somewhat prematurely, Sir John Craig pronounced the obsequies in his Chairman's Statement of May 1949. Colvilles Ltd., Annual Report and Accounts for 1948, pp. 10–11.
[95] See Burn's discussion of this point, *The Steel Industry*, pp. 264–8.

following the end of the war, capital expenditure exceeded £5 million (see Table 11.7) with no new shares, no debentures or loans, and no increase in dividends since 1946 (see Table 11.8).

TABLE 11.7

The Colville Group: Sales, Trading Profit, Capital Expenditure, and Dividend on Ordinary Shares, 1946–1966

Year	(1) Income from Sales (£'000s)	(2) Manufacturing & Trading Profit (£'000s)	(3) Capital Expenditure (£'000s)	(4) Ordinary Dividend (%)
1946	n.d.	n.d.	316	8·0
1947	n.d.	2,766	586	13·0
1948	n.d.	3,222	761	13·0
1949	n.d.	3,418	1,391	13·0
1950	n.d.	4,915	2,151	13·0
1951ᵃ	31,048	4,022	1,263	13·0
1952	42,136	4,639	1,660	13·0
1953	55,358	4,967	2,162	13·0
1954	52,234	4,618	1,827	13·0
1955	57,024	7,065	3,582	11·0ᵇ
1956	67,976	7,673	9,751	11·0
1957	77,055	9,018	13,499	13·0
1958	74,480	8,652	6,102	13·0
1959	56,542	9,352	5,870	14·0
1960	75,355	13,577	16,614	16·0
1961	75,202	10,923	33,095	16·0
1962	59,240	3,640	35,346	13·0
1963	59,767	2,200	11,259	12·0
1964	89,171	8,824	4,071	16·0
1965	96,658	5,637	5,920	16·0
1966	89,439	1,919	5,986	9·0

Notes:

ᵃ Nine months. Balancing date altered to the Saturday nearest 30 September in each year from this date.

ᵇ On reorganized capital.

Col. (2): These figures of manufacturing and trading profit include investment income and allow for 'normal depreciation'.

Col. (3): Until and including 1958, these figures represent the 'Additions to Fixed Assets (before depreciation)'; from 1959 onwards the table shows 'Expenditure on Fixed Assets'. The figure for 1958 has been estimated.

Source: Colvilles Ltd.: Annual Reports and Accounts.

Colvilles Ltd.: Capital Structure, 1945–1966

	SHARE CAPITAL[a]		LOAN CAPITAL			
	5½% Cumulative Preference Stock (£)	Ordinary (£)	4½% Debenture Stock, 1975–85 (£)	6% Convertible Debenture Stock, 1978–81 (£)	H.M. Government Loan (and accrued interest) (£)	Finance Corporation for Industry Ltd. Loan (£)
1945	2,000,000	3,919,550	—	—	—	—
1946	2,000,000	3,919,550	—	—	—	—
1947	2,000,000	3,919,550	—	—	—	—
1948	2,000,000	3,919,550	—	—	—	—
1949	2,000,000	3,919,550	—	—	—	—
1950	2,000,000	3,919,550	—	—	—	—
1951[b]	2,000,000	3,919,550	—	—	—	—
1952	2,000,000	3,919,550	—	—	—	—
1953	2,000,000	3,919,550	—	—	—	—
1954[c]	2,000,000	3,919,550	—	—	—	—
1955	4,000,000[d]	10,000,000	10,000,000[e]	—	—	—
1956	4,000,000[d]	10,000,000	10,000,000[e]	—	—	—
1957	4,000,000	10,000,000	10,000,000	—	—	—
1958	4,000,000	10,000,000	10,000,000	—	—	—
1959	4,000,000	10,374,796[f]	10,000,000	5,479,450	—	—
1960	4,000,000	13,915,116[f]	9,820,000	421,850	—	—
1961	4,000,000	19,451,230[g]	9,640,000	111,250	15,000,000	—
1962	4,000,000	19,505,383[f]	9,393,649	29,200	46,737,262	—
1963	4,000,000	19,508,647[f]	9,103,108	—	54,549,262	2,500,000
1964	4,000,000	19,508,647	8,901,818	—	55,061,764	2,500,000
1965	4,000,000	19,508,647	8,596,487	—	58,093,446	3,500,000
1966	4,000,000	19,508,647	8,271,994	—	59,833,812	6,000,000

Notes:
[a] Authorized and issued.
[a] Nine months. Balancing date altered to the Saturday nearest 30 Sept. in each year from this date.
[c] Capital reorganized and increased as from 21 Dec. 1954.
[d] £1,000,000 called up (i.e. 5s. per share).
[e] £10 per £100 paid.
[f] Increases due to holders of Convertible Debenture Stock exercising their rights to convert.
[g] 5,324,906 new shares were offered as a 3 for 8 rights issue at 57s. 6d. in July 1961 (85 per cent were left with the underwriters).

Source: Colvilles Ltd., Annual Reports and Accounts.

To Colvilles' chairman, such financial considerations served to reinforce his belief in the essential correctness of the company's policy.[96]

Thus, 'the major aim of the 1945 White Paper was not accomplished, but the subsidiary aims of works closure, plant specialization, fuel saving, and the greater use of hot metal, had been observed and partly realized'.[97] The whole episode illustrates the essential weakness of central planning in the immediate postwar period and the incompatibility of the aims of private enterprise and the public interest in an old-established industry, such as steel. As Heal has observed, 'To the outsider the Clydeside scheme had, and still has, great appeal in terms of grandeur and neatness, but it is clear that none of the people directly involved were anxious to face the upheaval that it would have created.'[98] The first Iron and Steel Board could do nothing to overcome this reluctance. Its control over the industry was essentially negative: it could tell particular firms what not to do, but not what to do. It was a lesson not lost on the advocates of nationalization.[99]

[96] As always, Burn has some trenchant comments. *The Steel Industry*, pp. 263–4.

[97] Heal's verdict. D. W. Heal, *The Steel Industry in Post-War Britain* (Newton Abbot: David & Charles, 1974), p. 53. Cf. Vaizey, *History of British Steel*, p. 142. Blochairn was to be closed down in 1952.

[98] Heal, *The Steel Industry*, p. 52. Cf. Kenneth Warren, 'Location Problems . . .', Part 2, *passim*. It is significant that the Iron and Steel Trades Confederation were against the Clydeside scheme. *Times Review of Industry*, December 1947, p. 29.

[99] See Ross, *The Nationalization of Steel*, p. 96.

XII

The Second Development Plan, 1951–1957: The Birth of Ravenscraig

1 Continuity Despite Politics

The refusal of the majority of the Iron and Steel Board to serve a further term of office in the autumn of 1948 coincided with the placing of the Iron and Steel Bill before Parliament. 'At long last, after three years of indecision and delay, the Labour Government intended to redeem the last of its major election promises.'[1] The Bill provided for the creation of an Iron and Steel Corporation of Great Britain. The principal function of this body would be to act as a holding company for all those firms producing specified quantities of iron ore, pig iron, or steel, whose shares were to be compulsorily acquired by the state, compensation being paid on the basis of Stock Exchange valuations prior to the introduction of the Bill.[2] It is important to recognize that it was intended that individual companies 'would be transferred to public ownership but would retain their identity and would, at any rate at the outset, continue to function as separate units subject to general supervision by [the Corporation], which would also have to exercise certain executive functions on behalf of the whole industry. [The Corporation] would itself be subject to ultimate control by the Minister of Supply.'[3] It was felt that among the advantages of adopting such a structure would be that it permitted the acquisition and continued operation of the various firms with the minimum of disturbance:

It was essential in the interests of efficient management that the publicly owned steel companies should be enabled not only to retain the services of

[1] Ross, *The Nationalization of Steel*, p. 87.
[2] The evolution of the Bill itself is described and explained by Sir Norman Chester, *The Nationalisation of British Industry, 1945–51* (London: H.M.S.O., 1975), pp. 172–9, 440–52.
[3] Ibid., p. 441; Burn, *The Steel Industry*, pp. 294–5.

the highly skilled executive staffs (including in many cases members of the boards of directors) but that the new regime should command from the start their full and wholehearted support. This would be the more easily achieved if those concerned knew that, subject to supervision in broad policy matters, they would continue to have a substantial measure of discretion and freedom of management in all day-to-day affairs serving, as heretofore, a particular company, and that they were not to become employees of a 'new and "soulless" state colossus'.[4]

There were disadvantages of taking over the iron and steel industry as a going concern, as it were, but it was confidently believed that these could be overcome. By retaining both the old company structure and even the directors in office, the impression might be given that there was very little real change, that the government was proceeding in a manner reminiscent of the company promoter rather than the revolutionary planner envisaged by the famous election manifesto 'Let us Face the Future'. But if it was emphasized that the Corporation would have the power to merge, wind up, or reorganize companies, establish functional authorities, and remove unco-operative officials, and if, moreover, the government expressed its clear intention of completely restructuring the entire industry on, for example, a geographical or product basis, after the transitional takeover period, then the fears of its left-wing supporters—disconcerted by the continuance of what appeared to be the old regime—and the anxieties of those who were more concerned with the long-term organizational needs of the industry, should be allayed.

Nevertheless, whatever the qualification—however much the initial form of the industry under public ownership might obscure the reality that power resided almost completely with the Corporation and the Minister of Supply—the fact remained that by the retention of the original companies, the government's nationalization scheme promised to make denationalization a comparatively easy process if, but only if, the Opposition could be returned to power before the Minister felt it expedient to embark on a programme of fundamental reorganization.

Another factor, too, strengthened the impression that the Act, when it was passed, would not immediately and irrevocably alter the industry's structure. The Bill, which its proponents hoped would forever shatter the power of Steel House—

[4] Chester, *The Nationalisation of British Industry*, p. 442.

the headquarters of the British Iron and Steel Federation—
said nothing about the Federation. This was, so it was argued,
because to have singled out the Federation for discriminative
action, would have run the risk of creating a 'hybrid Bill' which
might well have been subject to exceptionally prolonged
Parliamentary proceedings; so long, in fact, that the danger
existed that the Bill might still be progressing through the House
when the life of the 1945 Parliament came to an end. At all
events, the Bill would certainly have been held up, and many
felt that there had been delays enough with this measure
already.[5] It seemed best to proceed on the basis that the Corporation and the publicly-owned companies would 'have no
difficulty in coming to terms with the Federation [after
nationalization] and transferring or using the skill and expertise
of Steel House'.[6] Thus, here again, events conspired to preserve
an integral piece of the pre-nationalization structure of the iron
and steel industry.

When, after a stormy passage through Parliament[7]—during
the course of which the government was forced to postpone
vesting day until some time during 1951—the Iron and Steel
Bill was given the Royal Assent on 24 November 1949, it had
become inevitable that the Act could not be implemented until
after the General Election of 1950. This election gave the
Labour administration a precarious majority; so precarious, in
fact, that although the Iron and Steel Corporation of Great Britain was to come into being in October, the Minister experienced the utmost difficulty in recruiting its members. With the
Conservative Party, pledged to denationalize steel, likely soon
to be in power, ' "the best men suited for this responsible task"
were still understandably ... reluctant to commit themselves
... and throw up their present positions.'[8] In the event, the

---

[5] A 'hybrid' bill was a public bill which affected the rights of specific individuals or corporations within a class and not those of the entire class or group.
Hybrid bills were referable to a select committee after Second Reading to
hear the evidence of petitioners against them—petitioners who could not be
guillotined. The point is made clear by Ross, *The Nationalization of Steel*, pp.
86–7; see also Burn, *The Steel Industry*, p. 310, and Chester, *The Nationalisation
of British Industry*, pp. 178–9.
[6] Chester, *The Nationalisation of British Industry*, p. 181.
[7] A full account is given by Ross, *The Nationalization of Steel*, pp. 86–116.
[8] Burn, *The Steel Industry*, p. 311. See also Wilson, *A Man and His Times*,
pp. 30–1.

government finally induced Steven Hardie, Chairman of the British Oxygen Company and Vice-Chairman of Metal Industries Ltd., to become Chairman, and he was to be supported by Sir John Green (Labour Director of Firth Browns), J. W. Garton (Chairman of Brown Bayleys), General Sir James Steele, Sir Vaughan Berry, British Delegate to the Ruhr Authority, W. H. Stokes, an official of the Amalgamated Engineering Union, and A. R. McBain, an ex-Civil Servant. Even charitable observers believed this board was wildly unsuitable. With its own future so much in doubt, with the Federation's refusal to concede the Corporation any right to appoint members to its Council, Finance and Executive Committees, the new body was hamstrung almost from the outset. Lacking knowledge, given as much co-operation by its subsidiaries as was consistent with courtesy, and no more, it could not have any immediate or significant impact on the industry.

Nevertheless, the Corporation began formally to operate in October. On 9 October, the Minister of Supply ordered that vesting day was to be 15 February 1951. The day came and went, without excitement. As Ross puts it:

> If the 'Nation' owned the steel works, the worker saw only that his own bosses were the same after, as before nationalization ... boards of directors and higher management remained intact ... very little transfer of effective control to the Corporation occurred. As one observer [Aylmer Vallance in the *New Statesman and Nation*] viewed the situation, 'between now and a general election ... seats round every board-room table will be filled by men who see themselves as caretakers for private enterprise'.[9]

Eight months later the Conservatives returned to power, and on 13 November 1951 the new Minister of Supply, Mr. Duncan Sandys, issued a general directive forbidding the Corporation, without his consent, from making *inter alia* 'any alteration in the financial structure or management' of any of the publicly-owned companies. Whatever Hardie's plans for the industry may have been—and he apparently had envisaged a radical reorganization of the ninety-two nationalized firms into seven to ten large groups, in part regional and in part functional—they could not now be carried out.

The government had now simply to devise a scheme to return the industry to private enterprise. Although, as the

[9] Ross, *The Nationalization of Steel*, p. 138.

Financial Times pointed out as early as 1950, 'the unique arrangement chosen by the Socialists for steel nationalization, whereby the identity of the industry's individual units [was] maintained and the Steel Corporation [assumed] physical ownership of all the industry's share certificates, might have been expressly designed to facilitate unscrambling',[10] the process required careful timing and considerable ingenuity. The Iron and Steel Holding and Realization Agency was established to hold and dispose of the assets of the nationalized companies. No rigid timetable for this task was specified. The Agency was simply expected to sell shares as quickly as it thought possible at 'financially adequate' prices. Special priority was to be given to former shareholders who wished to buy back their holdings. This took a long time. Not until 1963 was the disposal operation essentially completed, and even then one large company, Richard Thomas & Baldwins, remained unsold. Meanwhile, the Agency supplied many firms with large loans to carry out their development plans. The other object of the Iron and Steel Act of 1953 was to establish a new Iron and Steel Board very similar to the Labour Government's Board both in composition and scope. It was, however, given additional powers, especially in respect to planning. First, it could recommend to the Minister that certain projects which appeared to be essential for the well-being of the industry as a whole, but which did not form part of the development plans of individual firms, be initiated and carried out by the Minister himself. And, second, the new Board was to be permitted to refuse its consent to any development proposal which would 'seriously prejudice the efficient and economic development of production facilities in Great Britain'. Furthermore, 'the Board was endowed with the function [through its ability to fix maximum home prices] of deciding profit margins ... with the possibility of varying them to help enforce their wishes in investment decisions ...'.[11] Thus, the Act of 1953 'was to preserve the continuity which, for fortuitous reasons, the Act of 1949 had not broken, continuity not merely in the composition of the firms

[10] *Financial Times*, 14 Nov. 1950, quoted by Ross, *The Nationalization of Steel*, p. 150.

[11] Burn, *The Steel Industry*, pp. 369–75. Wilson, *A Man and His Times*, pp. 33–4, provides an elegant summary of the powers of the new Board.

326   *The Second Development Plan, 1951–1957*

but in the I.D.A.C.-Federation policies of the thirties . . .'[12] This continuity was not to be finally broken until 1967, when the Labour Party's commitment to re-nationalize steel when the occasion presented itself was realized.

2 Colvilles' Proposed Contribution to the Second Development Plan

(a) *Its Formulation.* From a planning point of view, the two years 1949–50 constituted something of a breathing space for Colvilles, but shortly before vesting day, Colvilles had been requested by the British Iron and Steel Federation that its Advisory Committee on Development be notified of the company's 'general intentions . . . about development in relation to the Second Development Plan'.[13] This prompted a detailed review of the progress made in implementing past plans, a renewed examination of those schemes for which the details had not yet been fully agreed and a study of possible future projects.[14] On the basis of this information and after a further investigation of the raw material situation, Sir Andrew McCance prepared an outline of Colvilles' proposals for future development. This was submitted to the Federation for consideration by the Development Committee on 1 September 1951.

The latest proposals rested upon a number of assumptions; first that only scrap arising in this country would be available; second, and as a direct consequence of the first assumption, that a greater production of pig iron would be necessary; third, that no expansion of steel-making in Scotland based on cold metal practice (and high scrap consumption) would be permitted; and, finally, that with a national ingot output of 20 million tons, Colvilles' share should be 2,500,000 tons.[15] It followed that Colvilles' total requirements of pig iron would be 1,675,000 tons, and that with the exception of Glengarnock Works and No.

[12] Burn, *The Steel Industry*, p. 384.
[13] B. S. Keeling, Secretary, B.I.S.F., to Colvilles Ltd., 12 Jan. 1951.
[14] Colvilles Ltd., 'Notes on a Discussion held in the Technical Offices, 22 January 1951'; 'Development Schemes for the Colville Group', 30 Jan. 1951.
[15] Colvilles Ltd., 'Development Plan', 5 Sept. 1951, sections 1, 2, 11, pp. 1, 7, 8. The Report of the Advisory Committee on Development submitted to the Minister of Supply in November, 1952, set the target for home steel production at 20½ million tons. B.I.S.F., *Annual Report for 1952*, p. 34.

4 Melting Shop at Dalzell, where special qualities of steel were made, all the shops should be converted to hot metal practice. In addition, it was felt that the manufacture of alloy steel, 'which is always difficult to merge with that of mild steel', should be concentrated in one works. The estimated annual output required was 100,000 tons of ingots and it was decided that the Hallside Works of the Steel Company of Scotland, scheduled for closure, should be converted for this purpose.[16] It was proposed to meet the pig iron requirements by erecting a fourth blast furnace with a capacity of 5,000 tons per week

TABLE 12.1

Statistics Illustrating Certain Features of Colvilles' 1951 Development Plan

(i) *The Balance of Output envisaged:*

Works	Hot Metal	Cold Metal
Glengarnock	—	450,000 tons
Dalzell—No. 4 Shop	—	375,000
New Shop	450,000 tons	—
Clydebridge	750,000	—
Lanarkshire	375,000	—
Hallside (Alloy)	—	100,000
	1,575,000 tons	925,000 tons
TOTAL	2,500,000 tons	

(ii) *Scrap/Pig Iron Ratios:*

Cold Metal Shops:	Scrap	56%
	Pig Iron	44%
Hot Metal Shops:	Scrap	25·5%
	Pig Iron	74·5%
Overall Average:	Scrap	36·8%
	Pig Iron	63·2%

(iii) *Allocation of Pig Iron Production:*

Clyde Iron Works	850,000
Motherwell	825,000
	1,675,000 tons

Source: Colvilles Ltd., 'Development Plan', 1951, sections 4–5.

[16] Colvilles Ltd., 'Development Plan', 1951, section 4.

at Clyde Iron Works,[17] and two furnaces each with a capacity of 6,000 tons per week at the new Motherwell site. These developments, however, were dependent upon the availability of coking coal, 1,350,000 tons of which would be required, and it was feared that grave difficulties would be involved in obtaining this quantity without a change in the development plans of the National Coal Board. The iron ore required for the proposed increase in pig iron production also constituted a problem, especially when taken in conjunction with the corresponding expansion in the production of foundry and hematite iron which Bairds and Scottish Steel had finally been induced to undertake at Gartsherrie.[18] The quantity required—3,320,000 tons per annum[19]—made it impossible to delay the installation of unloaders at the General Terminus.

Colvilles proposed to meet the output targets by the methods outlined in their earlier survey of long-term developments. The various works were assigned their roles in the overall plan and any departures from previous submissions to the Federation fully explained. One argument, relating to the role of Clydebridge, is significant for the comprehension of subsequent events:

> It is recognized that the development of continuous strip rolling all over the world foreshadows ultimately the closing down of hand mills in this country.
>
> The sheet market in Scotland is catered for by our Subsidiary, Smith & McLean, and *it seems unlikely that the growth of local demand would justify their installing a fully continuous mill.* On the other hand, the standard of sheet quality is being improved to such an extent that it is unlikely that any customer will eventually be content with anything less than full continuous mill finish.
>
> We are therefore planning Clydebridge to make the installation of a 4-stand continuous mill the final stage of its development. In this extension to the 4-high mill, breakdowns in coils would be produced and sent to Smith & McLean's Works at Gartcosh, about 5 miles distant, where the hand mills are operating today. The necessary cold rolling plant would be installed there to handle these. This would preserve employment in this small village, which has practically no other industrial activity.[20]

[17] This furnace was to be supplied with coke made at Dixon's Ironworks. The blast furnaces at Dixon's, woefully insufficient, would be closed down. *Ibid.*, section 5.

[18] The Development Committee approved this project during 1951. B.I.S.F., *Annual Report for 1951*, pp. 25–6.

[19] Colvilles, 2,680,000 tons; Bairds, 640,000 tons. Colvilles Ltd., 'Development Plan', 1951, section 7.

[20] Ibid., section 9(c). Emphasis added.

(b) *Its Reception.* Colvilles' scheme was submitted to the Federation's Advisory Committee on Development in September 1951.[21] The ensuing report was distinctly cool, even sceptical.[22] It was couched in general terms and questioned the very basis of the company's long-term proposals. The key factor was demand:

During the 1945 discussions and subsequently it was thought that the future demand for steel in Scotland would not be so high as that in England and, therefore, the Scottish proportion of the national total would fall. This view arose because of the lower demand for heavy products, which form the bulk of Scottish production, compared with the very great demand for thin flat products and light material mainly produced in England. Recently, however, Colvilles Limited have re-assessed the market position and they now state that the demand in Scotland will be such as to maintain steel output in proportion to the rest of the country ... the steel output of the Colville Group has therefore been increased from 1·9 to 2·5 million tons.

To the Advisory Committee, it was '*not easy to see how the demand has changed so much in this short period of time, since there do not appear to be any new factors influencing the position which were not known three years ago*'.[23] Moreover, although 'Colvilles Limited state that the rise in demand is due to the rapid development of many new industrial estates and light industries and that the future export requirements will be considerably higher than at present', their explanation was not wholly consistent with 'the long-term proposals now submitted, which only envisage about 30–40 per cent of the total expansion going into light products'. It was also emphasized that 'during 1950 there was an export to England of approximately 500,000 tons (equivalent ingot tonnage) mainly in the form of plates and heavy products. It seems most unlikely that with the expansion and development of plants in England that this trade is likely to continue.' In the light of these arguments, it was felt that the maintenance of Scottish steel production even at its 1950

[21] This body, of which Sir Andrew McCance was a member, represented, in effect, a reconstitution of the panel of experts that had previously advised the Economic Efficiency Committee, a standing committee of the Federation from 1943 until its functions were taken over by the Development Committee in 1946. See Keeling and Wright, *The Development of the Modern British Steel Industry*, p. 146.
[22] B.I.S.F., 'Report of the Advisory Committee on Development on the Proposals submitted by Colvilles Ltd.', 3 Nov. 1951.
[23] Ibid., 'Steel Demand', section 2. Emphasis added.

level 'might be difficult'. The Advisory Committee clearly entertained grave suspicions that Colvilles were simply trying to keep up with the English—or Welsh—Joneses; that Colvilles were determined that Scotland's share of national output must not be allowed to fall. Having employed the inadequate demand argument as an integral part of their successful case against a riverside site, Colvilles were now claiming that demand conditions had been so transformed than an ingot production some 32 per cent above the 1948–9 submission was appropriate to national, particularly Scottish, requirements. It was too much for the Committee to swallow.[24]

As if this were not enough to damn the scheme, subsequent arguments emphasized that Colvilles' proposed steel output of 2·5 million tons implied, if a pig iron/scrap ratio of 63/37 was to be achieved, output of pig iron (based on imported ore) of 1,675,000 tons. That is, the Report commented wryly, no less than '2½ times the present production'. 'Was there sufficient raw material available?', asked the Committee. Was the available and proposed plant capable of achieving this target? Exactly what was the Federation being asked to commit itself to?

Take the case of Colvilles' fourth blast furnace at Clyde Iron Works, approval for which had already been given, 'since additional pig iron is urgently required for *existing* steel production'. 'Coke for this furnace is to be obtained from Dixon's coke ovens for which coking coal is available. These ovens are about 3 to 4 miles distant and, under an arrangement with the [Iron and Steel] Corporation [of Great Britain], are to be taken over by Colvilles Limited. They are in a very bad state of repair, however, and will require considerable rebuilding.' And even these developments would raise the annual output of basic iron at Clyde Iron to but 850,000 tons. Furthermore, coupled with the expansion and modernization of Bairds & Scottish Steel's Gartsherrie Works, this increase in pig iron capacity represented 'the maximum possible within the immediate future availability of coking coal'. Yet Colvilles were suggesting that an additional 825,000 tons of basic iron were required, from

---

[24] The point was emphasized by the inclusion of a summary of the various target figures envisaged by the plans submitted in 1945, 1948–9, and 1951, compared with the actual production in 1950 (see Table 12.2).

a new plant which would be 'entirely dependent on securing a further 1·2 million tons of coking coal' and enormous quantities of foreign ore! 'The coal is, in fact, in East Scotland, but the seams have not been opened up and the National Coal Board have no firm plans for sinking new shafts. Even if such work was begun now it would be several years before production could be increased to the required amount. The additional coking coal planned by the National Coal Board to be raised in Scotland amounts to 460,000 tons by 1962, less than half the extra needed.' Thus, even if Colvilles were able to convince the Federation that their ingot output was justifiable, it would be necessary to phase the complete scheme into two stages, only the first of which was 'immediately possible'. The second stage would depend entirely on the provision of additional coking coal.

And then there was the problem of providing sufficient iron ore. The total required for Stage I (intended to raise the pig iron output of Clyde Iron Works to 850,000 tons, and Gartsherrie to 375,000 tons) would be 1·85–2·00 million tons per annum. This alone represented an increase of 75–80 per cent over the tonnage currently handled.

TABLE 12.2

Scottish Steel Production: Target Figures Proposed in the Plans of 1945, 1948–9, and 1951, compared with Realized Output in 1950

Firm	1945 Plan	1948–9 Submission	1951 Submission	1950 Production[a]
Bairds & Scottish	110,000	110,000	110,000	109,607
Beardmore	85,000	85,000	85,000	84,875
Colville Group	1,875,000	1,900,000	2,500,000	1,888,534
Stewarts & Lloyds	160,000	165,000	180,000	163,073
Others	70,000	70,000	75,000	180,061[b]
Scottish Total	2,300,000	2,330,000	2,950,000	2,426,150
National Total	16,000,000	16,000,000	20,000,000	16,292,650
Scottish Proportion (%)	14·4	14·6	14·7	14·9

Notes:

[a] Compare with data contained in Table 11.6.

[b] This figure includes 112,000 tons produced at the Ministry of Supply's Linwood Works which went out of production at the end of 1950.

Source: B.I.S.F., 'Report of the Advisory Committee on Development', November 1951.

The main unloading point is Rothesay Dock situated on the North Bank of the River, immediately upstream from John Brown's Clydebank Yard; 85 per cent of the total tonnage is unloaded at this Dock. Smaller quantities are unloaded at Ardrossan (Ayrshire Coast), 10 per cent, and Grangemouth (Firth of Forth), 5 per cent. In its present condition Rothesay Dock could not handle the extra quantity of ore required. Nevertheless, when a number of ships are discharging it is known that the wagon handling arrangements at Clyde Iron Works cannot take the ore as fast as the Dock can unload.

This made it necessary, therefore, 'to expand and improve the ore handling and stock facilities at Clyde Iron Works, and improve the throughput of Rothesay Dock by the intensive use of larger wagons, longer working hours and replacement of some of the small capacity cranes, or provide new unloading equipment at some other point on the River'.

Overall, the raw material requirements for the first stage of Colvilles' proposals, taken in conjunction with the needs of the other Scottish steel-makers, meant that, *even to maintain* production levels 'within reach of the 1950 figure', home bought scrap could not be allowed to fall appreciably from current levels. This implied scrap imports at the rate of 2,500–3,000 tons per week. It was not certain that these conditions could be met.

The result of this disquieting analysis was that 'plans for the expansion and concentration of the existing steel plants and the question of further pig iron capacity [beyond] Stage I must, of necessity, be postponed until an analysis of the future demand has been studied and some progress with regard to coking coal has been made with the National Coal Board'. Only the first stage of the electrification of the Lanarkshire mills was given approval, since this would result in an improvement in efficiency and costs, but 'any further modernization involving re-siting of the mill stands and/or additional drives should be considered in relation to the future position when it has been clarified further'. Somewhat surprisingly, Sir Andrew's immediate reaction to this report was one of quiet confidence: 'I can quite understand the hesitancy which the Committee might have regarding our future target. The figure of 2·5 million tons is not, however, a guess figure: it has been prepared from a careful scrutiny of our existing business and the probable trend of its development.'[25]

[25] Sir Andrew McCance to R. M. Shone, 10 Nov. 1951. There exists, in fact, a lengthy memorandum prepared by T. R. Craig on the possible future

3 'The Fourth Blast Furnace'

At the same time as the implications of the Advisory Committee's Report on the company's proposed contribution to the Second Development Plan were being assessed,[26] Colvilles were grappling with the question of the fourth blast furnace at Clyde Iron Works. A fully-detailed investigation of this problem had begun in 1950, when Mr. R. P. Towndrow prepared the first of a series of lengthy reports on the subject.[27] Within three months, Sir Andrew McCance had enlisted the support of Mr. Robert Shone for the scheme. Such was the urgent need for improving the pig iron position at this time that the Federation's Director thought that 'there would be little difficulty in getting it approved quickly, particularly if it could be said that it was submitted without prejudice to the clearly longer-term question of pig iron development at Motherwell.[28] Having decided to build the new furnace with a hearth diameter of 25 feet 9 inches, which would give an output of approximately 1,000 tons a day, detailed planning began in 1951, when the estimated coke requirements for four blast furnaces at Clyde Iron were prepared, the gas balance calculated, ore requirements estimated, and transport needs assessed and discussed with British Railways. By the spring of 1952, detailed cost estimates (totalling some £2,527,000) had been prepared for both the furnace unit and the necessary ancillary plant (e.g. ore and coke handling equipment, boilers, and facilities).

The next step was to obtain the approval of the Iron and Steel Corporation of Great Britain, whose Chairman, Sir John Green, was sent a memorandum of the scheme, which had

---

demand for Colvilles' output by tonnage and by product, a revised copy of which, dated 13 Nov. 1951, was sent to R. M. Shone. Its principal finding was that 'Scottish consumption should at least increase at the same rate as the rest of Great Britain'.

[26] D. J. Falvey to Sir Andrew McCance, 13 Sept. 1952.

[27] R. P. Towndrow to Sir Andrew McCance, 5 Sept. 1950. R. P. Towndrow, M.Sc., had joined Colvilles as Works Manager, Clyde Iron Works, in December 1946. He had previously been with the blast furnace staff of Appleby Frodingham (1939–42), Dorman Long (1942–3), and Cargo Fleet (1943–6). He was appointed to the Executive Board of Colvilles in 1951 (*Colvilles' Magazine*, January–February 1952, p. 4), and was to join the main board in 1955 at the same time as William Barr, a member of the first executive board.

[28] R. M. Shone to Sir Andrew McCance, 28 Nov. 1950.

already been passed by the Federation's Development Committee.[29] It was pointed out that postwar changes in the scrap position had caused such serious difficulties in Scotland that in 1951 Colvilles' production of steel had been approximately 222,000 ingot tons less than 1950 (see Table 11.6). These difficulties could be met only by increasing iron production. This was the principal justification for the erection of a fourth blast furnace at Clyde Iron. It was not anticipated that any financial assistance for this scheme from outside sources would be necessary.

Sir John Green, entirely satisfied by Colvilles' argument, immediately sent the scheme to the Ministry of Supply who in turn approved it, as did the Steel Committee of the O.E.E.C. in Paris.[30] But no sooner had these hurdles been overcome and orders for the necessary plant placed with the makers, than it 'became clear that, owing to the shortage of coking coal in Scotland and the slow rate of development of new coking coal resources in [Scotland], the construction of another furnace at Clyde Iron Works was going to postpone for too long a period the opportunity of converting the steel works at Motherwell and Lanarkshire to hot metal practice'. Since this change was considered 'essential in view of the unlikelihood of this country being able to obtain supplies of imported scrap in future', Sir Andrew informed Sir John Green that 'it would be an advantage to the long term policy to build this fourth furnace at Motherwell instead of at Clyde Iron Works. It would permit the immediate construction of a new melting shop based on hot metal practice to replace the obsolete No. 3 Shop at our Dalzell Works and to restore the ingot production to its previous levels.'[31]

4 The Revision of Colvilles' Plan

The Federation prepared its Second Five Year Plan in the closing months of 1952 and Colvilles were required to submit their

---

[29] Sir Andrew McCance to Sir John Green, 10 Apr. 1952, enclosing memorandum entitled 'Colvilles Ltd., Clyde Iron Works, No. 4 Blast Furnace'. Sir John Green succeeded Mr. S. J. L. Hardie as Chairman of the Corporation when the latter resigned in February 1952.
[30] W. L. Hewlett to Sir Andrew McCance, 14 Oct. 1952.
[31] Sir Andrew McCance to Sir John Green, 12 Dec. 1952.

proposals. These were conceived in broad terms[32] and followed the lines of the memorandum submitted to the Advisory Committee on Development during the previous year. Significantly, Colvilles' annual target had been revised downwards. It was now proposed to produce 2,250,000 tons per annum (a quarter of a million tons less than the 1951 proposals), but as it had now been agreed that the national production of steel 'should have as its immediate target an ingot production of 18 million tons per annum', this revised target did not represent an acceptance of a lower proportion of the national output. With this more modest steel output, it was possible to aim at a somewhat lower production of pig iron (1,500,000 tons compared with 1,675,000 tons) without substantial alteration of the pig iron/ scrap ratio, which remained at about 66/34. This pig iron would be produced at Clyde Iron Works (750,000 tons) and at the new works at Motherwell (750,000 tons). But whereas all the preliminary planning had envisaged a fourth furnace at Clyde Iron it had 'now been decided to install this furnace at Motherwell in order that the production of steel from hot metal in these works could be proceeded with at as early a date as possible'.[33] This would be the first of a pair of furnaces, additional coke for which was now expected to be available during mid-1955. Because the unloading capacity at Glasgow Docks was already fully employed, Colvilles proposed to go ahead with the installation of modern unloading plant at the General Terminus, plans for which, they emphasized, had now received the 'provisional sanction' of both the Clyde Navigation Trust and British Railways. Only by beginning the construction of this plant immediately would it be completed in time for the new Motherwell furnaces. This determination to proceed with what Colvilles believed to be the logical and essential development of the Group is evident elsewhere in the revised plan. The 'schemes for which details had not yet been fully agreed', and those that were simply 'possible future projects' in 1951,[34] had now hardened into company policy. It was, the company's latest Development Plan implied, up to the Federation and the Iron and Steel Corporation to approve them.

[32] Colvilles Ltd., 'Development Plan', 30 Oct. 1952.
[33] Colvilles Ltd., 'Development Plan', 1952, section 3.
[34] See above, p. 326.

But however confidently the Plan was submitted to the Development Committee, 'the broad terms' in which it was couched did not immediately commend themselves to the members. Further information was demanded. How much would it all cost? This was a question which was anticipated and, had it not been for Sir Andrew's reluctance to quote figures which inflationary tendencies would render illusory, could have been satisfied earlier. What could hardly have been expected was the reappearance of the tidewater issue. It would seem that General Sir James Steele, a member of the Iron and Steel Corporation of Great Britain serving on the Federation's Development Committee, unfamiliar, like the public itself, with Colvilles' detailed objections to this moribund scheme, was encouraged to believe, perhaps by the Scottish Office and certainly by the joint Policy Committee, that a Clydeside works was still feasible.[35] Whatever the genesis of this frustrating resuscitation, Colvilles were once again asked to reconsider the deepwater proposals.

Sir Andrew McCance patiently redrafted the plan and prefaced it with a more convincing case for increasing Scotland's steel production than hitherto. Instead of emphasizing that Scotland's proportion of national output should not be allowed to fall, and hence giving the impression that Colvilles had determined their share and then attempted to justify it, the document began by stating that

The demand for steel in Scotland during the postwar period has shown a marked increase not only from the old-established consumers in the shipbuilding and engineering industries, but by new factories erected for English, American, and Canadian companies whose requirements of steel are of a substantial nature. The principal shortage has been in plates for shipbuilding, pipemaking, oil tanks, and wagons, and in fixing the target for the future great importance has been placed on the need to increase plate production.[36]

[35] Correspondence between Sir Andrew McCance and General Sir James Steele, May 1952. The Joint Policy Committee represented the Federation, the Joint Iron Council, and the National Council of Iron Ore Producers. See Burn, *The Steel Industry*, p. 303.
[36] Colvilles Ltd., 'Development Plan', 28 Jan. 1953, section 1. A new assessment of the Company's market for plates and sheets was made by Mr. T. R. Craig in January 1953, in which he argued that the earlier forecast of 860,00 tons was 'if anything, on the conservative side'. T. R. Craig to S. Thomson, 6 Jan. 1953.

It was clearly imperative that 'the production of steel ... be increased at the earliest possible date'. It followed that additional pig iron was required as 'no great increase in the amount of uprising scrap available for steel-making can be expected'. But any growth in pig iron production was determined by the availability of coking coal supplies and it was feared that the expansion contemplated by the National Coal Board would provide only enough coke by 1955–6 for an additional blast furnace providing 7,000 tons of pig iron per week, and then only if the obsolete coke ovens at Dixon's Ironworks Ltd. were closed within four years and the coal being used there was diverted to Motherwell.[37]

There followed a brief restatement of the company's objection to the proposed site on the Clyde, slightly refurbished by drawing attention to the increase of railway freights since the company's major investigation in the forties (which confirmed the cost disadvantages of Inchinnan), and an analysis of the company's proposed output based on Mr. T. R. Craig's earlier projections. The main body of the text was similar to, and often identical with, that of November 1952, although some details were altered. Where the redrafted Development Plan differed from its predecessor was in providing estimates of capital expenditure. These totalled £27·6 million. It was believed that if the ore handling scheme, the Motherwell blast furnace and coke ovens, the alterations at Clyde Iron, and the new melting shop at Dalzell were begun immediately, they could be in operation by 1957, by which time the major part of the Dalzell plate mill conversion would also be completed.

Although there was considerable controversy about the change in the location of Colvilles' new blast furnace—a change which created grave suspicions in the minds of 'the other makers'—the Federation's Development Committee approved both the plan and the estimated expenditure of £27·6 million.[38]

[37] In 1952 the total production of coking coal in Scotland was 2,800,000 tons. The National Coal Board planned for an increase of 310,000 tons in 1955–6 and another 50,000–60,000 tons in 1958–9. No further major increase would then take place until about 1965. Colvilles Ltd., 'Development Plan', January 1953, section 2.

[38] B.I.S.F., 'Minutes of the Meeting of the Development Committee of the British Iron and Steel Federation held on 24 March 1953', a copy of which was sent to Sir John Craig, as a member of the Development Committee, on 26 Mar. 1953.

TABLE 12.3

Colvilles Ltd.: Estimate of Increase in Annual Profits (before Depreciation and Taxation) in Connection with the Development Plan of 1953

1. Coke Ovens (Annual Output, 300,000 tons):
   (Profit on coke sales at 6s. per ton)   £ 90,000
2. Blast Furnaces (Annual Output, 350,000 tons in Pig Iron):
   (Profit on sales of pig iron to Group at 15s. 6d. per ton)   271,200
3. Saving in Electric Power Generation: 168,000
4. Saving in Manufacturing Costs of Ordinary Basic Billets and Plates (at Present Making Losses):   380,000
5. Profits on Additional Steel Output:

Products	Ingot Equivalent			Finished Weight (tons)	Profit Margins (per ton)	Increased Profit (£s)
	Output in 1952 (tons)	Output in 1957 (tons)	Increase (tons)			
(a) Billets, Blooms etc.	333,000	402,000	69,000	57,000	24s.	69,000
(b) Plates	761,000	950,000	189,000	126,000	35s.	220,500
(c) Heavy Sections and Rails	362,000	420,000	58,000	46,500	32s.	74,000
(d) Light Sections and Bars	164,000	223,000	59,000	47,000	18s.	42,300
(e) Electric Furnace Ingots and Castings	36,000	50,000	14,000	14,000	35s.	24,500
TOTALS	1,656,000	2,045,000	389,000	290,500		430,700

      430,700

      £1,339,900

Note: In September 1953, a revised estimate included a second item under Point 2: 'Saving in use of hot metal against cost of pig iron brought in ... £420,000', giving a new total of £1,759,900.

Source: Colvilles Ltd.: 'Estimate of Increase in Annual Profits before Depreciation and Taxation', 7 Apr. 1953. 9 Sept. 1953.

It was then considered by the Iron and Steel Corporation and Colvilles were asked to prepare a statement giving a detailed analysis of their estimated costs and profit margins at various stages of production, in order that 'the economic aspects of the proposals and the expected return might be examined'. In effect, the members of the Corporation sought to satisfy themselves on those aspects of the Plan which had previously been considered by the Iron and Steel Board. In addition, Colvilles were asked to explain how they expected to finance the scheme, 'showing particularly the sums which [they expected] to provide from retained profits during the next few years'.[39] Once again, Sir Andrew was being asked to provide figures which could, in his eyes, be little more than guesswork. However, as 'it has been agreed by the Government and everyone concerned that the Makers should on the average be able to obtain the Forbes margin on what they make', Sir Andrew used this margin, with all its imperfections,[40] to predict an increase in annual profits before depreciation and taxation of £1,339,900 (see Table 12.3). This represented a return of 4·84 per cent on the capital investment involved and, as Sir Andrew emphasized, it could 'not be considered . . . very attractive', but 'the necessity for the plant . . . really arises from the need to balance production and consumption of steel in Scotland. Without more pig iron, the total production in Scotland would be quite inadequate for her industries'. Because of this, it was implied the costs and returns of Colvilles' Development Plan of 1953 were largely irrelevant. Although several questions remained unresolved, Colvilles—clearly anticipating a favourable response from either the Iron and Steel Corporation of Great Britain (feverishly passing plans before it passed out of existence)[41] or

[39] W. L. Hewlett, I.S.C. of G.B., 25 Mar. 1953.

[40] 'I am aware that the Forbes margin, based as it is on the prewar cost of plant, is very inadequate as a return on the cost of plant today, and I think you will agree that the figures I am sending you . . . completely substantiate that. At the same time I can find no better basis of assessment at the moment.' Sir Andrew McCance to W. L. Hewlett, 16 Apr. 1953, see below, p. 342n. The question of margins in the industry's price-structure is discussed by Burn, *The Steel Industry*, pp. 214–17, 228–30, 238–42. Burn shows (p. 240) that Colvilles' profit per ingot ton was, like all the heavy steel-makers, comparatively low. See also R. M. Shone, 'Steel Price Policy', *Journal of Industrial Economics*, 1 (November 1952), 43–54.

[41] See Burn, *The Steel Industry*, p. 365.

the Second Iron and Steel Board,[42] and by the Steel Committee of O.E.E.C. and the Ministry of Supply—began active work on implementing the vast project at Motherwell, soon to be called 'Ravenscraig'.[43]

5 The Troubled Birth of Ravenscraig

(a) *False Labour.* Already, by mid-January 1953, Soil Mechanics Ltd. had completed a preliminary site investigation and topographical survey from which it appeared that the site was 'probably suitable'; only the mining engineer's confirmatory report was necessary before the final decision to proceed with construction could be taken.[44] Meanwhile, sub-committees under the chairmanship of Mr. S. Thomson and Mr. R. P. Towndrow were grappling with the technical problems of the scheme.[45] Provisional contracts had been entered into with Ashmore, Benson, Pease, & Company, a member of the Power Gas Group, for the blast furnace plant, and with Head, Wrightson, & Company Ltd. for gas cleaning plant, while the Woodall-Duckham Construction Company were preparing a tender for

[42] The members of the new Iron and Steel Board were appointed at the end of May 1953. Sir Andrew Forbes came back to be chairman of the second Board, Sir Lincoln Evans was also back, Mr. Robert Shone—translated from the B.I.S.F.—was to be the Board's other full-time member. The steel-makers were represented on the Board by Sir Andrew McCance and N. H. Rollason! Ibid., p. 537.

[43] In January 1953, T. R. Craig wrote to Sir Andrew McCance and observed that 'perhaps this is the time when we might consider what the new works at Motherwell are to be called. One suggestion is "Ravenscraig".' (T. R. Craig to Sir Andrew McCance, 19 Jan. 1953.) This name was formally adopted some eighteen months later (Sir Andrew McCance to T. J. Smith, 13 Sept. 1954). In this connection the advice of Major W. R. Brown, of Ashmore, Benson, Pease, & Co. (a major contractor for the project) is interesting: 'May I suggest that you bestow upon your Motherwell Developments a brief and incisive code name. I firmly believe that, by identifying the efforts of all and sundry under one particular symbol, a mental atmosphere is created which is of great benefit ... when (say) "Ravenscraig" is on the lips of the multitude, even the pot of paint for Ravenscraig is more important than the one for a less exalted destination.' Major W. R. Brown to Sir Andrew McCance, 2 Sept. 1954.

[44] Soil Mechanics Ltd.: 'Report No. 1353/1: Site Investigation and Topographical Survey for a Proposed Ironworks at Motherwell, Lanarkshire, Scotland (Preliminary Report)', January 1953, p. 2.

[45] These were summarized and embodied in a document entitled 'Technical Aspects of the Motherwell Development Scheme: Report to Sir Andrew McCance', 11 Feb. 1953.

the entire coke oven section. These companies, together with others, such as Babcock & Wilcox (boiler plant), Fraser & Chalmers (turbo-blowers and alternators), and Holst & Company (cooling towers), 'had been prepared to carry out a considerable amount of work and [had] accepted letters of intent for the required plant on a basis of free cancellation within a reasonable period of time'. This had 'been of considerable advantage in advancing the preparation of the job without commitment' to Colvilles.

Other major features of the scheme were receiving detailed attention. Mr. R. P. Towndrow was preparing a forecast of the sintering capacity that the company would require.[46] Negotiations between Colvilles and British Railways concerning the railway layout for the Ravenscraig and General Terminus sites, together with the rail connections with Clyde Iron, Dalzell, and Lanarkshire Works were nearing completion, and the Lanarkshire County Surveyor and Motherwell Town Planning Officer had been consulted on the road deviations necessary to keep the public from passing through the Ravenscraig site.

Public relations too were considered. A timetable of events, culminating in a press conference and press release, was prepared to provide full information for the B.B.C. and for editors of national and local newspapers, the entire programme being timed to synchronize with the announcement of the scheme by the Secretary of State for Scotland during the Scottish debate in the House of Commons. This was expected to take place on or about 2 July.[47] Until that date, however, and certainly not before the scheme had received official approval, Colvilles attempted to avoid all publicity. But, much to the company's chagrin, the Iron and Steel Corporation—'apparently desperately anxious to justify their existence'—prematurely

---

[46] R. P. Towndrow to Sir Andrew McCance, April 1953. For the general problems involved in sintering and the advantages of sinter to the pig iron producer, see B.I.S.F., *Statistical Bulletin*, vol. xxix, No. 4 (April 1954), pp. 7–10. Briefly, 'the sintering process converts ore fines (i.e. dust) and other finely divided iron-bearing material into a product suitable for use in the blast furnace. It thus makes it more economic to eliminate all fines from the iron ore before it is charged into a furnace—a process which improves the productivity of the furnace and reduces the coke consumption per ton of iron' (p. 7).

[47] Colvilles Ltd., 'Development Plan, Press Announcement', 26 Mar. 1953, and subsequent (undated) memo., 'Development Plan: Publication'.

disclosed all the information at a press conference in London.[48]

(b) *Further Examination.* This action, which was none of Colvilles' doing, might have been expected to have forced the hand of the new Iron and Steel Board, but Sir Archibald Forbes, back again as Chairman, was not so easily swayed. He required much more information on the financial implications of the scheme,[49] the capital expenditures involved and detailed flow diagrams of raw materials and finished products under various assumptions. The provision of these data, he commented somewhat unnecessarily, 'may well entail a considerable amount of work. But it seems to us to be vital to any proper consideration of [Colvilles'] development proposals.' What caused Sir Andrew most anxiety was the demand to prepare a 'flow sheet showing what the ultimate position of the Colville Group would be if the [blast furnace] scheme now under consideration was not proceeded with'. Sir Andrew could not see the point of preparing such a diagram. The need for additional pig iron was so obvious that the request seemed totally unnecessary. The consequence of preventing the company from erecting an additional blast furnace would be the closure of both Hallside and Blochairn, and so heavy a reduction of plate output that the shipbuilding industry would be severely affected. Indeed, so serious would be the repercussions on the Clyde that Colvilles would have to cease making special wire billets for the Sheffield trade and tube billets for Birmingham in order to 'cushion the blow'.[50] Nevertheless, Sir Andrew promised 'to do everything possible to expedite the preparation of all information that [might] be required', for he too was 'gravely concerned' at

[48] Sir Andrew McCance to Gordon Jackson, Ministry of Supply, 20 June 1953.

[49] Sir Archibald Forbes was particularly dubious of the calculations demonstrating that Colvilles' increased earnings under the scheme would be £1,339,000. (See above, p. 338.) All Colvilles had done, he commented, was to apply 'the standard margins to any increase in output in 1957 as compared with the output in 1952. These standard margins may very well be out of date since conditions have changed since they were presented in 1949. But apart from this, the margin was supposed to be applied to the average costs of all producers, and one cannot accept that Colvilles' results, either now or in the future, will be precisely on the basis of the operating costs equal to the average of the whole industry.' Sir Archibald Forbes to Sir Andrew McCance, 19 Aug. 1953.

[50] Sir Andrew McCance to Sir Archibald Forbes, 25 Aug. 1953.

Colvilles' inability to begin work on a scheme which was 'so urgently needed to maintain Scottish steel output'.

Sir Andrew's anxieties were not to be swiftly allayed. The Iron and Steel Board having received a report on Colvilles' Development Plan by the Ministry of Supply's accountants, Peat, Marwick, & Mitchell, decided to give the entire scheme 'further study'. The result was a demand for additional information on a whole range of specific issues and a request that previously agreed proposals be more adequately justified.[51] Colvilles' order of priorities was questioned; doubt was expressed on the assumptions underlying the company's future raw material requirements; and Colvilles' calculation of the financial results of the scheme flatly denied. As if this disquieting barrage of 'major points' was not enough, Sir Archibald insisted that Colvilles re-examine the possibility of transferring the scheme 'to a new site adjacent to a deepwater dock' since he was by no means convinced that Colvilles had destroyed the case for a riverside site.[52] Sir Archibald's closing shot was that the Iron and Steel Board 'continue to be handicapped by the very general and at times almost vague nature of your Company's proposals and the absence of information as precise as one is usually able to obtain in other cases'.

By the beginning of May, after a positive flood of statistical and other data had been sent to Mr. R. M. Shone and Dr. T. P. Colclough, Sir Andrew was becoming increasingly restive: 'It is now approaching twelve months since the Minister of Supply put the decision on our scheme into the hands of the Board ... Can anything be done to speed matters up?'[53] He had not much longer to wait. On 25 May 1954, Colvilles' development proposals were again considered by the Iron and Steel Board. It was a momentous meeting for whatever was decided would 'set the pattern of steel production in Scotland for many years to come'.[54]

[51] Sir Archibald Forbes to Sir Andrew McCance, 29 Dec. 1953.

[52] For example, 'The social and economic problems to which you refer are, I agree, important and would require serious consideration. They might of themselves be sufficiently serious to determine the matter. But they are not problems directly concerned with steel-making.' Ibid.

[53] Sir Andrew McCance to Sir Archibald Forbes, 12 May 1954.

[54] Sir Archibald Forbes, 'Notes on the Modernization and Development Proposals of Colvilles Ltd.', 22 May 1954, section 13.

As Sir Archibald saw the position, Colvilles were 'dependent to a quite unique degree on scrap obtained from outside their own area and also on pig iron purchased from other sources both inside and outside Scotland. This has long been regarded in most quarters as a fundamental weakness in the Scottish steel situation. Colvilles, however, for a long time withstood arguments to this effect in the belief that they could always rely on the necessary imported scrap. But it seems that they now accept that additional pig iron manufacture is essential. The present proposal envisages increasing the ratio of pig iron usage to about 50 per cent.' Unless this primary objective was fully appreciated, Sir Archibald believed that the economics of the proposals before the Board could not be understood:

It is not to be expected that heavy capital outlay on constructing a blast furnace and the coke ovens and other ancillary equipment and facilities which go with it can show an attractive return *per se* when this is not a replacement of an existing installation but is in part at least only a switchover from using scrap or bought-in pig iron (which needs relatively little capital equipment up to the charging stage) to using pig iron of own manufacture. One really has to consider whether the maintenance of the Colville steel production necessitates some such step and if it does whether the overall return from the whole of the Colville steel-making activities would still be satisfactory. It is believed that this would be so although unfortunately no precise figures as to this have yet been worked out. The alternative is to face some degree of contraction rather than expansion in the Colville steel output. This would not be catastrophic in the sense that judged only in relation to the present proposals the steel output instead of rising from the existing 1·85 m. tons to 2·05 m. tons would fall to say 1·7 m. tons. This in turn opens up consideration of whether it is economic to carry steel production in Scotland beyond a certain point as compared to manufacturing the excess in England. Production of pig iron in Scotland is, for the time being at least, at two disadvantages. The first is the relatively high cost of coking coal and the second the relatively higher cost of imported iron ore on which Scotland is wholly dependent since it is too far from the home orefields in England to make the transport of home ore at all economic.

One is really faced with considering the extent to which the demand for steel in Scotland will continue to grow and how far the extra cost of importing this steel into Scotland from England would offset the disadvantages of Scottish iron production. This question is of course affected by the varied nature of the demand for steel in relation to location of the production of different types of steel.

It does remain, however, for careful consideration whether accepting that more pig iron should be used in the manufacture of steel in Scotland it would be more economic to manufacture that pig iron in Scotland or to import it from England.[55]

To Sir Archibald this was the fundamental question that the Board had to answer. The capital investment necessitated by Colvilles' proposals was of the order of £30 million to £35 million. The sheer magnitude of this sum was such that it had given rise to 'considerable anxiety as to whether this is justified on an inland site or whether it would be preferable to take the bold step of constructing a new integrated works on a completely new site with its own deepwater facilities for discharging ore-carrying vessels. This is not a proposition which can be lightly dismissed although the majority opinion has concluded that the balance of judgement is against it on the grounds that it would be cheaper to proceed on the Motherwell site because of the continued usage of the facilities already existing there, and second the considerable social upheaval which would be caused by the transfer of operations away from Motherwell.'

With these 'observations' Sir Archibald introduced the formal papers[56] placed before the meeting of the Iron and Steel Board on 25 May 1954. How they were received is not known. Nor is it known how much time the Board devoted to considering such fundamental questions. The flat wording of the formal letter from the Board's secretary approving Colvilles' entire scheme gives but a hint of internal division: 'The Board, after weighing all the considerations involved, have concluded that on balance the arguments are in favour of developing pig iron production [at Motherwell] and they give their consent to the [company's] proposals . . . The Board have so informed the Iron and Steel Holding and Realisation Agency.'

(c) *Delivery.* Formal permission to proceed with the Ravenscraig project having been given, the entire scheme was publicly announced on 9 July 1954. It was now up to Colvilles to execute the plan. Construction began immediately, and with considerable prescience its progress was recorded on colour cine film.[57]

[55] Ibid., section 7.
[56] Cited by Sir Archibald as 'I.S.B. 64'', ibid., section 1.
[57] R. P. Towndrow to Sir Andrew McCance, 30 Oct. 1954. This film was later used in the production of the award-winning film, 'The Big Mill'.

The civil engineering work was of great magnitude. The first stage involved the moving of over three million cubic yards of earth to adjust the levels of the site. Many miles of railway track and graded siding yards were laid down and several miles of roads constructed. Road and rail bridges and numerous embankments had to be erected. The early days were not without bizarre incident. Dispossessed allotment holders took their troubles to the *Daily Express*.[58] The Lima cranes, ordered from America for the express purpose of erecting the melting shops, were carefully shepherded by road from Glasgow Docks to the site in the dead of night to avoid traffic obstruction, and in their first test promptly collapsed, causing an eleven-week delay to this part of the vast programme.[59] But the work went steadily ahead, despite occasional labour troubles and appalling conditions caused by heavy winter rainfall.

From Sir Andrew's office there flowed a stream of orders, advice, exhortations, and demands for information. Significantly, there was a flexibility about the details of the project which permitted the adoption of the most advanced iron- and steel-making practice within the parameters of the approved scheme. Sir Andrew refused to be bound by a rigid plan. If modifications were thought to be desirable, they were authorized. This is really the genesis of his adamant refusal to provide the Iron and Steel Board with more than an accurate outline of the company's proposals and of his failure to do more than indicate the probable cost. During 1956 many problems had been encountered—individual units of up to 60 tons in weight, immense girder splices involving many hundreds of holes and fitted bolts, handling difficulties, awkward delivery schedules—and had been overcome.[60] There had been natural difficulties too. With many of the buildings a hundred feet and more in height, the wind had become an increasingly important factor, and during the summer of 1956—the worst in a generation—gales and torrential rain had made the task of the steel erectors extremely hazardous. But such progress was maintained that

[58] *Scottish Daily Express*, 21 July 1954, and S. Thomson to Sir Andrew McCance, 26 July 1954.

[59] Colvilles Ltd., 'Report of test on Lima Type 703-SC crane on May 1955 at Ravenscraig, Motherwell'.

[60] The principal difficulties cited by Colville Constructional, *Colvilles' Magazine*, Summer 1956, p. 43.

early in 1957 Colvilles were able to announce the names of the men who were to take over the new iron and steel works at Ravenscraig when it went into production.[61] These men, all of whom had already attained senior positions within the Colville Group, were soon welded into a team by an active exchange of duties and information. In May discussions were taking place to determine the starting times of individual furnaces, the size of the labour force, and questions of steel quality and quantities. It was intended that Ravenscraig would replace No. 3 melting shop at Dalzell, but arrangements had to be made to keep the combined ingot output of the two works at a level consistent with the maintenance of existing plate output. At the same time, with the social awareness that had always characterized Colvilles' management, the men made redundant at Dalzell were as far as possible to be provided with similar jobs at Ravenscraig.[62]

In a sense, the majority of the decisions that the new team at Ravenscraig and Colvilles' parent and executive boards were called upon to make involved questions of *balance*: balance of plant, of men (in the boardroom, the works offices, and the shop floor), of products, and of raw materials. To attain equilibrium involved scrupulous attention to the timetable and flow diagrams that were the products of detailed planning. Hence the anxiety caused by the failure of a vital piece of machinery to arrive by the promised date, by the collapse of a crane, by an incipient or actual strike. And if the Iron and Steel Board had earlier remonstrated upon the vagueness that characterized parts of Colvilles' Development Plan of 1952, its members would have found difficulty in criticizing its execution, whatever private reservations lingered concerning the site.[63] Three years after Colvilles had taken over green fields, the new works opened, exactly on schedule. A £22·5 million investment started to make its stint of 400,000 tons of steel a year. The coke ovens were lit on Monday, 3 June, charged on Tuesday, 23 July, and made their first contribution to the blast furnace stock bins on the following day. A week later, after some

[61] *Colvilles' Magazine*, Spring 1957, pp. 30–1.
[62] S. Thomson to Dr. J. M. Ferguson, 6 May 1957; S. Thomson to Sir Andrew McCance, 19 June 1957.
[63] Burn, *The Steel Industry*, p. 557.

preliminary heating, the blast furnace was lit, and on 6 September the melting shop went into production.[64] It was a remarkable achievement.[65]

[64] *Colvilles' Magazine*, Autumn 1957, pp. 4–9.

[65] Cf. Burns's comment that 'it still took an astonishing long time to build new plant in Britain, and for a large works the [Iron and Steel] Board accepted five years as a minimum period'. *The Steel Industry*, p. 629.

XIII

The Last Decade of Private Enterprise, 1956–1967: The Ravenscraig Strip Mill

1 The Return to Private Enterprise

During the gestation and construction of Ravenscraig, Colvilles had returned to private ownership. In January 1955, the Iron and Steel Holding and Realisation Agency, having reorganized the firm's capital structure 'to bring it more into line with the capital employed in the business and to facilitate the financing of Ravenscraig' (see Table 11.8), sold 10 million £1 Ordinary shares to the public at 26s. per share.[1] The response to the Offer

[1] Preliminary work on the scheme for the sale of Colvilles to the public began in 1953. The negotiations between Colvilles and the Agency, which involved the reorganization of the firm's capital, were extremely complex, and Colvilles were advised by the firm of Morgan, Grenfell & Co. There was no disagreement concerning the magnitude of the ordinary share capital which would be offered to the public (£10·0 m). This was to be achieved by increasing the pre-nationalization Ordinary capital of Colvilles Ltd. of £3,919,550 by capitalizing £6,080,450 of reserves. But because this would seriously deplete the reserves of the parent company, the capital of the subsidiaries had in turn to be reorganized in order to make possible the transfer of over £3·0 m of their reserves to the balance sheet of the parent company by means of a special dividend. This arrangement caused no great difficulties; the differences turned on the price per share and the dividend which Colvilles thought could safely be promised, itself dependent upon the amount of maintainable profits the board were prepared to forecast. Colvilles' directors estimated the gross profits for the Group at £5·0 m which, after allowing £900,000 for depreciation, would make £4·1 m available for taxation, dividends, and reserves. Messrs. Peat, Marwick, & Mitchell, the chartered accountants advising the Agency, confirmed this figure, and on this basis the Agency suggested that Colvilles should be able to pay a dividend of 9 per cent. Colvilles objected that to do so would leave the company with too little profit for reserves and suggested a dividend of 8 per cent. The Agency believed that Colvilles were too pessimistic, but Colvilles would not budge until it became clear that there would probably be a downward adjustment in the ingot levy which promised to increase their future gross profits. Why the Agency was pressing for the higher dividend forecast was that it would increase the difference between the compensation paid in 1951 and the proceeds from the resale. Assuming the yield basis of 7½ per cent adopted in the discussions which

for Sale was remarkable. Nearly 160,000 applications were received for twelve times the number of shares available, and the Agency 'had to resort to a rationing system'. When the register was compiled, there remained nearly 50,000 shareholders, many of whom were employees who had been given financial assistance for the purchase of their shares. The Agency retained the 4 million $5\frac{1}{2}$ per cent £1 Cumulative Preference shares and all the $4\frac{1}{2}$ per cent Debenture stock.[2]

The manner in which the process of denationalization was carried out has been criticized. It has been argued that an opportunity to reconstruct the industry was thrown away.[3] 'Had the Agency been given powers to rationalize the industry prior to denationalization it could either have retained the small works and ultimately closed them, or, following the practice

---

took place in the third quarter of 1954, the position may be tabulated as follows:

	Agency's Proposals	Colvilles' Proposals
Compensation for Colvilles' Ordinary shares (£3,919,550 Ordinary stock at 38*s*.):		£7,447,145
Proceeds of Sale		
10,000,000 Ordinary shares at 24*s*.:	£11,500,000	
10,000,000 Ordinary shares at 22*s*.:		£10,625,000
'Profit' to the Agency	£ 4,052,855	£ 3,177,855

While Colvilles appreciated that the Agency was retaining the loan stock and the preference capital (the precise amount of which was also the subject of detailed discussion), they had the nagging suspicion that they were 'supplying all the profit to fill up other losses' (Colonel H. B. Spens to Sir John Craig, 27 July 1953). They were not wholly satisfied on this point until figures were drawn up in November 1954 showing the 'Apparent Profit to the Agency on Companies already Denationalized'. These were similar, though not identical, to those tabulated by Burn, *The Steel Industry*, p. 542. In the event, Colvilles Ordinary £1 shares were sold at 26*s*. per share, and the 'Offer for Sale' spoke of an anticipated dividend of 9 per cent. The principal sources on which this discussion is based are Colvilles Ltd.: 'Memorandum of Meeting with Sir George Erskine of Morgan, Grenfell & Co., 8 July 1953'; 'Résumé of Negotiations and Discussions with the Iron and Steel Holding and Realisation Agency and Messrs. Morgan, Grenfell & Co.', 12 Oct. 1954; 'Public Offer for Sale: Points for Decision', 29 Nov. 1954; correspondence between Sir John Craig and Sir George Erskine, July–October, 1954; Colvilles Ltd., Offer for Sale by the Iron and Steel Holding and Realisation Agency, 13 Jan. 1955.

[2] B.I.S.F., *Annual Report for 1955*, p. 46.

[3] For example, Vaizey, *History of British Steel*, p. 156; Heal, *The Steel Industry*, pp. 76–9.

of the salerooms, have included a small works in the same lot number as a choice item ... The major obstacle which prevented these alternatives from being given serious consideration was the continued existence of the original boards of directors ... and the evidence is that they were adamantly opposed to such changes. Some small works were offered to the major companies, but they could not be considered "tempting morsels".'[4] The general accuracy of Heal's observations is unquestionable. Nevertheless, Colvilles Ltd. did not return to private enterprise in quite its original form, for in August 1954, the company had acquired by transfer from the Agency the share capital of Dixon's Ironworks Ltd., and the Etna Iron & Steel Company Ltd.[5]

The genesis of this arrangement went back three years. In October 1951, Colvilles had been requested by Sir John Green of the Iron and Steel Corporation of Great Britain to take an interest in Dixon's Ironworks Ltd., 'as he was not satisfied with its supervision'.[6] Colvilles agreed and, on the resignation of Dixon's directors in March 1952, the board was reconstructed with Sir Andrew McCance as Chairman, and T. R. Craig, R. P. Towndrow, and T. Ritchie as directors. The works were in a very bad state of repair and, despite the efforts of R. P. Towndrow and his staff at Clyde Iron, little could be done with what was essentially obsolete plant. The furnaces were hand charged and the coke ovens inefficient. The works could 'only be regarded as having a limited life, probably not exceeding three to four years'. During the financial year ended 27 September 1952, the trading loss on pig iron production was equal to 36s. 1d. per ton, and it was believed that despite heavy expenditure on the rehabilitation of the works, this loss was likely to increase. There seemed to be no justification for incurring the very heavy capital expenditure which radical, cost-reducing reorganization would involve. In February 1953, Sir Andrew McCance discussed the position with Sir John Green who

pointed out that his Corporation was nearing the end of its existence and that the liabilities which they had carried would be taken over by the

[4] Heal, *The Steel Industry*, p. 77. See also Burn, *The Steel Industry*, p. 539.
[5] B.I.S.F., *Annual Report for 1954*, p. 44.
[6] Sir Andrew McCance, 'Memorandum on Dixon's Ironworks Ltd.', 26 Feb. 1953.

Realisation Agency. He felt it unlikely, in view of the position of Dixon's, that the Realisation Agency would wish to finance manufacturing operations in the way that he had done, and the position arising might be awkward. Sir John Green expressed the view that to close down Dixon's immediately after the passing of the Iron and Steel Bill might have a bad effect on public opinion and he suggested that it was to the interest of private enterprise not to have public opinion affected in this way. He suggested that our Board should consider taking over Dixon's Ironworks. [Indeed] it was more than likely that the Realisation Agency would wish to tie up Dixon's to Colvilles in order to assist the sale of the organization. He also expressed the opinion that our Board should also be seriously considering the absorption of Bairds & Scottish Steel Ltd. and the Etna Iron Works, as a similar suggestion might well come from the Realisation Agency whenever it was appointed.[7]

This is, in effect, what happened. In discussions between Sir Andrew McCance and Sir John Morison, chairman of the Iron and Steel Holding and Realisation Agency, preparatory to arranging for the public issue of Colvilles' shares, Sir Andrew reported to Colvilles' board that Sir John had told him that

... before our case could be put in its final form there were two little snags that he wanted to get over. He wanted us to take over Dixon's and Etna. The [Iron and Steel] Corporation [of Great Britain] and the Realisation Agency had lost a packet of money in both these cases, but that was their misfortune and they would just have to forget about it. He did not want to suggest anything to Colvilles that they would regard as a burden and the basis for the takeover he proposed was 'net liquid assets'. He was most anxious that these transactions should be completed as soon as ever possible so that when the public issue was made it could be announced as an accomplished fact with the minimum of indication as to how it had been arranged. In other words, he said he did not want to disclose, if it could be avoided, the losses entailed in the purchase and resale of these companies.[8]

Following a careful examination of the balance sheets of the two companies, Colvilles offered the Agency £625,000 for Dixon's Ironworks Ltd. (£425,000) and the Etna Iron & Steel Company Ltd. (£200,000), not, Sir Andrew emphasized, as a 'remunerative expenditure' but as 'a contribution to the general goodwill', and then only as a preliminary to 'regaining control of our own company'. Predictably, the original owners, to whom Sir John Morison was under an obligation to offer

[7] Sir Andrew McCance, 'Memorandum on Dixon's Ironworks Ltd.', sections 10 and 11.
[8] Colvilles Ltd., 'Scottish Pig Iron Development—Discussions with Agency and Steel Board', 23 June 1954.

these white elephants, happily waived their rights to repurchase them.[9]

Having taken over Dixon's, Colvilles kept the blast furnaces and coke ovens in operation until the recession of 1958 provided an opportunity to close the works. The Etna Iron & Steel Company survived ten years longer. Etna, formed in 1889 to acquire the Brandon Iron & Steel Works, Motherwell,[10] was one of the few Lanarkshire malleable iron to remain outside 'the combine' when the Scottish Iron and Steel Company was formed in 1912.[11] It continued to thrive in a modest way[12] and, as the market for malleable iron declined, built up a respectable business in the re-rolling of mild steel bars and sections. But its two hand-operated light section mills were increasingly uneconomic, and Colvilles would certainly have not taken over the firm had it not been for pressure by Sir John Green and subsequently, the Iron and Steel Holding and Realisation Agency.[13] Colvilles would not, however, 'absorb' Bairds & Scottish Steel. This was too great a burden. Several years later, in 1961, Colvilles toyed with the idea of buying the company jointly with Stewarts & Lloyds in order to prevent its control passing 'into troublesome hands'.[14] But the danger of Bairds being sold by the Agency to other than a syndicate of steel-makers soon faded, and, in the event, Bairds & Scottish Steel, Barrow Ironworks, Skinningrove, John Baker & Bessemer, and Gjers, Mills, & Company, were purchased in 1963 by a consortium of ten steel firms, one of whom was Colvilles.[15] Nor were Colvilles interested

[9] Colvilles Ltd., 'Memo on a Meeting with Sir John Morison on 21 July 1954, regarding Dixon's Ironworks and the Etna Iron & Steel Co.'; T. R. Craig to Sir John Craig, 17 Aug. 1954; 'Memorandum on Discussion with Mr. Palmar of Peat, Marwick, Mitchell, & Co.', 26 Aug. 1954.
[10] Etna Iron & Steel Co., 'Contract of Co-partnery between John Wotherspoon, Junior, and James Kerr, 1 January 1889'.
[11] See above, p. 100.
[12] During the original co-partnery which ran its full twenty-five years, something over 400,000 tons of wrought iron were produced. *Motherwell Standard*, 12 Feb. 1914.
[13] Sir John Green became a member of the Agency following the dissolution of the Corporation.
[14] Sir George Erskine to Sir Andrew McCance, 12 Jan. 1961; A. G. Stewart to Sir Andrew McCance, 18 Jan. 1961; Sir Andrew McCance to Lord Bilsland, 20 Jan. 1961 (from which letter the quotation is taken).
[15] In participating in this arrangement Colvilles were acting under a moral obligation to fulfil an undertaking entered into between the British Iron and Steel Federation and Sir Andrew Duncan that any unsaleable rump of com-

in Beardmores, which was spoken of as being unsaleable, and it may be conjectured that the company was greatly relieved when it was acquired by Firth Brown's who wanted 'more capacity cheaply and quickly'.[16]

2 Changes in the Boardroom: Sir John Craig Steps Down

Colvilles' board remained essentially unchanged during the brief episode of nationalization. In 1955 Sir John Craig was still chairman and joint managing director with Sir Andrew McCance, and they continued to be supported on 'the parent board' by Sir Frederick Rebbeck, Harry Yates, T. R. Craig, and Lord Bilsland, all of whom had first been appointed in 1936–7,[17] and Robert Marshall and Samuel Thomson, both of whom had been promoted from the executive board in 1950.[18] Lord Clydesmuir, grandson of David Colville and only son of John Colville, had returned to Colvilles in 1947 after a distinguished political career. Appointed to the board of David

panies after all the major companies had been denationalized would be taken over by a holding company in which the major companies would participate. Sir Andrew McCance to G. S. Nelson, Finance Corporation for Industry, 22 Oct. 1962; Sir Andrew McCance to Sir Dennis Proctor, 4 Oct. 1962.

[16] Burn, *The Steel Industry*, p. 539.

[17] See above, pp. 248–9. In 1949, Peter Baxter, who had come into Colvilles with the Lithgow brothers, had resigned on medical advice.

[18] Robert Marshall, after studying metallurgy at Coatbridge Technical College, began his career with the Waverley Iron and Steel Co. After two years, he moved to the Clydebridge Steel Co. Ltd. and was taken on to the staff of David Colville & Sons Ltd. when Clydebridge was acquired in 1916. In 1919, after being transferred to Dalzell, he became a sales representative of the company and was appointed Sales Manager in 1933. He was an original member of the Executive board of Colvilles Ltd. when this body was created in 1947. *Colvilles' Magazine*, January–February 1947, p. 13. In 1951 Robert Marshall was one of four expert advisers seconded to the Iron and Steel Corporation of Great Britain. For this episode, see Burn, *The Steel Industry*, p. 313; Ross, *Nationalization . . .*, pp. 140–1; Keeling and Wright, *Development . . .*, p. 175. Samuel Thomson, a director of the Lanarkshire Steel Co., was appointed to the Executive board of Colvilles Ltd. and made General Manager of both the Dalzell and Lanarkshire Works in August 1947. After attending Stirling High School, he started as a boy in the Dalzell Works of David Colville & Sons in 1906, where he was given a general office training. In 1916 he became Departmental Manager of the iron works mills at Dalzell. In 1929 he was appointed Mills Manager at Dalzell and, in 1935, Assistant Works Manager. Two years later, he became manager of the Lanarkshire Steel Co. In January 1947, he was promoted to the Lanarkshire board. *Colvilles' Magazine*, January–February 1947, p. 18; July–August 1947, p. 10.

Colville & Sons in 1920, he relinquished his salary shortly after
being elected to the Lanark County Council, because 'he
desired to be absent when required by his Council duties'.[19]
Thereafter, he devoted himself to public life. In 1929 he was
returned to Parliament as Member for the North Midlothian
division. Following a term of office as Parliamentary Secretary
to the Department of Overseas Trade, he became Under-Secre-
tary of State for Scotland (1935–6), Financial Secretary to the
Treasury (1936–8), and Secretary of State for Scotland (1938–
40). He relinquished this post on the formation of the Coalition
Government when he was appointed to the Army General Staff.
In March 1943, he became Governor of Bombay and until India gained independence was Acting Viceroy on four occasions.
Not until 1947, shortly after his elevation to the peerage, did
he 'feel himself free to rejoin the Company and accept a directorship' of Colvilles Ltd. As a member of the board he assumed
special responsibility for industrial welfare within the Group.
He died, aged 60, in 1954. Two new directors appointed at this
time, R. P. Towndrow and William Barr,[20] had previously been
members of the executive board, thereby reducing the number
of special directors, as they were now called, to three. Not
until 1957 was their number to be supplemented by the
appointments of John A. Kilby and John Guthrie, respectively
Chief Mechanical and Chief Electrical Engineers of the Group.

In the year following the return of Colvilles to private ownership, Sir John Craig stepped down from the chairmanship of
the company. He was now 82 and had been with Colvilles for
67 years. Many were the tributes paid to him and, in saying
that Sir John Craig had 'served the company in many spheres
of activity and in many positions, and to all of them he has
brought distinction and success', Sir Andrew McCance voiced
an almost universally-held opinion. The Colvilles may have
founded and established the firm, but its survival and growth
during the inter-war years was Sir John Craig's achievement.[21]

[19] D.C. & Sons: Minute Book IV, 9 Jan. 1923.

[20] *Colvilles' Magazine*, January–February 1948, p. 1; Winter 1955, pp. 6–8.

[21] Measured by ingot output, Colvilles was the second largest firm in the
industry in 1945 (Heal, *Steel Industry*, p. 12); in terms of net assets it was the
52nd largest quoted manufacturing company in the United Kingdom in 1948
(A. D. Chandler, 'The Development of Modern Management Structure in
the U.S. and U.K.', in Leslie Hannah (ed.), *Management Strategy* . . . , p. 42).

The problems the company had faced and overcome called for leadership of a high order combined with statesmanship, innate business ability, and, at times, incredible endurance. He enjoyed a remarkable career. There could have been few British industrialists of this period who had risen to a position of supremacy from such lowly origins: to have done so in the British iron and steel industry was extraordinary.[22] Luck played a part in it, but only driving energy and sheer ability permitted him to take advantage of the opportunities presented to him. He had already progressed far beyond what might have been regarded as his normal expectations when the Colville brothers died in 1916.[23] He emerged as chairman of the company as the choice of a relatively inexperienced board, and was promptly placed in a position of enormous power as the instrument by which Lord Pirrie controlled his steel interests. With the death of Lord Pirrie, Lord Kylsant—grappling with the financial problems of his vast, tottering shipping empire—left the conduct of the Colville Group almost entirely to John Craig. Meanwhile, Craig still regarded himself as the trustee of the Colville family and as such responsible to pass on the firm intact and even enlarged and strengthened. He was initially puzzled, even disappointed, that the third generation of Colvilles seemed not to share his own complete dedication.[24] Yet, years later, he was to write to one of Archibald Colville's daughters concerning her own son's decision not to enter the steel trade, that 'one feels that a young man should follow the lines of his liking, for otherwise his daily duties will not give him the pleasure which work is meant to give'.[25] This was a constant theme: repeated throughout his speeches and his correspondence. It was emphasized at his retirement, when he told a large gathering at

[22] See C. Erickson, *British Industrialists*, pp. 78, 200, and *passim*.

[23] One of the very old employees who had little sympathy for Sir John Craig told the author that 'Craig rose to the top on a stairway of coffins'.

[24] This is apparent in a series of letters between himself and David and Norman Colville and Norman Colville's mother, in which he made plain his determination that the third generation of Colvilles could not expect to be given positions of responsibility within the Group until they had thoroughly learned the trade. Nor would he use his growing influence to secure directorships for them in related companies (for example, in Lord Pirrie's shipping empire) until he believed they were able to make a positive contribution to the success of such companies. Sir John Craig, Personal Papers, 1919–30.

[25] Sir John Craig to Mrs. T. V. Booth-Jones (third daughter of Archibald Colville), 11 Nov. 1955.

Motherwell Town Hall that 'he did not want to lay down any principles, except possibly one: "Find your pleasure in your work and your work in your pleasure, and most problems will be solved." ' [26]

There was, of course, more in it than that. His strength was rooted in his religion. He became a very youthful elder of the Dalziel Free Church in 1901. He possessed 'a great love for his Church' and lived according to its precepts. His lifelong interest was in the Y.M.C.A., of the Scottish National Council of which, for many years, he was chairman and later President. The history of Colvilles under his chairmanship cannot fully be understood without appreciating that

> His religious sincerity reflected itself in his whole life and a career which might have received its original impetus from personal ambition, quickly resolved itself into one of service for his fellow men. Almost austere in his habits, asking little for his personal needs, he eagerly sought success for the works for which he was responsible, which was not so much measured by shareholders' dividends as by the substance and security for the thousands of Scottish families whose breadwinners toiled at its furnaces and mills.[27]

He knew the men. 'He had', Sir Andrew McCance observed, 'a natural interest in people':

> With everyone, irrespective of rank, he had the same friendly approach and the kindly manner that inspired confidence. His own friendliness was reflected in a multitude of friends. His memory for the details and ramifications of personal and family relationships was quite exceptional and often walking through the works he would stop and speak to one of the men, to ask some detail about his family or his own affairs—such questions arose to his mind without any striving or effort.[28]

The record of industrial relations in the steel industry and within the Colville Group was excellent. Despite the general strike, despite the long years of unemployment between the wars, despite the waxing and waning of enthusiasm for nationalization, there always existed a mutual respect between masters and men.[29] They seemed to see each others' problems

[26] *Colvilles' Magazine*, Spring 1956, p. 17. See above, p. 313n.
[27] Harry Douglas, General Secretary of the Iron and Steel Trades Confederation. *Colvilles' Magazine*, Spring 1957, p. 4.
[28] Ibid., p. 3.
[29] Sir John Craig frequently made this point in his speeches. See, for example, his Presidential Address to the West of Scotland Iron and Steel Institute. *Journal of the West of Scotland Iron and Steel Institute*, xxxiv (Session 1926–7), 19.

and the result was, as one Scottish steel worker put it, 'ours wasn't a hating trade, steel-making in Britain never has been a hating trade'.[30] The fact that it wasn't owes something to John Craig. Furthermore, the men were all conscious that in Colvilles 'you could move up'. Craig himself had done so, and he maintained a policy of internal promotion which operated at all levels. Furthermore, the widely-read *Colvilles' Magazine* went to considerable trouble to *show* that this policy operated at all levels. By enthusiasm, by sheer hard graft, by attending evening classes, by obtaining qualifications, one moved up. Some, the exceptionally able, could attain managerial positions, a few could and did become members of the executive board, and of them more than one rose to the parent board.[31] This was a most important element in Craig's strategy: managerial and entrepreneurial talent had to be fostered wherever it could be found (family connections meant little), but before bringing in an outsider he searched for what he wanted within the ranks of the organization. This policy ensured, he believed, a loyalty to the firm. There was an element of paternalism in all this. As he once said to the man who was to become the firm's Chief Labour Officer, the firm's only real resources are the trained men of Colvilles.[32] In a phrase reminiscent of that humane employer of the classic period of the Industrial Revolution, Samuel Greg, Craig believed he was 'creating a family: the Colville family'.

Perhaps because he himself had been given his chance by the Colville family, he sought to retain the old values. He possessed an innate understanding of the needs of large-scale enterprise. Until the last years of their lives, David and Archibald Colville had been concerned only with one, albeit very large, works, Dalzell. The strain of enlarging the scale of the enterprise by the absorption of Clydebridge and Glengarnock had contributed to their premature deaths. Craig promoted

[30] Patrick McGeown, *Heat the Furnaces Seven Times More* (London: Hutchinson, 1967), p. 116. Patrick McGeown was born in 1897 at Craigneuk in Lanarkshire. He began life as a manual labourer in a steel works and retired, forty years later, as a first-hand melter. On his retirement in 1962 he took a G.C.E. 'O' level in English language and, in addition to a number of articles in the *New Statesman*, *Man and Metal*, and *New Steel*, wrote his autobiography. It deserves to be read.
[31] See above, pp. 313–15.
[32] R. C. Dymock, personal communication.

experienced managers, brought in G. P. West, encouraged Dr. Andrew McCance, and linked the destiny of Clyde Alloy indissolubly with Colvilles. Disclaiming any technical knowledge, he had a unique ability 'to unite the common interest of the commercial man and the technical man',[33] and having appointed the latter, he gave him his head, as far as financial constraints would allow. And no one was better informed of the financial constraints. He inaugurated the provision of detailed monthly returns concerning production, marketing, employment, and costs from every works within the Group. He and his fellow members of the board had to see exactly what was happening in every sphere of activity. But at the same time as he developed a rational, objective, calculated approach to the business, he wanted to retain the loyalties and commitments that had existed in the small family partnership which had preceded his own chairmanship.[34]

And if Sir John Craig believed it was essential to promote harmony within the Group, he deemed it equally important to do so within the industry. 'The wisdom of his influence was always on the side of moderation. As one of the earlier Presidents of the British Iron and Steel Federation at a time when the idea of co-operating with your competitor had not yet sunk very deeply into the minds of a generation of steel-makers who had built up their businesses on strongly individualistic lines, Sir John Craig's wise counsel held the young organization together on more than one occasion.'[35] ' "Colvilles cannot

[33] In speaking to many organizations, Sir John Craig invariably prefaced his remarks by apologizing for his technical ignorance. A good example is provided by his Presidential Address to the West of Scotland Iron and Steel Institute, 8 Oct. 1926. *Journal of the West of Scotland Iron and Steel Institute*, xxxiv (Session 1926–7), 4. The quoted passage comes from the vote of thanks by James Mitchell, ibid., p. 9.

[34] There are many similarities between John Craig and P. S. du Pont. Indeed, some of the ideas of this paragraph have been inspired by A. D. Chandler, Jr., and Stephen Salsbury, *Pierre S. du Pont and the Making of the Modern Corporation* (New York: Harper & Row, 1971), esp. pp. 587–604.

[35] Sir Andrew McCance, *Colvilles' Magazine*, Spring 1957, p. 3. Sir John Craig was the third President of the National Federation of Iron and Steel Manufacturers and a member of the Executive Committee of the N.F.I.S.M. and of the B.I.S.F. continuously from 1918 to 1956, during which time he served on numerous of the sub-committees, boards, and councils established by industry's central organization. These facts were alluded to in a tribute paid to Sir John Craig by the Independent Chairman of the B.I.S.F. at a

prosper within an ailing industry", he once affirmed, "but decisions affecting the well-being and the future of the company are being taken in London. There I must go when occasion demands." Occasion demanded many, many times.'[36]

He was indefatigable. He might have retired at the beginning of the Second World War, but he stayed on. This, he used to say, was his 'war sacrifice'; he was giving up his retirement, but it is difficult not to believe that he did not want to go. The war provided an excuse, if excuse was needed, to go on working as hard as ever; though whether he could have been as effective as he had been in the past without his equally dedicated joint managing director, Sir Andrew McCance, is problematical. Not until the firm was safely back in private hands,[37] not until Ravenscraig was within a year of commissioning would he retire. He died a year later, and of all the obituaries that by David Graham, of the Dalzell Works, who knew him well, was possibly the most profound: 'The secret of his active and interesting career lay in the fact that he walked with God.'[38] In the middle of the twentieth century, it was an unusual and rare statement to make of a 'captain of industry'.

With Sir John's retirement—he was made Honorary President and retained his directorship—Sir Andrew McCance became chairman of Colvilles Ltd. Not until November 1958, were further appointments made to the board. In the month in which the retirement of Robert Marshall[39] was announced,

meeting of the Executive Committee of the Federation in April 1956. D. W. Lane, B.I.S.F., to Sir John Craig, 20 Apr. 1956.

[36] David Murray, *Sir John Craig: Sixty-Seven Years with Colvilles* (Commemorative Booklet commissioned by the Board of Colvilles Ltd., n.d. [*c.* 1956]), pp. 12–13.

[37] His passionate belief in co-operation within the industry did not preclude a vehement antipathy towards centralized control, which he felt would be extremely damaging to the national economy. He could not understand the desire of the government to nationalize the steel trade, 'except for purely partisan reasons'. Of nationalization he asked four questions: 'Will it produce more steel? Will it produce cheaper steel? Will it improve labour relations? Will it continue to make profits?' To all of them his answer was 'a definite negative'. See his statements prepared for the Sixteenth and Eighteenth Annual General Meetings of Colvilles Ltd., 29 May 1947, 27 May 1949. They are reprinted in *Colvilles' Magazine*, May–June 1947, pp. 2–4; May–June 1949, pp. 2–4.

[38] *Colvilles' Magazine*, Spring 1957, p. 7.

[39] To Robert Marshall was attributed the creation of a central Sales Department. Before he was appointed Sales Manager in 1933, 'each department

J. A. Kilby and T. J. Smith[40] were promoted from the special directorate and Ronald John Bilsland Colville, second Baron Clydesmuir, joined the main board,[41] having previously been managing director of the Steel Company of Scotland. Duncan Ferguson and E. W. Ferguson were appointed special directors.[42] Two years later Sir Andrew McCance assumed the title of Chairman and General Managing Director and T. R. Craig and R. P. Towndrow were appointed Managing Director (Sales) and Managing Director (Works) respectively. Promotion from the ranks of the special directors to the parent board, and from the various functional departments and from the works to the special directorate—where the policy inaugurated by the Colville brothers and formalized by Sir John Craig of appointing those who had shown their ability and energy in the service of the company, often by working up from the position of 'lads' or 'office boys', was continued—invariably had repercussions throughout the Group. Into the posts held by those who had moved upwards, were promoted others who possessed the necessary drive and expertise. The fact that the

in the Group virtually [decided] upon its own sales policy. There was little co-ordination. Works within the Group were frequently in competition with each other.' *Colvilles' Magazine*, Winter 1958, p. 19.

[40] It is worth noting that T. J. Smith, who was born in Motherwell, started work as a lad in Dalzell Works Office and spent his evenings studying for diplomas in Accountancy and commercial subjects before he came to specialize in the acquisition of raw materials. *Colvilles' Magazine*, Spring 1960, pp. 8–9.

[41] It had been intended that Lord Clydesmuir should join the company in 1939, having taken a degree in economics at Cambridge, but he was called up for military service in August 1939. He was evacuated from Dunkirk and his subsequent service took him to India, Persia, the Middle East, Sicily, Italy, and Germany. In 1947, Lord Clydesmuir started an intensive eighteen months' training in various departments of most of the firms in the Group. He then went to Head Office for over two years. In 1952 he joined the Steel Company of Scotland as assistant to James Aitken and subsequently became Managing Director. *Colvilles' Magazine*, Spring 1958, pp. 10–11.

[42] Duncan Ferguson was born in Motherwell and went straight from school to Dalzell as an office boy. From there he went to Head Office as a junior assistant in the Purchase Department where, apart from three years of works training at Dalzell and Clydebridge, he remained. He became purchasing manager in 1955. Ernest Ferguson was brought up in Motherwell and Glasgow, he became a junior at Head Office and, after spending nine months in the offices of a German iron works to gain experience, he joined the Home Sales Department at Colvilles and then moved to the Export Department. In 1940 he became export manager. *Colvilles' Magazine*, Winter 1960, pp. 10–11.

Group was constantly expanding facilitated this upward mobility, each stage of which was faithfully recorded in *Colvilles' Magazine*. It was a process that was to continue until 1967.[43]

On the eve of re-nationalization, Colvilles had been a managerial concern for half a century. Following the deaths of the Colville brothers, the members of the board and the senior management as a whole possessed but a handful of shares: ownership lay in the hands of the trustees who acted on behalf of the female dependants of the Colvilles. 'They did not know the business,' as one retired senior official who joined the staff as an office boy told the author, 'they *had to* trust John Craig.' John Craig, in turn, trusted and appointed those who, like himself, had gained their experience in the firm. They may, subsequently, have purchased shares but they did not owe their positions to their equity holdings. This point has already been discussed and need not be repeated.[44] What does deserve emphasis is the fact that even in 1943 94 per cent of the Ordinary shareholders held less than £1,000 stock (see Table 13.1 (a)), and of the big owners several were shipbuilding companies, themselves manager-controlled. In 1959, after denationalization, the Federation published an analysis of the ownership of the public companies. This showed that the number of shareholders was large and that most holdings were small. It is unnecessary to emphasize that a widespread ownership is not incompatible with effective control by a minority of very large shareholders, but this seems not to have been the case with Colvilles.[45] Certainly, of the twelve biggest steel companies in the British steel industry in 1959, Colvilles Ltd. was notable in having the smallest percentage of shares held by the ten largest shareholders (Table 13.1 (b)), and of these two were their old customers, John Brown & Company and Harland & Wolff.[46] Five years later, when the election of a Labour Government committed to the re-nationalization of the industry once again

[43] See below, pp. 410–11.
[44] See above, p. 242.
[45] This point is made by Burn, *The Steel Industry*, p. 544. For a general discussion of this issue see P. L. Payne, 'Industrial Entrepreneurship and Management in Britain, *c.*1760–1970', in Peter Mathias and M. M. Postan (eds.), *The Cambridge Economic History of Europe*, vii, Part 1, 211–13, 221–25. See also B.I.S.F., *Steel: The Facts* (London: B.I.S.F., n.d.) [*c.* 1965]), pp. 52–5.
[46] Correspondence between Sir John Craig and Sir John Morison, December 1954.

brought steel into the political arena, Sir Andrew McCance emphasized that 'There are no large holdings in private hands. Holdings of more than 5,000 [Colvilles'] shares are held to the extent of 98·6 per cent by pension funds, universities and religious institutions, insurance and investment companies.'[47]

3 The Development Plan of 1956

Ravenscraig was brought into being to increase Colvilles' output of pig iron and to make the Group more vertically integrated and less dependent upon scrap. But even while the site was still occupied by an army of contractors, consideration of Ravenscraig's eventual contribution to Colvilles' output was causing a complete reassessment of the allocation of productive capacity between the various works within the Group. This, of course, involved the prediction of the demand for the firm's

TABLE 13.1

Colvilles Ltd.: Some Details of Stockholdings, 1943, 1959, 1967

(a) Colvilles Ltd.: *March 1943*

Capital			
Authorized	Issued	Stock	No. of Stockholders
£2,000,000	£2,000,000	Preference	3,327
£4,000,000	£3,919,550	Ordinary	10,140
£6,000,000	£5,919,550		13,467

Ordinary Stockholders by Holding

	No. of Stockholders	Holding
£5,000 and over	81	£1,452,279
£1,000 to £4,999	506	£833,535
£999 and under	9,553	£1,633,736
	10,140	£3,919,550

It was noted that 94 per cent of the Ordinary stockholders held less than £1,000 stock, and that the bulk of the stockholders resided in the South of England.

Source: Colvilles Ltd., Directors' Minute Book III, 1 Apr. 1943.

[47] Sir Andrew McCance, Chairman's Statement, 5 Feb. 1965. Cf. B.I.S.F., *Steel: The Facts*, pp. 52–3.

(b) *Late 1958*

Percentage of shares held by Ten Largest Shareholders in Twelve British Steel Companies

Company	Per cent	Company	Per cent
Steel Co. of Wales	28·0	South Durham	14·5
Lancashire Steel	24·2	Dorman Long	11·3
John Summers	21·8	Consett	10·7
Whiteheads	20·5	Unified Steel	9·6
Firth Brown	15·2	Hadfields	9·5
Stewarts & Lloyds	15·2	Colvilles	9·3

Source: B.I.S.F., *Steel Review*, January 1959, quoted in Burn, *The Steel Industry*, p. 545.

(c) *Shareholdings in Colvilles Ltd., by size, Spring 1967*

No. of Ordinary shares held	No. of Shareholders	Proportion of Total No. of Shareholders (%)
1–100	15,963	46·95
100–500	15,239	44·82
500–1,000	2,119	6·22
1,000–5,000	349	1·03
5,000–10,000	108	0·32
10,000–50,000	175	0·51
50,000–100,000	32	0·09
Over 100,000	18	0·05
	34,003	100.00

Notes:

[a] There were no private individuals holding more than 100,000 shares; the biggest shareholders were all insurance companies, banks, and pension funds. This group held 21 per cent of all Ordinary shares.

[b] Although there were some individual shareholders in the 50,000–100,000 group, most of them were institutional holders.

Source: Colvilles' Magazine, Spring 1967, p. 15.

products not only in 1957—when production was to begin—but for many years ahead. Again, the basic problems were those of balance. Having made an assessment of future market demands, how were they to be satisfied? What raw material problems would be encountered? What technical difficulties would have to be overcome? How could the output be most efficiently allocated between the different works? What were the costs involved? How were they to be met? Ravenscraig would upset the current equilibrium: detailed planning was required to establish a new one at a more efficient and considerably higher level. At the same time, as the officials of the British Iron and Steel Federation and the Iron and Steel Board were keenly aware, to ensure an economically efficient *industry*, the companies' plans for the next five years must soon be assessed in order to achieve a proper *national* balance. They too had to make a market assessment and then adjudicate the often conflicting claims of the various steel-makers.

Colvilles' planning was already well advanced when the company was formally asked to submit to the Federation's Advisory Committee, a 'preliminary indication' of its 'general intentions or ideas in regard to future development'. This Advisory Committee, of which Sir Andrew McCance was a member, conceived its first task as being to formulate, in consultation with the various iron and steel Conferences, an estimate of the demand for steel in 1962. This, it was believed, might be 'of the order of 29 million tons'.[48] The companies were now being asked to provide their individual estimates of the level of iron and steel production they expected in 1962.

Colvilles were able to do this with some confidence. For over a year a Sub-Committee on Development had been planning the future growth of the Group 'in the light of present sales requirements for all products'. Its members were of the unanimous opinion that 'the immediate problem was the question of flat products and the necessity for meeting rising standards of quality and finish, viz. uniform gauge and flatness', and they felt that the Group's sheet position was 'most vulnerable'. The life of the existing hand mills was limited and it was believed that if Colvilles were to remain in the sheet trade 'early action must be taken'. Consequently, the sub-committee's principal recommendations were the provision of a modern four-high plate mill unit together with four four-high continuous stands

---

[48] Colvilles Ltd.: Special Report MB 45, 'Copy of the letter dated 30 December 1955, from the President of the British Iron and Steel Federation'. In the event, this estimate proved to be wildly inaccurate. British ingot steel production in 1962 was but 20·5 million tons, even less than the output attained in 1956 (see Table 11.6) and much nearer the figure predicted by Sir Andrew McCance in his Harold Wright Lecture to the Cleveland Scientific and Technical Institute in 1950. See above, p. 315 and Burn, *The Steel Industry*, p. 278.

for rolling light plates and sheet at Clydebridge, and the construction of a 44-inch slabbing mill at Ravenscraig to replace that at Dalzell. Initially, this slabbing mill would feed the existing 14-foot plate mill at Dalzell, but eventually a new wide plate unit would be built at Ravenscraig rather than on the confined site at Dalzell which was regarded as being 'quite unacceptable for modern outputs'.[49]

It was as well that Colvilles were already thinking on these lines for in June 1955, Sir Lincoln Evans, Deputy Chairman of the Iron and Steel Board, asked what increase in plate capacity was contemplated by Colvilles and whether their schemes included the installation of a four-high mill. If so, Colvilles' proposals would have to be considered in conjunction with the anticipated requests of both the Patent Shaft Company and the United Steel Company at Appleby Frodingham for similar equipment.[50] Sir Andrew's reply is interesting in the light of subsequent events. After outlining the plans for Clydebridge, Dalzell, and the further development of Ravenscraig, he explained that the four-high mill at Clydebridge was intended to handle lighter plates.

> We have thought it necessary to plan at this time a future extension of four continuous stands to enable sheet breakdowns in coils to be rolled at some future date. We cannot expect that our hand sheet mills in Scotland will escape the fate of those in other parts of the world, *nor can we expect to support the production from a full scale continuous mill.* Our problem has always been to devise a scheme that would deal economically with a limited, if growing Scottish consumption and we think we have now succeeded in finding a way out of this difficulty.

By the end of 1955 an exhaustive investigation had been made by the company's research and sales organization into the possible future demand for Colvilles' products. Mr. T. R. Craig believed that by 1962 the company should be producing 3·1 million ingot tons or about 50 per cent more than the 1957 target figure of 2,045 million tons, when the original Ravenscraig scheme would be completed. Although the calculation of this increase in capacity was based on predicted demands, notably on an expected doubling of plate sales, the suspicion

---

[49] This paragraph is based on Colvilles Ltd., 'Interim Report of the Sub-Committee on Development', 14 Feb. 1955.

[50] Correspondence between Sir Lincoln Evans and Sir Andrew McCance, June–July 1955.

is unavoidable that Colvilles were greatly influenced not so much by the anticipated future sales of the company's products as by a desire to make sure that Colvilles' relative position in the national steel industry did not worsen (see Table 11.6). The wording of a lengthy report by Mr. T. R. Craig to Sir Andrew McCance on the subject of sales forecasts is significant: 'The British requirements between 1958 and 1962 have been increased by 6,200,000 ingot tons. Our figures therefore require to be increased by approximately 10 per cent of this, to say a total of 3,100,000 tons per annum. *Provided the market conditions are suitable*, it is quite reasonable for us to claim at least this total...'[51] And, having done so, it was not too difficult to make out a realistic case for the division of this increased tonnage between products.

Sir Andrew received Mr. Craig's forecasts cautiously. He was inclined to favour the more conservative estimate of 2·5 million ingot tons put forward by Sam Thomson.[52] Unconvinced by Craig's argument for a doubling of plate output between 1955 and 1962, he called for additional market surveys, examined the cost implications of a greatly increased sales target, and estimated future ingot production from each of the different works and its allocation to different mills and different products. After the preparation and analysis of flow charts and a careful exploration of the technical issues involved (the yield of finished plates from ingots was harshly criticized),[53] it was decided to aim at a 1962 production of 2·5 million ingot tons of steel.[54]

Modest though it appears in relation to T. R. Craig's target of 3·1 million ingot tons, even an expansion of some 600,000 tons (1·9 million tons, 1955; 2·5 million tons 1962) involved major developments. At Ravenscraig it necessitated the building of a second blast furnace together with an additional battery

[51] T. R. Craig to Sir Andrew McCance, 9 Jan. 1956. Emphasis added.
[52] S. Thomson to Sir Andrew McCance, 9 Dec. 1955.
[53] 'At Dalzell they have allocated a finished output of plates of 4,750 tons per week. For this they require 7,550 tons of ingots—a yield of 62·9 per cent. Even taking account of their special qualities, I think this is much too low.' Sir Andrew McCance to T. R. Craig, 1 Mar. 1956. Nearly a year earlier Sir Andrew had compared the low yields 'about which Motherwell are so complacent' with those in Germany, where 'the new 4-high mill is getting a finished plate yield from ingot of 80 per cent ... [this is] what we are up against.' Sir Andrew McCance to S. Thomson, 25 Apr. 1955.
[54] Sir Andrew McCance to D. W. Lane, B.I.S.F., 30 Mar. 1956.

of 70 coke ovens and auxiliary plant, the extension of the melting shop to increase its capacity from 400,000 tons to 600,000 tons per annum, and the erection of a slabbing mill to replace the old cogging mill at Dalzell. At Dalzell, the plan involved the replacement of the existing two-high plate mill by a four-high plate mill, and at Clydebridge, the replacement of the existing three-high plate mill by two four-high stands in tandem plus provision for the future addition of stands for the production of light plates and sheet. Other elements in the overall scheme involved the continued modernization and rationalization of the section and bar mills at Glengarnock, Dalzell, Lanarkshire, and Hallside.[55] The total cost involved was estimated at £33 million. Such was the gist of Sir Andrew's reply to the Federation's request for an indication of the company's 'general intentions or ideas in regard to future developments',[56] and the essence of Colvilles' formal submission to the Federation's Development Committee and to the Iron and Steel Board but one week later.[57] Despite initial misgivings about the raw material balance, Colvilles' proposed contribution to the iron and steel industry's Third Development Plan was well received by both the Federation and the Board and was fully approved during the course of the summer.

4 The Strip Mill Question

With work on the first stage of the Ravenscraig project approaching completion and the acceptance of Colvilles' 1956 Development Plan,[58] the company's future growth seemed clearly charted for the next seven years. But under pressure of increased demand from Stewarts & Lloyds for additional supplies of plates for tubemaking (without which they believed

[55] These developments would further reduce the company's dependence on imported scrap. A second blast furnace with an annual capacity of 350,000 tons would bring Colvilles' output of pig iron to 1·4 million tons, or approximately 56 per cent of ingot production.
[56] See above, p. 365.
[57] Colvilles Ltd.: 'Development Proposals', 5 April. 1956.
[58] The plan was enthusiastically received and unanimously approved by the Iron and Steel Committee of the O.E.E.C. at its meetings in Paris in October: 'Of about twenty-five projects submitted for the United Kingdom, Belgium, Italy, France, and Germany, [it] aroused the most comment.' J. A. Kilby to Sir Andrew McCance, 30 Oct. 1956.

they would have to close down their Coatbridge works) and for sheet slabs and bars for rolling into light plates and sheet by their own subsidiary, Smith & McLean,[59] Colvilles were already contemplating the feasibility of a third blast furnace at Ravenscraig. Such a step would be imperative if Colvilles were to cease using imported scrap and to close down the increasingly costly, obsolete blast furnace plant at Dixon's Govan Works, currently capable of supplying some 100,000 tons of pig iron annually. But all these projected developments were to be superseded, if not dwarfed, by the possibility of Colvilles' undertaking the construction of a wide strip mill.

That growing demand for thin plates and breakdown coils was adequate to justify a modern plant in Scotland to produce such products was becoming increasingly evident. By the early months of 1956, complaints that Smith & McLean's Milnwood and Gartcosh Works were being starved by the parent company of sufficient sheet bars to sustain the expanding demand for sheets were becoming insistent.[60] In February Harry Yates claimed that if Smith & McLean were not to sustain an irrecoverable loss in light plate sales, he must have not less than 1,900 tons of sheet slabs and bars a week. But as providing this tonnage involved a diminution of the other products (particularly sections and rails) produced at Lanarkshire and Glengarnock, Smith & McLean's supply problem had temporarily to be solved by using billets from stock and by continued reliance on outside suppliers.[61] The position worsened in August when Stewarts & Lloyds indicated that they too anticipated considerably greater requirements of thin plate. Calculations indicated that these two sources of demand alone enabled a weekly output of 5,000–6,000 tons of thin flat rolled plates and coils to be envisaged.

[59] Sir Andrew McCance to Harry Yates, Smith & McLean, 1 Aug. 1956; Colvilles Ltd.: 'Special Report: Development: Colvilles/Stewarts and Lloyds Proposals', 3 Oct. 1956.
[60] Harry Yates to T. R. Craig, 1 Feb. 1956. Smith & McLeans were able to continue only by the purchase of sheet bars from Welsh, Continental, and even American suppliers. Should these supplies fail, 'orders . . . may be transferred to Germany, and therefore I think that nationally, not only from the relatively narrow point of view of Smith & McLean, it is vital that these requirements should be met'.
[61] Correspondence between T. R. Craig and Sir Andrew McCance, February–March 1956.

A demand of this magnitude was more than sufficient to warrant laying down new plant. Colvilles' preliminary investigations favoured a Steckel mill, a type of rolling mill best suited for firms which had neither the need nor the resources for a full-scale continuous strip mill.[62] Detailed discussions with Stewarts & Lloyds took place in January 1957, to determine the exact nature and magnitude of their requirements.[63] And, in the same week, the technical problems, the cost and the tentative delivery date of the plant was discussed with Davy & United Engineering Company Ltd. It was estimated that the complete cost of a Steckel mill, including foundations and buildings, would be about £8 million. Although a Steckel mill represented a good compromise for those areas, such as Scotland, which had 'neither the population nor the industries capable of absorbing the production of a wide strip mill', it was not without certain disadvantages. In comparison with a continuous mill, the Steckel mill produced a somewhat inferior surface finish and there were some variations in thickness along the length of a coil. Although such difficulties were being overcome by the installation of automatic control gear developed by the British Iron and Steel Research Association, the representatives of Davy-United were unable to recommend a Steckel mill for No. 1 quality automobile body sheets.[64]

This information, together with much additional data, was carefully considered by Colvilles' senior officials, but after the most searching examination, nothing came of the idea. The inhibiting factor was the supply of raw materials. As Sir Andrew

[62] This type of mill was developed in the U.S.A. by A. P. Steckel in the early thirties and was first used outside America at Westfalenhütte, Dortmund, where it was installed in 1938. Essentially, a hot Steckel mill consists of a four-high reversing mill which keeps the strip hot by means of furnaces placed on either side of it. The hot plate, of about ¾-inch thickness, is run through the mill, coiled *inside* the furnace at the other end, then reversed for the same process to take place on the opposite end. About five passes are needed to produce the finished strip. See B.I.S.F., *Monthly Statistical Bulletin*, xxviii, No. 7 (July 1953), pp. 5, 15; and B.I.S.F., *A Simple Guide to Technical Developments in the Iron and Steel Industry* (London, 1964), p. 26. Kenneth Warren, *The British Iron and Steel Sheet Industry since 1840*, pp. 195–6, discusses the advantages and disadvantages of the Steckel mill. The most important of the latter were relatively high operating costs and low yields.

[63] Colvilles Ltd., 'Record of Discussion with Stewarts & Lloyds, 21 January 1957'.

[64] Colvilles Ltd., 'Record of Discussions with Davy-United, 23 January 1957'. See also Warren, *Steel Sheet Industry*, p. 195.

McCance explained to Mr. A. Graham Stewart of Stewarts & Lloyds:

To feed the Steckel Mill properly with the minimum production of 5,000/6,000 tons per week, which was in mind, requires one half of the production of a second blast furnace at Ravenscraig. As you may know in connection with our development plan, we have promised both the Iron and Steel Board and the Federation that we would endeavour to increase our pig iron production to the extent that would make us independent of imported scrap by 1962. If one half of our second blast furnace output is allocated [to the Steckel mill], the other half is insufficient to fulfil this promise. [It] would also result in a curtailment of our plate production through the diversion of the raw material supplies. To contemplate now a marked slowing down in our plate production increase is not a thing that could be justified, and any [such] suggestion would cause considerable perturbation if it were known.

I have therefore somewhat reluctantly come to the conclusion that it would be unwise to site the new Steckel Mill in Scotland ... So far as I can see from the coal supply position, it will not be possible for us to build a third blast furnace at Ravenscraig until after 1962 and this, of course, is too far ahead to make any firm plans for it now.[65]

Not the least interesting feature of the abortive Steckel mill project was the reason for its abandonment. In the postwar years, the growth of the Colville Group was dependent upon adequate supplies of coking coal. Without these, the building and commissioning of additional blast furnace plant was prohibited, and the consequent chronic scarcity of pig iron retarded the expansion of ingot output and semi-finished steel products. This is what killed the promising Colvilles/Stewarts & Lloyds proposal. The significance of this was that if a 60- to 66-inch Steckel mill—with a theoretical annual capacity under European conditions of some 350,000–400,000 tons—was impractical in Scotland, how much more out of the question was a continuous or semi-continuous wide strip mill? Yet in October 1956, Sir John Morison, Chairman of the Iron and Steel Holding and Realisation Agency, had enquired of Sir Andrew McCance how Colvilles viewed a strip mill coming to Scotland, for already such a possibility—albeit remote—was being contemplated. Sir Andrew's reply was brief. There was, he said,

[65] Sir Andrew McCance to A. G. Stewart, 3 Apr. 1957. Sir Andrew's letter makes it clear that Stewarts & Lloyds were contemplating the erection of a Steckel mill at Corby, but they decided 'not to go ahead with it'. A. G. Stewart to Sir Andrew McCance, 5 Apr. 1957.

insufficient coking coal in Scotland for such a scheme.[66] Nevertheless, the murmurings continued: they were subsequently to become clamorous.

In the early 1950s there were three continuous hot strip mills in operation in Great Britain: those at Ebbw Vale (Richard Thomas & Baldwins), at Margam (Steel Company of Wales), and at Shotton (John Summers & Sons). Of these, the Abbey Works at Margam—which came into production in July 1951—was among the largest in the world, having a planned production for 1956 of some 1,800,000 tons, approximately double the outputs of each of the two other mills.[67] But such were the growing home and overseas demands for flat rolled products that it had been necessary to supplement the production of these mills (which were constantly being modified to achieve greater output)[68] by imports and by the continued operation of inefficient hand mills. This dependence on hand mills was clearly undesirable. Such mills—which in the early fifties were still supplying about 700,000 tons of sheet steel and tinplate a year—were uneconomic compared with the large-scale continuous mills, and their products possessed an inferior finish.[69] It was clear that a fourth strip mill was urgently required.[70] This was agreed by both the Iron and Steel Board and the Federation. Agreement on the site of the proposed new mill was, however, less easily arrived at, and from early in 1955 the claims of rival areas and firms were the subject of increasing public debate.[71]

The first firm formally to stake a claim for a new strip mill was Richard Thomas & Baldwins, though they did so tentatively

[66] Colvilles Ltd., 'Special Report: Development: Colvilles/Stewarts & Lloyds Proposals', report of a conversation that took place between Sir John Morison and Sir Andrew McCance in London on 2 Oct. 1956. Warren, *Steel Sheet Industry*, pp. 270–1, provides some of the background details. Richard Thomas & Baldwins made a show of examining a site near the River Carron, just north of Grangemouth, in 1956, but they had already decided to press for a fourth British strip mill at Newport. See below, p. 375.

[67] B.I.S.F., *Monthly Statistical Bulletin*, vol. xxviii, No. 7 (July 1953), pp. 5, 16.

[68] See, for example, B.I.S.F., *Annual Report for 1955* (April 1956), p. 18.

[69] Iron and Steel Board, *Development in the Iron and Steel Industry, 1953–1958* (February 1955), pp. 14–18.

[70] Its urgency seemed all the greater in the light of 'extraordinarily optimistic' forecasts of future demand. See Warren, *Steel Sheet Industry*, p. 256.

[71] Ibid., pp. 260–9, and Burn, *The Steel Industry*, pp. 639–43.

and only as a *possible* extension of a new integrated works at Newport designed for the manufacture of semi-finished steel.[72] The hesitant nature of Richard Thomas & Baldwins' proposals is partially to be explained by a downturn in home sheet demand in 1956[73] and partially by the fact that this firm still awaited denationalization. Its ownership remained in the hands of the Iron and Steel Holding and Realisation Agency, and it was believed that if the Agency agreed to commit the firm to an integrated strip mill its resale to private interests would be impossible.

The failure of the Agency and the Iron and Steel Board immediately to sanction Richard Thomas & Baldwins' proposals bolstered the hopes of the proponents of a wide strip mill in other areas and 'representations were made to the Government and to the Board by a number of Members of Parliament, local Authorities and other public bodies in favour of siting the capacity [elsewhere]'.[74] The sites receiving most vociferous support were Kidwelly and Swansea in South Wales, Grangemouth on the Forth estuary, and Immingham in Lincolnshire.[75] From an economic viewpoint the most serious contender was Immingham but, as Burn has emphasized, this area 'was supported by no pressure group (though there were local interests who hoped it would succeed). It was not sponsored by a firm. And as a politician involved prominently in the struggle remarked, "There was no Minister for England".'[76] The merits of the other possible sites were social rather than economic, and support for them was kept alive by politicians; politicians whose influence on the ultimate determination of the strip mill site was strengthened by the fact that it was becoming increasingly apparent that the government would have to assist in financing the project.[77] This being so, the final decision rested

[72] Iron and Steel Board, *Annual Report for 1957* (July 1958), p. 22, and see Burn, *The Steel Industry*, p. 640.
[73] Iron and Steel Board, *Development in the Iron and Steel Industry* (London: H.M.S.O., 1961), p. 31.
[74] Iron and Steel Board, *Annual Report for 1958*, p. 20.
[75] Warren, *Steel Sheet Industry*, pp. 254–69, clearly evaluates the various locations.
[76] Burn, *The Steel Industry*, p. 642.
[77] Burn, *The Steel Industry*, pp. 642–3, and see Iron and Steel Board, *Annual Report for 1957*, p. 21.

not with the steel-makers, not with the Iron and Steel Board, but with the Cabinet.

It was during the wrangling over these alternative sites that Sir Robert MacLean[78] spoke to a meeting of M.P.s in the House of Commons in May 1957. He argued not in favour of any particular location for a wide strip mill—though Grangemouth was clearly in his mind—but simply that, whatever the cost, Scotland should have one. 'Prewar Scottish production of steel was some 16 per cent of the U.K. total. As late as 1949, it was 15 per cent. Today it is 12 per cent.' Although 'much general industrial development' had taken place while Scotland's proportion of British steel output had been falling, '*unemployment in Scotland [was] still twice the U.K. average*'. To alleviate this situation he looked 'to the engineering and the new industries . . . for expansion and many of these industries are users, or potential users, of sheet or strip steel'. This argument, he believed, was worthy of elaboration:

> There are some 360 tenants on Scottish Industrial Estates Ltd. 83 of these, i.e. almost 1 in 4, use steel strip or sheet . . . as a *processing* material. The General Manager and myself as Chairman of the Estates, examined the position very recently to find out which 100 tenants were expanding or seem most likely to expand and we came to the conclusion that all 83 strip or sheet using firms were on the expansion list. The list comprised firms making refrigerators, stoves, clocks, vacuum cleaners and other household electrical equipment, a large range of typewriter, cash register, and accounting machines (a good deal of which is exported and to dollar markets too), electronic devices, electrical switch-gear, possibly railway carriages and so on. Since they became established in Scotland, many of these firms have more than doubled their factory space and their employees. This healthy expansion should be facilitated . . . If we had a modern strip mill in Scotland, it is almost certain that the strip-using industries in our midst would expand more quickly.

Sir Robert's conclusion epitomizes the arguments of all those bodies—such as the Scottish Council (Development and Industry) and the Scottish Trades Union Congress—and individuals pressing Scotland's case: 'This is not just a question of

[78] Sir Robert MacLean, C.A., was at this time chairman and managing director of A. F. Stoddard & Co., Carpet Manufacturers, of Elderslie, Johnstone, chairman of the Industrial Estates Management Corporation for Scotland, and among many other public offices president of the Glasgow Chamber of Commerce and chairman of the Export Committee of the Scottish Council (Development and Industry). In 1955 he was knighted for his services to industry.

the economics of a strip mill. It is part of the bigger problem of trying within reason to create a sound and balanced economy throughout Britain.' He urged therefore 'that the location of the new mill be considered not in isolation but as part of a wider national economy'.[79] The reaction of Sir Andrew McCance to such arguments was straightforward and brutally simple. The necessary coal for a new integrated plant and continuous strip mill was just not available.[80] This fact had repeatedly emerged from the raw material balances and flow charts which Colvilles had been drawing up throughout the previous decade.

By the spring of 1958, Richard Thomas & Baldwins Ltd. had submitted a second plan free of the ambiguities of the first. They wished to put down a continuous strip mill at Newport.[81] Still the Iron and Steel Board hesitated. Even the Federation's reaction was unenthusiastic. Whereas the need for a fourth strip mill by 1962 had appeared obvious in the early fifties, by 1958 the planners were not so sure.[82] Nevertheless, there was general agreement that Richard Thomas & Baldwins' new scheme was technically feasible. It was now up to the government.[83]

On 4 May 1958, Sir Andrew McCance received a visit from Mr. John S. Maclay, the Secretary of State for Scotland.[84] Mr. Maclay explained that the Cabinet was experiencing great difficulty in deciding upon the location of the new mill. There were, he said, 'two contending factions equally strong in their views': those in favour of Newport and those in favour of Scotland. The former group—'which included Lord Mills [the Minister of Power] and the Iron and Steel Board—

---

[79] Colvilles Ltd., 'Notes from which Sir Robert MacLean spoke at Mr. Walter Elliot's Meeting in the House of Commons on Wednesday, 15 May 1957'.
[80] *Glasgow Herald*, 25 July 1957. A month later the Scottish T.U.C was arguing: 'The General Council considers that assertions of insufficient coking coal and deposits of iron ore, *if not entirely irrelevant*, detract from the main issue', which was that a strip mill would provide an enormous stimulus to steel fabrication. The quotation, cited by Warren, *Steel Sheet Industry*, p. 271, is from the *Iron and Coal Trades Review*, 23 Aug. 1957, p. 417. Emphasis added.
[81] The details are given in Iron and Steel Board, *Annual Report for 1957*, pp. 20, 22.
[82] See, for example, Iron and Steel Board, *Special Report*, 1957, pp. 7, 59.
[83] Colvilles Ltd., 'Fourth Strip Mill: Notes taken at a meeting of the Development Committee of the B.I.S.F.', 15 April 1958'.
[84] Colvilles Ltd., 'Fourth Strip Mill: Report of a Meeting between Mr. Maclay and Sir Andrew McCance, 4 May 1958'.

[emphasized] that a market of approximately 600,000 tons already existed in South Wales. This was the production of the present hand mills which eventually must be closed down.'

Support for siting the mill in Scotland came from Mr. Iain Macleod [the Minister of Labour] and the arguments used were that Scotland was without facilities for producing high class sheet and strip and, so long as this lack of facility existed, they could not expect the motor car industry or other light industries to start up factories in Scotland when they could not get the steel materials they required. If the fourth strip mill went to South Wales, this state of affairs would be perpetuated indefinitely since it would be many years before a further strip mill would be required. The loss of this opportunity would therefore continue the lack of balance in the Scottish industrial area with its preponderance of shipbuilding and heavy engineering.

Significantly, Mr. Maclay did not mention the question of production costs. He did, however, recognize that a Scottish market for the products of a strip mill did not currently exist and apparently agreed with Sir Andrew 'that it would be many years before such a market could be developed. In the interval, a strip mill would make heavy losses in sending its products down to the consumer market in England.' This factor, combined with the paucity of coking coal, made a Scottish wide strip mill impractical.

'How then', Mr. Maclay asked, 'could the government get out of the dilemma in which they found themselves in regard to Scottish light industry expansion?' Sir Andrew suggested that Colvilles might obtain 'hot rolled strip from one or other of the existing strip mills and could reduce it in Scotland at the works of Smith & McLean Ltd.' Sir Andrew's memorandum on the meeting concluded:

Mr. Maclay asked whether Colvilles would be embarrassed if it were decided to [insist that Richard Thomas & Baldwins] build the strip mill in Scotland and what would be our attitude towards the project. I pointed out that we had no experience whatever of strip mill operation or construction and therefore could not be of any help in that direction. Nor had we the financial resources to face up to a project of this magnitude. At the same time, starting a new steel works in Scotland would inevitably have some implications for our trained steel-makers and our technical staff and to that extent might cause trouble. It was clearly necessary, if the mill were built in Scotland, that we would require to be associated in some way or another with the project in order that friction could be avoided. We could not offer very much help, but would certainly put no difficulties in the way and would lend all the assistance we could.

Nearly four weeks later, on 29 May, Sir Andrew received a telephone call from Sir Archibald Forbes, the chairman of the Iron and Steel Board, who explained that the 'extraordinary story had reached him that Colvilles were prepared to shoulder the construction of a strip mill in Scotland, either alone or with some outside help, and he wondered what truth there was in the statement which, he said, had come from a political source'.[85] Sir Andrew told him that 'the story was not correct', and that 'it had probably arisen from a misinterpretation of a conversation which [he] had had with Mr. Maclay'. It subsequently transpired that this was, in fact, the case but although both Sir Archibald Forbes and Lord Mills were in favour of the Newport site,

the Cabinet were very divided owing to the arguments which had been put forward strongly by Mr. Macleod, the Minister of Labour, and Sir David Eccles, the President of the Board of Trade. The force of their arguments rested on the unemployment position in Scotland. At the moment they had found the rising unemployment in Dundee and in Greenock very intractable and no project was in sight that would have any noticeable effect on Scottish unemployment. Support for the strip mill project, therefore, clearly arose from the idea that here was an opportunity of countering what was regarded as an inevitable rise in future unemployment in Scotland. It appeared at the present time that these arguments were having a powerful effect on the other members of the Cabinet and might well have a determining effect on the site issue.

Despite general agreement 'that the limited demand for sheets in Scotland would force the new strip mill to sell most of its products south of the border [and that] the heavy carriage and the heavy charges on a costly plant of this kind would preclude the new mill from competing with existing mills without making substantial losses' (estimated by Sir Andrew McCance to amount to £4 million to £5 million a year for many years to come), 'in the opinion of Mr. Macleod' these losses 'would be much less than the public assistance and unemployment benefit paid to men out of work in Scotland without such a development. He would face up willingly to losses on the strip mill because they would be substantially less than the aggregate unemployment payments, and the balance would be favourable to the general national economy.'

It was while Sir Andrew was pondering over the problems

[85] Colvilles Ltd., 'Fourth Strip Mill: Report of Discussions with Sir Archibald Forbes, 29 May, 3 June, and 6 June 1958'.

that might arise 'should a decision be taken on political grounds that a strip mill be sited in Scotland', that it occurred to him that a solution might lie in combining the production of light plates and hot rolled coil. 'In this way the limited demand for sheet in Scotland could be met in an economical way without the inevitable loss that would accompany a full strip mill meeting a demand much less than its latent capacity.' He elaborated on this idea at a meeting with Sir Archibald in June 1958.[86] Having 'gone into the question of the impact of a strip mill on Colvilles' development plans', Sir Andrew expressed the view that the only satisfactory solution 'would be to combine light plate and sheet production in a modified strip mill at Ravenscraig'. By reducing the current weekly output of the existing mills by approximately 5,000 tons of light plate (i.e. plates $\frac{3}{8}$-inch and under in thickness), the plant should be able to cope with the manufacture of medium ship plates with but minor modifications. This tonnage of light plates taken together with the current estimated weekly sheet consumption of 3,000 tons and a possible future growth of consumption by an additional 2,000 tons should make a semi-continuous strip mill with an annual output of 500,000 tons a viable economic proposition.

Nevertheless, 'from Colvilles' standpoint as a shareholding company, the return on the capital would not be good since the plant [would be] completely new, and present prices did not give an adequate return on new plant'. Because the company's 1956 development plan, already under way, 'had been based on improved and extended old plant', the return would be much better than could be expected from this new proposal. For this reason Colvilles would 'definitely not father the finance themselves'. 'It was impossible to get money from the City owing to the threat of re-nationalization and in any case, [Colvilles] might well be questioned for spending shareholders' money on a [project] which brought so poor a return.'[87] Sir Andrew's verdict on the economics of a full strip mill in Scot-

[86] Colvilles Ltd., 'Memorandum of Meeting with Sir Archibald Forbes on Wednesday, 11 June 1958'. The meeting was attended by Sir Lincoln Evans, Sir Robert Shone, Dr. A. H. Leckie, Mr. H. McArthur, and Mr. Turnbull.

[87] Directly after the meeting, Sir Andrew made 'a quick estimate of the profits' based on the conversion cost data with which he had been supplied. This gave a return of 6·2 per cent. When he gave this figure to Sir Archibald by telephone, the latter 'stated that the return on the Newport strip mill was

land was uncompromising. 'The development was the outcome of political pressure. [It] would be a financial disaster, and if the government were prepared to finance such a mill and were prepared to face up to a heavy annual loss for many years when it got to work, then a scheme which saved them such a loss merited some consideration in terms of favourable rates for financial loans to build it.'

Although it seemed to Sir Andrew that Sir Archibald 'was searching in his mind for arguments against [Colvilles' proposals because] of the initiative and support he had given during the past eighteen months to the R.T.B. scheme at Newport', Forbes was apparently 'impressed' by McCance's solution to what was fast becoming an apparently intractable problem. During the next two weeks, further talks on the technical and financial details took place between representatives of the Iron and Steel Board and Colvilles, and Sir Andrew's provisional estimate of the costs of the scheme (approximately £45·5 million at current prices, or £56 million if allowance were made for inflation and the provision of spare parts and additional rolls) broadly confirmed.[88] The return on this investment remained problematical. The Iron and Steel Board—basing their case on the evidence put forward in favour of the Newport strip mill—were much more optimistic than Sir Andrew, who expected lower selling prices than those assumed by the Steel Board's accountant and a *maximum* return of approximately 6·75 per cent. The new scheme would increase the annual capacity of the Colville Group to three million tons, and although Colvilles had not made any further enquiries concerning coal supplies, it was believed that, given government pressure on the National Coal Board, sufficient coal for the furnaces could be made available within the time required to construct the plant.

Almost a month after Sir Andrew had put forward his solution of a modified strip mill, he was again at the headquarters of the Iron and Steel Board, where he was to meet its full-time members and Sir Ernest Lever and Mr. H. Spencer of Richard

12 per cent, but I refused to take this seriously. When he [Sir Archibald] came down to earth, he would find it was even less than the 6·2 per cent I had calculated.' Sir Andrew McCance to Lord Mills, 14 Aug. 1958.

[88] Sir Andrew McCance to Sir Archibald Forbes, 25 June 1958.

Thomas & Baldwins.[89] Invited to express his ideas on the strip mill scheme, now that both sides 'had had a further opportunity of examining it', Sir Andrew was adamant. 'The return was not attractive and was much less than our own schemes. We could not therefore afford it. On the other hand, we could not allow someone else to build a strip mill in Scotland owing to the serious effect it would have on our own plans, firstly on the supplies of coal and secondly on the reduction of 5,000 tons a week of light plates which would go to the strip mill and leave our mills seriously underloaded.' Although Sir Andrew recognized that a strip mill would help to rectify the current industrial imbalance of Scotland, he wished to make it quite clear that the decision to build one could not be *economically* justified however socially desirable it might be. The representatives of Richard Thomas & Baldwins were then brought more fully into the discussion. Sir Ernest Lever was asked if his company's scheme could be modified on the lines of Colvilles' plan. That is, would Richard Thomas & Baldwins first put in a semi-continuous mill? 'Sir Ernest was reluctant to express an opinion, but [Henry] Spencer said that [they] certainly could . . . Indeed, there were some advantages in doing so. So long as R.T.B. could get 1,000,000 tons to put through the cogging mill, it would be economical. They could supply 300,000 tons of strip to be cold rolled at Ebbw Vale where [such] capacity was not fully used. The balance would replace the hand mill product in their group.' After an analysis of the possible future growth of sheet demand, it was decided that 'it *might* be that two *modified* mills . . . would be necessary—one in Wales to take care of the demand growth and one in Scotland to meet local requirements.'[90]

A month later, at the request of Sir Archibald Forbes, Sir Andrew went over the entire scheme again with Lord Mills, who was anxious to acquaint the Cabinet with the latest developments. Colvilles' proposals, it was agreed, were technically feasible.[91] More significant was the hardening of the idea

[89] Colvilles Ltd., 'Record of a Meeting at Norfolk House, 2 July 1958'. The Iron and Steel Board was represented by Sir Archibald Forbes, Sir Lincoln Evans, and Sir Robert Shone.

[90] Emphasis added.

[91] Colvilles Ltd., 'Memorandum of a Meeting [attended by Sir Archibald Forbes, Lord Mills, and Sir Andrew McCance] held on 6 August 1958'.

that two semi-continuous mills were required. The stumbling block was finance. Sir Andrew would not budge from his belief that it was unfair to expect Colvilles to make a substantial capital contribution. How, then, asked the Minister of Power, might a scheme of this magnitude be financed? Sir Andrew's ideas on this subject were, he admitted, only tentative, but he was thinking of a participating loan by the government with a low rate of interest ('say, 3 per cent') which would carry with it the right to participate in the profits eventually arising from the strip mill. Sir Andrew insisted that Lord Mills and the Cabinet understood that

> When Colvilles were denationalized, the Government had been a party to inducing the public to invest in a private enterprise. It was most essential therefore that neither the Government nor ourselves should do anything to diminish the value of the public holding in our company. We were contributing the benefit of substantial capital expenditure already incurred on the Ravenscraig site: we were also contributing a substantial portion of our present market in thin plates for the benefit of the new venture. These factors must be taken into account.

After a lengthy discussion, it was finally agreed that Sir Andrew should seek financial advice from Sir George Erskine of Morgan, Grenfell, & Company and that he should submit Colvilles' plan for a semi-continuous mill at Ravenscraig in more detail to Lord Mills and Sir Archibald Forbes.

It was evident that the Minister of Power was attracted by the scheme, and 'entertained a favourable view of its prospects'.[92] As requested, a week later Sir Andrew wrote to Lord Mills setting out in more detail the basis on which he believed that steel production by modern strip methods might advantageously be developed in Scotland.[93] The technical and economic features of the project were reiterated with great clarity and buttressed by numerous appendices. In addition, a number of points were made in greater detail than in previous papers on the subject: they concerned social, financial, and economic issues. The first concerned the role of Gartcosh (about six miles from Ravenscraig),

> It is a small village wholly dependent on Smith & McLean's activities and it has been a matter of concern that no alternative employment is available when the hand sheet mills close down, as inevitably they must. It is therefore

[92] Colvilles Ltd.: 'Memorandum of a Meeting held on 6 August 1958'.
[93] Sir Andrew McCance to Lord Mills, 14 Aug. 1958.

proposed that cold reduction mills for the production of high grade sheet would be installed on the site of Smith & McLean's works and that the coiled strip would be transferred by road from the hot strip mill at Ravenscraig. There would be little economic disadvantage in this since Gartcosh is nearer than Ravenscraig to Glasgow, the main consuming centre. Such a scheme would prevent this village becoming a derelict area and creating another social problem in Scotland.

The second emphasized that 'in considering the return to be expected from the strip mill extension' a distinction should be made between profits arising from additional production and profits arising from the transfer to the new plant of output already being produced by Colvilles. 'In particular, 250,000 tons per annum of thin plates are earning profits for Colvilles at the present time. If that output is made in the strip mill such profits cannot be credited as profits arising from the new capital expenditure: they have merely been transferred from Colvilles' present earnings. Only additional production made possible by the capital expenditure should be taken into account. This aspect will clearly require close consideration.' The third point dealt with the implications of the transfer to the new strip mill of Colvilles' current production of thin plates. This would require a readjustment of the company's 1956–62 development plan—a plan already approved by the Iron and Steel Board and the British Iron and Steel Federation—and would be achieved by concentrating the reduced plate output of the Blochairn Works and Clydebridge Works at the Clydebridge plate mill.

The report submitted to Lord Mills and the replies to a number of supplementary inquiries[94] were carefully considered by the Ministry of Power during the following month. On 20 September 1958, Lord Mills informed Sir Andrew that 'the plan for the new mill at Ravenscraig' had been approved by the Prime Minister, the Chancellor of the Exchequer, the Secretary of State for Scotland, and the President of the Board of Trade. It had also been discussed with the Minister for Wales. It was 'now only subject to satisfactory discussions in regard to finance'.[95] Sir Andrew's attitude was that Colvilles were

[94] Correspondence between Lord Mills and Sir Andrew McCance, 20 Aug. 1958–2 Sept. 1958.
[95] Colvilles Ltd., 'Special Report: Memorandum of a Conversation with Lord Mills on 20 September 1958'.

already making a profit out of their thin plate business and that this profit would continue even if they spent no further money on their plant. They were also making a profit out of the Ravenscraig Works, which they had built on their own initiative. The company were now being asked to undertake the construction and operation of what he expected to be an unprofitable strip mill with funds advanced by the government. Although Colvilles had agreed to do this, the company believed it to be only fair that the first charge on profits should be 6 per cent on the Ravenscraig capital. To this condition the Cabinet would not agree.

At this point there was complete deadlock. It was not even broken by Lord Mills's threat to authorize the Iron and Steel Board to build a new works in Scotland with government money 'and do the job themselves'. Beyond expressing the opinion that 'it would make a most interesting and expensive experiment', Sir Andrew refused to comment on this suggestion! Nevertheless, meetings continued to be held with representatives of the Ministry of Power, the Treasury, and the Iron and Steel Board. Throughout these negotiations (during which Sir Andrew was advised by Sir George Erskine), none of the suggestions put forward by Colvilles was acceptable to Lord Mills.[96] Not until the end of October had the issues been sufficiently clarified to make eventual agreement possible. On 6 November, Mr. P. D. Proctor, the Permanent Secretary to the Minister of Power, was able to set down the basic provisions which were subsequently to be embodied in the terms of a government loan, the maximum amount of which was to be £50 million. Only a number of details remained to be settled. The way was clear for the Prime Minister's dramatic announcement to the House of Commons on 18 November 1958, that there would be not one strip mill but two, each with appropriate steel-making and finishing capacity: one in South Wales, at Newport, and one in Scotland, at Ravenscraig.[97]

[96] As Mr. P. D. Proctor, the Permanent Secretary to the Ministry of Power, subsequently explained to Sir Andrew, the final settlement had to be one 'which the Government could defend as consistent with its general lending policy and which would not have embarrassing consequences in the steel industry'. P. D. Proctor to Sir Andrew McCance, 3 Nov. 1958.

[97] *Hansard*, 18 Nov. 1958, c. 1015.

5 The Strip Mill: Planning and Operation

(a) *Planning.* Whatever Sir Andrew's misgivings, Colvilles had, Lord Mills later declared, been 'persuaded' to 'a great act of faith'. There was no turning back. Immediately, a team of men was sent to visit existing strip mills to discuss with those possessing experience of such plant 'the pitfalls that must be avoided in a project of this kind',[98] and by April 1959, a formal statement setting out the details of the scheme had been prepared for submission to both the Iron and Steel Board and the British Iron and Steel Federation.[99]

Colvilles proposed to install a semi-continuous[100] hot strip mill at Ravenscraig with an initial output of 500,000 tons of coiled products, approximately half of which would be used to manufacture light plates and the remainder employed in the production of sheet. The hot coils for cold reduced sheet would be transferred to the Gartcosh Works of Smith & McLean Ltd., where the necessary finishing equipment would be installed. To increase Ravenscraig's ingot output to the necessary 1,000,000 tons required not less than 750,000 tons of pig iron, if the target pig iron/scrap ratio was to be attained. This output could be achieved by the two existing blast furnaces, but since the furnace lit in 1957 would have produced about 2 million tons of iron by 1962, it would 'most likely' have to be shut down for

[98] Sir Andrew McCance to Sir George Erskine, 10 Feb. 1959.
[99] Colvilles Ltd., 'Strip Mill Proposal', 9 April 1959.
[100] The difference between a continuous and semi-continuous strip mill may be explained as follows: In the former, slabs of steel, each of which may weigh up to 15 tons or more, pass continuously through a series of roll stands—usually ten in number—arranged in tandem, the slab being progressively reduced in thickness until it emerges from the last set of rolls as a thin strip of the required gauge. In the case of the semi-continuous mill, the number of stands of rolls can vary from five to seven, with a resultant saving in capital costs. The reduction in thickness which the slab undergoes in the first set of rolls of the semi-continuous mill has, however, to be greater than is the case in the fully continuous mill. This involves passing the slab to and fro in this first, or 'roughing', stand of rolls until it has been sufficiently reduced in thickness to permit passing it on to the subsequent or finishing stands, which operate in exactly the same way as a continuous mill. The reversing that takes place in the roughing stand means that the entire process of reducing slabs to strip takes longer in the semi-continuous mill than in the continuous type. The hot strip mill at Ravenscraig, which was planned to roll 60-inch finished strip, was to comprise continuous slab heating furnaces, a scale breaking stand, a reversing four-high roughing mill, and a six-stand continuous mill, together with all the necessary ancillary equipment.

re-lining at the very time that the strip mill was scheduled for completion. As a continuous supply of hot metal was essential, it was deemed necessary to construct a third blast furnace in order to maintain continuity. To obtain the necessary increase in steel output, it was proposed to build a fourth open-hearth furnace of 250 tons capacity at Ravenscraig and, after careful consideration, to install oxygen blown converters to operate the L.D. process with lime injection to provide the balance of the steel required.[101] This combination of open hearth and L.D. processes would, it was hoped, enable the desired annual ingot production of 1,000,000 tons to be achieved with a maximum degree of flexibility in the use of scrap and hot metal. Such was the intention. To realize it involved a major expansion of iron- and steel-making facilities, the estimated cost of which was approximately £47 million.

These proposals, together with additional information on raw material requirements, the anticipated output of the entire Group, and the estimated annual returns on the existing and proposed plant at Ravenscraig, was sent to the Iron and Steel Board and to the Federation in the third week of April 1959. There followed an intensive investigation of the scheme by both bodies. Colvilles' proposals were approved by the Federation's Development Committee on 12 May, but the Iron and Steel Board withheld their consent to two features of the overall scheme: those relating to the third blast furnace at Ravenscraig

[101] One of the three main oxygen steel-making processes (the others being the Kaldo and the Rotor), the L.D. process, named after the initial letters of Linz and Donawitz, the Austrian towns where it was first developed, is one in which oxygen is injected at high velocity on to the surface of the molten iron contained in a converter held stationary in a vertical position during the blow. About 2,000 cubic feet of oxygen is used for each ton of metal processed. The ensuing reactions result in rapid conversion and, as an end product, steel of high quality. One disadvantage of the method is that during the conversion dense clouds of red coloured iron oxide are emitted and these waste gases have to be collected, cooled, and cleaned. Another drawback was that initially the oxygen method could not be used with iron of more than about 0·4 per cent phosphorus. At first this seemed to rule out its widespread adoption, but the problem was overcome by a method of injecting lime powder with the oxygen (the L.D.–A.C., or Oxygen Lance Powder, process). This method of steel-making combines a good scrap-consuming capacity and a high rate of production with the comparatively low cost of the conventional Bessemer converter. Based on B.I.S.F., *A Simple Guide to Technical Developments in the Iron and Steel Industry*, pp. 15–16; and see *Colvilles' Magazine*, Spring 1964, pp. 2–5.

and to the provision of a second battery of coke ovens. The Board refused to believe that a third furnace was *essential* to the scheme.[102] The objection to the coke ovens was more serious. A second battery of coke ovens had already been sanctioned by the Board in August 1956; permission to build this plant had now been withdrawn. This caused considerable consternation. Colvilles believed that the Iron and Steel Board had been unduly influenced by the representatives of the National Coal Board on the Joint Carbonisation Committee who argued that Colvilles should consider obtaining coke from Durham, where the N.C.B. had surplus carbonisation capacity.

While Sir Andrew reluctantly agreed to postpone a decision on the third blast furnace for twelve months, when the question would be re-examined, he insisted on the second battery of coke ovens. He was so angry at the Board's decision that he talked of abandoning the entire strip mill project unless this part of the overall plan was approved.[103] Mr. R. T. Towndrow was asked to investigate the implications of the loss of this plant.[104] It appeared that to deliver Durham coke at Ravenscraig would cost at least £1 per ton more than the delivered price from the Scottish District. This not only meant an additional financial burden of approximately £510,000 a year, but a loss of revenue from gas sales of about £80,000. Nor was this all. Colvilles had no sidings to receive coke cars, nor had they any conveyors to transport the coke to the blast furnace bunkers. Annealing facilities at Gartcosh would, it was estimated, require from 10 to 12 million cubic feet of coke oven gas per week. It had always been intended to draw this quantity from the Scottish Gas Board's main and to replace it with an equivalent amount produced at Ravenscraig. Without the second battery of coke

[102] Sir Lincoln Evans thought that the provision of a third furnace was 'a rather heavy insurance policy ... [since] half the [steel-making] plant was open hearth [it] could presumably be fed with cold pig iron and scrap.' Iron and Steel Board, 'Notes of a Meeting at Norfolk House, 28 Apr. 1959'.

[103] Sir Andrew McCance to D. J. Falvey, 1 June 1959. To Sir Frederick Scopes, a director of Stewarts & Lloyds, chairman of its subsidiary, the Stanton Ironworks Co. Ltd., and a member of the Joint Carbonisation Committee, Sir Andrew wrote that 'the suggestion [that Colvilles use Durham coke] is a completely fatuous one and we are not going to agree to it in any circumstances'. Sir Andrew McCance to Sir Frederick Scopes, 27 May 1959.

[104] Colvilles Ltd., 'Steel Board Letter in Connection with Development Proposals', 27 May 1959; Sir Andrew McCance to S. Robinson, 27 May 1959.

ovens, Colvilles would be unable to supply *any* coke oven gas to the Gas Board, a gas plant would have to be erected at Gart-cosh, and (since the soaking pits at Ravenscraig had been designed to use coke oven gas) the company's energy balance would be upset. Furthermore, the cancellation of the second battery of coke ovens would reduce employment at Ravenscraig by about one hundred men and, by lowering Colvilles' coking coal requirements, involve a diminution in the manpower needs of the Scottish pits by approximately 1,400 men. Although no estimate of the real cost of these consequences of the Iron and Steel Board's decision was made, Sir Andrew 'suspect[ed] that the total cost to the company [alone] would fall not far short of the cost of the coke ovens themselves. We feel that you will not press this matter further.' Confronted with these arguments, the Joint Carbonisation Committee and the Iron and Steel Board capitulated. Consent was given to Colvilles' proposals for a second battery of coke ovens.[105]

While the debate over the formal acceptance of Colvilles' strip mill proposals by the Iron and Steel Board was going on, the technical and logistic details of the project were being examined. It soon became evident that the original idea of producing approximately 250,000 tons of sheet and 250,000 tons of light plate would lead to a very unbalanced plant which would make the operation of the sheet section unprofitable. At the same time, estimates made in 1959 by both Board and Federation indicated that by 1965 the market for sheets was likely to be greater than previous projections had indicated. The Iron and Steel Board was so concerned at the possibility that the industry might not be able to meet the rapidly rising demand for sheet, particularly from the car industry, that Sir Cyril Musgrave, Sir Archibald Forbes's successor at the Board, asked the four strip mill companies to submit suggestions for increasing their production.[106] The combination of these two factors induced Colvilles to revise their original plans. The Board itself suggested that Colvilles should produce an *additional* 250,000 tons of sheet and requested an estimate of the capital costs involved. While

[105] S. Robinson to Sir Andrew McCance, 24 June 1959.
[106] Harald Peake, Steel Company of Wales, to Sir Andrew McCance, 30 Oct. 1959. The four companies were Richard Thomas & Baldwins, John Summers, the Steel Company of Wales, and Colvilles.

somewhat hesitant to agree 'to start enlarging [the company's] original target when in the midst of setting the first one',[107] Sir Andrew saw that by agreeing to their suggestion he could force the Board's hand on the third blast furnace, the case for which, given an expansion of output, was significantly strengthened. It was made almost unanswerable by technical factors, hitherto not fully appreciated.

The revised submissions to the Board and to the Federation[108] explained that the changes had been necessitated by the possibility of a greatly increased local and national demand for sheet coupled with technical considerations. The first factor called for an expansion of the finishing plant; the second made a third blast furnace at Ravenscraig imperative. To attain the original target of approximately 230,000 tons of cold reduced sheets, it had been proposed to use two single-stand reversing mills and one temper mill, but discussions with Davy-United revealed that the capacity of this plant would be barely sufficient for the output envisaged and would certainly permit of no expansion. If, in fact, the future market had been underestimated, the company was likely to be in the 'very awkward' position of having capacity to roll the hot strip but inadequate cold rolling capacity to convert the hot strip into finished sheet. It was therefore proposed to install a four-stand four-high tandem mill at Gartcosh. This would provide flexibility in the various sheet gauges and increase the company's annual capacity from some 230,000 tons to a latent capacity of 700,000 tons, although the planned production was to be 400,000 tons per annum which, with a production of 100,000 tons of black sheets, would give the 500,000 tons required by the Board.

This expansion in sheet capacity necessitated a commensurate increase in both iron- and steel-making plant. Earlier in 1959, the company had conducted lengthy trials of making pig iron of the low sulphur quality required for strip production. These showed that the outputs obtainable from the blast furnaces making basic iron could not be attained when making pig iron of strip mill quality. This technical factor, coupled with the expansion of output contemplated in the revised plan, made the construction of a third stack, complete with coke ovens,

[107] Sir Andrew McCance to Harald Peake, S.C. of W., 5 Nov. 1959.
[108] Colvilles Ltd., 'Colvilles' Strip Mill Development', 2 Dec. 1959.

imperative. It was proposed to enlarge the steel-making capacity by increasing the size of the L.D. converters from 40–50 tons to 60–70 tons and by a corresponding adjustment in the liquid oxygen plant. No alteration in the hot strip mill itself was necessary since it already had a latent capacity approaching 1·5 million tons, but two additional oil-fired soaking pits would have to be built and the area of the slab-handling and dressing bay enlarged.

These and other relatively minor consequential changes in the original plan would cost an additional £11·3 million (£58·7 million compared with the original £47·4 million). It was planned to complete the cold reduction mill at Gartcosh by October 1961 and the hot strip mill by July 1962. By 1963 it was hoped that 'the production and quality difficulties inherent in starting up the new plant' would have been substantially overcome. This time the Board raised no objections to Colvilles' plan. Since it was at their request that the revision had been carried out, they were hardly in a position to do so. Whatever Sir Andrew's private doubts about the future course of sheet demand, estimates of which he considered 'excessive',[109] he seized the opportunity of exploiting the Board's anxieties to meet any future increase in sheet demand to obtain not only a third blast furnace at Ravenscraig but also much more efficient cold rolling equipment at Gartcosh.

(b) *Commissioning and Early Operations*. Despite a number of unforeseen difficulties the Gartcosh cold reduction plant was completed in November 1961, only a few weeks behind schedule. After various experimental tests, production began in December using hot strip purchased from English and Dutch strip mills. Colvilles had also accepted a substantial order to cold roll hot strip from Russia for re-export to the U.S.S.R.[110] Two months later, in February 1962, the Ravenscraig slabbing mill—the primary rolling mill to feed the strip mill—was commissioned, and by May about 80 per cent of the strip mill plant itself had been delivered and installed on its foundations.

[109] Sir Andrew McCance to Harald Peake, S.C. of W., 5 Nov. 1959: 'Certainly the figures submitted to the Federation do not justify all the excitement of the past fortnight.'
[110] Sir Andrew McCance to Sir Dennis Proctor, 28 Nov. 1961.

The vast mill was completed in the autumn, only two to three months behind the scheduled date, when initial trial runs of its different sections took place.[111] Meanwhile, under an agreement between Colvilles and the Republic Steel Corporation, one of the largest producers of strip steel in America, over thirty of Colvilles' key men had received instruction at works operated by Republic Steel and on their return from America had been made responsible for training Colvilles' own staff and operatives. Other officials of the Group gained experience at strip mills in this country and on the Continent. Certainly, everything was done to ensure that when the Ravenscraig mill was commissioned it would be manned by well-trained crews.[112]

The mill itself was regarded as being 'spectacular even in an industry used to spectacle'. Fed with slabs 25 feet long, it converted them into strips of steel up to 4,000 feet long, which, when they emerged from the six-stand four-high finishing train were travelling at nearly 30 miles per hour. A brief description of the sequence of events may be helpful in understanding the subsequent teething problems. The slabs, about 8 inches thick, produced in the massive new slabbing mill, were first reheated in a special furnace and then given a single pass through the vertical and horizontal scale-breakers. This was to remove the layer of iron oxide which covered the surface of the slab when it left the reheating furnace, for it was important that this 'scale' was not forced into the surface of the steel during the ensuing rolling processes. The scale-free slab then passed from three to seven times through the four-high reversing rougher until it was reduced to about one inch in thickness. Next came the six-stand four-high finishing train. It is at this stage that most of the major problems of producing strip at speed are encountered. Each stand of a finishing train is an ordinary four-high mill, but since the purpose of each stand is to contribute to the reduction of the thickness of the strip, each makes the strip longer before passing it on to its neighbour. The necessity for exact co-ordination will be apparent. Each of the six four-high mills in the train has to turn faster than the mill preceding it, just so much faster

[111] Colvilles Ltd., 'Memorandum on Colvilles' Ravenscraig Strip Mill', 28 May 1962, p. 8.
[112] Colvilles Ltd., Chairman's Statement for 1961, p. 6; *Colvilles' Magazine*, Spring 1962, p. 11.

that the strip will neither buckle nor break. By the use of complex automatic mechanisms the train is designed to cope with this problem, but two skilled men constantly watch the controls and adjust them as necessary. The strip, now moving at great speed, travels down the run-out table and is caught by one of the two coiling machines. The coiled strip is then either cut up into hot (or black) sheet or sent to the cold rolling plant to be reduced to the thinner gauges required by the manufacturers of car bodies and office and domestic equipment.[113]

It was in this way that the first black coil was rolled at the Ravenscraig strip mill on 4 December 1962.[114] For the next few months production was irregular and spasmodic. The company had to prove by the dispatch of trial orders that the quality of Colvilles' strip—marketed under the trade name 'Colcrest'—was acceptable to the users, and that the physical properties of the steel were comparable with those of the best products of other manufacturers. Not until the end of the year did Sir Andrew feel sufficiently confident to instigate an intensive sales campaign. It was very hard going. One consequence of setting themselves the highest metallurgical standards was a very high rejection rate. In 1963 the controls at the Ravenscraig mill were made up of between five and six thousand separate automatic units and a failure in any one of them could cause the rejection or down-grading of an entire batch of strip. The time taken to train employees and staff to run the strip mill and the Gartcosh cold rolling mill, and for maintenance engineers to become sufficiently familiar with the plant to be able to locate faults, took much longer than had been anticipated.[115] There were other problems. In planning the mill 'no marginal capacity could be provided to allow for the fluctuations in demand or for breakdown or other interruptions in production'.[116] But Colvilles soon discovered that there was a marked seasonality in the demand for cold reduced sheets which they had never

---

[113] This description is based on that given in *Colvilles' Magazine*, Autumn 1962, pp. 11–13; and see Colvilles Ltd., Chairman's Statement for 1963, p. 7.
[114] Colvilles Ltd., Chairman's Statement for 1962, p. 6.
[115] Colvilles Ltd., Chairman's Statement for 1962, p. 6; Sir Andrew McCance to Sir Cyril Musgrave, 1 Sept. 1964.
[116] Colvilles Ltd., 'Ravenscraig and Gartcosh Works: Development of Sheet Production'. Submission to the Iron and Steel Board, 27 May 1964.

encountered with their traditional heavy products. This necessitated the provision of additional capacity to meet peak demands considerably higher than the average weekly production. Customers expected prompt delivery at all times, yet to maintain the highest metallurgical standards, the manufacture of sheet steel had to proceed in an orderly and steady fashion. After a certain point in its production, any delay between processes caused a significant deterioration in finished quality. Conversely, Colvilles found that it was technically impossible to cope with periods of peak demand by a temporary acceleration of any of the processes. This too could be disastrous.[117] The consequence was that the outputs obtainable from certain items of plant were considerably lower than expected and that to obtain the specified annual output of 400,000 tons of cold reduced sheet involved the installation of additional equipment with a weekly capacity of 10,000–11,000 tons.[118]

As if these difficulties were not enough, the Ravenscraig–Gartcosh complex was plagued by labour troubles. Between 1 May and 30 September 1964, no fewer than thirty-two strikes took place, 'some of them from causes of unbelievable triviality'.[119] In August 1964, for example, a member of the Amalgamated Engineering Union whose job it was to remove the covers from the tanks in the continuous pickling line at Gartcosh was absent through illness, and the production men, members of the British Iron and Steel Confederation, did the job themselves. Immediately, they were accused by an A.E.U. shop steward of having transgressed the rules and 120 maintenance engineers walked out on unofficial strike. This caused Gartosh to be shut down for a week and all the sheet in process of manufacture had to be down-graded. So the problems accumulated. Those of technical nature were slowly overcome by research, by further training, by additional equipment. But when Sir Andrew McCance presented his last statement as Chairman of the company, he could foresee no diminution in industrial unrest.[120]

[117] 'High quality deep stamping sheet is not a mass production product in the ordinary sense . . . the processes cannot be hurried.' Sir Andrew McCance to Sir Cyril Musgrave, 1 Sept. 1964.
[118] Colvilles Ltd., 'Ravenscraig and Gartcosh Works . . .', 27 May 1964.
[119] Colvilles Ltd., Chairman's Statement for 1964, pp. 6–7.
[120] Sir Andrew McCance to Sir Cyril Musgrave, 1 Sept. 1964.

6 The Strip Mill: The Financial Burden

Negotiations to settle the details of the Government loan dragged on throughout the first nine months of 1959. By the beginning of September, Sir Andrew was becoming 'increasingly concerned at the delay in completing the formal agreement ... The election date is coming very near and I have stressed to Sir Dennis Proctor [the permanent Secretary to the Ministry of Power] the advisability of getting the agreement completed and signed before the election takes place ... The delay has been entirely due to the dilatory way in which the Treasury people have handled it.'[121] Lord Mills was made aware of Sir Andrew's anxieties and of 'how distasteful it would be [for him] to have to sign the formal agreement with representatives of another Government if something goes wrong with the Election'.[122] To these proddings, the Minister of Power reacted 'most energetically'. There ensued ten days of intensive consultation with the Treasury solicitors which culminated in the signing of the agreement on 29 September. Although Sir Andrew found that 'the atmosphere [had] hardened quite considerably from that existing at the beginning of the year, no doubt due to the imminence of the Election',[123] he felt that the agreement was 'a fair one'.[124] As Sir George Erskine observed, 'while the authorities have been a bit cheese-paring with some of the details, the Agreement, broadly speaking, conforms to the general basis which [had been] negotiated' before the Prime Minister's announcement in November 1958.[125]

The maximum amount to be advanced by the Ministry of Power was to be £50 million.[126] Despite the alternative suggestions put forward by Sir Andrew and Sir George Erskine, the advance took the form of a direct loan on standard terms

---

[121] Sir Andrew McCance to Sir George Erskine, 17 Sept. 1959.
[122] Sir Andrew McCance to G. H. Latham, Richard Thomas & Baldwins, 1 Oct. 1959; Sir Andrew McCance to Sir George Erskine, 30 Sept. 1959.
[123] Sir Andrew McCance to G. H. Latham, 1 Oct. 1959. 'The Treasury were adamant about any further concessions and I could readily see the political atmosphere behind it all.'
[124] Sir Andrew McCance to Sir George Erskine, 2 Oct. 1959.
[125] Sir George Erskine to Sir Andrew McCance, 5 Oct. 1959.
[126] Agreement between the Minister of Power and Colvilles Ltd., 29 Sept. 1959; Colvilles Ltd., 'Memorandum on Colvilles' Ravenscraig Strip Mill', 28 May 1962, p. 4.

repayable in twenty years at the 'going' rate of interest, although the government reserved the right to create a debenture charge on the whole assets of the Ravenscraig Works. One concession was made. Colvilles could elect to suspend the payment of any interest for a period of up to three years after strip production began, the amount owing being added to the sum advanced and bearing interest at the same rate.

At first all went well. The company was enjoying a period of prosperity. Earnings were good. Sir Andrew was not even greatly perturbed when it became apparent that no increase in the government loan could be expected to cover the enhanced cost of the revised scheme agreed upon in December 1959. Indeed, when the Minister of Power referred to the loan during the course of the debate on the Iron and Steel (Financial Provisions) Bill in February 1960,[127] no mention was made of the increased cost of the amended scheme and the impression was created that not all of the loan would be required.[128] Accidental though this may have been, it was not without some factual basis, since Sir Andrew had written to Sir Dennis Proctor at the time of the debate informing him of Colvilles' intention 'to take advantage of the loan to the smallest possible extent',[129] and this assurance was repeated to the Minister himself a month later.[130] It was not surprising therefore that Colvilles were subsequently pressed not to take up the entire loan as it was politically desirable to substantiate the general impression created by the debate. The more the loan was reduced the better it would be, but 'even if only £45 million [were] to be taken instead of the full £50 million, [the Minister] would regard the position as satisfactory from the political angle'.[131]

As Colvilles would need at least £50 million, the only way for the company to accede to the government's request was

[127] By this time Lord Mills had been succeeded as Minister of Power by Mr. Richard Wood.
[128] Colvilles Ltd., 'Memorandum of a Meeting with Sir Dennis Proctor, Ministry of Power, on 15 December 1960'; Colvilles Ltd., 'Memorandum on Colvilles' Ravenscraig Strip Mill', 28 May 1962.
[129] Sir Andrew McCance to Sir Denis Proctor, 8 Feb. 1960.
[130] Sir Andrew McCance to the Rt. Hon. Richard Wood, Minister of Power, 16 Mar. 1960.
[131] Colvilles Ltd., 'Memorandum of Meeting with Sir Dennis Proctor, Ministry of Power, 15 December 1960'; 'Minutes of a Meeting held in the Minister of Power's Room, 21 March 1961'.

to raise capital on the money market, a course urged on Sir
Andrew by Sir Dennis Proctor. Yet to do so might be difficult.
Sir George Erskine was very much against the idea. He felt that
Colvilles should 'not be too ready to modify the arrangements;
it is the old story that once they get you committed to go ahead
they are inclined to want to prune the terms'.[132] If Colvilles
were successful in raising 'new money from the public or the
shareholders'—which was by no means certain—it would
simply 'be taken in reduction of . . . Government borrowing',
leaving the company no better off. Sir Andrew remained unconvinced. He felt that steel shares were currently popular, and
he was 'apprehensive' that Colvilles 'might miss the boat' if the
company postponed putting its 'financial structure into better
shape until the strip mill was ready to commence operations'.[133]
Consequently, he suggested that Colvilles might make a 'rights'
issue similar to that announced by Stewarts & Lloyds in April
1961, for developments at Corby.

Sir George Erskine's reply was unenthusiastic. 'I think a
"rights" issue to raise about £15 million (1 for 3 at say 65*s*.)
would be about the maximum you would want to ask your
Shareholders to subscribe [but] it still seems to me that if you
do this now . . . you would in effect be raising money in relief
of H.M.G. and the benefit to you would be mainly in reducing
your gearing . . . [Nevertheless,] I agree that a "rights" issue
of the size I indicate should not be difficult.'[134] Sir Andrew
pondered over this problem for some time. By offering to try
to obtain finance from 'outside sources', he could perhaps induce the Government to accept a mere £5 million diminution
in the loan whatever the success of the 'rights' issue. So great
was the Government's anxiety 'to enable the call on public
funds to be reduced to a total of £45 million'[135] and 'so very
helpful would it be to the Minister' to be able to make an

[132] Sir George Erskine to Sir Andrew McCance, 20 Mar. 1961.

[133] Sir Andrew McCance to Sir George Erskine, 6 Apr. 1961. 'One never
knows when the popularity [of steel shares] may fade, and the recent
announcement by Harold Wilson of the Labour Party's determination
to re-nationalize the Steel industry might well have a bad effect on the
whole market if this policy is developed and made more definite at a later
date.'

[134] Sir George Erskine to Sir Andrew McCance, 7 Apr. 1961.

[135] Sir Dennis Proctor to Sir Andrew McCance, 2 May 1961.

announcement to this effect,[136] that Colvilles were to be permitted to use any balance raised from the shareholders over and above the £5 million concession to reduce their bank indebtedness, which promised to rise alarmingly over the next two years. This decided the point. Colvilles would make a 'rights' issue.

The financial arrangements were made by Morgan, Grenfell, & Company, who agreed to underwrite the issue. In May it had been expected that the new shares could be offered at 64*s*. each of which, if the company could sustain its current dividend of 16 per cent, would give a yield of 5 per cent, but by the end of June the market had fallen and the terms had had to be altered. On 3 July the price was fixed at 57*s*. 6*d*. a share and, in order to realize the necessary £15 million, the number of shares to be issued increased from 4,773,250 to 5,324,906. As a consequence, the offer to shareholders was changed to three new shares for every eight held with a corresponding adjustment in the offer to Convertible Debenture holders.[137] This price was below the quoted market price at the time but an international crisis unexpectedly blew up over Kuwait and share prices suffered a further decline. By 16 August only about a quarter of Colvilles' shareholders had accepted the offer: 808,142 shares had been taken up, leaving 85 per cent of the total issue in the hands of the underwriters.[138] Nevertheless, Colvilles had their £15 million.

From the beginning of the strip mill scheme, Colvilles made quarterly forecasts of the company's future financial position based on anticipated expenditures in relation to the cash expected to be available. These surveys continued to show a satisfactory position until the Autumn of 1961, when the impact of adverse factors, some of which had been discerned in the previous year, threatened to disrupt the company's predictions. The most important of these was that throughout the year the demand for steel continued to weaken and by September production had fallen considerably. 'What might have continued as a relatively slow rate of decline was accelerated ... by the

[136] Colvilles Ltd., 'Notes of a Meeting [between Sir Andrew McCance and Sir Dennis Proctor] 1 May 1961'.
[137] Colvilles Ltd., 'Special Report: Rights Issue', 29 June 1961.
[138] *Colvilles' Magazine*, Autumn 1961, p. 6.

measures the Government found it necessary to introduce to curb ... increasing inflation.'[139] Colvilles were particularly affected by the recession since the company was more dependent than those in other districts on the state of the shipbuilding industry, currently experiencing its own grave difficulties. The gross tonnage of merchant ships under construction during 1961 and 1962 was lower than at any time since 1938.[140] Ship plates had always constituted a large part of the company's output and the depression on the Clyde was, more than any other factor, responsible for the fact that throughout 1962 Colvilles were running at between only 58 and 63 per cent of capacity.[141]

The consequence of this serious diminution of demand was that the cash contribution which the company had been so confident of being able to make towards the cost of the strip mill scheme was materially reduced. This was but one aspect of a steadily deteriorating situation. An even more serious reduction in the company's cash flow was caused by the Iron and Steel Board's pricing policy, a cause of constant irritation to Sir Andrew. In 1961 the Board's method of determining prices was explained as follows. At periodic intervals, usually between two and three years, the Board made

a comprehensive assessment of the costs, both operating and capital, of a modern plant of optimum size well situated for materials, labour, and markets, and operated with a high degree of efficiency. From these assessments estimates [were] made of the prices that would be needed for the various steel products to meet the operating costs and the capital charges of the plant and to provide a reasonable return on the capital employed in operating it. While the prices so estimated [would] not necessarily be precisely those

[139] Colvilles Ltd., Chairman's Statement for 1961, p. 3.
[140] Iron and Steel Board and the British Iron and Steel Federation, *Annual Statistics*, 1956, Table 79, and 1966, Table 94. See also Iron and Steel Board, *Annual Report for 1962*, Table 2, p. 9.
[141] Colvilles Ltd., 'Memorandum on Strip Mill Finance', 28 Feb. 1962. The Iron and Steel Board estimated that during 1962 the industry as a whole was operating at about 74 per cent of capacity. 'Within this total, however, there were wide differences in the experience of the various sections of the industry. The lighter end, producing sheet and tinplate, did better than average, the heavier end, producing plates and heavy sections and mainly located in Scotland and on the North East Coast, fared badly. Thus the average level of operation was 87 per cent in the wide strip mills but only 68 per cent in the plate mills and 62 per cent in the mills producing constructional steel.' Iron and Steel Board, *Annual Report for 1962*, p. 2, para. 2.

appearing in the Board's statutory price determinations, they [were] the most important single factor in arriving at the determined prices.[142] In assessing the costs of this 'hypothetical new steel works' (as Sir Andrew always referred to it), the Board assumed that it possessed 'the most advanced type of plant in commercial operation in this country' (for which a twenty-five-year period of amortization was appropriate) and that it enjoyed a capacity utilization of 90 per cent. These factors, taken in conjunction with the need to permit reasonable interest and dividend payments, were those which determined what might be called the general level of steel product prices between the periodic reviews. But some flexibility was permitted by making provision for interim price adjustments to cover cost changes—particularly those outside the industry's control—which in the opinion of the Board were substantial and persistent.

In the closing months of 1960 and during the spring of 1961, the British iron and steel industry experienced a number of major cost increases of which the most important were rising wages and the tax on fuel oil, imposed by the Budget of April 1961. These and other increases, totalling an estimated £29·3 million and equivalent to 3 per cent of turnover, formed the basis of a claim by the British Iron and Steel Federation that the Board should make an interim price increase. Reluctantly accepting that cost increases of this magnitude had 'fallen on the industry', the Board believed that 'offsetting factors', such as the contemporaneous improvements in labour productivity and fuel efficiency, were sufficiently great to justify a price increase of only 1 per cent. The amount brought in by this price increase, which took effect in June 1961, was about £8·75 million. The Board's decision was bitterly criticized by the industry as being inadequate to meet the net increase in the industry's cost burden. The fact was, of course, that the beneficial influence of the 'offsetting factors'—particularly those ascribed to improvements in productivity—steadily diminished as the industry's capacity utilization fell from the 90 per cent assumed by the Board's formula (and, in fact, achieved during 1960) to barely 70 per cent in October 1961. As it became clear that the low level of working was not merely a temporary phenomenon, the Board, recognizing the validity of the complaints,

---

[142] Iron and Steel Board, *Annual Report for 1961*, pp. 18–19, para. 60.

undertook an entirely new assessment of the capital and operating costs of steel-making using modern plant working at 84 per cent of capacity. The result was that the prices of most iron and steel products were increased by an average of approximately 2½ per cent on 26 February 1962.[143]

This concession may have helped the industry as a whole, but Colvilles were in the difficult position of carrying a disproportionate share of the industry's rising costs. Not only was the company's plant working further below the optimum production level than any other major firm in the country,[144] largely because of its traditional dependence upon shipbuilding demands, but from 1 January 1962, Colvilles were saddled with an unexpected increase of about 10s. a ton in the delivered price of coking coal. Because this was a selective increase affecting only the National Coal Board's Scottish and North Western Divisions, it fell very heavily on Colvilles, who were unable to 'recover any part of it in [enhanced] steel prices'. It was estimated that the Coal Board's decision would cost the company an extra £900,000 a year in direct coal purchases from Scottish sources and greatly increase the cost of outside purchases of bricks and electricity.

The impact of the selective increase in the price of Scottish coking coal was immediate. In 1962, the company 'lost money in making pig iron at Ravenscraig for the first time since the works started'.[145] So serious was the position that an analysis was made of the economies that might be obtained by importing American coal. This revealed that coke made from American coal (at £5 13s. a ton delivered, the price quoted by four American colliery companies) would cost the company £1 18s. 6d. per ton less than coke produced from coal supplied by the

---

[143] Ibid., pp. 21–2; and B.I.S.F., *Annual Report for 1962*, p. 30.

[144] Colvilles Ltd.: 'Memorandum on Scottish Strip Mill Development, 4 April 1962'; and see Iron and Steel Board, *Annual Report for 1963*, p. 9. where the 'Average Rates of Utilization of Capacity for Crude Steel' are given by districts. The figures for Scotland and for the U.K. as a whole are as follows (per cent):

	1960	1961	1962	1963
All Districts	94·2	83·3	74·1	78·8
Scotland	89·5	73·9	60·3	64·7

[145] Colvilles Ltd., 'Strip Mill Finance', 28 Feb. 1962, para. 9.

N.C.B.[146] Alternatively, by using American coking coal the saving in making pig iron would be 25s. per ton and (assuming a ratio of pig iron to ingot steel of 44 per cent) about 15s. 8d. could be lopped off the production cost of a ton of plates and 16s. 2d. per ton off the cost of cold rolled strip. Persuasive though these figures were, the Minister of Power made it clear to Sir Andrew that there was 'little or no chance of getting permission to import American coal at the present time'.[147] It was politically inexpedient:[148] Colvilles could not look westward for relief.

All this meant that during 1961 and 1962 the company's cash resources were seriously depleted. It had 'been expected that in a year of full production the price increase granted by the Iron and Steel Board in February 1962, would bring about £1·8 million extra income' to the company.[149] But the whole of this

[146] The data may be tabulated as follows:

Source of Coal	Scotland	U.S.A.
Delivered price per ton	£6 6s. 9d.	£5 13s. 0d.
Content:	%	%
Moisture	12·0	4·0
Ash	7·4	5·0
Volatile matter	29·1	28·5
Fixed Carbon	51·5	62·5
Coal required to make one ton of coke	32·8 cwt	30·0 cwt
Cost of coke	£10 8s. 0d.	£8 9s. 6d.

Source: Sir Andrew McCance to The Minister of Power, 8 Feb. 1962.

[147] Ibid., and Colvilles Ltd., 'Memorandum of Meeting with Mr. R. W. Parker, Chairman of the Scottish Division, National Coal Board, at Edinburgh on 15 March 1962'.

[148] This was but the most recent of Colvilles' efforts to import American coking coal. Sir Andrew argued that to allow Colvilles to use this fuel would 'not only reduce the cost but prolong the active life of the Scottish coal fields. Conservative Governments had not the courage to agree, and Labour Governments thought it would reflect badly on nationalization. In any case, it was opposed by the trade unions.' Personal communication from Sir Andrew McCance.

[149] Colvilles Ltd.: 'Memorandum on Colvilles' Ravenscraig Strip Mill, 28 May 1962. These price increases were later stigmatized as being "inadequate" and "too late".' Colvilles Ltd., Chairman's Statement for 1962, p. 3.

increase was absorbed by the higher fuel costs and by an increase in local rates,[150] following revaluation of the works, of approximately £600,000.[151] This had a very damaging effect on the firm's profits. In the financial year ended 30 September 1962, 'a drop in turnover of approximately 20 per cent produced a fall in gross trading profit before depreciation of approximately 46 per cent'.[152] This in turn seriously affected the amount of cash the company could provide from its own resources towards the cost of the strip mill scheme.

In March 1962, when Colvilles' loan was formally reviewed by the Minister of Power, the company's latest cash forecast was examined and compared with previous quarterly surveys. It was estimated that the price increases granted by the Iron and Steel Board in June 1961, and February 1962, would add £2½ million to the company's annual income. Against this, however, their extra costs would be £4 million. It was obvious that Colvilles were confronted with a very serious cash deficiency during 1963. Originally, it had been calculated that this deficiency would reach a maximum of between £8 million and £9 million in March 1963, and arrangements had been made with the National Commercial Bank of Scotland to meet this amount by an overdraft. But by March 1962, when the position was clearer, the total cash deficit was expected to attain its maximum six months later than predicted and to amount to no less than £23 million, not more than £8 million of which could be covered by bank credit.[153]

The more the problem was discussed, the more intractable it seemed to become. Asked to restore the £5 million by which the original government loan had been reduced, the Minister of Power, Mr. Richard Wood, argued that it would be 'very embarrassing politically for him to have to go back to Parliament and say that the promises which both he and Sir Andrew

[150] The fuel oil tax of 2·2*d.* per gallon introduced in July 1961 added £385,000 to the company's costs, and the selective price increase in Scottish coking coal, not less than £900,000.

[151] Colvilles Ltd.: Chairman's Statement for 1963, p. 4. 'It would be ironical if the prevalent policy of using too large a proportion of the income from industrial rating to subsidize house rents, so impaired and reduced trade that there was no employment for the tenants.'

[152] Colvilles Ltd., Chairman's Statement for 1962, pp. 3–4.

[153] Colvilles Ltd., 'Special Report: Meeting at the Ministry of Power on 1 March 1962'.

had made could not be kept'. Furthermore, it 'might suggest a serious lack of confidence in the power of the steel industry in general, and of Colvilles in particular, to raise money in the market for their own capital expenditure—and thus throw doubt on the whole of the Government's denationalization policy'.[154] But if the government was not to help, what was the solution? Morgan, Grenfell, & Company were consulted on the possibility of raising money by a public issue of debentures or shares, but, 'after examining the records of our present depressed earning powers . . . they expressed the view that at the moment this would not be a feasible operation'.[155] The National Commercial Bank of Scotland was approached again and, after a full discussion, they agreed, without enthusiasm, to increase Colvilles' overdraft facilities to £10 million.[156] This was helpful, but even when the Government loan of £45 million was drawn, payment of interest postponed, and full advantage taken of bank overdraft facilities, Colvilles were still left with a deficit of at least £9·3 million.

A week after the formal review of the Loan Agreement, another meeting was held with representatives of the Ministry of Power and the Treasury.[157] With capital expenditure running at about £3 million a month, the company would exhaust its cash resources by December 1962. There was no alternative, argued Colvilles' representatives, but to stop construction of the strip mill. It was admitted that this would result in a 'heavy interest burden on instalments [of the loan that had] already been drawn' and which would, moreover, 'be payable on unproductive capital', but at least this action would save 'an established and profitable business from bankruptcy for the sake of an extension into a new trade which was admitted to need time for development'.[158] The possibility of an 'immediate cessation of construction' appalled the Ministry and Treasury officials and the company's representatives were left with the impression

[154] Ibid.
[155] Colvilles Ltd., 'The Scottish Strip Mill Development', 4 April 1962; Sir Andrew McCance to Sir Dennis Proctor, 23 Mar. 1962.
[156] Sir Andrew McCance to Sir Dennis Proctor, 2 Apr. 1962.
[157] Colvilles Ltd., 'Notes on the Review of the Loan Agreement with representatives of the Ministry of Power and the Treasury, 10 April 1962'; Ministry of Power: 'Notes of a Meeting at the Ministry of Power, 10 April 1962'.
[158] Colvilles Ltd., 'Notes on the Review of Loan Agreement . . ., 10 April 1962', para 8.

TABLE 13.2

Colvilles Ltd.: Trading Profit and Interest Payable on Loan Capital, 1956–1966
(in £'000s)

Financial Year ended c. 30 September	1956	1957	1958	1959	1960	1961	1962	1963	1964	1965	1966
Trading Profit	7,673	9,018	8,652	9,352	13,577	10,924	3,640	2,200	8,824	5,637	1,919
Interest Payable on Loan Capital	45	166	643	794	624	700	2,162	3,503	3,859	3,983	4,147

Source: Colvilles Ltd., Chairman's Statement, Annual Report and Accounts, 1965 and 1966.

that the government 'would do everything possible to prevent
[it], even to the extent of restoring the surrendered £5 million
of the loan, although that would be very much a last resort,
because of the political implications'.[159]

Relying on the accuracy of this impression, and grasping at
the possibility that 'Government encouragement would be
extended to ... an arrangement ... with the Finance Corporation for Industry', Colvilles formally applied for a loan of £10
million to £12 million from this source. At the same time, Sir
Andrew informed the Minister of Power that Colvilles were involved 'in private negotiations concerning possible ways of
meeting the cash deficiency'. If these approaches were unsuccessful a 'most serious position would arise' leaving 'only one
course of action open to the Board', the cessation of construction. 'Looking back on the causes of our present difficulties,' he added, 'it is evident that these would not have been
so aggravated had we been allowed to receive the full amount
of the Government loan originally agreed.'[160]

Although the company's application to the Finance Corporation for Industry was sympathetically received, the Corporation was 'reluctant to advance the £12 million which Colvilles required'. Instead, it was suggested that 'if the Ministry
were willing to restore the £5 million to the Government loan,
F.C.I. would be prepared to grant facilities up to £7 million'.[161]
After lengthy discussions at the Ministry of Power, Sir Dennis
Proctor promised to make a recommendation to his Minister
to revert to the terms of the original agreement.[162] The Finance
Corporation for Industry promptly approved a loan to Colvilles of up to £7 million. Four days later, after Sir Archibald
Forbes (now a member of the board of the Finance Corpora-
tion) had given 'tremendous help in arguing our case before
the Ministry',[163] the Minister of Power informed Parliament

[159] Colvilles Ltd., 'Notes on the Review of Loan Agreement ...', 10 April
1962', para 10. The Ministry of Power's official minute is very guarded on
these points.
[160] Sir Andrew McCance to Mr. Richard Wood, Minister of Power, 4 June
1962.
[161] Colvilles Ltd., 'Memorandum on a Meeting with Sir Dennis Proctor
at the Ministry of Power, 17 July 1962', para. 1.
[162] Ibid., para. 5.
[163] Sir Andrew McCance to Sir Archibald Forbes, 30 July 1962; J. E. H.
Collins, Morgan, Grenfell, & Co. to Sir Andrew McCance, 27 July 1962.

that he had restored the loan to Colvilles to the maximum figure of £50 million.[164] The immediate financial crisis was passed. An enormous debt burden remained (see Table 13.2).

7 The Final Years Under Private Enterprise

The strip mill at Ravenscraig was the last major capital development undertaken by Colvilles. It was officially commissioned on 1 May 1963, some nine weeks after the Minister of Power had 'come regretfully to the conclusion' that he must take up his security, lest in the event of liquidation his claim would rank merely with those of all the other unsecured creditors.[165] Sir Andrew's forebodings had come to pass. The mill, whatever its technical merits, had been a financial disaster. For nearly a century Colvilles had kept afloat, while others about them failed, by pursuing a conservative financial policy, by retaining as high a proportion of the profits as the board could get away with, and by acting within carefully calculated limits; the company had now been brought to its knees by undertaking a project 'that it had thought unwise'.[166] Colvilles was not the first firm, nor was it to be the last, to suffer crippling losses by succumbing to government pressure and constructing inappropriate plant at unsuitable locations,[167] but its experience was perhaps the most dramatic in the postwar history of the British steel industry.

The creation of the strip mill inevitably overshadowed contemporaneous developments elsewhere within the Group. Everywhere the plant was thoroughly modernized. A Universal Beam Mill was built at Lanarkshire, new slab heating facilities put down at Dalzell, and a four-high plate mill installed at Clydebridge. Hallside was completely rebuilt for the production of alloy steels, and at Ravenscraig itself the basic oxygen shop was commissioned early in 1964. Thereafter, the board trod warily; it had no alternative. A number of important capital

'I agree with you that [Sir Archibald] did more than any of us to get the thing through the Government.'
[164] *Hansard*, 23 July 1962.
[165] D. H. Crofton, Ministry of Power, to Sir Andrew McCance, 21 Feb. 1963.
[166] Vaizey's moderate expression, *History of British Steel*, p. 175.
[167] See *The Economist*, 3 Aug. 1974, pp. 70–1.

projects were undertaken or projected, but they nearly all arose from the need to balance up elements within the Ravenscraig complex or at Gartcosh to accommodate the changing nature of market demands and to exploit the firm's rapidly growing knowledge of strip technology. At other works, capital development was limited to replacing equipment which was nearing the end of its useful life or whose products could not meet the ever-rising standards of quality and finish demanded by consumers at home and overseas. Colvilles' Development Programme for the period 1965–70 (the Fifth Development Plan) envisaged only one new product: tinplate, for which the Iron and Steel Board believed there would be a shortage of capacity by 1970. The manufacture of tinplate in Scotland would give 'a better geographical distribution to the industry' and, more important, would provide a better loading (and hence lower production costs) of Colvilles' existing steel-making and rolling plant. The company's submission to the Iron and Steel Board mentioned, too, its experiments in continuous casting of plates and blooms, and vacuum degassing for special products. The successful application of these processes might affect certain details of the proposed development programme, the completion of which would give the Group a finished steel capacity of 3,215,000 tons and an ingot requirement of not less than 4,354,000 tons.[168]

Not that these figures were reached in the mid-sixties (see Table 11.6), but output started to rise again in 1963 to reach a new peak in 1965. It could have been higher had it not been for a series of labour disputes of unprecedented severity and complexity.[169] Of these, the most onerous were associated with the establishment of the 40-hour week, and what worried the company was that so many of the strikes were unofficial. Almost for the first time since the eighties of the previous century, several groups of employees refused to accept the decisions reached by independent adjudicators and attempted to achieve objectives which they were 'unable to secure at the negotiating table'. It is possible that this worsening in labour relations was related to the sheer growth of the Group (and of the individual

    [168] Colvilles Ltd., 'Development Programme', 12 July 1965.
    [169] Iron and Steel Board, *Annual Report for 1965*, p. 11. Colvilles Ltd., Chairman's Statement for 1965, pp. 21–2.

units within it) and the consequential weakening of the close personal contacts between management and men that had previously existed. However reluctant one may be to invoke an explanation in terms of individuals, it was perhaps not unconnected with the retirement in 1964 of Mr. R. C. Dymock, a special director and the Group's chief labour officer for many years. Born in Motherwell, Mr. Dymock began his career at Dalzell in 1906 as a pay clerk. He subsequently became divisional secretary of the Iron and Steel Trades Employers' Association and in 1960 president of that Association. Mr. Dymock built up an unparalleled knowledge of working conditions and rates of pay during a lifetime of direct contact with the men, and 'because he knew what he was talking about, men trusted him'.[170] He was one of the last of Colvilles' senior management whose service in the company reached back to the days of David Colville, jun. His departure from the firm— though he advised the company in a consultative capacity for several more years—marked the end of an epoch in labour relations.

New men were taking over in many spheres in these last few years of private enterprise in the steel industry. Mr. Harry Yates, former chairman and managing director of Smith & McLeans, and a member of the parent board of Colvilles since 1936, retired in 1961 and died, aged 83, a year later. Not the least of the many talents he had brought to the company was a clear conception of the importance of labour relations, born of his great interest in the welfare of the employees at Mavisbank, Port Glasgow, and Gartcosh. He too 'knew the men'. He had, after all, been brought up among them, having joined Smith & McLeans as a clerk at the age of 18, spending the days at work and the nights studying the theory and chemistry of the metal rolling and galvanizing processes. He had succeeded his father as works manager in 1907 and between them, father and son had an unbroken period of service of ninety-three years to Smith & McLeans.[171] Sir Frederick Rebbeck retired in 1962,

[170] *Colvilles' Magazine*, Winter 1964–5, pp. 27–8.

[171] Like Sir John Craig, Harry Yates's lifetime interest was with youth movements. He was a leading figure in the Boys' Brigade and 'his interest in young people was real and unbounded' (Sir Andrew McCance in *Colvilles' Magazine*, Winter 1962–3, p. 19), but he also took an active part in public affairs. A former president of the Glasgow Chamber of Commerce and of the

as did Mr. James Gibson, since 1956 special director in charge of Glengarnock and consultant to the Group on steel-making practice. Lord Bilsland, a member of the board since 1937, retired three years later, his last services to the company being the help he had given to Sir Andrew McCance in the financial negotiations over the strip mill.

It was the departure of these directors and, above all, the imminent retirement of Sir Andrew McCance, which provoked radical organizational changes in the Colville Group. Not only had the company become very large, judged by any standard (see above, p. 355n), but with the strip mill, its products had become increasingly diversified. The time had come for strategy to shape structure. The holding company form was inhibiting the company from taking full advantage of scale economies and the other advantage of size. The old administrative structure was, too, ceasing to provide the proper facilities needed to control, evaluate, and plan for the subsidiaries, whose position had been subtly altered by the capital reorganization involved in the denationalization procedure (see above, pp. 349n). A fundamental change had been wrought by the altered relationship between, for example, Colvilles Ltd. and Smith & McLeans. In the past, Colvilles had simply provided its sheet-making subsidiary with sheet bars which were processed in the 'hand mills' at Mavisbank and Gartcosh and sold by Smith & McLeans. Now, physically apart though the plants may have been, Ravenscraig and Gartcosh were essentially integrated into a sheet- and light plate-making complex. Furthermore, Harry Yates, who had worked so closely with Sir John Craig and Sir Andrew McCance, had gone. The close personal connection, now severed, had to be replaced by a more formal, structured relationship. It was the same elsewhere in the Group. The products that each unit manufactured were becoming more specialized, more differentiated. It was time for change. The new men rising to the board and to the special executive needed and demanded it; the new production and marketing methods required it. Above all, perhaps, Sir Andrew's successor, Mr. T. R. Craig, wanted it. The old administrative

Association of British Chambers of Commerce, he was a director of the Merchants' House of Glasgow and a trustee of the Clyde Navigation Trust for twelve years.

structure had worked because the men at the top were, it is clear, exceptionally talented autocrats. But it was not in Mr. Craig's nature to be an autocratic chairman. He saw himself as the leader of a team which thought and acted as a team. He believed, too, that the chairman of a company as complex as Colvilles had become, had to sit back a little from events and 'see them whole, concerning himself not with detail but with the big picture'. For this reason he refused 'to take on the chairmanship of the individual companies within the Group. He [felt that] the day to day events in which they would involve him should not be his concern.' Instead, he conceived his task as being 'to think, to meet the experts, to know the trends, to discuss, to initiate—and then to listen to the board'.[172]

It would be foolish to infer that the new chairman's predecessors did not do likewise, but T. R. Craig's regime promised to bring a different change of emphasis: a new style of management. Sir Andrew McCance thought; he met the experts; indeed, he himself was a metallurgist of genius; he discovered and analysed the trends, probably more accurately than the economists and commercial men on the staff of the Federation and the Iron and Steel Board; he discussed matters, but only with those whose opinions he valued and respected and even they were permitted few mistakes; and he initiated a whole series of brilliantly conceived technological projects. All the tasks which T. R. Craig spelled out, Sir Andrew did, but he did them on a different and higher plane than is implied by his successor's words. And whether he *listened* to the board, in the sense that he was prepared to be swayed by their arguments, is difficult to determine. The written record can, at best, only hint at a verdict on this question. It would appear that he was always prepared to consult his colleagues *individually* on matters in which they had acquired expertise: Lord Bilsland on finance, T. R. Craig on sales, Sam Thomson on steel-making practice, R. C. Dymock on labour relations, Harry Yates on conference agreements and sheet trade policies generally; but in the end he made the decision, not the board collectively. The 'right course' did not emerge from the board's discussions; what was to be done was suggested, on occasions even imposed, from above, so much so that the first task confronting his successor,

---

[172] *Colvilles' Magazine*, Spring 1965, p. 9; Spring 1967, p. 3.

as one of the last special directors to be appointed observed, was to teach the board how to direct, for it was a role which most of them had forgotten.[173]

Be that as it may, Colvilles had been fortunate in its chairmen. The company, as David Colville & Sons, had been driven into steel by the demonaic ambitions of David Colville, jun. who, by the eve of the First World War, had made the firm one of the largest concerns in the industry; it had been kept alive and, when conditions were right, expanded by Sir John Craig, a man of consummate diplomacy and commercial acumen; and it had been built into one huge, modernized, and integrated complex centred on Ravenscraig by the sheer technical virtuosity of Sir Andrew McCance. Between them they guided, some would say ruled, Colvilles for nearly a century. But, by the mid-sixties, 'the old days of the autocratic chairman [were] over. Modern industry', T. R. Craig believed, 'is too big for autocrats.'[174] And so, in the penultimate year of the chairmanship of Sir Andrew McCance, changes were introduced in the internal management structure and organization of the Group. Hitherto control and supervision had been centred in two bodies—'the Parent Board which, along with its overall responsibility, [had] concerned itself in detail with general policy, development, finance, and capital expenditure, and a Management Board of which each member [was] either a Director or a Special Director of the Company and to which [had] been delegated the regular examination and review of technical efficiency, production and production costs'. Now, there were to be four divisional executives responsible to the board:

a Heavy Steel Executive, under the chairmanship of Mr. T. R. Craig, Managing Director (Sales), to supervise the business of the Company in plates, sections, bars, and ancillary products, and a Strip Executive, under the chairmanship of Mr. R. P. Towndrow, Managing Director (Sheets), to supervise the production of sheets and all matters concerned with their manufacture. A Development Executive under Mr. J. A. Kilby will advise on plant and production development within the Group, and a Minerals Executive, under Mr. Duncan Ferguson, will co-ordinate the supply of raw materials and the operation of subsidiary companies like Shapfell Limestone Ltd. and Blanchland Fluor Mines Ltd. ... A Director is thus in charge of each Executive and, in addition to Special Directors who are members, representatives from

[173] Private communication to the author.
[174] *Colvilles' Magazine*, Spring 1967, p. 3.

senior management are included. It is intended by this change in the central structure to lessen the burden which each unit will be asked to carry while giving at the same time opportunities for wider experience to those who are taking an active part in the management of the Company.[175]

This multidivisional structure was refined when Mr. T. R. Craig became chairman and managing director. Within weeks of his appointment, he 'asked the Board to appoint certain of their colleagues as Assistant Managing Directors': Mr. Duncan Ferguson, from the commercial side, who became chairman of the Heavy Steel Division; Dr. Robert Hunter, a metallurgist long associated with Sir Andrew McCance at Clyde Alloy, and who succeeded him as chairman of that company, became head of the Alloy Steel Division; and Mr. J. A. Kilby, a mechanical engineer of considerable repute who had been deeply involved in the steel-making and rolling mill developments at Ravenscraig and Gartcosh, who became chairman of the Strip Division. In addition to these readily distinguishable product-related divisions, two further areas of activity concerning the entire Group were formally placed under the full-time supervision of a director. Thus, Mr. R. P. Towndrow became responsible for labour and personnel relations, and Lord Clydesmuir for public relations. These appointments made it desirable to strengthen the main board by promoting William Gillies from the ranks of the special directors, and to appoint several senior managers to the special directorate. The reorganization was radical. How well it would have functioned only time would tell, and time was not on the company's side. The legislation first proposed in the 1964 Parliament and long foreshadowed (see above, p. 395n) was confirmed by the 1966 election results and was then enacted.[176] Vesting day was 28 July 1967, when Colvilles and thirteen other large crude steel-producing companies passed into public ownership and were absorbed by the British Steel Corporation. This time there was to be no going back. In 1971 the new Conservative government made it clear that it would abide by the decision of its predecessors: there would not be another denationalization.

---

[175] Colvilles Ltd., Chairman's Statement for 1963, p. 6.
[176] Vaizey, *History of British Steel*, p. 180. See also B.I.S.F., *Annual Report for 1964*, v–vi; *Annual Report for 1965*, v–vi; *White Paper on Steel Nationalization* (Cmnd. 2651), April 1965; Colvilles Ltd., Chairman's Statements for 1965, pp. 20–1, and 1966, p. 22.

EPILOGUE

1967–1977

Epilogue: 1967–1977

The nationalization of the iron and steel industry in 1967
'differed significantly from that attempted nearly twenty years
before'. The Iron and Steel Act covered fewer firms, leaving
a substantial part of the industry (especially at the engineering
and specialist end) in private hands, dissolved the British Iron
and Steel Federation and the Iron and Steel Board, and left
to the Corporation the task of designing its own organization.[1]
These were fundamental differences, yet initially little seemed
to have been radically changed. This was an illusion created
by the continued existence of the names of the constituent companies. In its *First Report on Organisation*, issued only four days
after Vesting Day,[2] the Corporation revealed that it had been
decided to form 'four Groups, designed to reflect a combination
of geography, product links and economic considerations'.[3] In
effect, to organize the industry on the basis of individual firms,
grouped geographically. This was only marginally different
from what had happened in 1950. Indeed, the plan had a highly
respectable historical ancestry, being—as Vaizey has pointed
out—very much on the lines suggested by Brasserts to Montagu
Norman in 1930[4] and even more closely foreshadowed by C.
Bruce Gardner's elaborate Report of the same year.[5] Despite
a careful examination of possible alternatives,[6] the Organizing
Committee, set up in 1966 under the chairmanship of Lord
Melchett, had enjoyed too little time to formulate a more
fundamental scheme if the Corporation was to be able to fulfil
its objective of being *seen* to take immediate action on the pressing problem of internal organization.[7] Furthermore, proceeding by way of regional groupings was not without its advantages: it would 'simplify inter-works communications and

[1] Vaizey, *History of British Steel*, p. 180.
[2] British Steel Corporation (B.S.C.): *First Report on Organisation*, August
1967 (Cmnd. 3362).
[3] *British Steel*, April 1968, p. 9.
[4] Vaizey, *History of British Steel*, p. 181.
[5] C. Bruce Gardner, *Report on the Structure of the Iron and Steel Industry of Great
Britain incorporating Plans for Rationalisation*, 31 Dec. 1930.
[6] B.I.S.F., *Annual Report for 1966*, p. 1.
[7] *British Steel*, April 1968, p. 8.

would allow a sensible pattern of raw materials and products handling to develop'.[8] Nevertheless, the plan was clearly production oriented—whereas the Corporation itself emphasized the necessity of being 'market oriented'[9]—and in seeking, like the earlier nationalization, to enlist the full co-operation of management by retaining the original companies, it ran the very real risk of encouraging the survival of traditional loyalties rather than fostering 'a new loyalty with pride in the Corporation as a whole'.[10]

The choice of a regional model may also have reflected, as Heal has observed, 'a reluctance by the organizing committee to make full use of the powers which nationalization had provided, for the hope existed in some quarters, even within the committee, that in due course the industry would be returned once again to private enterprise. It would be a comparatively simple matter to restore complete autonomy to the regional groups.'[11] Whatever the precise reasons for the choice of the organizing committee, the result was that Colvilles became part of the Scottish and North-Western Group, under the managing directorship of Mr. T. R. Craig, along with John Summers Ltd. of North Wales, the Lancashire Steel Corporation, and the Monks Hall subsidiary of Richard Thomas & Baldwins. The almost inevitable reaction of *Colvilles' Magazine* was that 'it is clear that the Board [of the Corporation] values the goodwill of long-established company names, especially abroad, and will continue to use them . . .', adding, bravely, 'all of which suggests that Colville customers will continue to deal with Colvilles for a long time to come'.[12]

It was not to be. The creation of geographical groups was simply an interim measure, adopted because it presented the best opportunity of quickly initiating the process of control over what was, in effect, 'a massive merger, resulting in the largest steel business in the free world outside the U.S.A.'[13] It was all very reminiscent of the merger movement that had taken place

[8] Heal, *The Steel Industry*, p. 151.
[9] B.S.C., *Annual Report and Accounts, 1967–8*, p. 5.
[10] The words employed in British Steel Corporation, *Second Report on Organisation*, 11 Mar. 1969. House of Commons Paper No. 163.
[11] Heal, *The Steel Industry*, p. 152.
[12] *Colvilles' Magazine*, Summer 1967, p. 3.
[13] B.S.C., *Annual Report and Accounts, 1967–8*, pp. 5, 38–9.

in Britain at the turn of the century, when many of the 'giant firms' that had come into being were characterized by weak central direction and undeveloped organizational structures, and whose very existence was threatened by bitter internal rivalries.[14] So it was in the early days of the British Steel Corporation. The method of reorganization by regional grouping—given that the management personnel remained essentially unchanged—was not designed 'to dissolve the old parochialism'.[15] Indeed, it could serve to exacerbate it, especially when the organization committee itself declared that 'the spur of competition, other than price between the Groups and between the units below them is ... highly desirable ... The aim should be to create strong technical rivalry between the individual managements in order to secure the cheapest production by the best practices. It is by the reduction of costs and through the continuing improvement of service, quality, and productivity that the commercial success of the Groups will be judged.'[16] The Scottish and North-Western Group interpreted this admonition all too literally, choosing to forget, or even ignore, the ruling that 'individual development schemes submitted by [each Group] ... will be examined at the Head Office on behalf of the Corporation Board as a whole to ensure consistency with the Corporation's overall interest',[17] and in so doing planted a seed which, despite every discouragement, has taken firm root in Scotland's industrial strategy.

In the summer of 1968, only a few weeks after the industrial editor of the *Sunday Times*, in discussing the future of the British Steel Corporation, had observed that 'talk of Scottish projects raises no enthusiasm',[18] a press conference was held by the Scottish and North-Western Group. It was assumed that the purpose of this conference was to announce the findings of a detailed study into the possibility of building an ore terminal at Hunterston, on the Firth of Clyde, capable of handling vessels of up to 200,000 tons (compared with the 28,000-ton

---

[14] P. L. Payne, 'The Emergence of the Large-Scale Company in Great Britain, 1870–1914', *Economic History Review*, 2nd Series, xx (1967), especially pp. 527–36.
[15] To use Heal's apt expression, *The Steel Industry*, p. 154.
[16] *B.S.C., First Report on Organisation.*
[17] *British Steel*, April 1968, p. 9.
[18] *Sunday Times*, 23 June 1968.

TABLE E.1

Pig Iron Production, Output per Furnace and Coke Consumption per Unit of Output: United Kingdom and Scotland, 1955, 1965–1977

(in '000 tons up to and including 1970; thereafter in '000 tonnes)

Year	Production of Pig Iron			Pig Iron, Output per Furnace per Annum		Coke Consumed per Unit of Iron Produced	
	(1) U.K.	(2) Scot.	(3) Scot. % U.K.	(4) U.K.	(5) Scot.	(6) U.K.	(7) Scot.
1955	12,470·0	926·9	7·4	126·4	103·0	0·95	0·88
1965	17,459·9	1,674·8	9·6	262·9	305·6	0·68	0·62
1966	15,709·7	1,313·1	8·4	260·4	282·4	0·67	0·58
1967	15,153·0	1,251·2	8·3	275·1	317·4	0·66	0·57
1968	16,431·7	1,743·5	10·6	303·2	435·9	0·66	0·57
1969	16,389·7	1,908·1	11·4	299·4	414·8	0·65	0·54
1970	17,392·6	1,818·2	10·5	311·0	386·0	0·63	0·57
1971	15,416·3	1,664·3	10·8	302·8	179·9	0·61	0·56
1972	15,316·4	1,571·7	10·3	361·2	385·2	0·58	0·56
1973	16,838·3	1,818·2	10·8	374·4	363·6	0·58	0·55
1974	13,902·6	1,559·3	11·2	347·6	311·9	0·61	0·58
1975	12,131·0	1,000·4	8·2	346·6	333·5	0·61	0·59
1976	13,834·9	1,290·6	9·3	384·3	430·2	0·61	0·58
1977	12,231·8	1,207·3	9·9	382·2	424·3	0·60	0·58

Note: The tonne is the metric tonne of 1,000 kilogrammes = 0·9842 ton.
Source: Iron and Steel: Annual Statistics. (The figures in Cols. (3), (6), and (7) have been calculated from data drawn from this source.)

TABLE E.2

Crude Steel Production and Principal Materials Consumed: United Kingdom and Scotland; and Production by Process, Scotland, 1955, 1963–1977

(in '000 tons up to and including 1970; thereafter in '000 tonnes)

Year	Production of Crude Steel			Proportion (%) of Furnace Burden Composed of						Scottish Production by Process			
				Pig Iron				Scrap				Electric	
				Molten		Cold							
	(1) U.K.	(2) Scot.	(3) Scot./U.K. %	(4) U.K	(5) Scot.	(6) U.K.	(7) Scot.	(8) U.K.	(9) Scot.	(10) Open-Hearth	(11) L.D. Converter	(12) Arc	(13) Induction
1955	19,790·6	2,343·9	11·8	30·4	9·0	10·4	24·1	43·4	53·7	2,218·4	—	100·1	—
1963	22,520·2	2,067·7	9·2	39·5	18·4	6·0	14·8	39·9	53·9	1,856·5	—	205·1	4·8
1964	26,229·9	2,974·2	11·3	40·4	24·5	5·8	13·3	39·4	49·6	2,362·0	333·1	271·6	5·7
1965	27,006·1	3,053·0	11·3	40·5	24·8	5·8	14·6	40·2	48·5	2,217·2	533·5	294·7	5·8
1966	24,315·3	2,677·6	11·0	41·6	26·2	4·5	13·9	40·8	48·2	1,817·1	606·7	246·5	5·8
1967	23,895·2	2,599·7	10·9	41·7	25·5	4·1	13·3	41·5	50·2	1,728·7	623·5	240·5	6·0
1968	25,862·2	3,072·2	11·9	42·2	32·3	3·6	11·4	41·4	43·8	1,985·5	807·0	271·4	6·7
1969	26,422·3	3,296·3	12·5	40·7	32·2	4·2	11·3	42·8	44·7	2,095·6	886·8	307·3	5·0
1970	27,869·2	3,330·3	11·9	40·8	30·5	4·4	13·2	42·8	44·4	2,088·0	904·2	328·3	8·3
1971	24,173·5	2,986·3	12·4	42·9	33·3	4·0	11·2	41·8	44·0	1,721·7	1,035·0	221·9	6·6
1972	25,320·7	3,016·8	11·9	41·6	31·1	4·3	11·6	45·8	43·3	1,813·8	949·7	246·8	5·5
1973	26,649·4	3,250·7	12·2	44·1	42·2	3·8	4·7	41·8	43·1	1,829·6	1,121·2	293·1	6·6
1974	22,426·2	2,638·9	11·8	42·9	42·6	3·5	4·9	43·7	42·8	1,455·1	883·4	293·2	7·2
1975	20,197·9	1,965·4	9·7	41·7	36·4	4·2	4·2	44·7	50·2	1,040·8	549·0	368·6	7·0
1976	22,273·6	1,944·0	8·7	42·3	43·2	4·0	3·9	44·1	43·1	656·5	844·1	437·9	5·5
1977	20,410·7	1,944·7	9·5	42·3	44·2	4·0	5·0	44·2	40·9	976·2	494·0	468·7	5·8

Notes: The tonne is the metric ton of 1,000 kilogrammes = 0·9842 ton.

Col. (1) From and including 1976, the adoption of an amended definition of 'Crude Steel' produces output figures which are not absolutely comparable with those of earlier years, but the difference is not of great significance.

Cols. (4)–(9): Other materials consumed in the furnaces were Oxides, Finishings, Fluxes, and Fettling Materials.

Cols. (10)–(13): A number of processes of minor importance have been omitted.

Source: Iron and Steel: Annual Statistics. (The figures in Cols (3)–(9) have been *calculated* from data drawn from this source.)

vessels to which General Terminus Quay was restricted).[19] Instead, the meeting became the platform from which the Group announced its proposals for a £300 million fully integrated iron and steel works on an adjacent site, a plant with an ultimate capacity of some 5·0–6·0 million ingot tons, well beyond the 3·3 million tons a year which the Benson Committee had suggested was an appropriate size for the Scottish common steel industry in 1975.[20] The assumption underlying the scheme was that the Corporation's total capacity in 1983 would be a minimum of 35 million ingot tons and that Scotland should share in this expansion to the extent of producing at least 15–16 per cent of the national output. These ambitious proposals were totally unexpected.[21] They 'undoubtedly took the B.S.C. headquarters by surprise', and had they been accepted would have distorted the Corporation's maturing plans for a national and co-ordinated development strategy. Even at an 80 per cent operating rate an integrated works of the size contemplated would have been capable of supporting a finishing capacity well above the level of sales attained in the seventies (see Table E.2, Column 2, for actual ingot outputs; finished steel deliveries were, of course, commensurately lower, running at about 74 per cent of the ingot weight).[22] The implementation of the

[19] This episode has been examined by Heal, *The Steel Industry*, p. 154; K. Warren, 'Coastal Steelworks: A Case for Argument', *The Three Banks Review*, No. 82 (June 1969), pp. 36–7; and Chris Baur, 'The Future of Steel in Scotland', *British Steel*, Autumn 1974, pp. 16–17. This account rests on these sources.

[20] B.I.S.F., *The Steel Industry: The Stage I Report of the Development Co-ordinating Committee* [The Benson Committee] (July 1966), p. 79. The Benson Committee was set up by the Executive Committee of the B.I.S.F. to indicate how best the industry might be rationalized if it were to remain in private ownership. The report was given a qualified welcome by Colvilles. See *Colvilles' Magazine*, Autumn 1966, p. 7, and particularly Colvilles Ltd., Chairman's Statement for 1966, pp. 21–2. T. R. Craig emphasized that 'even at present Colvilles' annual ingot capacity approaches [the Benson Committee's estimate of Scotland's annual steel-making capacity of upwards of 3·3 million ingot tons] and with only marginal capital expenditure, the Group's annual capacity could be raised to more than 4 million tons ... It is a fact that additional modern ingot capacity could be provided by Colvilles at a lower capital cost than anywhere else in Britain.'

[21] It will be recalled that Colvilles' earlier development schemes were based on the assumption that Scottish ingot production should represent about 14 per cent of the national total and it was this figure with which Sir Robert MacLean prefaced his argument for a strip mill (see above, p. 374).

[22] See J. A. Allen, *Studies in Innovation in the Steel and Chemical Industries* (Manchester: Manchester University Press, 1967), pp. 216–17.

scheme would have been even more financially disastrous than the strip mill scheme and the social effects would have been incalculable. 'Unless very long hauls to the English market became more economical or the plant [had] such low overall costs that it [enjoyed] a large and profitable export business', construction of the new coastal works would have involved writing off 'most of the mid-Lanarkshire iron and steel complex where all but a fraction of the £116 million invested in Scottish steel between 1960 and 1966 was spent and which [employed] almost all the Scottish steelworkers.'[23] Any realistic assessment of future demand trends would have demonstrated that the scheme was just not feasible in the context of the late sixties and early seventies. Ever since the war, the Federation, the Iron and Steel Board and the individual firms had experienced the failure of sales to match the projected targets: capacity was perpetually well above the rates of utilization and nowhere more so than in Scotland.[24] Technically, there may have been much to commend the scheme but its principal weakness was its comparative neglect of demand factors,[25] transportation costs, and the social costs which had played such a major role in the assessment of previous projects.

It was only later—when Scottish, and indeed British, steel production obstinately failed to maintain the upward trend of the late sixties (see Table E.2)—that the unreality of the plan was fully exposed, but at the time of its announcement, the idea of a very large integrated steel works on the Ayrshire coast was seized upon by Scottish nationalists and by leading theoretical planners to become the centrepiece of a new grand strategy for the industrial renewal of Central Scotland. This concept is perhaps best exemplified by the 'Oceanspan' scheme propounded by the Scottish Council (Development and Industry) which

[23] Warren, 'Coastal Steelworks', p. 37.

[24] See *Report of the Benson Committee*, pp. 66–8; Iron and Steel Board, *Annual Report for 1965*, p. 11.

[25] Though even this was doubted by some, not unsympathetic observers. See J. Busby, *The British Steel Industry and its Expansion Plans in Scotland* (North Ayrshire Coastal Development Committee, October 1971), p. 4. John Busby was Convener of the North Ayrshire Coastal Development Committee's Technical Sub-Committee and a member of the staff of the Centre for Industrial Innovation at the University of Strathclyde. He claimed that the scheme could expect to lose up to £1,500 million over the period of operation, largely because it failed to exploit new processes such as direct reduction.

envisaged using the deepwater berthage of Hunterston to establish massive steel-making and oil-processing industries.[26] Sceptics may have been unconvinced but 'the idea could not be quietly dropped',[27] and to the infant British Steel Corporation it smacked of a pre-emptive bid calculated to enlist the vociferous support of all facets of Scottish opinion and harness the powerful political pressures which had contributed to the success of the campaign for a Scottish strip mill.

It is improbable that the Scottish and North-Western Group had anticipated such a furore. They had perhaps seen the *ore terminal* at Hunterston as a potent means of curing the 'mineral thrombosis' which had retarded Colvilles' growth and development for several decades and which annually was becoming more serious. With its raw material position secured, the Scottish steel industry had every prospect of forging ahead. It had every right to expect to do so. As a well informed commentator was later to argue,

Contrary to a common opinion, sedulously fostered in some quarters, the Scottish steel industry was by no means falling apart and held together with string when it was nationalized. It was in very good shape and well up to the then technological position ... the Scottish blast furnaces held the record as they still do in Britain for running out pig iron at the least cost in coke. And the steel furnaces were notable, as they still are, for their low conversion costs. Nor was it only that the works were better performers. The industry was far better 'rationalized', with all the works allotted appropriate duties, with no overlaps and redundancies, than the general in Britain. Moreover, by this time the industry had a very clear idea of where it was going.[28]

But other regions also entertained expensive ambitions. Within six months of the Hunterston announcement, the Midland Group unveiled its development programme: £312 millions would be spent at Scunthorpe, Sheffield, and Workington in what was in effect an enlarged version of the old United Steel Companies' 'Anchor' scheme.[29] These manifestations of

[26] Scottish Council (Development and Industry), *Oceanspan 2. A Study of Port and Industrial Development in Western Europe* (October 1971); C. Baur, 'The Future of Steel in Scotland', pp. 16–17.
[27] Warren, 'Coastal Steelworks', p. 37.
[28] David Murray, 'Scottish Steel. In the Melting Pot? Or the Graveyard?' *Scotland*, November 1972, p. 20. Murray had previously written at some length on the effects of the pricing policy of the National Coal Board on the Scottish iron and steel industry in *Colvilles' Magazine*, Winter 1962–3, pp. 2–6.
[29] For the Anchor scheme, see Heal, *The Steel Industry*, pp. 119–20.

regional exuberance sorely embarrassed the Corporation's head office and undoubtedly accelerated the work of its committee on reorganization, under the chairmanship of Dr. H. M. Finniston, who found that the system of multi-product groups 'impede[d] rationalization and the optimum utilization of the Corporation's assets'. It was felt that 'Development of new capacity must . . . be planned on a product basis' and that there was therefore a strong case for reorganizing the Corporation's activities and dissolving the company structure inherited under the Iron and Steel Act of 1967.[30] The Minister of Power readily agreed, and gave the proposals his blessing, if not his formal approval, which awaited the publication of a Third Report on Organisation. This duly appeared in December 1969 and received the Minister's statutory consent.[31] The group structure was to be replaced by a system of product divisions: General Steels, Special Steels, Strip Mills, Tubes, Constructional Engineering, and Chemicals; the old companies were swept away, their names were formally abolished[32] and the Corporation ceased to present separate financial accounts for what had been, in effect, its subsidiaries. With the creation of the new divisional structure, on 29 March 1970, Colvilles Ltd. passed out of existence and its works were parcelled out among the product divisions. As David Murray commented bitterly:

With the control of the strip mills gone to Cardiff, of the ordinary steel works to Middlesbrough, of the special steel works to Sheffield, and of the tube works to Corby, the steel industry in Scotland is now no more than a collection of operating dependencies. The big Colville combine which, in the nature of things, acted for the whole industry in many questions, is now be-headed and dismembered.[33]

And in saying this, Murray echoed the thoughts of many who had devoted their working lives to the firm established by David Colville nearly one hundred years earlier.

[30] B.S.C., *Second Report on Organisation*, March 1969, House of Commons Paper No. 163. See also *British Steel*, November 1969, pp. 2–3.
[31] B.S.C., *Third Report on Organisation*, December 1969. House of Commons Paper No. 60.
[32] By the Steel Companies (Vesting) Order, 1970, which came into operation on 29 Mar. 1970.
[33] David Murray, 'Scottish Steel', p. 22. In fact, the General Steels Division was based in Glasgow. See *British Steel*, October 1971, pp. 21–5.

Yet all had not been lost, as it might have been had the industry *not* been nationalized. Colvilles could not have continued in its old form carrying the suffocating debt incurred in the building of the strip mill; nor, it may be speculated, would there have been any overwhelming *economic* argument to do anything other than to permit the Group to wither away had there not been a strip mill and all the ancillary investment associated with that decision. In short, the future of the Colville Group under private enterprise—despite its acknowledged exploitation of the technological possibilities—must have been highly questionable. Warren has emphasized that

informed industry estimates, made in 1967, suggest that, although it will still be much the smallest of the five operations, Ravenscraig/Gartcosh will expand less between 1966 and 1975 than the rest of the strip mill industry. In the following five years its growth may be very much less. Strip mill output there in 1975 will probably be a little over ¾ million tons, about 38 per cent of the 1966 total of the Steel Company of Wales, and only just over 19 per cent of the four million tons suggested as desirable for the strip mill unit by the mid-seventies. Capital charges are lower than at Port Talbot or Newport, but the N.C.B. move to more realistic pricing has already pushed up Colvilles' fuel bill by £1 million, marketing hauls are long and the whole complex lies inland.[34]

Under these circumstances, it is difficult to believe that Colvilles would have been successful in going to the capital market for further funds, without which liquidation would have been almost inevitable. Yet under the Heritage Programme, the British Steel Corporation authorized the expenditure of about £60 million to Ravenscraig in the early seventies, and allotted to this works the twin roles of a major producer of hot rolled coil and of a supplier of ingots and slabs to the Scottish works in the General Steels Division.[35]

The B.S.C.'s Heritage Programme was designed to identify and remove the weakness in the inherited businesses and to develop those assets which were strong. Like the Corporation's initial organization, the original capital programme also represented a series of interim measures. The object was to keep

[34] K. Warren, *Steel Sheet Industry*, p. 294.
[35] The details are summarized in *British Steel*, January 1972, p. 17. By the end of March 1974, the cost of the implementation of the scheme was estimated at nearly £100 million. See B.S.C., *Annual Report and Accounts*, 1973–4, pp. 8–9.

things going and yet not to prejudice any long-term policy that might emerge from the deep-seated review that was contemplated from the outset and which took place in 1971–2. The results of this review were announced by the Secretary of State for Trade and Industry on 21 December 1972, and published in a White Paper two months later.[36] The steel industry in Scotland was to be modernized and expanded. All open-hearth furnaces at Clyde Iron/Clydebridge, Lanarkshire, Dalzell, Glengarnock, and Ravenscraig were to close by the end of the decade but investment in modern plant would raise B.S.C.'s steel-making capacity in Scotland from its current 3·7 million tonnes to $4\frac{1}{2}$ million tonnes by the early 1980s. The basic oxygen steel plant at Ravenscraig was to be brought up to a capacity of about 3·2 million tonnes a year; there was to be a progressive development of a new electric arc plant of up to 1 million tonnes capacity at Hallside and this plant would 'probably be supported at some stage by a direct reduction plant producing pelletized iron at Hunterston'. 'Substantial' investment at Clydesdale Tube Works and Dalzell's plate mill was contemplated, and finishing operations at Glengarnock were to continue. By these means, the hope was expressed that 'Scotland will ... remain an attractive location for engineering and other steel-using industries'.[37]

Such was the plan, and although its implementation is taking far longer than had originally been contemplated—largely because the industry has been passing through a period of deep depression (ingot production in 1975 was at its lowest level since the mid-fifties. See Tables 11.6 and E.2)—the Corporation has not deviated greatly from it, despite frighteningly escalating costs. In 1973 work started on the development of a terminal at Hunterston for discharging ore and coal designed to accept ore carriers of up to 350,000 tonnes capacity. The terminal is expected to become operational during the early part of 1978 in order to coincide with the completion of the key elements of the Ravenscraig expansion programme. In the same year, Britain's first direct reduction plants will be operating at Hunterston, thus enabling the Corporation 'to come to grips with a technology which is already the dominant iron-making

[36] B.S.C., *Ten Year Development Strategy*, 8 Feb. 1973 (Cmnd. 5226).
[37] Ibid., para. 44–5.

method in the developing countries of the world'.[38] Whether these and related developments at Hunterston[39] presage the ultimate fulfilment of the Scottish and North-Western Group's 1968 programme, it is too early to judge. Certainly, once established, the steel industry has always shown a stubborn antipathy to relocation. Hunterston can develop only at the cost of employment opportunities in Lanarkshire, and currently there seems to be considerable reluctance to pay such a price.[40] Even the phasing out of the open-hearth furnaces at Clydebridge, Dalzell, Lanarkshire, and Ravenscraig has been postponed, though Lord Beswick's second report on B.S.C.'s closure proposals broadly confirmed the Corporation's policy and restated the Corporation's long-term aim of developing Hunterston as an integrated works with blast furnaces, basic oxygen steel-making, continuous casting, and mills.[41]

Perhaps, after all, the Scottish steel industry will enjoy, in David Murray's words, a 'glorious resurrection'.[42] The hope that it might has undoubtedly been strengthened by yet another convulsive administrative reorganization whereby in March 1976, the structure of product divisions was superseded by a structure in which the Corporation's main iron- and steel-making activities were grouped into five manufacturing divisions, each based on one of the major steel-making areas under the B.S.C.'s *Ten Year Development Strategy*. One of these new divisions was the Scottish division. That which was torn

[38] Frank Fitzgerald, 'Direct Reduction at Hunterston', *British Steel*, Spring 1976, pp. 20–3. Direct reduction is a continuous process which reduces iron pellets and raw ore to a highly metallized product (over 90 per cent Fe) with a controlled carbon content, which can be charged directly to steel-making units.

[39] In 1974 Hunterston was being examined as a possible location for a £25–30 million electric arc furnace with a capacity of 1 million tonnes a year and some thought was being given to siting a £40–50 million product mill on the coast. Baur, 'The Future of Steel in Scotland', p. 18.

[40] *The Guardian*, 'Steel Complex May Be "White Elephant"', 14 Apr. 1975.

[41] Lord Beswick, Minister of State in the Department of Industry, announced his findings on the Corporation's closure policy on 6 Aug. 1975. The fullest reports were contained in *British Steel*, Autumn 1975, pp. 19–22, *Steel News*, 21 Aug. 1975, pp. 6–12. It attracted considerable press comment. The *Sunday Times*, 10 Aug. 1975, asked pertinently 'whether it is reasonable to expect the Corporation to bear the cost of delaying the closure [of open-hearth plant], and keeping open plants which it no longer really needs for "social reasons"'. Cf. above, p. 405.

[42] Murray, 'Scottish Steel', p. 21.

asunder in 1970 has essentially been reformed. 'A system of iron and steel divisions, each possessing its own commercial and plant loading responsibilities, is bound to encourage divisional managements to manufacture what is most convenient and profitable from their own point of view, rather than what the overall market situation dictates.'[43] The logic of Sir John Craig's policy has been reaffirmed, the separateness and versatility of the Scottish steel industry recognized by the Benson Committee in 1966 has once again been acknowledged. It must be a good omen.

[43] *British Steel*, Autumn 1975, pp. 12–14, Spring 1976, pp. 14–15; *Steel News*, 21 Aug. 1975, p. 4.

Select Bibliography

A. MANUSCRIPT COLLECTIONS

The majority of the surviving records of the companies which constituted the Colville Group were originally located and surveyed by the author in the early nineteen-sixties. They were then scattered among the various offices and works of the Group. With the nationalization of the iron and steel industry in 1967, the records passed into the possession of the British Steel Corporation and many of them are now held at the British Steel Corporation's Scottish Regional Record Centre in Glasgow.

B.S.C.: SCOTTISH REGIONAL RECORDS CENTRE

Among the more important items in this comprehensive collection, listed by companies, are:

David Colville & Sons, Ltd.

Minute books, 1895–1935; agenda books and papers relating to extraordinary and general meetings, 1895–1934, and to board meetings, 1925–36; private journals and ledgers, 1895–1928, balance sheets, 1882–1922, 1924, 1927, 1931; miscellaneous account and pay books, 1900–26; Dalzell steelworks erection account books, 1879–1909; steel works output books (Dalzell and Clydebridge), 1918–55; register of documents, 1871–1924; miscellaneous letter books, 1895–1916; income tax returns, schedules and statements, 1899–1914; register of shareholders, 1895–1935, share certificates, 1895–1934; and papers concerning the moratorium of 1931. Of great significance are the hundreds of accounts and papers relating to the establishment and acquisition of subsidiary companies and the purchases and amalgamations that resulted in the creation of Colvilles, Ltd. and what became known as the Colville Group in the nineteen-thirties. These include extensive files of memoranda, letters, agreements, and licences concerning Fullwood Foundry Co., Ltd., Clydebridge Steel Co., Ltd., the Glengarnock Iron and Steel Co., Ltd., Archibald Russell & Co., Ltd., the Clyde Alloy Steel Co., Ltd., Smith & McLean, Ltd., the Carnlough Lime Co., Ltd., the Clyde Ironworks of James Dunlop & Co., Ltd., the Steel Company of Scotland, Ltd., and the Lanarkshire Steel Co., Ltd. The acquisition by David Colville & Sons of Clydebridge and Glengarnock during the First World War generated a large correspondence with the Ministry of Munitions and a series of draft and final agreements between David Colville & Sons and the Ministry. The protracted negotiations that took place between the various English and Scottish steelmasters, the firm of H. A.

Brassert & Co., and C. Bruce Gardner, managing director of the Securities Management Trust, in the twenties and early thirties are covered by numerous files, not the least informative of which contain the correspondence between David Colville & Sons and their legal advisers, Maclay, Murray & Spens, and their bankers, the National Bank of Scotland.

Colvilles, Ltd.

Minute books, 1931–67; agendas and papers, 1931–47; production and cost charts, 1931–6; development files (these include copies of the company's development plans and the correspondence between the company and the British Iron and Steel Federation, the Iron and Steel Board, and the Ministry of Power to which the plans gave rise), 1938–70; and newspaper cutting books, 1936–7, 1938–9. In addition, many files (often labelled 'S.I.S.M.' [Scottish Iron and Steel Merger]) contain the papers generated by Colvilles' attempts to consolidate and rationalize the Scottish steel industry in the nineteen-thirties. Among the more important are those files containing the company's correspondence with Maclay, Murray & Spens, Sir William McLintock, C. Bruce Gardner, Sir James Lithgow, and Stewarts & Lloyds, Ltd.

Smith & McLean, Ltd.

Minute books, 1895–1900; private ledgers, 1895–1916; letter books 1895–1914; production and financial abstracts, 1880–1935; reports and accounts, 1894, 1896–1941; and papers relating to the purchase of Smith & McLean, Ltd. by David Colville & Sons, Ltd., in 1919.

Lanarkshire Steel Co., Ltd.

Minute books, 1889–1954; ledgers, 1897–1957; journals, 1897–1957; analysis of capital expenditure, 1898–1954. Bound in the minute books are miscellaneous agreements, special resolutions, and other memoranda.

Steel Company of Scotland, Ltd.

Minute books, 1872–1947; the company's first and fifth letter books, 1871–2, 1887–1909; copies of early legal agreements, including those with Charles William Siemens and Gilchrist Thomas for patent working, 1872–1880; production and inventory records (Blochairn), 1898–1939; sales records (Hallside and Blochairn), 1897–1925, and a collection of the company's printed notices and forms, together with press cuttings relating to the company, 1872–1934.

Board of Conciliation and Arbitration of the Manufactured Steel Trade of the West of Scotland

Minute books, 1890–1922.

UNIVERSITY OF GLASGOW ARCHIVES

William Dixon, Ltd.
 Ledgers and journals, 1931–52; production and sales records, 1929–58; private letter books, 1873–1906; numerous technical records containing analyses of fuels, pig iron, limestone, and blast furnace slags, and blast furnace report books, 1927–58.

Sir Andrew McCance
 Private papers, 1922–63 (these papers are closed until the death of Sir Andrew McCance).

BANK OF ENGLAND ARCHIVES

Numerous files among the archives of the Bank of England contain information on the negotiations conducted during the early thirties to achieve the rationalization of the Scottish steel industry. The majority of the more important documents are contained in the 'S.I.S.M.' files of Colvilles, Ltd., but the additional correspondence in the Bank of England files reveals more fully the Bank's role in encouraging the negotiations from which, in Scotland, reorganization ultimately emerged. The files most relevant to the Scottish iron and steel industry are as follows:

B.I.D. [Bankers Industrial Development Co.] 1/58: 'Steel—Scotland—Lithgow'.
B.I.D. 1/60: 'Scottish Iron and Steel Merger: Costs'.
B.I.D. 1/61: 'Scottish Steel Reorganisation—Colvilles, Lanarkshire Steel and the Steel Company of Scotland', 1931–4.
S.M.T. [Securities Management Trust] 2/56: 'Chairman's Papers: Bankers Industrial Development Co., Ltd., 3 April 1932–28 June 1945'.
S.M.T. 3/101: 'C. Bruce Gardner—Steel—Scottish'.

BRITISH LIBRARY OF POLITICAL AND ECONOMIC SCIENCE

Beatrice and Sidney Webb
 Trade Union MSS: Iron and Steel Trades, Collection E, Section A.23.

IN THE POSSESSION OF THE AUTHOR

H. A. Brassert
 Report to Lord Weir of Eastwood on the Manufacture of Iron and Steel by Wm. Baird & Co., Ltd., David Colville & Sons, Ltd., James Dunlop & Co., Ltd., Steel Company of Scotland, Ltd., and Stewarts & Lloyds, Ltd. by H. A. Brassert & Co., 16 May, 1929 [The Brassert Report]. (Lent by Sir Andrew McCance. A

copy of this report has been deposited in the British Steel Corporation's Scottish Regional Records Centre.)

Sir John Craig
Private papers, 1888–1950. (Lent by Mr. T. R. Craig.)

Etna Iron & Steel Co., Ltd.
Contract of co-partnery constituting the Etna Iron & Steel Co., 1889, and papers relating to the dissolution of the original co-partnery and the conversion of the firm into a private limited company, 1914. (Gift of Mr. James Kerr.)

C. Bruce Gardner
Report on the Structure of the Iron and Steel Industry of Great Britain, incorporating Plans for Rationalisation, 31 December, 1930. (Gift of Sir Andrew McCance.)

Lanarkshire Steel Co., Ltd.
Loose-leaf book of statistical and other data. (Lent by the late Mr. R. C. Dymock.)

B. OFFICIAL PUBLICATIONS

Board of Trade, *Report of the Departmental Committee on the Position of the Iron and Steel Trades after the War*, Cd. 9071, 1918.

Report of the Import Duties Advisory Committee on the Present Position and Future Development of the Iron and Steel Industry, Cmd. 5507, 1937.

Reports by the British Iron and Steel Federation and the Joint Iron Council to the Minister of Supply, Cmd. 6811, 1946.

British Steel Corporation, *First Report on Organisation*, Cmd. 3362, 1967.

C. BOOKS AND ARTICLES

ANDREWS, P. W. S., and ELIZABETH BRUNNER. *Capital Development in Steel: A Study of the United Steel Companies, Ltd.* Oxford: Blackwell, 1951.

BARNABY, N. 'On Iron and Steel for Shipbuilding', *Transactions of the Institution of Naval Architects*, xvi (1875).

BAUR, CHRIS. 'The Future of Steel in Scotland', *British Steel* (Autumn 1974).

BIRKETT, M. S. 'The Iron and Steel Trades During the War', *Journal of the Royal Statistical Society*, lxxxiii, Part III (1920).

BREMNER, DAVID. *The Industries of Scotland. Their Rise, Progress and Present Condition.* Edinburgh: A. & C. Black (1869).

BRITISH IRON AND STEEL FEDERATION. *Steel: The Facts.* London: B.I.S.F., n.d. (c. 1965).

—— *The Steel Industry: The Stage 1 Report of the Development Co-ordinating Committee* [The Benson Committee]. London: B.I.S.F., 1966.

BROWN, A. J. YOUNGSON. 'The Scots Coal Industry, 1854–1886.' D.Litt. Thesis, University of Aberdeen, 1952.

BURN, DUNCAN L. *The Economic History of Steel Making, 1867–1939.* Cambridge: Cambridge University Press, 1940.

—— *The Steel Industry, 1939–1959.* Cambridge: Cambridge University Press, 1961.

BURNHAM, T. H., and G. O. HOSKINS. *Iron and Steel in Britain, 1870–1930.* London: Allen & Unwin, 1943.

BYRES, T. J. 'The Scottish Economy during the "Great Depression", 1873–1896, with Special Reference to the Heavy Industries of the South-West'. B.Litt. Thesis, University of Glasgow, 1962.

CAMPBELL, R. H. 'Statistics of the Scottish Pig Iron Trade, 1830 to 1865', *Proceedings of the West of Scotland Iron and Steel Institute,* lxiv (1956–7).

—— 'Early Malleable Iron Production in Scotland', *Business History,* iv (1961–2).

—— *Carron Company.* Edinburgh: Oliver & Boyd, 1961.

CARNEGIE, A. QUINTIN. 'The Application of a Geared Steam Turbine to Rolling Mill Driving', *Journal of the West of Scotland Iron and Steel Institute,* xviii (1911).

CARR, J. C., and W. TAPLIN. *A History of the British Steel Industry.* Oxford: Blackwell, 1962.

CARVEL, J. L. *The Coltness Iron Company.* Edinburgh: privately printed for the Coltness Iron Co., 1948.

CHECKLAND, S. G. *The Mines of Tharsis.* London: Allen & Unwin, 1967.

—— *Scottish Banking: A History, 1695–1973.* Glasgow: Collins, 1975.

CHESTER, SIR NORMAN. *The Nationalisation of British Industry, 1945–51.* London: H.M.S.O., 1975.

CLAPHAM, SIR JOHN. *An Economic History of Modern Britain,* 3 volumes. Cambridge: Cambridge University Press, 1926–39.

CLAY, SIR HENRY. *Lord Norman.* London: Macmillan, 1957.

COLVILLE, DAVID, & SONS LTD., *Jubilee of David Colville & Sons Ltd., 1871–1921.* Glasgow, David Colville & Sons Ltd., 1921.

CORMACK, D. S. 'An Economic History of Shipbuilding and Marine Engineering (with Special Reference to the West of Scotland)'. Ph.D. Thesis, University of Glasgow, 1929.

CORRINS, R. D. 'The Great Hot-Blast Affair', *Industrial Archaeology,* vii (1970).

—— 'William Baird & Company, Coal and Iron Masters, 1830–1914.' Ph.D. Thesis, University of Strathclyde, 1974.

CUNNISON, J., and J. B. S. GILFILLAN (eds.). *The City of Glasgow (The Third Statistical Account of Scotland,* vol. v). Glasgow: Collins, 1958.

DAVIES, P. N. *The Trade Makers. Elder Dempster in West Africa, 1852–1972.* London: Allen & Unwin, 1973.

DAY, ST. JOHN V. 'The Iron and Steel Industries', in British Association, *Notices of Some of the Principal Manufactures of the West of Scotland*. Glasgow: British Association, 1876.

DENNY, WILLIAM. 'On Steel in the Shipbuilding Yard', *Transactions of the Institution of Naval Architects*, xxi (1880).

ERICKSON, CHARLOTTE. *British Industrialists: Steel and Hosiery, 1850–1950*. Cambridge University Press, 1959.

FAIRGRIEVE, J. G., and J. GIBSON. 'Basic Open Hearth Practice in Scotland', in Iron and Steel Institute, *Special Report*, No. 22 (1938).

GALE, W. K. V. *The British Iron and Steel Industry*. Newton Abbot: David & Charles, 1967.

GIBSON, I. F. 'The Economic History of the Scottish Iron and Steel Industry, 1830–1880.' Ph.D. Thesis, University of London, 1955.

——'The Establishment of the Scottish Steel Industry', *Scottish Journal of Political Economy*, v (1958).

HAMILTON, HENRY. *The Industrial Revolution in Scotland*. Oxford: Oxford University Press, 1932.

HAND, T. H. 'Progress in British Rolling-Mill Practice'. *Journal of the Iron and Steel Institute*, cxi (1925).

HANNAH, LESLIE. *The Rise of the Corporate Economy*. London: Methuen, 1976.

——(ed). *Management Strategy and Business Development*. London: Macmillan, 1975.

HATCH, F. H. *The Iron and Steel Industry of the United Kingdom under War Conditions*. London: privately published, 1919.

HEAL, D. W. *The Steel Industry in Post-War Britain*. Newton Abbot: David & Charles, 1974.

HODGE, JOHN. *Workman's Cottage to Windsor Castle*. London: Sampson Low, Marston & Co., 1931.

HUME, JOHN R., and MICHAEL S. MOSS. *Beardmore: The History of a Scottish Industrial Giant*. London: Heinemann Educational Books, 1979.

Iron and Coal Trades Review. *A Technical Survey of the Colville Group of Companies*. I.C.T.R., Special Supplement, undated (c. 1957).

Iron and Steel Board, *Development in the Iron and Steel Industry, 1953–1958*. London: H.M.S.O., 1955.

——*Development in the Iron and Steel Industry: Special Report, 1957*. London: H.M.S.O., 1975.

——*Development in the Iron and Steel Industry*. London: H.M.S.O., 1961.

KEELING, B. S., and A. E. WRIGHT. *The Development of the Modern British Steel Industry*. London: Longmans, 1964.

KILBY, J. A. 'The Production of Steel Plates in Scotland', *Journal of the Iron and Steel Institute*, clxvi (1950).

KOHN, C. FERDINAND. *Iron and Steel Manufacture: A Series of Papers ... with Descriptions of the Principal Iron and Steel Works in Great Britain and the Continent*. Glasgow and Edinburgh: William Mackenzie, 1869.

LAMBERTON, ANDREW. 'Improvements in Plate Rolling Mills', *Journal of the Iron and Steel Institute*, lxxvi (1908).

LANG, ERNEST F. 'The Old Lancashire Steel Company', *Memoirs and Proceedings of the Manchester Literary and Philosophical Society*, lxxxii (1937–8).

LUCAS, A. F. *Industrial Reconstruction and the Control of Competition: The British Experiments*. London: Longmans, 1937.

McCANCE, SIR ANDREW. 'Production in the Steel Industry: Its Growth, Distribution and Future Course.' Middlesbrough: Cleveland Scientific and Technical Institute, 1950.

McCLOSKEY, DONALD N. *Economic Maturity and Entrepreneurial Decline: British Iron and Steel, 1870–1913*. Cambridge, Mass.: Harvard University Press, 1973.

McLEAN, A. (ed.). *Handbook on the Industries of Glasgow and the West of Scotland*. Glasgow, British Association, 1901.

MACROSTY, H. W. *The Trust Movement in British Industry*. London: Longmans, 1907.

MARSHALL, JOHN D. *Furness and the Industrial Revolution*. Barrow-in-Furness: Barrow-in-Furness Library and Museums Committee, 1958.

MAXWELL, I. S. SCOTT. 'Clyde Iron Works Blast Furnaces', *Colvilles' Magazine* (Summer 1946).

MILLER, ANDREW. *The Rise and Progress of Coatbridge*. Glasgow: Robertson, 1864.

MILLER, T. R. *The Monkland Tradition*. London: Nelson, 1958.

MUIR, AUGUSTUS. *The Story of Shotts: A Short History of the Shotts Iron Co. Ltd.* Edinburgh: Shotts Iron Co. Ltd., n.d. (*c.* 1954).

MURRAY, DAVID. 'Scottish Steel. In the Melting Pot? Or the Graveyard?' *Scotland* (November 1972).

NORTH, G. A. *Teesside's Economic Heritage*. Cleveland: County Council of Cleveland, 1975.

PARKER, WILLIAM. 'Use of Mild Steel for Marine Boilers', *Transactions of the Institution of Naval Architects*, xix (1878).

——'On the Peculiarities of Behaviour of Steel Plates Supplied for the Boilers of the Imperial Russian Yacht, *Livadia*', *Transactions of the Institution of Naval Architects*, xxii (1881).

PARKINSON, J. R. *The Economics of Shipbuilding in the United Kingdom*. Cambridge: Cambridge University Press, 1960.

PAYNE, PETER L. (ed.). *Studies in Scottish Business History*. London: Cass, 1967.

——'Iron and Steel Manufactures' in D. H. Aldcroft (ed.), *The Development of British Industry and Foreign Competition, 1875–1914*. London: Allen & Unwin, 1968.

PERCY, JOHN. *Metallurgy: Iron and Steel*. London: Murray, 1864.

POLE, W. *The Life of Sir William Siemens*. London: John Murray, 1888.

PRICE, J. 'On Iron and Steel as Constructive Materials for Ships', *Proceedings of the Institution of Mechanical Engineers* (1881).

Select Bibliography 435

PUGH, SIR ARTHUR. *Men of Steel*. London: Iron and Steel Trades Confederation, 1951.

RAVENHILL, J. R. 'The Increased Use of Steel in Shipbuilding and Marine Engineering', *Transactions of the Institution of Naval Architects*, xxi (1880).

READER, W. J. *Imperial Chemical Industries: A History*. 2 vols. Oxford: Oxford University Press, 1971, 1975.

REID, J. M. *James Lithgow, Master of Work*. London: Hutchinson, 1964.

RICHARDSON, H. W., and J. M. BASS. 'The Profitability of the Consett Iron Company Before 1914', *Business History*, vii (1965).

RILEY, JAMES, 'On Steel for Shipbuilding as Supplied to the Royal Navy', *Transactions of the Institution of Naval Architects*, xvii (1876).

—— 'On Recent Improvements in the Method of the Manufacture of Open-Hearth Steel', *Journal of the Iron and Steel Institute* (1884).

—— 'The Rise and Progress of the Scotch Steel Trade', *Journal of the Iron and Steel Institute* (1885).

—— 'Presidential Address', *Journal of the West of Scotland Iron and Steel Institute*, i (1894).

—— 'Notes on Modern Steel-Works Machinery', *Proceedings of the Institution of Mechanical Engineers* (1895).

—— 'The Use of Fluid Metal in the Open-Hearth Furnace', *Journal of the Iron and Steel Institute*, lvii (1900).

ROSS, G. W. *The Nationalization of Steel*. London: MacGibbon & Kee, 1965.

SAYERS, R. S. *The Bank of England, 1891–1944*, 3 vols. Cambridge: Cambridge University Press, 1976.

SCOPES, SIR FREDERICK. *The Development of Corby Works*. Privately printed for Stewarts & Lloyds, 1968.

SCOTT, J. D. *Vickers: A History*. London: Weidenfeld & Nicolson, 1962.

SIMPSON, M. L. 'Steel Works—A Twenty-One Years' Review', *Journal of the West of Scotland Iron and Steel Institute*, xxi (1913–14).

STEWARTS & LLOYDS. *Stewarts and Lloyds, 1903–1953*. Privately printed for Stewarts & Lloyds, n.d. (*c.* 1954).

Tariff Commission. *Report of the Tariff Commission*, vol. i: *The Iron and Steel Trades*. London: Published for the Tariff Commission by P. S. King, 1904.

TEW, J. H. B. 'Costs, Prices, and Investment in the British Iron and Steel Industries, 1924–37. Ph.D. Thesis, University of Cambridge, 1941.

TEW, BRIAN. 'Reports on the Iron and Steel Industry', *Economic Journal*, lvi (1946).

THOMSON, GEORGE (ed.). *The County of Lanark (The Third Statistical Account of Scotland*, vol. viii). Glasgow: Collins, 1960.

VAIZEY, JOHN. *The History of British Steel*. London: Weidenfeld & Nicolson, 1974.

WARREN, KENNETH. 'The Sheffield Rail Trades, 1861–1930: An Episode in the Locational History of the British Steel Industry', *Transactions and Papers of the Institute of British Geographers*, Publication No. 34 (1964).

—— 'Locational Problems of the Scottish Iron and Steel Industry', *Scottish Geographical Magazine*, vol. lxxxi (1965).

—— 'Coastal Steelworks: A Case for Argument', *The Three Banks Review*, No. 82 (June 1969).

—— *The British Iron and Steel Sheet Industry Since 1840*. London: Bell, 1970.

WILSON, CHARLES. *A Man and His Times: A Memoir of Sir Ellis Hunter*. London: Newman Neame, n.d. (*c.* 1968).

Index

259n, 296, 305n; evidence to Tariff
Commission, 51
McCracken, John, 261, 314n
Macdiarmid, A. C., 182, 200, 207
McGavin & Thompson, 12
McGeown, Patrick, 258n
McGowan, Sir Harry, 167, 169
MacHarg, A. S., 183
McIntyre, John, 87, 88n
McKay, Donald, 250
McKenna, Reginald, 212, 213
Mackenzie, Thomas B., 87n, 107n, 191
McKinley Tariffs, 69
McLaren, Colin F., 100
Maclay, David Mowat, 87n, 132–4, 135n,
    140, 142, 190, 241
Maclay, David Thompson, 133
Maclay, John S., 375–7
Maclay, Murray, & Spens, 87, 133
McLean, Charles, 13
MacLean, Sir Robert, 374–5, 420n
MacLellan, Peter, 16
MacLellan, P. & W., 13, 15, 126n
MacLellan, Walter, 15
MacLellan, W. T., 126n
MacLeod, Iain, 376, 377
McLintock, Sir William, and problems of
    Royal Mail Group, 186–7, 213n; atti-
    tude towards Colville/Dunlop merger,
    188–9; plans for a Scottish iron and
    steel merger, 192, 196, 197–8, 201; and
    floatation of Colvilles' Ordinary shares,
    213–14; verdict on Craig's tenacity,
    215; crucial role in rationalization of
    Scottish steel industry, 243
Macrosty, H. W., 96, 97
McSkimming, James, 133

Napier, David, 10
Napier, J. S., 55–6, 59, 87; capital con-
    tributed to David Colville & Sons, 77;
    loans paid off, 79
Napier, James, 152n, 245
Napier & McIntyre, 87
Napier, Robert, & Sons, 6, 10, 88
National Bank of Scotland, 184, 188–9,
    210, 212, 235; credits granted to Col-
    villes, 185–6
National Coal Board, 328, 331, 332, 337,
    379, 386, 399–400, 422n, 424
National Commercial Bank of Scotland,
    overdraft to Colvilles Ltd., 401–2

National Committee (for iron and steel
    industry), 228
National Federation of Iron & Steel
    Manufacturers, 165, 228–9, 239, 359n
National Union of Blast Furnacemen, 311
Nationalization, 275, 277, 320; threat of
    re-nationalization and influence on
    capital market, 378, 395; the second
    nationalization (1967), 411, differs
    from first, 415
Neilson, the, family, 4, 9, 69n, 73; go into
    steel production, 45, 47–8
Neilson, Hugh, 133
Neilson, James Beaumont, hot-blast pro-
    cess, 3–4, 40
Neilson, James, 73, 93n
Neilson, Walter, 40
Neilson's Locomotive Works, 71n
Newport, as the site for fourth British strip
    mill, 373, 375–6, 379, 383
New Statesman and Nation, 324, 358n
Nimmo, Sir Adam, 170, 233n, 259
Nimmo, James, & Co., 170n, 233, 259
Nimmo & Dunlop, Ltd., 233n, 234, 259
Nobel's Explosives Company, 63
Noble, Sir Andrew, 91
Noble, Saxton, 91
Norman, Montagu, 180, 227, 229n, 243,
    415; attitude towards extending aid to
    Beardmores, 168–9; encourages Scott-
    ish steel merger, 192–3; evidence to
    Lord Sankey's sub-committee, 194;
    and the Securities Management Trust,
    194, 196n; and the Bankers' Industrial
    Development Co., 194, 196n; and
    Lithgow's purchase of Steel Company
    of Scotland, 209n
North Ayrshire Coastal Development
    Committee, 421n
North British Iron Works, 11, 16
North British Locomotive Co., 83
Northburn Steel Works, 163n, 164, 255
Northumberland Shipbuilding Co., Ltd.,
    147n, 153n

'Oceanspan' scheme, 421
Oil, as raw material for steel making, 312;
    cost increases, 398, 401n
Olga Iron Ore Co., 84n
Ord, L. C., 168
Ore, iron, 3, 46, 55, 69n, 71, 84, 171, 192,
    218, 259, 262–3, 310, 328, 331–2; diffi-
    culties in discharging imported, on

bald Forbes, 343–5; Heal's verdict on, 320; *see also*, Brassert

The Times, 196

Today, 60

Towndrow, R. P., 333, 340–1, 351, 355, 386; appointed Colvilles' Managing Director (Works), 361; role in multidivisional structure, 410–11

Trade Facilities Act, 198, 200

Tradeston Tube Co., 98n

Tradeston Works, Glasgow, 98n

Treasury, British, 135n, 186, 189, 210, 212n, 355, 383, 393, 402

Tropenas Process of steel casting, 96

Trow, Edward, 75

Tube Investment Group, 207

Tube Trade, 92–8, 103, 207–8

Tudhope, William, & Son Ltd, 100n

Tulloch & Denny, 71n

Turnbull, S. M., 210, 245

Turnbull, Grant & Co., 56

Union Bank, 248

Union Castle Mail Steamship Co., 243

Union Steamship Company of New Zealand, 35

Union Works, Coatbridge, 98n

United Dominions Trust, 248

United States Alloy Corporation, 267

United States Steel Corporation, 97n

United Steel Companies Ltd., 139, 165, 253, 364, 366, 422

Vallance, Aylmer, 324

Vacuum degassing, 406

Vaizey, John, 277, 313n, 314, 405, 415

Vickers, Albert, 89, 91

Vickers, Sons, & Maxim, Ltd., 89–91, 118

Victoria Iron & Steel Co., 100n

Vulcan Works, 96n

Wages, lower in English than Scottish steel works, 74–5

Wales, South, iron works in, 21; steel works in, 30n, 47; surpassed by Scotland in open-hearth steel industry, 75; output of open-hearth steel (1879–95), 76; output per active open-hearth furnace (1884–95), 76; Scottish iron and steel industry in late 1940's compared with position in, in the 1930's, 299; and market for steel strip, 376, 380; strip mill authorized, 383; *see also* Strip Mill

Wallace, David, 48

War, First World, impact of, on Scottish iron and steel industry, 125–38

War, Second World, 258–71; organization of control of iron and steel industry during, 258; exacerbation of inter-war weakness in steel industry during, 265

War Office, 260

Warren, Kenneth, 370n, 375n, 424

Watt, Alexander, 99n

Waverley Iron & Steel Co., 100n, 354n

Weir, William, 48

Weir, Lord, 167, 169–70, 171n, 180n, 184n; and genesis of Brassert Report, 170; involvement with housing, 266n, 267n

Wellman Charging Machine, 108

Wellman-Seaver-Morgan Engineering Co., 108n

West, G. P., 164, 190, 216, 241–2, 359; early career of, 191; appointed Director of Colvilles and made General Manager, 191; achievement of, 192

West Cumberland Steel Works, 31n

West of Scotland Iron and Steel Institute, 66, 115, 359n

West of Scotland Malleable Iron Company, 7, 9

West of Scotland Technical College, Glasgow, 132

Wheeler, C. R., 258n

Whitehead Iron & Steel Co., 364

Whitelaw, Alexander, 48

Williams, John, & Co., 45

Williams, Richard, 37n

Williamson, Thomas, 71, 110

Wilmot, John, 295, 311n

Wilson, David, 62

Wilson, George, & Co., 53

Wilson, Harold, 395n

Wilson, John, 4, 6, 8, 26, 62

Wilsons & Union Tube Co. Ltd., 98n

Wilsontown Colliery, 253

Wishaw Iron Company, 47, 70n

Wishaw Iron and Steel Works, 53, 70–2, 74, 83; scene of constant experiment, 110–12

Wood, Richard, 394, 400–5

Woodall-Duckham Construction Co., 340